D0212080

NOTABLE BRITISH NOVELISTS

NOTABLE BRITISH NOVELISTS

Volume 1

Richard Adams — Ford Madox Ford

1 – 350

edited by
CARL ROLLYSON

SALEM PRESS, INC.
Pasadena, California   Hackensack, New Jersey

R
820.903
N899s

Essays originally appeared in *Critical Survey of Long Fiction,
Second Revised Edition,* 2000; new material has been added.

∞ The paper used in these volumes conforms to the American
National Standard for Permanence of Paper for Printed Library Materials, Z39.48-1992 (R1997).

Library of Congress Cataloging-in-Publication Data
Notable British novelists / editor, Carl Rollyson
        p.   cm. — (Magill's choice)
    Includes bibliographical references and index.
ISBN 0-89356-204-1 (set : alk. paper). —
ISBN 0-89356-208-4 (v. 1 : alk. paper). —
ISBN 0-89356-209-2 (v. 2 : alk. paper). —
ISBN 0-89356-237-8 (v. 3 : alk. paper)
    1. English fiction—Bio-bibliography—Dictionaries. 2. Nov-
elists, English—Biography—Dictionaries. 3. English fiction— Dic-
tionaries I. Rollyson, Carl E. (Carl Edmund) II. Series.
PR821.N57   2001
820.9′0003—dc21
[B]   00-046380

First Printing

PRINTED IN THE UNITED STATES OF AMERICA

Contents – Volume 1

Publisher's Note

Notable British Novelists consists of biographical sketches and analyses of 104 of the best-known English, Scottish, and Irish writers of long fiction from the fifteenth through the twentieth centuries. The set's three volumes, which are a combination of new essays and updated essays from *The Critical Survey of Long Fiction, Second Revised Edition* (2000), examine the works most often studied in high school and undergraduate literature classes.

Notable British Novelists profiles eighty-nine English, six Scottish, and nine Irish writers. The Irish writers chosen for this set lived under British rule before the creation of the Irish Free State in 1922 or had careers that were closely associated with Great Britain; therefore, such modern Irish masters as James Joyce and Samuel Beckett are not included. *Notable British Novelists* examines novelists from the early fifteenth century, such as Sir Thomas Malory, to the present. Seventeenth century writers include Aphra Behn and Samuel Butler, and eighteenth century authors Fanny Burney, Henry Fielding, Ann Radcliffe, and Laurence Sterne are featured. Included in the discussions of nineteenth century writers are Wilkie Collins, George Eliot, Elizabeth Gaskell, Thomas Hardy, Mary Wollstonecraft Shelley, Robert Louis Stevenson, and Anthony Trollope. Authors of the twentieth century include Margaret Drabble, Aldous Huxley, Anthony Powell, and Virginia Woolf.

A range of genres and styles is explored in this set, from the gothicism of Charlotte and Emily Brontë and Matthew Gregory Lewis to the postmodernism of Anthony Burgess. Fantasy fiction is represented by Lewis Carroll, C. S. Lewis, and J. R. R. Tolkien, and the science fiction of Arthur C. Clarke and H. G. Wells is included. Among the detective and mystery writers featured are Agatha Christie, Arthur Conan Doyle, and P. D. James, and writers of satire include Jonathan Swift, Tobias Smollett, and Martin Amis. Also featured are the historical novels of Sir Walter Scott and Robert Graves and the feminist fiction of Dorothy Richardson, Jean Rhys, and Fay Weldon.

Each essay provides reference information at its beginning: the novelist's birth and death dates and a list of the principal works of long fiction, with publication dates. This is followed by "Other literary forms," which briefly looks at the author's works of drama, poetry, nonfiction, or short fiction, and "Achievements," which notes principal honors and awards. The major sections of the text follow: "Biography" offers a summary of the writer's personal and professional life, and "Analysis" looks at the author's work in detail. The longest section in the article, "Analysis" is divided into subsections focusing on the major individual works. These subsections offer a short summary of the work and illustrate the themes and techniques used by the novelist. "Other major works" follows "Analysis" and is a categorized list of major works in genres other than long fiction, with publication dates. Each essay ends with an updated, annotated bibliography. The majority of essays are accompanied by a portrait of the author.

The three-volume set is arranged alphabetically. Three helpful reference tools are featured at the end of volume 3: a glossary of "Terms and techniques," a time line of the novelists' birth dates and places, and an index. A list of contributing scholars and their affiliations appears at the beginning of volume 1.

List of Contributors

McCrea Adams
Independent scholar

Michael Adams
CUNY Graduate Center

Patrick Adcock
Henderson State University

S. Krishnamoorthy Aithal
Indian Institute of Technology

Jane Anderson Jones
Manatee Community College

Stanley Archer
Texas A&M University

Gerald S. Argetsinger
Rochester Institute of Technology

Bryan Aubrey
Independent scholar

James Barbour
Independent scholar

Carol M. Barnum
Southern College of Technology

David Barratt
Independent scholar

Kirk H. Beetz
Independent scholar

Todd K. Bender
University of Wisconsin, Madison

K. Bhaskara Rao
Physical Research Laboratory

Mary A. Blackmon
Hardin-Simmons University

Steve D. Boilard
Independent scholar

Mitzi M. Brunsdale
Mayville State College

C. F. Burgess
Independent scholar

John R. Clark
University of South Florida

Samuel Coale
Independent scholar

David W. Cole
University of Wisconsin Center-Baraboo

Deborah Core
Eastern Kentucky University

Carol I. Croxton
University of Southern Colorado

Marsha Daigle-Williamson
Spring Arbor College

Diane D'Amico
Independent scholar

J. Madison Davis
Pennsylvania State University

Frank Day
Clemson University

Paul J. deGategno
North Carolina Wesleyan Colllege

DeVitis, A. A.
Purdue University

Henry J. Donaghy
Kansas State University

David B. Eakin
University of Mississippi

Grace Eckley
Independent scholar

Wilton Eckley
Colorado School of Mines

Robert P. Ellis
Independent scholar

Ann Willardson Engar
Independent scholar

Kenneth Friedenreich
Independent scholar

Kristine Ottesen Garrigan
DePaul University

Peter W. Graham
Virginia Polytechnic Institute and State University

John R. Griffin
University of Southern Colorado

Stephen I. Gurney
Bemidji State University

Angela Hague
Middle Tennessee State University

Richard A. Spurgeon Hall
Methodist College

Melanie Hawthorne
Texas A&M University

William J. Heim
University of South Florida

Greig E. Henderson
University of Toronto

Erwin Hester
East Carolina University

Faith Hickman Brynie
Independent scholar

Nika Hoffman
Crossroads School for Arts & Sciences

John R. Holmes
Franciscan University of Steubenville

Mary Anne Hutchinson
Utica College of Syracuse University

Betty H. Jones
Rutgers University

Anna B. Katona
Independent scholar

Anne Kelsch Breznau
Independent scholar

Catherine Kenney
Independent scholar

John V. Knapp
Independent scholar

Grove Koger
Boise Public Library

Sarah B. Kovel
Independent scholar

Lawrence F. Laban
Independent scholar

Eugene Larson
Pierce College

William Laskowski
Jamestown College

Michael Lowenstein
Harris-Stowe State College

R. C. Lutz
University of the Pacific

James J. Lynch
Independent scholar

Fred B. McEwen
Waynesburg College

Richard D. McGhee
Arkansas State University

David W. Madden
California State University, Sacramento

Lois A. Marchino
University of Texas at El Paso

Patricia Marks
Valdosta State College

John L. Marsden
Indiana University of Pennsylvania

Charles E. May
California State University, Long Beach

Laurence W. Mazzeno
Alvernia College

Sally Mitchell
Temple University

Carole Moses
Independent scholar

Brian Murray
Youngstown State University

Allan Nelson
Caldwell College

Martha Nochimson
Independent scholar

William Peden
University of Missouri, Columbia

Robert C. Petersen
Middle Tennessee State University

Charles H. Pullen
Queens University

Rosemary M. Canfield Reisman
Charleston Southern University

Samuel J. Rogal
Illinois State University

Joseph Rosenblum
University of North Carolina, Greensboro

Dale Salwak
Citrus College

Vasant A. Shahane
University of New Hampshire

John C. Shields
Independent scholar

Marjorie Smelstor
University of Wisconsin - Eau Claire

Katherine Snipes
Independent scholar

George Soule
Carleton College

Brian Stableford
Independent scholar

Isabel Bonnyman Stanley
East Tennessee State University

William B. Stone
Independent scholar

Christopher J. Thaiss
George Mason University

Ronald G. Walker
Western Illinois University

John Michael Walsh
Hofstra University

Gary Westfahl
University of California, Riverside

Roger E. Wiehe
Independent scholar

Complete List of Contents

Contents—Volume 1

Contents—Volume 2

Contents—Volume 3

NOTABLE BRITISH NOVELISTS

Richard Adams

Born: Newbury, England; May 9, 1920

Principal long fiction · *Watership Down*, 1972; *Shardik*, 1974; *The Plague Dogs*, 1977; *The Girl in a Swing*, 1980; *Maia*, 1984; *Traveller*, 1988.

Other literary forms · Richard Adams has written two collections of short fiction, one of which, *Tales from Watership Down* (1996), is in part a sequel to his most famous novel. His other works include several illustrated children's books in verse; an illustrated series of nature guides; an account of a journey to Antarctica, *Voyage Through the Antarctic* (1982), cowritten with Ronald M. Lockley, the author of the factual basis for *Watership Down*; and an autobiography covering the first part of his life through his demobilization after World War II, *The Day Gone By* (1990).

Achievements · Called by English writer A. N. Wilson "the best adventure-story-writer alive," Richard Adams is most famous for taking the talking-animal story out of the genre of children's literature and informing it with mature concerns and interests, as in his first great success, *Watership Down*, which won the Carnegie Award and the *Guardian* award for children's fiction in 1972. He continued this transformation in *The Plague Dogs* and *Traveller*. Adams also made his mark in fantasy literature; his imaginary kingdom of Bekla is the backdrop for *Shardik* and *Maia*, novels whose main concerns, slavery and warfare, definitely remove them from the realm of children's literature. He also wrote a less successful full-length ghost story, *The Girl in a Swing*.

Biography · The youngest of three children, Richard Adams spent an idyllic childhood ("the happiest [days] of my life") growing up on the outskirts of Newbury, England. His father, a local doctor, transmitted his knowledge of and love for the flora and fauna of the region to his son, whose later devotion to animal welfare was also inspired by Hugh Lofting's Dr. Dolittle books. Adams's father also instilled in his son a lifelong interest in storytelling, which Adams later honed in bedtime tales told to roommates at prep school. Other important influences included the Uncle Remus stories of Joel Chandler Harris, *Uncle Tom's Cabin* (1852) by Harriet Beecher Stowe, *The Three Mulla-Mulgars* (1910) by Walter de la Mare, and the silent Rin-Tin-Tin films. All would later echo in his fiction.

While his time at prep school was often unpleasant, Adams thoroughly enjoyed his public school experience at Bradfield. The school put on a yearly play in its open-air theater, often a classical Greek drama, and Adams called the theater the place where he was "more consistently happy than anywhere else." Bradfield also encouraged his love of literature, the Greek and Roman classics, and history, the subject in which Adams won a scholarship to Worcester College, Oxford, in 1938. Adams was grateful to Oxford for its acceptance of what he called one's "fantasy potential."

Adams's Oxford years were interrupted, like those of so many others, by World War II. Adams chose to serve in the Royal Army Service Corps (RASC), which is mainly concerned with transport and communication duties, but later he volunteered for the airborne arm of the RASC and served in the Middle East and in Singapore. On his return to England, Adams was shocked to learn how many of his Oxford companions had died during the war.

    After demobilization, Adams soon met Elizabeth Acland, whom he would later marry and with whom he would have two daughters. In 1948 he joined the British Civil Service, but he never abandoned his love for storytelling. *Watership Down* began, like many other "children's" classics, as a story initially told by the author to his children (in this case to entertain them on a long car trip); two years after its publication, Adams was able to retire from the Civil Service and write full-time at his various homes in the south of England.

Analysis · In each of his novels, Richard Adams adopts a different individual narrative voice: easygoing and colloquial in *Watership Down* and *Maia*, stately and epic in *Shardik*, ironic and densely allusive in *The Plague Dogs*, and the very different first-person voices in *The Girl in a Swing* and *Traveller*. On the surface, Adams's natural gift as a storyteller is his strongest talent. Yet his novels deserve to be read more for his habitual concerns: a love for "the surface of the earth," as George Orwell called it, as manifested in the English countryside and the creatures who inhabit it; a hatred for the cruelties that human beings inflict on the other inhabitants of this world, as well as on themselves; and an acute awareness of the transitory nature of existence and the evanescence of friendship and love.

Watership Down · *Watership Down* burst on the literary scene in 1972, as unlikely a success as J. R. R. Tolkien's *The Lord of the Rings* (1955) had been two decades earlier. Its plot and character seemed those of a children's book: A group of rabbits leave their threatened burrow and make a dangerous journey to find a new home, as well as enough new rabbits to ensure its continuation. Yet in its length and often violent action it certainly went beyond the boundaries of a children's work, and it succeeded with many adults. It even led to some shameless imitations, such as William Horwood's mole epic, *Duncton Wood* (1980), but none had the imagination and freshness of the original.

    As Tolkien did with the hobbits, Adams made his exotic characters familiar by giving them an easily identifiable demotic speech. Hazel, Bigwig, and the others speak much like what the originals they are modeled on must have sounded like: Adams's companions in the 205th company of the RASC during World War II. (Hazel, according to Adams, is his commanding officer, John Gifford, and Bigwig is Paddy Kavanagh, who was killed in battle.) The rabbits, like their soldier counterparts, are believable everyday heroes. Their persistence in the face of daunting odds, their relatively unflappable demeanor as they are introduced into new and dangerous surroundings, their ingenuity in overcoming their difficulties—all recall the best qualities of those soldiers in the war.

    The familiar speech is also reproduced in the novel's narrative voice, which is often that of a good oral storyteller; as Adams said, "A true folk-tale teller is usually rather colloquial." This informality helps to disguise the classical underpinnings of the work, the main one of which is Vergil's *Aeneid* (c. 29-19 B.C.E.). There are also echoes of Xenophon's *Anabasis* (fourth century B.C.E.) and Homer's *Iliad* and *Odyssey* (both c. 800 B.C.E.), with Hazel as a more trustworthy Odysseus and Bigwig a less belligerent Achilles. These archetypal characters and plot devices are also supported by the scientific accuracy of the details of the rabbits' lives, which Adams culled from *The*

Private Life of the Rabbit by R. M. Lockley (1964). Familiar yet exotic characters, an epic story, and verisimilitude of milieu contribute to the lasting and deserved appeal of *Watership Down*. (*Tales from Watership Down*, in its latter half a sequel to the novel, also serves as an answer to those who accused the original of, among other charges, sexism.)

Shardik · Adams's next novel, *Shardik*, disappointed many of his readers, for while on the surface, like *Watership Down*, a fantasy, it was far removed from the first novel in setting, characters, and plot. Adams constructs the mythical land of Bekla, whose precarious peace is shattered by the emergence of a great bear, which is taken by many to be the avatar of the god Shardik. After a short rule by the bear's chief follower, Kelderek, the bear escapes, and Kelderek must learn the real meaning of the irruption of Shardik into the lives of so many people. For much of the book, the characters are unlikable, the setting is foreign without being exotic, and the plot seems to be nothing but one violent incident after another. The narration is also different from that in *Watership Down*, in this case, much more stately and epic in tone, with self-consciously Homeric similes interrupting the narrative flow.

Yet, in the end *Shardik* is satisfying, once the reader grasps the greater themes of the novel. Shardik's reign has allowed slavery to flourish once again in Bekla, and only by suffering and death can Shardik and Kelderek redeem themselves and society. Adams's own horror at slavery, both literary and real, echoes in the plot: The evil slaver Genshed is consciously modeled on Stowe's great villain in *Uncle Tom's Cabin*, Simon Legree, and the mutilated beggar boys seen by Adams from a troop train in India are reproduced in some Beklan slaves. Adams's own hatred of war causes the first half of the book almost to be anti-epic in its drive: The religious war it depicts is nasty, brutish, and long. Once the arc of the plot is evident, *Shardik* can be seen as an epic indictment of the horrors of epic war.

The Plague Dogs · *The Plague Dogs* is the most tendentious of Adams's novels. The title characters are trying to escape from a laboratory in England's Lake Country, where they have been subjected to cruel and unnecessary experiments. Although seemingly a return to the mode of his greatest success, the grown-up animal novel, it is much more a satire filled with savage indignation at the lengths to which humans will use and abuse other species, a satire which gains effect from Adams's experience working in government bureaucracies. Like *Shardik*, it is an investigation of cruelty, this time toward what the novel calls "animal slaves": "It's a bad world for the helpless," as one of its characters says. Once again Adams adopts a new narrative voice, particularly in the sections concerning humans, this one arch and packed with literary allusions. The novel is not totally one-sided, the case being made near the end for useful animal medical experimentation. Yet again it is in his animal portrayals that Adams best succeeds, particularly those of the dog Snitter, whose nonsense language, caused by a brain operation, echoes that of dramatist William Shakespeare's fools, and of the wild fox, whose feral otherness seems to be an answer to criticisms of Adams's cozy rabbits.

The Girl in a Swing · Adams's next two novels are major departures, explorations of the themes of sexuality and love, subjects he only tangentially touched on previously. *The Girl in a Swing* is nominally a ghost story, but more a depiction of the obsessive love that the hero, Alan Desland, feels for Käthe, a German girl whom he meets in

Copenhagen and swiftly marries, not knowing that she is trying to escape a ghost from her past. There are echoes of Emily Brontë's *Wuthering Heights* (1847)–Käthe as Cathy Earnshaw–but Alan is no Heathcliff, and while Adams's depictions of local scenery remain one of his strengths–much of the locale is again borrowed from Adams's childhood–the end of the novel is more deflationary than chilling. Adams said that ghosts in English horror writer M. R. James's short stories are knowingly artificial, but the one in *Girl in a Swing* is unfortunately no less an *umbra ex machina*, a ghost from the machine.

Maia · *Maia* returns to the fantasy world of Bekla which Adams created in *Shardik* to tell the story of the eponymous heroine who undergoes a transformation from literal sex slave to country matron, all described at sometimes tedious length, in more than twelve hundred pages. Adams's narrative style here is more familiar than that in *Shardik*, his similes shorter, homelier, and less epic. However, the reproduction of the girl's countrified speech becomes irritating, and anachronisms such as discussions of infection and primitive vaccination are annoying. The plot is basic: Girl meets boy; girl loses boy; girl gets boy. However, the girl does not even meet the boy until almost halfway through the novel, making for difficult reading. The underlying theme is much the same as *Shardik*'s, as the good side attempts to eradicate slavery in the Beklan empire, but this time the scenes of sadism that Adams describes become extremely uncomfortable. In *Shardik* such scenes had a moral point, but here their purpose seems cloudier: We know these characters are villains, so several scenes explicitly depicting their villainy are uncalled for. On the positive side, Adams once again depicts actions that undercut fantasy epic conventions: Maia's most heroic actions are undertaken to prevent, and not to further, violence and warfare. Yet at the end, when Maia has become a contented country wife and mother, the reader wonders how this matron grew out of the girl who, some nine hundred pages earlier, had realized she possessed "an exceptional erotic attitude" and proceeded to use and enjoy it.

Traveller · *Traveller* is basically the story of the Civil War seen through the eyes and told by the voice of Confederate general Robert E. Lee's famous horse. In this novel, Adams plays to all his strengths, including a new narrative voice, this one a modification of Joel Chandler Harris's in the Uncle Remus stories; a singular, believable animal persona through which the action is described; and a depiction of his favorite themes: hatred of war, admiration for those who must suffer through it, and sorrow over the ephemerality of comrades and friendship. The bravery of Lee's Army of Northern Virginia is, as Adams elsewhere said, a reflection of Adams's own pride in the gallantry of the British 1st Airborne Division in the battle of Arnhem. Lee is Adams's quintessential hero because he treats both animals and people with dignity and respect. Traveller, like satirist Jonathan Swift's Houyhnhnms (*Gulliver's Travels*, 1726), is aghast at humankind's capacity for cruelty, but he is not keen enough (or anachronistic enough) to see the cruelty that slavery commits. Traveller is, as another horse calls him, "thick": At Gettysburg, he thinks Pickett's charge succeeds, and at Appomattox, he thinks the Federals have surrendered to "Marse Robert." However, he gets the basic truth right: "Horses [are] for ever saying goodbye." It was the lesson Adams learned when he returned to Oxford after the war to learn of his friends' deaths, and it is the grave lesson that has informed his best fiction.

William Laskowski

Other major works

SHORT FICTION: *The Unbroken Web: Stories and Fables*, 1980 (originally *The Iron Wolf and Other Stories*); *Tales from Watership Down*, 1996.

NONFICTION: *Nature Through the Seasons*, 1975 (with Max Hooper); *Nature Day and Night*, 1978 (with Hooper); *Voyage Through the Antarctic*, 1982 (with Ronald M. Lockley); *A Nature Diary*, 1985; *The Day Gone By*, 1990.

CHILDREN'S LITERATURE: *The Tyger Voyage*, 1976; *The Adventures of and Brave Deeds of the Ship's Cat on the Spanish Maine: Together with the Most Lamentable Losse of the Alcestis and Triumphant Firing of the Port of Chagres*, 1977; *The Legend of Te Tuna*, 1982; *The Bureaucats*, 1985.

EDITED TEXT: *Sinister and Supernatural Stories*, 1978.

Bibliography

Bridgman, Joan. "The Significance of Myth in *Watership Down*." *Journal of the Fantastic in the Arts* 6, no. 1 (1993): 7-24. Demonstrates the influence of Walter de la Mare's *The Three Mulla-Mulgars* on the novel.

Chapman, Edgar. "The Shaman as Hero and Spiritual Leader: Richard Adams' Mythmaking in *Watership Down* and *Shardik*." *Mythlore* 5 (August, 1978): 7-11. Solid treatment of *Shardik* and myth; less reliable on *Watership Down*.

Kitchell, Kenneth. "The Shrinking of the Epic Hero: From Homer to Richard Adams's *Watership Down*." *Classical and Modern Literature* 7 (Fall, 1986): 13-30. Convincing argument that Adams's novel is a modern epic.

Meyer, Charles. "The Power of Myth and Rabbit Survival in Richard Adams' *Watership Down*." *Journal of the Fantastic in the Arts* 3, no. 4 (1994): 139-150. Shows the connections between the novel and R. M. Lockley's *The Private Life of the Rabbit*.

Miltner, Robert. "*Watership Down*: A Genre Study." *Journal of the Fantastic in the Arts* 6, no. 1 (1993): 63-70. Traces the various literary genres to which the novel belongs.

Kingsley Amis

Born: London, England; April 16, 1922
Died: London, England; October 22, 1995

Principal long fiction · *Lucky Jim*, 1954; *That Uncertain Feeling*, 1955; *I Like It Here*, 1958; *Take a Girl Like You*, 1960; *One Fat Englishman*, 1963; *The Egyptologists*, 1965 (with Robert Conquest); *The Anti-Death League*, 1966; *Colonel Sun: A James Bond Adventure*, 1968 (as Robert Markham); *I Want It Now*, 1968; *The Green Man*, 1969; *Girl, 20*, 1971; *The Riverside Villas Murder*, 1973; *Ending Up*, 1974; *The Crime of the Century*, 1975 (serial), 1987 (book); *The Alteration*, 1976; *Jake's Thing*, 1978; *Russian Hide-and-Seek*, 1980; *Stanley and the Women*, 1984; *The Old Devils*, 1986; *Difficulties with Girls*, 1988; *The Crime of the Century*, 1988; *The Folks That Live on the Hill*, 1990; *The Russian Girl*, 1992; *You Can't Do Both*, 1994; *The Biographer's Moustache*, 1995.

Other literary forms · Kingsley Amis is best known as a novelist, but readers have turned often to his other writings for the insight they give into the man and his fiction. Many of the themes that are explored in depth in his novels are expressed indirectly in the peripheral works. He published several collections of short stories, entitled *My Enemy's Enemy* (1962), *Collected Short Stories* (1980), and *Mr. Barrett's Secret and Other Stories* (1993). *Dear Illusion*, a novella, was published in 1972 in a limited edition of five hundred copies. His collections of poetry include: *Bright November* (1947), *A Frame of Mind* (1953), *A Case of Samples: Poems, 1946-1956* (1956), *The Evans Country* (1962), *A Look Round the Estate: Poems, 1957-1967* (1967), and *Collected Poems: 1944-1979* (1979). Amis published his opinionated *Memoirs* in 1991. His criticism covers an extremely wide range; in addition to studies of figures as diverse as Jane Austen and Rudyard Kipling, he published one of the first significant critical books on science fiction, *New Maps of Hell: A Survey of Science Fiction* (1960), a work that has done much to encourage academic study of the genre and to win recognition for many gifted writers. *The James Bond Dossier* (1965), *Lucky Jim's Politics* (1968), several volumes of collected science fiction, edited with Robert Conquest and entitled *Spectrum: A Science Fiction Anthology* (1961-1965), and *The King's English: A Guide to Modern Usage* (1997) offer further evidence of the extraordinary range of his work.

Achievements · Almost from the beginning of his career, Amis enjoyed the attention of numerous commentators. Because his works have been filled with innovations, surprises, and variations in techniques and themes, it is not surprising that critics and reviewers alike found it difficult to make a definitive statement about his achievements. The range of his work is extraordinary: fiction, poetry, reviews, criticism, humor, science fiction, and biography. Of all of his writings, however, his achievement depends most upon his novels.

Amis's early novels are considered by many critics to be "angry" novels of protest against the contemporary social, political, and economic scene in Britain. The themes include resentment of a rigid class stratification, rejection of formal institutional ties, discouragement with the economic insecurity and low status of those without money, loathing of pretentiousness in any form, and disenchantment with the past. Because many of Amis's contemporaries, including John Wain, John Osborne, John Braine, and Alan Sillitoe, seemed to express similar concerns, and because many came from working-class or lower-middle-class backgrounds, went to Oxford or Cambridge Universities, and taught for a time at a provincial university, journalists soon spoke of them as belonging to a literary movement. The "Angry Young Men," as their fictional heroes were called, were educated men who did not want to be conventional gentlemen. Kenneth Allsop called them "a new, rootless, faithless, classless class" lacking in manners and morals; W. Somerset Maugham called them "mean, malicious and envious . . . scum" and warned that these men would some day rule England. Some critics even confused the characters with the writers themselves. Amis's Jim Dixon (in *Lucky Jim*) was appalled by the tediousness and falseness of academic life;

©Washington Post; reprinted by permission of the D.C. Public Library

therefore, Dixon was interpreted as a symbol of anti-intellectualism. Dixon taught at a provincial university; therefore, he became a symbol of contempt for Cambridge and Oxford. Amis himself taught at a provincial university (Swansea); therefore, he and Dixon became one and the same in the minds of many critics. Like all literary generalizations, however, this one was soon inadequate. The most that can be said is that through Amis's early heroes there seemed to sound clearly those notes of disillusionment that were to become dominant in much of the literature of the 1950's.

Because it seems so artless, critics have also found Amis's fiction difficult to discuss. His straightforward plotting, gift for characterization, and ability to tell a good story, they say, are resistant to the modern techniques of literary criticism. Because Amis lacks the obscurity, complexity, and technical virtuosity of James Joyce or William Faulkner, these critics suggest that he is not to be valued as highly. In many of the early reviews, Amis is described as essentially a comic novelist, an entertainer, or an amiable satirist not unlike P. G. Wodehouse, the Marx Brothers, or Henry Fielding. Furthermore, his interest in mysteries, ghost stories, James Bond thrillers, and science fiction confirms for these critics the view that Amis is a writer lacking serious intent.

Looking beyond the social commentary and entertainment found in Amis's work, other critics find a distinct relationship between Amis's novels and the "new sincerity" of the so-called Movement poets of the 1950's and later. These poets (including Amis himself, Philip Larkin, John Wain, and D. J. Enright, all of whom also wrote fiction) saw their work as an alternative to the symbolic and allusive poetry of T. S. Eliot and his followers. In a movement away from allusion, obscurity, and excesses of style, the Movement poets encouraged precision, lucidity, and craftsmanship. They concentrated on honesty of thought and feeling to emphasize what A. L. Rowse calls a "businesslike intention to communicate with the reader." Amis's deceptively simple novels have been written with the same criteria he imposed on his poetry; one cannot read Amis with a measure suitable only to Joyce or Faulkner. Rather, his intellectual and literary ancestors antedate the great modernist writers, and the resultant shape is that of a nineteenth century man of letters. His novels may be appreciated for their commonsense approach. He writes clearly. He avoids extremes or excessive stylistic experimentation. He is witty, satirical, and often didactic.

Amis's novels after 1980 added a new phase to his career. One of the universal themes that most engaged Amis is the relation between men and women, both in and out of marriage. After 1980, he moved away from the broad scope of a society plagued by trouble to examine instead the troubles plaguing one of that society's most fundamental institutions—relationships—and the conflicts, misunderstandings, and drastically different responses of men and women to the world. Most of his characters suffer blighted marriages. Often they seem intelligent but dazed, as if there were something they had lost but cannot quite remember. Something has indeed been lost, and loss is at the heart of all of Amis's novels, so that he is, as novelist Malcolm Bradbury calls him, "one of our most disturbing contemporary novelists, an explorer of historical pain." From the beginning of his canon, Amis focused upon the absence of something significant in modern life: a basis, a framework, a structure for living, such as the old institutions like religion or marriage once provided. Having pushed that loss in societal terms to its absolute extreme in the previous novels, Amis subsequently studied it in personal terms, within the fundamental social unit. In *The Old Devils*, for example (for which he won the 1986 Booker Fiction Prize), his characters will not regain the old, secure sense of meaning that their lives once held, and Amis does not pretend that they will. What success they manage to attain is always partial. What, in the absence of an informing faith or an all-consuming family life, could provide purpose for living? More simply, how is one to be useful? This is the problem that haunts Amis's characters, and it is a question, underlying all of his novels, that came to the forefront near the end of his life.

In looking back over Amis's career, critics have found a consistent moral judgment quite visible beneath the social commentary, entertainment, and traditional techniques that Amis employs. Beginning in a world filled with verbal jokes, masquerades, and incidents, Amis's view of life grew increasingly pessimistic until he arrived at a fearfully grim vision of a nightmare world filled with hostility, violence, sexual abuse, and self-destruction. Critics, therefore, view Amis most significantly as a moralist, concerned with the ethical life in difficult times. Amis's response to such conditions was to use his great powers of observation and mimicry both to illuminate the changes in postwar British society and to suggest various ways of understanding and possibly coping with those changes. For all these reasons, one can assert that Amis has achieved a major reputation in contemporary English fiction, and, as is so often the case today, his is an achievement that does not depend upon any single work. It is rather the totality of his work with which readers should reckon.

Biography · Kingsley William Amis was born in London on April 16, 1922. His father, William Robert, was an office clerk with Coleman's Mustard and fully expected his only child to enter commerce. His son's intention, however, was to be a writer—a poet, really—though it was not until the publication of his rollicking and irreverent first novel, *Lucky Jim*, in 1954, that Amis achieved his goal.

By Amis's own account, he had been writing since he was a child. Writing became for him a means of coming to terms with certain fears. As a boy he suffered from the routine terrors of childhood, fear of the dark, fear of the future, fear of other children, fear of his parents' disapproval, but as he grew older the subjects of his fears changed. He was a complicated individual; depression alternated with laughter, and an inner loneliness counterbalanced his social charm. Typically, one fear involved his health. Like many of his characters, one of his strongest fears was the fear of loneliness. "Being the only person in the house is something I wouldn't like at all," he said, years later. "I would develop anxiety. By this I mean more than just a rational dislike of being alone and wanting company but something which means, for me, becoming very depressed and tense. I've always been terribly subject to tension. I worry a lot."

Kingsley Amis as an author and his characters themselves often seem to be running scared, playing out their lives while always looking over their shoulders, afraid that the truth of life's meaninglessness will catch up to them. Amis admitted that writing fiction encourages the illusion that there is some sense in life. "There isn't," he said, "but if that's all you thought, you'd go mad." In his fiction, if not in life, he was able to pretend that there is a pattern in events and that the suffering of his characters could be justified, or explained, or atoned for, or made all right. Such power to conjure up meaning where it otherwise may not exist brought with it the "wonderful feeling of being Lord of Creation."

Long before Amis was to experience this power, he was merely a schoolboy at St. Hilda's local fee-paying school. At St. Hilda's he learned French from Miss Crampton, and he also developed a crush on his English teacher, Miss Barr, "a tall, Eton-crowned figure of improbable eloquence." It is in these inauspicious surroundings, he said, humorously, that perhaps "we can date my first education into the glories of our literature." Perhaps because of Miss Barr but more probably because of his temperament and interests, he developed a fascination for anything to do with writing—pens, paper, and erasers.

His interest may have been piqued at St. Hilda's, but his first literary efforts occurred at Norbury College. There he was exposed to the vast entertainment that the days held for a British public school boy in the 1930's: Under the tutelage of his teachers, he began to write stories and poems. His first published work of fiction, a three-hundred-word adventure story called "The Sacred Rhino of Uganda," appeared in the school magazine. In the fall of 1934, he entered the "really splendid" City of London School, a day school of seven hundred boys that overlooked the Thames by Blackfriars Bridge. Amis read much during this period. He specialized in the classics until he was sixteen, then switched to English, but later would wish that he had been more interested in Scripture and divinity at the time and had been touched by the wings of faith, a wish that his fiction would ultimately demonstrate. He also read French. Early artistic delights included watercolors, Dadaism, and architecture. He especially loved to read poetry, and with his keen mind and quick sensibilities he could take in a considerable amount of material quickly.

In the prewar year of 1939, while he was in the sixth form, Amis and many of his school chums were suddenly surprised to find themselves being sent to Marlborough College in Wiltshire as evacuees; there he spent the next five terms. He found himself in the small country town of Marlborough, one of the most undisturbed countrysides remaining in the southwest of England. There, in vivid contrast to the suburbia he knew in Clapham, Amis was initiated into the beauties and mysteries of nature, and for the rest of his life he would carry images of Marlborough with him and re-create them in his fictional country scenes.

Amis's first novel, *The Legacy*, written while he attended St. John's College at the University of Oxford (1941-1942, 1945-1947), was rejected by fourteen publishers. Eventually Amis abandoned it altogether, having come to regard it as boring, unfunny, and derivative. Although his studies at Oxford were interrupted by the war, Amis persisted, earning his B.A. (with honors) and M.A. degrees in English.

Several factors influenced Amis's development into a writer whose stories and style are unique. His comic proclivities were encouraged by his father, a man with "a talent for physical clowning and mimicry." Amis described himself as "undersized, law-abiding, timid," a child able to make himself popular by charm or clowning, who found that at school he could achieve much by exploiting his inherited powers of mimicry. His school friends testified to Amis's capacity for making people laugh. Philip Larkin's description of their first meeting (1941), in the 1963 introduction to his own novel, *Jill*, suggests that it was Amis's "genius for imaginative mimicry" that attracted him: "For the first time I felt myself in the presence of a talent greater than my own." John Wain also recalled how, in the "literary group" to which they both belonged, Amis was a "superb mimic" who relished differences of character and idiom.

This period of "intensive joke swapping," as Larkin called it, continued when Amis entered the army in 1942. He became an officer, served in the Royal Signals, and landed in Normandy in June, 1944. After service in France, Belgium, and West Germany, he was demobilized in October, 1945. This period was to provide material for such stories as "My Enemy's Enemy," "Court of Inquiry," and "I Spy Strangers," but its immediate effect was to open his eyes to the world, to all sorts of strange people and strange ways of behaving.

Amis's status as an only child also contributed to his development as a writer, for he found himself looking at an early age for "self-entertainment." He satisfied this need by reading adventure stories, science fiction, and boys' comics. During these years, too, Amis became interested in horror tales. He recalled seeing the Boris Karloff version of *Frankenstein* (1931) and *The Mummy* (1932) and the Fredric March version of *Dr. Jekyll and Mr. Hyde* (1932). After that time, Amis was interested in what might be called the minor genres on grounds of wonder, excitement, and "a liking for the strange, the possibly horrific." Amis became aware that the detective story, various tales of horror or terror, and the science-fiction story provided vehicles for both social satire and investigation of human nature in a way not accessible to the mainstream novelist.

Along with his natural comic gifts, his interest in genre fiction, and his war experiences, Amis's development was influenced by his early exposure to an English tradition that has resisted the modernist innovations so influential in America and on the Continent at the time. His dislike for experimental prose may be traced in part to the influence of one of his tutors at Oxford, the Anglo-Saxon scholar Gavin Bone, and to his readings of certain eighteenth century novelists whose ability to bring immense variety and plentitude to their work without reverting to obscurity or stylistic excess appealed to the young Amis.

Amis attributed his personal standards of morality both to his readings in Charles Dickens, Henry Fielding, and Samuel Richardson and to the training in standard Protestant virtues he received while growing up at home. Both of his parents were Baptists, but in protest against their own forceful religious indoctrination, their visits to church became less and less frequent as they grew older. Any reader of Amis's works soon becomes aware that there is in his writings a clear repudiation of traditional Christian belief. Nevertheless, from his parents he received certain central moral convictions which crystallized a personal philosophy of life and art. Hard work, conscientiousness, obedience, loyalty, frugality, and patience—these lessons and others were put forward and later found their way into his novels, all of which emphasize the necessity of good works and of trying to live a moral life in the natural—as opposed to the supernatural—world.

Despite these convictions, however, Amis was not able to live his private life impeccably, as he himself would ultimately testify. His long-standing marriage to Hilary ("Hilly") Bardwell, which produced a daughter and two sons, including novelist Martin Amis, was marred by frequent infidelities and was ultimately destroyed by his romantic involvement with fellow novelist Elizabeth Jane Howard. Amis and Hilly were divorced in 1965. Amis's subsequent marriage to Howard was not happy, however, and the two separated in 1980. Misogynistic novels such as *Jake's Thing* and *Stanley and the Women* mirror his dissatisfaction with his relationship with Howard in particular and with relations between the sexes in general.

The sunnier aspect of Amis's final novels, especially *The Old Devils* and *The Folks That Live on the Hill*, owes its character to Amis's reconcilement (of sorts) with his first wife. In 1981 Amis, Hilly, and her third husband, Alistair Boyd (Lord Kilmarnock), set up housekeeping together. The arrangement was to last until Amis's death in late 1995. During this final period Amis was to win Britain's highest literary award, the Booker Prize, for *The Old Devils*. His unusual domestic arrangements are described in detail in Eric Jacobs's *Kingsley Amis: A Biography* (1995). Amis's final novel, *The Biographer's Moustache*, reflected his somewhat uneasy feelings over having his biography written. According to Jacobs, Amis remained a writer until his death in 1995. During his last illness he was busy compiling notes about hospital routines to be incorporated into yet another novel.

Analysis · Kingsley Amis's fiction is characterized by a recurring preoccupation with certain themes and concepts, with certain basic human experiences, attitudes, and perceptions. These persistent themes are treated with enormous variety, however, particularly in Amis's novels which draw on the conventions of genre fiction—the mystery, the spy thriller, the ghost story, and so on. Of the twenty novels Amis has published, his development as a seriocomic novelist is especially apparent in *Lucky Jim, Take a Girl Like You, The Anti-Death League, The Green Man, The Old Devils, The Folks That Live on the Hill*, and *The Russian Girl*, his most substantial and complex works, each of which is representative of a specific stage in his career. All these novels are set in contemporary England. Drawing upon a variety of traditional techniques of good storytelling—good and bad characters, simple irony, straightforward plot structure, clear point of view—they restate, in a variety of ways, the traditional pattern of tragedy: A man, divided and complex, vulnerable both to the world and to himself, is forced to make choices that will determine his destiny. Built into this situation is the probability that he will bring down suffering on his head and injure others in the process.

In *Lucky Jim*, for example, Amis establishes a comic acceptance of many of life's injustices in the academic world. The novel is distinguished by clear-cut cases of right and wrong, a simple irony, and knockabout farce. Because he has neither the courage nor the economic security to protest openly, the hero lives a highly comic secret life of protest consisting of practical jokes and rude faces, all directed against the hypocrisy and pseudointellectualism of certain members of the British establishment. While only hinted at in *Lucky Jim*, Amis's moral seriousness becomes increasingly evident beginning with *Take a Girl Like You*. Whereas in *Lucky Jim* the values are "hidden" beneath a comic narrative, gradually the comedy is submerged beneath a more serious treatment. Thus, *Take a Girl Like You* is a turning point for Amis in a number of ways: The characterization is more complex, the moral problems are more intense, and the point of view is not limited to one central character. Distinguished also by a better balance between the comic and the serious, the novel is more pessimistic than its predecessors, less given to horseplay and high spirits.

In later novels such as *The Anti-Death League* and *The Green Man*, Amis continues to see life more darkly, shifting to an increasingly metaphysical, even theological concern. Contemporary England is viewed as a wasteland of the spirit, and his characters try vainly to cope with a precarious world filled with madness and hysteria, a world in which love and religion have become distorted and vulgarized. Threatened with death and ugly accidents by a malicious God, Amis's characters feel powerless to change, and in an attempt to regain control of their lives, act immorally. Amis's ultimate vision is one in which all of the traditional certainties—faith, love, loyalty, responsibility, decency—have lost their power to comfort and sustain. Humanity is left groping in the dark of a nightmare world. In the later *The Old Devils*, Amis's study of a Wales and a Welshness that have slipped out of reach forever clearly shows a culmination of his increasing damnation of Western society, portrayed through the microcosm of human relationships. The final picture is one of the aimlessness of old age, the meaninglessness of much of life itself.

Lucky Jim · In *Lucky Jim*, a bumbling, somewhat conscientious hero stumbles across the social and cultural landscape of contemporary British academic life, faces a number of crises of conscience, makes fun of the world and of himself, and eventually returns to the love of a sensible, realistic girl. This is the traditional comic course followed by Amis's first three novels, of which *Lucky Jim* is the outstanding example. Beneath the horseplay and high spirits, however, Amis rhetorically manipulates the reader's moral judgment so that he or she leaves the novel sympathetic to the hero's point of view. By triumphing over an unrewarding job, a pretentious family, and a predatory female colleague, Dixon becomes the first in a long line of Amis's heroes who stand for common sense and decency, for the belief that life is to be made happy now, for the notion that "nice things are nicer than nasty things."

To develop his moral concern, Amis divides his characters into two archetypal groups reminiscent of the fantasy tale: the generally praiseworthy figures, the ones who gain the greatest share of the reader's sympathy; and the "evil" characters, those who obstruct the good characters. Jim Dixon (the put-upon young man), Gore-Urquhart (his benefactor or savior), and Christine Callaghan (the decent girl to whom Dixon turns) are among the former, distinguished by genuineness, sincerity, and a lack of pretense. Among the latter are Professor Welch (Dixon's principal tormentor), his son, Bertrand (the defeated boaster), and the neurotic Margaret Peele (the thwarted "witch"), all of whom disguise their motives and present a false appearance.

One example should be enough to demonstrate Amis's technique: the introduction to the seedy, absentminded historian, Professor Welch. In the opening chapter, Amis establishes an ironic discrepancy between what Welch seems to be (a scholar discussing history) and what he is in reality (a "vaudeville character" lecturing on the differences between flute and recorder). Although he tries to appear a cultured, sensitive intellecutal, all of the images point to a charlatan leading a boring, selfish life. His desk is "misleadingly littered." Once he is found standing, "surprisingly enough," in front of the college library's new-books shelf. Succeeding physical description undercuts his role-playing: He resembles "an old boxer," "an African savage," "a broken robot." What is more, his speech and gestures are mechanized by cliché and affectation. Professing to worship "integrated village-type community life" and to oppose anything mechanical, he is himself a virtual automaton and becomes more so as the novel progresses. Although Amis does not term Welch a ridiculous phony, the inference is inescapable.

Central to the novel's theme is Dixon's secret life of protest. Although he hates the Welch family, for economic reasons he dares not rebel openly. Therefore, he resorts to a comic fantasy world to express rage or loathing toward certain imbecilities of the Welch set. His rude faces and clever pranks serve a therapeutic function, a means by which Dixon can safely release his exasperations. At other times, however, Dixon becomes more aggressive: He fantasizes stuffing Welch down the lavatory or beating him about the head and shoulders with a bottle until he reveals why he gave a French name to his son.

In Amis's later novels, when the heroes' moral problems become more intense, even life-threatening, such aggressive acts become more frequent and less controlled. In this early novel, however, what the reader remembers best are the comic moments. Dixon is less an angry young man than a funny, bumbling, confused individual for whom a joke makes life bearable. There are, of course, other ways in which to react to an unjust world. One can flail at it, as does John Osborne's Jimmy Porter (*Look Back in Anger*, 1956). One can try to escape from it, as will Patrick Standish in *Take a Girl Like You*, or one can try to adapt to it. Like Charles Lumley's rebellion against middle-class values in John Wain's *Hurry on Down* (1953), Dixon's rebellion against the affectations of academia ends with an adjustment to the society and with a partial acceptance of its values. By remaining in the system, he can at least try to effect change.

Take a Girl Like You · Ostensibly another example of the familiar story of initiation, Amis's fourth novel, *Take a Girl Like You*, contains subtleties and ironies that set it apart from *Lucky Jim*. The characterization, the balance between the comic and the serious, and the emphasis on sexual behavior and the pursuit of pleasure blend to make this novel a significant step forward in Amis's development as a novelist.

The plot of this disturbing moral comedy is built around a variety of motifs: the travelogue and the innocent-abroad story, the theme of love-in-conflict-with-love, and the country-mouse story of an innocent girl visiting the big city for the first time. Jenny Bunn, from whose point of view more than half the novel is narrated, is the conventional, innocent young woman who has not been touched by deep experience in worldly matters. Like Jim Dixon, she finds herself in an unfamiliar setting, confronting people who treat her as a stranger with strange ideas. Out of a simpleminded zeal for the virtues of love and marriage, she becomes the victim of a plausible, nasty man.

Jenny carries out several artistic functions in the story. She is chiefly prominent as the perceptive observer of events close to her. Again like Dixon, she is able to detect fraud and incongruities from a considerable distance. When Patrick Standish first appears, for example, she understands that his look at her means he is "getting ideas about her." Amis draws a considerable fund of humor from Jenny's assumed naïveté. His chief device is the old but appropriate one of naïve comment, innocently uttered but tipped with truth. Jenny, a young girl living in a restrictive environment and ostensibly deferential toward the attitudes and opinions of the adults who compose that environment, yet also guided by her own instinctive reactions, may be expected to misinterpret a great deal of what she observes and feels. The reader follows her as she is excited, puzzled, and disturbed by Patrick's money-mad and pleasure-mad world–a world without fixed rules of conduct. Many of the "sex scenes" between them are built upon verbal jokes, comic maneuvers, digressions, and irrelevancies, all of which give life to the conventional narrative with which Amis is working.

Patrick Standish is the antithesis of the good, moral, somewhat passive Jenny. Like the masterful, selfish Bertrand Welch, he is a womanizer and a conscious hypocrite who condemns himself with every word he utters. In spite of Patrick's intolerable behavior and almost crippling faults, Amis maintains some degree of sympathy for him by granting him more than a surface treatment. In the earlier novels, the villains are seen from a distance through the heroes' eyes. In *Take a Girl Like You*, however, an interior view of the villain's thoughts, frustrations, and fears allows the reader some measure of understanding. Many scenes are rhetorically designed to emphasize Patrick's isolation and helplessness. Fears of impotence, cancer, and death haunt him. He seeks escape from these fears by turning to sex, drink, and practical jokes, but this behavior leads only to further boredom, unsatisfied longing, and ill health.

Also contributing to the somber tone of the novel are secondary characters such as Dick Thompson, Seaman Jackson, and Graham MacClintoch. Jackson equates marriage with "legalised bloody prostitution." MacClintoch complains that, for the unattractive, there is no charity in sex. Jenny's ideals are further diminished when she attends a party with these men. The conversation anticipates the emotional barrenness of later novels, in which love is dead and in its place are found endless games. Characters speak of love, marriage, and virtue in the same tone as they would speak of a cricket game or a new set of teeth.

With *Take a Girl Like You*, Amis leaves behind the hilarity and high spirits on which his reputation was founded, in order to give expression to the note of hostility and cruelty hinted at in *Lucky Jim*. Drifting steadily from bewilderment to disillusionment, Jenny and Patrick signal the beginning of a new phase in Amis's moral vision. Life is more complex, more precarious, less jovial. The simple romantic fantasy solution at the end of *Lucky Jim* is not possible here.

The Anti-Death League · *The Anti-Death League* represents for Amis yet another extension in philosophy and technique. The conventions of the spy thriller provide the necessary framework for a story within which Amis presents, from multiple viewpoints, a worldview that is more pessimistic than that of any of his previous novels. A preoccupation with fear and evil, an explicit religious frame of reference, and a juxtaposition of pain and laughter, cruelty and tenderness all go to create a sense of imminent calamity reminiscent of George Orwell's *Nineteen Eighty-Four* (1949). No longer does Amis's world allow carefree, uncomplicated figures of fun to move about, relying upon good luck and practical jokes to see them through their difficulties. Life has become an absurd game, and the players are suffering, often lonely and tragic individuals, caught in hopeless situations with little chance for winning the good life, free from anxieties, guilt, and doubts.

As the controlling image, the threat of death is introduced early in the novel in the form of an airplane shadow covering the principal characters. Related to this scene is an elaborate metaphor drawn from the language of pathology, astronomy, botany, and thermonuclear war. Part 1 of the three-part structure is entitled "The Edge of a Node"–referring to Operation Apollo, an elaborate project designed to destroy the

Red Chinese with a horrible plague. As the narrative progresses, the characters are brought to the edge or dead center of the node.

Related to this preoccupation with death is the sexual unhappiness of the characters. Jim Dixon's romps with Margaret are farcical and at times rather sad. Patrick Standish's pursuit and conquest of Jenny Bunn are disgusting and somewhat tragic. In *The Anti-Death League*, the characters' pursuit of love and sex leads only to unhappiness and even danger. Two disastrous marriages and several unhappy affairs have brought Catherine Casement to the brink of madness. An unfaithful husband and a possessive lover have caused Luzy Hazell to avoid any emotional involvement whatsoever. A desire to get away from love impels Max Hunter, an alcoholic and unabashed homosexual, to join the army.

Along with the inversion of love, Amis dramatizes an inversion of religion. In place of a benevolent, supreme being, Amis has substituted a malevolent God whose malicious jokes lead to death and tragic accidents. In protest, Will Ayscue, the army chaplain, declares war on Christianity as the embodiment of the most vicious lies ever told. Max Hunter writes a poem against God ("To a Baby Born Without Limbs"), organizes the Anti-Death League, and demolishes the local priory. James Churchill cites Max Hunter's alcoholism, the death of a courier, and Catherine's cancer as reasons for retreating from a world gone bad. While, in the preceding novels, laughter helps the heroes cope with specific injustices, in *The Anti-Death League*, laughter only intensifies the horror, the pain. Sometimes Amis shifts abruptly from laughter to pain to intensify the pain. A lighthearted moment with Hunter in the hospital is followed by a depressing scene between Catherine and Dr. Best. News of Catherine's cancer is juxtaposed with Dr. Best's highly comic hide-and-seek game.

Hysteria, depression, boredom: These are some of the moods in the army camp, bespeaking a malaise and a loss of hope from which neither sex nor religion nor drink offers any escape. Although the reader both condemns and laughs at the characters' foibles, he feels a personal involvement with them because he sees the suffering through the sufferers' eyes. Alone, trying to regain control of their lives, they act irresponsibly and immorally. Only Moti Naidu, like Gore-Urquhart, a moral voice in the novel, speaks truth in spite of the other characters' tragic mistakes. His recommendations that they aspire to common sense, fidelity, prudence, and rationality, however, go unheeded.

The Green Man · Although *The Green Man* offers the same preoccupation with God, death, and evil as *The Anti-Death League*, the novel is different from its predecessor in both feeling and technique. The work is, to begin with, a mixture of social satire, moral fable, comic tale, and ghost story. Evil appears in the figure of Dr. Thomas Underhill, a seventeenth century "wizard" who has raped young girls, created obscene visions, murdered his enemies, and now invaded the twentieth century in pursuit of the narrator's thirteen-year-old daughter. God also enters in the person of "a young, well-dressed, sort of after-shave lotion kind of man," neither omnipotent nor benevolent. For him, life is like a chess game whose rules he is tempted to break. A seduction, an orgy, an exorcism, and a monster are other features of this profoundly serious examination of dreaded death and all of its meaningless horror.

The novel is narrated retrospectively from the point of view of Maurice Allington. Like Patrick Standish and James Churchill, he spends most of his time escaping, or trying to escape, from himself, and for good reason. Death for him is a fearful mystery. Questions of ultimate justice and human destiny have been jarred loose of any religious or philosophical certainties. He suffers from "jactitations" (twitching of the limbs) as well as unpleasant and lengthy "hypnagogic hallucinations." What is more, problems with self extend to problems with his family and friends: He is unable to get along well with his wife or daughter, and his friends express doubts about his sanity. In fact, the only certainty Maurice has is that as he gets older, consciousness becomes more painful.

To dramatize Maurice's troubled mind, Amis also employs supernatural machinery as an integral part of the narrative. The windowpane through which Maurice sees Underhill becomes a metaphor for the great divide between the known, seen world of reality and the unknown, hence fearful world of the supernatural. Dr. Underhill, a *Doppelgänger*, reflects Maurice's own true nature in his selfish, insensitive manipulation of women for sexual ends. Also, Underhill's appearances provide Maurice with an opportunity to ennoble himself. In his pursuit and eventual destruction of both Underhill and the green monster, Maurice gains self-knowledge—something few of Amis's characters ever experience. He realizes his own potential for wickedness, accepts the limitations of life, and comes to an appreciation of what death has to offer as an escape from earthbound existence. For the first time in his life, Maurice recognizes and responds to the loving competence of his daughter, who looks after him when his wife leaves.

On one level, this elaborately created story is a superbly entertaining, fantastic tale. On another level, it is a powerful and moving parable of the limitations and disappointments of the human condition. Unlike *Lucky Jim* and *Take a Girl Like You*, both of which are rooted in the real world and are guided by the laws of nature, *The Green Man*—and to some extent *The Anti-Death League*—employs fantastic and surreal elements. Ravens, specters, vague midnight terrors, all associated with guilt and despair, provide fitting emblems for Maurice's self-absorbed condition.

The Old Devils · *The Old Devils* is not an easy book to read, but it is an almost irresistibly easy book to reread. It is one of Amis's densest novels, its many different characters and their stories diverging, interweaving, and dovetailing with a striking precision that requires the utmost concentration of the reader. The novel has no central hero-narrator; each of the major characters claims his (or her) own share of reader attention. Though their talks and thoughts wander from topic to topic casually, appearing aimless and undirected, actually the inner workings of the characters are carefully regulated, as are the descriptive comments by the omniscient narrator, to support, define, develop, and ultimately embody the novel's themes.

In terms of narrative, the story itself is painted in muted tones. Alun Weaver has chosen to retire from his successful television career in London as a kind of "professional Welshman" and third-rate poet and return after thirty years with his beautiful wife, Rhiannon, to South Wales. The novel explores, over a span of a few months, the effect of this return on their circle of old friends from university days. The old devils—a group of Welsh married couples all in their sixties and seventies—include Malcolm Cellan-Davies, an unsung local writer, and his wife, Gwen; Peter Thomas, a chemical engineer, and his wife, Muriel; Charlie Norris, the proprietor of a restaurant, and his wife, Sophie; Percy and Dorothy Morgan; and Garth Pumphrey, a former veterinarian who with his wife, Angharad, now attends to business at a local pub. Of the five couples, the first three have never left their hometown or accomplished anything very remarkable; their lives have passed them by. They are old now, retired from their professions, and do little else but drink heavily, a device Amis has often used to lower his characters' defenses and reveal their true emotional states. As Sophie says of her husband, "I never realised how much he drank till the night he came home sober. A revelation, it was."

The physical ill health the cronies worry about extends to the spiritual health of their marriages. With the exception of Rhiannon, her daughter Rosemary, and a few minor characters, the women in this novel not only are plain, hard, sharp, critical, or cross but also lack any reasonable relation with their husbands that would make significant communication possible. Only Alun and Rhiannon, married for thirty-four years, still seem to have an appetite for life and love as well as drink, and most of their misunderstandings lead only to teasing, not to disaster. Their arrival, however, arouses conflict among their old friends. "You know," says Muriel early in the novel, "I don't think that news about the Weavers is good news for anyone." The conflict comes in part because their return revives memories of various youthful liaisons and indiscretions, and also because the egotistical Alun immediately sets out to re-woo the three women with whom he had affairs in the old days.

Yet *The Old Devils* is about more than an aging present; it is also very much about the past and its impingements upon everyone. Many of the characters in *The Old Devils* are carrying scars from bitterness and regret because of something that happened in their lives long ago, something they hide carefully from the world, but on which their conscious attention is fixed. Past choices weigh heavily on all of them. These memories, like the memories of the aging characters in earlier novels, touch various notes, some sweet, some sour, some true, and others a bit off pitch. Indeed, these old devils are bedeviled by worries and fears of all kinds that deepen their uncertainty about life and increase their preoccupation with the past. Amis points out that one of the reasons old people make so many journeys into the past is to satisfy themselves that it is still there. When that, too, is gone, what is left? In this novel, what remains is only the sense of lost happiness not to be regained, only the awareness of the failure of love, only the present and its temporary consolations of drink, companionship, music, and any other diversions they might create, only a blind groping toward some insubstantial future. Neither human nor spiritual comfort bolsters their sagging lives and flagging souls; Malcolm speaks for all the characters, and probably for Amis himself, when he responds to a question about believing in God: "It's very hard to answer that. In a way I suppose I do. I certainly hate to see it all disappearing."

As in earlier novels, Amis finds in the everyday concerns of his ordinary folk a larger symbolic meaning, which carries beyond the characters to indict a whole country. By the end of the novel, one character after another has uncompromisingly attacked television, the media, abstract art, trendy pub decor, rude teenagers, children, shoppers, rock music, Arab ownership of shops and pubs, and anything that smacks of arty or folksy Welshness. The point, says Malcolm, sadly, is that Wales is following the trends from England and has found a way of destroying the country, "not by poverty but by prosperity." The decline and the decay, he says, are not the real problem. "We've faced that before and we've always come through." What he abominates is the specious affluence. "It's not the rubble I deplore," he says, "it's the vile crop that has sprung from it." Both extremes—decay and affluence—are suggested by the homes the characters occupy, and unhappiness characterizes either extreme. Amis's awareness of rooms, of houses, and of what they reveal about their inhabitants is a critical commonplace. Here, in each instance, the description of a character's personal environment is a means of rendering his or her appalled and irritated perception of the world.

Amis's characterization in *The Old Devils*, however, goes beyond a study of that final form of human deterioration. Rather, the novel examines an often debilitating process of moral and spiritual decay, a lessening of these people as human beings as life goes on and their hopes have dimmed along with their physical and mental powers. Perhaps Rhiannon, the most well-rounded of Amis's female characters in the novel, has kept her spiritual core more intact than any of the old devils. Without a doubt she holds a certain moral superiority over her husband in a way that is reminiscent of Jenny Bunn (in *Take a Girl Like You*), and the differences in husband and wife are played against each other. Rhiannon emerges as the voice of common sense in the novel, serene and utterly down-to-earth; Alun is condemned, by his actions and words, as a shallow, worldly, selfish man. In the end, he meets death, while Rhiannon survives and, in fact, looks ahead to future happiness. The two are unreconciled at Alun's death, no mention is made of her mourning, no homage is paid to his memory, and at the end of the novel she turns to Peter, her lover of forty years before. She finally forgives him for his long-ago abandonment, and the two begin to look forward to spending their last years together.

That event is one of two at the end of the novel that vitiate its undertone of pain, despair, and anxiety. The other positive event is the wedding of Rosemary, the Weavers' daughter, to William, the son of Peter and Muriel, suggesting the replacing of the older generation by the new, which in one sense is heralded by the author as a sign of progress and fulfillment. The reader feels that they will go on to live somewhat happy, placid lives. Despite the overriding negativism in the novel, there is some possibility of redemption. In *The Old Devils*, Amis pictures two relatively attractive people who show promise of living and working together peacefully, using their energy to make a new world instead of destroying an existing one.

The Folks That Live on the Hill · *The Folks That Live on the Hill* appeared only four years after *The Old Devils*, and while the two share certain similarities, especially the deployment of a wide, even panoramic, cast of characters, the latter novel exhibits a greater degree of acceptance of humankind's foibles. This attitude is displayed in particular by the novel's protagonist, Harry Caldecote, a retired librarian who cannot help caring about—and caring for—other people. These include a widowed sister who keeps house for him in the London suburb of Shepherd's Hill, a niece by marriage whose alcoholism is reaching catastrophic proportions, and a brother whose mediocre poetry Harry nevertheless shepherds toward publication. Providing a kind of running commentary on the novel's hapless characters are two immigrant brothers, a pair of bemused outsiders who see the follies of the "folks" all too clearly. When offered an attractive job in the United States, Harry chooses to remain where he is, partly through inertia but largely because he knows he is needed where he is. Yet Harry is recognizably an Amis character, and a distinctly male one at that. Twice-married and twice-divorced, he is largely intolerant of women, other classes, and their annoying patterns of speech.

The Russian Girl · *The Russian Girl* encapsulates many of Amis's perennial motifs and patterns, yet the gentler note sounded in *The Folks That Live on the Hill* remains. The novel's protagonist is Richard Vaisey, an opinionated professor of Russian literature and language, who is fighting to maintain the integrity of his subject in the face of academic progress. (It seems that Richard's considerable knowledge of his subject "dates" him.) Richard's wife Cordelia is perhaps the most harpy-like of all Amis's female characters, a rich, sexually attractive but wholly villainous creation noted for her absurd but attention-getting accent. The "girl" of the title is Anna Danilova, a visiting Russian poet who becomes involved with Richard. Their affair propels Richard from his comfortable, sheltered existence into a life of possibility.

Saving the novel's plot from a certain predictability is the fact that Anna, like Harry's brother Freddie in *The Folks That Live on the Hill*, is not a good poet. (To drive the point home, Amis reproduces an embarrassingly poor poem Anna has written in loving tribute to Richard.) This is a situation that Richard understands, yet ultimately chooses to accept. In turn, Anna senses Richard's true opinion of her work and accepts it as well. Although not his final novel, *The Russian Girl* represents in many ways the culmination of Amis's fictional career. More sharply focused than many of its predecessors, it forces its protagonist through very difficult moral and intellectual choices. Anna too achieves a kind of dignity because of, not despite, her very lack of talent and emerges as one of Amis's most gratifyingly complex female characters.

In retrospect, it is clear that Kingsley Amis is a moralist as well as a humorist. The early novels exhibit a richly comic sense and a considerable penetration into character, particularly in its eccentric forms. With *Take a Girl Like You*, Amis begins to produce work of more serious design. He gives much deeper and more complex pictures of disturbing and distorted people, and a more sympathetic insight into the lot of his wasted or burnt-out characters. In all of his novels, he fulfills most effectively the novelist's basic task of telling a good story. In his best novels—*Lucky Jim, Take a Girl Like You, The Anti-Death League, The Green Man, The Old Devils, The Folks That Live on the Hill*, and *The Russian Girl*—Amis tries to understand the truth about different kinds of human suffering, then passes it on to the reader without distortion, without sentimentality, without evasion, and without oversimplification. His work is based on a steadying common sense.

Dale Salwak, updated by Grove Koger

Other major works

SHORT FICTION: *My Enemy's Enemy*, 1962; *Collected Short Stories*, 1980; *We Are All Guilty*, 1991; *Mr. Barrett's Secret and Other Stories*, 1993.

POETRY: *Bright November*, 1947; *A Frame of Mind*, 1953; *A Case of Samples: Poems, 1946-1956*, 1956; *The Evans Country*, 1962; *A Look Round the Estate: Poems, 1957-1967*, 1967; *Collected Poems: 1944-1979*, 1979.

NONFICTION: *New Maps of Hell: A Survey of Science Fiction*, 1960; *The James Bond Dossier*, 1965 (with Ian Fleming); *What Became of Jane Austen? and Other Questions*, 1970; *On Drink*, 1972; *Tennyson*, 1973; *Kipling and His World*, 1975; *An Arts Policy?*, 1979; *Everyday Drinking*, 1983; *How's Your Glass?*, 1984; *Memoirs*, 1991; *The King's English: A Guide to Modern Usage*, 1997.

EDITED TEXTS: *Spectrum: A Science Fiction Anthology*, 1961, 1962, 1963, 1964, 1965 (with Robert Conquest); *Harold's Years: Impressions from the "New Statesman" and the "Spectator,"* 1977; *The Faber Popular Reciter*, 1978; *The New Oxford Book of Light Verse*, 1978; *The Golden Age of Science Fiction*, 1981; *The Great British Songbook*, 1986 (with James Cochrane); *The Amis Anthology*, 1988; *The Pleasure of Poetry: From His "Daily Mirror" Column*, 1990; *The Amis Story Anthology: A Personal Choice of Short Stories*, 1992.

Bibliography

Bradbury, Malcolm. *No, Not Bloomsbury*. London: Deutsch, 1987. Bradbury devotes a chapter to the comic fiction through *The Old Devils*, charting Amis's course from anger to bitterness. Bradbury notes Amis's moral seriousness, honesty, and humor. Includes a chronology and an index.

Bradford, Richard. *Kingsley Amis.* London: Arnold, 1989. This key study shows how Amis confounds customary distinctions between "popular" and "literary" fiction. Bradford argues that it is time to readjust the criteria for judging literary worth. Includes secondary bibliography and index.

Fussell, Paul. *The Anti-Egotist: Kingsley Amis, Man of Letters.* New York: Oxford University Press, 1994. An appreciation of Amis's versatile talents and accomplishments by a personal friend.

Gardner, Philip. *Kingsley Amis.* Boston: Twayne, 1981. This first full-length study of Amis's life and career treats his novels (through *Jake's Thing*) and nonfiction, paying particular attention to the recurrence of certain themes and character types, to his modes of comedy, and to the relationship between his life and fiction. Supplemented by a chronology, notes, selected primary and annotated secondary bibliographies, and an index.

Jacobs, Eric. *Kingsley Amis: A Biography.* New York: St. Martin's Press, 1998. A readable, sometimes painfully candid biography written with Amis's full cooperation. Includes photographs, notes, a primary bibliography, and an index. This American edition includes material that did not appear in the first (British) edition of 1995.

Laskowski, William. *Kingsley Amis.* New York: Twayne, 1998. Laskowski stresses Amis's overall accomplishment as a man of letters, divides his output into letters, genre fiction, and mainstream novels, and devotes equal consideration to each category. Published soon after Amis's death, this volume surpasses the coverage of Gardner's study (above), but does not replace it. Supplementary material is updated but otherwise similar.

McDermott, John. *Kingsley Amis: An English Moralist.* Basingstoke, England: Macmillan, 1989. This first British book-length study of Amis's work seeks to show that the novels are serious as well as funny, that they are distinctively English, and that they offer a wide range of approaches to significant aspects of human behavior. Includes substantial primary and secondary bibliographies and an index.

Mosley, Merritt. *Understanding Kingsley Amis.* Columbia: University of South Carolina Press, 1993. A short survey stressing Amis's accomplishments as a professional man of letters. Includes an annotated secondary bibliography and an index.

Salwak, Dale, ed. *Kingsley Amis: In Life and Letters.* New York: St. Martin's Press, 1990. Brings together the impressions, reminiscences, and judgments of twenty of Amis's friends and readers. The essays cover Amis's novels and poetry, his interest in science fiction, his tenures at various colleges and universities, his style, his changing social and moral attitudes, and his personality. Includes primary and secondary bibliographies, an index, and photographs.

Martin Amis

Born: Oxford, England; August 25, 1949

Principal long fiction · *The Rachel Papers*, 1973; *Dead Babies*, 1975 (also known as *Dark Secrets*, 1977); *Success*, 1978; *Other People: A Mystery Story*, 1981; *Money: A Suicide Note*, 1984; *London Fields*, 1989; *Time's Arrow: Or, The Nature of the Offence*, 1991; *The Information*, 1995; *Night Train*, 1997.

Other literary forms · *Invasion of the Space Invaders* (1982), a history of video games; *The Moronic Inferno: And Other Visits to America* (1986), a collection of journalistic pieces on America; and *Einstein's Monsters* (1987), a collection of short stories reflecting life in the shadow of nuclear weapons are among Martin Amis's other works. He also produced *Visiting Mrs. Nabokov and Other Excursions* (1993), essays on literature, politics, sports, and popular culture; *Heavy Water and Other Stories* (1998), another collection of short stories; and the nonfiction *Experience* (2000).

Achievements · Martin Amis has been a force on the modern literary scene since his first novel, *The Rachel Papers*, won the Somerset Maugham Award for 1974. Critical and popular acclaim accompanied his sixth novel, *London Fields*, which was a bestseller on both sides of the Atlantic. Amis has a powerfully comic and satiric vision of the ills of contemporary society, which he caricatures in a way that has reminded many reviewers of Charles Dickens. Amis spares his reader little in his depiction of low-life characters in all their physical grossness and emotional aridity. The emptiness and corruption inherent in a materialistic culture are recurring themes of his work. Yet in spite of the often-sordid subject matter, Amis's novels are illuminated by their stylistic exuberance and ingenuity. More than one critic has remarked on the American flavor of his work, and he is regularly compared to Tom Wolfe and Saul Bellow.

Biography · The son of the novelist Kingsley Amis, Martin Amis spent his early years in Swansea, in south Wales, where his father held a teaching position at Swansea University. The family spent a year in Princeton, New Jersey, in 1959, and then moved to Cambridge, England. Amis's parents were divorced when Amis was twelve, and this had a disruptive effect on his schooling: He attended a total of fourteen schools in six years. As a teenager he had a brief acting career, appearing in the film *A High Wind in Jamaica* (1965). In 1968 he entered Exeter College, Oxford, and graduated in 1971 with first-class honors in English. He immediately became editorial assistant for *The Times Literary Supplement* and began writing his first novel, *The Rachel Papers*. In 1975 Amis became assistant literary editor of the *New Statesman*, and his second novel, *Dead Babies*, was published in the same year.

In 1980, when Amis was a writer and reviewer for the London newspaper *The Observer*, he reported his discovery that the American writer Jacob Epstein had plagiarized as many as fifty passages from *The Rachel Papers* for his own novel *Wild Oats* (1979). The accusation created a storm in the literary world. Epstein quickly conceded that he had indeed copied passages from Amis's novel and others into a notebook which he had then inadvertently used for his own novel. Thirteen deletions

Cheryl A. Koralik

were made for the second American edition of Epstein's book, but Amis was infuriated because he thought that the revisions were not sufficiently extensive.

Martin Amis married Antonia Phillips, an American professor of aesthetics, in 1984, and they had two sons, Louis and Jacob. The controversy that has often accompanied Amis's writings spilled over into his private life from 1994 to 1996. First, he left his wife for American writer Isabel Fonseca. Then Amis fired his agent, Pat Kavanagh, when Kavanagh was unable to obtain a large advance from his publisher, Jonathan Cape, for his next novel, *The Information*. His new agent, the American Andrew Wylie, eventually made a deal with Harper-Collins, and the whole proceedings were reported in the British press with an intensity rarely given literary figures such as Amis. The controversy was compounded by the report that Amis spent part of his new earnings for extensive dental work in the United States. In 1996 it was revealed that he was the father of a twenty-year-old daughter from a 1975 affair. In 1999 he agreed to write three books and a screenplay for the multimedia company Talk Miramax.

Analysis · Martin Amis remarked in an interview that he wrote about "low events in a high style," and this comment gives a clue to the paradox his work embodies. Although the content of his novels is frequently sordid and nihilistic—dictated by the depressing absence in his characters of traditional cultural values—Amis's rich, ornate, and continually inventive style lifts the novels to a level from which they give delight. "I would certainly sacrifice any psychological or realistic truth for a phrase, for a paragraph that has a spin on it," Amis has commented. The result is that Amis's novels, in spite of the fact that they are often uproariously hilarious, do not make easy or quick reading. Indeed, Kingsley Amis has remarked that he is unable to get through his son's novels because of their ornate style, which he attributes to the influence of Vladimir Nabokov.

The Rachel Papers · Amis's first novel, *The Rachel Papers*, set the tone for most of his subsequent work, although his later novels, beginning with *Money*, have exhibited greater depth and range, as the force of his satire—his immense comic hyperbole—has steadily increased. Furthermore, one senses a sharp moral awareness in *Money* and *London Fields*, although Amis chooses not to offer any solutions to the individual and social ills he identifies so acutely.

The Rachel Papers is a lively but fairly innocuous satire about the turbulent adolescence of Charles Highway, the first-person narrator. Highway is a rather obnoxious young man, a self-absorbed intellectual studying for his Oxford examinations and aspiring to become a literary critic. The action takes place the evening before Highway's twentieth birthday and is filled out by extensive flashbacks. A substantial portion of Highway's intellectual and physical energy is devoted to getting his girlfriend Rachel into bed and to writing in his diary detailed descriptions of everything that happens when he succeeds. Amis's hilarious and seemingly infinitely inventive wordplay is never more effectively displayed than when Highway is describing his sexual adventures.

Dead Babies · *Dead Babies*, which chronicles the weekend debaucheries of a group of nine privileged young people, is considerably less successful than Amis's first novel, and Amis has since declared his own dislike for it. The theme seems to be a warning about what happens when traditional values (the dead babies of the title) are discarded. For the most part, however, the characters are too repulsive, and their indulgence in drugs, sex, alcohol, and violence too excessive, for the reader to care much about their fate.

Success · In *Success*, Amis chronicles a year in the lives of two contrasting characters. The handsome and conceited Gregory comes from an aristocratic family and appears to have all the worldly success anyone could want. He shares a flat in London with his foster brother Terry, who from every perspective is Gregory's opposite. Terry comes from the slums, he is physically unattractive and has low self-esteem, and he is stuck in a boring job which he is afraid of losing. The two characters take turns narrating the same events, which they naturally interpret very differently. As the year progresses, there is a change. Gregory is gradually forced to admit that his success is little more than an illusion. He has been fooling himself most of the time, and realization of his true ineptitude and childlike vulnerability causes him to go to pieces. Meanwhile, Terry's grim persistence finally pays off: He makes money, loses his self-hatred, and finally acquires a respectable girlfriend. For all of his crudity and loutishness, he is more in tune with the tough spirit of the times, in which traditional values are no longer seen to be of any value, and those who in theory represent them (like Gregory) have become effete.

Success is a clear indication of Amis's pessimism about life in London in the 1970's. Frequently employing extremely coarse language, the novel depicts some of the least attractive sides of human nature, and although this grimness is relieved (as in almost all Amis's books) by some ribald humor, on the whole *Success* is a depressing and superficial book. Indeed, it had to wait nine years after publication in Great Britain before an American publisher would take it on.

Other People · In Amis's fourth novel, *Other People: A Mystery Story*, he appears to have been trying to write something with more philosophical and existential depth than the satires that came before. This time the protagonist is a young woman, who suffers from total amnesia. Released from hospital, she wanders alone through alien city streets, viewing other people as a separate species and virtually unable to distinguish between animate and inanimate things. Taking the name Mary Lamb, she experiences life in complete innocence, having to relearn everything that being alive involves: not only who she is but also the purpose of everyday things such as shoes and money. She mixes with a range of people from drunks and down-and-outs to upper-class degenerates, at the same time edging closer to a discovery of her real identity. It transpires that her real name is Amy Hide and that everyone thinks that she was killed after being brutally attacked by a man. Adding to the surreal atmosphere of the novel is a mysterious character called Prince, whom Mary/Amy keeps encountering. Prince seems to fulfill many roles: He is a policeman, perhaps also the man who attacked her, and a kind of tutelary spirit, an awakener, under whose guidance she discovers her own identity.

Other People was written according to what is known in Great Britain as the Martian school of poetry, a point of view in which no knowledge about human life and society is assumed. This technique is intended to allow the most mundane things to be examined in a fresh light. Although Amis achieves some success in this area, the novel is spoiled by excessive obscurity. The novelist has simply not left enough clues to his intention, and the reader is left to grasp at bits of a puzzle without being able to construct an intelligible whole. Realizing that few people had grasped his meaning, Amis explained in an interview what his intention had been:

> Why should we expect death to be any less complicated than life? Nothing about life suggests that death will just be a silence. Life is very witty and cruel and pointed, and let us suppose that death is like that too. The novel is the girl's death, and her death is a sort of witty parody of her life.

This may not be of much help to readers who are especially puzzled by the novel's concluding pages. Perhaps the most rewarding parts of the novel are Amis's depictions of the characters Mary encounters; their physical and mental deformities are captured with merciless wit.

Money · In *Money: A Suicide Note*, Amis continued to devote attention to what he undoubtedly depicts best: people who have been deformed, who have failed to reach their full human growth, by the shallow materialism of the age. Yet the scope of *Money* is far wider and more impressive than anything Amis had produced before: Not only is it much longer, but it also fairly rocks with vulgar energy. Clearly, Amis has finished his writing apprenticeship and is moving into top gear.

The protagonist is John Self, a wealthy, early-middle-aged maker of television commercials who is visiting New York to direct what he hopes will be his first big motion picture. Yet the project runs into every difficulty imaginable, and after a series of humiliating experiences Self ends up back in London with nothing. The problem with Self is that although he is wealthy, he is uneducated and lacks all culture. He lives at a fast pace but spends his money and his time entirely on worthless things—junk food, alcohol, pornography, television. Satisfying pleasures continually elude him. Amis himself has commented on Self: "The world of culture is there as a sort of taunting presence in his life, and he wants it but he doesn't know how to get it, and all his responses are being blunted by living in the money world."

London Fields · Amis's attack on the "money world" continues in *London Fields*, although Amis's finest novel is far more than that. It is at once a comic murder-mystery and a wonderfully rich and varied evocation of the decline of civilization at the end of the millennium. Many of the comic scenes are worthy of Charles Dickens, and the plot is acted out against a cosmic, apocalyptic background, as the planet itself seems to be on the brink of disintegration.

Set in post-Thatcherite London in 1999, the plot centers on three main characters.

The first is the antiheroine Nicola Six. Nicola has a gift for seeing the future, and she has a premonition that on her next birthday, which happens to be her thirty-fifth, she will be murdered by one of two men she meets at a London pub called the Black Cross. She sets out to avenge herself in advance by using her sexual power to entice them and draw them to ruin. Nicola is a temptress of the first magnitude, and Amis employs comic hyperbole (as he does throughout the novel) to describe her: "Family men abandoned sick children to wait in the rain outside her flat. Semi-literate builders and bankers sent her sonnet sequences."

The second character, the possible murderer, is Keith Talent. Talent is probably Amis's finest creation, a larger-than-life character who might have stepped out of the pages of Dickens. He is a petty criminal, compulsive adulterer, wife-beater, and darts fanatic. He makes a living by cheating people, whether it be by selling fake perfume, running an outrageously expensive taxi service, or doing botched household repair jobs. He earns more money than the prime minister but never has any, because he loses it each day at the betting shop. Keith is not totally bad but wishes that he were: He regards his redeeming qualities as his tragic flaw. Obsessed with darts and television (which for him is the real world), his driving ambition is to reach the televised finals of an interpub darts competition. The miracle of the novel is that Amis has succeeded, as with John Self in *Money*, in making such a pathetic character almost likable.

The second possible murderer is Guy Clinch. Clinch is quite different from Keith Talent. He is a rich, upper-class innocent "who wanted for nothing and lacked everything." One of the things he lacks is a peaceful home life, after his wife, Hope, gives birth to Marmaduke, a ferocious infant who almost from birth is capable of acts of quite stunning malice and violence. (The only nurses who can cope with him are those who have been fired from lunatic asylums.) Once more the comedy is irresistible.

The convoluted plot, with its surprise ending, is narrated by a terminally ill American writer named Samson Young, who is in London on a house swap with the famous writer Mark Asprey. That the absent Asprey's initials are the same as those of Martin Amis is perhaps no coincidence. Young is in a sense the author's proxy, since he is himself gathering the material and writing the story of *London Fields* for an American publisher. To make matters even more subtle, a character named Martin Amis also makes an appearance in the novel, just as there had been a Martin Amis character in *Money*. Deconstructing his own fictions in this manner, Amis reminds the reader that in the manipulative world he depicts, he himself is the chief manipulator, but his own novel is only one fiction in a world of fictions.

The setting of *London Fields* is integral to the plot. The London of the near "future" (which 1999 was at the time of the novel's publication in 1989) possesses an oppressive, almost Blakean apocalyptic atmosphere. Not only has urban prosperity evaporated—parts of the city have sunk back into squalor—but the natural environment is in rapid decay also. Everyone is talking about the weather, but it is no longer simply small talk. Weather patterns are violently unstable; the sun seems to hang perpetually low in the sky, and rumors of impending cosmic catastrophe abound. The threat of a nuclear holocaust remains. When Nicola Six was a child, she invented two imaginary companions and called them Enola Gay and Little Boy. Enola Gay is the name of the airplane that dropped the first atom bomb, nicknamed Little Boy, on Hiroshima in 1945. Yet Samson Young, the narrator, calls nuclear weapons "dinosaurs" when compared to the environmental disasters that now threaten the earth. Eventually

Young refers to the situation simply as "The Crisis," a term that also well describes the human world that Amis ruthlessly exposes, in which love, decency, and genuine feeling have been superseded by violence, greed, and lust. Microcosm and macrocosm are joined in a kind of horrible, frenzied dance of death. The world of *London Fields*, in which people and planet hurtle helplessly toward disaster, is where all Amis's fiction has been leading.

Time's Arrow · *Time's Arrow* is an unusual departure for Amis. Not only does this most contemporary of writers deal with the past, but he also does so with a less realistic and more overtly moralistic approach than in his other novels. A Nazi doctor's life is told in reverse order from his death in the United States to his birth in Germany, though his true identity is not apparent until more than half of the way through the narrative. While many of Amis's narrators may not be completely reliable, the narrator of *Time's Arrow* is relatively innocent. The physician's reverse life is told by his alter ego, who stands outside the action until finally merging with the protagonist near the end.

Time's Arrow also deals with the question of identity in the twentieth century, as Tod Friendly progresses from an elderly, rather anonymous man into a Massachusetts physician; into another physician, this time in New York City, named John Young; into an exile in Portugal named Hamilton de Souza; into his true identity as Odilo Unverdorben, a concentration-camp doctor and protégé of the ominous Auschwitz monster he calls Uncle Pepi. In telling Friendly's increasingly complicated tale, Amis tries to encompass much of the history of the twentieth century, with particular attention to the Vietnam War era and the Cold War.

By telling the story backward, Amis also explores such themes as the banality of human communication, exemplified by conversations appearing with the sentences in reverse order: answers coming before questions. Amis gets considerable comic mileage out of the horrifying images of such acts as eating and excreting depicted backward. In this ironic, perverse universe, suffering brings about joy. The narrator, one of several Amis *Doppelgängers*, is alternately irritated and disgusted by Friendly's behavior, particularly his crude treatment of his longtime American lover, Irene. The narrator also professes his affection for and admiration of Jews before finally admitting that he and Unverdorben are one, a highly ironic means of accepting responsibility for one's actions.

Many critics have dismissed *Time's Arrow* as a narrative stunt. In an afterword, Amis acknowledges that other writers have also employed reverse narratives, mentioning the famous account of a bomb traveling backward to its origins underground in *Slaughterhouse-Five* (1969) by Kurt Vonnegut, Jr., as a particular influence. *Time's Arrow* is most notable for presenting less subtly Amis's moral concerns, which have often been compared to those of Saul Bellow.

The Information · With *The Information*, Amis returns to more typical themes. Two writers, best friends, are contrasted by their success, fame, and sex lives. Richard Tull, author of two little-read novels, edits *The Little Magazine*, a minor literary journal, serves as director of a vanity press, and writes reviews of biographies of minor writers. Gwyn Barry, on the other hand, has published a best-seller and is a major media figure. Married, with twin sons, Richard lusts after Lady Demeter, Gwyn's glamorous wife. Richard is not jealous of Gwyn's success so much as resentful that Gwyn's book is so universally beloved when it is completely without literary merit, an assessment with which both their wives agree. All of Richard's plans for revenge backfire, including hiring Steve Cousins, a mysterious criminal known as "Scozzy," to assault Gwyn.

In addition to addressing his usual topics—sex, violence, greed, and chaos—Amis presents a satirical view of literary infighting and pretensions. Richard creates primarily because of his need for love and attention. He perceives the world as an artist would, but he is unable to transform his vision into accessible literature: When editors read his latest effort, they become ill. Only the psychotic Scozzy seems to understand what he is trying to say. Richard cannot give up writing, however, because then he would be left with nothing but the tedium of everyday life. Gwyn is equally ridiculous. Obsessed by his fame, he reads newspaper and magazine articles about all subjects in hopes of seeing his name. The two writers are like a comic pair of mismatched twins.

The Information is also a typical Amis work in that it is highly self-conscious. The narrator who explains the warped workings of Scozzy's mind makes occasional appearances, first as "I," then as "M. A.," and finally as "Mart," yet another of Amis's cameo roles in his fiction. The narrator seems, as when he tries to explain that he cannot control Scozzy, to call attention to the artifice of the novel and to force the reader, as a willing participant in this satire, to share responsibility for the world's chaos.

Although some feminists have reservations about Amis's work (and it is true that most of his male characters treat their women with contempt), he is a formidable and critically acclaimed writer, certainly one of the most accomplished of the generation of English writers who came of age in the 1970's. Few others could have attempted a work on the scale of *London Fields*. Together with Salman Rushdie, Julian Barnes, and Peter Ackroyd—in their different ways—Amis has broken through the neat, middle-class boundaries of much contemporary English fiction and reached out toward a fiction that is more challenging and comprehensive in its scope.

Bryan Aubrey, updated by Michael Adams

Other major works
  NONFICTION: *Invasion of the Space Invaders*, 1982; *The Moronic Inferno: And Other Visits to America*, 1986; *Visiting Mrs. Nabokov and Other Excursions*, 1993; *Experience*, 2000.
  SHORT FICTION: *Einstein's Monsters*, 1987; *Heavy Water and Other Stories*, 1998.

Bibliography
Alexander, Victoria N. "Martin Amis: Between the Influences of Bellow and Nabokov." *Antioch Review* 52 (Fall, 1994): 580-590. Traces the influence of Saul Bellow and Vladimir Nabokov on Amis, showing how Amis's style represents a hybrid of Bellow's passion and Nabokov's coolness. Like his mentors, Amis is concerned with the decline of Western civilization.
Diedrick, James. *Understanding Martin Amis*. Columbia: University of South Carolina Press, 1995. The first book-length study of Amis examines his works through *The Information*. Argues that Amis's bad-boy image results from his challenging the genteel tradition dominating contemporary British fiction.
Finney, Brian. "Narrative and Narrated Homicides in Martin Amis's *Other People* and *London Fields*." Critique 37 (Fall, 1995): 3-15. Argues that in these two novels, by using manipulative, self-conscious narrators who victimize the other characters, Amis forces his readers to recognize how the characters are immersed both in and outside of the action.

Marowski, Daniel G., ed. *Contemporary Literary Criticism.* Vol. 38. Detroit, Mich.: Gale Research, 1986. Includes a summary of Amis's work and achievements up to *Money*, as well as extensive extracts from reviews of *Dead Babies, Success, Other People*, and *Money*, from both Great Britain and the United States. Volume 4 (1975) and volume 9 (1978) in the same series also have sections on Amis.

Moyle, David. "Beyond the Black Hole: The Emergence of Science Fiction Themes in the Recent Work of Martin Amis." *Extrapolation* 36 (Winter, 1995): 305-315. Shows how Amis adapts traditional science-fiction themes, such as time travel, concern about the end of the world, and a Doctor Frankenstein-like lack of regard for conventional morality, in *Time's Arrow* and *London Fields*.

Stout, Mira. "Martin Amis: Down London's Mean Streets." *The New York Times Magazine*, February 4, 1990, 32. A lively feature article, in which Amis, prodded by Stout, discusses a range of topics, including *London Fields*, his interest in the environment, his early life and career, his relationship with his father, the state of the novel as a form, the Thatcher government, middle age, and his daily work routine.

Jane Austen

Born: Steventon, England; December 16, 1775
Died: Winchester, England; July 18, 1817

Principal long fiction · *Sense and Sensibility*, 1811; *Pride and Prejudice*, 1813; *Mansfield Park*, 1814; *Emma*, 1815; *Northanger Abbey*, 1818; *Persuasion*, 1818; *Sanditon*, 1871 (fragment); *The Watsons*, 1871 (fragment).

Other literary forms · In addition to writing novels, Jane Austen was the author of various short juvenile pieces, most of them literary burlesques mocking the conventions of the eighteenth century novel. Her other works are *Lady Susan*, a story told in letters and written c. 1805; *The Watsons*, a fragment of a novel written about the same time; and *Sanditon*, another fragmentary novel begun in 1817 (all appended by J. E. Austen-Leigh to his 1871 *Memoir of Jane Austen*). All these pieces appear in *Minor Works* (vol. 6 of the *Oxford Illustrated Jane Austen*, 1954, R. W. Chapman, editor). Jane Austen's surviving letters have also been edited and published by Chapman.

Achievements · Austen, who published her novels anonymously, was not a writer famous in her time, nor did she wish to be. From the first, though, her novels written in and largely for her own family circle, gained the notice and esteem of a wider audience. Among her early admirers were the Prince Regent and the foremost novelist of the day, Sir Walter Scott, who deprecated his own aptitude for the "big Bow-Wow" and praised her as possessing a "talent for describing the involvements and feelings and characters of ordinary life which is to me the most wonderful I ever met with." Since the days of Scott's somewhat prescient praise, her reputation has steadily grown. The critical consensus now places Jane Austen in what F. R. Leavis has termed the "Great Tradition" of the English novel. Her talent was the first to forge, from the eighteenth century novel of external incident and internal sensibility, an art form that fully and faithfully presented a vision of real life in a particular segment of the real world. Austen's particular excellences–the elegant economy of her prose, the strength and delicacy of her judgment and moral discrimination, the subtlety of her wit, the imaginative vividness of her character drawing–have been emulated but not surpassed by subsequent writers.

Biography · Jane Austen's life contained little in the way of outward event. Born in 1775, she was the seventh of eight children. Her father, the Reverend George Austen, was a scholarly clergyman, the rector of Steventon in rural Hampshire, England. Mrs. Austen shared her husband's intelligence and intellectual interests, and the home they provided for their children was a happy and comfortable one, replete with the pleasures of country life, genteel society, perpetual reading, and lively discussion of ideas serious and frivolous. Jane Austen, who never married, was devoted throughout her life to her brothers and their families, but her closest relationship was with her older sister Cassandra, who likewise remained unmarried and whom Austen relied upon as her chief critic, cherished as a confidante, and admired as the ideal of feminine virtue.

On the rector's retirement in 1801, Austen moved with her parents and Cassandra to Bath. After the Reverend George Austen's death in 1804, the women continued to live for some time in that city. In 1806, the Austens moved to Southampton, where they shared a house with Captain Francis Austen, Jane's older brother, and his wife. In 1808, Edward Austen (who later adopted the surname Knight from the relations whose two estates he inherited) provided his mother and sisters with a permanent residence, Chawton Cottage, in the Hampshire village of the same name. At this house, Austen was to revise her manuscripts that became *Sense and Sensibility, Pride and Prejudice,* and *Northanger Abbey* and to write *Mansfield Park, Emma,* and *Persuasion.* In 1817, it became evident that she was ill with a serious complaint whose symptoms seem to have been those of Addison's disease. To be near medical help, she and Cassandra moved to lodgings in Winchester in May, 1817. Austen died there less than two months later.

Analysis · Jane Austen's novels—her "bits of ivory," as she modestly and perhaps half-playfully termed them—are unrivaled for their success in combining two sorts of excellence that all too seldom coexist. Meticulously conscious of her artistry (as, for example, is Henry James), Austen is also unremittingly attentive to the realities of ordinary human existence (as is, among others, Anthony Trollope). From the first, her works unite subtlety and common sense, good humor and acute moral judgment, charm and conciseness, deftly marshaled incident and carefully rounded character.

Austen's detractors have spoken of her as a "limited" novelist, one who, writing in an age of great men and important events, portrays small towns and petty concerns, who knows (or reveals) nothing of masculine occupations and ideas, and who reduces the range of feminine thought and deed to matrimonial scheming and social pleasantry. Though one merit of the first-rate novelist is the way his or her talent transmutes all it touches and thereby creates a distinctive and consistent world, it is true that the settings, characters, events, and ideas of Austen's novels are more than usually homogeneous. Her tales, like her own life, are set in country villages and at rural seats, from which the denizens venture forth to watering places or travel to London. True, her characters tend to be members of her own order, that prosperous and courteous segment of the middle class called the gentry. Unlike her novel-writing peers, Austen introduced few aristocrats into the pages of her novels, and the lower ranks, though glimpsed from time to time, are never brought forward. The happenings of her novels would not have been newsworthy in her day. She depicts society at leisure rather than on the march, and in portraying pleasures her literary preference is modest: Architectural improvement involves the remodeling of a parsonage rather than the construction of Carlton House Terrace and Regent's Park; a ball is a gathering of country neighbors dancing to a harpsichord, not a crush at Almack's or the Duchess of Richmond's glittering fête on the eve of Waterloo.

These limitations are the self-drawn boundaries of a strong mind rather than the innate restrictions of a weak or parochial one. Austen was in a position to know a broad band of social classes, from the local lord of the manor to the retired laborer subsisting on the charity of the parish. Some aspects of life that she did not herself experience she could learn about firsthand without leaving the family circle. Her brothers could tell her of the university, the navy in the age of Horatio Nelson, or the world of finance and fashion in Regency London. Her cousin (and later sister-in-law) Eliza, who had lost her first husband, the Comte de Feuillide, to the guillotine, could tell her of Paris during the last days of the old regime. In focusing on the manners and morals of rural middle-class English life, particularly on the ordering dance of matrimony that gives shape to society and situation to young ladies, Austen emphasizes rather than evades reality. The microcosm she depicts is convincing because she understands, though seldom explicitly assesses, its connections to the larger order. Her characters have clear social positions but are not just social types; the genius of such comic creations as Mrs. Bennet, Mr. Woodhouse, and Miss Bates is that each is a sparkling refinement on a quality or set of qualities existing at all times and on all levels. A proof of Austen's power (no one questions her polish) is that she succeeds in making whole communities live in the reader's imagination with little recourse to the stock device of the mere novelist of manners: descriptive detail. If a sparely drawn likeness is to convince, every line must count. The artist must understand what is omitted as well as what is supplied.

The six novels that constitute the Austen canon did not evolve in a straightforward way. Austen was, memoirs relate, as mistrustful of her judgment as she was rapid in her composition. In the case of *Pride and Prejudice*, for example, readers can be grateful that when the Reverend George Austen's letter offering the book's first incarnation, *First Impressions* (1797), to a publisher met with a negative reply, she was content to put the book aside for more than a decade. *Sense and Sensibility* was likewise a revision of a much earlier work. If Austen was notably nonchalant about the process of getting her literary progeny into print, one publisher with whom she had dealings was yet more dilatory. In 1803, Austen had completed *Northanger Abbey* (then entitled *Susan*) and, through her brother Henry's agency, had sold it to Crosby and Sons for ten pounds. Having acquired the manuscript, the publisher did not think fit to make use of it, and in December, 1816, Henry Austen repurchased the novel. He made known the author's identity, so family tradition has it, only after closing the deal. For these various reasons the chronology of Austen's novels can be set in different ways. Here, they will be discussed in order of their dates of publication.

Sense and Sensibility · *Sense and Sensibility*, Austen's first published novel, evolved from *Elinor and Marianne*, an epistolary work completed between 1795 and 1797. The novel is generally considered her weakest, largely because, as Walton Litz convincingly argues, it strives but fails to resolve "that struggle between inherited form and fresh experience which so often marks the transitional works of a great artist." The "inherited form" of which Litz speaks is the eighteenth century antithetical pattern suggested in the novel's title. According to this formula, opposing qualities of temperament or mind are presented in characters (generally female, often sisters) who despite their great differences are sincerely attached to one another.

In *Sense and Sensibility*, the antithetical characters are Elinor and Marianne Dashwood, the respective embodiments of cool, collected sense and prodigal, exquisite sensibility. In the company of their mother and younger sister, these lovely young ladies have, on the death of their father and the succession to his estate of their half brother, retired in very modest circumstances to a small house in Devonshire. There the imprudent Marianne meets and melts for Willoughby, a fashionable gentleman as charming as he is unscrupulous. Having engaged the rash girl's affections, Willoughby proceeds to trifle with them by bolting for London. When chance once again brings the Dashwood sisters into Willoughby's circle, his manner toward Marianne is greatly altered. On hearing of his engagement to an heiress, the representative of sensibility swoons, weeps, and exhibits her grief to the utmost.

Meanwhile, the reasonable Elinor has been equally unlucky in love, though she bears her disappointment quite differently. Before the family's move to Devonshire, Elinor had met and come to cherish fond feelings for her sister-in-law's brother Edward Ferrars, a rather tame fellow (at least in comparison with Willoughby) who returns her regard—but with a measure of unease. It soon becomes known that Ferrars's reluctance to press his suit with Elinor stems from an early and injudicious secret engagement he had contracted with shrewd, base Lucy Steele. Elinor highmindedly conceals her knowledge of the engagement and her feelings on the matter. Mrs. Ferrars, however, is a lady of less impressive self-control; she furiously disinherits her elder son in favor of his younger brother, whom Lucy then proceeds to ensnare. Thus Edward, free and provided with a small church living that will suffice to support a sensible sort of wife, can marry Elinor. Marianne—perhaps because she has finally exhausted her fancies and discovered her latent reason, perhaps because her creator is determined to punish the sensibility that throughout the novel has been so much more attractive than Elinor's prudence—is also provided with a husband: the rich Colonel Brandon, who has long loved her but whom, on account of his flannel waistcoats and his advanced age of five-and-thirty, she has heretofore reckoned beyond the pale.

The great flaw of *Sense and Sensibility* is that the polarities presented in the persons of Elinor and Marianne are too genuinely antithetical to be plausible or dynamic portraits of human beings. Elinor has strong feelings, securely managed though they may be, and Marianne has some rational powers to supplement her overactive imagination and emotions, but the young ladies do not often show themselves to be more than mere embodiments of sense and sensibility. In her second published novel, *Pride and Prejudice*, Austen makes defter use of two sisters whose values are the same but whose minds and hearts function differently. This book, a complete revision of *First Impressions*, the youthful effort that had, in 1797, been offered to and summarily rejected by the publisher Cadell, is, as numerous critics have observed, a paragon of "classic" literature in which the conventions and traditions of the eighteenth century novel come to full flowering yet are freshened and transformed by Austen's distinctive genius.

Pride and Prejudice · The title *Pride and Prejudice*, with its balanced alliterative abstractions, might suggest a second experiment in schematic psychology, and indeed the book does show some resemblances to *Sense and Sensibility*. Here again, as has been suggested, the reader encounters a pair of sisters, the elder (Jane Bennet) serene, the younger (Elizabeth) volatile. Unlike the Dashwoods, however, these ladies both demonstrate deep feelings and perceptive minds. The qualities alluded to in the title refer not to a contrast between sisters but to double defects shared by Elizabeth and Fitzwilliam Darcy, a wealthy and well-born young man she meets when his easygoing friend Charles Bingley leases Netherfield, the estate next to the Bennets' Longbourn. If so rich and vital a comic masterpiece could be reduced to a formula, it might be appropriate to say that the main thread of *Pride and Prejudice* involves the twin correction of these faults. As Darcy learns to moderate his tradition-based view of society and to recognize individual excellence (such as Elizabeth's, Jane's, and their Aunt and Uncle Gardiner's) in ranks below his own, Elizabeth becomes less dogmatic in her judgments, and in particular more aware of the real merits of Darcy, whom she initially dismisses as a haughty, unfeeling aristocrat.

The growing accord of Elizabeth and Darcy is one of the most perfectly satisfying courtships in English literature. Their persons, minds, tastes, and even phrases convince the reader that they are two people truly made for each other; their union confers fitness on the world around them. Lionel Trilling has observed that, because of this principal match, *Pride and Prejudice* "permits us to conceive of morality as style." Elizabeth and Darcy's slow-growing love may be *Pride and Prejudice*'s ideal alliance, but it is far from being the only one, and a host of finely drawn characters surround the heroine and hero. In Jane Bennet and Charles Bingley, whose early mutual attraction is temporarily suspended by Darcy and the Bingley sisters (who deplore, not without some cause, the vulgarity of the amiable Jane's family), Austen presents a less sparkling but eminently pleasing and well-matched pair. William Collins, the half-pompous, half-obsequious, totally asinine cousin who, because of an entail, will inherit Longbourn and displace the Bennet females after Mr. Bennet's demise, aspires to marry Elizabeth, but, when rejected, gains the hand of her plain and practical friend Charlotte Lucas. Aware of her suitor's absurdities, Charlotte is nevertheless alive to the advantages of the situation he can offer. Her calculated decision to marry gives a graver ring to the irony of the novel's famous opening sentence: "It is a truth universally acknowledged, that a single man in possession of a good fortune, must be in want of a wife." The last of the matches made in *Pride and Prejudice* is yet more precariously based. A lively, charming, and amoral young officer, George Wickham, son of the former steward of Pemberley, Darcy's estate, and source of many of Elizabeth's prejudices against that scrupulous gentleman, first fascinates Elizabeth, then elopes with her youngest sister, mindless, frivolous Lydia. Only through Darcy's personal and financial intervention is Wickham persuaded to marry the ill-bred girl, who never properly understands her disgrace—a folly she shares with her mother. Mrs. Bennet, a woman deficient in good humor and good sense, is—along with her cynical, capricious husband—the ponderous Collins, and the tyrannical Lady Catherine De Bourgh, one of the great comic creations of literature. Most of these characters could have seemed odious if sketched by another pen, but so brilliant is the sunny intelligence playing over the world of *Pride and Prejudice* that even fools are golden.

Mansfield Park · *Mansfield Park*, begun in 1811 and finished in 1813, is the first of Austen's novels to be a complete product of her maturity. The longest, most didactic, least ironic of her books, it is the one critics generally have the most trouble reconciling with their prevailing ideas of the author. Although *Mansfield Park* was composed more or less at one stretch, its conception coincided with the final revisions of *Pride and Prejudice*. Indeed, the critics who offer the most satisfying studies of *Mansfield Park* tend to see it not as a piece of authorial bad faith or self-suppression, a temporary anomaly, but as what Walton Litz calls a "counter-truth" to its immediate predecessor.

Pleased with and proud of *Pride and Prejudice*, Austen nevertheless recorded her impression of its being "rather too light, and bright, and sparkling"–in need of shade. That darkness she found wanting is supplied in *Mansfield Park*, which offers, as Trilling observes in his well-known essay on the novel, the antithesis to *Pride and Prejudice*'s generous, humorous, spirited social vision. *Mansfield Park*, Trilling argues, condemns rather than forgives: "its praise is not for social freedom but for social stasis. It takes full notice of spiritedness, vivacity, celerity, and lightness, only to reject them as having nothing to do with virtue and happiness, as being, indeed, deterrents to the good life."

Most of the action of *Mansfield Park* is set within the little world comprising the estate of that name, a country place resembling in large measure Godmersham, Edward Austen Knight's estate in Kent; but for her heroine and some interludes in which she figures, Austen dips into a milieu she has not previously frequented in her novels–the socially and financially precarious lower fringe of the middle class. Fanny Price, a frail, serious, modest girl, is one of nine children belonging to and inadequately supported by a feckless officer of marines and his lazy, self-centered wife. Mrs. Price's meddling sister, the widowed Mrs. Norris, arranges for Fanny to be reared in "poor relation" status at Mansfield Park, the seat of kindly but crusty Sir Thomas Bertram and his languid lady, the third of the sisters. At first awed by the splendor of her surroundings, the gruffness of the baronet, and the elegance, vigor, and high spirits of the young Bertrams–Tom, Edmund, Maria, and Julia–Fanny eventually wins a valued place in the household. During Sir Thomas's absence to visit his property in Antigua, evidence of Fanny's moral fineness, and the various degrees in which her cousins fall short of her excellence, is presented through a device that proves to be one of Austen's most brilliant triumphs of plotting. Visiting the rectory at Mansfield are the younger brother and sister of the rector's wife, Henry and Mary Crawford, witty, worldly, and wealthy. At Mary's proposal, amateur theatricals are introduced to Mansfield Park, and in the process of this diversion the moral pollution of London's Great World begins to corrupt the bracing country air.

Just how the staging of a play–even though it be *Lovers' Vows*, a sloppy piece of romantic bathos, adultery rendered sympathetic–can be morally reprehensible is a bit unclear for most twentieth century readers, especially those who realize that the Austens themselves reveled in theatricals at home. The problem as Austen here presents it lies in the possible consequences of role-playing: coming to feel the emotions and attitudes one presents on the stage or, worse yet, expressing rather than suppressing genuine but socially unacceptable feelings in the guise of mere acting. In the course of the theatricals, where Fanny, who will not act, is relegated to the role of spectator and moral chorus, Maria Bertram, engaged to a bovine local heir, vies with her sister in striving to fascinate Henry Crawford, who in turn is all too ready to charm them. Mary Crawford, though it is "her way" to find eldest sons most agreeable, has the good taste to be attracted to Edmund, the second son, who plans to enter the Church. Mary's vivacity, as evidenced by the theatricals, easily wins his heart.

Time passes and poor Fanny, who since childhood has adored her cousin Edmund, unintentionally interests Henry Crawford. Determined to gain the affections of this rare young woman who is indifferent to his charms, Crawford ends by succumbing to hers. He proposes. Fanny's unworldly refusal provokes the anger of her uncle. Then, while Fanny, still in disgrace with the baronet, is away from Mansfield Park and visiting her family at Portsmouth, the debacle of which *Lovers' Vows* was a harbinger comes about. The *homme fatal* Henry, at a loss for a woman to make love to, trains his charms on his old flirt Maria, now Mrs. Rushworth. She runs away with him; her sister, not to be outdone in bad behavior, elopes with an unsatisfactory suitor. Mary Crawford's moral coarseness becomes evident in her casual dismissal of these catastrophes. Edmund, now a clergyman, finds solace, then love, with the cousin whose sterling character shines brightly for him now that Mary's glitter has tarnished. Fanny gains all she could hope for in at last attaining the heart and hand of her clerical kinsman.

Emma · Austen's next novel, *Emma*, might be thought of as harmonizing the two voices heard in *Pride and Prejudice* and *Mansfield Park*. For this book, Austen claimed to be creating "a heroine whom no one but myself will much like," an "imaginist" whose circumstances and qualities of mind make her the self-crowned queen of her country neighborhood. Austen was not entirely serious or accurate: Emma certainly has her partisans. Even those readers who do not like her tend to find her fascinating, for she is a spirited, imaginative, healthy young woman who, like Mary Crawford, has potential to do considerable harm to the fabric of society but on whom, like Elizabeth Bennet, her creator generously bestows life's greatest blessing: union with a man whose virtues, talents, and assets are the best complement for her own.

Emma's eventual marriage to Mr. Knightley of Donwell Abbey is the ultimate expression of one of Austen's key assumptions, that marriage is a young woman's supreme act of self-definition. Unlike any other Austen heroine, Emma has no pressing need to marry. As the opening sentence of the book implies, Emma's situation makes her acceptance or rejection of a suitor an act of unencumbered will: "Emma Woodhouse, handsome, clever, and rich, with a comfortable home and happy disposition, seemed to unite some of the best blessings of existence; and had lived nearly twenty-one years in the world with very little to distress or vex her."

Free though circumstance allows her to be, Emma has not been encouraged by her lot in life to acquire the discipline and self-knowledge that, augmenting her innate intelligence and taste, would help her to choose wisely. Brought up by a doting valetudinarian of a father and a perceptive but permissive governess, Emma has been encouraged to think too highly of herself. Far from vain about her beauty, Emma has—as Mr. Knightley, the only person who ventures to criticize her, observes—complete yet unfounded faith in her ability to judge people's characters and arrange their lives. The course of *Emma* is Miss Woodhouse's education in judgment, a process achieved through repeated mistakes and humiliations.

As the novel opens, the young mistress of Hartfield is at loose ends. Her beloved governess has just married Mr. Weston, of the neighboring property, Randalls. To fill the newly made gap in her life, Emma takes notice of Harriet Smith, a pretty, dim "natural daughter of somebody," and a parlor-boarder at the local school. Determined to settle her protégé into the sort of life she deems suitable, Emma detaches Harriet from Robert Martin, a young farmer who has proposed to her, and embarks upon a campaign to conquer for Harriet the heart of Mr. Elton, Highbury's unmarried clergyman. Elton's attentiveness and excessive flattery convince Emma of her plan's success but at the same time show the reader what Emma is aghast to learn at the end of book 1: that Elton scorns the nobody and has designs upon the heiress herself.

With the arrival of three new personages in Highbury, book 2 widens Emma's opportunities for misconception. The first newcomer is Jane Fairfax, an elegant and accomplished connection of the Bates family and a girl whose prospective fate, the "governess trade," shows how unreliable the situations of well-bred young ladies without fortunes or husbands tend to be. Next to arrive is the suave Mr. Frank Churchill, Mr. Weston's grown son, who has been adopted by wealthy relations of his mother and who has been long remiss in paying a visit to Highbury. Finally, Mr. Elton brings home a bride, the former Augusta Hawkins of Bristol, a pretentious and impertinent creature possessed of an independent fortune, a well-married sister, and a boundless fund of self-congratulation. Emma mistakenly flatters herself that the dashing Frank Churchill is in love with her, and then settles on him as a husband for Harriet; she suspects the reserved Miss Fairfax, whose cultivation she rightly perceives as a reproach to her own untrained talents, of a clandestine relationship with a married man. She despises Mrs. Elton, as would any person of sense, but fails to see that the vulgar woman's offensiveness is an exaggerated version of her own officiousness and snobbery.

Thus, the potential consequences of Emma's misplaced faith in her judgment intensify, and the evidence of her fallibility mounts. Thoroughly embarrassed to learn that Frank Churchill, to whom she has retailed all her hypotheses regarding Jane Fairfax, has long been secretly engaged to that woman, Emma suffers the deathblow to her smug self-esteem when Harriet announces that the gentleman whose feelings she hopes to have aroused is not, as Emma supposes, Churchill but the squire of Donwell. Emma's moment of truth is devastating and complete, its importance marked by one of Jane Austen's rare uses of figurative language: "It darted through her, with the speed of an arrow, that Mr. Knightley must marry no one but herself!" Perhaps the greatest evidence of Emma's being a favorite of fortune is that Mr. Knightley feels the same as she does on this matter. Chastened by her series of bad judgments, paired with a gentleman who for years has loved and respected her enough to correct her and whom she can love and respect in turn, Emma participates in the minuet of marriage with which Austen concludes the book, the other couples so united being Miss Fairfax and Mr. Churchill and Harriet Smith (ductile enough to form four attachments in a year) and Robert Martin (stalwart enough to persist in his original feeling).

Emma Woodhouse's gradual education, which parallels the reader's growing awareness of what a menace to the social order her circumstances, abilities, and weaknesses combine to make her, is one of Austen's finest pieces of plotting. The depiction of character is likewise superb. Among a gallery of memorable and distinctive characters are Mr. Woodhouse; Miss Bates, the stream-of-consciousness talker who inadvertently provokes Emma's famous rudeness on Box Hill; and the wonderfully detestable Mrs. Elton, with her self-contradictions and her fractured Italian, her endless allusions to Selina, Mr. Suckling, Maple Grove, and the *barouche landau*. Life at Hartfield, Donwell, and Highbury is portrayed with complexity and economy. Every word, expression, opinion, and activity—whether sketching a portrait, selecting a dancing partner, or planning a strawberry-picking party—becomes a gesture of self-revelation. Emma demonstrates how, in Austen's hands, the novel of manners can become a statement of moral philosophy.

Northanger Abbey · *Northanger Abbey* was published in a four-volume unit with *Persuasion* in 1818, after Austen's death, but the manuscript had been completed much earlier, in 1803. Austen wrote a preface for *Northanger Abbey* but did not do the sort of revising that had transformed *Elinor and Marianne* and *First Impressions* into *Sense and Sensibility* and *Pride and Prejudice*. The published form of *Northanger Abbey* can therefore be seen as the earliest of the six novels. It is also, with the possible exception of *Sense and Sensibility*, the most "literary." *Northanger Abbey*, like some of Austen's juvenile burlesques, confronts the conventions of the gothic novel or tale of terror. The incidents of her novel have been shown to parallel, with ironic difference, the principal lines of gothic romance, particularly as practiced by Ann Radcliffe, whose most famous works, *The Romance of the Forest* (1791) and *The Mysteries of Udolpho* (1794), had appeared several years before Jane Austen had begun work on her burlesque.

Like *Emma*, *Northanger Abbey* is centrally concerned with tracing the growth of a young woman's mind and the cultivation of her judgment. In this less sophisticated work, however, the author accomplishes her goal through a rather schematic contrast. As an enthusiastic reader of tales of terror, Catherine Morland has gothic expectations of life despite a background most unsuitable for a heroine. Like the gothic heroines she admires, Catherine commences adventuring early in the novel. She is not, however, shipped to Venice or Dalmatia, but taken to Bath for a six-week stay. Her hosts are serenely amiable English folk, her pastimes the ordinary round of spa pleasures; the young man whose acquaintance she makes, Henry Tilney, is a witty clergyman rather than a misanthropic monk or dissolute rake. Toward this delightful, if far from gothic, young man, Catherine's feelings are early inclined. In turn, he, his sister, and even his father, the haughty, imperious General Tilney, are favorably disposed toward her. With the highest expectations, Catherine sets out to accompany them to their seat, the Abbey of the novel's title (which, like that of *Persuasion*, was selected not by the author but by Henry Austen, who handled the posthumous publication).

At Northanger, Catherine's education in the difference between literature and life continues. Despite its monastic origins, the Abbey proves a comfortable and well-maintained dwelling. When Catherine, like one of Radcliffe's protagonists, finds a mysterious document in a chest and spends a restless night wondering what lurid tale it might chronicle, she is again disappointed: "If the evidence of her sight might be trusted she held a washing-bill in her hand." Although Catherine's experience does not confirm the truth of Radcliffe's sensational horrors, it does not prove the world a straightforward, safe, cozy place. Catherine has already seen something of falseness and selfish vulgarity in the persons of Isabella Thorpe and her brother John, acquaintances formed at Bath. At Northanger, she learns that, though the general may not be the wife-murderer she has fancied him, he is quite as cruel as she could imagine. On learning that Catherine is not the great heiress he has mistakenly supposed her to be, the furious general packs her off in disgrace and discomfort in a public coach.

With this proof that the world of fact can prove as treacherous as that of fiction, Catherine returns sadder and wiser to the bosom of her family. She has not long to droop, though, for Henry Tilney, on hearing of his father's bad behavior, hurries after her and makes Catherine the proposal which he has long felt inclined to offer and which his father has until recently promoted. The approval of Catherine's parents is immediate, and the general is not overlong in coming to countenance the match. "To begin perfect happiness at the respective ages of twenty-six and eighteen is to do pretty well," observes the facetious narrator, striking a literary pose even in the novel's last sentence, "and . . . I leave it to be settled by whomsoever it may concern, whether the tendency of this work be altogether to recommend parental tyranny, or reward filial disobedience."

Persuasion · *Persuasion*, many readers believe, signals Austen's literary move out of the eighteenth century and into the nineteenth. This novel, quite different from those that preceded it, draws not upon the tradition of the novelists of the 1790's but on that of the lionized poets of the new century's second decade, Sir Walter Scott and Lord Byron. For the first time, Austen clearly seems the child of her time, susceptible to the charms of natural rather than improved landscapes, fields, and sea cliffs rather than gardens and shrubberies. The wistful, melancholy beauty of autumn that pervades the book is likewise romantic. The gaiety, vitality, and sparkling wit of *Pride and Prejudice* and *Emma* are muted. The stable social order represented by the great estate in *Mansfield Park* has become fluid in *Persuasion*: here the principal country house, Kellynch Hall, must be let because the indigenous family cannot afford to inhabit it.

Most important, *Persuasion*'s heroine is unique in Jane Austen's gallery. Anne Elliott, uprooted from her ancestral home, spiritually isolated from her selfish and small-minded father and sisters, separated from the man she loves by a long-standing estrangement, is every bit as "alienated" as such later nineteenth century heroines as Esther Summerson, Jane Eyre, and Becky Sharp. Anne's story is very much the product of Austen's middle age. At twenty-seven, she is the only Austen heroine to be past her first youth. Furthermore, she is in no need of education. Her one great mistake—overriding the impulse of her heart and yielding to the persuasion of her friend Lady Russell in rejecting the proposal of Frederick Wentworth, a sanguine young naval officer with his fortune still to make and his character to prove—is some eight years in the past, and she clearly recognizes it for the error it was.

Persuasion is the story of how Anne and Frederick (now the eminent Captain) Wentworth rekindle the embers of their love. Chance throws them together when the vain, foolish Sir Walter Elliott, obliged to economize or rent his estate, resolves to move his household to Bath, where he can cut a fine figure at less cost, and leases Kellynch to Admiral and Mrs. Croft, who turn out to be the brother-in-law and sister of Captain Wentworth. Initially cool to his former love—or rather, able to see the diminution of her beauty because he is unable to forgive her rejection—the Captain flirts with the Musgrove girls; they are sisters to the husband of Anne's younger sister Mary and blooming belles with the youth and vigor Anne lacks. The old appreciation of Anne's merits, her clear insight, kindness, high-mindedness, and modesty, soon reasserts itself, but not before fate and the Captain's impetuosity have all but forced another engagement upon him. Being "jumped down" from the Cobb at Lyme Regis, Louisa Musgrove misses his arms and falls unconscious on the pavement. Obliged by honor to declare himself hers if she should wish it, Wentworth is finally spared this self-sacrifice when the susceptible young lady and the sensitive Captain Benwick fall in love. Having discovered the intensity of his devotion to Anne by being on the point of having to abjure it, Wentworth hurries to Bath, there to declare his attachment in what is surely the most powerful engagement scene in the Austen canon.

Though the story of *Persuasion* belongs to Anne Elliott and Frederick Wentworth, Austen's skill at evoking characters is everywhere noticeable. As Elizabeth Jenkins observes, all of the supporting characters present different facets of the love theme. The heartless marital calculations of Mr. Elliott, Elizabeth Elliott, and Mrs. Clay, the domestic comforts of the senior Musgroves and the Crofts, and the half-fractious, half-amiable ménage of Charles and Mary Musgrove all permit the reader more clearly to discern how rare and true is the love Anne Elliott and her captain have come so close to losing. The mature, deeply grateful commitment they are able to make to each other is, if not the most charming, surely the most profound in the Austen world.

Peter W. Graham

Other major works
SHORT FICTION: *Minor Works*, 1954 (vol. 6 of the *Oxford Illustrated Jane Austen*; R. W. Chapman, editor).
NONFICTION: *Jane Austen's Letters to Her Sister Cassandra and Others*, 1952 (R. W. Chapman, editor).

Bibliography
Bush, Douglas. *Jane Austen*. New York: Macmillan, 1975. Addressed to students and general readers, this survey by an eminent scholar provides a straightforward introduction to Austen's work. Overviews of Austen's England, her life, and her early writings set the stage for chapter-length discussions of her six novels; two unfinished works, *The Watsons* and *Sanditon*, also receive a chapter each.
Copeland, Edward, and Juliet McMaster, eds. *The Cambridge Companion to Jane Austen*. Cambridge, England: Cambridge University Press, 1997. This collection of thirteen new essays on Austen is divided between those concerning her own world and those that address modern critical discourse, such as Claudia L. Johnson's "Austen Cults and Cultures." While some essays focus on Austen's novels, others deal with broad issues such as class consciousness, religion, and domestic economy. This excellent overview includes a chronology and concludes with an assessment of late twentieth century developments in Austen scholarship.
Grey, J. David, ed. *The Jane Austen Companion*. New York: Macmillan, 1986. An encyclopedic guide to Austen's life and works. Among the topics covered are "Characterization in Jane Austen," "Chronology of Composition," and "Editions and Publishing History." There are brief essays on "Dancing, Balls, and Assemblies," "Dress and Fashion," "Post/Mail," and many other aspects of everyday life in Austen's time. Each essay includes a bibliography. An indispensable resource.
Hardy, Barbara. *A Reading of Jane Austen*. New York: New York University Press, 1976. A thematic approach to Austen's fiction (Hardy does not discuss Austen's juvenilia or her fragmentary works). In the first chapter, "The Flexible Medium," Hardy argues that while Austen was not, on the surface, a radical innovator, she nevertheless transformed the genre in which she worked: "Indeed she may be said to have created the modern novel." Two later chapters provide a valuable study of Austen's handling of narrative point of view and of "telling and listening" in her novels. Lacks an index.
Lane, Maggie. *Jane Austen's England*. New York: St. Martin's Press, 1986. This fascinating book is full of illustrations which give Austen's readers a look at the world of her novels. Arranged chronologically, taking the reader to the places Austen would have gone, usually through contemporary paintings. The text is useful; the first chapter, "The England of Jane Austen's Time," gives a good basic summary of social conditions around the beginning of the nineteenth century. Includes references to the novels; for example, Lane quotes the Box Hill episode from *Emma* and

provides a painting of Box Hill. Also includes a map, a short bibliography, and an index.

Mooneyham, Laura G. *Romance, Language, and Education in Jane Austen's Novels.* New York: St. Martin's Press, 1986. Covers all six of Austen's complete novels, theorizing that a relationship exists among language, education, and romance. Asserts that the romance between heroine and hero is in itself educational for the heroine because romance offers the opportunity for open communication. This approach is provocative and useful, especially because it emphasizes Austen's own preoccupations. Each chapter discusses a separate novel, which may be useful for the study of one of Austen's works.

Myer, Valerie Grosvenor. *Jane Austen: Obstinate Heart.* New York: Arcade Publishing, 1997. This biography of Jane Austen emphasizes her self-consciousness, born of an inferior social position and constant money worries. Still, she would refuse the proposal of a wealthy suitor because, as Myer states, Austen's "obstinate heart" would only allow her to marry for love.

Nokes, David. *Jane Austen: A Life.* New York: Farrar, Straus and Giroux, 1997. Nokes attempts to uncover a more authentic Jane Austen than the saintly, censored image that her family presented to the public after her early death. His method is novelistic, in that he attempts, as much as possible, to present Austen's life from her own perspective.

Sulloway, Alison. *Jane Austen and the Province of Womanhood.* Philadelphia: University of Pennsylvania Press, 1989. Attempts to place Austen into a framework of "women-centered" authors from the tract-writers Mary Astell, Mary Wollstonecraft Godwin, and Catharine Macaulay, to novelists Fanny Burney, Maria Edgeworth, and Charlotte Smith. Counters early views of Austen as a conservative woman upholding the status quo in her novels. Suggests that Austen was a moderate feminist who sought reforms for women rather than outright revolution. Instead of reading Austen's novels separately, Sulloway focuses on themes which she calls "provinces": the ballroom (dancing and marriage), the drawing room (debate), the garden (reconciliation). A valuable book which is thought-provoking and not overly theoretical.

Tomalin, Claire. *Jane Austen: A Life.* New York: Knopf, 1998. This compelling account of Austen's life is exceedingly well written and, like Nokes's biography, attempts to tell the story from the subject's own perspective. Proceeding in chronological order, the book concludes with a postscript on the fates of Austen's family members and two interesting appendixes: a note of Austen's final illness and an excerpt from the diary of Austen's niece, Fanny.

J. G. Ballard

Born: Shanghai, China; November 15, 1930

Principal long fiction · *The Wind from Nowhere*, 1962; *The Drowned World*, 1962; *The Drought*, 1964 (later published as *The Burning World*); *The Crystal World*, 1966; *Crash*, 1973; *Concrete Island*, 1974; *High Rise*, 1975; *The Unlimited Dream Company*, 1979; *Hello America*, 1981; *Empire of the Sun*, 1984; *The Day of Creation*, 1987; *Running Wild*, 1988 (novella); *The Kindness of Women*, 1991; *Rushing to Paradise*, 1994; *Cocaine Nights*, 1996; *Super-Cannes*, 2000.

Other literary forms · J. G. Ballard has been a prolific short-story writer; there are more than twenty collections of his stories, though some are recombinations of stories in earlier collections, and the American and British collections constitute two series in which the same stories are combined in different ways. He has written occasional essays on imaginative fiction, and also on surrealist painting—he contributed an introduction to a collection of work by Salvador Dalí. Many of these essays are collected in *A User's Guide to the Millennium: Essays and Reviews* (1996). The best of his short fiction is to be found in two retrospective collections: *Chronopolis and Other Stories* (1971) and *The Best Short Stories of J. G. Ballard* (1978).

Achievements · Ballard is one of a handful of writers who, after establishing early reputations as science-fiction writers, subsequently achieved a kind of "transcendence" of their genre origins to be accepted by a wider public. This transcendence was completed by the success of *Empire of the Sun*, which was short-listed for the Booker Prize and won the Guardian Prize before being boosted to best-seller status by a film produced by Steven Spielberg. In 1997, maverick director David Cronenberg turned Ballard's cult classic *Crash* into an equally disturbing *film noir*, which quickly found a dedicated audience. For a time in the early 1960's, Ballard seemed to constitute a one-man avant-garde in British science fiction, and his influence was considerable enough for him to become established as the leading figure in the movement which came to be associated with the magazine *New Worlds* under the editorship of Michael Moorcock. His interest in science-fiction themes was always of a special kind; he is essentially a literary surrealist who finds the near future a convenient imaginative space. His primary concern is the effect of environment, both "natural" and synthetic—upon the psyche—and he has therefore found it appropriate to write about gross environmental changes and about the decay and dereliction of the artificial environment; these interests distance him markedly from other modern science-fiction writers and have helped him to become a writer *sui generis*.

Biography · James Graham Ballard was born and reared in Shanghai, China, where his father, originally an industrial chemist, was involved in the management of the Far East branch of a firm of textile manufacturers. The Sino-Japanese war had begun, and Shanghai was effectively a war zone by the time Ballard was seven years old; all of his early life was affected by the ever-nearness of war. After Japan's entry into World War II and its invasion of Shanghai, Ballard was interned in a prisoner-of-war camp.

41

This was in the summer of 1942, when he was eleven; he was there for more than three years.

Ballard has said that his experience of the internment camp was "not unpleasant"–it was simply a fact of life which, as a child, he accepted. Children were not generally mistreated by the guards, and the adults made sure that the children were adequately fed, even at their own expense. He has observed that his parents must have found the regime extremely harsh. Although his family was among the fortunate few who avoided malaria, his sister nearly died of a form of dysentery.

After his release, Ballard went to England in 1946. His family stayed in the Far East for a while, and his father did not return until 1950, when he was driven out of China by the Communist victory. Ballard has recalled that after spending his early years in "Americanized" Shanghai, England seemed very strange and foreign. He went to Leys' School in Cambridge for a while, then went to King's College, Cambridge, to study medicine. His ultimate aim at this time was to become a psychiatrist. At Cambridge he began writing, initially intending to maintain the activity as a hobby while he was qualifying. In fact, though, he dropped out of his course after two years and subsequently went to London University to read English. The university seems to have found him unsuitable for such a course, and he left after his first year.

He then embarked upon a series of short-term jobs, including working for an advertising agency and selling encyclopedias. Eventually, to end this aimless drifting, he enlisted in the Royal Air Force and was sent for training to Moosejaw, Saskatchewan, Canada. He was not suited to the air force either, but while in Canada he began reading magazine science fiction, and while waiting for his discharge back in England he wrote his first science-fiction story, "Passport to Eternity" (it was not published for some years). Shortly after this, in 1955, he married and worked in public libraries in order to support his family.

In 1956, Ballard began submitting short stories to Ted Carnell, editor of the British magazines *New Worlds* and *Science Fantasy*. Carnell was not only enthusiastic about Ballard's work but also helpful in finding Ballard a new job working on a trade journal. Eventually, Ballard became assistant editor of *Chemistry and Industry*, a job which he held for four years. He moved in 1960 to the small Thames-side town of Shepperton, where he would make his permanent home. By this time he had three children and was struggling to find time to devote to his writing. During a two-week annual holiday he managed to write *The Wind from Nowhere*, whose publication in America represented something of a breakthrough for him–the same publisher began to issue a series of short-story collections, and the income from these books allowed him to become a full-time writer. His wife died in 1964, when his youngest child was only five years old. As a result, he began to combine his career as a writer with the exacting pressures of being a single parent. The fame that followed the success of *Empire of the Sun* seems not to have disturbed his lifestyle at all.

For a reader curious about Ballard's life upon his move from China to England, his 1991 novel, *The Kindness of Women*, offers an enticing mix of autobiography and imagination. While real-life events are covered and include details such as Ballard's car crash, his subsequent exhibition of crashed cars at an avant-garde gallery in London, and his experimentation with hallucinogenic drugs in the 1970's, the novel should not be mistaken for a genuine autobiography. Composite characters and imagined or greatly exaggerated events abound, and most real-life characters are given new names, with the prominent exception of the protagonist, called Jim Ballard.

Unlike this novel's character, J. G. Ballard seems to have spent a lot of his creative energy on his imaginative writing. In addition to producing a steady output of original novels and short stories, Ballard has also been an active writer of essays and book reviews, which have made his a familiar voice in British literary circles.

Analysis · J. G. Ballard's first seven novels can be easily sorted into two groups. The first four are novels of worldwide disaster, while the next three are stories of cruelty and alienation set in the concrete wilderness of contemporary urban society. All of his novels are, however, linked by a concern with the disintegration of civilization on a global or local scale.

Ballard's early disaster stories follow a well-established tradition in British imaginative fiction. British science-fiction writers from H. G. Wells to John Wyndham always seem to have been fascinated by the notion of the fragility and vulnerability of the human empire, and have produced many careful and clinical descriptions of its fall. The earlier works in this tradition are didactic tales, insisting on the vanity of human wishes and reveling in the idea that when the crunch comes, only the tough will survive. Ballard, in contrast, is quite unconcerned with drawing morals—his disaster stories are not at all social Darwinist parables. His main concern is with the psychological readjustments which the characters are forced to make when faced with the disintegration of their world: He sees the problem of catastrophic change largely in terms of adaptation.

In one of his earliest essays on science fiction, a "guest editorial" which he contributed to *New Worlds* in 1962, Ballard committed the heresy of declaring that H. G. Wells was "a disastrous influence on the subsequent course of science fiction." He suggested that the vocabulary of ideas to which science-fiction writers and readers had become accustomed should be thrown overboard, and with them its customary narrative forms and conventional plots. It was time, he said, to turn to the exploration of inner space rather than outer space, and to realize that "the only truly alien planet is Earth." He offered his opinion that Salvador Dalí might be the most pertinent source of inspiration for modern writers of science fiction. The rhetorical flourishes which fill this essay caution readers against taking it all *too* seriously, but in the main this is the prospectus which Ballard has tried to follow. He has practiced what he preached, shaking off the legacy of H. G. Wells, dedicating himself to the exploration of inner space and the development of new metaphysical (particularly metapsychological) systems, and steering well clear of the old plots and narrative formulas. In so doing, he made himself one of the most original writers of his generation; such novels as *Empire of the Sun* and *The Day of Creation* do indeed demonstrate the essential alienness of the planet on which we live.

The Wind from Nowhere · In *The Wind from Nowhere*, which is considerably inferior to the three other disaster novels, a slowly accelerating wind plucks the human-made world apart. No one can stand firm against this active rebellion of nature—neither the American armed forces nor the immensely rich industrialist Hardoon, who seeks to secrete himself within a gigantic concrete pyramid, which the wind eventually topples into an abyss. *The Wind from Nowhere* has a whole series of protagonists and shows the catastrophe from several viewpoints. This was one of the well-tried methods of retailing disaster stories, but it was unsuited to Ballard's particular ambitions, and in the other novels of this early quartet he employed single protagonists as focal points—almost as measuring devices to analyze in depth the significance of parallel physical and psychological changes.

The Drowned World · In *The Drowned World*, Earth's surface temperature has risen and is still gradually rising. Water released by the melting of the ice caps has inundated much of the land, and dense tropical jungle has spread rapidly through what were once the temperate zones, rendering them all but uninhabitable. Ballard suggests that the world is undergoing a kind of retrogression to the environment of the Triassic period. The novel's protagonist is Robert Kerans, a biologist monitoring the changes from a research station in partly submerged London.

The psychological effects of the transfiguration first manifest themselves as dreams in which Kerans sees "himself" (no longer human) wandering a primitive world dominated by a huge, fierce sun. These dreams, he concludes, are a kind of memory retained within the cellular heritage of humankind, now called forth again by the appropriate stimulus. Their promise is that they will free the nervous system from the domination of the recently evolved brain, whose appropriate environment is gone, and restore the harmony of primeval proto-consciousness and archaic environment. Kerans watches other people trying to adapt in their various ways to the circumstances in which they find themselves, but he sees the essential meaninglessness of their strategies. He accepts the pull of destiny and treks south, submitting to the psychic metamorphosis that strips away his humanity until he becomes "a second Adam searching for the forgotten paradises of the reborn sun."

The Drowned World was sufficiently original and sophisticated to be incomprehensible to most of the aficionados of genre science fiction, who did not understand what Ballard was about or why. A minority, however, recognized its significance and its import; its reputation is now firmly established as one of the major works of its period.

The Drought · In *The Drought* (later published as *The Burning World*), the pattern of physical change is reversed: Earth becomes a vast desert because a pollutant molecular film has formed on the surface of the world's oceans, inhibiting evaporation. The landscape is gradually transformed, the concrete city-deserts becoming surrounded by seas of hot sand instead of arable land, while the seashore retreats to expose new deserts of crystalline salt. The soil dies and civilization shrivels, fires reducing forests and buildings alike to white ash. Ransom, the protagonist, is one of the last stubborn few who are reluctant to join the exodus to the retreating sea. From his houseboat he watches the river dwindle away, draining the dregs of the social and natural order. He lives surrounded by relics of an extinguished past, bereft of purpose and no longer capable of emotional response.

Eventually, Ransom and his surviving neighbors are driven to seek refuge in the "dune limbo" of the new seashore and take their places in a new social order dominated by the need to extract fresh water from the reluctant sea. Here, he finds, people are simply marking time and fighting a hopeless rear-guard action. In the final section of the story, he goes inland again to see what has become of the city and its last few inhabitants. They, mad and monstrous, have found a new way of life, hideous but somehow appropriate to the universal aridity, which is an aridity of the soul as well as of the land.

The Crystal World · In *The Crystal World*, certain areas of the earth's surface are subjected to a strange process of crystallization as some mysterious substance is precipitated out of the ether. This is a more localized and less destructive catastrophe than those in *The Drowned World* and *The Drought*, but the implication is that it will continue until the world is consumed. The initially affected area is in Africa, where the novel is set. The central character is Dr. Sanders, the assistant director of a leper colony, who is at first horrified when he finds his mistress and some of his patients joyfully accepting the process of cystallization within the flesh of their own bodies. Eventually, of course, he comes to realize that no other destiny is appropriate to the new circumstances. What is happening is that time and space are somehow being reduced, so that they are supersaturated with matter. Enclaves from which time itself has "evaporated" are therefore being formed–fragments of eternity where living things, though they cannot continue to live, also cannot die, but undergo instead a complete existential transubstantiation. Here, metaphors developed in *The Drought* are literalized with the aid of a wonderfully gaudy invention.

The transformation of the world in *The Crystal World* is a kind of beautification, and it is much easier for the reader to sympathize with Sanders's acceptance of its dictates than with Kerans's capitulation to the demands of his dreams. For this reason, the novel has been more popular within the science-fiction community than either of its predecessors. It is, however, largely a recapitulation of the same theme, which does not really gain from its association with the lush romanticism that occasionally surfaces in Ballard's work–most noticeably in the short stories set in the imaginary American west-coast artists' colony Vermilion Sands, a beach resort populated by decadent eccentrics and the flotsam of bygone star cults who surround themselves with florid artificial environments.

Crash · Seven years elapsed between publication of *The Crystal World* and the appearance of *Crash*. Although Ballard published numerous retrospective collections in the interim, his one major project was a collection of what he called "condensed novels"–a series of verbal collages featuring surreal combinations of images encapsulating what Ballard saw as the contemporary zeitgeist. In the world portrayed in these collages, there is a great deal of violence and perverted sexual arousal. Ubiquitous Ballardian images recur regularly: dead birds, junked space hardware, derelict buildings. Mixed in with these are secular icons: the suicide of entertainer Marilyn Monroe, the assassination of President John F. Kennedy, and other personalities whose fates could be seen as symbolic of the era in decline.

The theme of *Crash* is already well developed in the condensed novels (collected in the United Kingdom under the title *The Atrocity Exhibition*, 1969, and in the United States under the title *Love and Napalm: Export U.S.A.*). Cars, within the novel, are seen as symbols of power, speed, and sexuality–a commonplace psychoanalytic observation, to which Ballard adds the surprising further representation of the car crash as a kind of orgasm. The protagonist of the novel, who is called Ballard, finds his first car crash, despite all the pain and attendant anxiety, to be an initiation into a new way of being, whereby he is forced to reformulate his social relationships and his sense of purpose. Ballard apparently decided to write the book while considering the reactions of members of the public to an exhibition of crashed cars which he held at the New Arts Laboratory in London.

Although it is mundane by comparison with his previous novels–it is certainly not science fiction–*Crash* is by no means a realistic novel. Its subject matter is trauma and the private fantasization of alarming but ordinary events. The hero, at one point, does bear witness to a transformation of the world, but it is a purely subjective one while he is under the influence of a hallucinogen. He sees the landscapes of the city transformed, woven into a new metaphysics by the attribution of a new context of significance derived from his perverted fascination with cars and expressway architecture.

Concrete Island · The two novels which followed *Crash* retain and extrapolate many of its themes. *Concrete Island* and *High Rise* are both robinsonades whose characters become Crusoes in the very heart of modern civilization, cast away within sight and earshot of the metropolitan hordes but no less isolated for their proximity. In *Concrete Island*, a man is trapped on a traffic island in the middle of a complex freeway intersection, unable to reach the side of the road because the stream of cars is never-ending. Like Crusoe, he sets out to make the best of his situation, using whatever resources—material and social—he finds at hand. He adapts so well, in the end, that he refuses the opportunity to leave when it finally arrives.

High Rise · The high-rise apartment block which gives *High Rise* its title is intended to be a haven for the well-to-do middle class, a comfortable microcosm to which they can escape from the stressful outside world of work and anxiety. It is, perhaps, *too* well insulated from the world at large; it becomes a private empire where freedom from stress gives birth to a violent anarchy and a decay into savagery. If *Concrete Island* is spiritually akin to Daniel Defoe's *Robinson Crusoe* (1719), then *High Rise* is akin to William Golding's *Lord of the Flies* (1954), though it is all the more shocking in translocating the decline into barbarism of Golding's novel from a remote island to suburbia, and in attributing the decline to adults who are well aware of what is happening rather than to children whose innocence provides a ready excuse. As always, Ballard's interest is in the psychological readjustments made by his chief characters, and the way in which the whole process proves to be ultimately cathartic.

A major theme in the condensed novels, which extends into the three novels of the second group, is what Ballard refers to as the "death of affect," a sterilization of the emotions and attendant moral anesthesia, which he considers to be a significant contemporary trend induced by contemporary lifestyles. The greatest positive achievement of the characters in these novels is a special kind of ataraxia, a calm of mind rather different from the one Plato held up as an ideal, which allows one to live alongside all manner of horrors without being unusually moved to fear or pity.

The Unlimited Dream Company · Another gap, though not such a long one, separates *High Rise* from *The Unlimited Dream Company*, a messianic fantasy of the redemption of Shepperton from suburban mundanity. Its protagonist, Blake, crashes a stolen aircraft into the Thames River at Shepperton. Though his dead body remains trapped in the cockpit, he finds himself miraculously preserved on the bank. At first he cannot accept his true state, but several unsuccessful attempts to leave the town and a series of visions combine to convince him that he has a specially privileged role to play: He must teach the people to fly, so that they can transcend their earthly existence to achieve a mystical union with the vegetable and mineral worlds, dissolving themselves into eternity as the chief characters did in *The Crystal World*. Though the name of the central character is significant, the book also appears to be closely allied with the paintings of another artist: the eccentric Stanley Spencer, who lived in another Thames-side town (Cookham) and delighted in locating within its mundane urban scenery images of biblical and transcendental significance.

The kind of redemption featured in *The Unlimited Dream Company* is as ambivalent as the kinds of adaptation featured in earlier novels, and its promise does not carry the same wild optimism that similar motifs are made to carry in most science-fiction and fantasy novels. It is perhaps best to view *The Unlimited Dream Company* as one more novel of adaptation, but one which reverses the pattern of the earlier works.

Here, it is not Blake who must adapt to changes in the external world, but Shepperton which must adapt to him–and he, too, must adapt to his own godlike status. Blake is himself the "catastrophe" which visits Shepperton, the absolute at large within it whose immanence cannot be ignored or resisted. If the novel seems to the reader to be upbeat rather than downbeat, that is mainly the consequence of a change of viewpoint–and had the readers who thought *The Drowned World* downbeat been willing to accept such a change, they might have been able to find that novel equally uplifting.

Hello America · Although *The Unlimited Dream Company* does not represent such a dramatic change of pattern as first appearances suggest, *Hello America* is certainly, for Ballard, a break with his own tradition. There is little in the novel that seems new in thematic terms, although it recalls his short stories much more than previous novels, but there is nevertheless a sense in which it represents a radical departure. The plot concerns the "rediscovery" in the twenty-second century of a largely abandoned America by an oddly assorted expedition from Europe. What they find are the shattered relics of a whole series of American mythologies. The central character, Wayne, dreams of resurrecting America and its dream, restoring the mythology of technological optimism and glamorous consumerism to operational status. He cannot do so, of course, but there is a consistent note of ironic nostalgia in his hopeless ambition. What is remarkable about the book is that it is a confection, an offhand entertainment to be enjoyed but not taken seriously. From Ballard the novelist, this is totally unexpected, though his short fiction has frequently shown him to be a witty writer, and a master of the ironic aside.

Empire of the Sun · This change of direction proved, not unexpectedly, to be a purely temporary matter–a kind of brief holiday from more serious concerns. *Empire of the Sun* recovered all the mesmeric intensity of Ballard's earlier work, adding an extra turn of the screw by relating it to historically momentous events through which the author had actually lived. Although the book's young protagonist is named Jim and is the same age as Ballard was when he was interned by the Japanese, *Empire of the Sun* is–like *Crash* before it–by no means autobiographical in any strict sense. Jim's adventures are as exaggerated as the fictional Ballard's were, but the purpose of the exaggeration is here perfectly clear: What seems from an objective point of view to be a horrible and unmitigated catastrophe is to Jim simply part of the developing pattern of life, to which he must adapt himself, and which he takes aboard more or less innocently. From his point of view, given that the internment camp *is* the world, and not (as it is from the point of view of the adult internees) an intolerable interruption of the world, it is the behavior of the British prisoners which seems unreasonable and hostile, while the Japanese guards are the champions of order. The world does not begin to end for Jim until the war comes toward its close and the orderliness of camp life breaks down; that which others see as a source of hope and a possibility of redemption from their living hell is for Jim something else entirely, to which he reacts in characteristically idiosyncratic fashion. The frightful irony of all this is, as usual, overlaid and disguised by a straight-faced matter-of-factness which forbids the reader to cling to the conventional verities enshrined in an older, inherited attitude toward the war with Japan.

The Day of Creation · *The Day of Creation* returns to the Africa of *The Crystal World,* this time disrupted by the seemingly miraculous appearance of a new river whose "discoverer," Dr. Mallory of the World Health Organization, hopes that it may restore edenic life to territory spoiled for millennia by drought and ceaseless petty wars. Mallory's odyssey along the river upon which he bestows his own name might be seen as an inversion of Marlow's journey in Joseph Conrad's *Heart of Darkness* (1902), in which the mysteriously silent girl Noon is the hopeful counterpart of the soul-sick Kurtz; but the redemption promised by the river is a temporary illusion, and Noon herself may only be a figment of Mallory's imagination.

Running Wild · The novella *Running Wild,* thinly disguised as a mass-murder mystery in which the entire adult population of a small town is massacred, is another playfully ironic piece, though rather less gaudy than *Hello America*–appropriately, in view of its setting, which is a cozy suburban landscape of the Home Counties; it is a long short story rather than a short novel, but it carries forward the argument of *High Rise* as well as brief black comedies such as "The Intensive Care Unit."

The Kindness of Women · *The Kindness of Women* revisits Ballard's semiautobiographical subject matter, which he introduced with *Empire of the Sun.* The novel opens amid the Japanese invasion of Shanghai in 1937, an event Ballard himself witnessed as a boy. His protagonist's carefree adolescence is literally shattered by a bomb blast, when the Japanese air raid surprises a boy, again named Jim Ballard, as he strolls down the middle of Shanghai's amusement quarters. Moving from 1937 directly to Jim's arrival in post-World War II Great Britain, *The Kindness of Women* accompanies its protagonist to way stations modeled after significant events in the author's life, mixing imagination and autobiographical material. While *The Kindness of Women* covers terrain familiar to readers of Ballard's work, it nevertheless manages to shed fresh light on the author's recurring obsessions, themes, and symbols, such as the ubiquitous instances of downed aircraft, drained swimming pools, and concrete flyovers encircling Heathrow airport.

Rushing to Paradise · Ballard's next novel, *Rushing to Paradise,* has been marketed as a satire on the follies of the environmentalist movement, but it is a more complicated text than that. Antihero Dr. Barbara Rafferty is on a quest to establish a South Sea sanctuary for the albatross on an island wrested from the French government. The novel suggests that this is really a private attempt to build a murderous playground to live out psychosexual needs of her own. This boldly unconventional idea is obviously linked to Ballard's familiar suggestion of the dominance of the psychological over the material. The novel's invention of new psychological disorders and obsessions, and its iconoclastic depiction of an environmentalist physician who develops into a quasi commandant presiding over a disused airfield and ruined camera towers, clearly gives *Rushing to Paradise* the surrealist streak common to Ballard's fiction.

Perhaps not surprisingly, *Rushing to Paradise* largely failed to connect with a larger audience. Even though the novel's premise of renewed French nuclear testing in the South Seas uncannily anticipated the real-life development of such tests in the mid-1990's and thus predicted the future, something rarely accomplished by traditional science-fiction texts, many readers apparently did not forgive Ballard his choice of an environmentalist woman as the novel's surreal centerpiece. Ballard's idiosyncratic characters, who had alienated science-fiction fans when *The Drowned World* was published, managed again to distance his work from readers unwilling to engage the author on his own unique artistic grounds.

Cocaine Nights · *Cocaine Nights*, however, won great critical acclaim from British reviewers, who hailed the novel as Ballard's masterpiece for its fusion of surrealism and detective story. Ostensibly, *Cocaine Nights* tells of Charles Prentice's quest to exonerate his brother Frank, who is held in a Spanish jail and charged with a murder to which he has confessed. Utterly unconvinced that his brother has killed a wealthy family at a posh resort on the coast of southern Spain and believing his confession absurd, Charles tries to find the real culprit. His investigation quickly draws him into the orbit of Bobby Crawford, a rogue tennis instructor and self-appointed leader of a group of thrill-seeking English who fight terminal boredom by committing highly imaginative crimes and outrageous acts of vandalism.

With its emerging thesis that only the existence of crime can energize the somnolent resort community of terminally exhausted upper-middle-class retirees, Ballard's novel flies again in the face of the commonsense reader used to realistic fiction. Like his best work before, *Cocaine Nights* entices by its outrageously absurd proposal of the criminal as benefactor to humanity, and it confirms Ballard's position as one of England's most imaginative, original, and creative novelists.

Brian Stableford, updated by R. C. Lutz

Other major works

SHORT FICTION: *The Voices of Time*, 1962; *Billenium*, 1962; *The Four-Dimensional Nightmare*, 1963; *Passport to Eternity*, 1963; *The Terminal Beach*, 1964; *The Impossible Man*, 1966; *The Disaster Area*, 1967; *The Overloaded Man*, 1967; *The Atrocity Exhibition*, 1969 (also known as *Love and Napalm: Export U.S.A.*); *Vermilion Sands*, 1971; *Chronopolis and Other Stories*, 1971; *The Best Short Stories of J. G. Ballard*, 1978; *Myths of the Near Future*, 1982; *Memories of the Space Age*, 1988; *War Fever*, 1990.

NONFICTION: *A User's Guide to the Millennium: Essays and Reviews*, 1996.

Bibliography

Jones, Mark. "J. G. Ballard: Neurographer." In *Impossibility Fiction*, edited by Derek Littlewood. Amsterdam: Rodopi Press, 1996. Jones sees Ballard's fiction as characterized by the recurring theme of the author's description of the human mind as a kind of geographic landscape. Praises Ballard for his radical, surrealist descriptions of a new relationship between mind and reality.

Luckhurst, Roger. *"The Angle Between Two Walls": The Fiction of J. G. Ballard*. New York: St. Martin's Press, 1997. Most comprehensive study of Ballard's work. Thorough discussion and analysis of his fiction. Well-researched and extremely informative.

_____. "Petition, Repetition, and 'Autobiography': J. G. Ballard's *Empire of the Sun* and *The Kindness of Women*." *Contemporary Literature* 35, no. 4 (Winter, 1994): 688-708. Useful study of the historical veracity of Ballard's two novels. Luckhurst tries to discover methods and thematic and aesthetic strategies that have organized and informed Ballard's fictional work along with his autobiographical source material.

Pringle, David. *Earth Is the Alien Planet: J. G. Ballard's Four-Dimensional Nightmare*. San Bernardino, Calif.: Borgo Press, 1979. A monograph in Borgo's Milford series, featuring a biographical sketch and an excellent analysis of Ballard's work, by a critic who has followed the author's career very closely.

Re-Search: J. G. Ballard. San Francisco: Re-Search, 1983. A special issue of a periodical publication devoted to Ballard and his works, including an interview, critical articles, and some unusual items by Ballard; it views Ballard as an avant-garde literary figure rather than a science-fiction writer.

Stableford, Brian. "J. G. Ballard." In *Science Fiction Writers*, edited by E. F. Bleiler. New York: Charles Scribner's Sons, 1982. A competent overview of the author's work.

Julian Barnes

Dan Kavanagh

Born: Leicester, England; January 19, 1946

Principal long fiction · *Metroland*, 1980; *Duffy*, 1980 (as Dan Kavanagh); *Fiddle City*, 1981 (as Kavanagh); *Before She Met Me*, 1982; *Flaubert's Parrot*, 1984; *Putting the Boot In*, 1985 (as Kavanagh); *Staring at the Sun*, 1986; *Going to the Dogs*, 1987 (as Kavanagh); *A History of the World in 10½ Chapters*, 1989; *Talking It Over*, 1991; *The Porcupine*, 1992 (novella); *England, England*, 1998; *Love, etc.*, 2000.

Other literary forms · Julian Barnes has served as a journalist and columnist for several British newspapers and magazines. He has also published numerous essays and book reviews.

Achievements · Barnes is one of a number of British writers born after World War II who gravitated toward London and its literary scene. Reacting to the certainties and assumptions of the previous generation, they have often resorted to irony and comedy in viewing the contemporary world. Some have experimented with the form of the traditional novel. Barnes's early novels were narrative and chronological in approach, but his fifth book, *Flaubert's Parrot*, combined fact and fiction, novel and history, biography and literary criticism. For that work he was nominated for Great Britain's most prestigious literary award, the Booker Prize, and was awarded the Geoffrey Faber Memorial Prize. He has also won literary prizes in Italy and France, and he received the E. M. Forster Award from the American Academy of Arts and Letters. In *Staring at the Sun* and *A History of the World in 10½ Chapters*, Barnes continued his exploration of the novel and its form.

Biography · Born in the English Midlands city of Leicester just after World War II to parents who were French teachers, Julian Patrick Barnes studied French at Magdalen College, Oxford, from which he was graduated with honors in 1968 with a degree in modern languages. After leaving Oxford, his abiding interest in words and language led him to a position as a lexicographer for the *Oxford English Dictionary Supplement*. In 1972 Barnes became a freelance writer, preferring that parlous profession to the law. During the 1970's and 1980's, he wrote reviews for *The Times Literary Supplement* and was contributing editor to the *New Review*, assistant literary editor of *New Statesman*, and deputy literary editor of the *Sunday Times* of London. For a decade he served as a television critic, most notably for the London *Observer*, where his comments were witty, irreverent, and provocative.

Influenced by the French writer Gustave Flaubert, particularly his concern for form, style, and objectivity, Barnes's serious novels continued to exhibit his fascination with language and literary experiments, in contrast with the more traditional narrative approach and narrow subject matter of many twentieth century English novelists. Under the pseudonym Dan Kavanagh, Barnes also published a number of detective novels.

By the 1990's Barnes had become one of Britain's leading literary figures. His literary reviews appeared in many of the leading publications in both his own country and the United States. He also wrote brilliant journalistic pieces on various topics—political, social, and literary—some of them appearing in *The New Yorker*. Many of these essays were collected and published in *Letters from London* (1995). His long-standing fascination with France was revealed in his collection of short stories *Cross Channel* (1996), a series of tales about English men and women and their experiences of living and working in France.

In the mid-1990's Barnes accepted a one-year teaching position at The Johns Hopkins University, in part, he said, to increase his knowledge of American society, the United States being second only to France among Barnes's foreign fascinations. After a several-year novelistic hiatus, in 1998 he published *England, England,* which was widely reviewed and was short-listed for the Booker Prize, Britain's premier literary award, evidence that Barnes continued to be recognized as one of the most interesting novelists writing in English.

Analysis · In all of his works Barnes has pursued several ideas: Human beings question, even though there can be no absolute answers; humanity pursues its obsessions, often resulting in failure. Yet his novels have at the same time evolved in form and approach—the earliest are more traditional and conventional, the latter more experimental. Barnes's wit and irony, his use of history, literary criticism, myth, and fable, his melding of imagination and intellect, and his continuing risk in exploring new forms and methods make him one of the most significant English novelists of his generation.

Metroland · Barnes's first novel, *Metroland,* is orthodox in technique and approach; divided into three parts, it is a variation on the traditional *Bildungsroman,* or coming-of-age novel. In part 1, the narrator, Christopher Lloyd, and his close friend, Toni, grow up in 1963 in a north London suburb on the Metropolitan rail line (thus the title), pursuing the perennial adolescent dream of rebellion against parents, school, the middle class, and the establishment in general. Convinced of the superiority of French culture and consciously seeking answers to what they believe to be the larger questions of life, they choose to cultivate art, literature, and music in order to astound what they see as the bourgeoisie and its petty concerns.

Part 2, five years later, finds Christopher a student in Paris, the epitome of artistic bohemianism, particularly when compared to Metroland. It is 1968, and French students are demonstrating and rioting in the streets for social and political causes. None of this touches Christopher: He is more concerned about his personal self-discovery than about changing or challenging the wider world.

Nine years later, in part 3, set in 1977, Christopher is back in Metroland, married to Marion, an Englishwoman of his own class, with a child, a mortgaged suburban house, and a nine-to-five job. Toni, still a rebel, chides Christopher for selling out to the enemy. Ironically, however, Christopher is contented with life in Metroland. He consciously examines and questions his present circumstances but accepts their rewards and satisfactions. Questioning and irony are continuing themes in all Barnes's novels, as is the absence of significant character development except for the leading figure. Toni, Christopher's French girlfriend Annick, and Marion, his English wife, are not much more than supporting figures. Relationships are explored through Christopher's narration alone, and Christopher finds himself, his questions, and his life of most concern and interest to him.

Before She Met Me · *Before She Met Me* is also a story of an individual's attempt to relate
to and understand his personal world. Graham Hendrick, a forty-year-old professor
of history, has recently remarried. Now beginning a new life, happy with Ann, his
new wife, and outwardly contented, both personally and professionally, Hendrick
seems to be an older variation of Christopher and his self-satisfied middle-class
existence. As in his first novel, Barnes has included a bohemian writer, Jack Lupton,
as a foil for Hendrick's respectable conformity. Before they were married, Ann acted
in several minor films, and after viewing one of them, Hendrick, the historian, begins
to search out his wife's past. At first his quest seems based on simple curiosity; soon,
however, Ann's history begins to take over Hendrick's present life. Losing his
professional objectivity as a historian, succumbing to jealousy, compulsively immersing himself in Ann's past, blurring the distinction between the real Ann and her image
on the screen, Hendrick becomes completely obsessed. Seeing the present as a world
without causes, Hendrick finds his crusade in the past, and that crusade is no longer
public but private. Bordering on the melodramatic, *Before She Met Me* is the story of
the downward spiral of an individual who can no longer distinguish fantasy from
reality. Did the love affairs Ann had on the screen replicate her private life off camera?
Were her love affairs in the past continuing in the present?

Barnes poses the question, not only for Hendrick, caught up in his obsession, but
also for the reader: What is reality, and can one discover the truth? Like *Metroland*,
this novel has many comic and witty moments but ultimately ends tragically. Ann and
Lupton had an affair that has since ended, but Hendrick, in his obsessive quest, falsely
concludes that it continues; he murders Lupton and then, in Ann's presence, he takes
his own life. Although told in the third person, *Before She Met Me* centers on the plight
of a single figure questioning his world. Hendrick and his compulsions dominate the
novel: His first wife, their child, Ann, and Lupton are figures perceived through his
persona.

Flaubert's Parrot · With his third novel published under his own name, *Flaubert's
Parrot*, Barnes received considerable praise as a significant writer of fiction, less
parochial in form and technique than most English novelists of his time. His first book
published in the United States, *Flaubert's Parrot* was the recipient of numerous prizes.
It too is a novel of questions and obsessions, which unite the past and present. Yet in
its collage of literary techniques, it is not a traditional narrative novel, including as it
does fiction, biography, history, and literary criticism. As in his earlier works, here
Barnes focuses upon a single individual, Geoffrey Braithwaite, an English medical
doctor in his sixties, a widower, with a long-standing interest in the French writer
Gustave Flaubert. Barnes also has been a student of French and admirer of Flaubert,
and early in *Metroland* Christopher reads a work by Flaubert; several critics have
examined the possible relationships between the fictional figures, Braithwaite, Christopher, Hendrick, and the author.

Told in the first person, *Flaubert's Parrot* examines Braithwaite's attempt to discover
which of two different stuffed parrots on exhibit in competing Flaubert museums is
the one that sat on Flaubert's desk when he wrote his short story "Un Cœur simple"
("A Simple Heart"). In the story, an old servant, Félicité, is left after fifty years of
service with only a parrot as a companion. When the parrot dies, Félicité has it stuffed.
As her health fails, she confuses the parrot with the Holy Ghost, traditionally represented as a dove. On her deathbed she believes that she sees a giant parrot above her
head. Braithwaite's quest to determine the real parrot allows him, and Barnes, to

pursue with wit and irony numerous aspects of Flaubert's biography; his published works, including *Madame Bovary* (1857); his ideas for works he did not write; his travels; his use of animals in his writings; and his lovers. The novel includes chronologies, a dictionary, and an examination paper.

Yet the work is not concerned only with Braithwaite's interest in Flaubert's past and the two surviving stuffed parrots. As the doctor pursues Flaubert and his parrot, he also begins to reveal his own history. Braithwaite's wife had been frequently unfaithful to him, as Emma Bovary was to her husband Charles, and she had eventually committed suicide. As Braithwaite explores the relationship between Flaubert and his fiction, seeking to know which is the real parrot, he also attempts to understand the realities of his own life and his connection with the fictional Charles Bovary. He becomes obsessive about discovering the truth of the parrots, but he is also obsessive about discovering his own truth. The difficulty, however, is that truth and reality are always elusive, and the discovery of a number of small realities does not result in the illumination of absolute truth. In the course of his discussions, Braithwaite muses upon the incompetence even of specialists in ferreting out the truth; he criticizes a prominent Flaubertain scholar, whom he accuses of pronouncing French badly, of mistakenly identifying a portrait as Flaubert, and of being unable to specify the color of Emma Bovary's eyes.

Flaubert's parrot, too, is seen as a symbol of this dichotomy of fact and fiction. The parrot can utter human sounds, but only by mimicking what it hears; still, there is the appearance of understanding, regardless of whether it exists. Is a writer, such as Flaubert, merely a parrot, writing down human sounds and observing human life without understanding or interpretation? At the end of Braithwaite's search for the real stuffed parrot used by Flaubert while writing his short story, the doctor discovers that dozens of stuffed parrots exist which Flaubert could have borrowed and placed upon his desk. Thus Braithwaite's has been one of many quests with no resolutions, questions without final answers.

Staring at the Sun · *Staring at the Sun*, Barnes's fourth novel published under his own name, exhibits a stronger narrative line than *Flaubert's Parrot*, but as in the story of Braithwaite, narrative here is not the primary concern of the author; questions remain paramount. The central figure is a lower-middle-class woman, Jean Serjeant, significantly unlike earlier Barnes protagonists because she is naïve and unsophisticated, lacking any intellectual pretensions. The tone of Barnes's portrayal of Jean contrasts sharply with the wit and irony featured throughout *Flaubert's Parrot*. Yet even Jean asks questions, such as what happened to the sandwiches Charles Lindbergh did not eat when he flew over the Atlantic Ocean in 1927, and why the mink is so tenacious of life (a statement from a print that hung in her bedroom when she was a child). Those questions have no answers, and Jean muses that questions that do have answers are not real questions.

The novel begins in 1941, with a prologue set during World War II. Sergeant-pilot Prosser is flying back across the Channel to his English base from France, just before dawn. The sun rises from the waves on the eastern horizon, captivating Prosser's attention. Shortly after, he reduces his altitude when he sees the smoke from a steamship far below. As he flies at the lower altitude, the sun comes up again from the sea into his view, and for the second time in a single morning he watches the sun's ascent. He calls this event an ordinary miracle, but he never forgets it. Neither does Jean, after Prosser relates it to her a few months later while temporarily billeted in her parents' home. Prosser soon disappears from Jean's life but not from her memories: He kills himself, she later discovers, by flying directly into the sun. She marries Michael, a policeman who has no time for or interest in questions.

After twenty years of marriage, at the age of forty, Jean becomes pregnant for the first time. She leaves Michael in order to discover what she calls a more difficult, first-rate life; she is more on a quest for self than seeking an escape from her unsatisfactory husband. When her son, Gregory, is old enough to be left alone, Jean begins to travel widely, often by airplane. She pursues her own Seven Wonders of the World. While visiting Arizona's Grand Canyon, she observes an airplane flying below the canyon's rim. At first it seems to her to be against nature, but she concludes instead that it is against reason: Nature provides the miracles, such as the Grand Canyon and the double rising of the sun. As the novel proceeds, Jean becomes more like Barnes's other figures and less like her naïve and unsophisticated young self.

Gregory also parallels Barnes's earlier intellectual characters and their questions that can yield no conclusive answers. Afraid of death but contemplating suicide, he meditates upon God and His existence. He posits fourteen possible answers, but no final truth. The last part of the novel is set in the future, a world of intrusive and obtrusive computers. All the world's knowledge has been incorporated into the General Purposes Computer (GPC), open to everyone. Yet it cannot answer why minks are so tenacious of life. A special informational program, TAT (The Absolute Truth), is added to the GPC, but when Gregory asks TAT whether it believes in God, the computer answers that his question is not a real question, and when he asks why it is not a real question, TAT again responds that Gregory's second question is also not a real question. Only "real" questions, it appears, can be answered by computers. In what she believes will be the last incident in her long life, in 2021, Jean, at the age of ninety-nine, accompanied by Gregory, makes a final flight, observing the sun this time as it sets in the west rather than rising in the east, as it had done twice during Prosser's "ordinary miracle" so many years before.

A History of the World in 10½ Chapters · In *A History of the World in 10½ Chapters*, Barnes continued his experimentation in form and style. Unlike his earlier novels, this one has no central character. Instead, the reader is presented with a number of chapters or stories, ostensibly historical, which are loosely connected by several common themes. The first tale or fable is a revisionist account of the story of Noah and the ark. Narrated by a woodworm, the story portrays Noah as a drunk, humanity as badly flawed, and God and His plan as leaving much to be desired. Human beings fare equally poorly in the other chapters, and the ark returns in later stories: A nineteenth century English woman searches for the ark on Mount Ararat; a twentieth century American astronaut, also seeking the ark, finds a skeleton that he identifies as Noah's but that is really the bones of the woman explorer; another chapter discusses the ark in the form of the raft of the *Medusa*, painted by Théodore Géricault.

In this novel Barnes raises the question of how one turns disaster into art, or how one turns life into art. In a half chapter, or "Parenthesis," he discusses history and love: "History isn't what happened. History is just what historians tell us. . . . The history of the world? Just voices echoing in the dark, images that burn for a few centuries and then fade; stories, old stories that sometimes seem to overlap; strange links, impertinent connections." Barnes connects love to truth, but truth, objective truth, can never be found. Still, Sisyphus-like, one must constantly toil to find it. So it is with love: "We must believe in it, or we're lost." *A History of the World in 10½ Chapters* does not always succeed: The stories do not always successfully relate to one another, and the tone at times fails to achieve the ironic brilliance of *Flaubert's Parrot.*

Talking It Over · *Talking It Over* is superficially a less ambitious novel than *A History of the World in 10½ Chapters.* The novel features three characters: Stuart, a decent, dull banker; his wife, Gillian; and Stuart's old friend, Oliver, a flashy, "cultured" language instructor who falls in love with Gillian, who eventually leaves Stuart for Oliver. The characters are somewhat predictable, as is the eventual outcome, but Barnes's technique reveals the same events narrated by all three characters, who speak directly in monologues to the reader. Considered something of a minor work by critics, the novel again shows considerable verbal felicity, and in spite of the seeming predictability of the plot and the ordinariness of the characters, by the end the reader comes to appreciate their quirks and foibles.

England, England · It was several years before Barnes's next full-length novel appeared, in 1998, with *England, England.* In the interim he had written a novella, *The Porcupine,* set in an Eastern European country in the aftermath of the fall of Communism. In it Barnes notes how difficult it is to escape from the past, from history, and from its illusions and delusions, and he asks what one will escape to—to what new illusions and imaginings. *England, England* is also a meditation on history. A serious novel with a comedic and satirical core, it features Sir Jack Pitman, a larger-than-life, egocentric businessman who builds a historical Disneyland-style theme park on the Isle of Wight, off England's southern coast. Here tourists can enjoy and experience all of England's past and present at the same place, from the real king and queen, who have moved from the real England to "England, England," to a new Buckingham Palace, a half-sized Big Ben, cricket matches, William Shakespeare's wife Anne Hathaway's cottage, Stonehenge, poet William Wordsworth's daffodils, and every other event or place that in popular belief represents the English past. In time, this new England—"England, England"—becomes more successful, economically and in all other ways, than the country that inspired it.

Parallel to Pitman's story is that of Martha Cochrane, a leading member of his staff who briefly replaces him after discovering Pitman's unusual sexual proclivities. She, too, has had a difficult relationship with history, realizing that even personal reminiscences, like broader history, lack objective reality, and that even memories are constructs. The past becomes, perhaps, what we want it to be, or what we fear it was. Eventually, in old age, Cochrane escapes the present, returning to the former England, which itself has retreated into a largely preindustrial, rural past and is now called Anglia. The question becomes, can history go backward? Is Cochrane's Anglia any more authentic than Pitman's theme park; was old England itself ever more "real" than Pitman's "England, England," or was it too just an assembly of illusions and delusions?

Eugene Larson

Other major works
SHORT FICTION: *Cross Channel,* 1996.
NONFICTION: *Letters from London,* 1995 (essays).

Bibliography
Carey, John. "Land of Make-Believe." *The Sunday [London] Times*, August 23, 1998, p. 1. Carey, a leading British academic and a literary critic, discusses *England, England* as an unusual combination of the comic and the serious, a philosophical novel which posits important questions about reality.
Hulbert, Ann. "The Meaning of Meaning." *The New Republic* 196 (May 11, 1987): 37-39. Reviewing *Staring at the Sun*, Hulbert notes Barnes's continuing interest in the relationship between life and art; she comments on the differences in tone and technique between that novel and his earlier works, particularly *Flaubert's Parrot*.
Jenkins, Mitch. "Novel Escape." *The [London] Times Magazine*, January 13, 1996, p. 18. An interview with Barnes and a wide-ranging discussion of his life and works.
Kermode, Frank. "Obsessed with Obsession." *The New York Review of Books* 32 (April 25, 1985): 15. Kermode, an English literary critic, in his favorable review of *Flaubert's Parrot*, discusses some of the social and literary background of the younger generation of English novelists.
Locke, Richard. "Flood of Forms." *The New Republic* 201 (December 4, 1989): 40-43. Locke, a professor of comparative literature, places Barnes's interest in form and style in the context of modern literature, beginning with Flaubert. He summarizes all the novels, focusing particularly upon *A History of the World in 10½ Chapters*.
Lodge, David. "The Home Front." *The New York Review of Books* 34 (May 7, 1987): 21. Lodge is an English novelist, of the same generation as Barnes but generally less experimental in form. He finds *Staring at the Sun* less successful than *Flaubert's Parrot* and argues that Barnes attempted to incorporate too many elements into the former work.
Moseley, Merritt. *Understanding Julian Barnes*. Columbia: University of South Carolina Press, 1997. One of the volumes in the Understanding Contemporary British Literature series. Moseley finds Barnes to be one of the most intriguing and significant of modern British authors.

Aphra Behn

Born: England; July (?), 1640
Died: London, England; April 16, 1689

Principal long fiction · *Love Letters Between a Nobleman and His Sister*, 1683-1687 (3 volumes); *Agnes de Castro*, 1688; *The Fair Jilt: Or, The History of Prince Tarquin and Miranda*, 1688; *Oroonoko: Or, The History of the Royal Slave*, 1688; *The History of the Nun: Or, The Fair Vow-Breaker*, 1689; *The Lucky Mistake*, 1689; *The Nun: Or, The Perjured Beauty*, 1697; *The Adventure of the Black Lady*, 1698; *The Wandering Beauty*, 1698.

Other literary forms · As a truly professional writer, perhaps the first British female to have written for profit, Aphra Behn moved easily through the various literary genres and forms. Her plays include *The Forced Marriage: Or, The Jealous Bridegroom* (1670); *The Amorous Prince: Or, The Curious Husband* (1671); *The Dutch Lover* (1673); *The Town Fop: Or, Sir Timothy Tawdry* (1676); *Abdelazar: Or, The Moor's Revenge* (1676); *The Rover: Or, The Banished Cavaliers, Parts I and II* (1677, 1681); *Sir Patient Fancy* (1678); *The Roundheads: Or, The Good Old Cause* (1681); *The City Heiress: Or, Sir Timothy Treat-All* (1682); *The Lucky Chance: Or, An Alderman's Bargain* (1686); *The Emperor of the Moon* (1687); *The Widow Ranter: Or, The History of Bacon of Virginia* (1689); and *The Younger Brother: Or, The Amorous Jilt* (1696).

Although she enjoyed only mild success as a poet, her verse was probably no better or worse than that of a large number of second-rank versifiers of the Restoration. Behn's best poetry can be found in the song "Love in fantastic triumph sate" (1677), from her tragedy of *Abdelazar*, and in a metrical "Paraphrase on Oenone to Paris" for Jacob Tonson's volume of Ovid's *Epistles* (1680). The remainder of her verse includes a long, amorous allegory, *A Voyage to the Isle of Love* (1684); an adaptation of Bernard de Fontenelle's epic which she entitled *A Discovery of New Worlds* (1688); and two occasional pieces: "A Pindarick on the Death of Charles II" (1685) and "A Congratulatory Poem to Her Most Sacred Majesty" (1688).

Achievements · Behn's achievement as a novelist should be measured principally in terms of the modest gains made by that form in England during the seventeenth century. Prior to *Oroonoko*, the English novel lingered in the shadows of the theater. Thus, the small reading public contented itself with works such as John Lyly's *Euphues, the Anatomy of Wit* (1579), Sir Philip Sidney's *Arcadia* (1590), Thomas Lodge's *Rosalynde* (1590), Thomas Nashe's *The Unfortunate Traveler: Or, The Life of Jack Wilton* (1594), and Thomas Deloney's *Jack of Newbury* (1597)–all long, episodic stories, sprinkled with overly dramatic characterization and improbable plot structures. In *Oroonoko*, however, Behn advanced the novel to the point where her more skilled successors in the eighteenth century could begin to shape it into an independent, recognizable form.

Behn possessed the natural gifts of the storyteller, and her narrative art can easily stand beside that of her male contemporaries. A frankly commercial writer, she simply had no time, in pursuit of pleasure and the pen, to find a place in her narratives for intellectual substance. Nevertheless, she told a story as few others could, and the force of her own personality contributed both reality and a sense of immediacy to the still inchoate form of seventeenth century British fiction.

Biography · The details of Aphra Behn's birth are not known. The parish register of the Sts. Gregory and Martin Church, Wye, England, contains an entry stating that Ayfara Amis, daughter of John and Amy Amis, was baptized on July 10, 1640. Apparently, John Johnson, related to Lord Francis Willoughby of Parham, adopted the girl, although no one seems to know exactly when. Ayfara Amis accompanied her stepparents on a journey to Suriname (later Dutch Guiana) in 1658, Willoughby having appointed Johnson to serve as deputy governor of his extensive holdings there. Unfortunately, the new deputy died on the voyage; his widow and children proceeded to Suriname and took up residence at St. John's, one of Lord Willoughby's plantations. Exactly how long they remained is not clear, but certainly the details surrounding the time spent at St. John's form the background for *Oroonoko*.

Biographers have established the summer of 1663 as the most probable date of Behn's return to England. At any rate, by 1665 Behn was again in London and married to a wealthy merchant of Dutch extraction, who may well have had connections in, or at least around, the court of Charles II. In 1665 came the Great Plague and the death of Behn's husband; the latter proved the more disastrous for her, specifically because (again for unknown reasons) the Dutch merchant left nothing of substance for her—nothing, that is, except his court connections. Charles II, in the midst of the first of his wars against Holland, hired Aphra Behn as a secret government agent to spy upon the Dutch, for which purpose she proceeded to Antwerp. There she contacted another British agent, William Scott, from whom she obtained various pieces of military information, which she forwarded to London. Though she received little credit for her work, and even less money, Behn did conceive of the pseudonym Astrea, the name under which she published most of her poetry. The entire adventure into espionage proved a dismal failure for her; she even had to borrow money and pawn her valuables to pay her debts and obtain passage back to England. Once home, early in 1667, she found no relief from her desperate financial situation. Her debtors threat-

Library of Congress

ened prison, and the government refused any payment for her services. Prison followed, although the time and the exact length of her term remain unknown. Some of Behn's biographers speculate that she was aided in her release by John Hale (d. 1692)–a lawyer of Gray's Inn, a wit, an intellectual, a known homosexual, the principal subject of and reason for Behn's sonnets, and the man with whom she carried on a long romance. When she did gain her release, she determined to dedicate the rest of her life to writing and to pleasure, to trust to her own devices rather than to rely upon others who could not be trusted.

Behn launched her career as a dramatist in late December, 1670, at the new Duke's Theatre in Little Lincoln's Inn Fields, London. Her tragicomedy *The Forced Marriage* ran for six nights and included in the cast the nineteen-year-old Thomas Otway (1652-1685), the playwright-to-be only recently arrived from Oxford. Because of the length of the run, Behn, as was the practice, received the entire profit from the third performance, which meant that she could begin to function as an independent artist. She followed her first effort in the spring of 1671 with a comedy, *The Amorous Prince*, again at the Duke's; another comedy, *The Dutch Lover*, came to Drury Lane in February, 1673, and by the time of her anonymous comedy *The Rover*, in 1677, her reputation was secure. She mixed easily with the literati of her day, such as Thomas Killigrew, Edward Ravenscroft, the earl of Rochester, Edmund Waller, and the poet laureate John Dryden, who published her rough translations from Ovid in 1683. With her reputation came offers for witty prologues and epilogues for others' plays, as well as what she wanted more than anything–money. A confrontation with the earl of Shaftesbury and the newly emerged Whigs during the religious-political controversies of 1678, when she offended Charles II's opponents in a satirical prologue to an anonymous play, *Romulus and Hersilia*, brought her once again to the edge of financial hardship, as she was forced to abandon drama for the next five years.

Fortunately, Behn could fall back upon her abilities as a writer of popular fiction and occasional verse, although those forms were not as profitable as the London stage. Her series *Love Letters Between a Nobleman and His Sister* (1683-1687) and *Poems upon Several Occasions* (1684) were well received, but the meager financial returns from such projects could not keep pace with her personal expenses. When she did return to the stage in 1686 with her comedy *The Lucky Chance*, she met with only moderate success and some public abuse. *The Emperor of the Moon*, produced the following season, fared somewhat better, although by then the London audience had lost its stomach for a female playwright–and a Tory, at that. She continued to write fiction and verse, but sickness and the death of her friend Edmund Waller, both in October, 1688, discouraged her. Five days after the coronation of William III and Mary, on April 16, 1689, Behn died. She had risen high enough to merit burial in Westminster Abbey; John Hoyle provided the fitting epitaph: "Here lies proof that wit can never be/ Defense enough against mortality."

Analysis · In the early twentieth century, Vita Sackville-West, in trying to estimate Aphra Behn's contribution to English fiction, asked "what has she left behind her that is of any real value?" Sackville-West bemoaned Behn's failure in her fiction to reflect fully London life, London characters, London scenes; attention to exotic themes, settings, and characters merely debased and wasted her narrative gifts. Such a judgment, while plausible, fails to consider Behn's fiction in its historical and biographical context. Her tales abound with German princes, Spanish princesses, Portuguese kings, French counts, West Indian slaves, and various orders of bishops, priests, and nuns, yet, Behn's *real* world was itself highly artificial, even fantastic: the intrigue of the Stuart court, the ribaldry of the London stage, the gossip of the drawing room, the masquerade, and the card parlor. Behn, in her *real* world, took in the same scenes as did John Dryden, Samuel Pepys, and the earl of Rochester. Thus, to assert that her fiction neglects her actual experience in favor of fantastic and faraway window dressing may be too hasty a conclusion.

In *Agnes de Castro*, Behn lets loose various powers of love, with the result that her heroines' passions affect the fortunes of their lovers. Thus, Miranda (*The Fair Jilt*) reflects the raving, hypocritical enchantress whose very beauty drives her lovers mad; Ardelia (*The Nun*) plays the capricious lover, whose passion carries her through a series of men, as well as a nunnery; and Agnes de Castro presents a slight variation from the preceding, in that the titled character is a product of circumstance: She is loved by the husband of her mistress.

Another primary theme in Behn's work is the often discussed noble savage that has traditionally been assigned to *Oroonoko*, as has the subordinate issue of antislavery in that same novel. In 1975, Professor George Guffey suggested a withdrawal from the feminist-biographical positions (those from which the noble savage/antislavery ideals spring) and a movement toward "a hitherto unperceived level of political allusion." Guffey did not label *Oroonoko* a political allegory but did suggest that readers should look more closely at events in England between 1678 and 1688. Guffey maintains that the novelist deplores not the slavery of a black, noble savage but the bondage of a *royal prince*—again a reference to the political climate of the times. The interesting aspect of Guffey's analysis is that his approach lends substance to Behn's principal novel and to her overall reputation as a literary artist, and it parries the complaint that she failed to echo the sound and the sense of her own age.

In 1678, Sir Roger L'Estrange (1616-1704) published *Five Love Letters from a Nun to a Cavalier*, a translation of some fictional correspondence by the minor French writer Guilleraques. Behn used the work as a model for at least three of her prose pieces—*Love Letters Between a Nobleman and His Sister*, *The History of the Nun*, and *The Nun*. For the latter two, the novelist took advantage, at least on the surface, of the current religious and political controversies and set forth the usual claims to truth.

The History of the Nun · There may be some validity to the claim that *The History of the Nun* exists as one of the earliest examinations by a novelist into the psychology of crime and guilt. The events, at the outset, proceed reasonably enough but become less believable, and, by the novel's conclusion, the events appear to be exceedingly unreal. Despite this difficulty, the novel does have some value. Behn demonstrates her ability to develop thoroughly the key aspects of the weaknesses and the resultant sufferings of the heroine, Isabella. Behn immediately exposes the concept that "Mother Church" can take care of a girl's problems, can easily eradicate the desires of the world from her heart and mind, can readily transform a passionate maiden into a true, devoted sister of the faith. In addition, despite her wickedness, Isabella is still very much a human being worthy of the reader's understanding. At every step, the girl pays something for what she does; with each violation against the Church and each crime of passion, she falls deeper into the darkness of her own guilt. What she does, and how, is certainly contrived; how she reacts to her misdeeds reflects accurately the guilty conscience of a believable human being.

The Nun · The second "Nun" novel, not published until 1697, certainly leads the reader through a more complicated plot entanglement than the 1688 story, but it contains none of the virtue exhibited in the earlier work. The interesting aspect of *The Nun*'s plot is that Behn kills the heroine, Ardelia, first; only afterward do the principal rivals, Don Sebastian and Don Henriques, kill each other in a fight. The interest, however, is only fleeting, for those events do not occur until the end of the novel. All that remains of the bloody situation is Elvira, Don Sebastian's unfaithful sister. After weeping and calling for help, she is seized with a violent fever (in the final paragraph) and dies within twenty-four hours. Certainly, Behn's ingenuity in this piece demands some recognition, if for no other reason than her adeptness, according to James Sutherland, at "moving the pieces around the board."

Agnes de Castro · Because of the relative sanity of its plot, in contrast to the two previous tragedies, *Agnes de Castro* comes close to what Behn's feminist supporters expect of her. In other words, in this piece, pure evil or a series of tragic events cannot be blamed entirely on love or upon reckless female passion. Although Don Pedro genuinely loves his wife's maid-of-honor, Agnes, she, out of loyalty to her mistress, refuses to yield to his passion. Such action encourages the other characters to exhibit equal degrees of virtue. Constantia, Don Pedro's wife, seems to understand that the power of Agnes's charms, although innocent enough, is no match for her husband's frailty of heart over reason. Thus, she resents neither her husband nor her maid; in fact, she is willing to tolerate the presence of Agnes to keep her husband happy.

The novel, however, does not exist as a monument to reason. Something must always arise, either in politics or romance, to disrupt reasonable people's attempts at harmony. In the novel, a vengeful woman lies to Constantia and plants the rumor in her mind that Agnes and Don Pedro are plotting against her. Such a report breaks Constantia's trust in her husband and her maid, and the honest lady dies of a broken heart. The novel, however, remains believable, for Behn simply emphasizes the frailty of honor and trust in a world dominated by intrigue and pure hatred. Given the political and religious climates of the decade, the setting and the plot of *Agnes de Castro* are indeed flimsy façades for the court and coffeehouse of seventeenth century London.

The Fair Jilt · Although in *The Fair Jilt*, Behn continued to develop the conflict between love and reason, the novel has attracted critical attention because of its allusions to the writer's own experiences. Again, she lays claim to authenticity by maintaining that she witnessed parts of the events and heard the rest from sources close to the action and the characters. In addition, the events occur in Antwerp, the very city to which the novelist had been assigned for the performance of her spying activities for Charles II's ministers.

From the outset of the novel, Behn establishes the wickedness of Miranda, who uses her beauty to enchant the unsuspecting and even tempts the weak into commiting murder. Obviously, had Behn allowed her major character to succeed in her evil ways, nothing would have been gained from the novel. What results is the triumph of the hero's innate goodness; as weak as he is, he has endured. His loyalty and devotion have outlasted and, to a certain extent, conquered Miranda's wickedness.

Oroonoko · Behn's literary reputation today rests almost totally upon a single work, *Oroonoko*. The novel succeeds as her most realistic work, principally because she recounts the specifics of Suriname with considerable detail and force. Behn installs her hero amid the splendor of a tropical setting, a Natural Man, a pure savage untouched by the vices of Christian Europe, unaware of the white man's inherent baseness and falsehood.

In lashing out at the weaknesses of her society, Behn does not forget about one of her major concerns–love. Thus, Oroonoko loves the beautiful Imoinda, a child of his own race, but the prince's grandfather demands her for his own harem. Afterward, the monarch sells the girl into slavery, and she finds herself in Suriname, where Oroonoko is brought following his kidnapping. The prince embarks upon a term of virtuous and powerful adventures in the name of freedom for himself and Imoinda, but his captors deceive him. Thereupon, he leads a slave revolt, only to be captured by the white scoundrels and tortured. Rather than see Imoinda suffer dishonor at the hands of the ruthless white planters and government officers, Oroonoko manages to kill her himself. At the end, he calmly smokes his pipe–a habit learned from the Europeans–as his captors dismember his body and toss the pieces into the fire.

The final judgment upon Behn's fiction may still remain to be formulated. Evaluations of her work have tended to extremes. Some critics assert that her novels, even *Oroonoko*, had no significant influence on the development of the English novel, while others argue that her limited attempts at realism may well have influenced Daniel Defoe, Samuel Richardson, Henry Fielding, and others to begin to mold the ostensibly factual narrative into the novel as the twentieth century recognizes it. From Behn came the background against which fictional plots could go forward and fictional characters could function. Her problem, which her successors managed to surmount, was the inability (or refusal) to make her characters and events as real as their fictional environment. That fault (if it was a fault) lay with the tendencies and the demands of the age, not with the writer. Indeed, it is hardly a failure for a dramatist and a novelist to have given to her audience exactly what they wanted. To have done less would have meant an even quicker exit from fame and an even more obscure niche in the literary history of her time.

Samuel J. Rogal

Other major works

PLAYS: *The Forced Marriage: Or, The Jealous Bridegroom*, pr. 1670; *The Amorous Prince: Or, The Curious Husband*, pr., pb. 1671; *The Dutch Lover*, pr., pb. 1673; *Abdelazer: Or, The Moor's Revenge*, pr. 1676; *The Town Fop: Or, Sir Timothy Tawdry*, pr. 1676; *The Rover: Or, The Banished Cavaliers, Part I*, pr., pb. 1677, *Part II*, pr., pb. 1681; *Sir Patient Fancy*, pr., pb. 1678; *The Feigned Courtesans: Or, A Night's Intrigue*, pr., pb. 1679; *The Young King: Or, The Mistake*, pr. 1679; *The Roundheads: Or, The Good Old Cause*, pr. 1681; *The City Heiress: Or, Sir Timothy Treat-All*, pr., pb. 1682; *The Lucky Chance: Or, An Alderman's Bargain*, pr. 1686; *The Emperor of the Moon*, pr., pb. 1687; *The Widow Ranter: Or, The History of Bacon of Virginia*, pr. 1689; *The Younger Brother: Or, The Amorous Jilt*, pr., pb. 1696.

POETRY: *Poems upon Several Occasions, with a Voyage to the Island of Love*, 1684 (including adaptation of Abbé Paul Tallemant's *Le Voyage de l'isle d'amour*); *Miscellany: Being a Collection of Poems by Several Hands*, 1685 (includes works by others).

TRANSLATIONS: *Aesop's Fables*, 1687 (with Francis Barlow); *Of Trees*, 1689 (of book 6 of Abraham Cowley's *Sex libri plantarum*).

MISCELLANEOUS: *La Montre: Or, The Lover's Watch*, 1686 (prose and poetry); *The Case for the Watch*, 1686 (prose and poetry); *Lycidus: Or, The Lover in Fashion*, 1688 (prose and poetry; includes works by others); *The Lady's Looking-Glass, to Dress Herself By: Or,*

The Art of Charming, 1697 (prose and poetry); *The Works of Aphra Behn*, 1915, 1967 (6 volumes; Montague Summers, editor).

Bibliography

Goreau, Angeline. *Reconstructing Aphra: A Social Biography of Aphra Behn.* New York: Dial Press, 1980. Draws on Behn's own writings as well as contemporary comments about her, re-creating the life of the first professional female writer. Like Virginia Woolf, Behn is praised for providing a model for later women who took up the pen. The thirty-seven illustrations contribute to the reconstruction of the age. Little discussion of the fiction and later plays.

Guffey, George. "Aphra Behn's *Oroonoko:* Occasion and Accomplishment." In *Two English Novelists: Aphra Behn and Anthony Trollope: Papers Read at a Clark Library Seminar, May 11, 1974.* Los Angeles: Clark Library, 1975. Argues that *Oroonoko* is not an attack on slavery or a celebration of the natural man but rather a defense of James II, who is the model for the hero, as Suriname is made to resemble England.

Link, Frederick M. *Aphra Behn.* New York: Twayne, 1968. After a brief account of Behn's life, this book provides a critical survey of her works, devoting about half to her drama. Concludes with a survey of Behn's reputation since her death and includes a useful annotated bibliography of criticism.

O'Donnell, Mary Ann. *Aphra Behn: An Annotated Bibliography of Primary and Secondary Sources.* New York: Garland, 1986. After a detailed description of more than one hundred primary works, O'Donnell annotates 661 books, articles, essays, and dissertations written about Behn after 1666. These works are listed chronologically. Indexed.

Sackville-West, Vita. *Aphra Behn: The Incomparable Astrea.* New York: Viking Press, 1928. Sackville-West admires the woman more than the writing, though she finds the lyrics praiseworthy. Sympathetic and well written.

Todd, Janet, ed. *Aphra Behn Studies.* Cambridge, England: Cambridge University Press, 1996. Part 1 concentrates on Behn's plays, part 2 on her poetry, part 3 on her fiction, and part 4 on her biography. Includes an introduction outlining Behn's career and the essays in the volume and an index.

_____. *The Secret Life of Aphra Behn.* New Brunswick, N.J.: Rutgers University Press, 1996. The introduction summarizes efforts to study Behn's work and life, her place in literature, her ability to write in all the genres (except the sermon), and the biographer's efforts to overcome the paucity of biographical facts. In addition to a long, speculative narrative, Todd includes a bibliography of works written before 1800 and a bibliography of work published after 1800.

Woodcock, George. *The Incomparable Aphra.* London: Boardman, 1948. Behn is not only a good writer but also "a revolutionary influence on the social life and literature of her age."

Arnold Bennett

Born: Shelton, near Hanley, England; May 27, 1867
Died: London, England; March 27, 1931

Principal long fiction · *A Man from the North,* 1898; *Anna of the Five Towns,* 1902; *The Grand Babylon Hotel,* 1902 (pb. in U.S. as *T. Racksole and Daughter*); *The Gates of Wrath,* 1903; *Leonora,* 1903; *A Great Man,* 1904; *Teresa of Watling Street,* 1904; *Sacred and Profane Love,* 1905 (pb. in U.S. as *The Book of Carlotta*); *Hugo,* 1906; *Whom God Hath Joined,* 1906; *The Sinews of War,* 1906 (with Eden Phillpotts; pb. in U.S. as *Doubloons*); *The Ghost,* 1907; *The City of Pleasure,* 1907; *The Statue,* 1908 (with Phillpotts); *Buried Alive,* 1908; *The Old Wives' Tale,* 1908; *The Glimpse,* 1909; *Helen with the High Hand,* 1910; *Clayhanger,* 1910; *The Card,* 1911 (pb. in U.S. as *Denry the Audacious*); *Hilda Lessways,* 1911; *The Regent,* 1913 (pb. in U.S. as *The Old Adam*); *The Price of Love,* 1914; *These Twain,* 1915; *The Lion's Share,* 1916; *The Pretty Lady,* 1918; *The Roll-Call,* 1918; *Lilian,* 1922; *Mr. Prohack,* 1922; *Riceyman Steps,* 1923; *Elsie and the Child,* 1924; *Lord Raingo,* 1926; *The Strange Vanguard,* 1928 (pb. in U.S. as *The Vanguard,* 1927); *Accident,* 1928; *Piccadilly,* 1929; *Imperial Palace,* 1930; *Venus Rising from the Sea,* 1931.

Other literary forms · Besides fifteen major novels, Arnold Bennett published thirty-three other novels generally considered potboilers by his critics. Some of them Bennett himself regarded as serious works; others he variously called "fantasias," "frolics," "melodramas," or "adventures." His total published work exceeds eighty volumes, including eight collections of short stories, sixteen plays, six collections of essays, eight volumes of literary criticism, three volumes of letters, six travelogues, and volumes of autobiography, journals, and reviews, as well as miscellaneous short articles, introductions, pamphlets, "pocket philosophies," and a few poems. Much of his journal has never been published. Bennett collaborated in the production of five films and operas, three of which were adapted from his plays and novels. Four of his plays and novels were adapted for film by other screenwriters, and two of his novels were adapted for the stage.

Achievements · Although Arnold Bennett won only one major literary award, the James Tait Black Memorial Prize for *Riceyman Steps,* his contribution to the history of the novel exceeds that accomplishment. Bennett's early novels played an important role in the transition from the Victorian to the modern novel. A somewhat younger contemporary of Thomas Hardy, Henry James, and Joseph Conrad, he helped to displace the "loose, baggy" Victorian novel and to develop the realistic movement in England. With fine detail he portrayed the industrial Five Towns, his fictional version of the six towns of pottery manufacturing in Staffordshire County. His early career was strongly influenced by the aestheticism in form and language found in works by Gustave Flaubert, Guy de Maupassant, and Ivan Turgenev, and he admired the naturalism of Honoré de Balzac, Émile Zola, and Edmond and Jules de Goncourt. Later, however, he rejected what he called the "crudities and . . . morsels of available misery" of naturalism, and, while retaining an interest in form and beauty, he came to feel that aesthetics alone is an empty literary goal and that the novelist must combine "divine compassion," believability, and the creation of character with the "artistic shapely presentation of truth" and the discovery of "beauty, which is always hidden." With these aims in mind, he chose as the subject of his best works that which is beautiful and remarkable about the lives of unremarkable, middle-class people. Although his novels rarely sold well enough to earn his living, his best novels were highly regarded by critics and fellow authors. He carried on a correspondence of mutual encouragement and criticism with Conrad and H. G. Wells; some of these letters have been published. Conrad, a master of style, wrote: "I am . . . fascinated by your expression, by the ease of your realization, the force and delicacy of your phrases." Despite their acclaim for Bennett's best work, however, even his admirers regretted his propensity to write potboilers for money.

Because of the volume of his work, Bennett is remembered today as a novelist, but in his lifetime his income derived from his equally prodigious output of plays and journalism; his "pocket philosophies" and critical reviews also won him an enormous public prestige. During the 1920's he was virtually the arbiter of literary taste, a reviewer who could make or break a book's sales or a newcomer's career. He was among the first to praise the literary merits of such controversial newcomers as D. H. Lawrence, T. S. Eliot, William Faulkner, Virginia Woolf, and James Joyce. Bennett regarded himself less a novelist than a professional writer who should be able to, and did, undertake any genre with competence and craftsmanship. (The exception was poetry; he never wrote poetry to meet his own standards.) His reputation suffered in the latter part of his career for those very qualities, which too often fell short of genius and inspiration. He did reach the level of greatness occasionally, however, and his literary reputation is firmly established with the inclusion of *The Old Wives' Tale* in most lists of the great English novels.

Biography · Enoch Arnold Bennett was born on May 27, 1867, in Shelton, Staffordshire County, England, near the six towns that constitute the Potteries region in central England, the scene of much of Bennett's early work. His father, Enoch Bennett, was successively a potter, a draper, a pawnbroker, and eventually, through hard work and study, a solicitor. Bennett attended the local schools, where he passed the examination for Cambridge University. He did not attend college, however, because his autocratic father kept him at home as clerk in the solicitor's office.

As a means of escape from the grime and provincialism of the Potteries district, Bennett began writing for the *Staffordshire Sentinel* and studying shorthand. The latter skill enabled him to become a clerk with a London law firm in 1888. In London, he set about seriously to learn to write. He moved to Chelsea in 1891 to live with the Frederick Marriott family, in whose household he was introduced to the larger world of the arts. His first work published in London was a prizewinning parody for a competition in *Tit-Bits* in 1893; this work was followed by a short story in *The Yellow Book* and, in 1898, his first novel, *A Man from the North*. He became the assistant editor and later the editor of the magazine *Woman*, writing reviews pseudonymously as "Barbara," a gossip and advice column as "Marjorie," and short stories as "Sal Volatile." It is generally thought that this experience provided a good background for female characterization. As he became better known as a journalist, Bennett began writing reviews for *The Academy* and giving private lessons in journalism. His journalistic income allowed him in 1900 to establish a home at Trinity Hall Farm, Hockliffe, in Bedfordshire. He brought his family to Hockliffe after his father had been disabled by the softening of the brain which eventually killed him. Bennett wrote prodigiously

there, producing not only his admired *Anna of the Five Towns* but also popular potboilers and journalism, including the anonymous "Savoir-Faire Papers" and "Novelist's Log-Book" series for *T. P.'s Weekly*. This production financed some long-desired travel and a move to Paris in 1903.

Bennett lived in France for eight years, some of the busiest and happiest of his life. Shortly after his arrival, he observed a fat, fussy woman who inspired the thought that "she has been young and slim once," a thought that lingered in his mind for five years and inspired his masterwork, *The Old Wives' Tale*. Meanwhile, he continued writing for newspapers and magazines, including the first of his series "Books and Persons," written under the nom de plume "Jacob Tonson" for *The New Age*. Between 1903 and 1907 he also wrote ten novels. In 1907, he married Marguerite Soulié, an aspiring actress who had worked as his part-time secretary. From the beginning of the marriage, it was evident that the two were incompatible, but she did provide him with an atmosphere conducive to his undertaking the novel which had germinated for so long and which he felt beforehand would be a masterpiece. He determined that *The Old Wives' Tale* should "do one better than" Guy de Maupassant's *Une Vie* (1883), and his careful crafting of the book was recognized by critics, who immediately acclaimed it as a modern classic. Before moving back to England in 1913, he wrote six more novels, three of which are among his best: *Clayhanger, The Card,* and *Hilda Lessways.* In 1911, he traveled in the United States, where his books were selling well and were highly respected. After the tour, he moved to the country estate Comarques at Thorpe-le-Soken, Essex, where he had access to the harbor for a yacht, his means of gaining what relaxation he could.

The yacht was important to Bennett, because he had suffered since youth from a variety of ailments, mostly resulting from his high-strung temperament. He had a serious stammer or speech paralysis, which exhausted him in speaking; compulsive personal habits; and a liver ailment and chronic enteritis which restricted his diet and caused great discomfort when he ate incautiously. As he grew older, he suffered increasingly from excruciating neuralgia, headaches, and insomnia, almost without relief near the end of his life. Except for the yacht, his recreation was to write; he probably wrote his light works as a relief from the tension of the serious novels, yet he demanded good style from himself even for them. His craftsmanship was conscious and intense, and his drive to produce great quantity while still maintaining quality undoubtedly sapped his strength, both physically and psychologically, and contributed to his death at the age of sixty-three.

Bennett's physical maladies were probably exacerbated by World War I and the collapse of his marriage. Although he continued his usual pace of writing during the war—five more novels between 1914 and 1919—much of his energy was spent in patriotic activities ranging from entertaining soldiers to frontline journalism. From May 9, 1918, until the end of the war, he served as volunteer director of British propaganda in France. He refused knighthood for his services. After the war, he tried to restore his depleted finances by writing plays, which had been more remunerative than novels, but the later ones were unsuccessful. In 1921, he and Marguerite separated. He gave her a settlement so generous that for the rest of his life he was under pressure to publish and sell his writing. Contemporary critics believed that these years of low-novel production marked the end of his creativity.

Bennett surprised his critics, however, with *Riceyman Steps,* which was critically acclaimed and was awarded the James Tait Black Memorial Prize, Bennett's only literary award. This was followed by *Lord Raingo* and *Imperial Palace,* as well as six less distinguished novels and one unfinished at his death. This creative resurgence may have resulted in part from his relationship with Dorothy Cheston, who bore his only child, Virginia, in 1926. His journalistic career had never waned, and in the 1920's he continued his "Books and Persons" series in the *Evening Standard,* with a prestige that influenced the reading public and allowed him to promote the careers of many young authors. Bennett's health was steadily deteriorating, however, and in 1931 he died in his Chiltern Court flat from typhoid fever.

Analysis · As a self-designated professional author, Arnold Bennett not only wrote an extraordinary quantity in a great variety of genres but also created a broad range of themes and characters. A common approach or theme is difficult to detect in a corpus of forty-eight novels, which include fantasy, realism, romance, naturalism, satire, symbolism, comedy, tragedy, melodrama, Freudian psychology, allegory, economics, regionalism, cosmopolitanism, politics, medicine, and war. Nevertheless, in spite of this diversity, Bennett is generally esteemed for his realistic novels, which are considered his serious work. In most, if not all, of these fifteen novels, certain related themes recur, rising from his youthful experiences of growing up in Burslem under the domination of his father. His desire to escape the intellectual, aesthetic, and spiritual stultification of his Burslem environment led to a cluster of themes related to escape: rebellion against the ties of the home conflicting with love for one's roots, aspiration versus complacence and philistinism, fear of failure to escape and fear of failure after escape, and the problem of coping with success if it comes. Another cluster of themes relates to his conflict with his father and the shock of his father's debilitating illness and death: the generation gap, emotional repression by dominating parents, the cyclical influence of parents on their children, a soul parent who vies in influence with the natural parent, degeneration and illness, the pathos of decrepitude in old age, and awe at the purpose or purposelessness of life.

A Man from the North · *A Man from the North,* Bennett's first novel, includes the themes of aspiration, emotional repression, the soul parent, illness and death, and failure after escape. It is the story of Richard Larch, an aspiring writer from the Potteries, who goes to London to experience the greater intellectual and moral freedom of a cosmopolis. There he meets his soul father, Mr. Aked, a journalist and failed novelist who introduces Larch to the drama—the "tragedy"—of ordinary lives. Aked, however, is an unsuccessful guide; he dies. Larch is also unable to succeed; he eventually marries a woman he does not love and settles down to the sort of life Aked had described. It is the story of what Bennett himself might have been if he had not succeeded after leaving Burslem.

Anna of the Five Towns · *Anna of the Five Towns,* on the other hand, is the story of the failure to escape. Anna is repressed by her overbearing and miserly father; under the influence of her soul mother, Mrs. Sutton, she learns to aspire to a few amenities, such as new clothes for her wedding, but these aspirations come too late to change her life significantly. Accepting the values of the community rather than escaping them, she marries Henry Mynors, her more prosperous suitor, rather than Willie Price, the man she loves in her own way. While the themes of these books are similar, they differ in that Anna stays and copes with her environment with some success. She does not escape Bursley (Bennett's fictional name for Burslem), but she escapes her father's control and improves her perceptions of beauty and human relationships to some degree. The books also differ in that *A Man from the North* presents an unrelentingly grim memory of Burslem. Later, however, Bennett read George Moore's *A Mummer's Wife* (1884), and its section on Burslem showed him that "beauty, which is always hidden," could be found in the lives of its people and in art expressing those lives. Thus, Bennett returned to the locale for *Anna of the Five Towns,* and although the portrayal is still grim, Anna's life has tragic beauty. Anna rebels against the ties of home, but she also has some love for her roots there, in the person of Willie Price.

The Old Wives' Tale · Between *Anna of the Five Towns* and *The Old Wives' Tale,* Bennett wrote eleven minor novels, some of which were serious and some not, but all taught him something that contributed to the greatness of *The Old Wives' Tale.* Several of them were light comedies, and in writing these Bennett developed the assured comic touch which marks even his serious novels. Three of them were Five Towns novels about female characters from various segments of Bursley society; in these he developed those skills in characterizing women which were so admired in his finest novels. These skills were honed in France, where Bennett learned a great deal about the literary presentation of sex. During these years, Bennett said, he learned more about life than he had ever known before.

When Bennett was ready to write his masterpiece, *The Old Wives' Tale,* he had reached full artistic maturity and was at the height of his literary power. He had published one critically acclaimed novel and several others that had allowed him to improve his characterization, especially of women, to temper his realism with humor, and to perfect his themes in various plots. His dislike of Burslem's grime and provincialism had been balanced by compassion for its inhabitants and awareness of what beauty and aspiration could be found there. His personal involvement in the town had been modified by experience in London and Paris, so that he could be objective about the sources of his material. This balance of technique and emotion is reflected in the structure of *The Old Wives' Tale.* The novel counterpoints the lives of two sisters, Constance and Sophia Baines, the first of whom stays in Bursley, while the second leaves but later returns. Their stories parallel not only each other but also those of preceding and succeeding generations. In fact, the first section of the book is subtitled "Mrs. Baines" (the mother).

In section one, *The Old Wives' Tale* takes up in midcareer one generation's old wife, with a husband so ill that the wife is running his draper's business and rearing two young daughters. As the girls grow up, Mrs. Baines finds them increasingly hard to handle. During a town festival in which an elephant has to be executed for killing a spectator, Mr. Baines dies. Shortly afterward, Sophia elopes with Gerald Scales, a traveling salesman, and Constance marries Samuel Povey, the former shop assistant, whom Mrs. Baines considers "beneath" her. When Samuel and Constance take over the business, introducing progressive marketing methods, Mrs. Baines retires to live with her elder sister, and dies there. The story of Mrs. Baines, then, is the end of the life of a woman who "was young and slim once," although she is not depicted so and that part of her life is understood only by later comparison with the stories of her daughters.

The cycle of Mrs. Baines continues with Constance, who represents the person who stays in Bursley, held by the roots of the past. As Mrs. Baines's successor, Constance marries a husband whose aspiration is to improve, not to leave, Bursley, and they run the business with a combination of youthful progressiveness and family tradition. Constance and Samuel have a son, Cyril. After a scandal in which Samuel's cousin is executed for murdering his alcoholic wife, Samuel dies. Constance continues the business for a while, unresponsive to further progressive business practices, and spoils her son until he becomes hard for her to manage. She is finally forced to retire from business by changes in the business structure of Bursley, and Cyril escapes from her and Bursley to London to study art. As a result, Constance comes to depend emotionally on Cyril's cousin, Dick.

Sophia, the rebel against Bursley, finds a soul mother in the schoolteacher, who introduces her to a world of wider intellectual aspiration. In her eagerness to experience more than Bursley offers, however, she elopes with a salesman, who represents sophistication and romance to her. They go to France, where they squander their money and slip into mutual disillusionment and recrimination. After observing the public execution of the murderer of a courtesan, Sophia becomes ill and is abandoned by Gerald. She eventually acquires a boardinghouse in Paris, where she supports several dependents and survives the siege of Paris through single-minded hoarding and hard work. She becomes a reclusive fixture on her street, much like Constance on her square in Bursley. When she becomes ill and the business becomes hard for her to manage, she sells it and returns to Bursley to grow old and die.

Each daughter's life recapitulates Mrs. Baines's in certain respects. Each marries, loses a husband, succors children or other dependents, runs a business, gradually loses control over her life (the change marked in each case by a symbolic execution), loses health and strength, and retires to die as a burdensome old woman like the one Bennett saw in the Paris restaurant. Further, although they are not women, the two Povey young men, Cyril and his cousin Dick, recapitulate the early years of Sophia and Constance: Cyril, the rebel who leaves Bursley but does not succeed; and Dick, the stay-at-home progressive idealist. At the end, Dick is engaged to marry a slim, young counterpart to Constance, who will no doubt carry on the cycle. The thematic repetitions are not so obvious as they appear here, of course; the variations of individual character allow the reader a sense of more difference than similarity.

The variations also mark a further step in Bennett's use of his themes. Constance and Sophia are not so warped by Bursley as was Anna in *Anna of the Five Towns*; in fact, Sophia, who escapes, is warped more than Constance, who stays. Both have strength derived from their roots, and while neither can be said to escape or to achieve happiness or grace in living, both transcend Bursley more successfully than other townspeople. The theme of their decrepitude in old age is a separate one, also used in other novels, but not related to the escape and success themes. The Baineses are grouped in other Five Towns stories with those who succeed on Bursley's terms. Beginning in 1906 in *Whom God Hath Joined*, in the collection of short stories *The Matador of the Five Towns* (1912), and in *The Old Wives' Tale*, there is a growing emphasis upon those members of Burslem society who have some education, culture, and sophistication. Perhaps Bennett had been reassured by his personal success that his childhood in Burslem could be accepted.

Clayhanger · Whether it is true that Bennett had come to accept his past, it is certainly true that his next serious book, *Clayhanger*, was his most nearly autobiographical. After the completion of the trilogy of which *Clayhanger* was the first volume, Bennett turned from the Five Towns to London as the setting for his novels. The Clayhanger trilogy is the story of a man who at first is defeated in his desire to escape Bursley. Having been defeated, however, he learns from his soul father to rise above Bursley's philistinism. Over the years, he breaks one after another of his bonds to Bursley until he has succeeded in escaping intellectually, and, eventually, he completely abandons the Five Towns.

Much of this story occurs in the third volume of the trilogy, *These Twain*. *Clayhanger* itself is the story of the generational conflict between Edwin Clayhanger and his father Darius. The conflict is similar to the one between Anna and her father in *Anna of the Five Towns* and between Sophia and Mrs. Baines in *The Old Wives' Tale*, but in *Clayhanger* it is much more intense and more acutely observed. Edwin is sensitively introduced in the first two chapters; he has within him "a flame . . . like an altar-fire," a passion "to exhaust himself in doing his best." He is rebelling against his father, whose highest aspiration for his son is to have him take over his printing business. The advancement of the theme in *Clayhanger* over its treatment in the earlier novels is that the generational conflict is presented sympathetically on both sides. In chapters 3 and 4, Darius is portrayed as sensitively as Edwin has been previously. In an intensely moving chapter, his childhood of promise, stifled at seven years by poverty and abusive child labor, is described. Because Darius as a "man of nine" was unable to "keep the family," they were sent to the poorhouse. They were rescued from this degradation by Darius's Sunday school teacher (his soul father), who had recognized Darius's promise and who secured Darius a decent job as a printer's devil. This background of deprivation and emotional sterility prevents Darius from expressing his softer emotions, such as his love for Edwin; his total dedication to the business which he built and by which he supports his family is thoroughly empathetic to the reader. It is no wonder that he can conceive nothing nobler for Edwin than to carry on this decent business. Because Darius can never discuss these traumatic childhood experiences, Edwin never understands him any more than Darius understands Edwin.

In his desire to hold onto his son and keep him in the family business, Darius simply ignores and overrides Edwin's inchoate talent for architecture. Later, he uses Edwin's financial dependence to squelch his desire to marry Hilda Lessways, whom Edwin has met through the architect Osmond Orgreave. Although Edwin resents his father's domination, he cannot openly rebel; he feels inadequate before his father's dominance, and he looks forward to the day when he will have his vengeance. This day comes when Darius becomes ill with softening of the brain, the same ailment that killed Bennett's own father. The progression of the illness and Edwin's emotions of triumph, irritation, and compassion are exquisitely detailed. Even after Darius's death, however, Edwin is not free from his father's presence, for he becomes increasingly like his father, learning to take pride in the business and to tyrannize over his sisters and Hilda, with whom he is reconciled at the end of the book. *Clayhanger* thus concludes with the apparent defeat of aspiration by the cycle of parental influence.

Hilda Lessways · The hope of eventual success has been raised, however, by the death of Darius, that primary symbol of Bursley repression, and the return of Hilda, the symbol of aspiration. In *Hilda Lessways*, the second book of the trilogy, Bennett picks up her parallel story of generational conflict with her mother and cultural conflict with Turnhill, another of the Five Towns. Hilda's story is far less compelling than Edwin's, though, and adds little to the plot development. More important, its structure repeats what Bennett did successfully in *The Old Wives' Tale*: It contrasts two efforts to cope with Bursley, which provide for a double perspective on the problem, and then brings them together for the denouement made possible by that combined perspective. The double perspective also allows Bennett to maintain his characteristic objectivity and touch of humor.

These Twain · *These Twain* was the last Five Towns novel; it presents the marriage of Edwin and Hilda. Through a series of adjustments and small victories, the two are able to achieve a social success in the Five Towns, which allows them to wean themselves emotionally from the Potteries and leave forever. The *Clayhanger* trilogy thus deals with escape and success, rather than some aspect of failure as in the earlier novels.

In changing his fictional settings from Bursley to London or the Continent, Bennett also extended his themes from success or failure in escaping poverty and provincialism to success or failure in handling the accomplished escape. Perhaps that is another reason, besides the ones usually offered, for Bennett's long period of low productivity and substandard potboilers from 1915 to 1922. Between *Anna of the Five Towns* and *The Old Wives' Tale*, one should remember, there had been a similar period of low-quality work during which Bennett perfected skills that made the Five Towns novels great. Similarly, in his postwar characters Audrey Moze, George Cannon, G. J. Hoape, Lilian Share, and Mr. Prohack, Bennett experimented with stories of people who must cope with financial or social responsibilities for which they may have been poorly prepared. Also in these stories he experimented more boldly with varieties of sexual relationships: in *The Lion's Share*, implied lesbianism; in *The Pretty Lady*, prostitution; in *Lilian*, a mistress. Furthermore, although these next qualities do not show up clearly in the low-quality work of this period, the use of symbols and psychological insight must have been developing in Bennett's mind. These qualities emerge rather suddenly and very effectively in the novels beginning with *Riceyman Steps*. They may account for some of the high acclaim which that novel received after the period of reorientation, but the adapted themes were perfected by 1923, as well.

Riceyman Steps · The themes in *Riceyman Steps* are variations on those of the Five Towns novels, not departures which might seem necessary to a metropolitan setting. The decayed and grimy industrial area of Clerkenwell is in many respects Bursley resituated in London. Henry Earlforward, the miser, represents Bursley's industrial materialism. Henry, like Edwin Clayhanger, has succeeded in that environment; he has a well-respected bookstore that offers him financial self-sufficiency. Unlike Edwin, however, Henry's complacent rootedness to Clerkenwell progressively cuts him off from grace, beauty, then love, and finally even life. His wife, Violet, also has financial security, but because she fears the loss of her success, she has become almost as miserly as he. Both are described as sensual; Henry's rich red lips are mentioned several times, and Violet, formerly a widow, wears red flowers in her hat. Money, however, is the chief object of their eroticism. Henry's miserliness is his passion, and he gives Violet her own safe as a wedding gift. Violet becomes "liquid with acquiescence" after seeing the hoarded disorder of his house, and she urges him to bed after he has shown her the gold coins in his private safe. The passion for money soon overrides the related passion of human love. Henry especially, and Violet in acquiescence, lock doors more tightly about themselves to protect their treasures until each is figuratively shut into a private, iron-walled safe. Starving emotionally and intellectually in their isolation, they finally starve themselves physically as well, rather than spend money for adequate food. Here, aspiration gone awry, the fear of failure and the inability to cope with success become literally debilitating diseases. Violet dies of a tumor and malnutrition and Henry of cancer. After death, they are scarcely missed, the ultimate symbols of the stultification which Bennett's characters strive with varying success to escape.

Final Years · After *Riceyman Steps*, the next few novels—*Lord Raingo, Accident*, and *Imperial Palace*—continue the themes of coping with success, and the protagonists are given increasing ability to handle it. Much as Clayhanger finally overcomes the problems of escape, Evelyn Orcham in *Imperial Palace* is the culminating figure in the second cluster of themes. Ironically, Bennett died shortly after he had resolved the problems underlying the themes of his serious novels. All of Bennett's serious works are firmly rooted in the realistic tradition (although he used more symbolism than has generally been recognized), and he excelled in the presentation of detail that makes his themes and characters credible. In the late years of his career, he was criticized by Virginia Woolf for portraying people's surroundings, rather than the people themselves, and forcing his readers to do his imagining for him, even though he believed that character creating was one of the three most important functions of a novel. Woolf's criticism was sound enough to seriously damage Bennett's standing as a major novelist, and it has been the keystone of critical opinion ever since. Yet, a sense of environmental impact has always been accepted as an important means of characterization in realistic literature. Woolf's criticism says as much about changing styles in literature as it does about the merits of Bennett's fiction. More important, it was a criticism aimed at Bennett's total canon, since his potboilers had not yet died of their natural ailments when Woolf wrote. Sophia and Constance Baines, Edwin and Darius Clayhanger, and Henry Earlforward are finely articulated, memorable characters. It is, after all, for his best work that any artist is remembered. Bennett's sense of place, characters, and universality of themes combine to make his finest novels memorable; *The Old Wives' Tale* is sufficient to secure Bennett's stature as one of the outstanding novelists of his era.

Carol I. Croxton

Other major works

SHORT FICTION: *The Loot of Cities*, 1905; *Tales of the Five Towns*, 1905; *The Grim Smile of the Five Towns*, 1907; *The Matador of the Five Towns*, 1912; *The Woman Who Stole Everything*, 1927; *Selected Tales*, 1928; *The Night Visitor*, 1931.

PLAYS: *Polite Farces*, pb. 1899; *Cupid and Commonsense*, pr. 1908; *What the Public Wants*, pr., pb. 1909; *The Honeymoon: A Comedy in Three Acts*, pr., pb. 1911; *Milestones: A Play in Three Acts*, pr., pb. 1912 (with Edward Knoblock); *The Great Adventure: A Play of Fantasia in Four Sets*, pr. 1912; *The Title*, pr., pb. 1918; *Judith*, pr., pb. 1919; *Sacred and Profane Love*, pr., pb. 1919; *Body and Soul*, pr., pb. 1922; *The Love Match*, pr., pb. 1922; *Don Juan*, pb. 1923; *London Life*, pr., pb. 1924 (with Knoblock); *Flora*, pr. 1927; *Mr. Prohack*, pr., pb. 1927 (with Knoblock); *The Return Journey*, pr., pb. 1928.

NONFICTION: *Journalism for Women*, 1898; *Fame and Fiction*, 1901; *The Truth About an Author*, 1903; *How to Become an Author*, 1903; *Things That Interested Me*, 1906; *Things Which Have Interested Me*, 1907, 1908; *Books and Persons: Being Comments on a Past Epoch*, 1908-1911; *Literary Taste*, 1909; *Those United States*, 1912 (pb. in U.S. as *Your United States*); *Paris Nights*, 1913; *From the Log of the Velsa*, 1914; *The Author's Craft*, 1914; *Over There*, 1915; *Things That Have Interested Me*, 1921, 1923, 1926; *Selected Essays*, 1926; *Mediterranean Scenes*, 1928; *The Savour of Life*, 1928; *The Journals of Arnold Bennett*, 1929, 1930, 1932-1933.

Bibliography

Batchelor, John. *The Edwardian Novelists*. New York: St. Martin's Press, 1982. After quoting Virginia Woolf's reservations about Bennett's fiction, Batchelor goes on to compare the two novelists, especially in terms of their treatment of women as being socially conditioned. In addition to discussing *Clayhanger*, *A Man from the North*, *Anna of the Five Towns*, and *The Old Wives' Tale*, Batchelor examines Bennett's acclaimed short story "The Death of Simon Fuge."

Drabble, Margaret. *Arnold Bennett*. New York: Alfred A. Knopf, 1974. Drawing from Bennett's *Journals* and letters, this biography focuses on Bennett's background, childhood, and environment, which she ties to his literary works. Profusely illustrated, containing an excellent index (the entry under Bennett provides a capsule summary of his life) and a bibliography of Bennett's work.

Lucas, John. *Arnold Bennett: A Study of His Fiction*. London: Methuen, 1974. After a brief review of Bennett criticism, Lucas examines Bennett's fiction, devoting lengthy treatments to his major novels which are discussed in terms of character and plot. Ardently defends Bennett's realism, which is regarded as equal to that of D. H. Lawrence. This impressionistic study lacks documentation, except for copious quotations from Bennett's work.

Roby, Kinley. *A Writer at War: Arnold Bennett, 1914-1918.* Baton Rouge: Louisiana State University Press, 1972. Although primarily biographical, this book also offers valuable insights into Bennett's work during and after World War I. Defends Bennett's post-1914 work, contending that it was influenced by Bennett's exhaustion of his Five Towns material, by his steadily deteriorating relationship with his wife, Marguerite, and by the war itself. Contains works cited and an excellent index.

Squillace, Robert. *Modernism, Modernity, and Arnold Bennett.* Lewisburg, Pa.: Bucknell University Press, 1997. Squillace argues that Bennett saw more clearly than his contemporary novelists the emergence of the modern era, which transformed a male-dominated society to one open to all people regardless of class or gender. Very detailed notes and a bibliography acknowledge the work of the best scholars.

Wright, Walter F. *Arnold Bennett: Romantic Realist.* Lincoln: University of Nebraska Press, 1971. Sees Bennett as vacillating between the two extremes of Romanticism and realism and describes his novels as mildly experimental.

Elizabeth Bowen

Born: Dublin, Ireland; June 7, 1899
Died: London, England; February 22, 1973

Principal long fiction · *The Hotel,* 1927; *The Last September,* 1929; *Friends and Relations,* 1931; *To the North,* 1932; *The House in Paris,* 1935; *The Death of the Heart,* 1938; *The Heat of the Day,* 1949; *A World of Love,* 1955; *The Little Girls,* 1964; *Eva Trout,* 1968.

Other literary forms · The first seven of Elizabeth Bowen's novels were republished by Jonathan Cape in Cape Collected Editions between the years 1948 and 1954, when Cape also republished four of her short-story collections: *Joining Charles* (1929), *The Cat Jumps and Other Stories* (1934), *Look at All Those Roses* (1941), and *The Demon Lover* (1945). Other books of short stories are *Encounters* (1923), *Ann Lee's and Other Stories* (1926), *Stories by Elizabeth Bowen* (1959), and *A Day in the Dark and Other Stories* (1965). *The Demon Lover* was published in New York under the title *Ivy Gripped the Steps and Other Stories* (1946) and, as the original title indicates, has supernatural content which scarcely appears in the novels. Bowen's nonfiction includes *Bowen's Court* (1942), a description of her family residence in Ireland; *Seven Winters* (1942), an autobiography; *English Novelists* (1946), a literary history; *Collected Impressions* (1950), essays; *The Shelbourne: A Center of Dublin Life for More than a Century* (1951), a work about the hotel in Dublin; *A Time in Rome* (1960), travel essays; and *Afterthought: Pieces About Writing* (1962), broadcasts and reviews. A play, coauthored with John Perry and entitled *Castle Anna,* was performed in London in March, 1948.

Achievements · Considered a great lady by those who knew her, Bowen draws an appreciative audience from readers who understand English gentility, the calculated gesture and the controlled response. Bowen's support has come from intellectuals who recognize the values of the novel of manners and who liken her work to that of Jane Austen and Henry James. Her contemporaries and colleagues included members of the Bloomsbury Group and of Oxford University, where the classical scholar C. M. Bowra was a close friend. Many readers know Bowen best through her novel *The Death of the Heart* and her short stories, especially "The Demon Lover," "Joining Charles," and "Look at All Those Roses," which are frequently anthologized in college texts. Bowen was made a Commander of the British Empire in 1948, and she was awarded an honorary doctor of letters degree at Trinity College, Dublin, in 1949, and at Oxford University in 1957. She was made a Companion of Literature in 1965.

Biography · Although born in Ireland, Elizabeth Dorothea Cole Bowen came from a pro-British family who received land in County Cork as an award for fighting with Oliver Cromwell in 1649. The family built Bowen's Court in 1776—what the Irish call a "big house"—as a Protestant stronghold against the mainly Catholic Irish and lived there as part of the Anglo-Irish ascendancy. Bowen was educated in England and spent some summers at Bowen's Court. Not until after the Irish Rising in 1916 did she come to realize the causes of the Irish struggle for independence; and in writing

Bowen's Court, she admitted that her family "got their position and drew their power from a situation that shows an inherent wrong."

Her barrister father, when aged nineteen, had disobeyed warnings and carried home smallpox, which eventually killed his mother and rendered his father mad. Preoccupied with the desire for a son, the attempt to have one nearly killed his wife in 1904, and burdened with the debts of Bowen's Court, he suffered severe mental breakdowns in 1905 and 1906 and again in 1928. He was the cause of Elizabeth's removal to England, where, as an Irish outcast, her defense was to become excessively British. Living in a series of locations with her mother, she was kept uninformed of family circumstances; as an adult, her novels provided for her an outlet for her sense of guilt, the result of feeling responsible for the unex-

Library of Congress

plained events around her. Her lack of roots was intensified with the death of her mother in 1912.

Bowen studied art, traveled in Europe, and worked as an air-raid warden in London during World War II. In 1923, she married Alan Charles Cameron, who was employed in the school system near Oxford, and they lived there for twelve years. She inherited Bowen's Court in 1928 when her father died, and in 1952, she and her husband returned there to live. Bowen's husband, however, died that year. She sold the home in 1960 and returned to Oxford.

Bowen's career as novelist spanned years of drastic change, 1927 to 1968, and, except for *The Last September,* she wrote about the present; her war experiences are reflected in the short-story collection *The Demon Lover* and in the novel *The Heat of the Day.* After 1935, she also wrote reviews and articles for *The New Statesman* and other publications, the Ministry of Information during World War II, and *The Tatler* (in the 1940's), and she helped edit the *London Magazine* in the late 1950's. Afflicted with a slight stammer, Bowen lectured infrequently but effectively; two of her BBC broadcasts, "left as they were spoken," may be read in *Afterthought.* After a visit to Ireland in 1973, she died in London, leaving an unfinished autobiographical work, *Pictures and Conversations* (1975).

Analysis · Elizabeth Bowen had a special talent for writing the conversations of children around the age of nine, as she did in *The House in Paris*. Somewhat corresponding to her personal experience, her novels often present a homeless child (usually a girl), orphaned and shunted from one residence to another, or a child with one parent who dies and leaves the adolescent in the power of outwardly concerned but mainly selfish adults. Frequently, management by others prolongs the protagonist's state of innocence into the twenties, when the woman must begin to assert herself and learn to manage her own affairs. (At age twenty-four, for example, Eva Trout does not know how to boil water for tea.) On the other side of the relationship, the controlling adult is often a perfectly mannered woman of guile, wealthy enough to be idle and to fill the idleness with discreet exercise of power over others. The typical Bowen characters, then, are the child, the unwanted adolescent, the woman in her twenties in a prolonged state of adolescence, and the "terrible woman" of society. Young people, educated haphazardly but expensively, are culturally mature but aimless. Genteel adults, on the other hand, administer their own selfish standards of what constitutes an impertinence in another person; these judgments disguise Bowen's subtle criticism of the correct English.

Typical Bowen themes follow as "loss of innocence," "acceptance of the past," or "expanding consciousness." The pain and helplessness attendant upon these themes and the disguise of plentiful money make them unusual. Although she writes about the privileged class, three of her four common character types do not feel privileged. To handle her themes, Bowen frequently orders time and space by dividing the novels into three parts, with one part set ten years in the past and with a juxtaposition of at least two locations. The ten-year lapse provides a measure of the maturity gained, and the second location, by contrast, jars the consciousness into reevaluation of the earlier experience.

The Hotel · The fact that the Bowen women often have nothing to do is very obvious in *The Hotel*, set in Bordighera on the Italian Riviera, but, of greater interest it is, like Ireland, another place of British occupancy. Guests' activities are confined to walking, talking, taking tea, and playing tennis. Mrs. Kerr is the managing wealthy woman who feeds on the attentions of her protégé, Sydney Warren, and then abandons Sydney when her son arrives. At age twenty-two, Sydney, for lack of better purpose, studies for a doctorate at home in England. Back in Italy, she gets engaged to a clergyman as a means of achieving an identity and popularity, but her better sense forces reconsideration, and she cancels the engagement and asserts her independence.

The Last September · *The Last September*, set in 1920 when the hated British soldiers (the Black and Tans) were stationed in Ireland to quell rebellion, shows Sir Richard and Lady Myra Naylor entertaining with tennis parties at their big house. Like Bowen, who wrote in *Afterthought* that this novel was "nearest my heart," Lois Farquar is a summer visitor, aged nineteen, orphaned, asking herself what she should do. An older woman tells her that her art lacks talent. Almost engaged to a British soldier, Gerald Lesworth, she might have a career in marriage, but Lady Naylor, in the role of graceful-terrible woman, destroys the engagement in a brilliant heart-to-heart talk, in which she points out that he has no prospects.

As September closes the social season, Gerald Lesworth is killed in ambush, and as Lois—much more aware now and less innocent—prepares to depart for France, her home Danielstown is burned down, which signals her separation from the protected past.

To the North · After *Friends and Relations*, Bowen entered the most fruitful part of her career. Her next four novels are generally considered to be her best work. *To the North* has rather obvious symbolism in a protagonist named Emmeline Summers whose lack of feeling makes her "icy." She runs a successful travel agency with the motto "Travel Dangerously" (altering "Live Dangerously" and "Travel Safe"); the motto reflects both her ability to understand intellectually the feelings of others through their experience and her orphan state in homelessness. Emmeline tries to compensate for her weaknesses by imposing dramatic opposites: Without a home of her own, she overvalues her home with her widowed sister-in-law, Cecilia Summers; frequently called an angel, she has a fatal attraction to the devil-like character Markie Linkwater. When Cecilia plans to remarry (breaking up the home), when Markie (bored with Emmeline) returns to his former mistress, and when Emmeline's travel business begins to fail rapidly because of her preoccupation with Markie, she smashes her car while driving Markie north; "traveling dangerously" at high speeds, she becomes the angel of death.

The cold of the North suggested by the novel's title also touches other characters. Lady Waters, who offers Emmeline weekends on her estate as a kind of second home, feeds mercilessly on the unhappiness of failed loves and gossip. Lady Waters tells Cecilia to speak to Emmeline about her affair with Markie and thereby initiates the fateful dinner party, which leads to the accident. Pauline, the niece of Cecilia's fiancé, is the orphaned adolescent character on the verge of becoming aware of and embarrassed by sex. Bowen describes Emmeline as the "stepchild of her uneasy century," a century in which planes and trains have damaged the stability and book knowledge of sexual research (indicated by the reading of Havelock Ellis), thereby freeing relationships but failing to engage the heart. The travel and the lack of warmth make the title a metaphor for the new century's existence. With her tenuous hold on home, love, and career, Emmeline commits suicide.

The House in Paris · *The House in Paris* is set in three locations, which reflect different aspects of the protagonist, Karen Michaelis: England, the land of perfect society; Ireland, the land of awareness; and France, the land of passion and the dark past. Parts 1 and 3 take place in a single day in Paris; part 2 occurs ten years earlier, during four months when Karen was age twenty-three. The evils of the house in Paris become apparent in the flashback and can be appreciated only through recognition of the terrible woman who runs it, Mme Fisher, and the rootlessness of the foreign students who stay there. Among other students, Mme Fisher has had in her power Karen and her friend Naomi Fisher (Mme Fisher's daughter), and the young Max Ebhart, a Jew with no background. Ten years later, when Max wants to break his engagement with Naomi to marry another, Mme Fisher interferes, and he commits suicide.

The book begins and ends in a train station in Paris. In part 1, Leopold–age nine and the illegitimate child of Karen and Max Ebhart–and Henrietta Mountjoy, age eleven and the granddaughter of a friend of Mme Fisher, arrive on separate trains: Henrietta from England in the process of being shuttled to another relative, and Leopold from his adoptive parents in Italy to await a first acquaintance with his real mother. Leopold and Henrietta, meeting in the house in Paris, become symbolic of the possibility that, with Mme Fisher bedridden for ten years (since the suicide) and now dying, the future will be free of the mistakes of the past. Mme Fisher, in an interview with Leopold, tells him that the possibility of finding himself "like a young tree inside a tomb is to discover the power to crack the tomb and grow up to any height," something Max had failed to do.

Dark, egotistic, self-centered, and passionate like his father, Leopold constructs imaginatively a role for his unknown mother to play and then breaks into uncontrollable weeping when a telegram arrives canceling her visit. The mature and implacable Henrietta, orphaned like Leopold but accustomed to the vicissitudes of adult life, shows him how to crack out of the tomb of childhood. In part 3, quite unexpectedly, Ray Forrestier, who had given up diplomacy and taken up business to marry Karen in spite of her illegitimate child, urges a reunion with her son Leopold, takes matters into his own hands, and brings Leopold to Karen.

The Death of the Heart · The three-part structure of Bowen's novels is most fully realized in *The Death of the Heart*; the parts are labeled "The World," "The Flesh," and "The Devil," and follow the seasons of winter, spring, and summer. The world of Windsor Terrace, the Quaynes' residence in London, is advanced and sterile. Portia enters into this world at age fifteen, an orphan and stepsister to the present Thomas Quayne. Thomas's wife Anna, who has miscarried twice and is childless, secretly reads Portia's diary and is indignant at the construction Portia puts on the household events. Portia sees much "dissimulation" at Windsor Terrace, where doing the "right" thing does not mean making a moral choice. As one of Bowen's radical innocents who has spent her youth in hotels and temporary locations, Portia says no one in this house knows why she was born. She has only one friend in this, her first home: the head-servant Matchett, who gives Portia some religious training. Of the three male friends who wait upon Anna—St. Quentin Martin, Eddie, and Major Brutt—Portia fastens on the affections of Eddie.

Spring, in part 2, brings a much-needed vacation for the Quaynes. Thomas and Anna sail for Capri, and Portia goes to stay with Anna's former governess at Seale-on-Sea. At the governess's home, dubbed Waikiki, Portia is nearly drowned in sensuality—the sights, smells, sounds, and feelings of a vulgar and mannerless household. Portia invites Eddie to spend a weekend with her at Seale-on-Sea, which further educates her in the ways of the flesh.

Portia's more open nature, on her return to London in part 3, is immediately apparent to Matchett, who says she had been "too quiet." The Devil's works are represented both obviously and subtly in this section, and they take many identities. St. Quentin, Anna, Eddie, even the unloving atmosphere of Windsor Terrace make up the Devil's advocacy. St. Quentin, a novelist, tells Portia that Anna has been reading her diary, a disloyalty and an invasion of privacy with which, after some contemplation, Portia decides she cannot live. Herein lies the death of her teenage heart, what Bowen calls a betrayal of her innocence, or a "mysterious landscape" that has perished.

Summer at Windsor Terrace brings maturity to Portia, as well as others: Anna must confront her own culpability, even her jealousy of Portia; St. Quentin, his betrayal of Anna's reading of the diary; Thomas, his neglect of his father and his father's memory. Even Matchett takes a terrified ride in the unfamiliar cab, setting out in the night to an unknown location to pick up Portia. They all share in the summer's maturation that Portia has brought to fruition.

William Shakespeare's Portia preferred mercy to justice, paralleling the Portia in this novel. Bowen's Portia observes everything with a "political seriousness." The scaffolding of this novel supports much allusion, metaphor, and drama—all artfully structured. The world, the flesh, and the Devil as medieval threats to saintliness are reinterpreted in this context; they become the locations of the heart that has been thrust outside Eden and comprise a necessary trinity, not of holiness but of wholeness. This novel earns critics' accord as Bowen's best.

The Heat of the Day · In *The Death of the Heart*, ranked by many critics as a close second to *The Heat of the Day*, Bowen uses the war to purge the wasteland conditions that existed before and during the years from 1940 through 1945. Middle-class Robert Kelway has returned from Dunkirk (1940) with a limp that comes and goes according to the state of his emotions. At the individual level, it reflects the psychological crippling of his youth; at the national level, it is the culmination of the condition expressed by the person who says "Dunkirk was waiting there in us."

Upper-class Stella Rodney has retreated from the privileges of her past into a rented apartment and a war job. Having grown impassive with the century, divorced with a son (Roderick) in the army, she has taken Robert as her lover. She has become so impassive, in fact, that in 1942, a sinister and mysterious government spy named Harrison tells her that Robert has been passing information to the enemy, and she says and does nothing.

Critics have commented frequently on this novel's analogies to William Shakespeare's *Hamlet* (1600-1601), an obvious example being Holme Dene (Dane home), Robert Kelway's country home. Psychologically weak, Robert is ruled by his destructive mother, who also had stifled his father and planted the seeds of Robert's defection from English ways. While Stella visits Holme Dene and learns to understand Robert, her son visits a cousin who tells him that Stella did not divorce her husband, as was commonly thought, but rather was divorced by him while he was having an affair, although he died soon after the divorce. Roderick, however, has managed to survive Stella's homelessness with a positive and manly outlook and, when he inherits an estate in Ireland, finds that it will give him the foundation for a future.

Eva Trout · In *Eva Trout*, the various autobiographical elements of Bowen's work come to life: Bowen's stammer in Eva's reticence, the tragic deaths of both parents, the transience and sporadic education, the delayed adolescence, the settings of hotels and train stations. Eva Trout lives with a former teacher, Iseult Arbles, and her husband Eric while she waits for an inheritance. She turns twenty-four and receives the inheritance, which enables her to leave their home, where the marriage is unstable, to buy a home filled with used furniture. She also escapes the clutches of Constantine, her guardian who had been her father's male lover.

Eva discovers that a woman with money is suddenly pursued by "admirers," and Eric visits her in her new home. Eva subsequently lets Iseult think that Eric has fathered her child, whom she adopts in America. After eight years in American cities, where Eva seeks help for the deaf-mute child Jeremy, Eva and Jeremy return to England. From England, they flee to Paris, where a doctor and his wife begin successful training of Jeremy. Back in England, Eva attempts the next phase of reaching security and a normal life. She seeks a husband and persuades the son of Iseult's vicar to stage a wedding departure with her at Victoria Station. All her acquaintances are on hand to see the couple off, but Jeremy—brought from Paris for the occasion—playfully points a gun (he thinks a toy) at Eva and shoots her. In the midst of revelry, on the eve of her happiness, Eva drops dead beside the train.

Eva Trout makes a poignant and haunting last heroine for the Bowen sequence and a final bitter statement on the elusiveness of security and happiness.

Grace Eckley

Other major works

SHORT FICTION: *Encounters*, 1923; *Ann Lee's and Other Stories*, 1926; *Joining Charles*, 1929; *The Cat Jumps and Other Stories*, 1934; *Look at All Those Roses*, 1941; *The Demon Lover*, 1945 (pb. in U.S. as *Ivy Gripped the Steps and Other Stories*, 1946); *The Early Stories*, 1951; *Stories by Elizabeth Bowen*, 1959; *A Day in the Dark and Other Stories*, 1965; *Elizabeth Bowen's Irish Stories*, 1978; *The Collected Stories of Elizabeth Bowen*, 1980.

PLAY: *Castle Anna*, pr. 1948 (with John Perry).

NONFICTION: *Bowen's Court*, 1942; *Seven Winters*, 1942; *English Novelists*, 1946; *Collected Impressions*, 1950; *The Shelbourne: A Center of Dublin Life for More than a Century*, 1951; *A Time in Rome*, 1960; *Afterthought: Pieces About Writing*, 1962; *Pictures and Conversations*, 1975; *The Mulberry Tree: Writings of Elizabeth Bowen*, 1986.

CHILDREN'S LITERATURE: *The Good Tiger*, 1965.

Bibliography

Austin, Allan. *Elizabeth Bowen*. Rev. ed. Boston: Twayne, 1989. Emphasizes Bowen's ability to depict locale, as in her account of World War II London in *The Heat of the Day*. Her characters worry and react to events more with emotion than with reason. Bowen presents these characters in a distinctive and urbane style. After a survey of Bowen's general traits as an author, Austin follows with a detailed account of the novels and some of the shorter fiction.

Craig, Patricia. *Elizabeth Bowen*. London: Penguin Books, 1986. Most useful for those wishing to read a shorter biography of Bowen than Glendinning's. Written in a vigorous style and included in the Lives of Modern Women series. Like Glendinning, Craig emphasizes Bowen's extensive circle of literary friends. The depiction of events in Bowen's life is good-humored and blunt.

Glendinning, Victoria. *Elizabeth Bowen*. New York: Alfred A. Knopf, 1978. The standard biography of Bowen. Portrays Bowen as someone with a dominant personality, charming but at times overwhelming. Gives full coverage to Bowen's Anglo-Irish background and her wide circle of Oxford friends. Her devotion to her husband, which did not preclude extramarital affairs, emerges as a leitmotif of Bowen's rather uneventful life. Gives a detailed account of the genesis of each of the major novels.

Jordan, Heather Bryant. *How Will the Heart Endure: Elizabeth Bowen and the Landscape of War*. Ann Arbor: University of Michigan Press, 1992. Explores Bowen's contradictory responses to two world wars, and her view of literary modernism and contemporary events. Treats Bowen as an Anglo-Irish novelist with a strong grounding in history, asserting that she must be read in the context of the events she fictionalized. Includes notes and bibliography.

Lassner, Phyllis. *Elizabeth Bowen: A Study of the Short Fiction*. New York: Twayne, 1991. Section 1 treats Bowen's comedies of sex, manners, and terror, as well as her studies of the female character. Section 2 contains excerpts from Bowen's prefaces and essays. Section 3 provides a sampling of Bowen critics. Includes chronology and bibliography.

Lee, Hermione. *Elizabeth Bowen: An Estimation*. New York: Barnes & Noble Books, 1981. The most detailed critical study of Bowen. Places her in a tradition of Anglo-Irish writers and ranks *The Death of the Heart* as worthy of the highest praise. Considers not only Bowen's novels but her short stories and nonfiction writing as well. Lee ranks a number of the short stories, such as "Summer Night" and "The Cat Jumps," as outstanding.

Charlotte Brontë

Born: Thornton, Yorkshire, England; April 21, 1816
Died: Haworth, Yorkshire, England; March 31, 1855

Principal long fiction · *Jane Eyre*, 1847; *Shirley*, 1849; *Villette*, 1853; *The Professor*, 1857.

Other literary forms · The nineteen poems which Charlotte Brontë selected to print with her sister Anne's work in *Poems by Currer, Ellis, and Acton Bell* (1846) were her only other works published during her lifetime. The juvenilia produced by the four Brontë children–Charlotte, Emily, Anne, and Branwell, between 1824 and 1839 are scattered in libraries and private collections. Some of Charlotte's contributions have been published in *The Twelve Adventurers and Other Stories* (1925), *Legends of Angria* (1933), *The Search After Happiness* (1969), *Five Novelettes* (1971), and *The Secret and Lily Hart* (1979). A fragment of a novel written during the last year of Brontë's life was published as *Emma* in *Cornhill Magazine* in 1860 and is often reprinted in editions of *The Professor*. *The Complete Poems of Charlotte Brontë* appeared in 1923. Other brief selections, fragments, and ephemera have been printed in *Transactions and Other Publications of the Brontë Society*. The nineteen-volume Shakespeare Head Brontë (1931-1938), edited by T. J. Wise and J. A. Symington, contains all of the novels, four volumes of life and letters, two volumes of miscellaneous writings, and two volumes of poems.

Achievements · Brontë brought to English fiction an intensely personal voice. Her books show the moral and emotional growth of a protagonist almost entirely by self-revelation. Her novels focus on individual self-fulfillment; they express the sub-jective interior world not only in thoughts, dreams, visions, and symbols but also by projecting inner states through external objects, secondary characters, places, events, and weather. Brontë's own experiences and emotions inform the narrative presence. "Perhaps no other writer of her time," wrote Margaret Oliphant in 1855, "has impressed her mark so clearly on contemporary literature, or drawn so many followers into her own peculiar path."

The personal voice, which blurs the distance between novelist, protagonist, and reader, accounts for much of the critical ambivalence toward Brontë's work. Genera-tions of unsophisticated readers have identified with Jane Eyre; thousands of ro-mances and modern gothics have used Brontë's situations and invited readers to step into the fantasy. Brontë's novels, however, are much more than simply the common reader's daydreams. They are rich enough to allow a variety of critical approaches. They have been studied in relation to traditions (gothic, provincial, realistic, Roman-tic); read for psychological, linguistic, Christian, social, economic, and personal interpretations; analyzed in terms of symbolism, imagery, metaphor, viewpoint, narrative distance, and prose style. Because the novels are so clearly wrought from the materials of their author's life, psychoanalytic and feminist criticism has proved rewarding. In Brontë's work, a woman author makes significant statements about issues central to women's lives. Most of her heroines are working women; each feels the pull of individual self-development against the wish for emotional fulfillment, the tension between sexual energies and social realities, the almost unresolvable conflict between love and independence.

Biography · Charlotte Brontë was the third of six children born within seven years to the Reverend Patrick Brontë and his wife Maria Branwell Brontë. Patrick Brontë was perpetual curate of Haworth, a bleak manufacturing town in Yorkshire. In 1821, when Charlotte Brontë was five years old, her mother died of cancer. Three years later, the four elder girls were sent to the Clergy Daughters' School at Cowan Bridge—the school which appears as Lowood in *Jane Eyre*. In the summer of 1825, the eldest two daughters, Maria and Elizabeth, died of tuberculosis. Charlotte and Emily were removed from the school and brought home. There were no educated middle-class families in Haworth to supply friends and companions. The Brontë children lived with a noncommunicative aunt, an elderly servant, and a father much preoccupied by his intellectual interests and his own griefs.

In their home and with only one another for company, the children had material for both educational and imaginative development. Patrick Brontë expected his children to read and to carry on adult conversations about politics. He subscribed to *Blackwood's Edinburgh Magazine*, where his children had access to political and economic essays, art criticism, and literary reviews. They had annuals with engravings of fine art; they taught themselves to draw by copying the pictures in minute detail. They were free to do reading that would not have been permitted by any school of the time—by the age of thirteen Charlotte Brontë was fully acquainted not only with John Milton and Sir Walter Scott but also with Robert Southey, William Cowper, and (most important) Lord Byron.

In 1826, Branwell was given a set of wooden soldiers which the four children used for characters in creative play. These soldiers gradually took on personal characteristics and acquired countries to rule. The countries needed cities, governments, ruling families, political intrigues, legends, and citizens with private lives, all of which the children happily invented. In 1829, when Charlotte Brontë was thirteen, she and the others began to write down materials from these fantasies, producing a collection of juvenilia that extended ultimately to hundreds of items: magazines, histories, maps, essays, tales, dramas, poems, newspapers, wills, speeches, scrapbooks. This enormous creative production in adolescence gave concrete form to motifs that were later transformed into situations, characters, and concerns of Charlotte Brontë's mature work. It was also a workshop for literary technique; the young author explored prose style, experimented with viewpoint, and discovered how to control narrative voice. A single event, she learned, could be the basis for both a newspaper story and a romance, and the romance could be told by one of the protagonists or by a detached observer.

Because Patrick Brontë had no income beyond his salary, his daughters had to prepare to support themselves. In 1831, when she was almost fifteen, Charlotte Brontë went to Miss Wooler's School at Roe Head. After returning home for a time to tutor her sisters, she went back to Miss Wooler's as a teacher. Over the next several years, all three sisters held positions as governesses in private families. None, however, was happy as a governess; aside from the predictable difficulties caused by burdensome work and undisciplined children, they all suffered when separated from their shared emotional and creative life. A possible solution would have been to open their own school, but they needed some special qualification to attract pupils. Charlotte conceived a plan for going abroad to study languages. In 1842, she and Emily went to Brussels to the Pensionnat Héger. They returned in November because of their aunt's death, but in the following year Charlotte went back to Brussels alone to work as a pupil-teacher. An additional reason for her return to Brussels was that she desired to be near Professor Constantine Héger, but at the end of the year she left in misery after Héger's wife had realized (perhaps more clearly than did Charlotte herself) the romantic nature of the attraction.

In 1844, at the age of twenty-eight, Charlotte Brontë established herself permanently at Haworth. The prospectus for "The Misses Brontë's Establishment" was published, but no pupils applied. Branwell, dismissed in disgrace from his post as tutor, came home to drink, take opium, and disintegrate. Charlotte spent nearly two years in deep depression: Her yearning for love was unsatisfied, and she had repressed her creative impulse because she was afraid her fantasies were self-indulgent. Then, with the discovery that all three had written poetry, the sisters found a new aim in life. A joint volume of poems was published in May, 1846, though it sold only two copies. Each wrote a short novel; they offered the three together to publishers. Emily Brontë's *Wuthering Heights* (1847) and Anne Brontë's *Agnes Grey* (1847) were accepted. Charlotte Brontë's *The Professor* was refused, but one editor, George Smith, said he would like to see a three-volume novel written by its author. *Jane Eyre* was by that time almost finished; it was sent to Smith on August 24, 1847, and impressed him so much that he had it in print by the middle of October.

Library of Congress

Jane Eyre was immediately successful, but there was barely any time for its author to enjoy her fame and accomplishment. Within a single year, her three companions in creation died: Branwell on September 24, 1848; Emily on December 19, 1848; and Anne on May 28, 1849. When Charlotte Brontë began work on *Shirley*, she met with her sisters in the evenings to exchange ideas, read aloud, and offer criticism. By the time she finished the manuscript, she was alone.

Charlotte Brontë's sense that she was plain, "undeveloped," and unlikely to be loved seems to have been partly the product of her own psychological condition. She had refused more than one proposal in her early twenties. In 1852 there was another, from Arthur Bell Nicholls, curate at Haworth. Patrick Brontë objected violently and dismissed his curate. Gradually, however, the objections were worn away. On June 29, 1854, Charlotte Brontë and the Reverend Nicholls were married and, after a brief honeymoon tour, took up residence in Haworth parsonage. After a few months of apparent content—which did not prevent her from beginning work on another novel—

Charlotte Brontë died on March 31, 1855, at the age of thirty-eight; a severe cold made her too weak to survive the complications of early pregnancy.

Analysis · The individualism and richness of Charlotte Brontë's work arise from the multiple ways in which her writing is personal: observation and introspection, rational analysis and spontaneous emotion, accurate mimesis and private symbolism. Tension and ambiguity grow from the intersections and conflicts among these levels of writing and, indeed, among the layers of the self.

Few writers of English prose have so successfully communicated the emotional texture of inner life while still constructing fictions with enough verisimilitude to appear realistic. Brontë startled the Victorians because her work was so little influenced by the books of her own era. Its literary forebears were the written corporate daydreams of her childhood and the romantic poets she read during the period when the fantasies took shape. Certain characters and situations which crystallized the emotional conflicts of early adolescence became necessary components of emotional satisfaction. The source of these fantasies was, to a degree, beyond control, occurring in the region the twentieth century has termed "the unconscious"; by writing them down from childhood on, Brontë learned to preserve and draw on relatively undisguised desires and ego conflicts in a way lost to most adults.

The power and reality of the inner life disturbed Brontë after she had passed through adolescence; she compared her creative urge to the action of opium and was afraid that she might become lost in her "infernal world." When she began to think of publication, she deliberately used material from her own experience and reported scenes and characters in verifiable detail. In this way, she hoped to subdue the exaggerated romanticism—and the overwrought writing—of the fantasy-fictions. "Details, situations which I do not understand and cannot personally inspect," she wrote to her publisher, "I would not for the world meddle with." Her drawing from life was so accurate that the curates and the Yorkes in *Shirley* were recognized at once by people who knew them, and Brontë lost the protection that her pseudonym had provided.

The years of practice in writing fiction that satisfied her own emotional needs gave Brontë the means to produce powerful psychological effects. She uses a variety of resources to make readers share the protagonist's subjective state. The truth of the outside world is only that truth which reflects the narrator's feelings and perceptions. All characters are aspects of the consciousness which creates them: Brontë uses splitting, doubling, and other fairy-tale devices; she replicates key situations; she carefully controls the narrative distance and the amount of information readers have at their disposal.

The unquietness which Brontë's readers often feel grows from the tension between direct emotional satisfactions (often apparently immature) on one hand and, on the other, mature and realistic conflicts in motive, reason, and sense of self. Read as a sequence, the four completed novels demonstrate both Brontë's development and the story of a woman's relationship to the world. Brontë's heroines find identity outside the enclosed family popularly supposed to circumscribe nineteenth century women. Isolation allows the heroines' self-development, but it impedes their romantic yearning to be lost in love.

The Professor · At the beginning of *The Professor*, William Crimsworth is working as a clerk in a mill owned by his proud elder brother. He breaks away, goes to Brussels to teach English, survives a brief attraction to a seductive older woman, and then comes to love Frances Henri, an orphaned Anglo-Swiss lace-mender who had been his pupil.

Brontë's narrative devices supply shifting masks that both expose and evade the self. The epistolary opening keeps readers from identifying directly with Crimsworth but draws them into the novel as recipients of his revelations. The masculine persona, which Brontë used frequently in the juvenilia, gives her access to the literary mainstream and creates possibilities for action, attitude, and initiative that did not exist in models for female stories. The juvenile fantasies supply the feud between two brothers; the Belgian scenes and characters come from Brontë's own experiences. Although nominally male, Crimsworth is in an essentially female situation: disinherited, passive, timid. He has, furthermore, an exaggerated awareness and fear of the sexual overtones in human behavior.

Biographical details also go into the making of Frances Henri, the friendless older student working to pay for her lessons in the Belgian school. The poem that Frances writes is one Brontë had created out of her own yearning for Professor Héger. In *The Professor*, the dream can come true; the poem awakens the teacher's response.

Like the central figures in all Brontë novels, both Crimsworth and Frances enact a Cinderella plot. Each begins as an oppressed outcast and ends successful, confident, and satisfactorily placed in society. The details of Crimsworth's story work both symbolically and functionally. The imprisoning situations in the factory and the school reflect his perception of the world. At the same time, these situations are created by his own inner barriers. His bondage as a despised clerk is self-induced; he is an educated adult male who could move on at any time. In Belgium, he plods a treadmill of guilt because of Zoraïde Reuter's sexual manipulativeness—for which he is not responsible. His self-suppression is also seen through Yorke Hunsden, who appears whenever Crimsworth must express strong emotion. Hunsden voices anger and rebellion not permitted to the male/female narrator and becomes a voyeuristic alter ego to appreciate Frances and love.

The novel is weakest when it fails to integrate the biography, the emotion, and the ideas. True moral dilemmas are not developed. The heroine, seen through sympathetic male eyes, wins love for her writing, her pride, and her self-possession, and she continues to work even after she has a child. Brontë solves her chronic romantic dilemma (how can a strong woman love if woman's love is defined as willing subordination?) by letting Frances vibrate between two roles: She is the stately directress of the school by day, the little lace-mender by night.

Jane Eyre · In *Jane Eyre*, Brontë created a story that has the authority of myth. Everything which had deeply affected her was present in the book's emotional content. The traumatic experiences of maternal deprivation, the Clergy Daughters' School, and Maria's death create the events of Jane's early life. The book also taps universal feelings of rejection, victimization, and loneliness, making them permissible by displacement: The hateful children are cousins, not siblings; the bad adult an aunt, not a mother. Rochester's compelling power as a lover derives from neither literal nor literary sources—Rochester is the man Brontë had loved for twenty years, the duke of Zamorna who dominates the adolescent fantasies, exerting a power on both Jane and the reader that can hardly be explained by reason. Jane defied literary convention because she was poor, plain, and a heroine; she defied social convention by refusing to accept any external authority. Placed repeatedly in situations that exemplify male power, Jane resists and survives. At the end of the narrative, she is transformed from

Cinderella to Prince Charming, becoming the heroine who cuts through the brambles to rescue the imprisoned sleeper. Identification is so immediate and so close that readers often fail to notice Brontë's control of distance, in particular the points of detachment when an older Jane comments on her younger self and the direct addresses from Jane to the reader that break the spell when emotions become too strong.

Place controls the book's structure. Events at Gateshead, Lowood, Thornfield, and Moor House determine Jane's development; a brief coda at Ferndean provides the resolution. Each of the four major sections contains a figure representing the sources of male power over women: John Reed (physical force and the patriarchal family), Reverend Brocklehurst (the social structures of class, education, and religion), Rochester (sexual attraction), and St. John Rivers (moral and spiritual authority). Jane protects herself at first by devious and indirect means—fainting, illness, flight—and then ultimately, in rejecting St. John Rivers, by direct confrontation. Compelled by circumstances to fend for herself, she comes, at first instinctively, later rationally, to rely on herself.

The book's emotional power grows from its total absorption in Jane's view of the world and from the images, symbols, and structures that convey multiple interwoven reverberations. The red room—which suggests violence, irrationality, enclosure, rebellion, rebirth, the bloody chamber of emerging womanhood—echoes throughout the book. The Bridewell charade, Jane's paintings, the buildings and terrain, and a multitude of other details have both meaning and function. Characters double and split: Helen Burns (mind) and Bertha Mason (body) are aspects of Jane as well as actors in the plot. Recurring images of ice and fire suggest fatal coldness without and consuming fire within. Rochester's sexuality is the most threatening and ambiguous aspect of masculine power because of Jane's own complicity and her need for love. Her terrors and dreams accumulate as the marriage approaches; there are drowning images, abyss images, loss of consciousness. She refuses to become Rochester's mistress, finally, not because of the practical and moral dangers (which she does recognize) but because she fears her own willingness to make a god of him. She will not become dependent; she escapes to preserve her self.

As Jane takes her life into her own hands, she becomes less needy. After she has achieved independence by discovering a family and inheriting money, she is free to seek out Rochester. At the same time, he has become less omnipotent, perhaps a code for the destruction of patriarchal power. Thus, the marriage not only ends the romance and resolves the moral, emotional, and sexual conflicts but also supplies a satisfactory woman's fantasy of independence coupled with love.

Shirley · For the book that would follow *Jane Eyre*, Brontë deliberately sought a new style and subject matter. *Shirley*, set in 1812, concerns two public issues still relevant in 1848—working-class riots and the condition of women. Brontë did historical research in newspaper files. She used a panoramic scene, included a variety of characters observed from life, and added touches of comedy. *Shirley* is told in the third person; the interest is divided between two heroines, neither of whom is a persona. Nevertheless, Brontë is strongly present in the narrative voice, which remains objective only in scenes of action. The authorial commentary, more strongly even than the events themselves, creates a tone of anger, rebellion, suffering, and doubt.

The novel is clearly plotted, although the mechanics are at times apparent. Brontë shifts focus among characters and uses reported conversations to violate the time sequence so that she can arrange events in the most effective dramatic order. Robert Moore, owner of a cloth mill, arouses the workers' wrath by introducing machinery. Caroline Helstone loves Robert but her affection is not reciprocated. Although Caroline has a comfortable home with her uncle the rector, she is almost fatally depressed by lack of love and occupation. Property-owner Shirley Keeldar discovers that having a man's name, position, and forthrightness gives her some power but fails to make her man's equal; she is simply more valuable as a matrimonial prize. Louis Moore, Shirley's former tutor, loves her silently because he lacks wealth and social position. Eventually Robert, humbled by Shirley's contempt and weakened by a workman's bullet, declares his love for Caroline, who has in the meantime discovered her mother and grown much stronger. Shirley's union with Louis is more ambivalent; she loves him because he is a master she can look up to, but she is seen on her wedding day as a pantheress pining for virginal freedom.

The primary source of women's tribulation is dependency. Caroline Helstone craves occupation to fill her time, make her financially independent, and give her life purpose. Women become psychologically dependent on men because they have so little else to think about. Brontë examines the lives of several old maids; they are individuals, not stereotypes, but they are all lonely. Shirley and Caroline dissect John Milton, search for female roots, and talk cozily about men's inadequacies. They cannot, however, speak honestly to each other about their romantic feelings. Caroline must hold to herself the deep pain of unrequited love.

Although *Shirley* deliberately moves beyond the isolated mythic world of *Jane Eyre* to put women's oppression in the context of a society rent by other power struggles (workers against employers, England against France, Church against Nonconformity), the individualistic ending only partially resolves the divisions. Brontë's narrative tone in the final passage is bleak and bitter. She reminds readers that *Shirley*'s events are history. Fieldhead Hollow is covered by mills and mill housing; magic is gone from the world.

Villette · *Villette* is Brontë's most disciplined novel. Because *The Professor* had not been published, she was able to rework the Brussels experience without masks, as a story of loneliness and female deprivation, deliberately subduing the wish-fulfillment and making her uncompromising self-examination control form as well as feeling. Lucy Snowe is a woman without money, family, friends, or health. She is not, however, a sympathetic, friendly narrator like Jane Eyre. Her personality has the unattractiveness that realistically grows from deprivation; she has no social ease, no warmth, no mental quickness. Furthermore, her personality creates her pain, loneliness, and disengagement.

In the book's early sections, Lucy is not even the center of her narrative. She watches and judges instead of taking part; she tells other people's stories instead of her own. She is so self-disciplined that she appears to have neither feelings nor imagination, so restrained that she never reveals the facts about her family or the incidents of her youth that might explain to readers how and why she learned to suppress emotion, hope, and the desire for human contact. Despite—or perhaps because of—her anesthetized feeling and desperate shyness, Lucy Snowe drives herself to actions that might have been inconceivable for a woman more thoroughly socialized. Thrust into the world by the death of the elderly woman whose companion she had been, she goes alone to London, takes a ship for the Continent, gets a job as nursemaid, rises through her own efforts to teach in Madame Beck's school, and begins laying plans to open a school of her own.

The coincidental and melodramatic elements of the story gain authenticity because they grow from Lucy's inner life. When she is left alone in the school during vacation, her repressed need to be heard by someone drives her to enter the confessional of a Catholic church. Once the internal barrier is breached, she immediately meets the Bretton family. Realistically, she must have known they were in Villette; she knew that "Dr. John" was Graham Bretton, but she withheld that information from the reader both because of her habitual secretiveness and also because she did not really "know" the Brettons were accessible to her until she was able to admit her need to reach out for human sympathy. The characterization of Paul Emanuel gains richness and detail in such a manner that readers realize–before Lucy herself dares admit it–that she is interested in him. The phantom nun, at first a night terror of pure emotion, is revealed as a prankish disguise when Lucy is free to express feelings directly.

The novel's ending, however, is deliberately ambiguous, though not in event. (Only the most naïve readers dare accept Brontë's invitation to imagine that Paul Emanuel escapes drowning and to "picture union and a happy succeeding life.") The ambiguity grows from Lucy's earlier statement: "M. Emanuel was away for three years. Reader, they were the three happiest years of my life." In those years, Lucy Snowe prospered, became respected, expanded her school. Her happiness depends not on the presence of her beloved but rather on the knowledge that she is loved. With that knowledge, she becomes whole and independent. No longer telling others' stories, she speaks directly to the reader about her most private concerns. Only when her lover is absent, perhaps, can a woman treasure love and emotional satisfaction while yet retaining the freedom to be her own person.

Sally Mitchell

Other major works

POETRY: *Poems by Currer, Ellis, and Acton Bell,* 1846 (with Emily and Anne Brontë); *The Complete Poems of Charlotte Brontë,* 1923.

CHILDREN'S LITERATURE: *The Twelve Adventurers and Other Stories,* 1925 (C. K. Shorter and C. W. Hatfield, editors); *Legends of Angria,* 1933 (Fannie E. Ratchford, compiler); *The Search After Happiness,* 1969; *Five Novelettes,* 1971 (Winifred Gérin, editor); *The Secret and Lily Hart,* 1979 (William Holtz, editor).

MISCELLANEOUS: *The Shakespeare Head Brontë,* 1931-1938 (19 volumes; T. J. Wise and J. A. Symington, editors).

Bibliography

Barker, Juliet. *The Brontës.* New York: St. Martin's Press, 1995. This massive (more than one-thousand-page) study of the entire Brontë family sometimes overwhelms with detail, but it presents the most complete picture of one of English literature's most intriguing and productive families. Barker's analysis of the juvenilia, in particular, constitutes a major contribution to Brontë scholarship. Not surprisingly, she has more to say about Charlotte than about other members of the family, and she is honest in admitting that Emily remains an enigma.

Fraser, Rebecca. *The Brontës: Charlotte Brontë and Her Family.* New York: Crown, 1988. This thorough and engrossing biography of Charlotte Brontë and the Brontë family is carefully researched and annotated and offers a vividly written portrait of the Brontës and their world. Makes use of letters, published and unpublished manuscripts, and contemporary news sources to examine this complex literary family. Highly recommended.

Gaskell, Elizabeth C. *The Life of Charlotte Brontë.* 1857. Reprint. London: Penguin Books, 1975. Still an indispensable source for any student of Charlotte Brontë's life, Gaskell's biography offers the insights gained through her long friendship with Brontë. Herself a popular novelist of the time, Gaskell creates a memorable picture of Brontë as both a writer and a woman.

Gates, Barbara Timm. *Critical Essays on Charlotte Brontë.* Boston: G. K. Hall, 1990. The collection reprints some of the more provocative and salient evaluations of Charlotte Brontë's life and work, such as Adrienne Rich's "Jane Eyre: The Temptations of a Motherless Woman." The volume contains a set of five general essays grouped together under the rubric "Critical Perspectives on Brontë's Dualism," as well as eighteen devoted to Brontë's fiction.

Gordon, Lyndall. *Charlotte Brontë: A Passionate Life.* New York: W. W. Norton, 1994. Unlike Barker, Gordon had the blessing of the Brontë Society, which granted access to and permission to reproduce from its copious archives. Gordon makes good use of his materials, producing a readable account of Charlotte Brontë's life and literary output.

Lloyd Evans, Barbara, and Gareth Lloyd Evans. *The Scribner Companion to the Brontës.* New York: Charles Scribner's Sons, 1983. Provides an overview of the Brontë family as a whole. Includes the story of the Brontës' tragic history, sections on the young Brontës' juvenilia, discussions of Charlotte, Anne, and Emily's published works, and excerpts from criticisms written about those works at the time they were first published.

Emily Brontë

Born: Thornton, Yorkshire, England; July 30, 1818
Died: Haworth, Yorkshire, England; December 19, 1848

Principal long fiction · *Wuthering Heights*, 1847.

Other literary forms · *Poems by Currer, Ellis, and Acton Bell* (1846) contains poems by Charlotte, Emily, and Anne Brontë. Juvenilia and early prose works on the imaginary world of Gondal have all been lost.

Achievements · Emily Brontë occupies a unique place in the annals of literature. Her reputation as a major novelist stands on the merits of one relatively short novel which was misunderstood and intensely disliked upon publication; yet no study of British fiction is complete without a discussion of *Wuthering Heights*. The names of its settings and characters, particularly Heathcliff, have become part of the heritage of Western culture, familiar even to those who have neither read the novel nor know anything about its author's life and career. Several film versions, the two most popular in 1939 and 1970, have helped perpetuate this familiarity.

The literary achievement of *Wuthering Heights* lies in its realistic portrayal of a specific place and time and in its examination of universal patterns of human behavior. Set in Yorkshire in the closing years of the eighteenth century, the novel delineates the quality of life in the remote moors of northern England and also reminds the reader of the growing pains of industrialization throughout the nation. In addition, more than any other novel of the period, *Wuthering Heights* presents in clear dialectic form the conflict between two opposing psychic forces, embodied in the settings of the Grange and the Heights and the people who inhabit them. Although modern readers often apply the theories of Sigmund Freud and Carl Jung to give names to these forces, Brontë illustrated their conflict long before psychologists pigeonholed them. *Wuthering Heights* is so true in its portrayal of human nature that it fits easily into many theoretical and critical molds, from the historical to the psychological. The novel may be most fully appreciated, however, as a study of the nature of human perception and its ultimate failure in understanding human behavior. This underlying theme, presented through the dialectic structure of human perception, unites many of the elements that are sometimes singled out or overemphasized in particular critical approaches to the novel.

Brontë's skill is not confined to representing the world and the human forces at work within her characters, great as that skill is. She has also created a complex narrative structure built upon a series of interlocking memories and perceptions, spanning three generations, and moving across several social classes. Told primarily from two often unreliable and sometimes ambiguous first-person points of view, the structure of the novel itself illustrates the limitations of human intelligence and imagination. Faced with choosing between Lockwood or Nelly Dean's interpretation of Heathcliff's life, the reader can only ponder that human perception never allows a full understanding of another soul.

Biography · Emily Jane Brontë was born at Thornton, in Bradford Parish, Yorkshire, on July 30, 1818, the fifth child of the Reverend Patrick and Maria Brontë. Patrick Brontë had been born in County Down, Ireland, one of ten children, on March 17, 1777. He was a schoolteacher and tutor before obtaining his B.A. from Cambridge in 1806, from where he was ordained to curacies, first in Essex and then in Hartshead, Yorkshire. He married Maria Branwell, of Penzance, in Hartshead on December 19, 1812, and in 1817, they moved to Thornton. The other children at the time of Emily's birth were Maria, Elizabeth, Charlotte, and Patrick Branwell; another daughter, Anne, was born two years later. Charlotte and Anne also became writers.

In early 1820, the family moved to Haworth, four miles from the village of Keighley, where the Reverend Brontë was perpetual curate until his death in 1861. Maria Brontë died on September 15, 1821, and about a year later, an elder sister, Elizabeth Branwell, moved in to take care of the children and household. She remained with them until her own death in 1842.

Life at Haworth was spartan but not unpleasant. There was a close and devoted relationship among the children, especially between Charlotte and Emily. Reading was a favorite pastime, and a wide range of books, including the novels of Sir Walter Scott and the poetry of William Wordsworth and Robert Southey, as well as the more predictable classics, was available to the children. Outdoor activities included many hours of wandering through the moors and woods. Their father wanted the children to be hardy and independent, intellectually and physically, indifferent to the passing fashions of the world.

Maria, Elizabeth, and Charlotte had already been sent away to a school for clergymen's daughters, at Cowan Bridge, when Emily joined them in November, 1824. Emily was not happy in this confined and rigid environment and longed for home. Two of the sisters, Elizabeth and Maria, became ill and were taken home to die during 1825; in June, Charlotte and Emily returned home as well.

From 1825 to 1830, the remaining Brontë children lived at Haworth with their father and Miss Branwell. In June, 1826, their father gave them a set of wooden soldiers, a seemingly insignificant gift that stimulated their imaginative and literary talents. The children devoted endless energy to creating an imaginary world for these soldiers. During these years, Charlotte and her brother Branwell created in their minds and on paper the land of "Angria," while Emily and Anne were at work on "Gondal." Although all of these early prose works have been lost, some of Emily's poetry contains references to aspects of the Gondal-Angria creations.

In July, 1835, Emily again joined Charlotte, already a teacher, at the Roe Head school. She remained only three months, returning home in October. Three years later, she accepted a position as governess in a school in Halifax for about six months but returned to Haworth in December; Charlotte joined her there early in the following year. During 1839 and 1840, the sisters were planning to establish their own school at Haworth, but the plan was never carried through.

Charlotte left home again to serve as a governess in 1841, and in February, 1842, she and Emily went to Mme Héger's school in Brussels to study languages. They returned to Haworth in November because of Miss Branwell's death. Charlotte went back to Brussels to teach in 1843, but Emily never left Yorkshire again.

From August, 1845, the Brontë children were again united at Haworth. They did not have much contact with neighbors, whose educational level and intellectual interests were much inferior to theirs. They kept busy reading and writing, both fiction and poetry. *Wuthering Heights* was probably begun in October, 1845, and completed sometime in 1846, although it was not published until December, 1847, after the success of Charlotte's *Jane Eyre* (1847).

Meanwhile, the sisters published *Poems by Currer, Ellis, and Acton Bell* in May, 1846. Finding a press was very difficult, and the pseudonyms were chosen to avoid personal publicity and to create the fiction of male authorship, more readily acceptable to the general public. The reaction was predictable, as Charlotte reports: "Neither we nor our poems were at all wanted." The sisters were not discouraged, however, and they continued to seek publishers for their novels.

The first edition of *Wuthering Heights* was published in 1847 by T. C. Newby, with Anne's *Agnes Grey* as the third volume. It was a sloppy edition and contained many errors. The second edition, published in 1850, after the author's death, was "corrected" by Charlotte. The public reaction to *Wuthering Heights* was decidedly negative; readers were disturbed by the "wickedness" of the characters and the "implausibility" of the action. Until Charlotte herself corrected the misconception, readers assumed that *Wuthering Heights* was an inferior production by the author of *Jane Eyre.*

In October, 1848, Emily became seriously ill with a cough and cold. She suffered quietly and patiently, even refusing to see the doctor who had been called. She died of tuberculosis at Haworth on December 19, 1848. She was buried in the church alongside her mother, her sisters Maria and Elizabeth, and her brother Branwell.

These facts about Emily Brontë's life and death are known, but her character will always remain a mystery. Her early prose works have been lost, only three personal letters survive, and her poems give little insight into her own life. Most information about the Brontë family life and background comes from Mrs. Elizabeth Gaskell's biography of Charlotte and the autobiographical comments on which she based her work. Charlotte comments that Emily was "not a person of demonstrative character" and that she was "stronger than a man, simpler than a child." She had a nature that "stood alone." The person behind this mystery is revealed only in a reading of *Wuthering Heights.*

Analysis · *Wuthering Heights* is constructed around a series of dialectic motifs which interconnect and unify the elements of setting, character, and plot. An examination of these motifs will give the reader the clearest insight into the central meaning of the novel. Although *Wuthering Heights* is a "classic," as Frank Kermode points out in an essay, precisely because it is open to many different critical methods and conducive to many levels of interpretation, the novel grows from a coherent imaginative vision that underlies all the motifs. That vision demonstrates that all human perception is limited and failed. The fullest approach to Emily Brontë's novel is through the basic patterns that support this vision.

Wuthering Heights concerns the interactions of two families, the Earnshaws and Lintons, over three generations. The novel is set in the desolate moors of Yorkshire and covers the years from 1771 to 1803. The Earnshaws and Lintons are in harmony with their environment, but their lives are disrupted by an outsider and catalyst of change, the orphan Heathcliff. Heathcliff is, first of all, an emblem of the social problems of a nation entering the age of industrial expansion and urban growth. Although Brontë sets the action of the novel entirely within the locale familiar to her, she reminds the reader continually of the contrast between that world and the larger world outside.

Besides Heathcliff's background as a child of the streets and the description of urban Liverpool from which he is brought, there are other reminders that Yorkshire, long insulated from change and susceptible only to the forces of nature, is no longer as remote as it once was. The servant Joseph's religious cant, the class distinctions obvious in the treatment of Nelly Dean as well as of Heathcliff, and Lockwood's pseudosophisticated urban values are all reminders that Wuthering Heights cannot remain as it has been, that religious, social, and economic change is rampant. Brontë clearly signifies in the courtship and marriage of young Cathy and Hareton that progress and enlightenment *will* come and the wilderness *will* be tamed. Heathcliff is both an embodiment of the force of this change and its victim. He brings about a change but cannot change himself. What he leaves behind, as Lockwood attests and the relationship of Cathy and Hareton verifies, is a new society, at peace with itself and its environment.

It is not necessary, however, to examine in depth the Victorian context of *Wuthering Heights* to sense the dialectic contrast of environments. Within the limited setting that the novel itself describes, society is divided between two opposing worlds: Wuthering Heights, ancestral home of the Earnshaws, and Thrushcross Grange, the Linton estate. Wuthering Heights is rustic and wild; it is open to the elements of nature and takes its name from "atmospheric tumult." The house is strong, built with narrow windows and jutting cornerstones, fortified to withstand the battering of external forces. It is identified with the outdoors and nature and with strong, "masculine" values. Its appearance, both inside and out, is wild, untamed, disordered, and hard. The Grange expresses a more civilized, controlled atmosphere. The house is neat and orderly, and there is always an abundance of light–to Brontë's mind, "feminine" values. It is not surprising that Lockwood is more comfortable at the Grange, since he takes pleasure in "feminine" behavior (gossip, vanity of appearance, adherence to social decorum, romantic self-delusion), while Heathcliff, entirely "masculine," is always out of place there.

Indeed, all of the characters reflect, to greater or lesser degrees, the masculine and feminine values of the places they inhabit. Hindley and Catherine Earnshaw are as wild and uncontrollable as the Heights: Catherine claims even to prefer her home to the pleasures of heaven. Edgar and Isabella Linton are as refined and civilized as the Grange. The marriage of Edgar and Catherine (as well as the marriage of Isabella and Heathcliff) is ill-fated from the start, not only because she does not love him, as her answers to Nelly Dean's catechism reveal, but also because each is so strongly associated with the values of his or her home that he or she lacks the opposing and necessary personality components. Catherine is too willful, wild, and strong; she expresses too much of the "masculine" side of her personality (the animus of Jungian psychology), while Edgar is weak and effeminate (the anima). They are unable to interact fully with each other because they are not complete individuals themselves. This lack leads to their failures to perceive each other's true needs.

Even Cathy's passionate cry for Heathcliff, "Nelly, I *am* Heathcliff," is less love for him as an individual than the deepest form of self-love. Cathy cannot exist without him, but a meaningful relationship is not possible, because Cathy sees Heathcliff only as a reflection of herself. Heathcliff, too, has denied an important aspect of his personality. Archetypally masculine, Heathcliff acts out only the aggressive, violent parts of himself.

The settings and the characters are patterned against each other, and explosions are the only possible results. Only Hareton and young Cathy, each of whom embodies the psychological characteristics of both Heights and Grange, can successfully sustain a mutual relationship.

This dialectic structure extends into the roles of the narrators as well. The story is reflected through the words of Nelly Dean—an inmate of both houses, a participant in the events of the narrative, and a confidante of the major characters—and Lockwood, an outsider who witnesses only the results of the characters' interactions. Nelly is a companion and servant in the Earnshaw and Linton households, and she shares many of the values and perceptions of the families. Lockwood, an urban sophisticate on retreat, misunderstands his own character as well as others'. His brief romantic "adventure" in Bath and his awkwardness when he arrives at the Heights (he thinks Cathy will fall in love with him; he mistakes the dead rabbits for puppies) exemplify his obtuseness. His perceptions are always to be questioned. Occasionally, however, even a denizen of the conventional world may gain a glimpse of the forces at work beneath the surface of reality. Lockwood's dream of the dead Cathy, which sets off his curiosity and Heathcliff's final plans, is a reminder that even the placid, normal world may be disrupted by the psychic violence of a willful personality.

The presentation of two family units and parallel brother-sister, husband-wife relationships in each also emphasizes the dialectic. That two such opposing modes of behavior could arise in the same environment prevents the reader from easy condemnation of either pair. The use of flashback for the major part of the narration—it begins *in medias res*—reminds the reader that he or she is seeing events out of their natural order, recounted by two individuals whose reliability must be questioned. The working out of the plot over three generations further suggests that no one group, much less one individual, can perceive the complexity of the human personality.

Taken together, the setting, plot, characters, and structure combine into a whole when they are seen as parts of the dialectic nature of existence. In a world where opposing forces are continually arrayed against each other in the environment, in society, in families, and in relationships, as well as within the individual, there can be no easy route to perception of another human soul. *Wuthering Heights* convincingly demonstrates the complexity of this dialectic and portrays the limitations of human perception.

Lawrence F. Laban

Other major works

POETRY: *Poems by Currer, Ellis, and Acton Bell,* 1846 (with Charlotte and Anne Brontë); *The Complete Poems of Emily Jane Brontë,* 1941 (C. W. Hatfield, editor).

Bibliography

Berg, Maggie. *"Wuthering Heights": The Writing in the Margin.* New York: Twayne, 1996. Part of the Twayne Masterworks series, this volume provides a good introduction to Emily Brontë's masterpiece. A chronology of her life and works is followed by a section devoted to the literary and social context of the novel and a reading emphasizing the importance of the novel's "marginal spaces," such as the diary that Catherine keeps in the blank spaces of books.

Bloom, Harold, ed. *Heathcliff.* New York: Chelsea House, 1993. Part of the Major Literary Characters series, *Heathcliff* collects in one volume some of the most salient evaluations of Emily Brontë's hero. All have appeared previously elsewhere, but such an anthology between two covers is useful. *Heathcliff* includes both excerpts from longer works—starting with a passage from one of Charlotte Brontë's letters—and nine full-length essays. Harold Bloom offers an interesting introduction regarding "The Analysis of Character," which provides a framework for readers attempting to come to terms with Emily Brontë's most memorable literary creation.

Frank, Katherine. *A Chainless Soul: A Life of Emily Brontë.* Boston: Houghton Mifflin, 1990. Frank's book attempts to strike a balance between the "purple heather school of Brontë biography" and later accounts that present Emily Brontë as a victim.

Fraser, Rebecca. *The Brontës: Charlotte Brontë and Her Family.* New York: Crown, 1988. Although Fraser's central focus is Brontë's sister, Charlotte, her intelligent and exhaustively researched book offers much valuable material on Emily as well. Its portrait of the Brontës as a family evokes a vivid picture of life in the remote Yorkshire parsonage and its effect in shaping Emily's own work.

Gaskell, Elizabeth C. *The Life of Charlotte Brontë.* 1857. Reprint. London: Penguin Books, 1975. Although the central focus is Charlotte Brontë, this invaluable book is a necessary part of any thorough study of Emily. Gaskell's friendship with Charlotte provides this biography with a unique and informative perspective on the Brontës and their lives.

Hewish, John. *Emily Brontë: A Critical and Biographical Study.* New York: St. Martin's Press, 1969. Part biography and part literary analysis, this study of Brontë places her within the context of her time and society, examining her life and the critical and public reception her work received. Contains an extensive and exceptional bibliography of great use to any Brontë scholar.

Lloyd Evans, Barbara, and Gareth Lloyd Evans. *The Scribner Companion to the Brontës.* New York: Charles Scribner's Sons, 1983. Provides an overview of the Brontë family as a whole. Includes the story of the Brontës' tragic history, sections on the young Brontës' juvenilia, discussions of Charlotte, Anne, and Emily's published works, and excerpts from criticisms written about those works at the time they were first published.

Smith, Anne, ed. *The Art of Emily Brontë.* New York: Barnes & Noble Books, 1976. A collection of critical essays on Brontë's work, covering both her poetry and *Wuthering Heights.* Among the most interesting essays are Keith Sagar's comparison of Brontë and D. H. Lawrence, and Colin Wilson's thought-provoking comments on *Wuthering Heights,* which he views not as a great novel but as a "rough sketch for the masterpiece that should have followed."

Anita Brookner

Born: London, England; July 16, 1928

Principal long fiction · *A Start in Life,* 1981 (pb. in U.S. as *The Debut,* 1981); *Providence,* 1982; *Look at Me,* 1983; *Hotel du Lac,* 1984; *Family and Friends,* 1985; *The Misalliance,* 1986; *A Friend from England,* 1987; *Latecomers,* 1988; *Lewis Percy,* 1989; *Brief Lives,* 1990; *A Closed Eye,* 1991; *Fraud,* 1992; *A Family Romance,* 1993 (pb. in U.S. as *Dolly,* 1993); *A Private View,* 1994; *Incidents in the Rue Laugier,* 1995; *Altered States,* 1996; *Visitors,* 1997; *Falling Slowly,* 1998; *Undue Influence,* 1999.

Other literary forms · A distinguished historian of eighteenth and nineteenth century French art and culture, Anita Brookner wrote several books of nonfiction before she began to write novels. *Watteau* (1968) is an assessment of the early eighteenth century French artist Antoine Watteau. *The Genius of the Future, Studies in French Art Criticism: Diderot, Stendhal, Baudelaire, Zola, the Brothers Goncourt, Huysmans* (1971) is a collection of six essays on seven French writers; each writer is considered in the context of his time. The greatest space is given to Charles Baudelaire. *Greuze: The Rise and Fall of an Eighteenth-Century Phenomenon* (1972) is a study of the French painter Jean-Baptiste Greuze in a successful attempt to locate the background of a sentimental genre that is distinct from both rococo and classicism. *Jacques-Louis David* (1980), a biography of the foremost painter of the French revolutionary period, explores the relationship between David's life and work, places that work in the context of contemporary French painting, and details a career that spanned some of the most turbulent years in French history. *Soundings,* a collection of essays, was published in 1997, and *Romanticism and Its Discontents* was published in 2000. Brookner's translations include *Utrillo* (1960) and *The Fauves* (1962).

Achievements · Brookner suddenly began to write fiction during her middle years, while still an active teacher and scholar. Although she continued her academic career, she quickly found equal success as a novelist. With the publication of several novels, she gained an international following and widespread critical acclaim. In 1984, Great Britain's prestigious Booker Prize for fiction was awarded to *Hotel du Lac.* Brookner was praised for her elegant and precise prose, her acute sense of irony, and her subtle insights into character and social behavior. Her witty explorations of manners and morals suggest to many a literary kinship to Jane Austen and Barbara Pym. While Brookner's somber, more complex moral vision disallows any sustained comparison to Pym, Austen and Brookner undeniably share a common concern for intelligent, subtle, clever heroines who seek to satisfy both private sensibility and public expectations.

To regard Brookner's novels as simply traditional novels of manners, however, is to misconstrue her art. Brookner's intentions greatly exceed this conventional genre; her achievements, indeed, take her far beyond it. Perhaps it is more useful to note the singularity of her contribution to British letters. Her highly developed pictorial sense; her baroque diction, with its balance of reason and passion; and her allusive, richly textured narratives, haunting in their resonances, reflect at every turn her extensive knowledge of the materials and motifs of eighteenth and nineteenth century paintings and literature.

Her works have been generously admired, but some dissenting voices have been raised. She is occasionally brought to task for fictive worlds too narrow in scope and claustrophobic in their intensity, for overzealous, self-conscious, schematic fiction, and for excessive sentimentality that unfortunately evokes the pulp romance. Brookner's worlds, however, are invariably shaped toward significant moral revelations; technique rarely intrudes to the detriment of story; and her ability to maintain an ironic distance from her characters, one that allows her to reveal sentimentality, to make judgments dispassionately, is one of her greatest strengths as a writer.

Biography · Anita Brookner was born in London, England, on July 16, 1928, to Newsom and Maude Brookner. She was educated at James Allen's Girls' School; King's College, University of London; and received a Ph.D. in art history from the Courtauld Institute of Art in London in 1953. From 1959 to 1964, she was visiting lecturer at the University of Reading, Berkshire. In 1967-1968, she was Slade Professor at Cambridge University, the first woman to hold this position. From 1964 to 1988 she taught at the Courtauld Institute of Art, where she lectured on neoclassicism and the Romantic movement. She is a Fellow of New Hall of Cambridge University. In 1983, she became a fellow of the Royal Society of Literature, and in 1990 she was made a Commander, Order of the British Empire (CBE).

Brookner began her career as a novelist when she was more than fifty years old as an attempt, she hinted, to understand her own powerlessness after a grand passion went wrong. Between 1981 and 1997, she published a novel a year; *Hotel du Lac* won the prestigious Booker Prize. She has also written many articles, introductions, and reviews on art history and on both French and English literature. They have appeared in such publications as the *Burlington Magazine*, *The London Review of Books*, *The Times Literary Supplement*, *The Spectator*, *The Observer*, and *The Sunday Times*. Some of these pieces are collected in *Soundings*.

Analysis · Anita Brookner established her reputation as a novelist with four books published in rapid succession between 1981 and 1984. Written in austerely elegant prose, each of these four novels follows essentially the same course. Each centers on a scholarly, sensitive, morally earnest young woman who leads an attenuated life. None of these heroines has intended a life so circumscribed. As their stories begin, they seek change, liberation from boredom and loneliness. They seek connection to a wider world. While these women are intelligent, endlessly introspective, and possessed of a saving ironic wit, they do not know how to get the things they most desire: the love of, and marriage to, a man of quality. With compassion, rue, and infinite good humor, Brookner makes it abundantly clear that these worthy women, these good daughters, good writers, and good scholars are unknowing adherents to a romantic ideal. Like the shopgirls and "ultrafeminine" women they gaze upon with such wonder and awe, these intellectually and morally superior women accept without question the cultural assumption that marriage is a woman's greatest good. Consistently undervaluing their own considerable talents and professional achievements, these heroines look to love and marriage as a way of joining the cosmic dance of a rational, well-ordered society. Their intense yearning for a transforming love shapes their individual plots; in each case, the conflict between what the romantic imagination wants and what it indeed does get impels these narratives forward. Brookner's concern is to illuminate the worthiness, the loneliness, the longing of these heroines for love and a more splendid life.

Before their stories can end, these women must abandon sentiment and accept their solitary state. Their triumph lies in their ability to confront their fall from romantic innocence and recognize it for what it is. These novels build inexorably toward an ending that is both startling and profoundly moving. While Brookner's heroines must struggle with sentimentality, Brookner herself does not. Her vision is bleak, unsparing. In telling their stories, she raises several other themes: The most notable of these are filial obligation, the "romantic" versus the "realistic" apprehension of life, truth and its relationship to self-knowledge, the determination of proper behavior in society, and the small pleasures that attend the trivia of daily life. Brookner presents her major and minor themes against the background of fictive worlds so powerfully realized that her novels seem to be absorbed as much as read. These are novels of interior reality. Little that is overt happens; dramatic action rests in the consciousness of the heroine, who is always center stage.

The Debut · Brookner's first novel, *The Debut,* lacks the richness and gradation of tone that marks her later fiction, but is nevertheless well crafted. Set against Honoré de Balzac's *Eugénie Grandet* (1833), *The Debut* tells the story of Ruth Weiss, a scrupulous, thoughtful scholar, who finds herself at forty with a life "ruined" by literature. A passionate reader from an early age, now a professor of literature specializing in Balzac, Ruth leads a narrow life alternating between teaching students and caring for an aging father. She blames the tradition of filial duty she found in literature for her mostly cheerless state.

Like Frances Hinton of *Look at Me* and Kitty Maule of *Providence,* Ruth began with expectations. In her youth, she once cast aside the burden of an oppressive heritage, one best symbolized by the deep silence and heavy, dark furniture in the mausoleum of a house she shared with her parents, and fled England for France. Ostensibly, her goal was to write a dissertation on vice and virtue; in actuality, it was as much to seek air and space and light. Although she at first endured a sense of displacement and exile, a condition that at one time or another afflicts many of Brookner's heroines, over time Ruth's transplant into foreign soil proved successful. Away from her charming, eccentric, but infinitely demanding parents, Ruth flourished. She acquired polish, sophistication, lovers. Yet even as she gloried in her new life, Ruth, like many of Brookner's other heroines, engaged in a constant internal debate over the question of how life is best lived. Does vice or virtue bring victory? She concluded that a life of conventional virtue can spell disaster for one's hopes; regretfully, Balzacian opportunism cannot be discounted. It is better to be a bad winner than a poor loser. Even though she observed that conventional morality tales were wrong, however, Ruth lamented the triumph of vice.

Suddenly called back to England because of what proves to be a final deterioration in her mother's fragile health, Ruth is forced to leave the comfortable, satisfying life she built for herself. Her spirited adventure over, Ruth is unable to extricate herself once more. At forty, the long and beautiful red hair indicative of her youthful potential for rebellion now compressed into a tight chignon, Dr. Ruth Weiss is a felon recaptured. She is tender with her father, gentle with her students, and expects little more from life. She is the first of Brookner's heroines who learns to renounce. Ruth's story is told retrospectively, in a way that recalls the French novel of meditation. The bold configurations of her story suggest the quality of a fable. The narrative also gains a necessary solidity and weight by the many allusions to Balzacian characters and texts. These allusions create a substructure of irony that continues to reverberate long after Ruth's story is complete.

Providence · If Ruth is disheartened but finally resigned, Kitty Maule in *Providence*, Brookner's second novel, moves toward outright disillusionment. Kitty is also a professor of literature. Her interests lie in the Romantic movement; this novel, then, like the rest of Brookner's fiction, is filled with ideas, good talk, vigorous intellectual exchanges. Here, both Kitty's private musings and her running seminar on Benjamin Constant's *Adolphe* (1816) provide a context for the exploration of Romantic concerns. Brookner's use of Kitty as a teacher of the Romantic tradition is ultimately highly ironic, for Kitty cannot discern her own romanticism. Curiously, she has moments when she is almost able to see her romanticism for what it is. Yet in the end, she suppresses the would-be insights and retreats into her dreams and passionate longings. What Kitty longs for is love, marriage, and, perhaps, God. Her longing for God goes largely unrecognized; like her fellow Romantics, she requires a sign. Yet her longing for love, the love of one man in particular, is at the perceived center of her life.

The handsome, brilliant, but distant lover of the scholarly, sensitive woman in this novel is Maurice Bishop. Maurice, a professor of medieval history, is noted for his love of cathedrals and God. Well born, rich, confident in the manner of those accustomed to deference, Maurice is everything that Kitty wants in life: He is the very cultural ideal of England itself. To be his wife is Kitty's hope of heaven; to capture him, she brings to bear all of her weapons at hand: subtle intelligence, grace of manners, enduring patience, and abiding love. That Kitty's love for Maurice has the fervor of a religious acolyte is suggested by his surname. Maurice may be in love with the idea of a religious absolute, but Kitty's religion is romantic love. All of her repressed romanticism is focused on this elegant, remote man.

Kitty's extreme dependence upon Maurice as the repository of her hopes and dreams stems in large part from her sense of cultural displacement. The child of a French mother and a British father, both dead in their youth, Kitty was born in England and brought up there by her immigrant French grandparents. Despite her British birth, however, Kitty never feels at home in England. In the face of concerted and varied efforts to "belong," she retains a sense of exile. Nor is she truly considered English by her colleagues and acquaintances. The product of her doting French grandparents, Kitty is unaware of her true cultural allegiance; ironically, it is the French heritage that dominates in her English setting. Her manners, clothes, and speech belie her English father. In Maurice, Kitty seeks an attachment that anchors, a place to be. Here and elsewhere in Brookner's fiction, the recurrent theme of the search for a home acquires the force and weight of myth. So powerfully realized is Kitty's intense desire for love, acceptance, and liberation from loneliness that it comes as a shock when Kitty, who is expecting Maurice's proposal of marriage, instead learns of his sudden engagement to a woman who shares his aristocratic background. The novel concludes with Kitty's realization that she had indeed lived in a haze of romantic expectation; the truth is, she has been first, last, and always an outsider.

In addition to the major theme of the passive, excellent, but self-deceived young woman in the service of an illusory ideal, Brookner presents in *Providence* themes which are relevant to all of her works. Maurice's betrayal of Kitty, for example, establishes a motif that recurs in later novels, while Brookner's superbly comic depiction of bored and boring academics, a staple in her fiction, reaches perhaps its finest statement here. If Balzacian allusions underlie *The Debut* and give it additional power, allusions to many French writers, but especially to Constant's *Adolphe* are used to provide ironic commentary on and foreshadowings of Kitty's fate. Most important, however, Kitty Maule herself is arguably the quintessential Brooknerian heroine. Like her fictional sisters, Ruth Weiss of *The Debut,* Frances Hinton of *Look at Me,* Edith Hope of *Hotel du Lac,* and Mimi Dorn of *Family and Friends,* Kitty waits patiently for her life to begin. She is blind to her own worth and discounts her singular achievements; longs for order, a place in a rational world; finds joy in the chores, duties, and routines of everyday life; is sensitive, compassionate, morally deserving. Finally, her final inevitable loss of a man morally her inferior leaves her stripped of all romantic illusions, a convert to reality.

Look at Me · By her own admission a relentless observer, Frances Hinton, the heroine of *Look at Me,* Brookner's third novel, tells her own compelling story. To be sure, all of Brookner's heroines are detached observers, though probably none records and stores information so clinically as does Frances. All of Brookner's heroines suffer, yet perhaps none suffers more intensely than Frances. Like other Brooknerian heroines, Frances is virtuous, sensitive, bright, and in need of a more marvelous life. Like other Brooknerian heroines also, she does not know how to get the things she wants. Frozen into inaction, her intense melancholia is mirrored in the images of death and desolation that surround her. A medical librarian who catalogs prints and engravings of disease through the ages, Frances comments ironically on the scenes of madness, nightmare affliction, and death she must sort and mount. She lives in a tomb of a house where her mother has died; Brookner's use of Frances's house recalls her uses of houses elsewhere: They are symbols of oppressive traditions that constrain and weigh heavily upon those who inhabit them. For Frances, the world is somber, dark. The glittering, stylish couple who offer temporary access to a dazzling social world prove cruelly false. In an act of betrayal so profound that Frances cannot but withdraw from the world she has long sought, the beautiful Nick and Alix Fraser hold Frances up to public ridicule. Her brief liberation from solitariness and the eternal prison of self ends abruptly. Always self-analytic, self-deprecatory, Frances sees her failure to find a place in the world as a failure of egotism or will. She observes that others advance through egotism, but she cannot mimic them. She decides to become a writer. Writing will allow her both to comment on life and to retreat from it.

As is usual in Brookner's works, the dramatic action is largely inner. Hers are novels of the interior; the terrain surveyed is that of the soul. Frances presents a commanding narrative voice as she sorts, gathers, and finally reassembles the fragments of her experience into a unified whole. In fullest voice, she provides useful insights into the processes of the creative, transforming imagination. From the detritus of her daily life she, as writer-at-work, will abstract significant form. If Brookner here provides a mirror of herself busy fashioning art from the materials of the ordinary, the details of eating or dressing or chatting that receive so much attention in her novels, she also repeats the characteristic fusion of the comic and the sad that lends such poignancy to her works. Further, the influence of the pictorial is reflected here as well; characters are often framed in an action, presented with a consciousness of scene or setting. Finally, Frances's long commentary on her experience that is the text of *Look at Me* again evokes the French novel of meditation, a literary form that subtly influences and pervades Brookner's fiction. Notably, as Frances begins to write on the last page of the novel, she is free of self-pity. Solitude may be her lot, but art will vindicate her. Art will represent the triumph of the unvanquished self.

Hotel du Lac · Edith Hope, the heroine of *Hotel du Lac*, Brookner's fourth novel and the winner of the 1984 Booker Prize, is also a writer. Edith writes pulp romances for a living. Yet until she learns better, she believes that romance is only her business, not her frame of mind. Brookner's fiction, however, reveals her tendency sometimes to use names to signal character traits or habits of thought. Such is the case here: Edith is indeed a romantic, although an unknowing one. Edith begins her stay at the Hotel du Lac in ignorance of her true nature; she leaves enlightened as to the deeper, more recessed aspects of her moral being.

It was not Edith's choice to leave England and travel to Switzerland, the setting of *Hotel du Lac*. Edith was sent away because of her severe breach of social decorum: She chose not to appear at her own wedding, thus profoundly humiliating a good man and eminently suitable husband. Her action was shocking to all, including Edith herself. Modest, unassuming, and usually anxious to please, Edith is in many ways a typical Brooknerian heroine. She, too, spends too much time alone, condemned to her own introspection. Her marriage would have broken that isolation. Edith's revolt and subsequent removal to Switzerland provide a context for the discussion of numerous moral and psychological questions. While Edith's story is always foremost, the novel itself alternates between first-and third-person narratives, with philosophical positions being argued, accepted, or dismissed. The central fact that emerges about Edith is her passionate love for a married man whom she only seldom sees. Like his fictional predecessors, Edith's David is exceedingly handsome, elegant, intelligent, and re-mote. For love of him, Edith jilted her dull but safe fiancé. At the Hotel du Lac, Edith's interactions with the other residents move her to a greater understanding of truth, self-knowledge, and the differences between romance and reality. Numerous other themes are present here as well, including that of "ultrafeminine" as opposed to "feminist" women. Edith understands these women as models of feminine response to feminine experience. In relative isolation at this Swiss hotel, she studies these models and rejects both. The will to power, the utility of egotism as a serviceable instrument in the world, a recurrent Brooknerian theme, also receives much discussion here.

What Edith eventually learns as she evaluates her exchanges and relationships with her fellow guests is accorded significant status by the mythological underpinnings of this novel. Inside the hotel, characters are both particular and types, acting out self-assigned roles in a grand comedy of manners. All the inhabitants exhibit a theatrical sense of themselves; they "present" themselves to this community con-sciously, deliberately. Such attention to the pictorial, personal presentation is a constant of Brookner's fiction. The details of clothes, manners, and mannerisms convey aspects of self and morality in Brookner's works as they do in the works of Henry James, to whom Brookner alludes in this novel. If inside the hotel the characters are on parade, making their statements with dress, or gesture, once outside the hotel, they are subsumed into the mythicized landscape. Gray mist, conveying a sense of menace and oppression, surrounds everything. Characters make journeys that are important only for their mythic impact. Much movement against this dreary landscape takes place as characters are directed toward crucial, definitive moral choices. The landscape helps Edith to perceive her dilemmas; she is finally able to reject a diabolical figure who offers marriage without love. He forces Edith to recognize her romanticism for what it is. At least in the end, however, when she returns to England and her married lover, Edith knows that she has chosen a cold and solitary path. Her self-determination represents a triumph for her and for this book. Edith is finally transformed by her successful journey to knowledge.

Having laid claim with her first four novels to a sharply defined fictional territory, Brookner has shown in subsequent books a willingness to extend her range. In *Latecomers*, for example, she centers her story for the first time on two male figures, close friends, both of whom were refugees brought from Germany to England as children during World War II. *Lewis Percy* features a single protagonist, again a man, in some ways the counterpart of Brookner's earlier heroines.

Family and Friends · The book with which Brookner departed most radically from the pattern established in her first four novels was *Family and Friends*; perhaps because it violated readers' expectations, it was sharply criticized by some reviewers. Written in the historical present with virtually no dialogue, *Family and Friends* is an extended meditation on the French tradition. It stems from the ruminations of a narrator who quickly disappears, makes only glancing reappearances, and is curiously never identified. Here, Brookner's concern is not with a particular heroine, but with the Dorn family, rich, most likely German immigrants who fled to England before the start of World War II. The war, when it comes, receives but scant attention; the novel focuses always on the small, interior world of the Dorn family. Little seems to exist outside the family and their immediate interests, sparking again charges of a work too narrow in range.

The lives of the Dorn family and their associates are followed over a period of time. Sofka, the gentle but strong matriarch of the family, is the moral center of the work. Widowed early in life, she rejects the idea of remarriage, directing her loving attentions to her family instead. Mimi and Betty are her two daughters. While Betty is selfish, willful, theatrical, tricking her family into giving her an independent life quite early, she is nevertheless the child Sofka secretly loves best. Sofka, beautiful and contained, admires her younger daughter's spirit. Mimi is virtuous, dreamy, passive, frozen into inertia in young womanhood when an early feeble attempt to reach out for love is unsuccessful. Mimi languishes for years afterward, until her mother urges her into marriage, and thereby respectability, with a gentle, good man who would normally be her social inferior. Also playing a significant part in the novel are Sofka's two sons: the sensitive, intelligent, responsible Alfred and his handsome, charming brother Frederick. Interestingly, it is Alfred's plight that mirrors the situation of the usual Brooknerian heroine. It is he who is trapped by filial obligation into a life he had not intended; it is he who suffers forever afterward from an unsatisfying search for love and a desire for a larger, more extended world. It is also he who ultimately becomes inured to long-established habits of insularity.

This, then, is the saga of a family whose interior lives and moral relations are acutely realized. Important themes here include familial relations, especially filial obligation; the search for a transcendent love; the need to venture, to dare, if one is to "win" in life. Structured around four wedding pictures, the novel impresses with its unity and intensity of tone; the pervasive, elegant irony; the discerning moral judgments; and the engrossing character portraits. Especially effective also is the novel's lament for the loss of youthful promise, energy, and innocence. The once-vibrant Betty, trapped in middle-aged stasis, is a case in point. Dominating this entire work is a rich narrative voice, stern, compassionate, and often sad. The Dorn family seems to exist in a twilight, dreamlike world outside time. Yet this world, while admittedly narrow, is nevertheless mesmerizing.

Altered States · Brookner writes novels in both the first and third person, and most of her novels center on women. *Altered States* represents a first: a novel told by a man, Alan Sherwood, in the first person. In *Hotel du Lac*, Brookner divides women into hares (happy winners in life's game) and tortoises (losers, for whom romance novels are written). In *Altered States*, Sherwood is a male tortoise; he is obsessed with a hare, the flashy and sexy Sarah Miller. As usual in Brookner, Alan the tortoise figure is a dull person, dutiful and bound to a parent. He is wheedled into marriage by another tortoise, Angela, and he is tortured by guilt after he betrays her and seemingly causes her death.

Altered States is different from other Brookner novels in other ways. Sarah is cruder, sexier, more selfish, and more anarchistic than any of Brookner's other hares; she embodies most of the seven deadly sins. Her lovemaking with Alan is more purely sexual than similar encounters elsewhere in Brookner. Alan, on the other hand, is not simply a tortoise; he *knows* he is a tortoise. He knows that he is dull and that he represents not just dullness but also civilized order. By the end of the novel, Alan not only learns about himself and the other people in his life, but he also has a small triumph over Sarah. He convinces her to step outside her character and perform a generous act.

Visitors · In *Visitors*, the central character is once more a woman: Thea May, age seventy. She is perhaps Brookner's most inert and solitary tortoise—until a crisis makes her take a hare into her home. The hare is named Steve Best, a young friend of someone about to marry into Thea's late husband's family. The contrast could not be greater. Thea is a lonely, apprehensive, static old woman; Steve is a gregarious, wandering, confident young man. Her reaction to him is complicated. She responds to his presence and even coddles him, but at the same time she feels that her home has been violated, and she wishes he would leave.

Visitors is about understanding. Many characters, such as Thea's husband's self-centered family and the rude and charmless young people, understand each other hardly at all. They certainly do not understand Thea. However, as the novel proceeds, Thea displays a talent for understanding all of them and is even able to act on that understanding on a climactic occasion. As she is drawn out of her usual routine, Thea thinks more and more about her past. Since childhood she has harbored a secret fear of intruders—hares such as Steve and even her husband. By the end of the novel, Thea seems to come to terms with her anxieties. She acknowledges her affection for her husband's family and feels more receptive to daily joys.

Betty H. Jones, updated by George Soule

Other major works

NONFICTION: *Watteau*, 1968; *The Genius of the Future, Studies in French Art Criticism: Diderot, Stendhal, Baudelaire, Zola, the Brothers Goncourt, Huysmans*, 1971; *Greuze: The Rise and Fall of an Eighteenth-Century Phenomenon*, 1972; *Jacques-Louis David*, 1980; *Soundings*, 1997; *Romanticism and Its Discontents*, 2000.

TRANSLATIONS: *Utrillo*, 1960 (of Waldemar George's biography); *The Fauves*, 1962 (of Jean Paul Crespelle's book).

Bibliography

Baxter, Gisèle Marieks. "Cultural Experiences and Identity in the Early Novels of Anita Brookner." *English* 42 (Summer, 1993): 125-139. Three central characters of early Brookner novels attempt (unsuccessfully) to find the formulas of literary romance in their lives. They aspire, not to the traditional aristocracy or even to the world of the gentry, but to the financially secure ideal of Prime Minister Margaret Thatcher's era.

Fisher-Wirth, Ann. "Hunger Art: The Novels of Anita Brookner." *Twentieth Century Literature* 41 (Spring, 1995): 1-15. At first glance, Brookner's heroines seem to be women trapped in a patriarchal world who accept their humiliation. A closer reading reveals that Brookner treats the universal human situation.

Haffenden, John. *Novelists in Interview.* London: Methuen, 1985. Includes a lively interview with Anita Brookner (pages 57-75) in which she discusses her novels, the ideas behind her writing, and the existential dilemmas of her characters. A substantial interview that provides a useful background to her works.

Hosmer, Robert E., Jr. "Paradigm and Passage: The Fiction of Anita Brookner." In *Contemporary British Women Writers: Narrative Strategies.* New York: St. Martin's Press, 1993. Brookner's central characters, like Brookner herself, are in the tradition of exile figures, from the Bible to contemporary times.

Sadler, Lynn Veach. *Anita Brookner.* Boston: Twayne, 1990. The first full-length study of Brookner's work, which discusses her first seven novels. Sadler compares Brookner to Barbara Pym and Margaret Drabble but also shows why Brookner has her own voice in feminist fiction. Analyzes Brookner's heroines and gives insight into the author's use of irony.

Skinner, John. *The Fictions of Anita Brookner: Illusions of Romance.* New York: St. Martin's Press, 1992. Skinner speculates on the close relationship of Brookner's novels to her life. He also discusses the novels in the light of contemporary narrative theory.

John Bunyan

Born: Elstow, England; November, 1628
Died: London, England; August 31, 1688

Principal long fiction · *Grace Abounding to the Chief of Sinners*, 1666; *The Pilgrim's Progress from This World to That Which Is to Come*, Part I, 1678; *The Life and Death of Mr. Badman*, 1680; *The Holy War*, 1682; *The Pilgrim's Progress from This World to That Which Is to Come, the Second Part*, 1684.

Other literary forms · Between 1656 and 1688, John Bunyan published forty-four separate works, including prose narratives and tracts, sermons, and verse; ten posthumous publications appeared in a folio edition of 1692, which the author himself had prepared for the press. A nearly complete edition, in two volumes, was printed between 1736 and 1737, another in 1767 by George Whitefield, and a six-volume Edinburgh edition in 1784. The best of Bunyan's verse can be found in a small collection (c. 1664) containing "The Four Last Things," "Ebal and Gerizim," and "Prison Meditations." In addition, he wrote *A Caution to Stir Up to Watch Against Sin* (1664), a half-sheet broadside poem in sixteen stanzas; *A Book for Boys and Girls: Or, Country Rhymes for Children* (1686); and *Discourse of the Building, Nature, Excellency, and Government of the House of God* (1688), a poem in twelve parts.

Achievements · The spirit of seventeenth century Protestant dissent burst into flame within the heart and mind of Bunyan. He attended only grammar school, served in the parliamentary army at age sixteen, and returned to Bedfordshire to undergo religious crisis and conversion. Imprisoned after the Restoration of Charles II for refusing to obey the laws against religious dissent, he turned to his pen as the only available means of performing his divinely ordained stewardship. He wrote his most significant work, the vision of *The Pilgrim's Progress*, while in jail, and the piece became a companion to the Scriptures among lower-class English Dissenters. His limited education came from two sources: the *Actes and Monuments* (1563) of John Foxe, containing the accounts of the martyrdom of sixteenth century English Protestants; and the Authorized Version of the Bible, the content and style of which he skillfully applied to his own prose.

Bunyan's art grew out of his natural abilities of observation and analysis. He was a Puritan and a product of the Puritan movement, yet, as can be seen clearly from the autobiographical *Grace Abounding to the Chief of Sinners*, he was chiefly interested in actual human experience, not in religious doctrine for its own sake. His allegorical characters—Mr. Timorous, Mr. Talkative, Mrs. Diffidence, Mr. By-ends, Lord Turnabout, Mr. Smooth-man, Mr. Facing-bothways—originated in everyday life. Similarly, the Valley of Humiliation, the Slough of Despond, Vanity Fair, and Fair-speech can be found by all people everywhere, no matter what their culture or religion. In *The Pilgrim's Progress*, Bunyan universalized his Puritanism, depicting every earnest Christian's search for salvation, every upright person's attempt to achieve some degree of faith. He wrote to awaken conscience, to strengthen faith, and to win souls—the last being the true object of his evangelical mission. At the same time, he managed to write tracts and narratives worthy of recognition as *literature*—even, in certain instances, as masterpieces.

Biography · John Bunyan was born in the village of Elstow, in Bedfordshire (one mile south of Bedford) in November, 1628. The parish register of Elstow records his baptism on November 30. His father, Thomas Bunyan, a native of Elstow, married three times between January, 1623, and August, 1644; John Bunyan was the first child of his father's second marriage, on May 23, 1627, to Margaret Bentley, also of Elstow. The boy's father was a "whitesmith," a maker and mender of pots and kettles, although by the time the son adopted the same vocation, the job reference had changed to "tinker." Young Bunyan attended a nearby grammar school (either the one at Bedford or another at Elstow), where he learned to read and write—but little else. In fact, what he did learn he promptly forgot after his father removed him from school to help in the family forge and workshop. When, in 1644, his mother died and the elder Bunyan promptly remarried, Bunyan lost all interest in his family; he entered the parliamentary army in November, at age sixteen, and remained until the disbanding of that force in 1646. He then returned to Elstow and the family trade.

At the end of 1648 or the beginning of 1649, Bunyan married a pious but otherwise unidentified woman who bore him four children, one of whom, Mary, was born blind. He spent some four years wrestling with his finances and his soul, and in 1653 joined a dissenting sect that met at St. John's Church, Bedford. Shortly after his removal to that city in 1655, his wife died, and two years later he was called upon to preach by the Baptist sect whose church he had joined. In 1659, he married again, to a woman named Elizabeth, who spent considerable time rearing his children, bearing him two more, and trying to secure her husband's release from a series of prison terms.

Bunyan's career as a writer cannot be separated from his difficulties immediately preceding and during the Restoration of Charles II. The period of Cromwell's Commonwealth produced a number of dissenting preachers, both male and female, who achieved their offices through inspiration rather than ordination; they professed to be filled with inner light and the gifts of the Holy Spirit rather than with learning. Charles II had promised to tolerate these preachers, but the established Church, in November, 1660, set about to persecute and to silence them. Thus, Bunyan, who chose imprisonment rather than silence, spent all but a few weeks of the next eleven years in jail in Bedford, where he preached to his fellow prisoners, made tagged laces, and wrote religious books—the most noteworthy being his spiritual autobiography, *Grace Abounding to the Chief of Sinners.* He was freed in September, 1672, when Charles II, through his Declaration of Indulgence, suspended all penal statutes against Nonconformists and papists.

Upon his release from prison, Bunyan returned to his ministerial duties at St. John's Church in Bedford, this time with a license (given to him by royal authority) to preach. By 1675, however, he was again imprisoned in Bedford, the result of refusing to declare formal allegiance to Charles II (against whom he had no real objection) and the Church of England. While serving this particular sentence, Bunyan produced his most significant piece of prose, *The Pilgrim's Progress.* Bunyan's major prose works were written within the last ten years of his life, the period during which he both suffered from intolerance and received honors from the intolerant. In the last year of his life, he served as the unofficial chaplain to Sir John Shorter, the Lord Mayor of London. Indeed, Bunyan endured the entire tide of religious and political trauma of the middle and late seventeenth century: parliamentary acts, ministerial

changes, popish plots, the rebellious factions. His work bears testimony to that endurance, to the patience of a nonpolitical yet deeply pious man who lost much of his freedom to the impatience of a supposedly pious but terribly political religious establishment.

Bunyan died on August 31, 1688, at the London house of his friend, John Strudwick, a grocer and chandler. Supposedly, in order to settle a dispute between a father and his son, he rode through heavy rain and caught a severe cold that led to his death. He was buried in Bunhill Fields, the burial ground of London Dissenters.

Analysis · John Bunyan viewed his life as a commitment to Christian stewardship, to be carried on by gospel preaching and instructive writing. Although practically everything that he wrote reflects that commitment, he possessed the ability to create interesting variations on similar themes, keeping in mind the needs of his lower-class audience. Thus, *The Pilgrim's Progress* is an allegory of human life and universal religious experience. In *The Life and Death of Mr. Badman*, Bunyan abandoned allegory and developed a dialogue between Mr. Wiseman and Mr. Attentive through which he publicized the aims and methods of the late seventeenth century bourgeois scoundrel, whose lack of principle and honesty was well known among Bunyan's readers (the victims of Mr. Badman). Finally, his first major work, *Grace Abounding to the Chief of Sinners*, is a "spiritual autobiography" which presents adventures and experiences not unlike those undergone by any human being at any moment in history who must wrestle with the fundamental questions of life. The function of Bunyan's prose in every case was to spread the Word of God and to establish a holy community of humankind in which that Word could be practiced. Once the Word took hold, Bunyan believed, the world would become a veritable garden of peace and order.

Grace Abounding to the Chief of Sinners · Published in 1666, *Grace Abounding to the Chief of Sinners* remains one of the most significant spiritual autobiographies by an English writer. Bunyan's style is perhaps more formal in this piece than in *The Pilgrim's Progress*, although he did well to balance the heavy phrasing of Scripture (as it appeared in the Authorized Version) with picturesque, colloquial English. A richly emotional work in which such highly charged experiences as the Last Judgment and the tortures of Hell become as clear as the mundane experiences of daily existence, Bunyan's autobiography is a narrative of spiritual adventure set against the backdrop of a real village in Britain. Although he omitted specific names and dates, obviously to universalize the piece, he did not forget to describe what he had seen after his return from the army: the popular game of "cat," with its participants and spectators; the bellringers at the parish church; the poor women sitting, in sunlight, before the door of a village house; the puddles in the road. Woven into this fabric of reality are the experiences of the dreamer; the people of Bedford appear as though in a vision on the sunny side of a high mountain, as the dreamer, shut out by an encompassing wall, shivers in the cold storm. Such interweaving of reality and fantasy was to take place again, with greater force and allegorical complexity, in the first part of *The Pilgrim's Progress*.

Bunyan's intention in *Grace Abounding to the Chief of Sinners* was to point the way by which average Christians, convinced of their own sins, can be led by God's grace to endure the pain of spiritual crisis. He determined to record how, as an obscure Bedfordshire tinker, he had changed his course from sloth and sin to become an eloquent and fearless man of God. Of course, when he wrote the work, he had been in prison for ten years, and (as stated in the preface) he set about to enlighten and assist those from whom he had, for so long a period, been separated.

From the confinement of his prison cell, Bunyan felt the desire to survey his entire life—to grasp his soul in his hands and take account of himself. Thus, *Grace Abounding to the Chief of Sinners* emerged from the heart and the spirit of a man isolated from humankind to become not merely one more testimonial for the instruction of the faithful, but a serious, psychological self-study—one so truthful and so sincere (and also so spontaneous) that it may be the first work of its kind. Bunyan's language is simple and direct, and his constant references to Scripture emphasize the typicality of his experiences as a struggling Christian. His fears, doubts, and moments of comfort are filtered through the encounter between David and Goliath and God's deliverance of the young shepherd, while his lively imagination gathers images from the Psalms and the Proverbs and reshapes them to fit the context of his spiritual experiences.

The Pilgrim's Progress · Bunyan's ability to universalize his experience is supremely evident in *The Pilgrim's Progress*, perhaps the most successful allegory in British literature. *The Pilgrim's Progress* has as its basic metaphor the familiar idea of life as a journey. Bunyan confronts his pilgrim, Christian, with homely and commonplace sights: a quagmire, the bypaths and shortcuts through pleasant country meadows, the inn, the steep hill, the town fair on market day, the river to be forded. Such places belong to the everyday experience of every man, woman, and child; on another level, they recall the holy but homely parables of Christ's earthly ministry, and thus assume spiritual significance. Those familiar details serve as an effective background for Bunyan's narrative, a story of adventure intended to hold the reader in suspense. Bunyan grew up among the very people who constituted his audience, and he knew how to balance the romantic and the strange with the familiar. Thus, Christian travels the King's Highway at the same time that he traverses a perilous path to encounter giants, wild beasts, hobgoblins, and the terrible Apollyon, the angel of the bottomless pit with whom the central character must fight. Other travelers are worthy of humorous characterization, as they represent a variety of intellectual and moral attitudes, while Christian himself runs the gamut of universal experience, from the moment he learns of his sins until the account of his meeting with Hopeful in the river.

As always, Bunyan molds his style from the Authorized Version of the Bible. By relying upon concrete, common language, he enables even the simplest of his readers to share experiences with the characters of *The Pilgrim's Progress*. Even the conversations relating to complex and tedious theological issues do not detract from the human and dramatic aspects of the allegory: Evangelist pointing the way; Christian running from his home with his fingers stuck in his ears; the starkness of the place of the Cross in contrast to the activity of Vanity Fair; the humorous but terribly circumstantial trial. It is this homely but vivid realism that accounts for the timeless appeal of Bunyan's allegory. *The Pilgrim's Progress* reveals the truth about humankind–its weakness, its imperfection, its baseness–but also its search for goodness and order.

The Life and Death of Mr. Badman · *The Life and Death of Mr. Badman* represents Bunyan's major attempt at a dialogue, a confrontation between the Christian and the atheist, between the road to Paradise and the route to Hell. Mr. Wiseman, a Christian, tells the story of Mr. Badman to Mr. Attentive, who in turn comments upon it. Badman is an example of the reprobate, one whose sins become evident during childhood. In fact, he is so addicted to lying that his parents cannot distinguish when he is speaking the truth. Bunyan does not place much blame upon the parents, for they indeed bear the burden of their son's actions; they even attempt to counsel him and to redirect his ways. The situation becomes worse, however, as Badman's lying turns to pilfering and then to outright stealing. All of this, naturally, leads to a hatred of Sunday, of the Puritan demands of that day: reading Scripture, attending conferences, repeating sermons, praying to God. Wiseman, the defender of the Puritan Sabbath, maintains that little boys, as a matter of course, must learn to appreciate the Sabbath; those who do not are victims of their own wickedness. Hatred of the Sabbath leads to swearing and cursing, which become as natural to young Badman as eating, drinking, and sleeping.

Badman's adult life is painstakingly drawn out through realistic descriptions, anecdotes, and dialogue. He cheats and steals his way through the world of debauchery and commerce and creates misery for his wife and seven children. Growing in importance, he forms a league with the devil and becomes a wealthy man by taking advantage of others' misfortunes. When the time comes for his end, he cannot be saved–nor does Bunyan try to fabricate an excuse for his redemption and salvation. As Mr. Wiseman states, "As his life was full of sin, so his death was without repentance." Throughout a long sickness, Badman fails to acknowledge his sins, remaining firm in his self-satisfaction. He dies without struggle, "like a chrisom child, quietly and without fear."

The strength of *The Life and Death of Mr. Badman* derives in large part from Bunyan's ability to depict common English life of the mid- and late seventeenth century. The details are so accurate, so minute, that the reader can gain as much history from the piece as morality or practical theology. Bunyan places no demands upon the reader's credulity by providential interpositions, nor does he alter his wicked character's ways for the sake of a happy ending. In portraying Badman's ways, Bunyan concedes nothing, nor does he exaggerate. Badman succeeds, gains wealth and power, and dies at peace with himself. Bunyan creates a monstrous product of sin and places him squarely in the center of English provincial life. The one consolation, the principal lesson, is that Badman travels the direct route to everlasting hellfire. On his way, he partakes of life's pleasures and is gratified by them as only an unrepentant sinner could be. For Bunyan, the harsh specificity of Badman's life is a sufficient lesson through which to promote his version of positive Christianity.

Beneath the veil of seventeenth century British Puritanism, for all its seeming narrowness and sectarian strife, there was something for all persons of all eras–the struggle to know God, to do his will, to find peace. If Bunyan's first major prose work was a spiritual autobiography, then it is fair to state that the principal efforts that followed–*The Pilgrim's Progress* and *The Life and Death of Mr. Badman*–constituted one of the earliest spiritual histories of all humankind.

Samuel J. Rogal

Other major works

POETRY: *A Caution to Stir Up to Watch Against Sin*, 1664; *A Book for Boys and Girls: Or, Country Rhymes for Children*, 1686; *Discourse of the Building, Nature, Excellency, and Government of the House of God*, 1688.

NONFICTION: *Some Gospel Truths Opened*, 1656; *A Vindication . . . of Some Gospel Truths Opened*, 1657; *A Few Signs from Hell*, 1658; *The Doctrine of the Law and Grace Unfolded*, 1659; *Profitable Meditations Fitted to Man's Different Condition*, 1661; *I Will Pray with the Spirit*, 1663; *A Mapp Shewing the Order and Causes of Salvation and Damnation*, 1664; *One Thing Is Needful*, 1665; *The Holy City: Or, The New Jerusalem*, 1665; *A Confession of My Faith and a Reason for My Practice*, 1671; *A New and Useful Concordance to the Holy Bible*, 1672; *A Defence of the Doctrine of Justification by Faith*, 1672; *The Strait Gate: Or, The Great Difficulty of Going to Heaven*, 1676; *Saved by Grace*, 1676; *A Treatise of the Fear of God*, 1679; *A Holy Life, the Beauty of Christianity*, 1684; *Solomon's Temple Spiritualized: Or, Gospel Light Fecht Out of the Temple at Jerusalem*, 1688; *The Jerusalem Sinner Saved*, 1688.

Bibliography

Collmer, Robert G. *Bunyan in Our Time.* Kent, Ohio: Kent State University Press, 1989. A collection of distinguished literary criticism and appraisals of Bunyan. Includes essays on his use of language, satire and its biblical sources, and *The Pilgrim's Progress* as allegory. Of particular interest are the essays on Marxist perspectives on Bunyan and a comparison between Bunyan's quest and C. S. Lewis's quest in *The Pilgrim's Regress* (1933).

Harrison, G. B. *John Bunyan: A Study in Personality.* New York: Archon Books, 1967. A short study that traces the mind and personality of Bunyan as shown in his writings. Discusses his conversion, his imprisonment, and his roles as pastor and writer. The close analysis of minor works makes this an important critical source.

Kelman, John. *The Road: A Study of John Bunyan's "Pilgrim's Progress."* 2 vols. Port Washington, N.Y.: Kennikat Press, 1912. These volumes are intended as a commentary or textbook, to be read point by point with *The Pilgrim's Progress.* An evangelical approach to Bunyan, filled with praise for his work. Gives close analysis of the text from a strongly Christian point of view.

Newey, Vincent. *"The Pilgrim's Progress": Critical and Historical Views.* Liverpool, England: Liverpool University Press, 1980. Brings together critical essays on *The Pilgrim's Progress* to provide fresh, detailed, and varied approaches to this work. Discusses the tension between allegory and naturalism and Bunyan's handling of the language and values of the people. Indispensable to the serious scholar of this work.

Sadler, Lynn Veach. *John Bunyan.* Boston: Twayne, 1979. A useful introduction to beginning readers of Bunyan. Discusses his life, his religious milieu, and his works. Places *Grace Abounding to the Chief of Sinners* in the genre of "spiritual autobiography." Most of the literary criticism goes to *The Pilgrim's Progress,* but there is also discussion of *The Life and Death of Mr. Badman* and *The Holy War.* Also includes a selected bibliography.

Spargo, Tamsin. *The Writing of John Bunyan.* Brookfield, Mass.: Ashgate, 1997. A detailed exploration of how Bunyan established his authority as an author. Includes notes and detailed bibliography. Recommended for advanced students and scholars.

Anthony Burgess

John Anthony Burgess Wilson

Born: Manchester, England; February 25, 1917
Died: London, England; November 25, 1993

Principal long fiction · *Time for a Tiger*, 1956; *The Enemy in the Blanket*, 1958; *Beds in the East*, 1959; *The Doctor Is Sick*, 1960; *The Right to an Answer*, 1960; *Devil of a State*, 1961; *One Hand Clapping*, 1961 (as Joseph Kell); *The Worm and the Ring*, 1961; *A Clockwork Orange*, 1962 (reprinted with final chapter, 1986); *The Wanting Seed*, 1962; *Honey for the Bears*, 1963; *Inside Mr. Enderby*, 1963 (as Joseph Kell); *The Eve of Saint Venus*, 1964; *Nothing Like the Sun: A Story of Shakespeare's Love-Life*, 1964; *The Long Day Wanes*, 1965 (includes *Time for a Tiger*, *The Enemy in the Blanket*, and *Beds in the East*); *A Vision of Battlements*, 1965; *Tremor of Intent*, 1966; *Enderby*, 1968 (includes *Mr. Enderby* and *Enderby Outside*); *Enderby Outside*, 1968; *MF*, 1971; The Clockwork Testament: Or, Enderby's End, 1974; *Napoleon Symphony*, 1974; *Beard's Roman Woman*, 1976; *Moses: A Narrative*, 1976; *Abba, Abba*, 1977; *1985*, 1978; *Man of Nazareth*, 1979; *Earthly Powers*, 1980; *The End of the World News*, 1983; *Enderby's Dark Lady*, 1984; *The Kingdom of the Wicked*, 1985; *The Pianoplayers*, 1986; *Any Old Iron*, 1989; *A Dead Man in Deptford*, 1993; *Byrne*, 1995.

Other literary forms · In addition to his novels, Anthony Burgess published eight works of literary criticism. He paid tribute to his self-confessed literary mentor, James Joyce, in such works as *Re Joyce* (1965) and *Joysprick: An Introduction to the Language of James Joyce* (1972). His book reviews and essays were collected in *The Novel Now* (1967, revised 1971), *Urgent Copy* (1968), and *But Do Blondes Prefer Gentlemen? Homage to Qwert Yuiop and Other Writings* (1986). His fascination with language and with the lives of writers led to such works as *Language Made Plain* (1964), *Shakespeare* (1970), and *Flame into Being: The Life and Work of D. H. Lawrence* (1985). An autobiographical work, *Little Wilson and Big God*, was published in 1987 (part of which was republished in 1996 as *Childhood*), and a collection of short fiction, *The Devil's Mode*, in 1989. A posthumous volume of his uncollected writings, *One Man's Chorus* (1998), includes a variety of essays divided into sections on travel, contemporary life, literary criticism, and personality sketches.

Achievements · In his novels, Burgess extended the boundaries of English fiction. His inventive use of language, his use of symphonic forms and motifs, his rewriting of myths and legends, his examination of cultural clashes between the Third World and the West, and his pursuit of various ways to tell a story established him as one of the chief exemplars of postmodernism. His novels are studied in contemporary fiction courses, and he also achieved popular success with such works as *A Clockwork Orange* and *Earthly Powers*, for which he received the Prix du Meilleur Livre Étranger in 1981. Stanley Kubrick's controversial film *A Clockwork Orange* (1971) further established Burgess's popular reputation.

Biography · John Anthony Burgess Wilson was born in Manchester, England, on February 25, 1917. His mother and sister died in the influenza epidemic of 1918. Of Irish background, his mother had performed in the music halls of the period and was known as "the Beautiful Belle Burgess." His father performed as a silent-film pianist and when he remarried, played piano in a pub called "The Golden Eagle," owned by his new wife; Burgess himself began to compose music when he was fourteen. Burgess graduated from the Bishop Bilsborrow School and planned to study music at Manchester University. When he failed a required physics entrance exam there, he changed his focus to literature and graduated from Xaverian College in Manchester; in 1940, he wrote his senior honors thesis on Christopher Marlowe, while Nazi bombs fell overhead.

In October, 1940, Burgess joined the army and was placed in the Army Medical Corps. He was later shifted to the Army Educational Corps–a prophetic move, since he became a teacher for nearly twenty years afterwards. In 1942, Burgess married Llewela Isherwood Jones, a Welsh fellow student. He spent three years, from 1943 to 1946, with the British army on Gibraltar, during which time he wrote his first novel, *A Vision of Battlements* (which was not published until 1965).

Burgess left the army as a sergeant major and as a training college lecturer in speech and drama in 1946 to become a member of the Central Advisory Council for Adult Education in the armed forces. He lectured at Birmingham University until 1948, when he served as a lecturer in phonetics for the Ministry of Education in Preston, Lancashire. From 1950 until 1954, he taught English literature, phonetics, Spanish, and music at the Banbury grammar school in Oxfordshire.

Throughout these years, Burgess was painfully aware of his Irish heritage and Catholic religion. Though he had renounced Catholicism early, the Irish-Catholic stigma remained with him in rigorously Protestant England. His decision to apply for the job of education officer for the Colonial Service may have had something to do with his desire to leave England and his need to exile himself physically from a homeland that had already exiled him in spirit. From 1954 to 1957, he was the Senior Lecturer in English at the Malayan Teachers Training College in Kahta Baru, Malaya. There, he had more leisure time to write, and he published his first novel, *Time for a Tiger*, in 1956 under his middle names, Anthony Burgess. Members of the Colonial Service were not allowed to publish fiction under their own names.

Burgess continued working for the Colonial Service as an English-language specialist in Brunei, Borneo, from 1957 to 1959 and published two more novels, which, with his first, eventually constituted his Malayan trilogy, *The Long Day Wanes.* The clash between the manners and morals of East and West became the major focus of his early novels.

Apparent tragedy struck in 1959, when Burgess collapsed in his Borneo classroom. After excruciating medical tests, he was diagnosed with an inoperable brain tumor. He was given a year to live and was returned to England. Unable to teach, virtually penniless, Burgess set himself to writing as much as he could in order to provide for his wife. Not only had she already shown signs of the cirrhosis of the liver that was eventually to kill her, but also she had attempted suicide. In the next three years, Burgess wrote and published nine novels, including *A Clockwork Orange* and *Enderby.*

On the first day of spring, March 20, 1968, Llewela Burgess finally died. That October, Burgess married Liliana Macellari, a member of the linguistics department at Cambridge, intensifying the scandal that originally developed when their affair produced a son, Andreas, in 1964. The personal guilt involved with his first wife's death always haunted Burgess and provided one of the major underlying themes of his fiction. "Guilt's a good thing," Burgess once said, "because the morals are just ticking away very nicely." In fact, persistent guilt shadows all of his characters and consistently threatens to overwhelm them completely.

Burgess, Liliana, and Andrew left England in October, 1968; they moved to Malta, to Bracciano in Italy, and eventually settled in Monaco. Burgess's life changed dramatically in 1971, when director Stanley Kubrick filmed *A Clockwork Orange*, making Burgess a celebrity. Regardless of his continuous production of new works in several genres, Burgess lived in the shadow of his 1962 novel. In 1980, he published *Earthly Powers*, a long and ambitious novel on which he had been working for more than ten years. He continued to compose symphonies and write reviews and articles for major newspapers and periodicals. He also became a skilled dramatic writer, with credits that include a version of Edmond Rostand's *Cyrano de Bergerac* (1897), produced on Broadway in 1972, the screenplay for Franco Zeffirelli's 1977 extravaganza *Jesus of Nazareth*, and *A Clockwork Orange 2004*, produced at the Barbizon Theater, London, in 1990. Burgess's production never slackened. In the last decade of his life, he produced six more novels, his last, *A Dead Man in Deptford*, being published just before his death, due to cancer, in 1993.

Analysis · Anthony Burgess shares with many postmodernist writers an almost obsessive awareness of his great modernist predecessors—particularly James Joyce. The vision that Burgess inherited from modernism is informed by the anguish of a sensitive soul lost in a fragmented, shattered world. Each of Burgess's novels reveals one central character virtually "at sea" in a landscape of battered, broken figures and events. Burgess conveys this fragmented worldview by means of many of the literary devices of his modernist predecessors. Often he employs a stream-of-consciousness narration, in which his main characters tell their own stories; he also has used what T. S. Eliot, reviewing Joyce's *Ulysses* (1922), called the "mythic method," in which contemporary chaos is compared with and contrasted to heroic myths, legends, religious ceremonies, and rituals of the past. As Eliot remarked, the mythic method "is simply a way of controlling, of ordering, of giving a shape and significance to the intense panorama of futility and anarchy which is contemporary history."

Like many postmodernists, convinced that most literary forms are serious games devised to stave off approaching chaos and collapse, Burgess delights in the play of language for its own sake. Here again, Joyce is a prime source of inspiration: surprising images, poetic revelations, linguistic twists and turns, and strange evocative words nearly overwhelm the narrative shape of *Ulysses* and certainly overwhelm it in *Finnegans Wake* (1939). Burgess's best novels are those in which language for its own sake plays an important role, as in *Enderby*, *Nothing Like the Sun*, *A Clockwork Orange*, and *Napoleon Symphony*.

At the heart of his vision of the world lies Burgess's Manichean sensibility, his belief that there is "a duality that is fixed almost from the beginning of the world and the outcome is in doubt." God and the Devil reign over a supremely divided universe; they are equal in power, and they will battle to the end of the world. In the Manichean tradition—most notably, that of the Gnostics—Burgess sees the world as a materialistic trap, a prison of the spirit and a place devised by the Devil to incarcerate people until their death. Only art can break through the battlelines; only art can save him. The recasting of a religious commitment in aesthetic terms also belongs to the legacy of modernism. Burgess's Manichean vision produces such clashes of opposites as that between East and West, between the self and the state, and between a single character and an alien social environment. These recurring polarities structure Burgess's fiction.

The Right to an Answer · This principle of polarity or opposition is evident in the early novel *The Right to an Answer*, in which J. W. Denham, businessman and exile, returns to his father's house in the suburban British Midlands and finds a provincial, self-satisfied community engaged in wife-swapping, television-viewing, and pub-crawling. He remains a detached observer, longing for a kind of communion he cannot find, and in his telling his own tale, he reveals himself as friendless, disillusioned, and homeless.

The wife-swapping quartet at the Black Swan pub is disturbed by the entrance of Mr. Raj, a Ceylonese gentleman, interested in English sociology and in satisfying his lust for white women. He plays by no rules but his own and espouses a kind of deadly Eastern realism that threatens the suburban sport. Moving in with Denham's father, he unfortunately kills the old man by "currying" him to death with his hot dishes. The upshot of this clash of cultural and social values is that Raj kills Winterbottom, the most innocent member of the *ménage à quatre*, and then kills himself.

Throughout the novel, Burgess explores both Denham's point of view and Raj's within the seedy suburban landscape. Their viewpoints reflect the irreconcilable differences between East and West, between black and white, between sex and love, and between true religion and dead ritual. Denham's stream-of-consciousness narration eventually reveals his own spirit of exile, which he cannot overcome. He remains disconnected from both worlds, from England and the East, and epitomizes the state of lovelessness and isolation that has permeated modern culture. This early novel clearly explores Burgess's main themes and narrative forms.

Tremor of Intent · In the guise of a thriller à la James Bond, *Tremor of Intent* explores a world of "God" and "Not-God," a profoundly Manichaean universe. Soviet spies battle English spies, while the real villains of the novel, the "neutralists," play one camp off against the other purely for personal gain. Burgess derides the whole notion of the spy's realm, but he insists that taking sides is essential in such a world, whether ultimate good or evil is ever really confronted.

Denis Hillier, aging technician and spy, writes his confessional memoirs in the light of his possible redemption. His Catholic sense of original sin never falters for an instant, and he is constantly in need of some higher truth, some ultimate communion and revelation. In the course of the novel, he fights every Manichaean division, drinks "Old Mortality," sees himself as a "fallen Adam," and works his way toward some vision of hope. Finally, he abandons the spy game and becomes a priest, exiling himself to Ireland. From this new perspective, he believes that he can approach the real mysteries of good and evil, of free will and predestination, beyond the limiting and limited categories of the Cold War.

Hillier's opposite in the novel is Edwin Roper, a rationalist who has jettisoned religious belief and who hungers for an ultimately unified universe based on scientific truth and explanation. Such rationalism leads him to the Marxist logic of Soviet ideology, and he defects to the Russian side. Hillier has been sent to rescue him. One section of the novel consists of Roper's autobiographical explanation of his actions; its flat, logical prose reflects his methodical and disbelieving mind, in contrast to Hillier's more religious sensibility.

Within the complicated plot of the novel, self-serving scoundrels such as Mr.

Theodorescu and Richard Wriste set out to destroy both Hillier and Roper and gather information to sell to the highest bidder. They fail, owing largely to the actions of Alan and Clara Walters, two children on board the ship that is taking Hillier to meet Roper. The children become initiated into the world of double agents and sexual intrigue, and Theodorescu and Wriste are assassinated.

Burgess displays his love of language for its own sake in exotic descriptions of sex, food, and life aboard a cruise ship. Such language intensifies the Manichaean divisions in the book, the constant battle between the things of this world and the imagined horrors of the next. The very language that Hillier and Roper use to tell their own stories reveals their own distinctly different personalities and visions.

Tremor of Intent insists on the mystery of human will. To choose is to be human; that is good. Thus, to choose evil is both a good and a bad thing, a Manichaean complication that Burgess leaves with the reader. In allegorical terms the novel presents the problems of free will and its consequences, which underlie all of Burgess's fiction.

Nothing Like the Sun · *Nothing Like the Sun,* Burgess's fanciful novel based on the life of Shakespeare, showcases every facet of his vision and technique as a novelist. Shakespeare finds himself caught between his love for a golden man and a black woman. Sex feeds the fires of love and possession, and from these fires grows his art, the passion of language. From these fires also comes syphilis, the dread disease that eventually kills him, the source of the dark vision that surfaces in his apocalyptic tragedies. Shakespeare as a writer and Shakespeare as a man battle it out, and from that dualistic confrontation emerges the perilous equilibrium of his greatest plays.

In part, Burgess's fiction is based on the theories about Shakespeare's life which Stephen Dedalus expounds in *Ulysses.* Dedalus suggests that Shakespeare was cuckolded by his brother Richard, that Shakespeare's vision of a treacherous and tragic world was based on his own intimate experience. To this conjecture, Burgess adds the notion that the Dark Lady of the sonnets was a non-Caucasian and that Shakespeare himself was a victim of syphilis. All of these "myths" concerning Shakespeare serve Burgess's Manichaean vision: Sex and disease, art and personality are ultimately at war with one another and can only be resolved in the actual plays that Shakespeare wrote.

Nothing Like the Sun is written in an exuberant, bawdy, pseudo-Elizabethan style. It is clear that Burgess relished the creation of lists of epithets, curses, and prophecies, filled as they are with puns and his own outrageous coinings. Burgess audaciously attempts to mime the development of Shakespeare's art as he slowly awakens to the possibilities of poetry, trying different styles, moving from the sweet rhymes of "Venus and Adonis" to the "sharp knives and brutal hammers" of the later tragedies.

The book is constructed in the form of a lecture by Burgess himself to his Malayan students. He drinks as he talks and explains his paradoxical theories as he goes along. His passing out from too much drink at the novel's end parallels Shakespeare's death. He puns also with his real last name, Wilson, regarding himself as in fact "Will's son," a poet and author in his own right.

Enderby · *Enderby* is prototypic of Burgess's preoccupation with the duality of forces that influence life: the struggle between society's capacity to do good and the dilemma that human nature inevitably leads to evil. Originally conceived as a whole, *Enderby* was written as two independent novels, *Mr. Enderby* and *Enderby Outside,* for the pragmatic reason that Burgess wanted to tell at least half the tale before he died from his supposed brain tumor. One of Burgess's most popular characters, the flatulent poet F. X. Enderby, was spawned in a men's room when the author thought he saw a man feverishly writing poetry as he purged his bowels. *Enderby* is teeming with opposites, juxtaposing the sublime with the ridiculous. Enderby is catapulted into life-transforming situations as the outside world continually plays on and alters the poet's sensibilities. Burgess, the writer, examines his creation, a writer, whom he happens to admire in spite of his foibles.

Mr. Enderby and *Enderby Outside* depict the difference between transformations that originate within the individual and those that society imposes upon the individual. In the first novel, the very private poet is lured into marriage with Vesta Bainbridge, who leads him into a pop-art world that strips away his integrity and identity. Enderby achieves some success by prostituting his talent, but he is ultimately outraged when a rival poet gains fame and fortune by stealing his ideas, transforming them into a horror film. Enderby escapes from his wife and public life but is despondent and intellectually withered. He is taken to Wapenshaw, a psychologist, who "cures" him by destroying his poetic muse. Enderby is transmuted into Piggy Hogg, a bartender and useful citizen.

Enderby Outside is the mirror image of *Mr. Enderby*, transforming Hogg back into Enderby through a series of parallel experiences. Bainbridge has married a pop singer, Yod Crewsey, whose success is the result of poems stolen from Enderby. When the singer is shot, Enderby is accused of the murder and flees, confronting the chaos and confusion of the modern world and falling prey to another woman, the sensuous Miranda Boland. During sexual intercourse with Boland, inspiration finally strikes Enderby. In the end, he meets a sibylline girl, Muse, who leads him to his art. Enderby is as he began, alone and free, but a poet.

The Clockwork Testament and Enderby's Dark Lady · In *Enderby*, Burgess shows that the master must come to peace with both his body and society before he can indulge in the intellectual. Shortly after the film version of *A Clockwork Orange* was released, Enderby returned in *The Clockwork Testament: Or, Enderby's End*, which satirized the writer reduced to production assistant by the film industry. Enderby dies of a heart attack when he sees the violent, pornographic film made from his novel. Just as British detective novelist Arthur Conan Doyle was forced to return Sherlock Holmes to life, Burgess resurrects his antihero in *Enderby's Dark Lady*. Enderby travels to Indiana, where he writes the libretto for a ridiculous musical about Shakespeare. Burgess directs his satire at American culture, but his exploration of the poetic muse is sacrificed for the comic adventure.

Earthly Powers · *Earthly Powers*, Burgess's longest novel, features perhaps his most arresting first sentence: "It was the afternoon of my 81st birthday, and I was in bed with my catamite when Ali announced that the archbishop had come to see me." Thus begin the memoirs of Kenneth Toomey, cynical agnostic and homosexual writer, a character based loosely on Somerset Maugham.

Toomey's memoirs span the twentieth century—its literary intrigues, cultural fashions, and political horrors. Toomey is seduced on June 16, 1904, that Dublin day immortalized by Joyce in *Ulysses*, revels in the Paris of the 1920's, the Hollywood of the 1930's, and the stylish New York of the 1940's and 1950's; his old age is spent in exotic exile in Tangier and Malta in the 1970's. During his long life he writes plays and film scenarios, carries on with a host of male secretary-lovers, and experiences the traumas of Nazism and Communism. He abhors the state-controlled collective soul, which he sees as the ultimate product of the twentieth century.

Burgess's huge, sprawling novel displays a plot crowded with coincidence and bursting with stylistic parodies and re-creations. A priest on his way to becoming pope saves a dying child, only to see him grow up to be the leader of a fanatical religious cult akin to that of Jim Jones in Guyana. An American anthropologist and his wife are butchered during a Catholic mass in Africa: The natives there take the commands of the ceremony all too literally and swallow their visitors.

Toomey believes that evil lies firmly within all people and that his experiences of the twentieth century prove that the world is a murderous place. His Manichean opposite in faith is his brother-in-law, Carlo Campanati, the gambler-gourmet priest who becomes Pope Gregory XVII. Evil remains external to humanity, the pope maintains; humankind is essentially good. In Burgess's jaundiced view of things, such misconceived idealism produces only further evils. Any similarities between Gregory and John XXIII are strictly intentional.

The world of *Earthly Powers* is Toomey's world, a bright place with clipped, swift glimpses of fads and fashion. Librettos, snippets of plays, even a re-creation of the Garden of Eden story from a homosexual point of view appear in this modernist memoir. The style itself reflects Burgess's conception of the "brittle yet excruciatingly precise" manner of the homosexual.

Earthly Powers wobbles. More than six hundred pages of bright wit can cloy. Verbal surfaces congeal and trail off into trivial documentation. The pope's spiritual observations impede the novel's progress, encased as they are in lectures, sermons, and tracts. Indeed, Gregory is as thin a character as Toomey is an interesting one.

The book proves that Toomey is right: Things are rotten. No amount of linguistic fun, modernist maneuverings, or Manichaean machinations can change the fact that this is the worst of all possible worlds. Chunks of smart conversation cannot hide that fact; they become stupefying and evasive in the end. The nature of free will, however, and its legacy of unquestionable evil in the twentieth century pervade Burgess's fat book and linger to undermine any "safe" position the reader may hope to find.

A Clockwork Orange · Burgess's Manichaean nightmare in *A Clockwork Orange* occupies the center of his most accomplished book. The language of *nadsat* in its harsh, Russian-accented diction, the ongoing battle between the State and Alex the *droog*, the vision of an urban landscape wracked with violence and decay, the mysterious interpenetration of Beethoven and lust, and the unresolved issues of good and evil reflect and parallel one another so completely that the novel emerges as Burgess's masterpiece.

The issue raised is an increasingly timely one: Can the state program the individual to be good? Can it eradicate the individual's right to freedom of choice, especially if in choosing, he or she chooses to commit violent and evil acts? Burgess replies in the negative. No matter how awful Alex's actions become, he should be allowed to choose them.

Since the novel is written from Alex's point of view, the reader sympathizes with him, despite his acts of rape and mayhem. Alex loves Beethoven; he "shines artistic"; he is brighter than his ghoulish friends; he is rejected by his parents. He is in all ways superior to the foul futuristic landscape that surrounds him. When the state brain-washes him, the reader experiences his pain in a personal, forthright manner. The violence in the rest of the book falls upon outsiders and remains distanced by the very language Alex uses to describe his actions.

Burgess's slang creates a strange and distant world. The reader approaches the novel as an outsider to that world and must try diligently to decode it to understand it. Never has Burgess used language so effectively to create the very atmosphere of his fiction. The Russian-influenced slang of the novel is a tour de force of the highest order and yet functions perfectly as a reflection of Alex's state of mind and of the society of which he is a rebellious member.

The world of *A Clockwork Orange* recognizes only power and political force. All talk of free will dissolves before such a harrowing place of behaviorist psychologists and social controllers. Individual freedom in such a world remains a myth, not a reality, a matter of faith, not an ultimate truth. Everyone is in some sense a clockwork orange, a victim of his or her society, compelled to act in a social order that celebrates only power, manipulation, and control.

Even the cyclical form of *A Clockwork Orange* reveals a world trapped within its own inevitable patterns. At first, Alex victimizes those around him. He in turn is victimized by the state. In the third and final part of the novel, he returns to victimize other people once again: "I was cured all right." Victimization remains the only reality here. There are no loopholes, no escape hatches from the vicious pattern. The frightening cityscape at night, the harsh language, the paradoxical personality of Alex, the collaborationist or revolutionary tactics of Alex's "friends," and the very shape of the novel reinforce this recognition of utter entrapment and human decay. "Oh, my brothers," Alex addresses his readers, as Eliot in *The Waste Land* (1922) quoted Charles Baudelaire: *"Hypocrite lecteur, mon semblable, mon frère."*

Despite Burgess's pessimistic vision of contemporary life and the creative soul's place in it, the best of his novels still reveal a commitment to literature as a serious ceremony, as a game which the reader and the writer must continue to play, if only to transcend momentarily the horrors of Western civilization in the twentieth century.

Samuel Coale, updated by Gerald S. Argetsinger

Other major works
SHORT FICTION: *The Devil's Mode*, 1989.
SCREENPLAY: *Jesus of Nazareth*, 1977.
TELEPLAY: *Moses the Lawgiver*, 1976.
NONFICTION: *English Literature: A Survey for Students*, 1958 (as John Burgess Wilson); *The Novel Today*, 1963; *Language Made Plain*, 1964; *Here Comes Everybody: An Introduction to James Joyce for the Ordinary Reader*, 1965 (pb. in U.S. as *Re Joyce*, 1965); *The Novel Now*, 1967, rev. ed. 1971; *Urgent Copy: Literary Studies*, 1968; *Shakespeare*, 1970; *Joysprick: An Introduction to the Language of James Joyce*, 1972; *Ernest Hemingway and His World*, 1978; *On Going to Bed*, 1982; *This Man and Music*, 1983; *Flame into Being: The Life and Work of D. H. Lawrence*, 1985; *But Do Blondes Prefer Gentlemen? Homage to Qwert Yuiop and Other Writings*, 1986 (also known as *Homage to Qwert Yuiop*, 1985); *Little Wilson and Big God*, 1987 (partly reprinted as *Childhood*, 1996); *You've Had Your Time*, 1990; *A Mouthful of Air: Languages, Languages, Especially English*, 1992; *One Man's Chorus: The Uncollected Writings*, 1998.
CHILDREN'S LITERATURE: *A Long Trip to Teatime*, 1976.
TRANSLATIONS: *The Man Who Robbed Poor-Boxes*, 1965 (of Michel Servin's play); *Cyrano de Bergerac*, 1971 (of Edmond Rostand's play); *Oedipus the King*, 1972 (of Sophocles' play).
MISCELLANEOUS: *On Mozart: A Paean for Wolfgang*, 1991.

Bibliography
Aggeler, Geoffrey, ed. *Critical Essays on Anthony Burgess.* Boston: G. K. Hall, 1986. A collection of well-regarded criticism on Burgess, with particular attention given to his "linguistic pyrotechnics." Aggeler's introduction presents an overview of Burgess's work and discussion of his novels, followed by a *Paris Review* interview with Burgess.

Bloom, Harold, ed. *Modern Critical Views: Anthony Burgess.* New York: Chelsea House, 1987. A compilation of fine critical essays, including an essay by the eminent critic of James Joyce, Robert Martin Adams, who considers Joyce's influence on Burgess. In the introduction, Bloom presents his views on Burgess's writing, citing *Inside Mr. Enderby* as one of the most underrated English novels of this era.

Boytinck, Paul W. *Anthony Burgess: An Annotated Bibliography and Reference Guide.* New York: Garland, 1985. A checklist of Burgess's works up to 1984, including bibliographical background on Burgess and extracts from reviews, essays, and articles on his work. An excellent and informative resource for both the beginning reader and scholar of Burgess.

Critique: Studies in Modern Fiction 27 (Fall, 1981). This special issue gathers together seven critical essays on Burgess, some of which are appreciative, "Burgess is clearly in command of his material," in reference to *Earthly Powers,* and others which are less favorable–"Burgess' plots have a tendency to twitch and gyrate."

Keen, Suzanne. "Ironies and Inversions: The Art of Anthony Burgess." *Commonweal* 121 (February 11, 1994). This is an examination of the "Catholic quality" in Burgess's fiction and nonfiction. Focuses primarily upon the autobiographies, the literary criticism of Joyce's works, and Burgess's final novel, *A Dead Man in Deptford.*

Mathews, Richard. *The Clockwork Orange Universe of Anthony Burgess.* San Bernardino, Calif.: Borgo Press, 1978. This admiring monograph traces the thematic and temporal concerns that led Burgess to write his futuristic novels, including *A Clockwork Orange.* Mathews discusses ten novels that fit the metaphor of "clockwork universe."

Stinson, John J. *Anthony Burgess Revisited.* Boston: Twayne, 1991. This is particularly valuable for biographical information and critical analysis of the later works. Particular attention is given Burgess's increasing reputation as a public intellectual and the use of language, the importance of moral choice, and the conflict between the Pelagian and Augustinian philosophies in his works.

Fanny Burney

Born: King's Lynn, England; June 13, 1752
Died: London, England; January 6, 1840

Principal long fiction · *Evelina: Or, The History of a Young Lady's Entrance into the World,* 1778; *Cecilia: Or, Memoirs of an Heiress,* 1782; *Camilla: Or, A Picture of Youth,* 1796; *The Wanderer: Or, Female Difficulties,* 1814.

Other literary forms · In addition to editing the memoirs of her father, the noted organist, composer, and music historian Dr. Charles Burney (1726-1814), Fanny Burney wrote an *Early Diary, 1768-1778* (1889) and then a later *Diary and Letters, 1778-1840* (1842-1846). The first work, not published until 1889, contains pleasant sketches of Samuel Johnson, James Boswell, David Garrick, and Richard Brinsley Sheridan. Notable figures from government and the arts march across the pages of the early diary, which scholars have claimed surpasses her fiction in literary quality. The latter diary and correspondence appeared between 1842 and 1846; the seven volumes are notable for the record of the writer's meeting in her garden with the insane George III of England, the account of her glimpse of Napoleon I, and the recollections of her chat with the weary Louis XVIII of France.

Of her eight dramatic productions, three are worthy of mention: *The Witlings* (never published); *Edwy and Elgiva,* written in 1790, performed at Drury Lane on March 21, 1795, and withdrawn after the first night; and *Love and Fashion,* written in 1800, accepted by the manager at Covent Garden, but never performed. Finally, Burney published, in 1793, a political essay entitled *Brief Reflections Relative to the French Emigrant Clergy,* an address to the women of Great Britain in behalf of the French emigrant priests.

Achievements · Most critics tend to place the reputation of Burney within the shadow of her most immediate successor, Jane Austen. Reasons for this assessment are not immediately clear, especially in the light of responses to the novels from contemporary readers. Burney's problem during the past two centuries, however, has not concerned popularity, subject matter, or even literary style; rather, certain personal circumstances under which she wrote seriously reduced her artistic effectiveness and considerably dulled her reputation. Essentially, Burney produced fiction at a time in history when a lady of means and social standing could not easily write fiction and still be considered a lady. Adding to that inhibition was the aura of her noted and influential father and his circle of even more influential friends: Samuel Johnson, Mrs. Hester Lynch Thrale Piozzi, Oliver Goldsmith, and Sir Joshua Reynolds. Both her father and his friends held literary standards not always easy for a self-educated young woman to attain. She burned her early manuscript efforts, wrote secretly at night, and published anonymously; she labored under the artistic domination of her father and the advice of his friends; she remained cautious, intimidated by and dependent on elderly people who served as guardians of her intellect.

Nevertheless, Burney succeeded as a novelist and achieved significance as a contributor to the history and development of the English novel. She brought to that

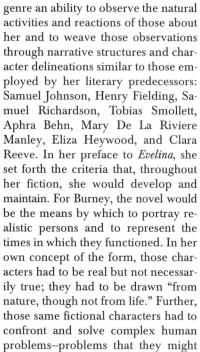

Library of Congress

genre an ability to observe the natural activities and reactions of those about her and to weave those observations through narrative structures and character delineations similar to those employed by her literary predecessors: Samuel Johnson, Henry Fielding, Samuel Richardson, Tobias Smollett, Aphra Behn, Mary De La Riviere Manley, Eliza Heywood, and Clara Reeve. In her preface to *Evelina*, she set forth the criteria that, throughout her fiction, she would develop and maintain. For Burney, the novel would be the means by which to portray realistic persons and to represent the times in which they functioned. In her own concept of the form, those characters had to be real but not necessarily true; they had to be drawn "from nature, though not from life." Further, those same fictional characters had to confront and solve complex human problems—problems that they might avoid for a time but eventually would be forced to encounter.

Although Burney's four novels were published anonymously, the sophisticated readers of the day recognized the woman's point of view and immediately set the works apart from those of their contemporaries. The female readership, especially, both appreciated and praised the woman's view of the contemporary world; on the other hand, the young dandies of the late eighteenth century and the pre-Victorian age scoffed at the novels' heroines as comic sentimentalists, products of blatant amateurism, and characteristic examples of a sex that would continue to be dominated by men.

The real basis on which to place Burney's popularity, however, rests with the ability of the novelist to develop fully the effects of female intelligence upon and within a society dominated by men and to convince her audience that coexistence between the sexes was far more beneficial than the dominance of one over the other. The essential difference between Fanny Burney and her female predecessors (Aphra Behn is the most obvious example) is the extent to which the issue of feminism was developed and then thrust forward as a major consideration.

As a woman writing about women, Burney could not cling too long to the models that the past century had provided for her. Despite the mild increase in the numbers of female novelists during the last quarter of the eighteenth century, Burney had little guidance in developing the woman's point of view. She had, essentially, to find her own way within the confines of a limited world and even more limited experience. Thus, she determined early to purge her fictional environment of masculine influence. In its place, she would establish the importance of her titled characters as working parts in the machinery of eighteenth century British society. Burney's heroines do not convey appearances of being rebels, radicals, or social freaks; rather, their creator has drawn each one of them with a fine and firm hand. As a group, they are indeed meant to be carbon copies of one another; individually, each portrays a young lady in pursuit of traditional goals: marriage, money, and the discovery of the self.

Biography · Fanny (Frances) Burney, later Madame D'Arblay, the third of six children of Charles Burney and Esther Sleepe Burney, was born on June 13, 1752, at King's Lynn, Norfolk, where her father served as church organist while recuperating from consumption. In 1760, his health completely restored, Burney moved his family to London, where he resumed his professional involvements in teaching, composition, and music history. Upon the death of Esther Burney on September 28, 1761, two of the children (Esther and Susannah) went to school in Paris, while Frances remained at home. Apparently, Dr. Burney feared that his middle daughter's devotion to her grandmother (then living in France) would bring about the child's conversion to Catholicism. He seemed prepared to change that point of view and send Frances to join her sisters, when, in 1766, he married Mrs. Stephen Allen. Thus, the fourteen-year-old girl remained at home in London, left to her own educational aims and directions, since her father had no time to supervise her learning. She had, at about age ten, begun to write drama, poetry, and fiction; on her fifteenth birthday, she supposedly burned her manuscripts because she felt guilty about wasting her time with such trifles.

Still, she could not purge her imagination, and the story of Evelina and her adventures did not die in the flames of her fireplace. Her brother, Charles, offered the first two volumes of *Evelina* to James Dodsley, who declined to consider an anonymous work for publication; Thomas Lowndes, however, asked to see the completed manuscript. After finishing *Evelina* and then securing her father's permission, Burney gave the work to the London publisher, who issued it in January, 1778, and paid the writer thirty pounds and ten bound copies. Its success and popularity owed some debt to Dr. Burney, who passed the novel on to Mrs. Thrale, a prominent figure in London's literary society. From there, it made its way to the select seat of London's intellectual empire, presided over by Dr. Johnson, Joshua Reynolds, and Edmund Burke. Shortly afterward, Fanny Burney met Mrs. Thrale, who took the new novelist into her home at Streatham (south of London) and introduced her to Johnson, Reynolds, Sheridan, and Arthur Murphy—all of whom pressed her to write drama. The result took the form of *The Whitlings*, a dramatic piece that, principally because of her father's displeasure over the quality of the work, she never published.

Returning to the form that produced her initial success, Burney published *Cecilia* in the summer of 1782, further advancing her literary reputation and social standing. She met Mary Delany, an intimate of the royal family, who helped secure for her an appointment in July, 1786, as second keeper of the Queen's robes, a position worth two hundred pounds per year. Her tenure at court proved to be more of a confinement than a social or political advantage because of the menial tasks, the rigid schedule, and the stiffness of the Queen and her attendants.

The activities and events at court, however, did contribute to the value of Burney's diaries, though her health suffered from the extreme physical demands of her labors. She continued in service until July, 1791, at which time she sought and gained permission to retire on a pension of one hundred pounds per annum. Then followed a period of domestic travel aimed at improving her health, followed by her marriage, on July 31, 1793, to General Alexandre D'Arblay, a comrade of the Marquis de Lafayette and a member of the small French community living at Juniper Hall, near

Mickleham (north of Dorking, in Surrey). The couple's entire income rested with Madame D'Arblay's pension, and thus she sought to increase the family's fortunes through her writing. A tragedy, *Edwy and Elgiva*, lasted but a single night at Drury Lane, but a third novel, *Camilla*, generated more than three thousand pounds from subscriptions and additional sales, although the piece failed to achieve the literary merit of *Evelina* or *Cecilia*.

In 1801, General D'Arblay returned to France to seek employment but managed only a pension of fifteen hundred francs. His wife and son, Alexander, joined him the next year, and the family spent the succeeding ten years at Passy, in a state of quasi exile that lasted throughout the Napoleonic Wars. Madame D'Arblay and her son returned to England in 1812, and there, the novelist attended her aged father until his death in April, 1814. Her last novel, begun in France in 1802 and entitled *The Wanderer*, appeared early in 1814. Again, the financial returns far exceeded the literary quality of the piece; there were considerable buyers and subscribers but extremely few readers. After Napoleon's exile, the novelist returned to her husband in Paris; she then went to Brussels after the emperor's return from Elba. General D'Arblay, meanwhile, had been seriously injured by the kick of a horse, which brought about an immediate end to his military career. The family returned to England to spend the remainder of their years: General D'Arblay died on May 3, 1818, and Alexander died on January 19, 1837–less than a year after having been nominated minister of Ely chapel. In November, 1839, Madame D'Arblay suffered a severe illness and died on January 6, 1840, in her eighty-seventh year.

Analysis · Despite the relative brevity of her canon, Fanny Burney's fiction cannot be dismissed with the usual generalizations from literary history: specifically that the author shared the interests of her youthful heroines in good manners. She possessed a quick sense for the comic in character and situation, and those talents distinctly advanced the art of the English novel in the direction of Jane Austen. From one viewpoint, she indeed exists as an important transitional figure between the satiric allegories of the earlier eighteenth century and the instruments that portrayed middle-class manners in full flourish during the first quarter of the nineteenth century.

Burney's contemporaries understood both her method and her purpose. Samuel Johnson thought her a "real wonder," one worth being singled out for her honest sense of modesty and her ability to apply it to fiction, while Edmund Burke seemed amazed by her knowledge of human nature. Three years after her death, Thomas Babington Macaulay proclaimed that the author of *Evelina* and *Cecilia* had done for the English novel what Jeremy Collier, at the end of the seventeenth century, did for the drama: maintain rigid morality and virgin delicacy. Macaulay proclaimed that Fanny Burney had indeed vindicated the right of woman "to an equal share in a fair and noble promise of letters" and had accomplished her task in clear, natural, and lively "woman's English."

Nevertheless, Fanny Burney contributed more to the English novel than simply the advancement of her sex's cause. Her heroines are mentally tormented and yet emerge as wiser and stronger human beings. The fictional contexts into which she placed her principal characters are those that readers of every time and place could recognize: situations in which the proponents of negative values seem to prosper and the defenders of virtue cling tenaciously to their ground. Burney's women must learn the ways of a difficult world, a society composed of countless snares and endless rules; they must quickly don the accoutrements for survival: modesty, reserve, submission, and (above all else) manners. What makes Burney's depiction of women in society particularly poignant is the knowledge that the author herself had to endure trials of survival. An awareness of the author's accounts of actual struggles for social survival, then, becomes a necessity for understanding and appreciating the problems confronted by her fictional characters.

Evelina · In Burney's first novel, *Evelina*, the title character brings with her to London and Bristol two qualities most difficult for a young provincial girl to defend: her sense of propriety and her pure innocence—the latter quality not to be confused with ignorance. In London, Evelina stumbles into false, insecure situations because she does not comprehend the rules of the social game. During the course of eighty-five epistles, however, she learns. The learning process is of utmost importance to Burney, for it serves as both plot for her fiction and instruction for her largely female readership. Once in London, life unfolds new meanings for Evelina Anville, as she samples the wares of urbanity: assemblies, amusements, parks and gardens, drawing rooms, operas, and theaters. Accompanying the activities is a corps of sophisticates by whose rules Evelina must play: Lord Orville, the well-bred young man and the jealous lover; Sir Clement Willoughby, the obnoxious admirer of Evelina who tries (through forged letters) to breach the relationship between Orville and Evelina; Macartney, the young poet whom Evelina saves from suicide and against whom Orville exercises his jealous streak; Captain Mirvan, the practical joker who smiles only at the expense of others; Mrs. Beaumont, who would have the heroine believe that good qualities originate from pride rather than from principles; Lady Louisa Larpent, the sullen and distraught (but always arrogant) sister of Lord Orville who tries to separate her brother from Evelina; Mr. Lovel, a demeaning fop who constantly refers to Evelina's simple background; the Watkins sisters, who chide Evelina because they envy her attractiveness to young men.

Despite these obstacles of situation and character, however, Evelina does not lack some protection. The Reverend Arthur Villars, her devoted guardian since the death of her mother, guides and counsels the seventeen-year-old girl from his home in Dorsetshire. Villars receives the major portion of Evelina's letters; in fact, he initally advises her to be wary of Lord Orville but then relents when he learns of his ward's extreme happiness. Since Evelina cannot count on immediate assistance from Villars, she does rely on several people in London. Mrs. Mirvan, the amiable and well-bred wife of the captain, introduces Evelina to a variety of social affairs, while their daughter, Maria, becomes the heroine's only real confidante, sharing mutual happiness and disappointment. Finally, there is the Reverend Villars's neighbor, Mrs. Selwyn, who accompanies Evelina on a visit to Bristol Hot Wells. Unfortunately, the one person closest to Evelina during her London tenure, her maternal grandmother, Madame Duval, proves of little use and even less assistance. A blunt, indelicate, and severe woman, she is bothered by her granddaughter's display of independence and vows that the young lady will not share in her inheritance.

Villars emerges as the supporting character with the most depth, principally because he is ever present in the letters. From the novel's beginning, the heroine reaches out to him for guidance and support, scarcely prepared "to form a wish that has not [his] sanction." The local clergyman, Villars serves as parent for a motherless and socially fatherless young lady who, for the first time, is about to see something of the world. Thus, Villars's caution and anxiety appear natural, for he knows the bitter effects of socially unequal marriages, as in the cases of Evelina's own parents and grandparents. He naturally mistrusts Lord Orville and fears the weakness of the young girl's imagination. Everyone knows that as long as Evelina remains obedient to Villars's will, no union between her and Orville can occur. Once the girl's father, Sir John Belmont, repents for his many years of unkindness to his daughter and then bequeaths her thirty thousand pounds, however, the guardian cleric no longer remains the dominant influence. Lord Orville proceeds to put his own moral house in order and supplants his rivals; the reserve felt by Evelina because of the Reverend Villars's fears and anxieties gradually disintegrates, and the romance proceeds towards its inevitable conclusion.

The process may be inevitable, but it is sufficiently hampered by a series of struggles and conflicts, as is typical of the late eighteenth century novel of manners. Both her grandmother and Mrs. Mirvan provide Evelina with fairly easy access to fashionable society, but the socialites in that society involve the girl in a number of uncomfortable and burdensome situations. For example, Biddy and Polly Branghton and Madam Duval use Evelina's name in requesting the use of Lord Orville's coach. Evelina realizes the impropriety of the request and knows that Orville's benevolence would never permit him to refuse it. Furthermore, Tom Branghton, an admirer of Evelina, solicits business from Orville also by relying on Evelina's name; he does so after damaging the borrowed vehicle. Evelina's innocence forces her to bear the responsibility for her relatives' actions and schemes, although she opposes all that they attempt. Fortunately, the fierce determination with which she advances her innocence and honesty enables her to endure such problems until rescued, in this case, by Lord Orville and Mrs. Selwyn. Vulgarity (Madam Duval), ill breeding (the Branghtons), and impertinence (Sir Clement Willoughby) eventually fall before the steadfastness and the force of Evelina's emerging wisdom and strength. Burney here demonstrates the specific means by which an eighteenth century woman could surmount the perplexities of that era.

Cecilia · If Evelina Anville must defend her innocence and honesty against the social vultures of London and Bristol, Cecilia Beverley, the heroine of *Cecilia*, carries the added burden of retaining a fortune left to her by an eccentric uncle. She must withstand assaults upon her coffers from a variety of attackers. One of her guardians, Mr. Harrel, draws heavily upon Cecilia's funds to repay the moneylenders who underwrite his fashionable existence. At the other extreme, Mr. Briggs, the third legally appointed guardian, manages Cecilia's money during her minority. Although wealthy in his own right, Briggs evidences obvious eccentricity and uncouthness; he is a miser who wants the heroine to live with him to conserve money. In the middle stands another guardian, Compton Delvile, who has priorities other than money; however, he can hardly be recommended as an asset to the development of his ward. Simply, Delvile cares only to preserve the family name, and beneath his pride lie hard layers of meanness. Against such onslaughts upon her morality and her fortune Cecilia must rebel; she is both angry and bewildered at what Burney terms as "acts so detrimental to her own interest."

Unlike Evelina, who has many opportunities to address and receive concerns from a surrogate parent, Cecilia has few people and even less guidance upon which to rely. *Cecilia* revealed to the world not only a trio of impotent guardians but also a number of irritating male characters who devote considerable time to tormenting her. Obviously bent upon revealing the grotesqueness and instability of London life, Burney created a variety of grotesque and unstable supporting players: Harrel, Dr. Lyster,

Mrs. Wyers, and Mrs. Hill are some examples. Clearly, Burney's characters in *Cecilia* were total strangers to the mainstream of the late eighteenth century fictional world, even though they truly belonged to reality. While at times creating humorous scenes and incidents, these ugly characters nevertheless produced a disturbing effect upon the novelist's reading audience. Unfortunately, from a social or historical perspective, that audience was not yet ready for significant action to effect social change, which meant that much of the novel's force was lost amid the apathy of its audience.

Camilla · The publication of *Camilla*, eighteen years after *Evelina* and fourteen following *Cecilia*, marked the reappearance of a young lady entering society and enduring shameful experiences. Like her immediate predecessor, Cecilia Beverley, Camilla Tyrold has money problems, only hers involve involuntary indebtedness. Also like *Cecilia*, the novel contains several grotesque minor characters, whose manners and actions play psychological havoc with Camilla's attempts to overcome her distress. Particularly vulgar are Mr. Dubster and the mercenary Mrs. Mittin, aided by the overscholarly Dr. Orkborne and the foppish Sir Sedley Clarendel. A major problem, however, is that these characters are pulled from the earlier novels. On the surface, *Camilla* gives evidence that Burney has matured as a writer and as a commentator on the affairs of women, but that maturity did not broaden her literary experience. If anything, there are signs of regression, for Camilla definitely lacks Evelina's common sense and her instinct toward feminine resourcefulness.

Camilla further suffers from its length; Burney barely holds the plot together through countless episodes, intrigues, misunderstandings, all in front of a backdrop of drollery and absurdity. Stripped of its comic elements, the novel is no more than an overstrained romance. Burney's motive, however, was to draw the exact conditions that brought about Camilla's collection of debts and thus contributed to her highly anxious state of mind. Burney rises to her usual level of excellence in detailing the plight of a woman distracted and deprived by misfortune not of her own doing. For late eighteenth century women, especially, such misfortune carried with it an underlying sense of shame. Thus, Burney gave to English prose fiction a sense of psychological depth not always apparent in the works of her female counterparts or in those fictional efforts written by men but concerned with women.

The Wanderer · Burney's last novel, *The Wanderer*, appeared in 1814 and became lost in the new sensibility of Jane Austen and Maria Edgeworth. The work, however, reveals Burney's determination that the nineteenth century should not forget its women. Her heroine—known variously as L. S. (or Ellis), Incognita, Miss Ellis, and Juliet—determines that the cause of her suffering points directly to the fact that she was born a woman, which automatically places her on the lowest rung of the social order. The woman's lot contains little beyond the usual taboos, disqualifications, discomforts, and inconveniences; the novelist, through the various predicaments of Juliet Granville, rarely allows her readers to forget the degree to which her heroine must suffer because of society's insensitivity and stupidity. *The Wanderer*, like Burney's previous novels, has a number of supporting characters; some of these, while they do not always understand Juliet's plight, at least try to help her through her difficulties. Others, such as Mrs. Ireton and Miss Arbe, represent the tyranny, frivolity, and insensitivity of the times and thus merely compound Juliet's problems.

The strength of *The Wanderer*, however, lies in its thematic relationship to the three earlier novels. Although Burney tends to repeat herself, particularly through her minor characters–and again the plot hardly deserves the length of the narrative–her ability to depict the misgivings of those who are driven by external circumstances to earn a livelihood through unaccustomed means is powerful. In coming to grips with an obvious and serious problem of her time, she demonstrated how her major fictional characters and she herself, as a character from the real world, could indeed rely successfully upon the resources endowed upon all individuals, female as well as male. If nothing else, the novelist showed her society and the generations that followed not only how well women could function in the real world but also how much they could contribute and take advantage of opportunities offered them. In a sense, Burney's compositions belong to social history as much as to literature, and they serve as some of the earliest examples of a struggle that has yet to be won.

Samuel J. Rogal

Other major works
    PLAYS: *Edwy and Elgiva: A Tragedy*, pr. 1795; *Love and Fashion*, pr. 1800; *The Complete Plays of Frances Burney*, pb. 1995 (2 volumes).
    NONFICTION: *Brief Reflections Relative to the French Emigrant Clergy*, 1793; *Diary and Letters, 1778-1840*, 1842-1846 (7 volumes; Charlotte Frances Barrett, editor); *The Early Diary of Frances Burney, 1768-1778*, 1889 (Anne Raine Ellis, editor).
    EDITED TEXT: *Memoirs of Dr. Charles Burney*, 1832.

Bibliography
Bloom, Harold, ed. *Fanny Burney's "Evelina": Modern Critical Interpretations*. New York: Chelsea House, 1988. This group of essays, written between 1967 and 1988, focuses on Burney's first novel. Included are essays by Ronald Paulson, Susan Staves, Patricia Meyer Spacks, Judith Lowder Newton, Mary Poovey, Jennifer A. Wagner, and Julia L. Epstein. Bloom's introduction disparages the feminist tendency of recent Burney criticism, even though this volume includes primarily feminist approaches to Burney's work. This collection of focused essays provides an illuminating look at current critical opinion of *Evelina*.
Epstein, Julia L. *The Iron Pen: Frances Burney and the Politics of Women's Writing*. Madison: University of Wisconsin Press, 1989. Takes a feminist approach, focusing primarily on the violence, hostility, and danger in Burney's work. Finds these parts of her novels to be generally controlled, but occasionally bursting forth into rage. This study meshes moments of physical and emotional danger and pain from Burney's life with similar images in her novels. Epstein's interest lies in Burney's construction of a self-image that plays down danger and violence but that she is frequently unable to control. The bibliography and index are excellent and quite helpful.
Simons, Judy. *Fanny Burney*. Totowa, N.J.: Barnes & Noble Books, 1987. Contains a condensed look at Burney's life. The introductory biographical essay places Burney in a tradition of other women writers, such as Elizabeth Inchbald, Mary Wollstonecraft Godwin, and Eliza Haywood, and discusses these women's views on their roles in society. Includes a chapter on the heroines of Burney's novels; a chapter on each of her four best-known works, *Evelina, Cecilia, Camilla*, and *The Wanderer*; and one on her journals and plays. The bibliography is short but helpful, especially since it includes a section on works about women's history in the eighteenth century.

Straub, Kristina. *Divided Fictions: Fanny Burney and Feminine Strategy*. Lexington: University Press of Kentucky, 1987. Examines the "ambiguous social definition of the woman novelist at mid-century," specifically as it related to Burney. A feminist approach grounded in eighteenth century cultural history. Devotes three chapters to *Evelina*, one to *Cecilia*, and one to both *Camilla* and *The Wanderer*. Straub's introductory chapter, "Critical Methods and Historic Contexts," is excellent and useful, as well as the chapter "The Receptive Reader and Other Necessary Fictions," which makes intriguing points about Burney's reaction to the publicity of being a novelist and part of the literary circles of her day.

Zonitch, Barbara. *Familiar Violence: Gender and Social Upheaval in the Novels of Frances Burney*. Newark: University of Delaware Press, 1997. Chapters on *Evelina*, *Cecilia*, *Camilla*, and *The Wanderer*. See especially Zonitch's introduction, "Social Transformations: The Crisis of the Aristocracy and the Status of Women." Includes detailed notes and excellent bibliography.

Samuel Butler

Born: Langar Rectory, England; December 4, 1835
Died: London, England; June 18, 1902

Principal long fiction · *Erewhon*, 1872; *The Fair Haven*, 1873; *Erewhon Revisited*, 1901; *The Way of All Flesh*, 1903.

Other literary forms · The Shrewsbury editions of Samuel Butler's works, published between 1923 and 1926, reveal the breadth of his interests. Butler's fiction was perhaps less important to him than his work in other fields, notably his theorizing on religion and evolution. He was also an art critic (*Ex Voto*, 1888; *Alps and Sanctuaries of Piedmont and the Ticino*, 1881); a literary critic (*The Authoress of the "Odyssey,"* 1897; *Shakespeare's Sonnets Reconsidered*, 1899); the biographer of his famous grandfather, Dr. Samuel Butler; a letter-writer; and a poet. An age which produces "specialists" may find Butler to be a talented dabbler or dilettante, but his unifying philosophy gives a center to all his work.

Achievements · Butler was a figure of controversy during his lifetime, and perhaps his greatest achievement resides in his ability to challenge: He contended with Charles Darwin and Darwinism; he took on the established scholars of William Shakespeare, classical literature, and art; and he was part of the nineteenth century revolt against traditional religion. He approached all of these areas in such a way that his opponents could not ignore him; whether he was right or wrong, any subject benefited by his treatment, which opened it up to new and candid thought.

Of his four works which may be labeled as fiction, by far the greatest is *The Way of All Flesh*. Virginia Woolf, in *Contemporary Writers* (1965), described this novel as a seed from which many others developed—a biological image which would have pleased Butler. In earlier novels, indifferent or cruel families had been portrayed as agents of the hero's youthful unhappiness—witness Charles Dickens's *David Copperfield* (1849-1850)—but only in *The Way of All Flesh* did the oppressiveness and cruelty of family life become a theme in itself, worthy of generation-by-generation treatment.

Biography · Samuel Butler was born in 1835, the son of a clergyman who wished him to go into the Church. After a successful career at Cambridge University, Butler prepared for a career in the Church but found himself unable to face the prospect of that life. Letters between Butler and his father show the young man to be considering a half-dozen plans at once: art, the army, cotton-growing, and bookselling among them. Finally, father and son agreed that the young man should emigrate to New Zealand and try his fortune there, with Butler's father providing capital. Both father and son hoped that the experience would "settle" Butler and build his character.

Butler arrived in New Zealand in January of 1860, remaining there for four years. It was a useful time: He made money, which freed him of his family, at least financially, and he saw an unusual country which gave him a subject and setting for his later writings. New Zealand, however, was too rough a land to be his permanent home. His "hut" there was an island of comfort and civilization, where Butler devoted himself to music and study. His optimistic letters home became the basis of *A First Year in Canterbury Settlement* (1863), a book assembled and published by Butler's father.

Returning to England in 1864, Butler settled at Clifford's Inn in London, which would be his home for the rest of his life. He began to study art; his paintings had some success. He wished to do something greater, however—something which would express his developing ideas. Out of this desire grew *Erewhon*, a satire which was published anonymously in 1872 at the author's own expense. By that time, Butler was already at work on *The Fair Haven*. This book may or may not be considered fiction; it is a dispute over the validity of Christianity, but the dispute is conducted in a fictional frame.

The following year, 1873, was an important one for Butler. *The Fair Haven* was published, his mother died, he made a risky financial investment, and he began *The Way of All Flesh*. All of these events shaped his later years. *The Fair Haven*, following on the heels of *Erewhon*, marked him as a belligerent enemy of traditional religion. His mother's death caused him some grief, but it spurred him to begin *The Way of All Flesh*, the work for which he is most remembered. That work was slowed, though, by financial troubles. Butler invested his New Zealand fortune in a Canadian venture which soon failed. He salvaged less than a quarter of his investment and had to seek help from his father. Not until 1886, when his father died, was Butler wholly free of financial pressures.

The next several years were occupied by work on evolution and religion. In 1882, Butler returned to *The Way of All Flesh*, completing it the following year. He felt, however, that the book should not be published while anyone who could be hurt by it was still alive; therefore it did not appear until a year after his own death.

In 1883, Butler began to write music. Music and music criticism were to occupy him intermittently for several years, interspersed with art criticism. The last decade of his life was filled with the study of literature, culminating in his publications on Shakespeare's sonnets and his translations of the *Iliad* (1898) and the *Odyssey* (1900). These works were characterized by the combativeness that to some degree sums up Butler's life. He was always the rebellious, contradictory son.

Butler's life was shaped by a number of intense relationships. His relationship with his family was unresolved; the work (*The Way of All Flesh*) which might have laid the ghosts to rest was haunted by another ghost, Butler's lifelong friend Eliza Mary Ann Savage. A fellow art student, she gave the writer friendship, friendly criticism, advice, and approval. Her own understanding of the relationship can never be known, but Butler feared she wished to marry him. His implicit rejection disturbed him deeply after her death. Other friendships were equally ambiguous. Charles Paine Pauli consumed much of Butler's attentions and resources from their first meeting in New Zealand until Pauli's death in 1897, when Butler discovered that Pauli had been supported by two other men. The perhaps sexual ambiguities of this relationship were repeated in Butler's affection for a young Swiss, Hans Faesch, and to a lesser degree in his long-lasting bonds with Henry Festing Jones and Alfred Emery Cathie. Butler's emotional makeup seems similar to that of Henry James. Both men formed passionate attachments to other men; both appreciated women more as memories than as living beings.

Analysis · On his deathbed, Samuel Butler spoke of the "pretty roundness" of his career, beginning with *Erewhon* and ending, thirty years later, with *Erewhon Revisited.*

Erewhon · *Erewhon* must be understood first of all as a satire rather than as a novel. It is in the tradition of Jonathan Swift's *Gulliver's Travels* (1726) and Samuel Johnson's *Rasselas, Prince of Abyssinia* (1759), works that sacrifice unity and development to a vision of the writer's society in the guise of an imaginary foreign land. Like Rasselas and Gulliver, Higgs of *Erewhon* is a young man, ready for adventure, out to learn about the world. He quickly reveals his image of himself as sharp, cunning, and bold. Before he tells his story, he lets the reader know the things he will hold back so that no reader will be able to find Erewhon and thus profit financially from Higgs's exploration.

His story begins as he is working on a sheep farm in a colony, the name of which he will not reveal. Intending to find precious metals or at least good sheep-grazing land, he journeys alone inland, over a mountain range. On the other side, he finds a kingdom called Erewhon (Nowhere), which looks very much like England. Higgs's point of reference is England; all aspects of Erewhonian life he measures by that standard.

Many such satires work through the narrator's quick judgment that his new land is either much better or much worse than his native country: The narrator's rather simple view plays against the author's more complex perspective. In *Erewhon*, however, the narrator is not quite so naïve. His own failings, rather than his naïveté, become part of the satire, which thus has a dual focus, much like book 4 of *Gulliver's Travels*. Higgs, like many good Victorian heroes, is out to make money. It is this prospect which motivates him most strongly. Coexisting with his desire for fortune is his religiosity. Here, Butler's satire upon his character is most pronounced and simplistic. Higgs observes the Sabbath, but he seduces Yram (Mary) with no regret. He plans to make his fortune by selling the Erewhonians into slavery, arguing that they would be converted to Christianity in the process; the slaveholders would be lining their pockets and doing good simultaneously. Thus, Butler exposes, to no one's great surprise, the mingled piety and avarice of British colonialists.

Butler satirizes European culture through the Erewhonians more often than through his hero, Higgs, gradually unfolding their lives for the reader to observe. Their lives are, on the surface, peaceful and pleasant; they are a strikingly attractive race. Only through personal experience does Higgs learn the underpinnings of the society: When he is ill, he learns that illness is a crime in Erewhon, while moral lapses are regarded in the same way as illnesses are in England. When his pocket watch is discovered, he learns that all "machines" have been banned from Erewhon. Erewhonian morality is based on reversals: The morally corrupt receive sympathy, while the ill are imprisoned; a child duped by his guardian is punished for having been ignorant, while the guardian is rewarded; children are responsible for their own birth, while their parents are consoled for having been "wronged" by the unborn. This pattern of reversals is of necessity incomplete, a problem noted by reviewers of *Erewhon* in 1872.

"The Book of the Machines" is the section of the satire which has drawn the most attention, because of its relationship to Darwinian thought. It may well be, as it has often been considered, a *reductio ad absurdum* of Darwinism, but the chapter also takes on reasoning by analogy as a less complex target of satire. "The Book of the Machines" is Higgs's translation of the Erewhonian book which led to the banning of all mechanical devices. Its author claimed that machines had developed–evolved– more rapidly than humankind and thus would soon dominate, leaving humans mere slaves or parasites. He argued that machines were capable of reproduction, using humans in the process as flowers use bees. The arguments proved so convincing that all machines in Erewhon were soon destroyed, leaving the country in the rather primitive state in which Higgs found it.

The purpose of "The Book of the Machines" becomes clearer in the following two chapters, which detail Erewhonian debates on the rights of animals and the rights of vegetables. At one point in the past, insistence on the rights of animals had turned Erewhon into a land of vegetarians, but the philosophers went a step further and decreed that vegetables, too, had rights, based upon their evolving consciousness. Again, Butler plays with argument by analogy, as the philosophers compare the vegetables' intelligence to that of a human embryo.

The Erewhonians who believed in the rights of vegetables were led nearly to starvation by their extremism, and it is this same extremism which causes Higgs to leave Erewhon. Fearful that disfavor is growing against his foreign presence, he plans to escape by balloon, taking with him his beloved Arowhena. The perilous escape takes place, and the hero, married to Arowhena and restored to England, becomes a fairly successful hack writer. His account of Erewhon, he says at the end, constitutes an appeal for subscriptions to finance his scheme to return to Erewhon.

Erewhon Revisited · The broad, traditional satire of *Erewhon* is abandoned in its sequel. Written years later, *Erewhon Revisited* reflects the maturity of its author, then in his sixties. In the later work, Butler treats Erewhon as a habitation of human beings, not satiric simplifications. *Erewhon Revisited* is thus a novel, not a satire; its focus is on human relationships. Butler had already written (though not published) *The Way of All Flesh*, and the preoccupations of that work are also evident in *Erewhon Revisited*. Both works grew out of Butler's fascination with family relationships, especially those between father and son.

The narrator of *Erewhon Revisited* is John Higgs, the son of George Higgs and Arowhena. He tells of his mother's early death and of his father's desire to return to Erewhon. This time, though, Higgs's desire is sentimental; he has grown past his earlier wish to profit from the Erewhonians. He goes to Erewhon, returns in ill health, tells the story of his adventure to John, and dies. The book in this way becomes John's tribute to his father.

Although *Erewhon Revisited* may be identified as a novel rather than as a satire, it does have a satiric subject as part of its plot. Upon reentering Erewhon, Higgs discovers that his ascent by balloon has become the source of a new religion. The Erewhonians revere his memory and worship him as the "Sun Child." Higgs is horrified to find that there are theologians of Sunchildism fighting heretics. Unfortunately, Sunchildism has not made the Erewhonians a better or kinder people. Here is the heart of Butler's satire: that a religion based upon a supernatural event will divide people, place power in the wrong hands, and humiliate reason.

In *Erewhon*, Higgs was a pious and hypocritical prig, a target of satire himself. In the sequel, he is a genial, loving humanist, appalled by the "evolution" of his frantic escape into the ascent of a god. Much of *Erewhon Revisited* develops his plans to deflate Sunchildism, to reveal himself as the "Sun Child" and tell the truth about his "ascent."

Higgs has a special motive which transcends his disgust with Sunchildism. Upon arriving in Erewhon, he meets a young man whom he soon recognizes as his own son, a son he did not know he had. The young man is the product of Higgs's brief romance with Yram, the jailer's daughter. Higgs keeps his identity from his son (also named George) for a while, but eventually the two are revealed to each other in a touching and intense scene. To earn his newfound son's respect, Higgs determines to deflate

Sunchildism. Thus, the process of satire in *Erewhon Revisited* is rooted in its human relationships.

Higgs's son John, the narrator of the novel, feels no jealousy toward his half brother. Instead, he shares the elder Higgs's enthusiasm for young George. Following his father's death, John goes to Erewhon himself to meet George and to deliver a large gift of gold to him. This legacy exemplified one of Butler's tenets about parent-child relations: that the best parents are kind, mostly absent, and very free with money. This theme is repeated throughout *The Way of All Flesh*. In *Erewhon Revisited*, however, it has a simpler expression. The relationship of Higgs and his two sons forms the emotional center of the novel and creates the impetus for some of its plot, but it is distinct from the satire on religion which makes up much of the book.

The Fair Haven · It is fitting that Butler's last work, *Erewhon Revisited*, should have presented a genial hero determined to strip away what he saw as ridiculous supernatural beliefs. Much of "Sunchildism" is a response to the religious foment of the nineteenth century with which Butler had begun contending early in his career. *The Fair Haven* was his first satire concerned with Christian belief. This work is "fiction" only in a very limited sense: Butler creates a persona, John Pickard Owen, whose arguments in favor of Christianity are in fact the vehicle for Butler's satire against it. *The Fair Haven* begins with a fictional memoir of John Pickard Owen by his brother. The memoir reveals that Owen moved from faith to disbelief to faith, and that his efforts to prove the validity of his religion pushed him to mental exhaustion and, eventually, death.

The Way of All Flesh · The characters of *The Fair Haven* are forerunners of the Pontifex family in *The Way of All Flesh*, Butler's fullest and most characteristic work. *The Way of All Flesh* encompasses all of Butler's concerns: family life, money, sexual attitudes, class structure, religion, and art. This novel too is a satire, but in it Butler does not portray an Erewhon; much more disturbingly, he keeps the reader at home.

The Way of All Flesh is Ernest Pontifex's story, but it does not begin with Ernest. Butler the evolutionist shows Ernest as the product of several generations of social changes and personal tensions. The genealogical background, as well as the title and biblical epigraph, "We know that all things work together for good to them that love God," helps to create the ironic treatment of religion which will permeate the novel. What is the way of all flesh? The biblical echo suggests sin and decay; Butler's fiction, however, reminds the reader that the way of all flesh is change, for better or worse.

Ernest is the product of three generations of upward mobility. His great-grandfather is a simple, kind craftsman who sends his only son into the city. The son, George Pontifex, becomes successful as a publisher and even more successful as a bully. He chooses the Church as a career for his second son, Theobald, who revolts briefly, then acquiesces and evolves into the image of his father. Butler is careful to show personalities as products of environment. George's bullying is only that of an egotistical, self-made man; Theobald's is more harsh, the product of his own fear and suppressed anger. The unfortunate object of this anger is Theobald's firstborn son, Ernest Pontifex.

Ernest's childhood is dominated by fear of his father. His mother, Christina, is of little help; Butler portrays her as the product of her own family life and the larger social system, both of which make marriage a necessity for her. Like Theobald, Christina becomes a hypocrite pressed into the service of "what is done." Much later in life, Ernest reflects that the family is a painful anachronism, confined in nature to the lower species. His opinion is shared by Overton, the narrator of the novel, an old family friend who takes an interest in young Ernest and becomes his lifelong friend and adviser. The two of them, in fact, eventually come to constitute a kind of family–an evolved, freely chosen family, not one formed by mere biological ties.

This outcome occurs only after long agony on Ernest's part. As a child, he believes all that is told: that he is, for example, a wicked, ungrateful boy who deserves Theobald's frequent beatings. His young life is lightened, however, by the interest taken in him by his aunt Alethea and by Overton, who has known all of the Pontifexes well and who tells their story with compassion.

Ernest is still an innocent and unformed young man when he goes to Cambridge to prepare for a career in the Church. Near the end of his peaceful, happy years there, he comes under the influence of an Evangelical group which alters his perceptions of what his life as a clergyman ought to be. Instead of stepping into a pleasant rural parish, Ernest becomes a missionary in the slums of London. He falls under the spell of the oily clergyman Nicholas Pryor, who "invests" Ernest's money and eventually absconds with it. Pryor, the Cambridge enthusiasts, and Theobald Pontifex all represent the clerical life; they are radically different kinds of people, and they are all portrayed negatively. Butler took no prisoners in his war on the clergy; his use of the genial Overton as a narrator partially masks this characteristic.

Sexual ignorance, imposed (and shared) by Theobald and his kind, provides Butler with his next target for satire. In despair over his religious life, Ernest seeks a prostitute and approaches the wrong woman, the eponymous Miss Snow. Ernest's ignorance lands him in prison and cuts him off forever from mere gentility. It redeems him, however, from a life circumscribed by his father: Ironically, Theobald's strict control over Ernest liberates Ernest at last. In prison, stripped of all his former identity, Ernest begins to come to terms with what his life has been and may be. A long illness serves to clarify his mind; he rejects traditional religion, society, and his family's condescending offers of help. Overton alone stands by Ernest, and it is at this point in Ernest's development that they become fast friends. Overton takes on the role of the ideal father–fond, genteel, and moneyed.

It is in this last area that Overton's role is most important to the events of the book: He keeps Alethea's substantial bequest in trust for Ernest, allowing him knowledge of it and access to it, according to Alethea's wish, only when he judges that Ernest is prepared to use it wisely. Ernest's ill-advised marriage and his decision to work as a tailor cause Overton to hold the money back. Eventually, Ernest's maturity evolves to a level acceptable to Overton, and the two of them lead a pleasant life of wealth and, on Ernest's side at least, accomplishment: He has become a writer who, like Butler, writes thoughtful, theoretical books.

In his role as a father, Ernest also has evolved. The children of his marriage to Ellen are reared by simple country people and grow up free of the pressures of Ernest's childhood. After four generations, the Pontifexes have returned to the peaceful and happy life of Ernest's great-grandfather.

Liberal amounts of money, however, keep Ernest's son and daughter from any want that ordinary country folk might experience. Ernest's son wants to be a riverboat captain: Ernest buys him riverboats. This scenario is nearly as idealized a version of country life as was Marie Antoinette's. What makes this vision disconcerting is that Ernest's attitudes are clearly shared by Butler. Early in the novel, Ernest the bullied child is the object of the reader's pity. As a student and young cleric, his life creates a sense of pity but also humor. The more fully Ernest evolves, however, the less appealing the reader is likely to find him. The Ernest who finally comes into his aunt's fortune is a rather dull prig, who, upon learning of his wealth, considers how his emotion might be rendered in music. He tells Overton that he regrets nothing—not his parents' brutality, not prison—because everything has contributed to his evolution away from the "swindle" of middle-class expectations. Unfortunately, this self-satisfied view makes his character seem shallow, consisting only of words and affectations.

In spite of this problem, Butler's achievement is considerable. *The Way of All Flesh* is an immensely ambitious book, and much of it succeeds. Butler articulated fully and convincingly the varied stresses of family life, and that aspect alone would make the novel worthwhile. *Erewhon* and *Erewhon Revisited* share some of that evocative power. They also express Butler's optimism. For all his satirical vision and contentiousness, Butler does offer happy endings: Higgs's successful escape from Erewhon with his beloved, the reunion of the brothers in *Erewhon Revisited,* and the pleasant life of Ernest and Overton in *The Way of All Flesh.* Though societies may often be in the wrong, Butler seems to tell the reader, there is hope in freely chosen human relationships.

Deborah Core

Other major works

NONFICTION: *A First Year in Canterbury Settlement,* 1863; *Life and Habit,* 1877; *Evolution, Old and New,* 1879; *God the Known and God the Unknown,* 1879; *Unconscious Memory,* 1880; *Alps and Sanctuaries of Piedmont and the Ticino,* 1881; *A Psalm of Montreal,* 1884; *Luck or Cunning,* 1887; *Ex Voto,* 1888; *The Life and Letters of Dr. Samuel Butler,* 1896; *The Authoress of the "Odyssey,"* 1897; *Shakespeare's Sonnets Reconsidered,* 1899; *The Note-books,* 1912 (H. Festing Jones, editor).

TRANSLATIONS: *Iliad,* 1898 (Homer); *Odyssey,* 1900 (Homer).

Bibliography

Bekker, W. G. *An Historical and Critical Review of Samuel Butler's Literary Works.* 1925. Reprint. New York: Russell & Russell, 1964. A full-length study of Butler written by a native of Holland, where *Erewhon* found popularity and immediate acceptance. Bekker argues for the unity in Butler's works.

Cole, G. D. H. *Samuel Butler and "The Way of All Flesh."* London: Home & Van Thal, 1947. An appreciative study of Butler's novel *The Way of All Flesh.* Contains some discussion of his other works, including *Erewhon.* Also includes valuable background material on Butler, such as his upbringing and his relationship to Darwinism.

Holt, Lee E. *Samuel Butler.* Rev. ed. Boston: Twayne, 1989. Updates this introductory study, first published in 1964. Holt takes into account new scholarships and criticism and new editions of Butler's work. There are chapters on Butler's major fiction, a chronology, and an annotated bibliography.

Jones, Joseph. *The Cradle of "Erewhon": Samuel Butler in New Zealand.* Austin: University of Texas Press, 1959. A valuable account of Butler's five years in New Zealand and the origins of his later *Erewhon* books.

Raby, Peter. *Samuel Butler: A Biography.* Iowa City: University of Iowa Press, 1991. A comprehensive scholarly biography, with detailed notes and bibliography.

Lewis Carroll

Charles Lutwidge Dodgson

Born: Daresbury, Cheshire, England; January 27, 1832
Died: Guildford, Surrey, England; January 14, 1898

Principal long fiction · *Alice's Adventures in Wonderland*, 1865; *Through the Looking-Glass and What Alice Found There*, 1871.

Other literary forms · Before and after writing his novels for children, Lewis Carroll published volumes in his primary vocation, mathematics: *A Syllabus of Plane Algebraical Geometry, Systematically Arranged, with Formal Definitions, Postulates, and Axioms* (1860), *An Elementary Treatise on Determinants* (1867), *Curiosa Mathematica* (Part I, 1888; Part II, 1893), and *Symbolic Logic, Part I: Elementary* (1896). His gift for light verse, demonstrated in his novels, also led to four books of poems, with some duplication of content: *Phantasmagoria: And Other Poems* (1869), *The Hunting of the Snark* (1876), *Rhyme? and Reason?* (1883), and the posthumous *Three Sunsets and Other Poems* (1898). His literary and mathematical sides were fused in *A Tangled Tale* (1885), a series of mathematical word problems in the form of short stories, and *Euclid and His Modern Rivals* (1879) a closet drama in which Euclid is defended by various scholars and spirits.

Achievements · In 1898, a few months after Carroll's death, the *Pall Mall Gazette* published a survey of the popularity of children's books, and the overwhelming front-runner was *Alice's Adventures in Wonderland*. Queen Victoria enjoyed *Alice's Adventures in Wonderland* so much that she asked Carroll to dedicate his next book to her (ironically, his next book, *An Elementary Treatise on Determinants*, proved to be nothing like the whimsical adventure the Queen had admired).

Carroll encouraged the stage versions of the *Alice* books that appeared in his lifetime, though he was dismayed at his lack of legal control over adaptations. The *Alice* books have been translated into dozens of languages and are quoted more often than any English work, after that of William Shakespeare. *Alice's Adventures in Wonderland* is noteworthy for more than its popularity, however; it was the first work of literature for children that did not have an overtly didactic or moralistic nature. In fact, Carroll parodied didactic children's works in verse, such as "You Are Old, Father William" in *Through the Looking-Glass and What Alice Found There* and characters such as the Duchess in *Alice's Adventures in Wonderland*. Writers as abstruse and complex as British philosopher Ludwig Wittgenstein and Irish novelist James Joyce were drawn to the deeper implications of Carroll's work, especially the lighthearted sense of play and the role of nonsense in human thought. The absurdist writers of the twentieth century saw Carroll as their prophet, and a few of his nonsense words, such as "Boojum," "Jabberwocky," and "chortle," have become a seemingly permanent part of the English language. His term for a particular method of coining compound words, "portmanteau," has since become a standard linguistic name for the process.

Biography · Charles Lutwidge Dodgson was the third of eleven children and the eldest son of the Reverend Charles Dodgson and Frances Jane Lutwidge. The younger Charles Dodgson was left-handed and spoke with a stutter, an affliction from which he would suffer his whole life. With eight younger siblings, Dodgson very early developed the knack of amusing children, an ability he would keep as an adult. He wrote and drew little magazines for their amusement, which demonstrated the whimsy of his Alice books. Some of the verses in the Alice books received their first audition in these family magazines.

At age twelve, Dodgson attended Richmond Grammar School, and the following year, the famous public school at Rugby. Nearly four years at Rugby, which he later recalled with displeasure, prepared him for Oxford University: He entered Christ Church College there on January 24, 1851. He distinguished himself in mathematics and classics, though difficulty with philosophy and history kept him in the lower third of his class. On December 18, 1854, he received his A.B. with first-class honors in mathematics. He stayed on at Christ Church as a tutor and lecturer. At this time his earliest stories and poems appeared in periodicals at Oxford and Whitby.

Early in 1856 Dodgson acquired his first camera, then a relatively rare and complicated device restricted to use by specialists. A large number of his photographs, mostly of young girls, survive, and one historian of photography has declared Dodgson the most outstanding child photographer of the nineteenth century. A month after purchasing the camera, one young model, the four-year-old daughter of an Oxford dean, caught Dodgson's eye. Her name was Alice Liddell. Six years later he would extemporize, on a boating expedition, a story about Alice that was to become the famous *Alice* stories. However, until then, Dodgson's energies went into his vocations of mathematics and the Church: He published his first book on mathematics in 1860, and he was ordained a deacon just before Christmas of 1861.

By February of 1863, Dodgson had committed to paper the story from the 1862 excursion with the Liddell sisters. He published it in 1865 (though it did not appear until 1866) as *Alice's Adventures in Wonderland.* Dodgson used the pseudonym Lewis Carroll for his publications, a name seemingly derived from the names Lutwidge and Charles. In 1867 Dodgson made the only voyage of his lifetime away from England, touring the Continent (mostly Russia). He had already begun his sequel to *Alice's Adventures in Wonderland,* which appeared near Christmas, 1871, as *Through the Looking-Glass and What Alice Found There.* When his father died in 1868, Dodgson moved his siblings to Guildford, and he moved into rooms at Tom Quad, Oxford, where he remained the rest of his life. In 1881 his income from writing was sufficient for him to resign his lectureship in mathematics, although he remained at Oxford. The following year he was elected curator of the Senior Common room, a post he held for ten years. He continued writing until his death in 1898, though he never equalled the success of the *Alice* books.

Analysis · Lewis Carroll's first great contribution to children's literature is that he freed it from the heavy didacticism of previous children's books. The second is his legitimizing of nonsense in children's literature, though in this claim he is preceded by fellow Victorian Edward Lear, whose *A Book of Nonsense* (1846) preceded the *Alice* books by two decades. It is perhaps in his nonsense that we can see the connection between Reverend Dodgson, the mathematician, and Lewis Carroll, the writer. Nonsense is self-referential; that is, it lacks "sense," if sense means a relationship to the world outside of the work of nonsense. Thus, it is like certain mathematical systems or logic games. Carroll's works are in fact games, which is one of the reasons for their appeal to children.

Alice's Adventures in Wonderland · Carroll's first novel, *Alice's Adventures in Wonderland,* successfully creates and maintains a dream-consciousness. Its dreamlike quality is revealed not merely in its conventional ending, with Alice waking up to discover her adventures in Wonderland were "all a dream"; its episodic movements are dreamlike in that one episode melts into the other and has no necessary logical connection to the previous. Identities constantly shift: A baby turns into a pig; the Cheshire cat fades away into a grin. Because the logic of dreams, as the logic of

Wonderland, is closed, internal, and self-referential, *Alice's Adventures in Wonderland* resists interpretations that attempt to "explain" the novel by connecting its elements to structures outside it, such as biographical, historical, psychoanalytic, or political interpretations.

The story begins with Alice drowsing while her sister reads a boring book. Her attention is arrested by a white rabbit, whom she follows, only to fall down a rabbit hole, where she finds a world where nothing is like the world she left. When she eats and drinks the Wonderland foods, she changes drastically in size, becoming small as a mouse, then large as a house. When small, she finds her way into a garden, where she meets a caterpillar, rescues a baby from a mean duchess, attends a mad tea party, plays croquet with the Queen of Hearts, listens to a mock turtle's life story, and attends the trial of the Knave of Hearts. When the angry subjects of the Queen rush at Alice, she awakens to find them to be only, in the real world, falling leaves.

The novel is narrated in the third person, but with limited omniscience, allowing us to view Wonderland from Alice's perspective. The creation of the Alice character (though it must be remembered that she is modelled after a real girl of the author's acquaintance) is one of Carroll's most stunning achievements. It is seen immediately in the opening paragraph, presenting her thoughts as she peers into a book her sister is reading, which bores her because it has no pictures or conversations. This is clearly a child's perspective. Even Alice's precipitous changes in size reflect the point of view of children who are given contradictory messages: that they are too big for some things and too little for others. Alice is the most fully realized of the characters in the book, all others being functionally flat. The flatness of the characters is essential to the humor of the book, particularly the slapstick elements, for the whimsy of the Mad Hatter and the March Hare dunking the Dormouse in a teapot is lost if we sympathize with him as a real character with feelings.

Through the Looking-Glass and What Alice Found There · Carroll's second novel is a sequel to the first, with the same main character. This time the "wonderland" is the looking-glass world, the world we see when we look in the mirror, a reverse image of our own world. As a photographer, needing to visualize a finished photograph from its negative image, Carroll had an intuitive understanding of the implications of a "reverse" world. The consciousness of his "abnormality" of being a left-handed boy may also have played into the creation of *Through the Looking-Glass and What Alice Found There*.

In the opening chapter, Alice enters the looking-glass to find a house precisely the reverse of her own. She goes out into the garden, where she meets the Red Queen, then to the surrounding country where she encounters strange insects, Tweedledee and Tweedledum, the White Queen, Humpty Dumpty, the lion and the unicorn, and the White Knight. In chapter 9, Alice becomes queen, and she upsets the board of chess pieces in a transition from dream to waking precisely like that of the first *Alice* book. The transition is handled in two truncated chapters, one of fifty-nine words, in which Alice shakes the Red Queen, and one of only six words, in which the Red Queen turns out to be Alice's kitten, and she is awake. The final chapter is an epilogue, in which Alice poses an unanswered question on the relation of dream to reality.

Sylvie and Bruno · Carroll's last two novels were not as successful commercially as the *Alice* books, and according to their earliest critics, they were unsuccessful artistically as well. Carroll continues to play with dream-reality in the *Sylvie and Bruno* books, but this time waking and dream realities are interlaced in alternating chapters. In place of Wonderland or the looking-glass world, *Sylvie and Bruno* puts forth "the eerie state," in which one becomes aware of fairies.

Thus, *Sylvie and Bruno* has two parallel plots: In the waking world, which Carroll's introduction calls "the ordinary state," there is a love triangle. The noble and selfless Dr. Arthur Forester loves Lady Muriel Orme but believes that she loves her cousin, Captain Eric Linden. The cousins, in fact, become engaged, but there is a grave religious impediment: Eric is not a Christian. The novel ends with Arthur accepting a medical post in India so as not to stand in Eric's way. Simultaneously in the fairy or "eerie" realm parallel to the human one of Arthur, Eric, and Muriel, Sylvie and Bruno are innocent fairy children of the Warden of Outland. This plot is a version of the ancient myth and fairy-tale motif of the disguised god or king. The Warden temporarily abandons his rule in order to travel the kingdom disguised as a beggar. In his absence his wicked brother Sibimet conspires with his wife and selfish son Uggug to take over Outland.

Sylvie and Bruno Concluded · In the sequel to *Sylvie and Bruno*, the interaction between the fairy realm of Outland and the human realm of Arthur and Muriel are more causally connected, as Sylvie and Bruno work "behind the scenes" to bring the true lovers together. Sylvie, in fact, appears to be the fairyland identity of Muriel. Through the invisible ministry of Sylvie and Bruno, Arthur and Muriel are married, but shortly after the wedding Arthur must go off to combat a plague in a nearby town. Muriel reads a false account of the death of Arthur in the plague, who, ironically, is rescued by Eric, who has come to accept the Christian faith and sees his assistance to a would-be rival as divinely directed. Meanwhile, the Warden (Arthur's counterpart) returns to Outland, thwarts Sibimet (Eric's counterpart), who repents, and regains his kingdom.

Perhaps it is no surprise that the human characters in both *Sylvie and Bruno* books are the least believable. They are the hackneyed stock characters of sentimental romance, though no worse than others of the same genre. As in the *Alice* books, the title characters, Sylvie and Bruno, are the more remarkable creations, though readers may have difficulty with the cloying baby talk of the fairies and the effusive affection they lavish on one another. Sylvie and Bruno are emblems of childlike innocence, which Carroll also tried to capture in *Alice* and in his photography.

John R. Holmes

Other major works

SHORT FICTION: "Bruno's Revenge," 1867.

POETRY: *Phantasmagoria*, 1869; *The Hunting of the Snark*, 1876; *Rhyme? and Reason?*, 1883; *Three Sunsets and Other Poems*, 1898.

NONFICTION: *A Syllabus of Plane Algebraical Geometry*, 1860; *An Elementary Treatise on Determinants*, 1867; *Euclid and His Modern Rivals*, 1879; *Twelve Months in a Curatorship*, 1884; *Three Years in a Curatorship*, 1886; The *Game of Logic*, 1887; *Curiosa Mathematica*, Part I, 1888; Part II, 1893; *Symbolic Logic*, 1896.

CHILDREN'S LITERATURE: *A Tangled Tale*, 1885; *Sylvie and Bruno*, 1889; *Sylvie and Bruno Concluded*, 1893.

Bibliography

Bloom, Harold, ed. *Modern Critical Views on Lewis Carroll.* New York: Chelsea House, 1987. Part of a standard series of literary essays, the selections are good but contain specialized studies that may not help the beginner. Bloom's brief introduction is a good starting point in critically assessing Carroll.

Cohen, Morton Norton. *Lewis Carroll: A Biography.* New York: A. A. Knopf, 1995. A good, updated biography of Carroll.

Fordyce, Rachel, ed. *Lewis Carroll: A Reference Guide.* Boston: G. K. Hall, 1988. An exhaustive annotated bibliography of primary and secondary material on Carroll.

Gray, Donald J., ed. *Alice in Wonderland.* New York: Norton, 1992. This Norton Critical Edition is an ideal starting point for the beginner, not only because of the nearly two hundred pages of background and critical essays, but also because of the helpful annotations on the two *Alice* novels. Many of the best essays from other collections are reprinted here, making it a reference work of first resort.

Guiliano, Edward, ed. *Lewis Carroll: A Celebration.* New York: Clarkson N. Potter, 1982. A collection of essays in honor of Carroll's one hundred fiftieth birthday, this book is notable for two essays that restore the critical reputation of *Sylvie and Bruno.*

Hudson, Derek. *Lewis Carroll: An Illustrated Biography.* New York: New American Library, 1978. One of the best biographies available, offering a much-needed corrective to the spate of amateur psychological studies of Carroll's life.

Kelly, Richard Michael. *Lewis Carroll.* Boston: Twayne, 1990. A solid study of Carroll for the beginning student. Includes index and bibliographical references.

Angela Carter

Born: Eastbourne, Sussex, England; May 7, 1940
Died: London, England; February 16, 1992

Principal long fiction · *Shadow Dance*, 1966 (pb. in U.S. as *Honeybuzzard*, 1967); *The Magic Toyshop*, 1967; *Several Perceptions*, 1968; *Heroes and Villains*, 1969; *Love*, 1971, rev. 1987; *The Infernal Desire Machines of Doctor Hoffman*, 1972 (pb. in U.S. as *The War of Dreams*, 1974); *The Passion of New Eve*, 1977; *Nights at the Circus*, 1984; *Wise Children*, 1991.

Other literary forms · Angela Carter is nearly as well known for her short fiction as she is for her novels. Her short-story collections include *Fireworks: Nine Profane Pieces* (1974), *Black Venus* (1985; published in U.S. as *Saints and Strangers*, 1986), the highly praised *The Bloody Chamber and Other Stories* (1979), which contains her transformations of well-known fairy tales into adult tales with erotic overtones, and *American Ghosts and Old World Wonders* (1993). She also wrote a number of fantastic stories for children, including *Miss Z, the Dark Young Lady* (1970), *The Donkey Prince* (1970), and a translated adaptation of the works of Charles Perrault, *The Fairy Tales of Charles Perrault* (1977). In 1978, she published her first book of nonfiction, *The Sadeian Woman: And the Ideology of Pornography*, a feminist study of the Marquis de Sade that remains controversial among both literary and feminist critics. Other nonfiction essays have been published by British journals; *Nothing Sacred: Selected Writings* (1982) is a collection of her journalistic pieces, and *Shaking a Leg: Journalism and Writings* (1997) reprints other essays and reviews. She also cowrote, with Neil Jordan, the screenplay for the British film *The Company of Wolves* (1984), based on her short story of the same title.

Achievements · With the publication of her first novels in the late 1960's, Carter received wide recognition and acclaim in Great Britain for blending gothic and surreal elements with vivid portrayals of urban sufferers and survivors. She was awarded the John Llewellyn Rhys Memorial Prize for *The Magic Toyshop* and the Somerset Maugham Award for *Several Perceptions*. Critics have praised her wit, inventiveness, eccentric characters, descriptive wealth, and strongly sustained narrative while sometimes questioning her depth of purpose and suggesting a degree of pretentiousness. Her imaginative transformation of folkloric elements and examination of their mythic impact on sexual relationships began to be fully appreciated on the appearance of *The Bloody Chamber and Other Stories*, which received the Cheltenham Festival of Literature Award. *Nights at the Circus*, recipient of the James Tait Black Memorial Prize, helped to establish firmly for Carter a growing transatlantic reputation as an extravagant stylist of the Magical Realist school. Following her untimely death in 1992–which enabled her establishment in the syllabus of British universities traditionally reluctant to venerate living writers–Carter was immediately hailed as the most important English fantasist of her generation. Her critical writings, which add a robust and sometimes scathing rhetoric to the lucid prose of her fiction, also attracted new attention.

Biography · Angela Carter (née Stalker) was born in Eastbourne, Sussex, England, on May 7, 1940. After working as a journalist from 1958 to 1961 in Croyden, Surrey, she attended Bristol University, from which she received a B.A. in English literature in 1965. While married to Paul Carter between 1960 and 1972 she traveled widely and lived for several years in Japan. From 1976 to 1978, she served as Arts Council of Great Britain Fellow in Creative Writing at Sheffield University. She was a visiting professor at Brown University, the University of Texas, Austin, and the University of Iowa. She spent the last years of her life in London, living with Mark Pearce, the father of her son Alexander, who was born in 1983. She died of lung cancer in London on February 16, 1992.

Analysis · The search for self and for autonomy is the underlying theme of most of Angela Carter's fiction. Her protagonists, usually described as bored or in some other way detached from their lives, are thrust into an unknown landscape or enter on a picaresque journey in which they encounter representatives of a vast variety of human experience and suffering. These encountered characters are often grotesques or exaggerated parodies reminiscent of those found in the novels of Charles Dickens or such southern gothic writers as Flannery O'Connor. They also sometimes exhibit the animalistic or supernatural qualities of fairy-tale characters. The protagonists undergo a voluntary or, more often, forced submission to their own suppressed desires. By internalizing the insights gained through such submission and vicariously from the experiences of their antagonists and comrades or lovers, the protagonists are then able to garner some control over their own destinies. This narrative structure is borrowed from the classic folk- and fairy tales with which Carter has been closely associated. Carter does not merely retell such tales in modern dress; rather, she probes and twists the ancient stories to illuminate the underlying hierarchical structures of power and dominance, weakness and submission.

In addition to the folkloric influence, Carter draws from a variety of other writers, most notably Lewis Carroll, Jonathan Swift, the Marquis de Sade, and William Blake. The rather literal-minded innocent abroad in a nightmarish wonderland recalls both Alice and Gulliver, and Carter acknowledges, both directly and obliquely, her borrowings from Carroll's *Alice's Adventures in Wonderland* (1865) and Swift's *Gulliver's Travels* (1726). She was also influenced by the Swiftian tool of grotesque parody used in the service of satire. It is through Swiftian glasses that she read Sade. While deploring the depradations on the human condition committed by both the victims and victimizers in Sade's writings, she interprets these as hyperbolic visions of the actual social situation, and she employs in her novels derivatively descriptive situations for their satiric shock value. Finally, the thematic concerns of Blake's visionary poetry—the tension between the contrarieties of innocence and experience, rationality and desire—are integral to Carter's outlook. The energy created by such tension creates the plane on which Carter's protagonists can live most fully. In Blake's words and in Carter's novels, "Energy is Eternal Delight."

Although Carter's landscapes range from London in the 1960's (*The Magic Toyshop, Several Perceptions, Love*) to a postapocalyptic rural England (*Heroes and Villains*) or a sometime-in-the-future South America (*The Infernal Desire Machines of Doctor Hoffman*), a United States whose social fabric is rapidly disintegrating (*The Passion of New Eve*), or London and Russia at the turn of the century (*Nights at the Circus*), certain symbolic motifs appear regularly in her novels. Carter is particularly intrigued by the possibilities of roses, wedding dresses, swans, wolves, tigers, bears, vampires, mirrors, tears, and vanilla ice cream. Menacing father figures, prostitute mothers, and a kaleidoscope of circus, fair, and Gypsy folk inhabit most of her landscapes. It is unfair, however, to reduce Carter's novels to a formulaic mode. She juggles traditional and innovative elements with a sometimes dazzling dexterity and is inevitably a strong storyteller.

The Magic Toyshop · At the opening of *The Magic Toyshop*, fifteen-year-old Melanie is entranced with her budding sexuality. She dresses up in her absent mother's wedding gown to dance on the lawn in the moonlight. Overwhelmed by her awakening knowledge and the immensities of possibilities the night offers, she is terrified and climbs back into her room by the childhood route of the apple tree—shredding her mother's gown in the process. Her return to childhood becomes catastrophic when a telegram arrives announcing the death of Melanie's parents in a plane crash. Melanie, with her younger brother and sister, is thrust from a safe and comfortable existence into the constricted and terrifying London household of her Uncle Philip Flower, a toy maker of exquisite skill and sadistically warped sensibility. He is a domestic tyrant whose Irish wife, Margaret, was inexplicably struck dumb on her wedding day. The household is also inhabited by Margaret's two younger brothers, Finn and Francie Jowle; the three siblings form a magic "circle of red people" which is alternately seductive and repulsive to Melanie. Uncle Philip is a creator of the mechanical. He is obsessed by his private puppet theater, his created world to which he enslaves the entire household. In aligning herself with the Jowle siblings, Melanie asserts her affirmation of life but becomes aware of the thwarted and devious avenues of survival open to the oppressed. The growing, but ambivalent, attraction between her and Finn is premature and manipulated by Uncle Philip. Even the love that holds the siblings together is underlined by a current of incest. Finn is driven to inciting his uncle to murder him in order to effect Philip's damnation. The crisis arises when Uncle Philip casts Melanie as Leda in a puppet extravaganza. Her symbolic rape by the immense mechanical swan and Finn's subsequent destruction of the puppet release an orgiastic, yet purifying, energy within the "circle of red people." The ensuing wrath of Uncle Philip results in the conflagration and destruction of the house. Finn and Melanie are driven out, Adam-and-Eve-like, to face a new world "in a wild surmise."

In fairy-tale fashion, Melanie is threatened by an evil father figure, protected by the good mother, and rescued by the young hero. Even in this early novel, however, Carter skews and claws at the traditional fabric. The Jowle brothers, grimy, embittered, and twisted by their victimization at the hands of Philip Flower, are as dangerous as they are endangered. They are unable to effect their own freedom. Melanie's submission to Uncle Philip's swan catalyzes not only her own rescue but also, indeed, the release of the Jowle siblings. Melanie's sacrifice breaks the magic spell that held the Jowles imprisoned.

Several Perceptions · *Several Perceptions*, Carter's third novel, depends less on such folkloric structure. In this novel, her evocation of the late 1960's counterculture is so finely detailed that she manages to illuminate the thin line between the idealism and solipsism of that era, without denigrating the former or disguising the latter. The clarity of observation is achieved by viewing the culture through the eyes of Joseph Harker, a classic dropout. He has failed at the university, been dumped by his Jane Austen-reading lover, is disheartened by his job caring for dying old men, despises the contentment of his hippie peers, and, early in the novel, bungles a suicide attempt. Joseph, like his biblical namesake, is a dreamer of dreams: He dreams in the violent images of Vietnam atrocities, the self-immolation of Buddhist monks, and assassinations. His schizophrenic perceptions are colored by shattered images from the books in his room, *Alice's Adventures in Wonderland* and Anne Gilchrist's *Life of William Blake* (1863), by memories of his grandfather, visions of his psychiatrist, the purring of his pregnant cat, Anne Blossom's custard, and the vanilla ice-cream breasts of Mrs. Boulder. The novel narrates Joseph's slow crawl back into the world of the living. Despite a tough-minded acknowledgment of the grubby and quite desolate lives of the characters, the novel is written with a gentle touch and ends on an affirmative note. The Christmas party that takes place at the end of the novel, in which Joseph symbolically reenters society, stands as a classic description of a hippie-generation party, just as F. Scott Fitzgerald's description of Gatsby's party stands as the image for the flapper generation. The connected-disconnected flow, the costumes, the easy sexuality, the simple goodwill, the silliness, and the sometimes inspired personal insights are vividly re-created. Carter wrote the novel as this lifestyle was being played out, and it is much to her credit that she succumbed neither to sentimentality nor to parody.

Heroes and Villains, The Infernal Desire Machines of Doctor Hoffman*, and *The Passion of New Eve · Parody and satire are, however, major elements in Carter's three novels that are often classified as science fiction or science fantasy. In *Heroes and Villains, The Infernal Desire Machines of Doctor Hoffman*, and *The Passion of New Eve*, Carter's protagonists dwell in societies which are described in metaphysical iconography. Carter seems to be questioning the nature and values of received reality. Marianne's world in *Heroes and Villains* is divided into high-technology enclaves containing Professors, the Soldiers who protect them, and the Workers who serve them. Outside the enclaves, in the semijungle/semicesspool wildernesses, dwell the tribes of nomadic Barbarians and the Out-people, freaks created by nature gone awry. Marianne, the daughter of a Professor, motivated mainly by boredom, escapes from her enclave with Jewel, a young Barbarian chieftain, during a raid. In *The Infernal Desire Machines of Doctor Hoffman*, the aging Desiderio narrates his heroic exploits as a young man when he saved his City during the Reality War. Doctor Hoffman besieges the City with mirages generated from his Desire Machines. Sent by the Minister of Determination to kill Doctor Hoffman, Desiderio is initiated into the wonders of desires made manifest, Nebulous Time, and the juggled samples of cracked and broken reality. His guide is Hoffman's daughter, Albertina, who appears to Desiderio as an androgynous ambassador, a black swan, the young valet of a vampiric count, and finally as his one true love, the emanation of his whole desire.

The United States in *The Passion of New Eve* is torn apart by racial, class, and sexual conflicts. Evelyn, a young British teacher, travels through this landscape and is re-created. The unconsciously exploitive and disinterestedly sadistic narrator suffers a wild revenge when captured by an Amazonlike community of women. He is castrated, resexed, raped, forcibly wed and mated, and ultimately torn from his wife's love by a gang of murderous Puritanical boys. Each of these protagonists experiences love but only seems to be able to achieve wholeness through the destruction of the loved one. Symbolically, the protagonists seem to consume the otherness of the loved ones, reincorporating these manifest desires back into their whole beings. Each, however, is left alone at the end of the novel.

Symbolic imagery of a harshly violent though rollicking nature threatens to overwhelm these three novels. The parody is at times wildly exaggerated and at times cuts very close to reality (for example, in *The Passion of New Eve*, the new Eve is incorporated into a polygamous family which closely resembles the Manson cult). Although some critics have decried Carter's heavy reliance on fantasies, visions, and zany exuberance, it is probably these qualities that have appealed to a widening audience. It must also be given to Carter that, within her magical realms, she continues to probe and mock the repressive nature of institutionalized relationships and sexual politics.

Nights at the Circus · With *Nights at the Circus*, Carter wove the diverse threads of her earlier novels into brilliantly realized tapestry. This novel has two protagonists—Fevvers, the Cockney Venus, a winged, six-foot, peroxide blonde aerialist, who was found "hatched out of a bloody great egg" on the steps of a benevolent whorehouse (her real name is Sophia) and Jack Walser, an American journalist compiling a series of interviews entitled "Great Humbugs of the World," who joins Colonel Kearney's circus, the Ludic Game, in order to follow Fevvers, and who is "Not hatched out, yet . . . his own shell don't break, yet." It is 1899, and a New World is about to break forth. The ambivalent, tenuous attraction between Fevvers and Walser is reminiscent of that between Melanie and Finn in *The Magic Toyshop* or Marianne and Jewel in *Heroes and Villains*, but it is now mature and more subtly complex. The picaresque journeyings from London to St. Petersburg and across the steppes of Russia recall the travels in *The Infernal Desire Machines of Doctor Hoffman* and *The Passion of New Eve* but are more firmly grounded in historical landscapes. The magic in this novel comes in the blurring between fact and fiction, the intense unbelievability of actual reality and the seductive possibilities of imaginative and dreamlike visions. Are Fevvers's wings real or contrived? Do the clowns hide behind their makeup and wigs or only become actualized when they don their disguises? As in most Magical Realist fiction, Carter is probing the lines between art and artifice, creation and generation, in a raucous and lush style.

Here, after a long hiatus from the rather bleak apocalyptic visions of her 1970's novels, in which autonomous selfhood is only achieved through a kind of self-cannibalization of destroyed love, Angela Carter envisions a route to self-affirmation that allows sexual love to exist. With shifting narrative focuses, Carter unfolds the rebirths of Walser and Fevvers through their own and each other's eyes. Walser's shells of consciousness are cracked as he becomes a "first-of-May" clown, the waltzing partner to a tigress, the Human Chicken, and, in losing consciousness, an apprentice shaman to a primitive Finno-Urgic tribe. As star of Kearney's circus, Fevvers is the toast of European capitals: an impregnable, seductive freak, secure in and exploitive of her own singularity. On the interminable train trek through Siberia, she seems to mislay her magnificence and invulnerability. She becomes less a freak and more a woman, but she remains determined to hatch Walser into her New Man. As he had to forgo his socially conditioned consciousness in order to recognize Sophia, however, so she has to allow him to hatch himself. It is as confident seers that Sophia/Fevvers and Jack Walser love at the close of the novel.

Wise Children · The fact that Carter produced only one novel during the last eight years of her life has more to do with the claims made on her time and attention by her son Alexander than the depredations of the cancer that killed her. This was a sore point—her much younger partner, Alexander's father, did not keep promises he made to take primary responsibility for childcare—and some of that soreness is evident in the pages of the satirical comedy *Wise Children*, in which disowned and abandoned children are extravagantly featured. The story comprises a century-spanning memoir written by Dora Chance, one of the "lucky Chance" twins fathered–but swiftly disowned–by the Shakespearean actor Melchior Hazard in advance of the first of his three marriages.

Dora recalls that the identical Chance twins are indeed lucky, first by virtue of being informally adopted by Melchior's more colorful but less successful fraternal twin Peregrine, and second by virtue of developing a career as dancers in music halls. (Music halls were Britain's primary form of vulgar popular entertainment from the turn of the century to the end of World War II.) It subsequently transpires that Peregrine is the biological father of Melchior's supposedly legitimate identical twin daughters by his first marriage, Saskia and Imogen. The paternity of the fraternal twins of Melchior's third marriage, Gareth and Tristan, is never formally disputed, although Dora and her sister Nora cannot help but wonder why it is that one bears a far stronger physical resemblance to Peregrine.

The intricate comparisons and contrasts drawn between the fortunes and pretensions of the legitimate Hazards and the illegitimate Chances mirror and embody the fortunes and pretensions of "legitimate" theater and the music-hall tradition, as both are swallowed up by new media–first by Hollywood films (the most hilarious chapter describes the brief reunion of the Chances with their father on the set of a chaotic film version of William Shakespeare's *A Midsummer Night's Dream*) and then by television. The contemporary events that surround Dora's recollections involve the effects of television game-show host Tristan's simultaneous sexual involvement with his much older half sister Saskia and the Chances' protégé Tiffany (significantly nicknamed "Our Tiff"). The paradoxes of Melchior's theatrical career are summed up by the juxtaposition of his eventual knighthood with his attachment to the cardboard crown that was the chief legacy he received from his father, also a redoubtable Shakespearean actor.

Although *Wise Children* is far more sentimental than the bleakly dark fantasies Carter penned while her own marriage was failing in the early 1970's, it is to some extent a revisitation of their themes. (The revised version of *Love*, which she prepared while struggling to find the time to write *Wise Children*, also softens the self-mutilatory aspects of the original, but only slightly.) What Carter's final novel adds to her jaundiced view of family life, however, is the legacy of her midperiod preoccupation with the processes by which the substance of childhood dreams and unfathomable experiences can be transmuted into high and low art. Beneath the surface of its comic exuberance, *Wise Children* achieves considerable intensity in its celebration of theatrical magic and its accounts of the redemption of wounded personalities by spirited performances.

Jane Anderson Jones, updated by Brian Stableford

Other major works

SHORT FICTION: *Fireworks: Nine Profane Pieces*, 1974; *The Bloody Chamber and Other Stories*, 1979; *Black Venus*, 1985 (pb. in U.S. as *Saints and Strangers*, 1986); *American Ghosts and Old World Wonders*, 1993; *Burning Your Boats*, 1995.

SCREENPLAYS: *The Company of Wolves*, 1985 (with Neil Jordan); *The Magic Toyshop*, 1987.

RADIO PLAYS: *Vampirella*, 1976; *Come unto These Yellow Sands*, 1979; *The Company of*

Wolves, 1980; *Puss in Boots,* 1982; *Come unto These Yellow Sands: Four Radio Plays,* pb. 1985 (includes previous four plays).

NONFICTION: *The Sadeian Woman: And the Ideology of Pornography,* 1978; *Nothing Sacred: Selected Writings,* 1982; *Expletives Deleted: Selected Writings,* 1992; *Shaking a Leg: Journalism and Writings,* 1997.

CHILDREN'S LITERATURE: *Miss Z, the Dark Young Lady,* 1970; *The Donkey Prince,* 1970; *Moonshadow,* 1982.

TRANSLATION: *The Fairy Tales of Charles Perrault,* 1977; *Sleeping Beauty and Other Favourite Fairy Tales,* 1982 (translation and adaptation of Perrault's tales).

EDITED TEXTS: *Wayward Girls and Wicked Women,* 1986; *The Virago Book of Fairy Tales,* 1990 (pb. in U.S. as *The Old Wives' Fairy Tale Book*).

Bibliography

Lee, Alison. *Angela Carter.* New York: G. K. Hall, 1997. A good biographical and critical book-length study of Carter. Includes bibliographical references and an index.

Palumbo, Donald, ed. *Erotic Universe: Sexuality and Fantastic in Literature.* London: Greenwood Press, 1986. A compilation of essays on feminist literature. The chapter by Brooks Landon looks at sexuality and the reversal of expectations in Carter's novels, in particular *Heroes and Villains.* Discusses the feminist mythology of this novel and Carter's confrontation of sexual stereotypes.

Peach, Linden. *Angela Carter.* New York: St. Martin's Press, 1998. Part of the Modern Novelists series, this book offers a good examination of Carter's life and work.

Punter, David. "Angela Carter: Supersessions of the Masculine." *Critique: Studies in Modern Fiction* 25 (Summer, 1984): 209-222. Describes Carter as charting the unconscious processes of Western society and addresses the sexual themes in her novels, such as the struggle between Eros and Thanatos in *The Infernal Desire Machines of Doctor Hoffman.* Also includes some commentary on *The Passion of New Eve* and *The Sadeian Woman.* A thoughtful essay on Carter.

Sage, Lorna, ed. *Flesh and the Mirror: Essays on the Art of Angela Carter.* London: Chatto & Windus, 1994. A collection of thirteen essays on various aspects of Carter's work, which comprise an intelligent and wide-ranging commentary.

Smith, Joan. Introduction to *Shaking a Leg: Collected Writings by Angela Carter.* London: Chatto & Windus, 1997. A good essay on Carter's critical work, linking her social commentary to major themes in her long fiction.

Joyce Cary

Born: Londonderry, Ireland; December 7, 1888
Died: Oxford, England; March 29, 1957

Principal long fiction · *Aissa Saved*, 1932; *An American Visitor*, 1933; *The African Witch*, 1936; *Castle Corner*, 1938; *Mister Johnson*, 1939; *Charley Is My Darling*, 1940; *A House of Children*, 1941; *Herself Surprised*, 1941; *To Be a Pilgrim*, 1942; *The Horse's Mouth*, 1944, 1957; *The Moonlight*, 1946; *A Fearful Joy*, 1949; *Prisoner of Grace*, 1952; *Except the Lord*, 1953; *Not Honour More*, 1955; *The Captive and the Free*, 1959 (Winnifred Davin, editor); *Cock Jarvis*, 1974 (A. G. Bishop, editor).

Other literary forms · All of Joyce Cary's short stories published under his own name are contained in *Spring Song and Other Stories* (1960, Winnifred Davin, editor). Ten early stories published under the pseudonym Thomas Joyce are not included. More than half a dozen of these stories, which deal with bohemian life in Paris, Cary sold to the *Saturday Evening Post* (1920) in order to support his serious writing. Cary's self-admitted formula for these "potboilers" was a little sentiment, a little incident, and surprise.

Cary also published three booklets of verse and many essays, the latter appearing in such places as *Harper's Magazine*, *The New Yorker*, and the *Sunday Times*. The most significant pieces of Cary's occasional writing have been gathered by A. G. Bishop into a volume of *Selected Essays* (1976). This volume is of interest to the literary student because it includes some samples of Cary's practical criticism and of his views on the theory and practice of writing, as well as interesting material about his background and political views. *Art and Reality* (1958) is a sequence of meditations on aesthetics that Cary composed for the 1956 Clark Lectures at Cambridge University but was too ill to deliver.

Cary's other nonfiction mainly articulates his views on the philosophy and practice of politics, concerning itself with such issues as history, imperialism, and war. These works include *Power in Men* (1939), *The Case for African Freedom* (1941; reprinted with other essays about Africa in 1962), *Process of Real Freedom* (1943), and *Memoir of the Bobotes* (1960). These works shed light upon Cary's treatment of ethical and political issues in his fiction. A collection of Cary's unpublished manuscripts, papers, letters, and diaries is in the possession of the Bodleian Library at Oxford University.

Achievements · Cary's major artistic achievements—*Mister Johnson* and the novels *Herself Surprised*, *To Be a Pilgrim*, and *The Horse's Mouth* composing a trilogy—are realistic books that reflect social, moral, and historical change as well as technical performances that embody the formal and linguistic innovations of literary modernism. This distinctive mixture of traditional realism and modernist style is Cary's principal legacy as a novelist. Although he experiments with techniques such as stream of consciousness, interior monologue, disrupted chronology, shifting point of view, and present-tense narration, he consistently rivets the action—past or present—to a particular historical and social context. The continuity of exterior events never completely disintegrates, though it is sometimes difficult to reconstruct. To be sure, the various novels offer the reader different perspectives and interpretations of social reality. The intention, however, is not to obscure that reality or to render it relative to the subjectivity of the narrator, but rather to layer it, to augment its texture. Cary's perspective, therefore, is not nihilistic. His experiments in the trilogy form enhance the reader's sense of dwelling in a shared or intersubjective reality, even though each novel in the series adroitly captures the idiosyncratic perspective of its first-person narrator. Cary refuses to endorse any sort of feckless relativism (he was repelled by the moral defeatism and philosophical pessimism of such post-World War I writers as Aldous Huxley) and yet manages to incorporate into his writing the innovations of modernism. His self-proclaimed comedy of freedom ex-

Library of Congress

tends the range of traditional realism and offers new possibilities for the form of fiction.

Recognition of Cary's literary merit came only late in his life. Under the pseudonym Thomas Joyce, he published in the *Saturday Evening Post* several stories based on his youthful experiences of bohemian life in Paris, but he considered these efforts to be potboilers rather than serious pieces of fiction. The journal, in fact, rejected his subsequent stories for being too "literary." Not unitl 1932, when Cary was forty-three, was his first novel, *Aissa Saved,* published. It was not a commercial success. He continued to produce novels, and finally, in 1941, after the publication of *A House of Children,* his seventh novel, he won his first literary award: the James Tait Black Memorial Prize for the best British novel of the year.

After this award, Cary's reputation increased steadily. In 1950, *The Adam International Review* devoted a special issue to his work, and in 1953, Walter Allen's seminal study of his work, *Joyce Cary,* appeared. Cary enjoyed a successful lecture tour in the United States (1951), and he was asked to deliver the 1956 Clark Lectures at Cambridge University. During his lifetime, he was praised by such prestigious critics as Allen, John Dover Wilson, and Barbara Hardy. Since his death in 1957, Cary scholarship has grown steadily. In 1963, *Modern Fiction Studies* devoted a special issue to his work, and there are numerous books, articles, and theses dealing with Cary's achievements.

Biography · Arthur Joyce Lunel Cary was born in Londonderry, Ireland, on December 7, 1888. His ancestors had been Irish landlords since the early seventeenth century. The Arrears Act of 1882, however, plunged his grandfather into ruinous debt, and his father, Arthur Cary, a prospective civil engineer, moved the family to London shortly after Cary's birth. There the nexus of traditional family life was Cromwell House, owned by Cary's Uncle Tristam. Cary never lost contact with his Irish roots and the legacy of his family history, spending childhood vacations at his grandparents' cottages in Ireland and gaining familiarity with Devon, England, the point of his family's origin. These settings, along with the familial stability and continuity they represented, were important to Cary's fiction. *Castle Corner* deals with a half century of life in Ireland, England, and Africa, moving from the 1870's to the brink of World War I; *Charley Is My Darling* deals with the World War II evacuation of thousands of London children to Devon; *A House of Children* is a poetical evocation of childhood based on Cary's recollections of his Irish vacations; and *The Moonlight* and his two trilogies are set mainly in Devon.

A tragic note entered Cary's life when his mother died in 1898, and his sense of life's miseries was compounded when his stepmother died five years later. His performance as a student at Hurstleigh and Clifton was average at best, though he did show interest in telling stories and writing poetry. In 1904, at the age of fifteen, he went on a sketching trip with his aunt to France, which was his first exposure to Impressionist painting. Two years later, he went to Paris as an art student and experienced bohemian life. He then went to Edinburgh for formal artistic training; at the age of twenty, he decided that he was not good enough to be a first-rate painter: Writing would be his vocation and painting his hobby. *Verses by Arthur Cary*, a decidedly mediocre effort, was published in 1908.

These early experiences were later exploited in his fiction. The first fictional pieces he published were short stories which dealt with bohemian life in Paris, and *The Horse's Mouth*, his portrait of the artist, not only draws some of its material from his life in Paris and Edinburgh but also bases its style on a literary approximation of Impressionism. Cary's highly developed visual imagination is evident throughout his writings.

In accordance with his choice of vocation, Cary went to Oxford University in 1909 to take a degree in law, intending to provide himself with an alternate career should his literary attempts fail. His fourth-class degree, however, the lowest one possible, debarred him from pursuing a gainful career in either the civil service or the field of education. In 1912, the Balkan War erupted, and Cary decided to go to the aid of Montenegro, Yugoslavia, feeling that the firsthand experience of war would offer a writer valuable material. *Memoir of the Bobotes* is a nonfictional account of his Montenegrin sojourn. He returned to England in 1913, entered the Nigerian service in 1914, and fought against the Germans in West Africa. In 1916, in England on leave from Nigeria, he married Gertrude Ogilvie, whom he had met in Oxford. He returned to Nigeria before the end of the year.

Cary's African years (1914-1919) had a formative influence on the shape of his fiction. *Aissa Saved* deals with the collision between Western religion and African paganism; *An American Visitor* explores the difference between the Western idealization of the noble savage and the African reality of tribal life; *The African Witch* reveals the prejudices of some Britons in Africa; *Mister Johnson* depicts the vibrantly imaginative existence of a young black clerk with "civilized" aspirations and his tragicomic relationship with District Officer Rudbeck; and *Cock Jarvis* dramatizes the experience of a "Joseph Conrad character in a Rudyard Kipling role," a morally sensitive liberal whose paternalistic and imperialistic attitudes do not coincide with the historical situation in twentieth century Africa. Without his experience as an assistant district officer in Nigeria–a position which required him to work as a policeman, tax collector, judge, administrator, census taker, mapmaker, and road builder, not to mention someone capable of dealing tactfully with the mysteries of witchcraft and juju–Cary would not have developed the sympathetic imagination that allowed him to understand and record the African point of view with sensitivity and knowledge. Not surprisingly, his long residence in Africa put some strain on his marriage; his first two children, born in England during his absence, were virtual strangers to him. Despite occasional outbreaks of tempestuous disagreement, Cary and his wife shared a love that carried them through several adversities and the birth of three more children. Gertrude died in 1949. Cary's ability to render vividly the perspectives of women is particularly evident in *Herself Surprised, The Moonlight, A Fearful Joy,* and *Prisoner of Grace*; in part, this ability derives from the depth and intensity of his relationship with his wife.

In 1920, Cary returned to England, and he, his wife, and their two sons moved to a house in Oxford, where Cary lived until his death. After the publication of his first novel, *Aissa Saved,* in 1932, he produced novels at the impressive rate of almost one a year. His literary reputation increased steadily after he won the James Tait Memorial Prize in 1941.

Analysis · The entirety of Joyce Cary's fiction is, as the author himself suggests, about one world–the world of freedom, "the active creative freedom which maintains the world in being . . . the source of moral responsibility and of good and evil . . . of injustice and love, of a special comedy and a special tragic dilemma which can never be solved." It is "a world in everlasting conflict between the new idea and the old allegiances, new arts and new inventions against the old establishment." Cary sees human beings as condemned to be free and society as perpetually poised between the extremes of anarchy and totalitarianism. Because creative imagination is of the highest value, the individual must rebel against the forces that threaten to trammel or stultify the free expression of his imagination, whether the forces be those of the established church, the state, tribalism, nationalism, conventional morality, or whatever. Throughout his novels, Cary dramatizes the tension between the intuitive and the analytical, the imaginative and the conceptual, the concrete and the abstract, and the vital and the mechanical.

Cary's romanticism, however, is not naïve. He is acutely aware that the tension between freedom and authority is necessary, that the will to create is continually in conflict with the will to preserve. His first trilogy, for example, sympathetically portrays a survivalist, a conservative, and a rebel. Yet even radically different characters must enact their lives and secure their salvation or damnation in the moral world of freedom, imagination, and love.

In *Joyce Cary* (1973), R. W. Noble conveniently divides Cary's novels into five categories, according to their subject matter: Africa and empire; youth and childhood; women and social change; the artist and society; and politics and the individual. The novels of Africa and empire are substantial achievements but not major novels of the twentieth century, save for *Mister Johnson.*

Cock Jarvis · *Cock Jarvis,* Cary's first effort, was abandoned in 1937; it was published posthumously. The problem with the novel was that Cary could not construct a plot adequate to encompass the character of Cock Jarvis, for at this point Cary had not assimilated the modernist style. Without recourse to first-person narration or stream of consciousness, his eminently interesting character was locked into a melodramatic and conventional plot structure. Whether Jarvis was to murder his wife and her lover, forgive them, or commit suicide, Cary never decided; none of the resolutions would solve the essential problem, which is technical.

Aissa Saved · *Aissa Saved*, with its seventy or more characters, has so many cultural conflicts, disconnected episodes, and thematic concerns that the aesthetic experience for the reader is congested and finally diffuse. Its analysis of the transforming powers of religious conversion, however, is penetrating and ironic. The juxtaposition of Aissa, an African convert who understands the sacrifice of Christ in a dangerously literal way and ingests Him as she would a lover, and Hilda, an English convert, is effective. Though the backgrounds of the two converts are divergent, they both end by participating in gruesome blood sacrifices. The novel as a whole, however, suffers from two problems. First, its central action, which revolves around attempts to end a devastating drought, cannot unify the manifold details of the plot: the cultural, religious, and military conflicts between Christians, pagans, and Muslims. Second, its tone is somewhat ambiguous. It is not clear whether the novel is meant to be an outright attack on missionaries and thus an ironic and cynical treatment of Aissa's so-called salvation or a more moderate assessment of the transforming powers of religious conversion.

An American Visitor · *An American Visitor* has more manageable intentions. The book effectively dramatizes the difference between practical and theoretical knowledge and concrete and abstract knowledge. The preconceptions of the American visitor, Marie Hasluck, are not experientially based and are contrasted with the practices of the local district officer, Monkey Bewsher, who strives to strike a balance between freedom and authority. Even though reality forces Marie to abandon some of her pseudoanthropological beliefs, utopianism is so much a part of her psychological complex that she turns to religious pacifism for compensation, a turning that has tragic consequences for the pragmatic, imaginative, and somewhat self-deluded officer.

The African Witch · *The African Witch* is more panoramic in scope. It deals with the social, political, and religious life of both Europeans and Africans. The plot revolves around the election of a new emir: The Oxford-educated Aladai is pitted against Salé, a Muslim. Aladai's Western demeanor offends many of the Europeans; they prefer Africans to be noble savages rather than liberal rationalists. In the end, the forces of juju and political corruption prevail. Aladai is rejected and chooses a self-sacrificial death, presumably abandoning his rationalism and lapsing into stereotype. The conclusion of the novel is not convincingly wrought.

Castle Corner · *Castle Corner* is part of a projected trilogy or quartet of novels which Cary decided not to continue. Covering a half century of life in Ireland, England, and Africa, the novel moves from the 1870's to the brink of World War I. Because of its congeries of characters and variety of themes, the book resists summary. In general, however, it puts the world of individual freedom and responsibility in collision with the world of historical change, but it has too much explicit debate and attitudinizing to be dramatically effective.

Generally, Cary's novels of Africa and empire are competent but not exceptional fiction. More materially than formally satisfying, they suffer finally from a lack of cohesion and unity; the form is not adequate to the content, which is rich and detailed. Nevertheless, these novels well delineate the everlasting conflict between new ideas and the old allegiances, the necessary tension between freedom and authority, reflecting Cary's characteristic preoccupation with the struggle for imaginative freedom on a personal, moral, social, religious, and political level.

Mister Johnson · *Mister Johnson* is an exceptional piece of fiction. The character from whom the novel takes its title, as Cary points out in the preface, is a young clerk who turns his life into a romance, a poet who creates for himself a glorious destiny. Johnson is a supreme embodiment of imaginative vitality and, as such, a prototype for the picaresque heroes in Cary's later novels. Even though Johnson's fate is ultimately tragic, his mind is full of active invention until the end.

The novel occupies a pivotal moment in the dialectic of Cary's art, for not only is the content exceptional—Mr. Johnson is an unforgettable character; his adventures indelibly impress themselves upon the reader—but also the innovative form is adequate to that content. In *Mister Johnson*, Cary deploys third-person, present-tense narration. He notes in the preface that he chose this style because it carries the reader unreflectingly on the stream of events, creating an agitated rather than a contemplative mood. Because Johnson lives in the present and is completely immersed in the vibrant immediacy of his experience, he does not judge. Nor does the reader judge, since the present-tense narration makes him swim gaily with Johnson on the surface of life.

Cary's choice of third-person narration, which he does not discuss in the preface, is equally strategic. The first-person style that he uses so effectively in some of his later novels would have been appropriate. By using the third-person style, he is able not only to give the African scene a solidity of local detail but also to enter into the mind of Rudbeck, so that the reader can empathize with his conscientious decision to shoot Johnson, a personal act, rather than hanging him, an official act. The impact of the tragic outcome is thereby intensified.

The novel traces the rise and fall of Mr. Johnson, chief clerk of Fada in Nigeria. A southerner in northern Nigeria and an African in European clothes, he has aspirations to be civilized and claims to be a friend of District Officer Rudbeck, the Wazirin Fada, the King of England, and anyone who vaguely likes him. Johnson's aspirations, however, are not in consonance with his finances, and his marriage, machinations, schemes, stories, parties, petty thefts, capital crime, and irrepressible good spirits become part of the exuberant but relentless rhythm of events that lead to his death. For Johnson, as Cary suggests, life is simply perpetual experience, which he soaks into himself through all five senses at once and produces again in the form of reflections, comments, songs, and jokes. His vitality is beyond good and evil, equally capable of expressing itself anarchistically or creatively.

Rudbeck, too, is a man of imagination, though not as liberated from constraint as Johnson. His passion for road building becomes obsessive once Johnson's imagination further fuels his own. He goes so far as to misappropriate funds in order to realize his dream. Without the infectious influence of Johnson's creativity, Rudbeck would never have rebelled against the forces of conservatism. The completed road demonstrates the power of creative imagination.

The road, however, brings crime as well as trade, and in his disillusionment, Rudbeck fires Johnson for embezzlement. In the end, Johnson murders a man and is sentenced to death by Rudbeck. Johnson wants his friend Rudbeck to kill him personally, and Rudbeck eventually complies with his clerk's wish, putting his career as district officer in jeopardy by committing this compassionate but illegal act.

Charley Is My Darling · After *Mister Johnson*, Cary chose domestic settings for his novels. His novels of youth and childhood, *Charley Is My Darling* and *A House of Children*, are set in Devon and Ireland. The former deals with the evacuation of thousands of London children to Devon during World War II; the latter is a poetical evocation of childhood vacations in Ireland.

In *Charley Is My Darling*, the main character, Charley, like Mr. Johnson, is thrust into an alien world, and the urban values he represents are contrasted with the rural values represented by Lina Allchin, the well-intentioned supervisor of the evacuees. Charley, whose head is shaved as part of a delousing process, is isolated from his peers and consequently channels his imaginative energies into crime and ultimately into anarchistic destruction in order to gain acceptability. Because neither school nor society offers him any outlet for his creative individuality, it expresses itself in violence, an expression which is perhaps a microcosmic commentary on the causes of war.

A House of Children · *A House of Children* is autobiographical. Technically innovative, it has no omniscient point of view and relies instead on one central consciousness, which narrates the story in the first person. This was to become Cary's characteristic narrative style. The novel has a poetic rather than a linear coherence, depending on a series of revelations or epiphanies rather than on plot. Cary obviously learned a great deal from James Joyce's *A Portrait of the Artist as a Young Man* (1916), which he had read in Africa.

The Moonlight and *A Fearful Joy* · *The Moonlight* and *A Fearful Joy* are two novels about women and social change. The former, a response to Leo Tolstoy's interpretation of women in *The Kreutzer Sonata* (1890), deals with the familiar theme of law and order versus personal freedom; Ludwig van Beethoven's "Moonlight Sonata" represents romantic love and womanhood. The latter chronicles Tabitha Baskett's life from 1890 to 1948 and is set in southeast England and the Midlands. The roguish Bonser, one of her paramours, is a memorable character.

These novels were followed by Cary's masterpiece, a trilogy that focuses on the artist and society. Cary designed the trilogy, he said, to show three characters, not only in themselves but also as seen by one another, the object being to get a three-dimensional depth and force of character. Each novel adapts its style to the perceptual, emotive, and cognitive idiosyncrasies of its first-person narrator. *Herself Surprised*, the narrative of Sara Monday, is reminiscent of Daniel Defoe's *Moll Flanders* (1722), and its autobiographical style is ideally suited to dramatize the ironic disparity between Sara's conventional moral attitudes and her "surprising," unconventional behavior. *To Be a Pilgrim*, the narrative of Tom Wilcher, is akin to a Victorian memoir, and the formal politeness of its language reflects the repressed and conservative nature of its narrator. *The Horse's Mouth*, the narrative of Gulley Jimson, uses stream of consciousness and verbally imitates the Impressionist style of painting, an imitation which strikingly reveals the dazzling power of Gulley's visual imagination. The entire trilogy is a virtuoso performance, underscoring Cary's talent for rendering characters from the inside.

Herself Surprised · Sara Monday is the eternal female—wife, mother, homemaker, mistress, and friend. In accordance with her working-class position as a cook, she consistently describes her world in domestic images and metaphors—the sky for her is as warm as new milk and as still as water in a goldfish bowl. Her desire to improve her socioeconomic lot is a major motivating factor in her life, and this desire often encourages her to operate outside the bounds of morality and law. Sara, however, is not a moral revolutionary; her values mirror her Victorian education. In her terms, she is constantly "sinning" and constantly "surprised" by sin, but in terms of the reader's understanding of her, she is a lively and sensuous being with an unconscious genius for survival who succumbs, sometimes profitably, sometimes disastrously, to immediate temptation. Her language of sin, which is vital and concrete, belies her language of repentance, which is mechanical and abstract. Nevertheless, Sara, unlike Moll Flanders, does not seem to be a conscious opportunist and manipulator.

Sara betters her socioeconomic status by securing a middle-class marriage to Matthew Monday. The marriage, however, does not prevent her from having affairs with Hickson, a millionaire, and Jimson, an artist. (The narrative description of these "surprises" is exquisitely managed.) Though she sincerely believes in conventional morality, that morality is no match for her joy of life. Cary also shows the negative aspects of Sara's mode of being. Like other characters in his fiction, she is a creative being whose imaginative vitality borders on the anarchistic and irresponsible. She virtually ruins her first husband and makes little effort to keep contact with her four daughters.

After her violent relationship with Gulley Jimson, Sara becomes a cook for the lawyer Wilcher and is about to marry him when his niece has Sara jailed for theft. She had been stealing in order to purchase art supplies for Gulley and to pay for his son's education. Her will to live is thus an implicit critique of the conventional morality that her conscious mind mechanically endorses. She is a survivalist par excellence.

To Be a Pilgrim · Unlike the events in *Herself Surprised,* those in *To Be a Pilgrim* are not presented chronologically. The narrative is layered, juxtaposing Wilcher's present situation of imminent death with the social, political, and religious history of his times. The disrupted chronology poignantly accentuates Wilcher's realization, which comes too late, that he ought to have been a pilgrim, that possessions have been his curse. Now his repressed energies can only counterproductively express themselves in exhibitionism and arson. Marriage to Sara Monday, which might have been a redemptive force in his life, is now impossible, for she has already been incarcerated for her crimes.

In the present time of the novel, Wilcher is a virtual prisoner at Tolbrook Manor, the family home. His niece Ann, a doctor and the daughter of his dead brother Edward, a liberal politician whose life Wilcher tried to manage, is his warden. She marries her cousin Robert, a progressive farmer devoted to the utilitarian goal of making the historic manor a viable commercial enterprise, much to Wilcher's chagrin. Ultimately, Wilcher is forced to recognize that change is the essence of life and that his conservative fixation with tradition, the family, and moral propriety has sapped him of his existential energy, of his ability to be a pilgrim.

The Horse's Mouth · *The Horse's Mouth,* a portrait of the artist as an old man, is justly celebrated as Cary's most remarkable achievement. (Although the Carfax edition of Cary's novels is complete and authoritative, the revised Rainbird edition of *The Horse's Mouth,* 1957, illustrated by the author, includes a chapter—"The Old Strife at Plant's"—which Cary had previously deleted.) Its reputation has been enhanced by the excellent film version in which Alec Guiness plays the role of Gulley Jimson.

Gulley Jimson is a pilgrim; he accepts the necessity of the fall into freedom with joy and energy, conceiving of it as a challenge to his imagination and thereby seeking to impose aesthetic order on experiential chaos. For Gulley, anything that is part of the grimy reality of the contingent world—fried-fish shops, straw, chicken boxes, dirt, oil, mud—can inspire a painting. The Impressionist style of his narrative reflects his vocation, for he mainly construes his world in terms of physical imagery, texture, solidity, perspective, color, shape, and line, merging Blakean vision with Joycean stream of consciousness. Gulley's sensibility is perpetually open to novelty, and his life affirms the existential value of becoming, for he identifies with the creative process rather than with the finished product. His energies focus on the future, on starting new works, not on dwelling on past accomplishments. Even though he is destitute, he refuses to paint in the lucrative style of his Sara Monday period.

Gulley is also a born con artist, a streetwise survivor. He is not adverse to stealing, cheating, swindling, blackmailing, or even murdering if his imaginative self-expression is at stake. He is completely comfortable in a brutal, violent, and unjust world. His vision, therefore, has limitations. His pushing Sara down the stairs to her death shows the anarchistic irresponsibility implicit in regarding life as merely spiritual fodder for the imagination. Moreover, Gulley lacks historical consciousness. Even though the novel chronicles his life before and after the beginning of World War II, Gulley seems to have no conception of who Adolf Hitler is and what he represents.

For the most part, this novel clearly champions the creative individual and criticizes the repressive society that inhibits him, although Cary is always fairminded enough to imply the limitations of his characters. Gulley Jimson remains a paradigm of energetic vitality, an imaginative visionary who blasts through generation to regeneration, redeeming the poverty of the contingent world and liberating consciousness from the malady of the quotidian. The entire trilogy is a masterpiece; the created worlds of the three narrators mutually supplement and criticize one another, stressing the difficulty of achieving a workable balance between the will to survive, to preserve, and to create.

Prisoner of Grace · Cary's second trilogy—*Prisoner of Grace, Except the Lord*, and *Not Honour More*—deals with politics and the individual. It is a commentary on radical liberalism, evangelicalism, and crypto-Fascism, moving from the 1860's to the 1930's and involving the lives of three characters (Nina Nimmo/Latter, Chester Nimmo, and Jim Latter) whose lives are inextricably enmeshed, unlike those of the characters of the first trilogy.

In *Prisoner of Grace*, Nina Nimmo (Nina Latter by the end of her narrative) tries to protect and defend both her lovers: the radical liberal politician Nimmo, maligned for his alleged opportunism and demagoguery, and the crypto-Fascist Latter, a military man obsessed by a perverted notion of honor. The time span of the novel covers the Boer War, the Edwardian reform government, the World War I victory, the prosperous aftermath, and the 1926 General Strike. The action takes place mainly in Devon, where Chester Nimmo makes his mark as a politician and becomes a member of Parliament, and in London, where Nimmo eventually becomes a cabinet minister.

Nina, carrying the child of her cousin Jim Latter, marries the lower-class Chester Nimmo, who is handsomely remunerated for rescuing the fallen woman in order to secure a respectable future for the child. Nina never loves Nimmo but is converted to his cause by his political and religious rhetoric. She writes her account in order to anticipate and rebut criticism of his conduct.

Thrust into the duplicitous and morally ambiguous world of politics, she succumbs both to Chester's ideals, values, morals, and beliefs and to his lusts, lies, schemes, and maneuverings, seemingly incapable of distinguishing the one from the other, as is the reader, since he can only rely on Nina's unreliable account. Unlike the disingenuousness of Sara Monday in *Herself Surprised*, which the reader can easily disentangle–Sara's sensuous vitality gives the lie to the maxims of conventional piety she mechanically utters–Nina's disingenuousness is a fundamental part of her character. Nina, like Chester, is both sincere and hypocritical, genuinely moral and meretriciously rhetorical, an embodiment of the political personality. Even the politics of their marriage parallel in miniature the politics of the outside world.

Nina is a prisoner of grace once she has converted to the belief that Chester's being is infused with grace and that his religious and political beliefs enjoy moral rectitude by definition. Her love for Jim is also a grace that imprisons her and ultimately impels her to divorce Chester and marry Jim. The reader, too, is a prisoner of grace, since he cannot get outside of Nina's "political" point of view and thus cannot separate truth and falsity, the authorial implication being that the two are necessarily confused and interdependent in the political personality. Like Sara, Nina is a survivalist, and after she becomes adulterously involved with Nimmo, she, like Sara, is murdered by a man whom she had helped. Survivalism has limits.

Except the Lord · *Except the Lord*, the story of Nimmo's childhood and youth, takes place in the 1860's and 1870's. It is the history of a boy's mind and soul rather than one of political events. Like *To Be a Pilgrim*, it takes the form of a Victorian memoir in which the mature narrator explores the events and forces that caused him to become what he is. Nurtured in an environment of poverty, fundamentalist faith, and familial love, Nimmo becomes in turn a radical preacher, labor agitator, and liberal politician.

According to the first verse of Psalm 127, "Except the Lord build the house, they labour in vain that would build it; except the Lord keep the city, the watchman waketh but in vain." Since this novel stops before the events of *Prisoner of Grace* and *Not Honour More* begin, and since it principally induces a sympathetic response to Nimmo, the reader has a difficult time interpreting the significance of the title. He tends to see Nimmo differently after having read the account of the latter's youth, but he is still uncertain whether Nimmo is a knight of faith or an opportunistic antinomian. The trilogy as a whole seems to suggest that Chester is both.

Not Honour More · *Not Honour More* is the story of a soldier, Jim Latter, who sees the world in dichotomous terms and cannot accept the necessarily ambiguous transaction between the realms of freedom and authority. The novel is a policewoman's transcript of Jim's confession; it is dictated as he awaits execution for the murder of Nina, provoked by his discovery of her adulterous relationship with Nimmo, her ex-husband. His language is a combination of clipped military prose, hysterical defensiveness, and invective against both the decadence of British society around the time of the 1926 General Strike and the corruption of politicians such as Nimmo.

Latter believes in authority, in imposing law and order on the masses. He has no sense of the moral ambiguity of human behavior, no sense of the complexity of human motivation. A self-proclaimed spiritual descendent of the Cavalier poet Richard Lovelace, Jim believes that his murder of Nina proves that he loves honor more. He conceives of the murder as an execution, a moral act, whereas it is in reality a perversion of honor, a parody of the code that Lovelace represents. District Officer Rudbeck, of *Mister Johnson*, is by comparison a truly honorable man: He personalizes rather than ritualizes Mr. Johnson's death. Because Jim believes in the rectitude of authoritarians with superior gifts, he is a crypto-Fascist. The best that can be said of him is that he has the courage of his misplaced convictions.

Throughout his novels, Cary focused his creative energies on human beings who are condemned to be free, to enact their lives somewhere between the extremes of anarchism and conformity. His achievement demonstrates that it is possible for a novelist to be at once stylistically sophisticated, realistically oriented, and ethically involved.

Greig E. Henderson

Other major works

SHORT FICTION: *Spring Song and Other Stories,* 1960 (Winnifred Davin, editor).

POETRY: *Verses by Arthur Cary,* 1908; *Marching Soldier,* 1945; *The Drunken Sailor,* 1947.

NONFICTION: *Power in Men,* 1939; *The Case for African Freedom,* 1941, 1962; *Process of Real Freedom,* 1943; *Britain and West Africa,* 1946; *Art and Reality,* 1958; *Memoir of the Bobotes,* 1960; *Selected Essays,* 1976 (A. G. Bishop, editor).

Bibliography

Adams, Hazard. *Joyce Cary's Trilogies: Pursuit of the Particular Real.* Tallahassee, Fla.: University Presses of Florida, 1983. Adams attempts to rescue Cary from what he views as misplaced critical emphasis by focusing on the particularity of Cary's two trilogies. Whereas, he says, earlier critics have attempted to interpret Cary's fiction by using the abstract ideas found in his nonfiction as a guide, Adams saves his theorizing until the last chapter. The book also includes two appendixes devoted to chronologies of the trilogies.

Echeruo, Michael J. *Joyce Cary and the Novel of Africa.* London: Longman, 1973. Echeruo places Cary's African novels in the tradition of the foreign novel and argues that they have a special place in this genre. Provides new insights into the growth of Cary's art as well as valuable criticism of Cary's African novels.

Foster, Malcolm. *Joyce Cary: A Biography.* London: Michael Joseph, 1969. Written in four parts, this is an exhaustive and informative study of Cary; Foster had access to the Cary collection at the Bodleian Library in Oxford, England. Critical discussion of each novel is brief and incomplete; however, Foster offers some new insights into Cary's novels.

Hall, Dennis. *Joyce Cary: A Reappraisal.* London: Macmillan, 1983. Makes the point that there are two Carys: one the thinker and the other the artist. This full-length study discusses all of Cary's novels with conscientious thoroughness. Hall is sympathetic to Cary, but notes the unevenness of his work and concludes that Cary is "his own worst enemy." Contains a helpful bibliography for the Cary scholar.

Levitt, Annette S. *The Intertextuality of Joyce Cary's "The Horse's Mouth."* Lewiston, N.Y.: E. Mellen Press, 1993. A thorough examination of Cary's novel. Includes bibliographical references and an index.

Majumdar, Bimalendu. *Joyce Cary: An Existentialist Approach.* Atlantic Highlands, N.J.: Humanities Press, 1982. A scholarly study of Cary devoted to critical appraisal of his work. Majumdar focuses on the central existential theme in Cary's novels: the uniqueness of the individual who "refuses to fit into some system constructed by rational thought."

O'Brien, Colin Joseph. *Art and Reality in the Novels of Joyce Cary.* New Delhi: Commonwealth, 1990. An excellent critical study of Cary. Includes bibliographical references.

Roby, Kinley E. *Joyce Cary.* Boston: Twayne, 1984. After providing an overview of Cary's biography, this brief volume surveys Cary's fiction, all of which, Roby declares, is concerned with the "unchangeable changeableness of life." Roby also gives glancing attention to Cary's literary criticism and journalism. The book includes a chronology and a selected bibliography.

G. K. Chesterton

Born: London, England; May 29, 1874
Died: Beaconsfield, England; June 14, 1936

Principal long fiction · *The Napoleon of Notting Hill,* 1904; *The Man Who Was Thursday: A Nightmare,* 1908; *The Ball and the Cross,* 1909; *Manalive,* 1912; *The Wisdom of Father Brown,* 1914; *The Flying Inn,* 1914; *The Incredulity of Father Brown,* 1926; *The Return of Don Quixote,* 1927; *The Secret of Father Brown,* 1927; *The Floating Admiral,* 1931 (with others); *The Scandal of Father Brown,* 1935.

Other literary forms · G. K. Chesterton was a prolific writer, and besides novels he produced works in numerous other genres. Throughout his life he wrote poetry; his first two published books were poetical works. He also produced short fiction, especially detective stories. In addition he wrote plays, but he was not always comfortable in this medium since he was at heart an essayist. He published a large number of nonfiction works in such areas as autobiography, biography, essays, history, and literary criticism.

Achievements · Among the primary achievements of Chesterton's long writing career are the wide range of subjects written about, the large number of genres employed, and the sheer volume of publications produced. Chesterton was primarily a journalist and essayist who wrote articles, book reviews, and essays for newspapers and periodicals. Yet he also wrote poetry, biographies, plays, history, and literary criticism as well as novels and short stories.

In his approach to fiction Chesterton rejected the "modern realistic short story" and the realistic novel. Instead, in the first instance, he turned to the detective short story and wrote extensively on its legitimacy as a literary art form. Chesterton himself helped to develop the definition of the detective story; he contended that it was the sole popular literary structure expressing "some sense of the poetry of modern life," and he popularized detective fiction in his fifty-one Father Brown stories and short novels.

As a novelist, Chesterton argued that "sensational novels are the most moral part of modern fiction." He liked tales about death, secret groups, theft, adventure, and fantasy. There was no genre in his day that embraced his ideas and so he crafted his own literary structure, the "fantastic novel." In his novels Chesterton stressed such themes and issues as family, science versus religion, moral and political integrity, and local patriotism versus empire building. There are also subthemes such as the common man, nature, and womanhood. Above all, Chesterton's novels illustrate his "love of ideas."

Biography · Gilbert Keith Chesterton's family was middle class. His father, Edward, was an estate agent who liked literature and art, and his mother, Marie, was the daughter of a Wesleyan lay preacher. Both parents were Unitarians but baptized their son in the Anglican Church. Chesterton attended the Colet Court Preparation school and then in 1887 went to St. Paul's School. His academic record was not good, but

he finally began to demonstrate literary capability as a member of the Junior Debating Club, which he and some of his fellow students established during the summer of 1890. Two years later he won the Milton Prize for his poem "St. Francis Xavier."

Between 1892 and 1895 he attended the Slade School to study art and took some courses in French, English, and Latin at University College, London. However, except for English, he did not do well, and he left the Slade School in 1895 without taking a degree. For the next six years he worked in publishing houses reading authors' manuscripts, and at night he did his own writing. In 1900 his first two books appeared, *Greybeards at Play: Literature and Art for Old Gentlemen—Rhymes and Sketches* and *The Wild Knight and Other Poems,* both works of poetry. The next year he began to submit articles regularly to the *Speaker* and the *Daily News* and thus started a career as a journalist that was to last until his death. He became known for his opposition to the Boer War and his support of small nations.

In 1901 Chesterton married Frances Blogg after a courtship of five years. The couple lived first in London, and then in 1909 they moved to Beaconsfield, forty miles outside London. They had no offspring, but they enjoyed the company of the children of their friends, relatives, and neighbors.

In 1904 Chesterton's first novel, *The Napoleon of Notting Hill* was published, and by 1914 he had written five more novels and numerous other works, including biographies (*Robert Browning*, 1903, and *Charles Dickens: A Critical Study*, 1906) as well as *Heretics* (1905), which criticized what he saw as the mistakes of some contemporary writers, *Orthodoxy* (1908), a defense and support of Christianity, and a study of his friend and disputant, *George Bernard Shaw* (1909). In 1911 the first of his volumes of detective stories appeared, featuring a Catholic priest, Father Brown, as the sleuth.

Chesterton wrote his best work prior to 1914; in November of that year he became gravely ill with a form of dropsy, and it was not until June that he recovered. During the years after World War I, he traveled, visiting Palestine, the United States, Poland, and Italy. In 1922 he became a Roman Catholic, a faith which had attracted him for some time, as is reflected in his writing. The most notable works of his later years are *The Everlasting Man* (1925) and another biography, *St. Thomas Aquinas* (1933). Chesterton's health declined during the first half of 1936, and on June 14 he died in Beaconsfield.

Analysis · Between 1904 and 1927 G. K. Chesterton wrote six full-length novels (not including the long Father Brown mysteries). All of them stressed the sensational, and they illustrated life as a fight and a battle. Chesterton thought that literature should portray life as perilous rather than as something listless. Tales of death, robbery, and secret groups interested him, and he did not think that what he called the "tea table twaddle" type of novels approached the status of significant art. The sensational story "was the moral part of fiction."

Fantasy was an important part of Chesterton's novels, and the methodology used in his long fiction emphasized adventure, suspense, fantasy, characterization, satire, narrative technique, and humor. He needed a medium to employ these techniques, so he produced the "fantastic novel." Fanstasy also involves ideas, and in all Chesterton's novels ideas are a central, indispensable feature.

Chesterton's novels served as a vehicle for the dissemination of whatever were his political and social ideas at the time, and to this extent they were propagandistic. His critics have had difficulty in deciding the merits of his various writings in terms of separating propaganda from literary art. Often he used allegory as a device for conveying his controversial ideas. Critic Ian Boyd calls Chesterton's long fiction "political fables, parables, and allegories or more simply and conveniently . . . novels."

In Chesterton's novels, the state of bachelorhood predominates; this situation is appropriate, since this status is a fundamental element of adventure. Moreover, women rarely appear in any significant roles in his long fiction. There is no female character in his first novel, *The Napoleon of Notting Hill*, while the woman in *The Man Who Was Thursday* is a passing character. In *The Ball and the Cross* and *The Flying Inn*, women are minor figures, but they do play significant roles in *Manalive* and *The Return of Don Quixote*, works that are more involved with the family and society.

The weakest of Chesterton's nondetective novels are perhaps *Manalive*, published in 1912, and *The Return of Don Quixote*, which appeared in 1927. In *The Return of Don Quixote*, Chesterton concludes that the only good future for England involves "a remarriage" of the country with the Catholic Church, as was the case in the Middle

Ages. The first three of Chesterton's novels, published between 1904 and 1909, are widely considered his best.

The Napoleon of Notting Hill · *The Napoleon of Notting Hill* is Chesterton's first novel. The first two chapters are distinct from the main plot, the first being an essay on prophecy showing the author working in a genre that was always congenial to him. The next chapter concerns a luncheon discussion between three government clerks and the former president of Nicaragua, Juan del Fuego. The content of their talk brings out one of the main themes of the novel, "the sanctity of small nations," a concept dear to Chesterton that stemmed from his opposition to the Boer War.

The subsequent death of del Fuego eliminates him from the work, but one of the three clerks, Auberon Quin, a zany individual and joker, is subsequently selected king in the futuristic utopian England of 1984, where a mild political despotism exists. The monarch is chosen by lot. Once crowned as king, Quin reorganizes the sections of London into separate municipalities and thus re-creates the smallness of medieval cities, complete with costumes and heraldry. Quin then encounters Adam Wayne, first as a youth and then as the serious-minded provost of Notting Hill, one of the municipalities; Wayne has embraced the king's "Charter of Cities" wholeheartedly.

Wayne, however, much to the dismay of the provosts of other London municipalities, refuses to give up a street in his domain, Pump Street, which contains several shops, so that a thoroughfare connecting three boroughs can be built. The result is a war, which Wayne wins by encouraging the patriotism of Pump Street residents and by following excellent strategy, despite being outnumbered by the opposing forces. Quin with his "Charter of Cities" and Wayne in his defense of Notting Hill both illustrate Chesterton's small-nation theme. The concluding chapters of the novel concern London twenty years later when the powerful and dominant Notting Hill has become corrupt; the corruption causes a revolt of subject municipalities. Wayne fights in the second war but realizes that there is no longer a noble cause involved. Conflict in the novel lies in the confrontation between Wayne and Quin, the fanatic and the joker. Wayne's opponents had accused him of being mad, but Quin asserts that the only sane individuals are himself and Wayne. The last chapter is a discussion between the two men, now dead and in the afterlife, in which Wayne argues that in order to be complete both men needed each other since the joker was without seriousness and the fanatic lacked laughter.

The Man Who Was Thursday · Chesterton's second novel, *The Man Who Was Thursday: A Nightmare*, has been described by some critics as his best. Ronald Knox called it "an extraordinary book written as if the publisher had commissioned him to write something rather like the *Pilgrim's Progress* in the style of the *Pickwick Papers*." Chesterton himself called it a protest against the pessimism of the 1880's, and this protest gives rise to one of two allegories in the novel, a personal one. The other is a public or political allegory concerning an individual's clash with a world conspiracy that does not really exist. The story concerns a young poet, Gabriel Syme, who, wishing to fight a gigantic conspiracy supposedly being plotted by anarchists, joins the police and becomes a member of an undercover squad of detectives.

As a result of a bit of trickery and luck, he becomes a member of the top anarchist council, called the Council of Seven Days because each member has the name of a day of the week. Syme's name is Thursday. The council's leader, named Sunday, is an ambiguous figure. While working to stop a bombing planned for Paris, Thursday discovers that, except for Sunday, all his fellow council members are undercover police detectives. Each had been interviewed by a figure whom nobody saw in a dark room at Scotland Yard. By the conclusion of the novel, it is revealed that Sunday is both the head of the detectives and the leader of the anarchists. Some critics seem to think that Chesterton is condoning evil in the novel, but as he later asserted, he is attempting to discover if everything is evil and whether one can find good in the pessimism of the age.

The Ball and the Cross · A review published a year after the publication of *The Ball and the Cross* stated that the novel was about two individuals dueling over "the most vital problem in the world, the truth of Christianity." This work definitely deals with religion and the nature of good and evil, subjects either ignored or ambiguously dealt with in Chesterton's first two novels. The book opens with Professor Lucifer depositing a captured Bulgarian monk, Michael, from a flying machine atop the cross and ball of St. Paul's Cathedral in London.

The plot continues with a confrontation between a Catholic highland Scot, Evan McIan, and another Scot, John Turnbull, an atheist and publisher of works on atheism. The two fight a duel over what McIan perceives as an insult to the Virgin Mary. The duelists are constantly interrupted, however; they go through a series of adventures and ultimately become friends. The book ends with the two men in an insane asylum, which is set on fire by a satanic figure. The inmates are led out by the monk, Michael, who had been a prisoner there. Ultimately Turnbull becomes a Christian. The novel contains much symbolism and many allegories. The ball on St. Paul's dome, for example, is the rational and independent world, while the cross represents religion. Martin Gardner views the work as reflecting the clash between St. Augustine's City of God, which in Chesterton's view is the Catholic Church, and the City of Man, which is dominated by Satan. The novel also attacks modern science and accuses modern culture of being "luke warm."

Allan Nelson

Other major works

NONFICTION: *The Defendant,* 1901; *Twelve Types,* 1902 (revised as *Varied Types,* 1903, and also known as *Simplicity and Tolstoy*); *Thomas Carlyle,* 1902; *Robert Louis Stevenson,* 1902 (with W. Robertson Nicoll); *Leo Tolstoy,* 1903 (with G. H. Perris and Edward Garnett); *Charles Dickens,* 1903 (with F. G. Kitton); *Robert Browning,* 1903; *Tennyson,* 1903 (with Richard Garnett); *Thackeray,* 1903 (with Lewis Melville); *G. F. Watts,* 1904; *Heretics,* 1905; *Charles Dickens: A Critical Study,* 1906; *All Things Considered,* 1908; *Orthodoxy,* 1908; *George Bernard Shaw,* 1909, rev. ed. 1935; *Tremendous Trifles,* 1909; *What's Wrong with the World,* 1910; *Alarms and Discursions,* 1910; *William Blake,* 1910; *The Ultimate Lie,* 1910; *Appreciations and Criticisms of the Works of Charles Dickens,* 1911; *A Defence of Nonsense and Other Essays,* 1911; *The Future of Religion: Mr. G. K. Chesterton's Reply to Mr. Bernard Shaw,* 1911; *The Conversion of an Anarchist,* 1912; *A Miscellany of Men,* 1912; *The Victorian Age in Literature,* 1913; *Thoughts from Chesterton,* 1913; *The Barbarism of Berlin,* 1914; *London,* 1914 (with Alvin Langdon Coburn); *Prussian Versus Belgian Culture,* 1914; *The Crimes of England,* 1915; *Letters to an Old Garibaldian,* 1915; *The So-Called Belgian Bargain,* 1915; *Divorce Versus Democracy,* 1916; *Temperance and the Great Alliance,* 1916; *A Shilling for My Thoughts,* 1916; *Lord Kitchener,* 1917; *A Short History of England,* 1917; *Utopia of Usurers and Other Essays,* 1917; *How to Help Annexation,* 1918;

Irish Impressions, 1920; *The Superstition of Divorce*, 1920; *Charles Dickens Fifty Years After*, 1920; *The Uses of Diversity*, 1920; *The New Jerusalem*, 1920; *Eugenics and Other Evils*, 1922; *What I Saw in America*, 1922; *Fancies Versus Fads*, 1923; *St. Francis of Assisi*, 1923; *The End of the Roman Road: A Pageant of Wayfarers*, 1924; *The Superstitions of the Sceptic*, 1924; *The Everlasting Man*, 1925; *William Cobbett*, 1925; *The Outline of Sanity*, 1926; *The Catholic Church and Conversion*, 1926; *A Gleaming Cohort, Being from the Words of G. K. Chesterton*, 1926; *Social Reform Versus Birth Control*, 1927; *Culture and the Coming Peril*, 1927; *Robert Louis Stevenson*, 1927; *Generally Speaking*, 1928 (essays); *Do We Agree? A Debate*, 1928 (with George Bernard Shaw); *The Thing*, 1929; *G. K. C. as M. C., Being a Collection of Thirty-seven Introductions*, 1929; *The Resurrection of Rome*, 1930; *Come to Think of It*, 1930; *The Turkey and the Turk*, 1930; *At the Sign of the World's End*, 1930; *Is There a Return to Religion?*, 1931 (with E. Haldeman-Julius); *All Is Grist*, 1931; *Chaucer*, 1932; *Sidelights on New London and Newer York and Other Essays*, 1932; *Christendom in Dublin*, 1932; *All I Survey*, 1933; *St. Thomas Aquinas*, 1933; *G. K. Chesterton*, 1933 (also known as *Running After One's Hat and Other Whimsies*); *Avowals and Denials*, 1934; *The Well and the Shallows*, 1935; *Explaining the English*, 1935; *As I Was Saying*, 1936; *Autobiography*, 1936; *The Man Who Was Chesterton*, 1937; *The End of the Armistice*, 1940; *The Common Man*, 1950; *The Glass Walking-Stick and Other Essays from the "Illustrated London News," 1905-1936*, 1955; *Lunacy and Letters*, 1958; *Where All Roads Lead*, 1961; *The Man Who Was Orthodox: A Selection from the Uncollected Writings of G. K. Chesterton*, 1963; *The Spice of Life and Other Essays*, 1964; *Chesterton on Shakespeare*, 1971.

SHORT FICTION: *The Tremendous Adventures of Major Brown*, 1903; *The Club of Queer Trades*, 1905; *The Perishing of the Pendragons*, 1914; *The Man Who Knew Too Much and Other Stories*, 1922; *Tales of the Long Bow*, 1925; *Stories*, 1928; *The Sword of Wood*, 1928; *The Moderate Murder and the Honest Quack*, 1929; *The Poet and the Lunatics: Episodes in the Life of Gabriel Gale*, 1929; *Four Faultless Felons*, 1930; *The Ecstatic Thief*, 1930; *The Paradoxes of Mr. Pond*, 1936.

POETRY: *Greybeards at Play: Literature and Art for Old Gentlemen—Rhymes and Sketches*, 1900; *The Wild Knight and Other Poems*, 1900, rev. 1914; *The Ballad of the White Horse*, 1911; *A Poem*, 1915; *Poems*, 1915; *Wine, Water, and Song*, 1915; *Old King Cole*, 1920; *The Ballad of St. Barbara and Other Verses*, 1922; *Poems*, 1925; *The Queen of Seven Swords*, 1926; *Gloria in Profundis*, 1927; *Ubi Ecclesia*, 1929; *The Grave of Arthur*, 1930.

EDITED TEXTS: *Thackeray*, 1909; *Samuel Johnson*, 1911 (with Alice Meynell); *Essays by Divers Hands*, 1926.

MISCELLANEOUS: *Stories, Essays, and Poems*, 1935; *The Coloured Lands*, 1938.

Bibliography
Boyd, Ian. *The Novels of G. K. Chesterton: A Study in Art and Propaganda*. New York: Barnes and Noble, 1975. A good study of Chesterton's six major novels, as well as his collections of short stories. Discusses the novels in four periods: early, the eve of World War I, postwar (Distributist), and late.

Carol, Sister M. *G. K. Chesterton: The Dynamic Classicist*. Delhi, India: Motilal Banarsi Dass, 1971. Contains a chapter on Chesterton as a short-story writer as well as an insightful chapter analyzing his novels.

Clipper, Lawrence. *G. K. Chesterton*. New York: Twayne, 1974. Contains an insightful analysis of Chesterton's thought and writing in an assortment of areas. Includes a chapter entitled "Detectives and Apocalypses" that discusses his detective short stories and each of his novels.

Lauer, Quentin. *G. K. Chesterton: Philosopher Without Portfolio*. New York: Fordham

University Press, 1988. Lauer analyzes the philosophical and theological dimensions of Chesterton's work.

Pearce, Joseph. *Wisdom and Innocence: A Life of G. K. Chesterton.* San Francisco: Ignatius Press, 1996. A scholarly and well-written biography of Chesterton. Contains many quotes from his works and good analysis of them, as well as useful data on his family and friends.

Tadie, Andrew A., and Michael H. Macdonald, eds. *Permanent Things: Toward the Recovery of a More Human Scale at the End of the Twentieth Century.* Grand Rapids, Mich.: William B. Eerdmans, 1995. This volume includes a fairly thorough discussion of Chesterton's writing, along with works of T. S. Eliot and C. S. Lewis, looking primarily at its ethical and religious components.

Ward, Maisie. *Gilbert Keith Chesterton.* New York: Sheed and Ward, 1943. One of the best biographies of Chesterton. Written by a friend of Gilbert and Frances Chesterton who knew and interviewed individuals in their circle. Published seven years after his death, it contains firsthand accounts and data.

Agatha Christie

Born: Torquay, England; September 15, 1890
Died: Wallingford, England; January 12, 1976

Principal long fiction · *The Mysterious Affair at Styles: A Detective Story*, 1920; *The Secret Adversary*, 1922; *The Murder on the Links*, 1923; *The Man in the Brown Suit*, 1924; *The Secret of Chimneys*, 1925; *The Murder of Roger Ackroyd*, 1926; *The Big Four*, 1927; *The Mystery of the Blue Train*, 1928; *The Seven Dials Mystery*, 1929; *The Murder at the Vicarage*, 1930; *Giants' Bread*, 1930 (as Mary Westmacott); *The Sittaford Mystery*, 1931 (pb. in U.S. as *The Murder at Hazelmoor*); *The Floating Admiral*, 1931 (with others); *Peril at End House*, 1932; *Lord Edgware Dies*, 1933 (pb. in U.S. as *Thirteen at Dinner*); *Murder on the Orient Express*, 1934 (pb. in U.S. as *Murder on the Calais Coach*); *Murder in Three Acts*, 1934; *Why Didn't They Ask Evans?*, 1934 (pb. in U.S. as *Boomerang Clue*, 1935); *Unfinished Portrait*, 1934 (as Westmacott); *Death in the Clouds*, 1935 (pb. in U.S. as *Death in the Air*); *The A. B. C. Murders: A New Poirot Mystery*, 1936; *Cards on the Table*, 1936; *Murder in Mesopotamia*, 1936; *Death on the Nile*, 1937; *Dumb Witness*, 1937 (pb. in U.S. as *Poirot Loses a Client*); *Appointment with Death: A Poirot Mystery*, 1938; *Hercule Poirot's Christmas*, 1939 (pb. in U.S. as *Murder for Christmas: A Poirot Story*); *Murder Is Easy*, 1939 (pb. in U.S. as *Easy to Kill*); *Ten Little Niggers*, 1939 (pb. in U.S. as *And Then There Were None*, 1940); *One, Two, Buckle My Shoe*, 1940 (pb. in U.S. as *The Patriotic Murders*, 1941); *Sad Cypress*, 1940; *Evil Under the Sun*, 1941; *N or M? The New Mystery*, 1941; *The Body in the Library*, 1942; *Five Little Pigs*, 1942 (pb. in U.S. as *Murder in Retrospect*); *The Moving Finger*, 1942; *Death Comes in the End*, 1944; *Towards Zero*, 1944; *Absent in the Spring*, 1944 (as Westmacott); *Sparkling Cyanide*, 1945 (pb. in U.S. as *Remembered Death*); *The Hollow: A Hercule Poirot Mystery*, 1946; *Murder Medley*, 1948; *Taken at the Flood*, 1948 (pb. in U.S. as *There Is a Tide . . .*); *The Rose and the Yew Tree*, 1948 (as Westmacott); *Crooked House*, 1949; *A Murder Is Announced*, 1950; *Blood Will Tell*, 1951; *They Came to Baghdad*, 1951; *They Do It with Mirrors*, 1952 (pb. in U.S. as *Murder with Mirrors*); *Mrs. McGinty's Dead*, 1952; *A Daughter's a Daughter*, 1952 (as Westmacott); *After the Funeral*, 1953 (pb. in U.S. as *Funerals Are Fatal*); *A Pocket Full of Rye*, 1953; *Destination Unknown*, 1954 (pb. in U.S. as *So Many Steps to Death*, 1955); *Hickory, Dickory, Dock*, 1955 (pb. in U.S. as *Hickory, Dickory, Death*); *Dead Man's Folly*, 1956; *The Burden*, 1956 (as Westmacott); *4:50 from Paddington*, 1957 (pb. in U.S. as *What Mrs. McGillicuddy Saw!*); *Ordeal by Innocence*, 1958; *Cat Among the Pigeons*, 1959; *The Pale Horse*, 1961; *The Mirror Crack'd from Side to Side*, 1962 (pb. in U.S. as *The Mirror Crack'd*, 1963); *The Clocks*, 1963; *A Caribbean Mystery*, 1964; *At Bertram's Hotel*, 1965; *Third Girl*, 1966; *Endless Night*, 1967; *By the Pricking of My Thumb*, 1968; *Hallowe'en Party*, 1969; *Passenger to Frankfurt*, 1970; *Nemesis*, 1971; *Elephants Can Remember*, 1972; *Postern of Fate*, 1973; *Curtain: Hercule Poirot's Last Case*, 1975; *Sleeping Murder*, 1976 (posthumous).

Other literary forms · Agatha Christie published approximately thirty collections of short stories, fifteen plays, a nonfiction book (*Come Tell Me How You Live*, 1946), and many omnibus editions of her novels. Under the pen name Mary Westmacott, Christie published six romantic novels. At least ten of her detective works were made into motion pictures, and *An Autobiography* (1977) was published because, as Christie told *Publishers Weekly* (1966), "If anybody writes about my life in the future, I'd rather they got the facts right." Sources disagree on the total number of Christie's publications because of the unusual quantity of titles, the reissue of so many novels under different titles, and especially the tendency to publish the same book in England and America under differing titles.

Achievements · Among her many achievements, Christie bears one unusual distinction: She is the only writer whose main character's death precipitated a front-page obituary in *The New York Times*. Christie was a Fellow in the Royal Society of Literature; received the New York Drama Critics' Circle Award for Best Foreign Play of the year in 1955 (*Witness for the Prosecution*); was knighted Dame Commander, Order of the British Empire, 1971; received the Film Daily Poll Ten Best Pictures Award, 1958 (*Witness for the Prosecution*); and was made a doctor of literature at the University of Exeter.

Biography · Mary Clarissa Agatha Miller was born at Torquay, England, on September 15, 1890; the impact of this location on her was enormous. Near the end of *An Autobiography*, Christie indicates that all other memories and homes pale beside Ashfield, her parents' home in Torquay. "And there you are again—remembering. 'I remember, I remember, the house where I was born. . . .' I go back to that always in my mind. Ashfield." The roots of Christie's self-contained, quiet sense of place are found in her accounts of life at Ashfield. The love of peace, routine, and order was born in her mother's well-ordered household, a household cared for by servants whose nature seemed never to change, and sparked by the sudden whims of an energetic and dramatic mother. Christie's father was Fred Miller, an American, many years older than her English mother, Clara. They were distant cousins and had an exceptionally harmonious marriage because, Christie says, her father was an exceptionally agreeable man. Nigel Dennis, writing for *Life* (May, 1956), says that Christie is at her best in "orderly, settled surroundings" in which she can suddenly introduce disruption and ultimately violence. Her autobiographical accounts of days upon days of peace and routine followed by sudden impulsive adventures initiated by her mother support the idea that, as she says, all comes back to Ashfield, including her mystery stories at their best.

In writing her autobiography, Christie left a detailed and insightful commentary on her works. To one familiar with her autobiography, the details of her life can be found in the incidents and plots of her novels. Frequently, she barely disguises them. She writes, for example, of a recurring childhood dream about "the Gunman," whose outstanding characteristics were his frightening eyes appearing suddenly and staring at her from absolutely any person around her, including her beloved mother. This dream forms almost the entire basis for the plot of *Unfinished Portrait*, a romantic novel written under the pen name "Mary Westmacott." That dream may have been the source of her willingness to allow absolutely any character the role of murderer. No one, including her great Hercule Poirot, is exempt from suddenly becoming the Gunman.

Christie was educated at home chiefly by her parents and her nurse. She taught herself to read before she was five and from then on was allowed to read any available book at Ashfield. Her father taught her arithmetic, for which she had a propensity and which she enjoyed. She hated spelling, on the other hand, because she read by word sight and not by the sound of letters. She learned history from historical novels and

a book of history that her mother expected her to study in preparation for
a weekly quiz.

A stay in France at about age seven
and an ensuing return with a French
woman as her companion resulted in
her speaking and reading French easily. She also had piano and voice tutors and a weekly dancing class. As
she grew older, she attended the theater
weekly, and, in her teens, she was sent
to a boarding school in France.

She was always allowed to use her
imagination freely. Her sensible and
beloved nurse went along with her
early construction of plots and tales
enlisting the nurse as well as dolls and
animals to be the characters. She carried on a constant dialogue with these
characters as she went through her
days. The absence of playmates and
the storytelling done within the family
also contributed to the development
of her imagination. Her mother invented ongoing bedtime tales of a dra-

Library of Congress

matic and mysterious nature. Her elder sister, Madge, liked to write, and she repeatedly told Agatha one particular story: It was the "Elder Sister" tale. Like the Gunman,
the Elder Sister became a frequent personage in her later novels. As a child, Agatha
would ask her sister, feeling a mixture of terror and delight, when the elder sister was
coming; Madge would indicate that it would be soon. Then a few days later, there
would be a knock on Agatha's door and her sister would enter and begin talking in
an eerie voice as if she were an elder, disturbed sister who was normally locked up
somewhere but at large for the day. The pattern seems similar to that of the Gunman:
the familiar figure who is suddenly dangerous. One book in particular, *Elephants Can
Remember*, concerns a crazy identical twin sister who escapes from a mental institution,
kills her twin, and takes her place in marriage to a man they had both known and
loved as young girls.

Besides her sister, Madge, Agatha had an elder brother, Monty, whom she adored.
He allowed her to join him frequently in his escapades and was generally agreeable,
but, like her father, did not amount to much otherwise and was managed and even
supported by his sisters later in his life. "Auntie Grannie" was another strong figure
in Agatha's early life. She was the aunt who had reared Clara Miller and was also
Fred's stepmother. Many critics see in her the basis for the character of Miss Marple.

The picture emerging of Christie is of a woman coming from an intensely female-
dominated household where men were agreeable and delightful but not very effective. Female servants and family members provided Agatha with her rigorous, stable
values and independent behavior. She grew up expecting little of men except affection
and loyalty; in return, she expected to be sensible and self-supporting when possible.
Another possible explanation for Christie's self-sufficiency is the emotional support

that these surrounding females provided for her. Even after her mother's death in the late 1920's, Christie always sought the companionship of loyal female servants and secretaries who, in the British Victorian fashion, then became invaluable to her in her work and personal life. Especially in her marriage to Archibald Christie, she relied on her female relatives and servants to encourage, assist, and even love her. The Miss Marples of her world, the Constance Sheppards (*The Murder of Roger Ackroyd*), and the servants were her life's bedrock.

In 1914, Agatha Miller married Colonel Archibald Christie in a hasty wartime ceremony. They had one daughter, Rosamund, whom Agatha adored but considered an "efficient" child. She characterized Rosamund in "Mary Westmacott's" novel *A Daughter's a Daughter.*

Agatha started writing on a dare from her sister but only began writing novels seriously when her husband was away in World War I and she was employed as a chemist's (pharmacist's) assistant in a dispensary. Finding herself with extra time, she wrote *The Mysterious Affair at Styles.* Since she was familiar with both poisons and death because of her hospital and dispensary work, she was able to distinguish herself by the accuracy of her descriptions. Several other books followed, which were increasingly successful, until *The Murder of Roger Ackroyd* became a best-seller in 1926.

The death of her mother and a divorce from Archie Christie took place about the same time as her success. These sent her into a tailspin which ended in her famous eleven-day disappearance. She reappeared at a health spa unharmed but, to her embarrassment, the object of a great deal of attention; the public was outraged at the large expense of the search.

In 1930, she married Sir Max Mallowan, an archaeologist, perhaps a more "agreeable" man. Certainly her domestic life after the marriage was peaceful; in addition, she was able to travel with Mallowan to his archaeological dig sites in the Middle East. This gave her new settings and material for her books and enabled her to indulge in one of her greatest pleasures: travel.

In 1930, *The Murder at the Vicarage* was published; it introduced her own favorite sleuth, Miss Jane Marple, who was village spinster and observer of the village scene. By this time, Christie was an established author, and in the 1940's, her books began to be made into plays and motion pictures. In 1952, *The Mousetrap* was launched in London theater and eventually became one of the longest-running plays in that city's history. The film version of *Witness for the Prosecution* received awards and acclaim in the early 1950's. *Murder on the Calais Coach* became *Murder on the Orient Express,* a popular American film.

Producing approximately one book per year, Christie has been likened to an assembly line, but, as her autobiography indicates, each book was a little puzzle for her own "grey cells," the conceiving of which gave her great enjoyment and the writing of which took about six to twelve weeks and was often tedious. In 1971, she was knighted Dame Agatha Christie by Queen Elizabeth II and had what she considered one of her most thrilling experiences, tea with the Queen. In 1975, she allowed the book *Curtain: Hercule Poirot's Last Case* to be published and the death of her chief sleuth, Hercule Poirot, to occur. This was of sufficient interest to warrant a front-page obituary in *The New York Times.*

By the time of her own death in 1976, Ellsworth Grant in *Horizon* (1976) claimed that Christie's writings had "reached a wider audience than those of any author who ever lived." More than 400 million copies of her novels and short stories had been sold, and her works had been translated into 103 languages.

Analysis · Agatha Christie's trademarks in detective fiction brought to maturity the classical tradition of the genre, which was in its adolescence when she began to write. The tradition had some stable characteristics, but she added many more and perfected existing ones. The classical detective hero, for example, from Edgar Allan Poe on, according to Ellsworth Grant, is of "superior intellect," is "fiercely independent," and has "amusing idiosyncrasies." Christie's Hercule Poirot was crafted by these ground rules and reflects them in *The Mysterious Affair at Styles* but quickly begins to deplore this Sherlock Holmes type of detecting. Poirot would rather think from his armchair than rush about, magnifying glass in hand, searching for clues. He may, by his words, satirize classical detection, but he is also satirizing himself, as Christie well knew.

Christie's own contributions to the genre can be classified mainly as the following: a peaceful, usually upper-class setting into which violence intrudes; satire of her own heroes, craft, and genre; a grand finale in which all characters involved gather for the dramatic revelation of truth; the careful access to all clues; increased emphasis on the "who" and the "why" with less interest in the "how"; heavy use of dialogue and lightning-quick description, which create a fast-paced, easy read; a consistent moral framework for the action; and the willingness to allow absolutely any character to be guilty, a precedent-setting break with the tradition. Her weakness, critics claim, is in her barely two-dimensional characters and in their lack of psychological depth.

Christie created, as Grant puts it, a great many interesting "caricatures of people we have met." Grant excuses her on the grounds that allowing every character to be a possible suspect limits the degree to which they can be psychologically explored. One might also attribute her caricatures to her great admiration for Charles Dickens, who also indulged in caricatures, especially with his minor characters. Christie herself gives a simple explanation. She judged it best not to write about people she actually knew, preferring to observe strangers in railroad stations and restaurants, perhaps catching a fragment of their conversation. From this glimpse, she would make up a character and a plot. Character fascinated her endlessly, but, like Miss Marple, she believed the depths of human iniquity were in everyone, and it was only in the outward manifestation that people became evil or good. "I could've done it," a juvenile character cries in *Evil Under the Sun.* "Ah, but you didn't and between those two things there is a world of difference," Poirot replies.

Death Comes in the End · In spite of Christie's simplistic judgment of human character, she manages, on occasion (especially in her novels of the 1940's and later), to make accurate and discerning forays into the thought processes of some characters. In *Death Comes in the End,* considerable time is spent on Renisenb's internal musings. Caught in the illiterate role which her time (Egypt, 2000 B.C.E.) and sex status decree for her, Renisenb struggles to achieve language so she can articulate her anxieties about evil and good. Her male friend, Hori, speaks at great length of the way that evil affects people. "People create a false door, to deceive," he says, but "when reality comes and touches them with the feather of truth—their truth self reasserts itself." When Norfret, a beautiful concubine, enters a closed, self-contained household and threatens its stability, all the characters begin to behave differently. The murderer is discovered precisely because he is the only person who does *not* behave differently on the outside. Any innocent person would act guilty because the presence of evil touches self-doubts and faults; therefore, the one who acts against this Christie truth and remains normal in the face of murder must, in fact, be guilty.

The Mysterious Affair at Styles · Although *The Mysterious Affair at Styles* is marred by overwriting and explanations that Christie sheds in later books, it shows signs of those qualities that will make her great. The village of Styles St. Mary is quiet, and Styles House is a typical country manor. The book is written in the first person by Hastings, who comes to visit his old friend John Cavendish and finds him dealing with a difficult family situation. His mother married a man who everyone agrees is a fortune hunter. Shortly afterward, she dies of poison in full view of several family members, calling her husband's name. Hastings runs into Hercule Poirot at the post office; an old acquaintance temporarily residing at Styles, he is a former police inspector from Belgium. Christie's idea in this first novel seems to be that Hastings will play Watson to Poirot's Holmes, although she quickly tires of this arrangement and in a later book ships Hastings off to Argentina.

Every obvious clue points to the husband as the murderer. Indeed, he *is* the murderer and has made arrangements with an accomplice so that he will be brought to a speedy trial. At the trial, it would then be revealed that the husband had an absolute alibi for the time when the poison must have been administered; hence, he and his accomplice try to encourage everyone to think him guilty. Poirot delays the trial and figures out that the real poison was in the woman's own medicine, which contained a substance that would only become fatal if released from other elements. It then would settle to the bottom of the bottle and the last dose would be lethal. Bromide is an ingredient that separates the elements. Bromide was added at the murderer's leisure, and he had only to wait until the day when she would take the last dose, making sure that both he and his accomplice are seen by many people far distant from the household at the time she is declared to have been poisoned. The plot is brilliant, and Christie received congratulations from a chemists' association for her correct use of the poisons in the book.

The Murder of Roger Ackroyd · By the publication of *The Murder of Roger Ackroyd*, her sixth book, Christie had hit her stride. Although Poirot's explanations are still somewhat lengthy, the book is considered one of her best. It is chiefly noted for the precedent it set in detective fiction. The first-person narrator, Dr. Sheppard, turns out to be the murderer. The skill with which this is revealed and concealed is perhaps Christie at her most subtle. The reader is made to like Dr. Sheppard, to feel he or she is being taken into his confidence as he attempts to write the history of Roger Ackroyd's murder as it unwinds. Poirot cultivates Dr. Sheppard's acquaintanceship, and the reader believes, because he hears it from Dr. Sheppard, that Poirot trusts him. In the end, Dr. Sheppard is guilty. Christie allows herself to gloat at her own fiendish cleverness through the very words that Sheppard uses to gloat over his crime when he refers back to a part of his narrative (the story itself is supposedly being written to help Poirot solve the crime) where a discerning reader or sleuth ought to have found him out.

The Body in the Library · *The Body in the Library*, executed with Christie's usual skill, is distinctive for two elements: the extended discussions of Miss Marple's sleuthing style and the humorous dialogue surrounding the discovery of the body of an unknown young woman in the library of a good family. Grant says of Jane Marple that she insists, as she knits, that human nature never changes. O. L. Bailey expands upon this in *Saturday Review* (1973): "Victorian to the core," he writes, "she loves to gossip, and her piercing blue eyes twinkle as she solves the most heinous crimes by analogy to life in her archetypal English village of St. Mary Mead."

Marple, as well as the other characters, comments on her methods. Marple feels her success is in her skeptical nature, calling her mind "a sink." She goes on to explain that "the truth is . . . that most people . . . are far too trusting for this wicked world." Another character, Sir Henry, describes her as "an old lady with a sweet, placid, spinsterish face and a mind that has plumbed the depths of human iniquity and taken it as all in the day's work."

Through a delightfully comic conversation between Mr. and Mrs. Bantry, the possibility of a dead body in the library is introduced, and, once it is discovered, the story continues in standard sleuth style; the opening dialogue, however, is almost too funny for the subject matter. Ralph Tyler in *Saturday Review* (1975) calls this mixture of evil and the ordinary a distancing of death "by bringing it about in an upper-middle-class milieu of consummate orderliness." In that milieu, the Bantrys' dialogue is not too funny; it is quite believable, especially since they do not yet know the body is downstairs.

The Secret Adversary · Perhaps a real Christie aficionado can be identified by his reaction to Tommy and Tuppence Beresford of *The Secret Adversary*, an engaging pair of sleuths who take up adventuring because they cannot find work in postwar England. Critics dismiss or ignore the pair, but Christie fans often express a secret fondness for the two. In Tommy and Tuppence, readers find heroes close to home. The two blunder about and solve mysteries by luck as much as by anything else. Readers can easily identify with these two and even feel a bit protective of them.

Tommy and Tuppence develop a romance as they establish an "adventurers for hire" agency and wait for clients. Adventure begins innocently when Tommy tells Tuppence he has overheard someone talking about a woman named Jane Finn and comments disgustedly, "Did you ever hear such a name?" Later they discover that the name is a password into an international spy ring.

The use of luck and coincidence in the story is made much of by Christie herself. Christie seems to tire of the frequent convenient circumstances and lets Tommy and Tuppence's romance and "high adventure" lead the novel's progress. When Tommy asks Mr. Carter, the British spy expert, for some tips, Carter replies, "I think not. My experts, working in stereotyped ways, have failed. You will bring imagination and an open mind to the task." Mr. Carter also admits that he is superstitious and that he believes in luck "and all that sort of thing." In this novel, readers are presented with a clever story, the resolution of which relies on elements quite different from deductive reasoning or intuition. It relies on those qualities which the young seem to exude and attract: audacity and luck.

N or M? The New Mystery · In *N or M? The New Mystery*, Tommy and Tuppence (now married and some twenty years older) are again unemployed. Their two children are both serving their country in World War II. The parents are bemoaning their fate when a messenger from their old friend Mr. Carter starts them on a spy adventure at the seacoast hotel of Sans Souci. They arrive with the assumed names Mr. Meadowes and Mrs. Blenkensop. Mrs. Blenkensop, they agree, will pursue Mr. Meadowes and every now and then corner him so they can exchange information. The dialogue is amusing and there is a good deal of suspense, but too many characters and a thin plot keep this from being one of Christie's best.

At times, it seems that Christie withholds clues; the fact that all evidence is presented to the reader is the supreme test of good detective fiction. Mrs. Sprot, adopted mother of Betty, coolly shoots Betty's real mother in the head while the woman is holding Betty over the edge of a cliff. The reader cannot be expected to know that the woman on the cliff is Betty's real mother. Nor can the reader be expected to decipher Tuppence's mutterings about the story of Solomon. In the story of Solomon, two women claim the same baby, and Solomon decrees that the woman who is willing to give up her child rather than have it killed is the real mother. Since both women in this scene *appear* willing to jeopardize the baby's life, the reader is likely, justifiably, to form some wrong conclusions. This seems less fair than Christie usually is in delivering her clues.

Sleeping Murder · In *Sleeping Murder*, written several years before its 1976 publication date, Christie achieves more depth in her portrayal of characters than before: Gwenda, her dead stepmother, Dr. Kennedy, and some of the minor characters such as Mr. Erskine are excellent examples. The motivation in the book is, at least, psychological, as opposed to murder for money or personal gain, which are the usual motives in Christie's novels. There seems, in short, to be much more probing into the origin and motivation of her characters' actions.

Her last novel, *Sleeping Murder* ends with the romantic young couple and the wise old Miss Marple conversing on the front porch of a hotel in, of all places, Torquay, Christie's beloved birthplace. Christie came full circle, celebrating her romantic and impulsive youth and her pleasant old age in one final reunion at home in Torquay, England.

Anne Kelsch Breznau

Other major works
SHORT FICTION: *Poirot Investigates*, 1924; *Partners in Crime*, 1929; *The Mysterious Mr. Quin*, 1930; *The Thirteen Problems*, 1932 (pb. in U.S. as *The Tuesday Club Murders*, 1933); *The Hound of Death and Other Stories*, 1933; *The Listerdale Mystery and Other Stories*, 1934; *Parker Pyne Investigates*, 1934 (pb. in U.S. as *Mr. Parker Pyne, Detective*); *Murder in the Mews and Other Stories*, 1937 (pb. in U.S. as *Dead Man's Mirror and Other Stories*); *The Regatta Mystery and Other Stories*, 1939; *The Labours of Hercules: Short Stories*, 1947 (pb. in U.S. as *Labors of Hercules: New Adventures in Crime by Hercule Poirot*); *The Witness for the Prosecution and Other Stories*, 1948; *Three Blind Mice and Other Stories*, 1950; *Under Dog and Other Stories*, 1951; *The Adventures of the Christmas Pudding, and Selection of Entrées*, 1960; *Double Sin and Other Stories*, 1961; *Thirteen for Luck: A Selection of Mystery Stories for Young Readers*, 1961; *Star over Bethlehem and Other Stories*, 1965 (as A. C. Mallowan); *Surprize! Surprize! A Collection of Mystery Stories with Unexpected Endings*, 1965; *Thirteen Clues for Miss Marple: A Collection of Mystery Stories*, 1965; *The Golden Ball and Other Stories*, 1971; *Hercule Poirot's Early Cases*, 1974.
PLAYS: *Black Coffee*, pr. 1930; *Ten Little Niggers*, pr. 1943 (pb. in U.S. as *Ten Little Indians*, pr. 1944); *Appointment with Death*, pr., pb. 1945; *Murder on the Nile*, pr., pb. 1946; *The Hollow*, pr. 1951; *The Mousetrap*, pr. 1952; *Witness for the Prosecution*, pr. 1953; *The Spider's Web*, pr. 1954; *Towards Zero*, pr. 1956 (with Gerald Verner); *The Unexpected Guest*, pr., pb. 1958; *Verdict*, pr., pb. 1958; *Go Back for Murder*, pr., pb. 1960; *Afternoon at the Seaside*, pr. 1962; *The Patient*, pr. 1962; *The Rats*, pr. 1962; *Akhnaton*, pb. 1973 (also known as *Akhnaton and Nefertiti*).
POETRY: *The Road of Dreams*, 1925; *Poems*, 1973.
NONFICTION: *Come Tell Me How You Live*, 1946; *An Autobiography*, 1977.

Bibliography

Bargainnier, Earl F. *The Gentle Art of Murder: The Detective Fiction of Agatha Christie.* Bowling Green, Ohio: Bowling Green University Popular Press, 1980. A scholarly study which provides a literary analysis of Christie's writings. Individual chapters focus on settings, characters, plots, and so on. Contains a very useful bibliography.

Cade, Jared. *Agatha Christie and the Eleven Missing Days.* London: Peter Owen, 1998. Questions Christie's disappearance. Includes bibliographical references, a list of works, and an index.

Gill, Gillian. *Agatha Christie: The Woman and Her Mysteries.* New York: The Free Press, 1990. This short and highly readable biography is definitely of the popular, rather than critical, variety, employing as chapter titles seven different names used at one time or another by the mystery writer (including the assumed name Christie used during her infamous disappearance in 1926). Still, Gill goes out of her way to emphasize Christie's dedication to her art and the discipline of her life.

Riley, Dick, and Pam McAllister, eds. *The Bedside, Bathtub, and Armchair Companion to Agatha Christie.* New York: Frederick Ungar, 1979. Containing more than two hundred illustrations, this handbook also provides plot summaries of all Christie's novels, plays, and many of her short stories arranged chronologically by first date of publication.

Robyns, Gwen. *The Mystery of Agatha Christie.* Garden City, N.Y.: Doubleday, 1978. Provides a well-written and well-rounded popular biography of Christie. Richly illustrated and contains an appendix with a chronological listing of all Christie's writings. Perhaps the best place to begin a further study of Christie.

Shaw, Marion, and Sabine Vanacker. *Reflecting on Miss Marple.* London: Routledge, 1991. After a brief chronology of Christie's life, Shaw and Vanacker devote four chapters to one of her most memorable detectives, in the course of which they make a case for viewing Miss Marple as a feminist heroine. They do so by reviewing the history of women writers and the golden age of detective fiction, as well as the social context of Christie's Miss Marple books. The spinster Miss Marple, they conclude, is able to solve her cases by exploiting prejudice against unmarried older women.

Sova, Dawn B. *Agatha Christie A to Z: The Essential Reference to Her Life and Writings.* New York: Facts on File, 1996. Provides information on all aspects of Christie's life and career.

Toye, Randall. *The Agatha Christie's Who's Who.* New York: Holt, Rinehart and Winston, 1980. Toye has compiled a dictionary of more than two thousand, out of a total of more than seven thousand, important characters appearing in Christie's 66 mystery novels and 147 short stories. For each entry, he attempts to give the character's importance to the story, as well as some memorable characteristics.

Wagoner, Mary S. *Agatha Christie.* Boston: Twayne, 1986. A scholarly but readable study of Christie and her writings. A brief biography of Christie in the first chapter is followed by analytical chapters focusing on the different genres of her works, such as short stories. Also contains a good bibliography, an index, and a chronological table of Christie's life.

Arthur C. Clarke

Born: Minehead, Somerset, England; December 16, 1917

Principal long fiction · *Prelude to Space*, 1951; *The Sands of Mars*, 1951; *Against the Fall of Night*, 1953, 1956 (revised as *The City and the Stars*); *Childhood's End*, 1953; *Earthlight*, 1955; *The Deep Range*, 1957; *Across the Sea of Stars*, 1959; *A Fall of Moondust*, 1961; *From the Ocean, from the Stars*, 1962; *Glide Path*, 1963; *Prelude to Mars*, 1965; *"The Lion of Comarre" and "Against the Fall of Night,"* 1968; *2001: A Space Odyssey*, 1968; *Rendezvous with Rama*, 1973; *Imperial Earth*, 1975; *The Fountains of Paradise*, 1979; *2010: Odyssey Two*, 1982; *The Songs of Distant Earth*, 1986; *2061: Odyssey Three*, 1987; *Cradle*, 1988 (with Gentry Lee); *Rama II*, 1989 (with Lee); *The Ghost from the Grand Banks*, 1990; *Beyond the Fall of Night*, 1990 (with Gregory Benford); *The Garden of Rama*, 1991 (with Lee); *The Hammer of God*, 1993; *Rama Revealed*, 1993 (with Lee); *Richter 10*, 1996 (with Mike McQuay); *3001: The Final Odyssey*, 1997; *The Light and Other Days*, 2000 (with Stephen Baxter).

Other literary forms · Best known for his novels, Arthur C. Clarke has also written numerous science-fiction stories, which are available in several collections; two of them, "The Star" and "A Meeting with Medusa," won major awards. Clarke is noted for scientific essays and books for general readers, usually about outer space or the ocean, and he published a few loosely structured autobiographies.

Achievements · Beginning in the 1950's, Arthur C. Clarke became acknowledged as a major science-fiction author, winning several Hugo and Nebula Awards for his works, and he earned the Kalinga Prize in 1961 for science writing. He garnered greater renown in 1968 as author of the novel *2001: A Space Odyssey* and as a screenwriter of the Stanley Kubrick film of the same name, which led to an Academy Award nomination; a year later, he joined newscaster Walter Cronkite as a television commentator on the Apollo 11 space mission to the Moon. From the 1970's on, his novels were best-sellers, the most successful being his sequels to *2001*. In the 1980's, he hosted two documentary series about strange phenomena, *Arthur C. Clarke's Mysterious World* (1981) and *Arthur C. Clarke's World of Strange Powers* (1984), and in 1998, he was knighted by the British government for his contributions to literature.

Biography · Clarke first displayed his interests in science fiction and science as a child, reading pulp magazines and conducting his own experiments. By the late 1930's, he was living in London, working for the British Interplanetary Society and publishing scientific articles. During World War II, he helped develop a system for radar-assisted airplane landings, an experience fictionally recounted in *Glide Path*. In 1945, he published a now-famous article that first proposed communications satellites. After the war, he graduated from college and worked as assistant editor of *Physics Abstracts* before quitting to pursue a writing career.

In the 1950's, Clarke grew fascinated with the sea and, in 1956, moved to the island of Sri Lanka, which became his permanent residence. His 1953 marriage to Marilyn Mayfield ended with divorce in 1964. After the success of *2001*, Clarke signed a million-dollar contract to write *Rendezvous with Rama, Imperial Earth,* and *The Fountains of Paradise,* once announced as his final work. Clarke continued writing novels, though many were disappointed by a flurry of collaborations: *Cradle, Rama II, The Garden of Rama,* and *Rama Revealed,* all cowritten with Gentry Lee; *Beyond the Fall of Night,* cowritten with Gregory Benford; and *Richter 10,* cowritten with Mike McQuay. In these works, Clarke's participation was presumed to be minimal.

Analysis · Clarke's fiction consistently displays tremendous scientific knowledge combined with a boundless imagination, often touching upon the mystical, and flashes of ironic humor. One specialty of Clarke is the novel that, with meticulous realism, describes near-future events, such as the first space flight (*Prelude to Space*), humans living under the sea (*The Deep Range*), lunar settlements (*Earthlight, A Fall of Moondust*), colonies on Mars (*The Sands of Mars*), and efforts to raise the *Titanic* (*The Ghost from the Grand Banks*). While these novels are involving, Clarke's determination to be plausible can make them less than dramatic, and they are rarely celebrated. More noteworthy to most readers are the novels that envision incredible engineering accomplishments (*Rendezvous with Rama, The Fountains of Paradise*), venture far into the future (*Against the Fall of Night, The Songs of Distant Earth*), or depict encounters with enigmatic aliens (*Childhood's End, 2001* and its sequels). Few writers can match Clarke's ability to take a broad perspective and regard vast expanses of space and time as mere episodes in a vast cosmic drama inaccessible to human understanding.

Critics frequently complained about Clarke's undistinguished prose style and wooden characters, but he steadily improved in these areas, and if his fiction of the 1980's and 1990's brought no spectacular new visions, the writing is generally more impressive than that of the 1950's and 1960's. *The Ghost from the Grand Banks,* for example, effectively employs short chapters that jump forward and backward in time and reveal Clarke's skill in crafting superb opening and closing lines. Many observed the previously underdeveloped Heywood Floyd and Frank Poole evolve into realistic characters in the sequels to *2001.* While commentaries often focus more on the earlier works, Clarke's later novels also merit attention.

Against the Fall of Night · Clarke's first major novel features Alvin, a restless young man, in Diaspar, a city in Earth's distant future where machines provide for all needs. Alvin quickly disrupts the placid, unchanging lives of Diaspar's nearly immortal residents with his remarkable discoveries. An underground vehicle transports him to Lys, a previously unknown civilization where people choose agrarian lifestyles aided by telepathic powers rather than machines. There, an old man's strange robot reveals the location of a spaceship, in which Alvin journeys to a faraway planet, where he encounters a disembodied intelligence named Vanamonde. Back on Earth, Alvin and the elders of Lys deduce humanity's history: After humans worked with aliens to create pure intelligences, their first product, the Mad Mind, went insane and unleashed its destructive energies throughout the galaxy. After creating other, sane intelligences like Vanamonde, humans left the universe entirely, leaving behind a few who preferred to remain on Earth. Dispatching a robot to search for the departed humans, Alvin stays behind to solve other mysteries of human history.

Overflowing with ideas, presented with breathless haste, *Against the Fall of Night* commands attention for its evocative and imaginative portrayal of decadent future humans haunted by a misunderstood heritage, and the arrogance with which Alvin dominates and upsets their sterile existence may reflect the self-confidence of a young author who felt destined to accomplish great things. However, a dissatisfied Clarke soon took the unusual step of writing an extensive revision, published as *The City and the Stars*. While this new version offered fascinating new details about life in Diaspar, many preferred the youthful exuberance of the original story, and a consensus developed that the first version was superior. Thus, in continuing Alvin's story, writer Gregory Benford chose to follow the original version, republished together with Benford's sequel as *Beyond the Fall of Night* in 1989.

Childhood's End · Sometimes considered Clarke's masterpiece, *Childhood's End* begins when Earth is peacefully taken over by the benevolent alien Overlords. Concealing themselves because they resemble devils, the Overlords govern through human intermediaries such as the Secretary General of the United Nations, whom they effortlessly rescue when he is kidnapped by rebels who oppose the Overlords. When they finally reveal their appearance fifty years later, humanity is enjoying a golden age of peace and prosperity thanks to the Overlords' wise rule and advanced technology. However, streaks of rebelliousness persist, and a man named Jan Rodricks stows away on a starship to visit the Overlords' homeworld. Later, on Earth, George and Jean Greggson are upset when their son begins dreaming about other worlds and their daughter manifests telekinetic powers. An Overlord now explains the true motives behind their takeover. Certain races, such as humans, have the capacity to achieve a higher level of evolution by merging into a group mind and joining the mysterious Overmind that controls the universe; the Overmind assigns the Overlords, who paradoxically lack this potential, to supervise these races during the transitional stage. Soon, all human children have mentally united and seem like aliens to their distraught parents. While the adults, their dreams shattered, commit suicide in various ways, Rodricks returns to Earth to observe its final moments, as the children employ psychic powers to disintegrate their world and merge with the Overmind.

Perhaps perturbed by his own prophecy, Clarke adds this introductory comment: "The opinions expressed in this book are not those of the author." Certainly, *Childhood's End* stirs strong and conflicting emotions in its final portrait of Earth's children seemingly reduced to naked savages engaged in senseless activities, even while the reader is assured that they represent a glorious new stage in human evolution. If not wholly satisfactory in style and character development, the novel persuasively presents its unsettling developments and, decades after publication, inspires heated discussion.

2001 · Clarke's novel *2001: A Space Odyssey* differs from the film based on it both in major details and in its overall tone, which is clear and explanatory in contrast to Kubrick's directorial mystification. Clarke develops the character of Moon-Watcher, the ape-man of the distant past who first notices the alien monolith that teaches Moon-Watcher and his companions to use tools. Next, in the near future, Heywood Floyd visits the Moon to examine another monolith, which suddenly emits a powerful radio signal toward Saturn (not Jupiter, as in the film). The spaceship *Discovery* is sent to investigate, though the crewmen who are not placed in hibernation, David Bowman and Frank Poole, know nothing about the monolith. Driven insane by contradictory commands to cooperate with Bowman and Poole while concealing their real mission, the onboard computer HAL kills Poole in space and attempts to kill Bowman by opening the ship's airlocks, exposing him to the vacuum of space. Finding an emergency shelter with a spacesuit, Bowman disables HAL and proceeds to Saturn, where another monolith waits on the surface of Saturn's moon Japetus. An alien transportation system then takes Bowman to a distant planet and a crude replica of an Earth hotel, where he is transformed into a baby with immense powers who returns to Earth and destroys its nuclear weapons.

2010, 2061, and 3001 · *2001* stands on its own as a masterful saga of human evolution and exploration. The later sequels do not enhance its impact, however. In *2010: Odyssey Two*, Floyd returns to Jupiter (following the film version) to discover Bowman's fate, meets a ghostly Bowman (now cast more as a messenger for the aliens than as the harbinger of a new human race), and flees when Jupiter becomes a star, with its moons offered to humanity as new homes (except Europa, declared off-limits by the aliens). In *2061: Odyssey Three*, Floyd journeys to Halley's Comet but accidentally lands on Europa, while in *3001: The Final Odyssey*, a revived Poole helps to disable the monoliths, now likened to out-of-control computers. Though readers may enjoy meeting old friends, the sequels never reveal the unseen aliens or their final plans for humanity, which is perhaps as it should be.

Rendezvous with Rama · Clarke's first novel after *2001* begins with the discovery of a gigantic cylindrical object, clearly artificial in origin, approaching the Sun. William Norton, commanding the spaceship *Endeavour*, leads an investigation of the object, named Rama. Entering through an airlock, Norton and his crew observe a huge interior landscape divided by a Cylindrical Sea, with clusters of buildings dubbed "cities" and other inexplicable objects. As they descend to the surface, massive lights suddenly illuminate Rama, as if it were coming to life. When a crewman crosses the Cylindrical Sea in a glider and investigates strange formations, he notices the first of many "biots"–biological robots manufactured to perform functions such as observation and removal of debris. The people of Mercury, fearing Rama is hostile, launch a nuclear missile to destroy it, but another crewman disables the bomb. As the humans depart, the biots destroy themselves and the lights go out, signaling that Rama has finished its work. Rama then absorbs energy and matter from the Sun before leaving the solar system–though a scientist notes, "The Ramans do everything in threes," suggesting other alien vehicles may arrive soon.

Despite weak characterization, Clarke's unique ability to evoke the bizarre with straightforward exposition is well displayed in this story, which intrigues readers with its narrative unpredictability and unanswered questions. *Rendezvous with Rama* earned the Hugo and Nebula Awards as the best science-fiction novel of 1973. Clarke later continued the story in three sequels cowritten with Gentry Lee–*Rama II, The Garden of Rama*, and *Rama Revealed*–describing the coming of another Raman spaceship and the astronauts who stay on board for a cosmic journey. Despite revealing new data about the Ramans and their goals, the sequels leave many mysteries unresolved, ultimately adding little to the original novel.

The Fountains of Paradise · Projected as the capstone of Clarke's career, *The Fountains of Paradise* describes a future engineer, Vannevar Morgan, planning to construct an enormous "space elevator" to connect the surface of Earth to a geosynchronous satellite, providing cheap and safe transportation into space. His story is interwoven with that of another great builder, Kalidasa, the ancient king of Taprobane (an island analogous to Sri Lanka) who built the magnificent Fountains of Paradise at the mountain where Morgan wishes to build his space elevator. When the monks inhabiting the mountain abandon their home after an old prophecy is fulfilled, Morgan begins work, and soon the tower is slowly being constructed from a point between Earth and space. When scientists are stranded on the incomplete tower, Morgan pilots a transport vehicle to bring supplies, though the effort strains his weak heart and causes his death. In an epilogue set further in the future, an alien visiting Earth marvels at its "Ring City," with Morgan's tower as only one spoke in an immense wheel of satellites circling the globe, all linked to each other and to the ground.

Inspired by the history and traditions of Sri Lanka, Clarke's adopted homeland, *The Fountains of Paradise* seems one of his most personal works, blending reverence for ancient accomplishments with dreams of futuristic space exploration. Like *Rendezvous with Rama*, it earned both the Hugo and Nebula Awards. The concluding chapters describing Morgan's rescue may be the most gripping sequence Clarke has ever written, but its awe-inspiring vision of a world transformed by cosmic engineering makes the novel memorable.

Gary Westfahl

Other major works

SHORT FICTION: *Expedition to Earth*, 1953; *Reach for Tomorrow*, 1956; *Tales from the White Hart*, 1957; *The Other Side of the Sky*, 1958; *Tales of Ten Worlds*, 1962; *The Nine Billion Names of God*, 1967; *Of Time and Stars: The Worlds of Arthur C. Clarke*, 1972; *The Wind from the Sun*, 1972; *The Best of Arthur C. Clarke, 1937-1971*, 1973; *The Sentinel: Masterworks of Science Fiction and Fantasy*, 1983; *Dilemmas: The Secret*, 1989; *Tales from Planet Earth*, 1989; *More than One Universe: The Collected Stories of Arthur C. Clarke*, 1991.

NONFICTION: *Interplanetary Flight*, 1950; *The Exploration of Space*, 1951 (revised 1959); *The Exploration of the Moon*, 1954; *Going into Space*, 1954; *The Coast of Coral*, 1956; *The Making of a Moon*, 1957; *The Reefs of Taprobane*, 1957; *Voice Across the Sea*, 1958; *The Challenge of the Spaceship*, 1959; *The Challenge of the Sea*, 1960; *The First Five Fathoms*, 1960; *Indian Ocean Adventure*, 1961 (with Mike Wilson); *Profiles of the Future*, 1962; *Man and Space*, 1964 (with others); *Indian Ocean Treasure*, 1964 (with Wilson); *The Treasure of the Great Reef*, 1964; *Voices from the Sky*, 1965; *The Promise of Space*, 1968; *First on the Moon*, 1970 (with others); *Into Space*, 1971 (with Robert Silverberg); *Report on Planet Three*, 1972; *Beyond Jupiter*, 1972 (with Chesley Bonestall); *The Lost Worlds of 2001*, 1972; *The View from Serendip*, 1977; *1984: Spring, a Choice of Futures*, 1984; *Ascent to Orbit: A Scientific Autobiography*, 1984; *Arthur C. Clarke's July 20, 2019: Life in the 21st Century*, 1986; *The Odyssey File*, 1985 (with Peter Hyams); *Astounding Days: A Science*

Fictional Autobiography, 1989; *How the World Was One: Beyond the Global Village,* 1992; *By Space Possessed,* 1993; *The Snows of Olympus: A Garden of Mars,* 1994; *Greetings, Carbon-Based Bipeds! Collected Essays, 1934-1998,* 1999.

CHILDREN'S LITERATURE: *Islands in the Sky,* 1952; *Dolphin Island,* 1963.

Bibliography

Hollow, John. *Against the Night, the Stars: The Science Fiction of Arthur C. Clarke.* San Diego: Harcourt Brace Jovanovich, 1983. An analysis of major themes in Clarke's fiction.

McAleer, Neil. *Arthur C. Clarke: The Authorized Biography.* Chicago: Contemporary Books, 1992. A definitive account of Clarke's career, written with Clarke's cooperation.

Reid, Robin Anne. *Arthur C. Clarke: A Critical Companion.* Westport, Conn.: Greenwood Press, 1997. An accessible study of Clarke focusing on major novels after 1970.

Samuelson, David N. *Arthur C. Clarke: A Primary and Secondary Bibliography.* Boston: G. K. Hall, 1984. A complete bibliography of Clarke's works from the 1930's to early 1980's.

Slusser, George Edgar. *The Space Odysseys of Arthur C. Clarke.* San Bernardino, Calif.: Borgo Press, 1978. A brief but provocative commentary on Clarke's fiction.

Wilkie Collins

Born: London, England; January 8, 1824
Died: London, England; September 23, 1889

Principal long fiction · *Antonina: Or, The Fall of Rome*, 1850; *Basil: A Story of Modern Life*, 1852; *Hide and Seek*, 1854; *The Dead Secret*, 1857; *The Woman in White*, 1860; *No Name*, 1862; *Armadale*, 1866; *The Moonstone*, 1868; *Man and Wife*, 1870; *Poor Miss Finch: A Novel*, 1872; *The New Magdalen*, 1873; *The Law and the Lady*, 1875; *The Two Destinies: A Romance*, 1876; *A Rogue's Life*, 1879; *The Fallen Leaves*, 1879; *Jezebel's Daughter*, 1880; *The Black Robe*, 1881; *Heart and Science*, 1883; *I Say No*, 1884; *The Evil Genius: A Dramatic Story*, 1886; *The Legacy of Cain*, 1889; *Blind Love*, 1890 (completed by Walter Besant).

Other literary forms · Wilkie Collins produced a biography of his father in 1848 as well as travel books, essays and reviews, and a number of short stories. He also wrote and adapted plays, often in collaboration with Charles Dickens.

Achievements · Collins's reputation nearly a century after his death rests almost entirely on two works—*The Woman in White*, published serially in *All the Year Round* between November 26, 1859, and August 25, 1860; and *The Moonstone*, published in 1868. About this latter work, Dorothy Sayers said it is "probably the finest detective story ever written." No chronicler of crime and detective fiction can fail to include Collins's important contributions to the genre; simply for the ingenuity of his plots, Collins earned the admiration of T. S. Eliot. *The Woman in White* and *The Moonstone* have also been made into numerous adaptations for stage, film, radio, and television. Yet, for an author so conscientious and industrious—averaging one "big" novel every two years in his maturity—to be known as the author of two books would hardly be satisfactory. The relative obscurity into which most of Collins's work has fallen cannot be completely attributed to the shadow cast by his friend and sometime collaborator, Charles Dickens, nor to his physical infirmities and his addiction to laudanum, nor to the social vision which led him to write a succession of thesis novels. Indeed, the greatest mystery Collins left behind concerns the course of his literary career and subsequent reputation.

Biography · A pencil drawing survives, entitled "Wilkie Collins by his father William Collins, R. A." It shows a pretty, if serious, round face. The features beneath the end of the boy's nose are shaded, giving especial prominence to the upper face and forehead. The viewer at once is drawn to the boy's eyes. They are large, probing, mysterious, hardly the eyes of a child. Perhaps the artist-father sought to impart to his elder son some of his own austere, pious nature. William Collins (1788-1847), whose life began on the verge of one great European revolution and ended on the verge of another, was no revolutionary himself, nor the bohemian others of his calling imagined themselves. Instead, William Collins was a strict Sabbatarian, an individual who overcame by talent and perseverance the disadvantages of poverty. The novelist's paternal grandfather was an art dealer, a restorer, a storyteller who lovingly trained and cajoled his son in painting and drawing. William Collins did not begin to taste success until several years after the death of his father in 1812, but gradually commissions and patrons did come, including Sir Robert Peel. Befriended by noted artists such as Sir David Wilkie and Washington Allston, William Collins was at last elected to the Royal Academy in 1820. Two years later, he married Harriet Geddes. The names of both of their sons, born in 1824 and 1828, respectively, honored fellow artists: William Wilkie Collins and Charles Allston Collins.

Little is known of Wilkie Collins's early years, save that they appear to have been relatively tranquil. By 1833, Collins was already enrolled at Maida Hill Academy. In 1836, William Collins elected to take his family to Italy, where they remained until the late summer of 1838. The return to London required taking new lodgings at Regent's Park, and the fourteen-year-old Wilkie Collins was sent to boarding school at Highbury. By the close of 1840, he was presumably finished with school. His father's health began to fail, and the senior Collins made known his wish that Wilkie take holy orders, though the son apparently had no such inclinations. The choice became university or commerce. Wilkie Collins chose business, and he became an apprentice to the tea merchants Antrobus and Company in 1841. Collins performed well and was able to take a leave in order to accompany his father to Scotland the following summer. While still an apprentice, Collins began to write occasional pieces, and in August, 1843, *The Illuminated Magazine* published his first signed story, "The Last Stage Coachman." A novel about Polynesia was also written but discarded. In 1844, Collins traveled to Paris with his friend Charles Ward, and he made a second visit in 1845. While William Collins's health began to deteriorate more rapidly, his son was released from his apprenticeship and decided upon the study of law. In February, 1847, William Collins died.

Wilkie Collins emulated his father's self-discipline, industry, and especially his love of art and beauty, yet if one judges by the series of self-serving religious zealots who populate Collins's fiction, one must assume that, while he respected his father's artistic sensibilities, he did not admire his pious ardor. Instead, Wilkie Collins seems in most things to have taken the example of his mother, a woman of loving good nature and humor with whom both he and his brother Charles remained close until her death. Nevertheless, William Collins near the end of life had asked Wilkie to write his biography, providing the opportunity for the young man's first published book, *Memoirs of the Life of William Collins, R. A.*, published in 1848 in two volumes. While the narrator tends toward self-effacement and burdens his readers with minute detail, the work is nevertheless a formidable accomplishment. Researches on the book led Collins into correspondence with the American writer Richard Henry Dana and with a circle of established and rising artists, including E. M. Ward (brother of his friend Charles), Augustus Egg, John Everett Millais, Holman Hunt, and the Rossettis. At this time, Collins completed his historical novel *Antonina*, filled with gothic violence and adventure, a work that attracted the serious attention of John Ruskin. It was published in 1850, the same year in which Collins made his first public stage appearance in *A Court Duel*, which he had adapted from the French. With the success of his first dramatic work and the surprisingly positive reception of *Antonina*, Collins began to enjoy a rising reputation.

Richard Bentley published Collins's account of a Cornwall hiking trip taken during the summer of 1850 in January, 1851, as *Rambles Beyond Railways*. Two months later, Egg introduced the twenty-seven-year-old Collins to Dickens, and the initial contact resulted in Collins taking part in Dickens's theatrical, *Not So Bad as We Seem*, written by Edward Bulwer-Lytton. (Until Dickens's death in 1870, he and Collins remained staunch friends, though there remains some indication of friction following Collins's success with *The Moonstone* and Dickens's supposed attempt to outdo his junior in his incomplete novel, *The Mystery of Edwin Drood,* 1870.) In 1852, after having tried to sell the version of a story that would become "Mad Monkton" to Dickens, Collins published "A Terribly Strange Bed," anthologized often since, in *Household Words* (1850-1859). The following years saw considerable collaboration between the two authors, not the least of which were Collins's stories for the Christmas annuals such as *Mr. Wray's Cash-Box: Or, The Mask and the Mystery* (1852); the collaboration *The Seven Poor Travellers* (1854); *The Wreck of the Golden Mary* (1856), a work often attributed to Dickens until the late twentieth century; the novel *The Dead Secret* (1857); and numerous other stories and articles. In 1853, Collins, Dickens, and Egg traveled together in Italy and Switzerland. Four years later, Dickens produced Collins's play *The Frozen Deep,* later noting that the self-sacrifice of the central character, Richard Wardour (played by Dickens), provided the germ for *A Tale of Two Cities* (1859). Although never published as a play, *The Frozen Deep* was published in 1874 as a collection of short stories.

The impact each had on the writing of the other has long been a topic of controversy and speculation for critics and biographers; generally unchallenged is the influence of Collins's meticulous plotting on his senior. In turn, Dickens often corrected and refined by suggestion Collins's fiction, although he never agreed with Collins's practice of including prefaces which upbraided critics and the public alike. When Collins published *Basil* (having included for Bentley's publication in book form the first of those vexing prefaces), he forwarded the volumes to Dickens. After a two-week silence, there came a thoughtful, admiring reply: "I have made Basil's acquaintance," wrote Dickens at the end of 1852, "with great gratification, and entertain high respect for him. I hope that I shall become intimate with many worthy descendants of his, who are yet in the limbo of creatures waiting to be born." Collins did not disappoint Dickens on that count over their years of friendship and collaboration; indeed, they became "family" when Charles Allston Collins married Dickens's daughter Kate.

Household Words faded in 1859 along with Dickens's association with the publishers Bradbury and Evans. Dickens's new periodical, *All the Year Round* (1859-1870), began auspiciously with the publication of *A Tale of Two Cities.* After its run, he needed something to keep public interest in the new magazine from abating, and Collins provided it with *The Woman in White.* Its monumental success put Collins into that rarest literary circle: that of well-to-do authors. Its success also coincided with other important events—personal ones—in Collins's life.

Collins had lived the life of a bachelor, residing with his brother and mother at least into his early thirties. Their house was often open to guests. On one such evening, the author and his brother escorted home the artist Millais through then rural North London. Suddenly, a woman appeared to them in the moonlight, attired in flowing robes, all in white. Though distraught, she gained her composure and vanished as quickly as she had appeared. The author was most astounded, and insisted he would discover the identity of the lovely creature. J. G. Millais, the painter's son, who narrates this anecdote in a life of his father, does not reveal the lady's ultimate identity: "Her subsequent history, interesting as it is, is not for these pages." The woman was Caroline Elizabeth Graves, born 1834, mother of a little girl, Harriet. Her husband, G. R. Graves, may or may not have been dead. Of him, only his name is known.

Clearly, however, the liaison between Caroline Graves and Wilkie Collins was fully under way when he began to write *The Woman in White*. From at least 1859, the couple lived together in a secret relationship known only to their closest friends, until the autumn of 1868, when for obscure reasons Caroline married the son of a distiller, John C. Clow. Collins, not one to waste time, started a new liaison with Martha Rudd. This union produced three children: Marian (1869), Harriet Constance (1871), and William Charles (1874). The children took the surname Dawson, but Collins freely admitted his paternity. By this time, too, Caroline and her daughter returned, and Harriet Graves for a time served as her mother's lover's amanuensis; Collins adopted her as his daughter. A lover of hearty food, fine champagne, and good cigars, Collins appears to have lived in private a life that would have shocked many of his readers. Still, Collins treated his "morganatic family" quite well: He provided handsomely for his natural and adopted children and for their mothers. When she died in 1895 at sixty-one, Caroline Elizabeth Graves was interred beside the author of *The Woman in White*.

As Collins's private life began taking on its unconventional proportions in the 1860's, his public career grew more distinguished. His output for *All the Year Round* in shorter forms declined; he simply did not need the money. In March, 1861, a didactic novel about inheritance, *No Name*, began its run; it was published in volume form in December, 1862. A year later, Collins resigned his editorial assignment for Dickens's periodical and also published, with Sampson Low, Son, and Company, *My Miscellanies*, bringing together, in two volumes, work that had first appeared in the two Dickens periodicals. After about seven years of almost obsessive productivity, Collins relented, but only for a time; he began *Armadale* in the spring of 1864, for serial publication in *The Cornhill Magazine* in Britain and *Harper's Monthly* in the United States. This exploration of inherited and personal guilt remains one of Collins's most adept and popular novels; it is also his longest. He wrote a dramatic version of the novel in 1866, but not until it appeared as *Miss Gwilt* (1876) was it produced.

In 1867, Collins and Dickens began their last collaboration, *No Thoroughfare*, an adventure set in the Alps and perhaps not unaffected by their shared Swiss journey many years before. By this time, too, Collins began to suffer tremendously from the good living he had long enjoyed—gout of the areas around the eyes drove him into excruciating pain, requiring the application of bandages for weeks at a time. To allay the ache, Collins developed a habit for laudanum, that tincture of opium that fills the darker recesses of middle Victorian culture. It was in this period of alternating pain and bliss that Collins penned *The Moonstone*, for *All the Year Round*, beginning in January, 1868. It was an uncontestable triumph; Collins himself thought it wonderfully wrought.

Yet *The Moonstone* had hardly begun its run when Collins's mother died, and later that same year, Caroline married Clow. When the novel was finished, Collins again turned to the stage, writing *Black and White* with his actor-friend Charles Fechter, which successfully opened in March, 1869. At the end of the year, the serialization of *Man and Wife* began in *Harper's Weekly* and in January, 1870, in *Cassell's Magazine*. Posterity has judged *Man and Wife* more harshly than did its first readers. It was a different kind of novel from *The Moonstone*: It attacked society's growing obsession with athleticism and castigated marital laws which Collins believed to be cruel, unfair, and unrealistic. Collins's "standard" modern biographer, Kenneth Robinson, sees *Man and Wife* as the turning point in Collins's career, the start of the "Downhill" (his chapter title) phase of the writer's life. It sold well after its serialization; Collins also wrote a four-act dramatic version, although it did not appear onstage until 1873.

At the same time, Collins adapted *No Name* for the theater, and in 1871, *The Woman in White*. This play opened at the Olympic Theatre in October and ran for five months before going on tour. The same year saw the beginning of a new novel in serial, *Poor Miss Finch*, about a blind woman who falls in love with an epileptic whose cure turns him blue. When she is temporarily cured of her affliction, she finds herself in a dilemma about her blue lover, whose healthy twin also desires her love. A year later the indefatigible Collins published *The New Magdalen* in a magazine called *Temple Bar*, whose heroine, a virtuous prostitute, outraged contemporary critics. Its dramatization (1873) was greeted with enthusiasm.

As his work increasingly turned to exposing social hypocrisies, Collins sought to regulate as a writer of established repute the body of his published work. Since *Basil*, wholesale piracy had angered him and hurt his finances. By the early 1870's, he had reached agreement with the German publisher Tauchnitz, with Harper and Brothers in America, and, by 1875, with Chatto & Windus in Britain. Chatto & Windus not only bought all extant copyrights to Collins's work but also became his publisher for the rest of his life. This arrangement was finalized in the year after Collins, like his friend Dickens before him, had undertaken a reading tour of the United States and Canada. Apparently, while in New York, his gout had relented sufficiently for him to demand only brut champagne.

The years 1875 and 1876 saw the publication of two popular but lesser novels, *The Law and the Lady* and *The Two Destinies*. The next year was marked, however, by the successful dramatization of *The Moonstone* and the beginning of Collins's friendship with Charles Reade. In 1879, Collins wrote *The Haunted Hotel* for *The Belgravia Magazine*, a ghost story fresh in invention that extends one's notions about the genre. Meanwhile, however, Collins's health became less certain and his laudanum draughts became more frequent and potent. The decade took away many close friends, beginning with Dickens, and later, his brother Charles, then Augustus Egg.

In the last decade of his life, Collins became more reclusive, though not much less productive. He adapted his 1858 play, *The Red Vial*, into a novel *Jezebel's Daughter*. He also began, for serialization in *The Canadian Monthly*, the novel *The Black Robe*, whose central figure is a priest plotting to encumber the wealth of a large estate. The work has been regarded as the most successful of his longer, late novels. It was followed by a more controversial novel, *Heart and Science*, a polemic against vivisection that appeared in 1883. The same year saw Collins's last theatrical, *Rank and Riches*, an unqualified disaster that brought the leading lady to tears before the first-act curtain and which led her leading man, G. W. Anson, to berate the audience. Collins thereafter gave up writing for the stage, save a one-performance version of *The Evil Genius* (1885), quickly recast as a novel that proved his single most lucrative publication.

Although 1884 saw the passing of Reade, Collins's closest friend of the time, he continued to write steadily. *The Guilty River* made its appearance in the *Arrowsmith Christmas Annual* for 1886; in 1887, Chatto & Windus published *Little Novels*, collecting earlier stories. Two works also appeared that ended the battle Collins had long waged with critics. A young man, Harry Quilter, published an encomiastic article for *The Contemporary Review*, "A Living Story-Teller." Collins himself wrote "How I Write My Books" for *The Globe*, an account of composing *The Woman in White*. As his health at last began to fail precipitously in 1888, Collins completed his final serial novel, *The Legacy of Cain*. It appeared in three volumes the following year, at a time when he was finished writing *Blind Love* for *The Illustrated London News*. On the evening of June 30, 1889, Collins suffered a stroke. He requested Walter Besant, then traveling in the north, to return and complete the tale. Collins had long ago befriended Dickens's physician and neighbor, Frank Beard. Beard did what little could be done to comfort Collins in his final days. Just past mid-morning, on September 23, 1889, Wilkie Collins died, Beard at his bedside.

Four days following his death, Collins was buried at Kensal Green; his procession was headed by Caroline Graves, Harriet Graves, and his surviving literary, theatrical, and household friends. Despite infirmities, Collins had lived a life long and full, remaining productive, industrious, and successful throughout his career.

Analysis · At its best, Wilkie Collins's fiction is characterized by a transparent style that occasionally pleases and surprises the reader with an apt turn of word or phrase; by a genius for intricate plots; by a talent for characterization that in at least one instance must earn the epithet "Miltonic"; and by an eye for detail that seems to make the story worth telling. These are the talents of an individual who learned early to look at things like a painter, to see the meaning, the emotion behind the gesture or pose–a habit of observation which constituted William Collins's finest bequest to his elder son.

Little Novels · The transparency of Collins's style rests on his adherence to the conventions of the popular fiction of his day. More so than contemporaries, he talks to readers, cajoles them, often protesting that the author will recede into the shadows in order that the reader may judge the action for himself. The "games"–as one current critic observes–that Collins plays with readers revolve about his mazelike plots, his "ingenuous" interruptions of the narrative, and his iterative language, symbolic names, and metaphors. Thus, at the beginning of "Mrs. Zant and the Ghost," published in *Little Novels*, the narrator begins by insisting that this tale of "supernatural influence" occurs in the daylight hours, adding "the writer declines to follow modern examples by thrusting himself and his opinions on the public view. He returns to the shadow from which he has emerged, and leaves the opposing forces of incredulity and belief to fight the old battle over again, on the old ground." The apt word is "shadow," for certainly, this story depicts a shadow world. At its close, when the preternatural events have occurred, the reader is left to assume a happy resolution between the near victim Mrs. Zant and her earthly rescuer, Mr. Rayburn, through the mood of the man's daughter:

> Arrived at the end of the journey, Lucy held fast by Mrs. Zant's hand. Tears were rising in the child's eyes. "Are we to bid her good-bye?" she said sadly to her father.
> He seemed to be unwilling to trust himself to speak; he only said, "My dear, ask her yourself."
> But the result justified him. Lucy was happy again.

Here, Collins's narrator has receded like Mrs. Zant's supernatural protector, leaving the reader to hope and to expect that Mrs. Zant can again find love in this world. This kind of exchange–direct and inferred–between author and reader can go in other directions. Surely, when near the middle of *The Woman in White*, one realizes that Count Fosco has read–as it were–over one's shoulder the diary of Miss Halcolmbe, the author intends that one should feel violated, while at the same time forced into collusion with the already attractive, formidable villain.

The Woman in White and ***The Moonstone*** · Because Collins's style as narrator is so frequently self-effacing, it sustains the ingenuity of his plots. These are surely most elaborate in *The Woman in White* and *The Moonstone*. In both cases, Collins elects to have one figure, party to the main actions, assemble the materials of different narratives into cohesive form. It is a method far less tedious than that of epistolary novels, and provides for both mystery and suspense. Although not the ostensible theme in either work, matters of self-identity and control over one's behavior operate in the contest between virtue and vice, good and evil. Thus, Laura Fairlie's identity is obliterated in an attempt to wrest from her her large fortune; thus, Franklin Blake, heavily drugged, unconsciously removes a gem that makes him the center of elaborate investigation. In each novel, the discovery of the actual circumstances restores identity to these characters. The capacity to plot allows Collins to surprise his readers profoundly: In *The Woman in White*, one is astounded to be confronted by Laura Fairlie standing in the churchyard, above her own grave. In *The Moonstone*, one is baffled when the detective, Sergeant Cuff, provides a plausible solution to the theft of the diamond which turns out to be completely incorrect.

The novels of the 1860's find Collins having firmly established his transparent detachment from the subjects at hand, in turn giving full scope to his meticulous sense of plot. *No Name* and *Armadale* are no less complex in their respective actions than their more widely read counterparts. Interestingly, though, all of these novels explore matters of identity and motive for action; they attest Collins's ability to relate popular tales that encompass more serious issues.

Because he had a painter's eye for detail, Collins was a master of characterization, even when it appears that a character is flat. Consider, for example, this passage from "Miss Dulane and My Lord" published in *Little Novels*:

> Mrs. Newsham, tall and elegant, painted and dyed, acted on the opposite principle in dressing, which confesses nothing. On exhibition before the world, this lady's disguise asserted she had reached her thirtieth year on her last birthday. Her husband was discreetly silent, and Father Time was discreetly silent; they both knew that her last birthday had happened thirty years since.

Here an incidental figure in a minor tale remains fixed, the picture of one comically out of synchronization with her own manner; before she has uttered a syllable, one dislikes her. Consider, on the other hand, the initial appearance of a woman one will grow to like and admire, Marian Halcolmbe, as she makes her way to meet Walter Hartright in *The Woman in White*:

> She turned towards me immediately. The easy elegance of every movement of her limbs and body as soon as she began to advance from the far end of the room, set me in a flutter of expectation to see her face clearly. She left the window—and I said to myself, The lady is dark. She moved forward a few steps—and I said to myself, The lady is young. She approached nearer—and I said to myself (with a sense of surprise which words fail me to express), The lady is ugly!

Not only does this passage reveal Collins's superb sense of pace, his ability to set a trap of astonished laughter, but also it reveals some of Hartright's incorrect assumptions about the position he has taken at Limmeridge House; for example, that the two young women he will instruct are pampered, spoiled, and not worth his serious consideration. Preeminently, it shows the grace of Marian Halcombe, a grace that overcomes her lack of physical beauty in conventional senses and points to her indefatigable intelligence and loyalty so crucial to future events in the novel. Marian is, too, a foil for her half sister, Laura Fairlie, the victim of the main crimes in the book. While one might easily dismiss Laura Fairlie with her name—she is fair and petite and very vulnerable—she also displays a quiet resilience and determination in the face of overwhelming adversaries.

The most memorable of Collins's characters is Count Fosco in the same novel, whose name immediately suggests a bludgeon. To Marian Halcombe, Collins gives the job of describing the Count: "He looks like a man who could tame anything." In his characterization of Fosco, Collins spawned an entire race of fat villains and, occasionally, fat detectives, such as Nero Wolfe and Gideon Fell. One is not surprised that Sydney Greenstreet played both Fosco and his descendant, Caspar Gutman, in film versions of *The Woman in White* and Dashiell Hammett's *The Maltese Falcon* (1930). In one of his best speeches, Fosco reveals the nature of his hubris, his evil genius:

> Crimes cause their own detection, do they? . . . there are foolish criminals who are discovered, and wise criminals who escape. The hiding of a crime, or the detection of a crime, what is it? A trial of skill between the police on one side, and the individual on the other. When the criminal is a brutal, ignorant fool, the police in nine cases out of ten win. When the criminal is a resolute, educated, highly-intelligent man, the police in nine cases out of ten lose.

In pitting decent people against others who manipulate the law and social conventions to impose their wills, Collins frequently creates characters more interesting for their deficiencies than for their virtues. His novels pit, sensationally at times, the unsuspecting, the infirm, or the unprepossessing, against darker figures, usually operating under the scope of social acceptance. Beneath the veneer of his fiction, one finds in Collins a continuing struggle to legitimize the illegitimate, to neutralize hypocrisy, and to subvert the public certainties of his era.

Kenneth Friedenreich

Other major works

SHORT FICTION: *Rambles Beyond Railways*, 1851; *Mr. Wray's Cash-Box: Or, The Mask and the Mystery*, 1852; *The Seven Poor Travellers*, 1854; *After Dark*, 1856; *The Wreck of the Golden Mary*, 1856; *The Queen of Hearts*, 1859; *Miss or Mrs.? and Other Stories*, 1873; *The Frozen Deep*, 1874; *The Haunted Hotel: A Mystery of Modern Venice*, 1879; *The Guilty River*, 1886; *Little Novels*, 1887; *The Lazy Tour of Two Apprentices*, 1890 (with Charles Dickens).

PLAYS: *No Thoroughfare*, pr., pb. 1867 (with Charles Dickens); *The New Magdalen*, pr., pb. 1873; *Man and Wife*, pr. 1873; *The Moonstone*, pr., pb. 1877.

NONFICTION: *Memoirs of the Life of William Collins, R. A.*, 1848 (2 volumes); *The Letters of Wilkie Collins*, 1999 (edited by William Baker and William M. Clarke).

MISCELLANEOUS: *My Miscellanies*, 1863; *The Works of Wilkie Collins*, 1900, 1970 (30 volumes).

Bibliography

Gasson, Andrew. *Wilkie Collins: An Illustrated Guide*. New York: Oxford University Press, 1998. A well-illustrated, alphabetical guide to characters, titles, and terms in Collins. Includes a chronology, the Collins family tree, maps, and a bibliography.
Nayder, Lillian. *Wilkie Collins*. New York: Twayne, 1997. A good introductory study of the author. Includes biographical information and literary criticism.

O'Neill, Philip. *Wilkie Collins: Women, Property, and Propriety.* New York: Macmillan, 1988. Seeks to move the discussion of Collins away from popularist categories by using modern feminist criticism deconstructively to open up a more considered version of his thematic material. Contains a full bibliography.

Page, Norman. *Wilkie Collins.* Boston: Routledge & Kegan Paul, 1974. One of the Critical Heritage series, this is a full anthology of Collins's critical reception from 1850 through 1891. Contains a short bibliography.

Peters, Catherine. *The King of Inventors: A Life of Wilkie Collins.* Princeton, N.J.: Princeton University Press, 1991. A comprehensive biography, with detailed notes and bibliography.

Pykett, Lyn, ed. *Wilkie Collins.* New York: St. Martin's Press, 1998. An excellent place for the beginning student to begin. Includes bibliographical references and an index.

Taylor, Jenny. *In the Secret Theatre of Home: Wilkie Collins, Sensation Narrative, and Nineteenth Century Psychology.* New York: Routledge, 1988. The subtitle of this study suggests its perspective. However, it deals as fully with social structures and how these shape the structures of Collins's major fiction. Contains full notes and an excellent select bibliography of both primary and secondary material.

Ivy Compton-Burnett

Born: Pinner, England; June 5, 1884
Died: London, England; August 27, 1969

Principal long fiction · *Dolores*, 1911; *Pastors and Masters*, 1925; *Brothers and Sisters*, 1929; *Men and Wives*, 1931; *More Women than Men*, 1933; *A House and Its Head*, 1935; *Daughters and Sons*, 1937; *A Family and a Fortune*, 1939; *Parents and Children*, 1941; *Elders and Betters*, 1944; *Manservant and Maidservant*, 1947 (pb. in U.S. as *Bullivant and the Lambs*, 1948); *Two Worlds and Their Ways*, 1949; *Darkness and Day*, 1951; *The Present and the Past*, 1953; *Mother and Son*, 1955; *A Father and His Fate*, 1957; *A Heritage and Its History*, 1959; *The Mighty and Their Fall*, 1961; *A God and His Gifts*, 1963; *The Last and the First*, 1971.

Other literary forms · Ivy Compton-Burnett is known only for her novels.

Achievements · Compton-Burnett is a novelist's novelist, much appreciated by her peers. She has been compared by her partisans to figures as various as Jane Austen, Jean Racine, Henry James, Leo Tolstoy, George Eliot, Anton Chekhov, the Elizabethan tragedians, William Congreve, Oscar Wilde, George Meredith, Elizabeth Gaskell, Harold Pinter, and the cubists. Her appeal is to a growing circle of admirers, although her work has enjoyed neither popular adulation nor widespread critical attention. Her novels require slow and attentive reading and make heavy demands upon the reader, yet they do not offer the inviting depths of works such as James Joyce's *Ulysses* (1922) and William Faulkner's *The Sound and the Fury* (1929). Compton-Burnett's modernism is of a different kind: Her works present hard and brittle surfaces, and her style reaches its purest expression in pages of unbroken dialogue, highly stylized and crackling with suppressed emotion. Her uncompromising artistry won for her a small but permanent place in twentieth century world literature.

Biography · Ivy Compton-Burnett always thought she would write, even when she was quite young. She came from a well-to-do family: Her father, James Compton Burnett (no hyphen), was a doctor and direct descendant of the ecclesiastical writer Bishop Gilbert Burnett. Ivy adored her father and from him inherited a love of words and of nature. Her mother, Katharine Rees Compton-Burnett, was the second wife of her father: Katharine became stepmother to five children at marriage and mother of seven more, of whom Ivy was the oldest. Katharine seems to have been the prototype for several of the tyrants in Compton-Burnett's works: She was beautiful, autocratic, indifferent to her stepchildren and distant to her own. The real mother to the children was their nurse Minnie. Olive, the eldest of all the children, was bitterly jealous of her stepmother and of Ivy for her close relationship with their father.

Compton-Burnett's closest companions were her two younger brothers, Guy and Noel (Jim). The three were educated together, first by a governess, then by a tutor, and Compton-Burnett always remained proud that she had had a boy's education. She loved Latin and Greek. In 1902, she entered Royal Holloway College, London

University; in 1904, she was awarded the Founder's Scholarship; in 1906, she passed the bachelor of arts honors examination in the classics. Her love of the classics appears clearly in her works: Her plots, with their recurring motifs of incest and family murder, seem straight from Greek tragedy; her characters often allude to Greek tragedy; her view of life as cruel and ironic is the tragic view of the Greek dramatists, skewed by modern experience and by her own temperament.

Compton-Burnett claimed to have written very little before her first novel, *Dolores*, was published. She discounted *Dolores* entirely in later life, uncertain which parts were hers and which were the work of her overly enthusiastic brother Noel. Between the publication of *Dolores* and *Pastors and Masters*, her second novel, is a gap of fourteen years which was filled with family turbulence. After the death of both her parents, Ivy became head of the household and a bit of a tyrant herself. Her four younger sisters and Minnie moved out and set up their own household which they refused to let Ivy visit. Compton-Burnett's only remaining brother, Noel (Guy had died earlier), was killed in World War I, and the author cared for his widow after she took an overdose of sleeping pills. Around the same time, Ivy's two youngest sisters committed suicide. She herself had a bout with Spanish influenza which drained her energy for some years.

In the early 1920's, Compton-Burnett settled in a flat in London with her friend, Margaret Jourdain, an authority on Regency furniture, with whom she lived for thirty years. Jourdain was the more famous and remained the dominant of the pair. The two women traveled abroad together every year, where Compton-Burnett pursued her passion of collecting wildflowers. Every odd-numbered year, with only a few exceptions, she produced a novel. World War II disturbed her greatly: She and Jourdain fled to the country to escape the bombing. When Jourdain died in 1951, Compton-Burnett felt betrayed by her "desertion."

In her later years, many honors were bestowed upon Compton-Burnett. She was made a Commander of the Order of the British Empire in 1951; she was awarded the James Tait Black Memorial Prize in 1956; in 1960, she received an honorary doctor of letters degree from the University of Leeds; in 1967, she was made a Dame Commander of the British Empire.

Compton-Burnett dedicated her life to her art, reading and working continually. She had little wish to reveal the details of her private life, "I haven't been at all deedy"—and believed that all she had to offer the world could be found in her books.

Analysis · Ivy Compton-Burnett has no wide range of style or subject in her twenty novels. Like Jane Austen, she limits her characters to a few well-to-do families in the country. The action takes place in the late Victorian era, though there are few indications of any time period. Scenery is almost nonexistent, and no heavy Victorian furnishings clutter the scene.

Compton-Burnett concentrates entirely on her characters, not in describing them but in having them reveal (and sometimes betray) themselves in what they do and do not say. Her novels demand more of the ear than of the eye. They have been likened to plays in their spareness of description, narration, exposition, and their concentration on talk. Dialogue indeed is the reason why her novels draw readers and is her chief contribution to the art of the novel. Each chapter contains one event, which is discussed in detail by one family, and then perhaps another, or by the masters in the house and then the servants. Although Compton-Burnett as an omniscient author does not comment on or analyze her characters or their motives, her chorus of servants, children, neighbors, and schoolmistresses do so incessantly. In this way, she achieves many points of view instead of only one.

Compton-Burnett's novels do have plots—melodramatic and sometimes implausible ones with murders, incest, infidelity, and perversions of justice. At times, she drops enough clues for the reader to know what will happen; at other times, events occur arbitrarily. Shipwrecked characters often reappear; documents are stolen or concealed only to turn up later. Eavesdroppers populate her novels. Several people, for example, coincidentally walk into a room when they are being slandered. Although the events themselves are often too coincidental, the highly crafted conversations about them prove Compton-Burnett's talent as a writer. These witty and ironic conversations insist on the revelation of truth, on the precise use of language, making Compton-Burnett's novels memorable. Language insulates people against the primitive forces, the unmentionable deeds of which they are capable. Her witty dialogue tends to anesthetize the reader's response (and the characters' as well) to horrendous crimes of passion.

Compton-Burnett's novels explore all the tensions of family life—between strong and weak, between generations, between classes. Power is her chief subject, with love, money, and death as constant attendants. Her main foes are complacency, tyranny, and hypocrisy. Compton-Burnett deplores sloppy thinking and dishonesty, whether with oneself or with others. Her novels clearly indicate her view of human nature. She believes that wickedness is often not punished and that is why it is prevalent. When wickedness is likely to be punished, most people, she thinks, are intelligent enough to avoid it. She also sees very few people as darkly evil; many people, when subjected to strong and sudden temptation without the risk of being found out, yield to such an urge. Even her bad characters have some good in them. Although the good points of the tyrants can be recognized, their cruelty can never be forgiven. Yet, ironically, their cruelty often produces good results. The victims build up bravery, loyalty, and affection as defenses against the wicked and cruel. Compton-Burnett's novels, above all, elicit concern for human suffering.

Though she does believe in economic and hereditary forces, Compton-Burnett also believes in free will. She is one of the rare novelists whose good-hearted characters are credible as well as likable. The good and innocent characters in her novels, particularly the children, are not corrupted and usually remain unharmed. They conquer by truth, affection, and, most important, by intelligence. Compton-Burnett shows the great resilience of the human spirit; her characters survive atrocities and then settle down to resume their everyday lives. In her novels, the greatest crimes are not crimes of violence, but crimes against the human spirit: one person beating down, wounding, or enslaving another's spirit. Yet her novels do not end with a feeling of despair. They end, rather, with a feeling of understanding. The good characters see the faults of the tyrants yet continue to love them and gallantly pick them up when they have fallen. The good characters realize that evil and good are inextricable.

Compton-Burnett's strengths and weaknesses as a novelist are both suggested by the fact that she has no masterpiece, no best or greatest novel. Her oeuvre has a remarkable consistency, the product of an unswerving artistic intelligence yet also evidence of a certain narrowness and rigidity. By general consensus, her strongest works are those of her middle period, including *Brothers and Sisters, More Women than Men, A Family and a Fortune,* and *Manservant and Maidservant.*

Brothers and Sisters · *Brothers and Sisters,* Compton-Burnett's third novel, is distinguished by the appearance of the first of many tyrannical women in her oeuvre.
Sophia Stace (who, like the later tyrants, is a tragic figure as well) wants attention and
affection, but she is never willing to give in return. She never sees beyond herself or
acts for anyone but herself. Her daughter Dinah succinctly comments: "Power has
never been any advantage to Sophia. . . . It has her worn out, and everyone who would
have served her."

Sophia's self-absorption leads to disaster. Thinking her father's instructions, which
are locked in a desk, will cut her and her adopted brother out of his will, Sophia leaves
them there unread, marries her adopted brother (who is really her half brother), and
bears three children. Her husband dies of a heart attack after finding out the truth
about his and Sophia's parentage, and Sophia reacts to his death by imprisoning
herself in her home. Intending to draw attention to herself, Sophia dramatizes her
grief. When her children attempt to resume life as usual, she moans that they feel no
affection for her: "I don't know whether you like sitting there, having your dinner,
with your mother eating nothing?" Like other Compton-Burnett tyrants, she turns
mealtime into domestic inquisition.

The only one who can control Sophia, modeled on Compton-Burnett's mother
Katharine, is Miss Patmore, modeled on Compton-Burnett's own nurse Minnie. The
children love and respect "Patty" as a mother since their own is incapable of giving
love. When Sophia herself finds out the truth, she has no feeling for what the revelation
will do to her children. They meet the tragedy with characteristic wittiness to cover the
pain: "Well if we are equal to this occasion, no other in our lives can find us at a loss.
We may look forward to all emergencies without misgiving." The children, though they
have been Sophia's victims, are able to realize after her death that she, more than
anyone else, has been her own victim: "The survey of Sophia's life flashed on them,
the years of ruthlessness and tragedy, power and grief. Happiness, of which she held
to have had so much, had never been real to Sophia. They saw it now." Power thus eats
away at the powerful while their victims rise to a higher moral plane of understanding.

Brothers and Sisters has many of the standard Compton-Burnett plot ingredients:
incest, illegitimacy, domestic torture, and the family secret that becomes public
knowledge. What gives the novel added strength is the subplot of Peter Bateman and
his children, another example of a parent who blithely torments his children. Socially
gauche, Peter's vicious stupidity inflicts painful embarrassment on his skulking son
Latimer and his self-effacing daughter Tilly. He determinedly pigeonholes his children into demeaning positions.

While the bond between parents and children in the novel is a brutal one, the bond
between brothers and sisters becomes a saving one. Sophia's children, Andrew,
Robin, and Dinah, support one another, and they are not the only brothers and sisters
in the novel to do so. There are three other sets of brothers and sisters: Edward and
Judith, Julian and Sarah, and Gilbert and Caroline, all friends of the Stace children.
At various points in the novel, Andrew and Dinah are engaged to Caroline and
Gilbert, then to Judith and Edward, and finally Julian proposes to Dinah but is
rejected. The Stace children and their friends change romantic partners as if they were
merely changing partners at a dance, partly in reaction to the tragic secrets that are
revealed, and partly because Compton-Burnett has little faith in marriage or in
romantic love. Her marriages are matters of convenience, timing, and location; none
of her husbands and wives grow together in a fulfilling relationship. The strongest
love bond is always the fraternal bond.

More Women than Men · Like Compton-Burnett's first two novels, *More Women than Men* is a school novel. The schoolmistresses of Josephine Napier's girls' school function as the villagers do in Compton-Burnett's manor novels: They serve as a chorus for the main action and provide comic relief from the main tragic action (Miss Munday, the senior teacher, is particularly good at this). The schoolmistresses, however, have less freedom than the villagers: In a society where unmarried or widowed women have few options in supporting themselves, they are bound to the tyrant Josephine.

More Women than Men, like *Men and Wives* and *A House and Its Head*, the novels that immediately preceded and followed it, is a very somber work. Josephine is morally, though not legally, guilty of murder; she exposes her nephew Gabriel's wife, who is deathly ill with pneumonia, to cold blasts of air. She is also a hypocrite par excellence. When her husband Simon dies, she affects ostentatious mourning and claims, "I am not a person to take a pride in not being able to eat and sleep," yet she does exactly that. In reality, she feels little at his death. Gabriel, her morose victim, is also one of the few people who stands up to her. When she makes such claims as "I am not an ogress," Gabriel flatly replies, "Well, you are rather." His standing up to her, though, cannot prevent his wife's murder.

There are two other important elements in Josephine's complex personality: sexual repression and dominance. Indeed, *More Women than Men* is preoccupied with the psychology of sex and with gender differences. Men and women are attracted both to women and to men. Josephine, for example, many years before the book begins, has stolen Simon from Elizabeth Giffard; she disposes of Ruth Giffard so she can reclaim her nephew Gabriel's affections; she thrusts herself on Felix Bacon and, when rejected, accepts the love of Miss Rossetti, Gabriel's natural mother. For Josephine, sex is purely an expression of power.

Josephine's cruel oppression is counterbalanced by another sexually amorphous character, the comic Felix Bacon. Felix begins the novel as the homosexual companion of Josephine's brother, inherits a manor and a fortune in the course of the novel, and marries the intelligent young heroine Helen Keats at the end. He triumphs in that he escapes Josephine's smothering affection and is able to be master of his own world, yet he still feels a longing for the old situation. One can never break completely free from the stranglehold of the tyrant.

Gender differences are explored in many of Compton-Burnett's novels. In *Pastors and Masters*, she had already dealt with the relative merits of men and women. Emily Herrick, the novel's main character, had maintained that men are egotistical and "devious." In *More Women than Men*, Compton-Burnett raises the problem of the shoddy attention women receive. Felix, for example, wryly remarks that parents express surprise that their daughters' education should be taken seriously. "It is a good thing that they entrust it to other people . . . they don't seem to give any real thought to their being the mothers of the race." Although never an ardent supporter of feminist causes, Compton-Burnett did object to the unequal treatment women received, especially in terms of education.

A Family and a Fortune · *A Family and a Fortune* is one of Compton-Burnett's kindliest novels. Matty Seaton, the tyrant, is not like the tyrants of earlier novels: She has neither the highly dramatic and tragic sense of Sophia Stace nor the magnetizing and suffocating attraction of Josephine Napier. She wants to be needed by others and craves power, but her tyranny is limited because she is a maiden aunt (not a mother), because she is financially dependent on her sister's family, because she cannot actively move about (she was crippled in a riding accident), and because she lives in a lodge separated from the main family in the manor. With these limitations, she becomes a study of frustrated tyranny. Compton-Burnett introduces her thus: "Her energy seemed to accumulate and to work itself out at the cost of some havoc within her." All that is left of her youthful attractiveness is her overpowering self-regard. She tries to make herself needed by cutting down others with recrimination and guilt, but all her maneuvers are transparent. She releases her frustration by browbeating her paid companion Miss Griffin, whom she even drives out into the cold one night.

While Matty's energies are loosed into negative and destructive channels, her niece Justine releases her own similar energies in positive and constructive routes. Justine is one of the best of the strong-minded, clear-seeing, female characters whom Compton-Burnett uses to balance her tyrants (Patty in *Brothers and Sisters* and Rachel in *Men and Wives* are other examples). Justine is the one who patches the leaky boat of family life with her optimistic matter-of-factness. Self-effacing and comic, she is "utterly honest" with herself, particularly about her own potential weaknesses. She busies herself about everyone's business but never lapses into tyranny and willingly yields her power when her father remarries. Though a bit officious, she brings a positive force to the family and the novel, insisting that life has meaning: "All human effort must achieve something essential, if not apparent," she explains. She is one of the few Compton-Burnett characters who is morally good and truthful, but not cynical (nor very witty). It is she who makes the ending of the novel happy—with the two brothers Edgar and Dudley once again arm in arm—happy because she insists it is.

Another remarkable character in the novel is Aubrey, Justine's fifteen-year-old retarded brother. Compton-Burnett first introduced children into her novels in *Daughters and Sons*, and they never left her novels thereafter. Children prove useful to Compton-Burnett in the contrast they make with their parents; in the choric comments they can make on the action; in the helpless victims they provide for the tyrants; and in themselves, because Compton-Burnett knows the difficult and sometimes fearful world of children. Aubrey senses his inadequacies and is always trying to reassure himself by saying how much he is like someone else in the family. His dialogue brings out real family resemblances: At times he is peevish like his grandfather, at other times he consciously (and sometimes unconsciously) imitates his uncle Dudley's clearheaded, mannered speech. Aubrey's attempts to be normal constitute some of the most moving scenes in Compton-Burnett's fiction.

One important theme of *A Family and a Fortune* is that to be "normal" is to be flawed. Matty Seaton treats her devoted companion brutally; her nephew Clement Gaveston hoards gold coins in his bedroom; and Dudley Gaveston, the generous bachelor uncle who inherits the fortune, leaves the manor in a jealous rage when his brother Edgar steals his fiancé. Dudley sums up their behavior by saying that all have their ridiculous moments.

Dudley and Edgar have the very close fraternal relationship so common in Compton-Burnett novels. They almost exclude Blanche, Edgar's first wife, from close communion, and the greatest threat in the novel is not murder or incest as in the early novels, but that the brotherly bond will be broken. At the end of the novel, though, it is clear that Edgar will return to Dudley.

Manservant and Maidservant · *Manservant and Maidservant* has been the most popular of all Compton-Burnett's novels; some critics have named it as their favorite, and

Compton-Burnett even said it was one that she particularly liked. It is less spare than the other novels, with more exposition, more sense of place (a smoking fireplace begins and ends the novel, for example), and fully drawn characters. A story of reformation, it shows strong bonds of affection among Horace Lamb, his cousin Mortimer, and his counterpart in the servants' world, Bullivant, the butler.

Horace, a penny-pincher who makes his children do calisthenics to keep warm in winter, is one of Compton-Burnett's crotchety male tyrants. He often looks aside in apparent abstraction as "punishment to people for the nervous exasperation that they produced in him, and must expiate." His wife Charlotte and his cousin Mortimer plan to run away and take the children with them to save them from suffering. Horace finds a letter detailing their plans and becomes Compton-Burnett's first and only tyrant who attempts to reform. His reformation does not erase the past (his children, in particular, point this out); in fact, it makes the children suffer more because he inevitably has lapses. The ups and downs of being nourished, then starved, torture the children far more excruciatingly than would consistent oppression. Yet Horace draws forth deep love from Mortimer and devoted service from Bullivant. Mortimer explains the tyrant's appeal: "Is there something in Horace that twines itself about the heart? Perhaps it is being his own worst enemy." The wise characters may be victims of the tyrants, but they also understand and pity them.

Mortimer, like Dudley Gaveston, is an example of Compton-Burnett's unmarried, rather impotent characters who attach themselves to their richer relatives in the manor. Like Dudley, Mortimer cares more about the children than their own father does. It is these dependent characters who have the strength to challenge the tyrant's ruthlessness, who speak with caustic honesty to expose the tyrant's pretentiousness. They act courageously, even though they must mortify themselves (thus Mortimer's name) and expose their own weakness in the cause of truth. The exploiter needs the exploited, and vice versa.

Manservant and Maidservant introduces an important new element in Compton-Burnett's novels: the servants. Like the children, they can mirror their masters or can serve as a chorus discussing the action. The characters of Compton-Burnett's servants are never better than in this novel: the timid maid; the motherly, nonconformist cook; George, the workhouse boy with grandiose pretensions; and Bullivant, the wonderfully comic butler. Bullivant holds both upstairs and downstairs together with his wry wit and firm hand. He knows everything that has transpired and anticipates what will come. He is also a character of great tenderness and protectiveness, though he hides it under a mask of strict propriety. His devotion to Horace is almost that of an elder brother, though he is always careful to keep his place.

Two important themes of *Manservant and Maidservant* are the conflict between instinct and social conventions and the pernicious effects of do-gooders' meddling. Compton-Burnett had no belief in God, but she was a great supporter of social conventions as necessary restraints on man's primitive instincts. The decent majority of men create social and moral rules; the unscrupulous minority violate them. Horace claims that civilized life consists in suppressing one's instincts, but his wife Charlotte corrects him by saying that all life consists in fulfilling them. Charlotte expresses the complexity of Compton-Burnett's vision: "There is so much truth on all the different sides of things."

Compton-Burnett first sounded the theme of meddling do-gooders in *Pastors and Masters*, in which one character remarks, "I think it's rather terrible to see it [good] being done." In *Manservant and Maidservant*, Mortimer breaks his engagement to

Magdalen because of her interference: "At any time you might act for my good. When people do that, it kills something precious between them." Like Charles Dickens in *Bleak House* (1852-1853), Compton-Burnett believes that do-gooders are usually thinly veiled tyrants. Yet the novel ends happily with an act of goodness: The maid will teach Miss Buchanan, the illiterate shopkeeper, to read.

A God and His Gifts · After *Manservant and Maidservant*, Compton-Burnett's novels weaken, showing signs of strain, repetition, melodrama, and lack of inventiveness. One exception to this is *A God and His Gifts*, in which the tyrant Hereward Egerton overflows with sexual and artistic energy. Through his character, Compton-Burnett reflects on the nature of the artist: his essential and consuming egoism and his godlike creativity.

The most telling criticism leveled against the novels of Compton-Burnett is their sameness. The plots of her novels tend to become indistinguishable after many are read; the speech of all her characters, no matter what their social class or background, is witty and stylized, and her characters themselves become habitual types. Such charges have a degree of validity, yet Compton-Burnett's novels must be accepted on their own terms. She was not interested in realistic dialogue; she was concerned with speech as a means of revealing human character. Her tyrants tend to be careless in their discourse, relying on clichés or using words inexactly, just as they are careless in the way they trample moral laws and people. They pretend to be open, but their speech incriminates them for lack of self-knowledge and candor. Their victims, who seek truth, always correct the tyrants' misuse of language by questioning the real meaning of the words they use.

Whatever her flaws as a novelist, Compton-Burnett was an artist of uncommon intelligence, originality, and control. Her work might best be described in a phrase from one of her own novels, *More Women than Men*: "Like agate, beautiful and bright and hard."

Ann Willardson Engar

Bibliography

Baldana, Frank. *Ivy Compton-Burnett*. New York: Twayne, 1964. Packs much information into a short space. Offers brief characterizations of all the novels, organized around common themes such as home and family. Also "criticizes the critics," giving an analysis of the major evaluations of Compton-Burnett available at that time. Baldana regards Compton-Burnett as the foremost contemporary novelist.

Burkhart, Charles. *I. Compton-Burnett*. London: Victor Gollancz, 1965. Classes Compton-Burnett as an eccentric novelist and offers a psychological account of this type of writer. Presents themes found in Compton-Burnett's works, such as conventions, secrets, people and power, and ethos, devoting a chapter to each. Concludes with a summary of each of the novels, ranking *Manservant and Maidservant* as the most brilliant.

Gentile, Kathy Justice. *Ivy Compton-Burnett*. New York: St. Martin's Press, 1991. A shrewd feminist rereading with chapters on Compton-Burnett's "ethic of tolerance," her early novels, her treatment of mothers and martyrs, her view of civilization, her later novels, her reading of human character, and the responses of her critics. A very thorough study, with notes and bibliography.

Nevius, Blake. *Ivy Compton-Burnett*. New York: Columbia University Press, 1970. This short study presents a general account of the novelist. Her works stress the conflict of passion and duty and are situated in an enclosed space. Their peculiar form, consisting almost entirely of dialogue, has led many to dismiss Compton-Burnett as an eccentric. Although her characters are static, her theme of the abuse of power has contemporary relevance.

Sprigge, Elizabeth. *The Life of Ivy Compton-Burnett*. New York: George Braziller, 1973. Devoted to Compton-Burnett's life much more than her works, but includes some literary analysis. Sprigge denies that the novels are all alike: Each one is a separate creation. The main theme of Compton-Burnett's work is that the truth behind a family's relationships will eventually come to light. Sprigge is extremely favorable to her subject and accepts what Compton-Burnett claims at face value.

Spurling, Hilary. *Ivy: The Life of I. Compton-Burnett*. New York: Alfred A. Knopf, 1984. The most comprehensive account of Compton-Burnett's life, based on exhaustive research and conversations with Compton-Burnett's friends. The novelist's severely repressed life as a child in the late Victorian era dominates the first half of the book. After the death of her two sisters by suicide in 1917, her life was outwardly uneventful. Her childhood experiences influenced her stories and novels, all of which are discussed at length.

Joseph Conrad

Jósef Teodor Konrad Nałęcz Korzeniowski

Born: Near Berdyczów, Poland; December 3, 1857
Died: Oswalds, Bishopsbourne, England; August 3, 1924

Principal long fiction · *Almayer's Folly*, 1895; *An Outcast of the Islands*, 1896; *The Nigger of the "Narcissus,"* 1897; *Heart of Darkness*, 1899 (serial), 1902 (book); *Lord Jim*, 1900; *The Inheritors*, 1901 (with Ford Madox Ford); *Romance*, 1903 (with Ford); *Nostromo*, 1904; *The Secret Agent*, 1907; *Under Western Eyes*, 1911; *Chance*, 1913; *Victory*, 1915; *The Shadow-Line*, 1917; *The Arrow of Gold*, 1919; *The Rescue*, 1920; *The Rover*, 1923; *The Nature of a Crime*, 1909 (serial), 1924 (book; with Ford); *Suspense*, 1925 (incomplete).

Other literary forms · Joseph Conrad's many short stories were published in seven collected editions. The majority of the stories appeared earlier in magazine form, especially in *Blackwood's Magazine*, a magazine that Conrad referred to as "Maga." Of the short stories, three—"Youth," "The Secret Sharer," and "An Outpost of Progress"—have been widely anthologized and are generally recognized as classics of the genre. Two memoirs of Conrad's years at sea, *The Mirror of the Sea* (1906) and *A Personal Record* (1912) are prime sources of background information on Conrad's sea tales. Conrad wrote three plays: *The Secret Agent* (1921), a four-act adaptation of the novel which enjoyed a brief success on the London stage; and two short plays, *Laughing Anne* (1923) and *One Day More* (1905), which had no success. His oeuvre is rounded out by two books of essays on widely ranging topics, *Notes on Life and Letters* (1921) and *Last Essays* (1926); a travel book, *Joseph Conrad's Diary of His Journey Up the Valley of the Congo in 1890* (1926); and the aborted novel *The Sisters*, left incomplete at his death in 1924, but published in fragment form in 1928.

Achievements · In the late twentieth century, Conrad enjoyed an extraordinary renaissance in readership and in critical attention. Readers and critics alike have come to recognize that although one of Conrad's last novels, *The Rover*, was published in the early 1920's, he is the most modern of writers in both theme and technique.

Conrad is, in fact, the architect of the modern psychological novel with its emphasis on character and character analysis. For Conrad, people in plot situations, rather than plot situations themselves, are the primary concern. Indeed, Conrad once professed that he was incapable of creating "an effective lie," meaning a plot "that would sell and be admirable." This is something of an exaggeration, but the fact remains that Conrad's novels center around the solitary hero who, either by chance or by choice, is somehow alienated and set apart from his fellow people. This theme of isolation and alienation dominates Conrad's novels and spans his work from the early sea tales to the political novels to what Conrad called his "romances."

Conrad's "loners" are manifest everywhere in his work—Jim in *Lord Jim*, Kurtz in *Heart of Darkness*, Razumov in *Under Western Eyes*. This emphasis on the alienated and isolated figure has had a considerable impact on the direction of the twentieth century novel, and Conrad's influence may be discerned in such disparate writers as Stephen Crane, F. Scott Fitzgerald, and T. S. Eliot.

Conrad made another contribution in shaping the modern novel: He was the forerunner (although hardly the originator) of two techniques which have found much favor and wide employment in the twentieth century novel. Conrad was among the first of the modern novelists to employ multiple narrators, or shifting points of view, as he does in *Heart of Darkness* and *Lord Jim*. This technique enabled Conrad to make the probing analyses of characters and their motivations which are the hallmarks both of his work and of the work of so many others to follow. The reader sees both Kurtz and Jim, for example, through several pairs of eyes, some sympathetic, some not, before both tales are turned over to Charlie Marlow, who does his best to sort out the conflicting testimonies and to give the reader an objective and a rounded view of both men.

Library of Congress

The extensive use of the flashback in the contemporary novel and, indeed, the contemporary film, is another technique which Conrad pioneered. In Conrad's case, as is the case with all writers who employ the technique, the flashback creates suspense; but it also serves another and more important function in his work, enabling him to examine more thoroughly the minds and the motivations of his characters. Having presented the crisis or the moment of action or the point of decision, Conrad then goes back in time, in an almost leisurely fashion, and retraces step by step the psychological pattern which led to the crisis, to the action, or to the decision.

Finally, Conrad finds a place and a role among the moderns in still another way. He is one of the great Symbolists in English literature. Conrad's use of thoroughly unconventional symbols, related in some way to the metaphysical metaphors to be found in much modern poetry, has had an inestimable influence on the modern novel.

Biography · Joseph Conrad was born Jósef Teodor Konrad Nałęcz Korzeniowski on December 3, 1857, near the rural village of Berdyczów in Poland, under Russian domination. Conrad's mother, Ewa Bobrowski, came from an affluent and influential family of landowners who had made their peace, as best they could, with their Russian overlords. Conrad's father, Apollo Korzeniowski, was a would-be poet, a dedicated patriot, and a translator of William Shakespeare into Polish who found no peace in Russian Poland. The marriage of Apollo and Ewa was frowned upon by the Bobrowskis, who felt that Ewa had married beneath herself, and Ewa's brother, Tadeusz, a prominent lawyer and member of the landed gentry, seldom missed an opportunity to remind his nephew, Józef, that he bore the tainted Nałęcz blood.

Apollo Korzeniowski devoted all his energies and, ultimately, his life to the Polish freedom movement. As a result of his political activities, he was labeled an enemy of the state and exiled to Vologda in northern Russia. The five-year-old Józef and his mother followed Apollo into exile. Three years later, her health ruined by the fierce Russian winters, Ewa Korzeniowski died, and Apollo, equally weakened by the ordeal, succumbed four years after his wife. There is little doubt that Conrad's own lifelong precarious physical state had its genesis in these years in exile.

From these blighted early years, two convictions were impressed in Conrad's consciousness which surfaced in his work: a continuing hatred for all things Russian and for autocratic regimes; and a strong sense of man as victim, instilled by his father's fate, and of man's essential loneliness and isolation, instilled by his own orphanage at the age of twelve. The victimization of the innocent lies at the heart of Conrad's political novels, especially *Under Western Eyes* and *The Secret Agent*, and is a major theme in *Heart of Darkness*. The alienated figure, forced to cope as best he can alone, is the essential Conrad.

With the deaths of Apollo and Ewa Korzeniowski, Conrad came under the tutelage of his concerned but somewhat demanding maternal uncle, Tadeusz Bobrowski. Bobrowski, a man of many affairs and very positive ideas and ideals, sent his young ward to St. Anne's School in Kraków for a brief term and later provided Conrad with a tutor and companion in the hope of creating a proper Polish gentleman. These few years constituted the extent of Conrad's formal education. An avid reader from his early childhood, Conrad was largely self-educated, and the wide knowledge of English, French, and Russian literature apparent in his works (especially in his critical essays) was acquired through his own efforts.

Bobrowski's hopes and plans for Conrad's becoming an accepted member of the right circles in Polish society were not to be realized. Chafing under the regimen of his oversolicitous uncle and, perhaps, convinced that there was no place for Apollo Korzienowski's son in Russian Poland, Conrad finally persuaded his reluctant uncle that his future lay elsewhere: at sea, a dream with which Conrad had been obsessed since seeing the Adriatic during a walking tour of northern Italy in 1873.

In 1874 Conrad left Poland for the port city of Marseilles, France, and the seaman's life to which he would devote the next twenty years. He carried with him his uncle's begrudging blessing and, more important, considerable financial support. The break with his native land was to be more complete than Conrad may have realized at the time, since he returned to Poland on only three occasions during the remainder of his life.

Conrad's adventures and misadventures during his four years in and about Marseilles provided the material, many years later, for the almost lyrical memoir *The Mirror of the Sea* and the novel *The Arrow of Gold*, the latter of which has been the subject of much critical dispute. With his uncle's backing, Conrad acquired, during that time, part ownership of the bark *Tremolino*, which was then employed in smuggling arms for the Spanish Pretender, Don Carlos. It was a period of much intrigue, and Conrad appears to have been at the center, enjoying it hugely.

What is not clear about the Marseilles years, unless one accepts Conrad's highly fictionalized version of the events in *The Arrow of Gold*, is how his ventures at that time all came to a disastrous end. Conrad apparently invested a considerable sum of money in a quixotic mining venture. Moreover, if the Doña Rita of *The Arrow of Gold* did, in fact, exist as Conrad describes her in the novel, then a particularly painful and hopeless love affair complicated Conrad's desperate financial straits. In any event, in February, 1878, Conrad attempted suicide and almost succeeded by placing a bullet in his chest, very near the heart.

Uncle Tadeusz made a hasty trip to Marseilles and restored some kind of order to Conrad's tangled affairs, and, on April 24, 1878, Conrad signed on the British ship *Mavis*, bound from Marseilles to England. Conrad's career as a seaman and, more particularly as a British seaman, had begun. In the next twenty years, sailing on a variety of ships on passages which encompassed half the globe, Conrad accomplished an incredible feat. An alien from a landlocked country, bearing an unpronounceable foreign name and speaking English with a pronounced Slavic-French accent, Conrad rose from able seaman to master mariner in the British Merchant Service. Conrad took great pride in being addressed as Captain Korzeniowski, just as he took great pride in his British citizenship, acquired in 1885.

Many of the ships on which Conrad sailed make an appearance in his works. For example, there actually was a *Narcissus* on which Conrad sailed from Bombay to Dunkirk and a *Palestine* which became the *Judea* of "Youth" and the SS *Roi des Belges*, the counterpart of Marlow's "tinpot" steamboat in *Heart of Darkness*. In similar fashion, many of Conrad's characters are based on real-life prototypes, men whom Conrad had encountered or of whom he had heard while at sea. There *was* a "Jim"; there *was* a "MacWhirr"; there *was* an "Almayer"; there *was* an "Axel Heyst"; there *was* a "Tom Lingard"; and there *was* a "Charlie Marlow," born Jósef Korzeniowski.

In 1889, while between ships in London, Conrad began work on the strange tale of Kaspar Almayer. The work continued sporadically during Conrad's six-month tour in the Belgian Congo in 1890, a sojourn which later provided the material for his first major work, *Heart of Darkness*, and also succeeded in further undermining his already unstable health. In 1893, Conrad, then first mate of the ship *Torrens*, showed the nine completed chapters of *Almayer's Folly* to an English passenger and was encouraged to finish the book. *Almayer's Folly* was published in 1895, to be followed by *An Outcast of the Islands* in 1896, *The Nigger of the "Narcissus"* in 1897, *Heart of Darkness* in 1899, and *Lord Jim* in 1900.

Conrad enjoyed almost immediate critical acclaim, but despite the string of critical successes, he had only a modest public following. In fact, Conrad did not have a best-seller until 1913, with *Chance*. Ironically, the reading public did not find Conrad until after he had written his best work.

Given this limited popular success, Conrad did not feel secure enough to devote himself entirely to a writing career, and, for a six-year period, 1889 to 1895, he vacillated between the safety of a master's berth aboard ship and the uncertainty of his writing table. Even as late as 1898, when he was well established with a publisher and several reputable magazines were eager for his work, Conrad seriously considered returning to the sea.

With his marriage to Jessie George in 1894, Conrad had, in effect, returned from the sea and settled down to a life of hectic domesticity and long, agonizing hours of writing. Jessie, an unassuming, maternal woman, was the perfect mate for the often unpredictable, volatile, and ailing Conrad, and she cheerfully nursed him through his frequent attacks of malaria, gout, and deep depression. The marriage produced two sons, Borys and John, and lasted until Conrad's death.

Except for a brief trip to his native Poland in 1914, a few holidays on the Continent, and an even briefer trip to the United States in 1923, Conrad was resigned to the endless hours at his desk and content to live the life of an English gentleman in his adopted land. The Conrads were something of a nomadic family, however, moving frequently whenever Conrad tired of one of their rented dwellings. His last five years were spent at Oswalds, Bishopsbourne, near Canterbury.

After World War I, the acclaim and the recognition which he had so richly earned finally came to Conrad—an offer of knighthood (which he declined) and the friendship and the respect of many of the literary greats of the time. Essentially a very private man, Conrad, while never denying his Polish origins or renouncing his Roman Catholic faith, tried to live the quiet life of the quintessential English country squire. There was always, however, something of the foreigner about him—the monocle, the Continental-style greatcoat, the slightly Asian eyes, the click of the heels and the formal bow from the waist—which did not go unnoticed among his English friends and neighbors. Like so many of the characters in his novels, Conrad remained somehow apart and alienated from the mainstream of the life about him.

On August 3, 1924, Conrad succumbed to a massive heart attack at his home near Bishopsbourne. He is buried in the cemetery at Canterbury, in—according to the parish register of St. Thomas's Church—"that part reserved for Catholics." Even in death, Conrad, like so many of his fictional creations, found himself alone and apart.

Analysis · Three themes are dominant among Joseph Conrad's sea tales, considered by most critics as his best work. The first of these themes is an unremitting sense of loyalty and duty to the ship, and this quality is exemplified by Conrad's seamen who are successful in practicing their craft. In *The Mirror of the Sea*, Conrad, in propria persona, and through Singleton, the exemplar of the faithful seaman in *The Nigger of the "Narcissus,"* summarized this necessity for keeping faith in observing, "Ships are all right. It's the men in them." The note of fidelity is struck again in *A Personal Record*, when Conrad says of his years at sea: "I do not know whether I have been a good seaman, but I know I have been a very faithful one." Conversely, it is the men who break faith—Jim is the prime example—who fail and who are doomed to be set apart.

A second major theme in Conrad's sea tales, noted by virtually all of his critics, is the therapeutic value of work. To Conrad, the ancient adage "Idle hands are the devil's workshop" was not a cliché but a valid principle. The two most damning words in Conrad's lexicon are "undisciplined" and "lazy," and, again, it is the men whose hands and minds are without meaningful employment who get into difficulties, who fail, and who suffer the Conradian penalty for failure, alienation and isolation. Kurtz, in *Heart of Darkness*, is Conrad's chief exemplar here, but Jim's failure, too, partially results from the fact that he has very little to do in the way of work during the crucial passage aboard the *Patna*.

Finally, a sense of tradition, of one's place in the long continuum of men who have gone to sea, is a recurring theme in Conrad's sea tales. Marlow expresses this sense of tradition best when he speaks of the faithful seamen who band together and are bonded together in what he calls "the fellowship of the craft." The Jims, on the other hand, the captains who display cowardice, the seamen who panic under stress, all those who bring disgrace on the men who have kept faith and do keep faith, are dismissed from the fellowship and are set apart, isolated and alienated. Conrad, then, played a central role in setting the stage for the alienated, solitary figures and, ultimately, the rebels-at-arms who people the pages of the modern novel.

Heart of Darkness · In *Heart of Darkness*, the first of Conrad's recognized masterpieces and one of the greatest novellas in the language, a number of familiar Conradian themes and techniques coalesce: his detestation of autocratic regimes and their special manifestation, colonialism; the characteristic Conradian alien figure, isolated and apart; the therapeutic value of work; and the use of multiple points of view and of strikingly unconventional symbols.

Charlie Marlow, the ostensible narrator of the story, finds himself (as Conrad did on occasion during his sea career) without a ship and with few prospects. As a last resort, he signs on to command a river steamboat for a Belgian trading company, then seeking ivory in the Congo. In a curious way, Marlow's venture into the Congo represents a wish fulfillment, since, Marlow recalls, as a child he had placed his finger on a map of Africa and said, "Someday, I will go there," "there" being the Congo. (This is "autobiography as fiction" again in that Conrad himself had once expressed such a desire and in exactly the terms Marlow employs.)

The mature Marlow, however, has few illusions about what he is undertaking. He characterizes his "command" as "a two-penny-half-penny river-steamboat with a penny whistle attached," and he is quite aware that he will be working for a company whose chief concern is turning a profit, and a large one at that. Moreover, the Company's success will come only at the expense of the innocent and helpless natives who have the misfortune of living in an area that has immense possibilities as a colony.

Marlow, like Conrad, abhors the concept of one people dominating another unless, as he says, the colonizing power is faithful to the "idea" which provides the sole rationale for colonialism, that is, the "idea" of actually bringing the benefits of civilization to the colonized. He believes that only in the British Crown Colonies is the "idea" being adhered to, and he has grave reservations about what he will find in the Congo. Despite these reservations, Marlow is hardly prepared for what awaits him.

Marlow finds in the Congo disorder bordering on lunacy, waste, intrigue, inefficiency, and the cruelest kind of exploitation. The "pilgrims of progress," as Marlow calls them, go about their aimless and pointless tasks while the steamboat he is to command sits idle in the river with a hole in her bottom. Mountains are leveled to no purpose, while equipment and supplies rust or rot in the African sun or never reach their destination. As long as the ivory flows from the heart of darkness, however, no one is overly concerned. Marlow is appalled by the hypocrisy of the situation. An entire continent is being ruthlessly ravaged and pillaged in the name of progress, when, in fact, the real motivation is sheer greed. Nor is there the slightest concern for the plight of the natives in the Company's employ. Marlow sees once proud and strong tribesmen, divorced from their natural surroundings and from all that is familiar to them, sickened and weakened, sitting passively in the shade waiting to die.

Herein is Marlow/Conrad's chief objection to colonialism. By taking people from their normal mode of life and thrusting upon them a culture which they neither want nor understand, colonialism places people in isolation and makes them aliens in their own land. The cannibals who serve as woodcutters for Marlow's steamboat have lost their muscle tone and belong back in the jungle practicing the peculiar rites that, however revolting by other standards, are natural for them. The native fireman on the steamboat, "an improved specimen," Marlow calls him, watches the water gauge on the boiler, lest the god inside become angry. He sits, his teeth filed, his head shaved in strange patterns, a voodoo charm tied to his arm, a piece of polished bone inserted through his lower lip. He represents the perfect victim of the white man's progress, and "he ought to have been clapping his hands and stamping his feet on the bank."

The evil that colonialism has wrought is not, however, confined to the natives. The whites who seek adventure or fortune in the Congo are equally uprooted from all that is natural for them, equally isolated and alienated. The doctor who gives Marlow a perfunctory examination in the Company's headquarters in Brussels asks apologetically for permission to measure Marlow's head while, at the same time, noting that the significant changes will occur "inside." To some degree or other, such changes have come to the whites whom Marlow encounters in Africa. The ship on which Marlow sails to the Congo passes a French gunboat firing aimlessly into the jungle as an object lesson to the natives. The accountant at the Central Station makes perfectly correct entries in his impeccable ledgers while just outside his window, in the grove of death, the mass of displaced natives is dying of fever and malnutrition. The Company's brickmaker makes no bricks because there has been no straw for more than a year, but he remains placid and unconcerned.

Marlow's summation of what he has seen in the Congo is acerbic, withering in its emotional intensity, but it is also an accurate statement of Conrad's feelings toward this, the cruelest exercise of autocratic power. Marlow says, "It was just robbery with violence, aggravated murder on a great scale . . . and with no more moral purpose at the back of it than there is in burglars breaking into a safe." The voice is Charlie Marlow's, but the sentiments are Joseph Conrad's.

One man alone among the Company's disreputable, if not depraved, white traders appears to be an exception, a man who is faithful to the "idea" and is bringing progress and betterment to the natives in exchange for the ivory he gathers. Kurtz is by far the Company's most productive trader, and his future in Brussels seems assured. At the same time, Kurtz is both hated and feared by all the Europeans in the Company's employ. He is hated because of the unconventional (an ironic adjective) methods he has adopted, and he is feared because these methods are apparently working.

With the introduction of Kurtz into the tale, Conrad works by indirection. Neither Marlow nor the reader is allowed to see Kurtz immediately. Rather, one is exposed to Kurtz through many different viewpoints, and, in an effort to allow the reader to see Kurtz from all perspectives, other narrators are brought forth to take over the story briefly: the accountant; the brickmaker; the manager of the Central Station; the Russian; penultimately, Marlow himself; and ultimately, Kurtz's fiancé, the Intended. In addition to these many shifting points of view which Conrad employs, it should be noted that the story, from beginning to end, is told by a dual narrator. Charlie Marlow speaks, but Marlow's unnamed crony, the fifth member of the group gathered on the fantail of the *Nellie*, is the actual narrator of the story, retelling the tale as he has heard it from Marlow. In some sense, then, it is difficult to say whether *Heart of Darkness* is Kurtz's story or Marlow's story or the anonymous narrator's story, since Marlow's tale has obviously had a significant impact on the silent listener.

Marlow is fascinated by Kurtz and what his informants tell him of Kurtz, and throughout the long journey upriver to the Inner Station, he is obsessed with meeting this remarkable man, but he is destined for a shocking disappointment. Kurtz is perhaps the extreme example among all the isolated and alienated figures to be found in Conrad's works. Philosophically and spiritually alienated from the "pilgrims of progress," he is also physically isolated. He is the only white man at the Inner Station, and, given the steamboat debacle, nothing has been heard from or of him for months. He has been alone too long, and the jungle has found him out. He is, in Marlow's words, "a hollow man" with great plans and hopes but totally lacking in the inner resources vital for survival in an alien environment. As a result, he has regressed completely to the primitive state; he has become a god to the natives, who worship him in the course of "unspeakable rites." He has taken a native woman as a consort, and the Russian trader who tried to befriend him has been relegated to fool and jester in Kurtz's jungle court. Kurtz exercises absolute power of life and death over the natives, and he punishes his enemies by placing their severed heads on poles about his hut as ornaments. The doctor in Brussels, Marlow recalls, was fearful of what physical and spiritual isolation might do to people's minds, and on Kurtz, the effect has been devastating. Kurtz is mentally unbalanced, but even worse, as Marlow says, "His soul was mad."

Marlow has confessed that he, too, has heard the appeal of "the fascination of the abomination," the strange sounds and voices emanating from the banks of the river as the steamboat makes its way to Kurtz. Meaningless and unintelligible as the sounds and voices are, they are also somehow familiar to Marlow and strike deep at some primordial instinct within him. Yet, while Kurtz is destroyed, Marlow survives, "luckily, luckily," as he observes. The difference between the two men is restraint, a recurrent term in the novel: With restraint, a man can survive in isolation. The cannibals on the steamboat have it, and Marlow is at a loss to explain the phenomenon. The manager at the Central Station also has it, largely the result of his unfailing good health which permits him to serve, virtually unscathed, term after term in the darkness. The accountant has restraint by virtue of concentrating on his correct entries in his meticulous ledgers and, at the same time, by forfeiting his humanity and closing his mind to the chaos around him.

Chiefly, however, restraint (in Conrad's *Weltanschauung*) is a function of work, and Conrad's major statement of the redeeming nature of work comes in *Heart of Darkness*. Marlow confesses that, like most human beings, he does not like work per se. He does, however, respond to "what is in the work," and he recognizes its salutary effect, "the chance to find yourself." Indeed, the fact that Marlow has work to do in the Congo is his salvation. The steamboat must be salvaged; it must be raised from the bottom of the river. No supplies are available, and the boiler is in disrepair. Marlow needs rivets and sheeting to patch the gaping hole in the boat. The task seems hopeless, but Marlow attacks it enthusiastically, almost joyously, because his preoccupation with rescuing his "two-penny, half-penny" command effectively shields him from "the fascination of the abomination." Later, during the trip upriver to the Inner Station, it is again the work of piloting the vulnerable steamboat around and through the myriad rocks and snags of the convoluted river and the intense concentration required for the work that shut Marlow's eyes and, more important, his mind to the dangers to psyche and spirit surrounding him. Marlow does not leave the Congo completely untouched; he has paid a price, both physically and mentally, for venturing into the darkness, but he does escape with his life and his sanity. As he later recognizes, he owes his escape to the steamboat, his "influential friend," as he calls it, and to the work it provided.

Symbols abound in *Heart of Darkness*, many of them conventional: the interplay of light and darkness throughout the novel, for example, carrying essentially the traditional symbolic meanings of the two terms, or the rusting and decaying equipment Marlow comes across at the Central Station, symbolizing the callous inefficiency of the Company's management. More striking, however, is Conrad's use of thoroughly unconventional symbols; dissimilar images are yoked together in a startling fashion, unique in Conrad's time. Kurtz's totally bald head, for example, is compared to a ball of ivory, and the comparison moves beyond metaphor to the realm of symbol, adumbrating the manner in which the lust for and preoccupation with ivory have turned flesh-and-blood human beings into cold, lifeless ivory figures. There are also the shrunken heads fixed as ornaments on the fence posts surrounding Kurtz's hut. These are Kurtz's "rebels" and, notably, all but one are facing inward, so that, even in death, they are compelled to worship their god. The one facing outward, however, is irretrievably damned and without hope of salvation.

Lord Jim · Similar in many ways to *Heart of Darkness*, *Lord Jim* is considered by many critics to be not only Conrad's greatest sea tale but also his greatest novel. *Lord Jim* is not a sea tale, however, in the purest sense, since most of the action of the novel takes place on land. *Lord Jim* is one of Conrad's psychological studies; Jim's mind and his motivations are searched and probed in meticulous detail in an effort to "see Jim clearly." In making this effort, Conrad employs two characteristic techniques: shifting, multiple points of view and the extensive use of flashbacks.

The narrative begins conventionally with an unnamed third-person narrator who brings the reader to the point of Marlow's first encounter with Jim at the Board of Inquiry investigating the strange case of the pilgrim ship *Patna*. At this point, Marlow takes over the tale, recounting his meeting with Jim. Marlow's account, however, is filtered through the consciousness of the anonymous narrator, much as is the case in *Heart of Darkness*. The manipulation of the narrative voices in *Lord Jim* is much more complex, however, since Jim speaks through Marlow and Marlow through the ultimate narrator.

Again, as in *Heart of Darkness*, other narrators enter the scene briefly, and Marlow gives way to a series of speakers, each of whom is qualified to tell the reader something more about Jim. Montague Brierly, captain of the crack ship *Ossa*, is troubled by Jim's failure to meet the demands of "the fellowship of the craft" and is also troubled by his doubts about his own ability to meet those demands. The French Lieutenant who boarded the abandoned *Patna* and brought it safely to port is a bit more sympathetic toward Jim's moment of cowardice, but is also more rigid in his condemnation of Jim's loss of honor. At the opposite end of the scale, Chester, the preposterous seaman-at-large, dismisses Jim's canceled mate's certificate as nothing more than "a bit of ass's skin" and solicits Marlow's aid in involving Jim in Chester's lunatic scheme of extracting guano from an island that is totally inaccessible. In Chester's view, Jim is the right man for the job, since he is now good for nothing else. Through Chester as interim narrator, Marlow recognizes how desperate Jim's plight is and how equally desperate Jim is for his help.

Marlow does help by putting Jim in touch with Mr. Denver, the owner of a rice mill, and Jim thrives for a time, becoming, in essence, a surrogate son to his employer. The specter of the *Patna* affair overtakes Jim, however, in the form of the fated ship's second engineer, who comes to work at the rice mill. Through Denver; through Egström, who employs Jim briefly as a water clerk; and finally, through the seedy Schomberg, proprietor of an equally seedy hotel in Bangkok, Marlow learns of Jim's gradual decline and his erratic flight from the *Patna* or, as Marlow puts it, his flight "from himself."

In an attempt to help Jim, Marlow turns to Stein, an extraordinary trader and shrewd judge of both butterflies and people. Stein's eminently "practical" solution is to send Jim to Patusan, virtually the end of the earth, where the *Patna* has never been heard of and from where Jim need run no more.

Marlow's visit to Patusan and to Jim is relayed, as is the bulk of the novel, through the unnamed listener among Marlow's small circle of friends gathered over their evening cigars, to whom Marlow has been addressing his tale. In the final chapters,

Conrad's tour de force of narrative technique takes yet another twist. The disaster in Patusan is recounted through the medium of a lengthy letter which Marlow writes to the ultimate narrator, the narration thus coming full circle from third-person narrator, to Marlow, to a series of intermediate narrators, and finally returning to the speaking voice which began the tale.

Adding to the difficulties which Conrad's dizzying shift of narrators presents for the reader is his frequent use of time shifts in the narrative. Jim's long colloquy with Marlow in Marlow's room at the Malabar House, for example, takes the reader back in time to the events aboard the *Patna*, which occurred several months earlier. While observing the seemingly bored Brierly in the courtroom at the Board of Inquiry, Marlow abruptly moves ahead in time to Brierly's suicide, which follows a week after the end of the trial, and then ahead again some two years for the mate's detailed account of Brierly's methodical leap over the side of the *Ossa*. Marlow's letter, which Conrad employs to bring the novel to its close, represents yet another flashback. Examples of this movement back and forth in time in the novel could be multiplied.

Conrad's complex manipulation of his narrators and of the disjointed time sequence of the events of the novel have a single purpose: to give the reader a complete view of a psychologically complex figure. It is an effort, as Marlow insists several times, to "see Jim clearly." Yet, for all Conrad's (and Marlow's) efforts, Jim remains an enigma. Marlow, in fact, confesses at the end of his letter that Jim continues to be "inscrutable."

Chiefly, there are two problems which have plagued critics in coming to grips with Jim. Stein, on whom Marlow relies for enlightenment, pronounces Jim "a romantic," which Stein says is "very bad . . . and very good too." In attempting to resolve the problem of how a romantic may cope with reality, Stein uses the metaphor of a man falling into the sea (the overtones of Jim's leap from the *Patna* are obvious here). Stein continues, "The way is to the destructive element submit yourself, and with the exertions of your hands and feet in the water make the deep, deep sea keep you up." The trouble here is that Stein does not make clear whether it is Jim's dream of heroes and heroics which is the "destructive element" or whether it is the practical and mundane world in which he must endeavor to carry out this dream which is destructive. Does Jim immerse himself in the dream yet keep his head above "water" in the world of reality, or immerse himself in the world of reality and yet keep the dream alive directly above the surface? The critical controversy which Stein's cryptic advice has provoked continues.

Critics are also divided on the meaning of the end of the novel. When Jim presents himself to the old nakhoda, Doramin, and suffers the pistol shot which ends his life, is this the act of a man who has finally accepted that he is capable of failure and who "has mastered his destiny," or is it merely the desperate act of a man who has simply run out of options? The distinction may seem fine, since in any case, Jim's gesture is a positive act, but it governs the reader's final judgment on whether Marlow is correct in accepting Jim as "one of us."

If Jim is not "one of us," he is clearly one of "them," them being the familiar Conradian figures, the isolated and alienated solitaries, and he is so both spiritually and physically. In abandoning the *Patna*, Jim has violated a cardinal principle of the seaman's code, placing his own safety above that of the pilgrims who have entrusted themselves to him. As Brierly puts it, "we are trusted," and he is unforgiving of Jim's dereliction, as is Marlow, although Marlow is willing to admit mitigating circumstances. To the seamen whom Jim encounters, who raise the specter of the *Patna*, Jim is a pariah who has broken the bond of "the fellowship of the craft." Jim himself is quite conscious of his alienation. When he sails aboard Marlow's ship from Bangkok, he takes no interest in the passage as a seaman would, but instead, in Marlow's words, skulks below deck, "as though he had become a stowaway."

Jim is also isolated physically. In a moving passage, Marlow speaks with great feeling of the seaman's ties with and affection for his native land, for home. Jim, however, can never go home; he has, in effect, no home, and his destiny lies everywhere and anywhere but in the village in Essex where he came into being.

On Patusan, Jim's physical isolation is complete. Except for the unspeakable Cornelius, he is the only white man for hundreds of miles. With the *Patna* safely behind him, as he supposes, Jim thrives in isolation, bringing order and security to the troubled land, and is called by the natives "Tuan Jim," "which is to say, Lord Jim." The years of unparalleled success take their toll. Jim is convinced that "nothing can touch me," and his egotism proves fatal when Gentleman Brown finds him out. Jim's last hours are spent isolated and alone, and he dies alone.

In addition to the alienated hero, another familiar Conradian motif may be observed in *Lord Jim*: Conrad's continuing insistence on the redeeming nature of work. Earlier in the novel, the unnamed narrator makes an attempt to sum up Jim, and it comes in the form of Jim's failure to accept or to appreciate the nature of the demands of life at sea. The narrator says that "the only reward [one may expect in the seafaring life] is in the perfect love of the work. This reward eluded him." Notably, throughout the novel, Jim is most vulnerable when he is without work. During his long stay in the hospital at Singapore, he is infected by the malaise of the seamen ashore who have been in the East too long and who have given up all thought of returning to the more demanding Home Service. Under this debilitating influence, Jim takes the fateful step of signing aboard the *Patna*. The ship's passage is deceptively uneventful and undemanding, and Jim has so little to do as mate that his "faculty of swift and forestalling vision," as Marlow calls it, is given free reign. Thus, in the emergency, Jim sees with his imagination rather than with his eyes. In like fashion, after the initial heroics on Patusan, the demands on Jim are minimal. In the absence of anything practical for Jim to do, except carry out his role as "Tuan Jim," he is again vulnerable. Gentleman Brown is enabled, as a result, to catch Jim off guard, to find the "weak spot," "the place of decay," and Jim's idyllic but precarious world comes crashing down.

Conrad the Symbolist may also be observed in *Lord Jim*. Again, as in *Heart of Darkness*, some of the symbols are conventional. Jim's retreat from the *Patna*, for example, is always eastward toward the rising sun, and Jim has bright blue eyes–the eyes, one assumes, of the romantic which darken in moments of stress–and Jim wears immaculate white attire during his climactic confrontation with Gentleman Brown across the creek in Patusan.

As in *Heart of Darkness*, however, some of the symbols in *Lord Jim* are thoroughly original. In pronouncing Jim a "romantic," Stein is, in part, also pronouncing judgment on himself. Stein's romanticism, though, is mixed with a strong alloy of the practical, and he is prepared, as Jim is not, to act or to react immediately when action is called for, as is evident when he is ambushed and defends himself with skill and daring. Thus, Stein the romantic collects butterflies, while Stein the practical man collects beetles. The ring which Doramin gives his old "war-comrade" Stein as a talisman of the bond between white and native ultimately assumes symbolic import. Stein, in turn, gives the ring to Jim as his entrée to Patusan, and Jim wears it proudly during his brief days of glory. In the midst of the Gentleman Brown affair, Jim sends the ring to Doramin's son, Dain Waris, as a token of the white man's faith. In the closing scene of the novel, the ring, taken from the finger of the dead Dain Waris and placed in Doramin's lap, falls to the ground at Jim's feet. Jim glances down at it, and, as he raises his head, Doramin shoots Jim. The ring, then, paradoxically, is both a symbol of faith and of a breach of faith.

Victory · *Victory*, one of Conrad's later novels, was published in 1915. As such, it represents in one sense a Conrad who had mastered the techniques of the genre he had made his own, the novel, and in another sense a Conrad in decline as a creative artist. The early experimentation in narrative technique—the multiplicity of narrators and the complex, and sometimes confusing, manipulation of chronology—is behind Conrad. *Victory* is a linear narrative, told by a single, first-person speaking voice without interruption of the forward chronological thrust of the tale. For the noncritical reader, this straightforward handling of his material on Conrad's part was a boon and may very well account for the fact that not until *Chance*, in 1913, and *Victory*, two years later, did Conrad enjoy a genuine popular success.

At the same time, Conrad made a stride forward in narrative technique and in command of the language in the fifteen years between *Lord Jim* and *Victory*. This step took him past clarity to simplicity. *Victory* is, perhaps, too straightforward a tale, freed of occasional confusion and of the varied and variable speaking voices, but also lacking the richness and the range contributed by those same voices. Confined as Conrad is to one point of view, the extensive searching and probing of his characters, seen in Kurtz and Jim, are denied him. Axel Heyst is an interesting character, but he is only that. He is not, like Kurtz and Jim, a provocative, puzzling, and ultimately enigmatic figure.

The other characters in the novel are similarly unimpressive. Heyst finds the heroine, Alma, or Lena, a thoroughly intriguing young woman, but the reader is at a loss to understand the fascination, even the appeal, she seems to have for Heyst. Other than the commitment Heyst has made to Lena in rescuing her from the odious Schomberg, the tie between the two is tenuous. Many critics have noted that Conrad's women are generally lifeless, and it is true that, with the possible exception of Doña Rita in *The Arrow of Gold* (and here Conrad may have been writing from direct emotional involvement), women generally remained mysteries to him. As his greatest work attests, he was essentially a man's writer.

The three other principal characters in *Victory*, however, are male; yet they, too, are wooden and artificial. Much has been made of "plain Mr. Jones," Ricardo, and Pedro's representing Conrad's most searching study of evil. In this construct, Jones stands for intellectual evil, Ricardo for moral (or amoral) evil, and Pedro for the evil of force. On the whole, however, they emerge as a singularly unimpressive trio of thugs. The lanky, emaciated Jones, called the "spectre," is indeed a ghostlike figure whose presence is observed but scarcely felt. Ricardo, with his bluster and swagger, is almost a comic character, and some of his lines are worthy of a nineteenth century melodrama. Pedro's chief function in the novel appears to be his availability to be bashed on the head and suffer multiple contusions. Compared to Gentleman Brown, "the show ruffian of the Australian coast" in *Lord Jim*, they are theatrical, and while they may do harm, the evil they represent pales beside that ascribed by Conrad to Brown, "akin to madness, derived from intense egoism, inflamed by resistance, tearing the soul to pieces and giving factitious vigor to the body."

Victory is a talky novel with long passages devoted to inconclusive conversations between Heyst and Lena. It is relevant here to contrast the lengthy exchange between Jim and Marlow in the Malabar House and the "getting to know one another" colloquies in which Heyst and Lena engage. In the former, every line is relevant and every word tells; in the latter, the emotional fencing between the two ultimately becomes tedious.

Gone, indeed, in *Victory* are the overblown passages of the earlier works, which can make even the most devout Conradian wince. Gone too, however, are the great passages, the moments of magic in which by the sheer power of words, Conrad moves, stirs, and thrills the reader. On the whole, the style in *Victory*, like the format of the novel itself, is straightforward; the prose is clear, but the interludes of splendor are sadly missing, and missed.

Whatever differences are to be found in the later works in Conrad's technical handling of the narrative and in his style, one constant remains. Heyst, like Kurtz, Jim, and so many of the figures who fill Conrad's pages—is an alien, isolated and apart, both spiritually and physically. He does differ somewhat from his counterparts, however, in that he stands alone by choice. Heyst, following the dying precept of his gifted but idealistic father—"Look-on—make no sound"—proposes to spend his life aloof and divorced from humankind; in this way, he believes, nothing can ever touch him. In general, except for his brief involvement with the unfortunate Morrison, Heyst manages to maintain his role of the amused and detached skeptic, living, as Conrad puts it, an "unattached, floating existence." He accommodates himself to all people but makes no commitments to anyone. Thus, chameleon-like, he is known under many guises; he is called, for example, "Enchanted Heyst" because of his expressed enchantment with the East and, on other occasions by would-be interpreters, "Hard Facts Heyst," "the Utopist," "the Baron," "the Spider," and "the Enemy." A final sobriquet, "the Hermit," is attached to Heyst when, with the collapse of the Tropical Belt Coal Company, he chooses to remain alone on the deserted island of Samburan. Heyst's physical isolation is now of a piece with his spiritual isolation.

The encounter with Lena changes this attitude. With his commitment to Lena, Heyst is no longer the detached observer of the world, and with the flight to Samburan, his wanderings come to an end. Paradoxically, this commitment brings about both his spiritual salvation and his physical destruction. It is a redeemed Heyst, freed at last from the other enchantment of his life (the living presence of his dead father), who, at Lena's death, is able to assert, "Woe to the man whose heart has not learned while young to hope, to love—and to put its trust in life!" Thus, Heyst differs from Conrad's other alien spirits in that he "masters his destiny," as Jim could not and Kurtz, perhaps, would not.

In still another way, Heyst "masters his destiny" as Jim and Kurtz do not. Kurtz dies the victim of his own excesses and of the debilitating effect of the jungle; Jim places his life in the hands of Doramin. Heyst, however, governs his own fate and chooses to die with Lena, immolating himself in the purgative fire which he sets to destroy all traces of their brief idyll on Samburan, a fire that, ironically, blazes over the ruins of a defunct coal company.

Other echoes of the earlier Conrad may be seen in *Victory*. For example, albeit to a lesser degree than in *Lord Jim*, *Heart of Darkness*, *The Arrow of Gold*, and *Almayer's Folly*, *Victory* is another instance of Conrad's writing "autobiography as fiction." In the Author's Note to the novel, Conrad speaks of a real-life Heyst whom he remembers with affection, but also with a sense of mystery. So too, Mr. Jones, Ricardo, and Pedro come from Conrad's store of memories, although he encountered each individually and not as the trio they compose in the book. The character of Lena is drawn from a brief encounter in a café in the south of France with a group of entertainers and with one girl in the company who particularly caught Conrad's eye. The settings of *Victory*, exotic names such as Malacca, Timor, and Sourabaya, were, of course, as familiar to the seagoing Conrad as the streets of London, and there is no reason to doubt that somewhere in the tropics, the fictional Samburan has its counterpart.

Finally, in *Victory*, Conrad the Symbolist may again be seen. Noticeably, however, in this later novel, just as Conrad's narrative technique and his style have become simplified and his ability to create vivid characters has declined, the symbols he employs lack the freshness and the depth of those of the earlier novels. Conrad makes much of the portrait of the elder Heyst which dominates the sparse living room on Samburan, just as the subject of the portrait has dominated Heyst's existence. In fact, Conrad makes too much of the portrait as a symbol, calling attention to it again and again until the reader can virtually predict that each time Heyst enters the room, the portrait will be brought to his and to the reader's attention. As a symbol, then, the portrait is overdone, overt, and obvious. Similarly, the darkening storm which threatens Samburan as the events of the novel reach their climax is a bit heavy-handed and hardly worthy of Conrad at his best.

Even so, there is a brief moment of the genuine Conrad shortly before the climactic violence that brings about both Heyst's redemption and destruction. Conrad writes: "The thunder growled distantly with angry modulations of its tremendous voice, while the world outside shuddered incessantly around the dead stillness of the room where the framed profile of Heyst's father looked severely into space." Here, the two symbols coalesce in a telling and effective manner. Regrettably, telling and effective instances such as this are rare in *Victory*. Conrad's work as a whole, however, with its stylistic and narrative innovations, testifies to the quality of his contribution to twentieth century literature.

C. F. Burgess

Other major works

SHORT FICTION: *Tales of Unrest*, 1898; *Youth: A Narrative, and Two Other Stories*, 1902; *Typhoon, and Other Stories*, 1903; *A Set of Six*, 1908; *'Twixt Land and Sea, Tales*, 1912; *Within the Tides*, 1915; *Tales of Hearsay*, 1925; *The Complete Short Stories of Joseph Conrad*, 1933.

PLAYS: *One Day More: A Play in One Act*, pr. 1905; *The Secret Agent: A Drama in Four Acts*, pb. 1921; *Laughing Anne: A Play*, pb. 1923.

NONFICTION: *The Mirror of the Sea*, 1906; *Some Reminiscences*, 1912 (pb. in U.S. as *A Personal Record*); *Notes on Life and Letters*, 1921; *Joseph Conrad's Diary of His Journey Up the Valley of the Congo in 1890*, 1926; *Last Essays*, 1926; *Joseph Conrad: Life and Letters*, 1927 (Gérard Jean-Aubry, editor); *Joseph Conrad's Letters to His Wife*, 1927; *Conrad to a Friend*, 1928 (Richard Curle, editor); *Letters from Joseph Conrad, 1895-1924*, 1928 (Edward Garnett, editor); *Lettres françaises de Joseph Conrad*, 1929 (Gérard Jean-Aubry, editor); *Letters of Joseph Conrad to Marguerite Doradowska*, 1940 (John A. Gee and Paul J. Sturm, editors); *The Collected Letters of Joseph Conrad: Volume I, 1861-1897*, 1983; *The Collected Letters of Joseph Conrad: Volume II, 1898-1902*, 1986; *The Collected Letters of Joseph Conrad: Volume III, 1903-1907*, 1988.

Bibliography

Bohlmann, Otto. *Conrad's Existentialism.* New York: St. Martin's Press, 1991. Bohl-mann interprets six of Conrad's major works in the light of the philosophical musings of theoreticians such as Søren Kierkegaard and Friedrich Nietzsche and practitioners such as Jean-Paul Sartre and Albert Camus.

Davis, Laura L., ed. *Conrad's Century: The Past and Future Splendour.* New York: Columbia University Press, 1998. Examines Conrad and his times. Includes bibliographical references and an index.

Gekoski, R. A. *Conrad: The Moral World of the Novelist.* New York: Barnes & Noble Books, 1978. Explores the novels in terms of the apparent contradiction between personal autonomy, with its attendant alienation, and social responsibility. Devotes separate chapters to Conrad's major fiction. Gekoski's analyses are studded with quotations from the works and with plot summaries. Contains a selected bibliography and an index.

Gibson, Andrew, and Robert Hampson, eds. *Conrad and Theory.* Atlanta: Rodopi, 1998. Essays include "Conrad and the Politics of the Sublime," "The Dialogue of *Lord Jim,*" and "Conrad, Theory and Value."

Guerard, Albert J. *Conrad the Novelist.* Cambridge, Mass.: Harvard University Press, 1958. A pioneering critical study of Conrad's major fiction.

Jordan, Elaine, ed. *Joseph Conrad.* New York: St. Martin's Press, 1996. An excellent introductory study of Conrad and his works.

Karl, Frederick Robert. *A Reader's Guide to Joseph Conrad.* Rev. ed. Syracuse, N.Y.: Syracuse University Press, 1997. A good handbook for students. Provides bibliographical references and an index.

Orr, Leonard, and Ted Billy, eds. *A Joseph Conrad Companion.* Westport, Conn.: Greenwood Press, 1999. A good manual, complete with bibliographical references and an index.

Ressler, Steve. *Joseph Conrad: Consciousness and Integrity.* New York: New York University Press, 1988. Devotes separate chapters to Conrad's major fiction: *Heart of Darkness, Lord Jim, Nostromo,* "The Secret Sharer," and *Under Western Eyes.* Ressler's focus is the conflict between the characters' self-affirming possibilities of action and the necessary test of moral substance. Claims that *Under Western Eyes* is Conrad's greatest artistic and moral success; the later *Victory* is dismissed, along with Conrad's other late fiction.

Stape, J. H., ed. *The Cambridge Companion to Joseph Conrad.* Cambridge, England: Cambridge University Press, 1996. This companion to Conrad's life and works is intended primarily for the layperson, rather than the specialist. A three-and-a-half-page chronology is followed by twelve essays—each written by a different author and each devoted to a different work or set of works, and to analyses of Conrad's narrative technique, his attitude toward British imperialism, his literary modernism, and his influence on other writers and artists. Each essay includes a bibliography, and the volume concludes with suggestions for further reading.

Swisher, Clarice, ed. *Readings on Joseph Conrad.* San Diego: Greenhaven Press, 1998. Contains essays by J. B. Priestley, Robert Penn Warren, and Richard Adams about many of Conrad's works.

A. J. Cronin

Born: Cardross, Scotland; July 19, 1896
Died: Gilon, near Montreux, Switzerland; January 6, 1981

Principal long fiction · *Hatter's Castle*, 1931; *Three Loves*, 1932; *The Grand Canary*, 1933; *The Stars Look Down*, 1935; *The Citadel*, 1937; *The Keys of the Kingdom*, 1941; *The Green Years*, 1944; *Shannon's Way*, 1948; *The Spanish Gardener*, 1950; *Beyond This Place*, 1953; *A Thing of Beauty*, 1956 (also known as *Crusader's Tomb*); *The Northern Light*, 1958; *The Judas Tree*, 1961; *A Song of Sixpence*, 1964; *A Pocketful of Rye*, 1969; *Desmonde*, 1975 (also known as *The Mistral Boy*); *Lady with Carnations*, 1976; *Gracie Lindsay*, 1978; *Doctor Finlay of Tannochbrae*, 1978.

Other literary forms · In addition to the many novels he has published, A. J. Cronin has also written one play, *Jupiter Laughs*, which was produced in Glasgow and New York in 1940. His autobiography, *Adventures in Two Worlds* (1952), remains the best account of his formative years as well as an engaging vehicle for many of his opinions. In 1926, he also wrote two studies entitled *Report on First-Aid Conditions in British Coal Mines* and *Report on Dust Inhalation in Haematite Mines*. The outcome of his journeys to investigate the conditions said to prevail there became the fictional account of the mining communities found in *The Stars Look Down* and *The Citadel*.

Achievements · In the spring of 1930, a tall, sandy-haired, genial physician sold his London practice and home, moved with his family to an isolated farmhouse near Inverary, Scotland, and at the age of thirty-four wrote a novel for the first time in his life. *Hatter's Castle*, published the following year by Victor Gollancz, became an immediate success. It was the first novel to be chosen by the English Book Society for the Book-of-the-Month Club. It was later translated into many languages, dramatized, and made into a Paramount motion picture starring James Mason and Deborah Kerr. Before long, critics hailed Cronin as a new and important author, whose writing was comparable in content and style to that of Charles Dickens, Thomas Hardy, and Honoré de Balzac.

Cronin and his wife moved to a small apartment in London and then on to a modest cottage in Sussex, where he went to work on another novel, *Three Loves*. His popularity continued to increase following *The Grand Canary* and *The Stars Look Down*; the ex-physician became something of a literary lion, in demand at dinners, bazaars, and book fairs. His writing launched him upon a literary career with such impetus that, once and for all, he "hung up [his] stethoscope and put away that little black bag–[his] medical days were over."

The physician-novelist is of course by no means an unfamiliar literary figure. Arthur Conan Doyle, W. Somerset Maugham, C. S. Forester, Oliver Goldsmith, and the poet laureate of England, Robert Bridges, among others, had rich medical backgrounds into which they reached for ideas for their books. None of these examples, however, can quite parallel the dual career of Cronin. Medicine with him was not a stopgap or a stepping-stone. He was an outstanding professional and financial success; moreover, he was ambitious, desperately tenacious, and single-minded in his pursuit of that success. It was hard won and well deserved. His second success, in an entirely different field, was equally substantial. Twenty novels (several of which were adapted to the cinema), a play, an autobiography, and one of the longest-running British television series represent a career that spans one-half of the twentieth century—1930 to 1978—and a life that was itself as engrossing and multifaceted as Cronin's fiction.

Perhaps just as remarkable as the extraordinary commercial success of the novels is the fact that most of them are much more than highly readable potboilers. Like Emily Brontë, Dickens, and Hardy, three writers with whom he is often compared, Cronin was a natural-born storyteller who transcended the category of "academic" fiction writer. His novels are realistic, purporting to present the actual experiences of actual people. They present life not in the vacuum of timelessness, but in the timely flux of ordinary experience. They rely on a specific sense of place—interiors and exteriors—and reflect a rapid mastery of the different settings and environments to which Cronin's travels had taken him. Even in his most extreme formal experimentation—as in *The Stars Look Down*—Cronin's fiction retains accessibility and readability.

Although Cronin's popularity has somewhat waned, he was for many years one of the best-known and most controversial of British writers; through a number of books remarkable for their honesty and realism, he helped entertain and educate a generation of readers. As a writer, he was always promoting tolerance, integrity, and social justice. His favorite theme was that people should learn to be creative rather than acquisitive, altruistic rather than selfish.

Biography · Before Archibald Joseph Cronin's books can be appreciatively read, the reader must have a reasonable acquaintance with his life. This is not necessarily true in the case of many writers, whose private lives are less clearly reflected in their work than are those of writers such as Dickens and Maugham, to whom Cronin bears a resemblance in this matter. Throughout his career as a novelist, Cronin drew heavily on his memories of what he had actually observed. Henry James's argument that the writer of fiction should be "one upon whom nothing is lost" received an emphatic embodiment in the life of Cronin, whose experiences as a child, a medical student, and a physician are woven inextricably into the fabric of his novel.

As is the case with so many of his fictional characters, life for young Cronin was by no means idyllic. He was born in Cardross (Dumbartonshire), Scotland, on July 19, 1896, the only child of a middle-class family whose fortunes were soon to decline rapidly. His mother, Jessie Montgomerie, was a Scottish Protestant woman who had defied her family—and a host of ancestors—by marrying an Irishman and turning Catholic. His father, Patrick Cronin, was a mercantile agent who until his death was able to offer his family a fairly comfortable existence. After the death of his father, however, Cronin was forced to retreat with his penniless mother to the bitter and poverty-stricken home of her parents.

To most neighbors and relatives in the small, strictly moral, and sternly Protestant town of Cardross, Jessie Montgomerie's marriage and conversion were considered a disgrace, and upon young Cronin they inflicted the inevitable ridicule and persecution. On one hand, there was sectarian antagonism, not far short of that which has erupted in the late twentieth century in Northern Ireland as violence. On the other hand, there was the stern Protestant morality. Cronin was permanently marked by an environment that was noisy, quarrelsome, profoundly unhappy, and emotionally dramatic—a source of endless tension and grief for the growing boy and of endless material for the future novelist.

Cronin's delight in reading and learning perhaps compensated for his frustrations. Among the authors he read were Robert Louis Stevenson (an only child like himself and a firm favorite right to the end of his life), Sir Walter Scott, Guy de Maupassant, Dickens, Maugham, and Samuel Butler—whose *The Way of All Flesh* (1903) Cronin cited as his favorite book. At Cardross Village School and later at the Dumbarton Academy, where literature was his best subject, the boy became something of a prodigy, repeatedly winning prizes and discovering in himself that love for learning which would be a source of stability all his life. Both as a student and, later in life, as a physician-writer, he spent enormous stretches of time at his desk, wrestling with his work. This compulsiveness, combined with his intelligence and his eagerness, won Cronin the approbation of his uncle—a poor, kindly Catholic priest who helped secure for him his education and who later became the model for Father Chisholm in *The Keys of the Kingdom*—and of his great-grandfather, who later became the model for Alexander Gow in *The Green Years*.

Yet Cronin's talent also meant he would suffer the emotions of premature loneliness that so often afflict an unusually bright boy. He was highly regarded by his teachers; however, other students—and their parents—sometimes resented his abilities. One father, whose young hopeful was beaten by Cronin in an important examination, became so enraged that years later *Hatter's Castle* took shape around his domineering personality. The theme, "the tragic record of a man's egotism and bitter pride," suggests the dark and often melodramatic atmosphere of Cronin's early novels. In them, some characters are drawn with humorous realism, but for the most part humor is dimmed by gloomy memories of his own neglected childhood, and sensational scenes are shrouded in an atmosphere genuinely eerie and sinister. Inevitably, Cronin clung to the notion that between the life of the mind and the life of the senses, between a disciplined commitment to scholarship and a need to share in the common pleasures of humankind, there is an irremediable conflict.

The religious bigotry, the family's unceasing poverty, the interest in learning—this trio of forces worked at shaping the young Cronin. A shy, sensitive, lonely boy, aware of his peculiarities yet hungry for the town's acceptance, he developed, like Robert Shannon of *The Green Years*, an overt mistrust of organized religion. Until his father's death, Cronin had been devout, and the question of his becoming a clergyman may have been considered, but if Cronin had entertained any such ambitions, his increasing indifference, which emerges very clearly in his novels, must have caused him to abandon such plans. Instead, he decided he would become a doctor—the only other thing for an ambitious poor boy living in Scotland to do—and in 1914 he entered Glasgow University Medical School.

Cronin had begun his medical studies when World War I took him into the Royal Navy Volunteer Reserve as a surgeon sublieutenant. Back at the university, he was struck forcefully by the contrast between his sincere idealism and the cynicism, selfishness, and muddled incompetency of many of the students and doctors he met. This conflict later found expression in his fiction, in which his idealized heroes' enthusiasm is contrasted sharply with the satirical descriptions of other doctors, civic officials, and small-town bigots. In *The Stars Look Down*, *The Citadel*, *The Green Years*, and *Shannon's Way*, for example, every aspect of the medical profession is criticized: medical schools, small-town practice, public health, fashionable clinics, and even research centers.

Having been graduated M.B., Ch.B. with honors in 1919, Cronin was appointed physician to the outpatients in Bellahouston war pensions hospital, and later medical superintendent at Lightburn Hospital, Glasgow. Two years later, he married Agnes Mary Gibson, also a medical school graduate, and entered into general practice in a mining area of South Wales from 1921 until 1924. In the latter year, he became a medical inspector of mines for Great Britain. In 1925, he took his M.D. degree with honors; a year later he prepared a report on first-aid conditions in British coal mines and another report on dust inhalation in haematite mines. After his service with the ministry of mines was completed, Cronin moved to London and built a practice in London's West End. Throughout these experiences and contacts with people of every kind, he continually thought of stories he could create. His patients and colleagues provided him with a dramatic cast of characters, a ready-made network of complex relationships, and a complete set of thunderous emotions. In all of this, he was not only an active participant but also, as the trusted doctor, an advantaged spectator.

"It has been said that the medical profession proves the best training ground for a novelist," Cronin wrote, "since there it is possible to see people with their masks off." Certainly, in his own writings, Cronin drew heavily upon his experiences as a doctor. The Glasgow medical school environment; the touch-and-go associations with mental patients at a suburban asylum; the medical practice in a Welsh mining village with its calls in the night and impromptu surgery on the kitchen tables and in mine shafts; the drama, pathos, and cynical worldliness that passed under his eyes as a medical practitioner in London—all these episodes were used as material for his novels.

The richest source of material for his novels, however—especially the later ones, beginning with *The Keys of the Kingdom*—was his newfound faith. At the height of financial prosperity and great reputation, in good health and with his work flowing smoothly and abundantly, Cronin felt a deep malaise, a feeling of emptiness and "interior desolation." For years he had ignored matters of the spirit; then, almost coinciding with the end of one career and the start of a new, even more successful one, he found himself confronted with a fundamental fact of existence. He had been born a Catholic, observing the outward practice of his faith, but had gradually drifted into a position where religion was something entirely outside his inner experience. In the years after World War II, he took his wife on pilgrimages to Vienna, Italy, and France, in particular Normandy. Each trip to war-battered Europe provided experiences which further crystallized Cronin's maturing faith. The source of his renewed strength can be summed up in a few words: "No matter how we try to escape, to lose ourselves from our divine source, there is no substitute for God." This is a simple statement of sincere faith by a man whose adventures in various environments were marked by a steady development in spirit and in art.

Analysis · Everything that A. J. Cronin wrote was stamped by his personality, his sincerity, his direct concern with ethical issues, his seemingly instinctive knowledge of ordinary people, and his tremendous gift for storytelling. An examination of five of his most popular novels, *Hatter's Castle*, *The Stars Look Down*, *The Citadel*, *The Keys of the Kingdom*, and *The Green Years*, reveals a consistent commitment to the value of the individual—the personal—and a remarkable development in narrative technique.

Hatter's Castle · *Hatter's Castle* was in many ways a happy accident, securing for its author laudatory reviews and substantial earnings and establishing him as a writer of great promise. In its hero, readers found an outstanding personality; a hatter in

Levenford, in strongly characterized surroundings, who lived through a destiny of suffering and tragedy. Readers were also treated to a return to the English novel in the grand tradition. Its themes of the rejected family, the struggle against poverty, the desire for wealth, the illusion of limitless opportunity, and the conflict between personal desire and conventional restraint were recurring ones throughout Cronin's fiction.

To develop the plot of *Hatter's Castle*, Cronin used the familiar Victorian conventions available to all aspiring writers of the time: a straightforward linear chronology unfolded through the agency of the omniscient third-person narrator, with an emphasis on melodrama and horror. Added to these conventions is one of the most familiar themes of Greek tragedy, the retribution that attends overweening pride. James Brodie is a man whose inordinate self-love and unusually strong physique have made him the most feared person in town as well as the tyrant of a trembling household. He has deluded himself into believing that his hat shop is a thriving business, that his house is a romantic castle, and that he himself is related to the aristocracy. The novel proceeds almost consecutively from its beginning, with the hero at the "peak" of his power, to his decline into futility, frustration, and finally, alienation.

Woven through the book are patterns of developing images and symbols which serve important structural functions: They relate and unify the individual lives presented in the book; they support and embody its themes; and they are the means by which the texture of an event or feeling is conveyed. One cluster of these images grows out of the title, which refers, of course, literally to the house, and also to James Brodie himself and his career. The "castle," at once a physical structure and symbol of the Brodie family, is pictured early in the novel in terms that both symbolize the owner's pride and prophesy the dreadful environment and outcome of the story. It is a place of gloom and solitude, "more fitted for a prison than a home," "veiled, forbidding, sinister; its purpose likewise 'hidden and obscure.'" The pompous dignity of the gables greets the visitor with "cold severity." The parapet embraces the body of the house like a "manacle." Its windows are "secret, close-set eyes [which] grudgingly admitted light." Its doorway is "a thin repellent mouth." This description not only provides a haunting counterpoint to the action of *Hatter's Castle* but also establishes the essential character of Brodie well before he appears, before he is even named.

The members of the Brodie family share with the house a condition of imminent collapse. Typical of so many novelists, Cronin's device, here and elsewhere, is to put his minor characters in dire straits at the outset of the action so that they can be tested against the hardships life has to offer. This strategy he accomplishes by introducing the family members as they wait for Brodie, moving from grandmother to elder daughter, from younger daughter to mother, and each picture is presented as a miniature scene in a continuous drama of frustration. All along, the reader notes a strange absence of the usual signs of domesticity in a large country household.

The driving force of the book, however, is the portrayal of the successive disasters that Brodie brings upon himself and his family. Margaret, his feeble, downtrodden wife, is reduced to abjection and dies horribly of cancer. Mary, his elder daughter, is a lovely, gentle girl not quite able to cope with her father. She becomes pregnant, is thrown out of the house into a raging storm, and eventually marries the young doctor whom Brodie hates. Nessie, the younger daughter, is driven to insanity and suicide by Brodie's morbid determination that she shall win a scholarship and go to college. Matthew, Brodie's weakling son, robs his mother, lies to both of his parents, and runs off with his father's mistress. By the end of the novel, therefore, any manifestations of

Brodie's supposed supremacy have vanished. Not only has he lost his family, but he has lost his business and has become a drunkard. He is left shattered, with no companion but his tragic, greedy old mother, and with no hope but death.

Although *Hatter's Castle* is in many ways a conventional novel, there are ideas, themes, and techniques in it which reappear in Cronin's later, more mature work. The characters are typical of Cronin: paradoxical mixtures of good and bad, weak and strong. Possessiveness, to the point of the pathological, is used as a catalyst to introduce a conflict and action, and, as in his later novels, it is always expressly condemned. The unrequited love theme which appears so often in Cronin's writing is present in the form of Mary's plight. Also, the central idea of rebellion against social pressures anticipates the kinds of revolt that motivate so many Cronin characters, including artists, seekers, and criminals.

Perhaps a legitimate criticism of the plot is that the sheer number of misfortunes suffered by Brodie and his family seems excessive and implausible. Possibly, but it seems to be a part of Cronin's philosophy that troubles never come singly, and, certainly, all of Brodie's misfortunes can be convincingly traced to his character and actions. "Character is Fate," quotes Thomas Hardy in *The Mayor of Casterbridge* (1886), and his nemesis works unerringly through Brodie's own glaring defects. Imaginative belief in Brodie compels belief in what happens to him. As one critic observed, "The plot may creak, but Brodie lives."

The Stars Look Down · Cronin's fourth novel, *The Stars Look Down*, surpasses its predecessors by many standards. It develops in greater depth his major preoccupations—a concern with the chaos of life, its bitterness and desolation—but keeps under restraint the tendency toward melodrama without weakening the force of his instinct for drama. Characters reflect the special types to which Cronin is attracted, but the theme of the futility of the British working class against the greed and selfishness of the moneyed overlords receives fuller treatment here.

With action ranging over much of England, the novel takes place in the period from 1903 to 1933. The story's center is the Neptune coal mine in Ryneside County. The plot moves back and forth between two families, the Fenwicks and Barrases, adding constantly to their widening circle of acquaintances. Working primarily (although not exclusively) within the minds of his characters, Cronin maintains a tightly unified texture as he changes focus from one character to another. The six main characters are rather schematically drawn: One character is paired off with another, usually to show contrasting versions of a general type. The six major characters fall into three pairs: David Fenwick and Joe Gowlan; Laura Millington and Jenny Sunley; and Arthur Barras and his father, Richard. David, Laura, and Arthur are the generally praiseworthy characters in the novel, the ones who gain the greatest share of the reader's sympathy. The "evil" ones, or those who obstruct the good characters, are Joe, Jenny, and Richard. The good are characterized by genuineness, sincerity, and a general lack of pretense; the bad, on the other hand, continually disguise their motives and present a false appearance.

If the six main characters have obvious symbolic import, so has the title of the novel. Subject to their own laws and compulsions, heeding little outside them, the stars look down upon a scene of chaos and social revolution and go on looking, unperturbed. "Did you ever look at the stars?" asks the fat man in Robert Louis Stevenson's *The Merry Men* (1887). "'When a great battle has been lost or a dear friend is dead, when we are hipped or in high spirits, there they are, unweariedly shining overhead.' 'I see,' answered Will. 'We are in a mousetrap.'" This is the idea Cronin suggests in the title and acts out through his characters, intending to convey something of the aloofness of eternity compared to the chaos of the earth below.

Cronin conveys the atmosphere of a typical mining community by piling up factual detail upon factual detail in an attempt to re-create the very look, texture, and smell of the life of the miner. Frequently, he uses the slangy, ungrammatical language of these people even in descriptive or explanatory passages when the omniscient narrator is speaking. A work on a subject as technical as coal mining is bound to have a somewhat specialized vocabulary, and a reader without firsthand knowledge of life in the pits must search for the meanings of such words as "collier," "hewer," "getter," "breaker," "pickman," and "pikeman." To come to grips with the actualities of life in the mine, Cronin describes scenes such as the gaunt, unfriendly landscape, perpetually shrouded in grit; the silent and laconic manner of the miners; and the pervasive atmosphere of grim suffering and endurance. The town's very name–"Sleesdale," suggesting "sleazy"–is emblematic. This, then, is the backdrop to the human drama Cronin reconstructs, a drama about defeat and disappointment, about how people are victims of the greed and selfishness of others in power.

The Citadel · Set partly in the same atmosphere as *The Stars Look Down*–the dusky, dirty towns of the English coal-mining region–Cronin's fifth novel, *The Citadel,* is the savage and fiercely idealistic story of a young physician's struggle to achieve success in life. To many readers, doctors particularly, the novel's main interest lay in Cronin's indictment of both the unethical practices of the medical profession and the system under which the miners lived and worked. To other readers, the interest lay in the unmistakable similarity between the hero's personal philosophy and Cronin's own opinions. There is the same integrity of character, the same effort to focus public attention on social forces which are responsible for many of the ills of his patients, and the same deep concern as an individual for lessening human disaster. In the hero, these readers welcomed the titillating sense of being "inside" the medical profession. Reading Cronin, they enjoyed the especially comforting thought that they were being educated as well as entertained.

If there is any single clue as to Cronin's intention in *The Citadel,* it is in the title. This simultaneously tragic and romantic novel was first called *Manson, M.D.,* after its hero, but it was felt that the title finally chosen was a better expression of the underlying meaning of the novel. Andrew Manson is a man who in spite of great odds tries and ultimately succeeds in freeing himself from materialistic influences. The word "citadel" stands for medical competency and medical integrity, the ideals to which Manson aspires. That this symbol is central to the plot of the novel is made clear when Chris Manson tells her husband: "Don't you remember how you used to speak of life, that it was an attack on the unknown, an assault uphill . . . as though you had to take some castle that you knew was there, but could not see, on the top?" At the end of the story, as Manson leaves Chris's grave, he sees in the sky before him a bank of clouds "bearing the shape of battlements." The reader is left to assume that Manson will once more assault the battlements, and that the conquest of them will be the greatest of all his achievements.

A large part of the novel's impressiveness stems from the way it functions throughout on a realistic level. Having grown out of Cronin's years as a physician and his experiences in Wales and London from 1921 to 1930, *The Citadel* may be read autobiographically, but with great caution. The reader may be sure that the greedy

Mrs. Edward Page, the bitter Philip Denny, the incompetent but fashionable Doctors Ivory, Freedman, and Hampton, and a score of others had their living counterparts in Cronin's own experience. From a full spectrum of professional men and women, Cronin tells of the jealousies of the assistants and the scheming rivalries of their supervisors, of questionable medical practices, unsanitary conditions, hostile patients, rejected treatments, ephemeral successes and horrifying failures, and always the drudgery of endless plodding hackwork.

Significantly, these supporting characters remain stereotypes, since Cronin's main point is that, except for Denny, they ease through life, think and talk mostly of fees, and scheme to get ahead. The lazy among them learn little and continue to prescribe routine drugs and treatments. The ambitious think up tricks to entice rich patients, prompting them to believe they are sick whether or not they are. These antagonists—the nonprogressive, materialistic doctors—are mostly figures of straw, their outlines only vaguely discernible through the young doctor's self-concern. Relative to Manson's vigor and vitality, these characters appear flat and insipid.

Another striking achievement of the book is the solid underlayer of fact. Almost all of Cronin's books, including the poor ones, have this foundation, giving them a satisfying density and bulk. In *The Citadel*, the details of Manson's experiences—without the use of abstruse technical terms and too many scientific explanations—are tremendously appealing to the reader. His restoration to life of Joe Morgan's stillborn baby, his coal-pit amputation of a miner's arm in the perilous tunnel, his restoration to consciousness of hysterical Toppy Le Roy, and the shocking butchery of the operation by Dr. Ivory, all of these scenes rouse the emotions as a means of persuading the mind. With its sober factuality, it is not difficult to understand why this novel has been enormously popular in both the United States and Great Britain.

While *The Citadel* has much to say about a society which seems unwilling to allow Manson to do his best work, while it dilates upon the evil practices of other physicians, it is also an unusual love story, with Andrew and Chris Manson at the center. Chris is effectively presented as a frank, well-educated, levelheaded young woman whose instinctive enjoyment of life is the counterpart of Andrew's integrity and determination. She knows the secret of turning hardships into fun, of forgetting irritation in laughter. Hard work and poverty do not scare her. The passionate integrity her husband brings to his science she brings to human relations—above all to her husband. From him, she refuses to accept any compromise of principle, even though this course leads them for a time to obscurity and poverty. She is strongly opposed to materialism and its shabby, cheapening results. She fights as best she can against every influence which she thinks will hurt her husband either as a scientist or as a man.

If one demands purity of conception and unflagging precision of execution in a novel, then *The Citadel* is clearly disappointing. Cronin, however, surmounts these flaws as an artist to represent seriously, and at times movingly, some of the significant problems of his day. To one concerned with literary movements, part of the interest of the book lies in its representation of the many facets of its cultural and social milieu. It contains elements of Romantic optimism, of realistic appraisal, and of naturalistic pessimism. In attempting to trace in *The Citadel* the progression of his own attitudes toward life, Cronin makes a comment about human experience that frequently strikes home with compelling force.

The Keys of the Kingdom · Perhaps his most popular novel, *The Keys of the Kingdom* emphasizes with incisiveness the problems encountered when a religious man rebels against the human-made rules, limitations, and barriers that are continually thrust between human beings and their God. Its merit lies precisely in its analysis of the conflicts between kindliness, sincere faith, and human understanding on one side, and smugness, intolerance, bigotry, and assumed piety on the other side. Francis Chisholm is the medium through which Cronin presents his conception of what has been called the most difficult subject in the world: religion.

In *The Keys of the Kingdom*, it is not the profession of medicine but that of the priesthood which is held up to examination. The verdict, however, is much the same as that found in *The Citadel*. The priest who serves God according to the teachings of Christ, viewing himself as the selfless shepherd and servant of man, accepting poverty, humility, and perhaps even martyrdom, is likely to be misunderstood, undervalued, and cruelly censored by his brethren. The more worldly priest, on the other hand, will win the power and the glory that the Church has to bestow. Cronin's priest, like Cronin's doctor, is an individualist with the courage to accept the guidance of his conscience rather than his self-interest. In the Church, as in the medical profession, such courage may put one at a disadvantage, often bringing disappointment and disillusionment. *The Keys of the Kingdom*, therefore, is an entrancing story, but also an expression of personal faith.

The title for this novel comes from the words of Christ to Peter—"And I will give to thee the keys of the kingdom of heaven"—and the central theme comes from Geoffrey Chaucer's famous description of the poor parson of the town, which ends, "But Christes' lore and his apostles twelve/ He taught, but first he followed it himself." Thus, the keys, according to Cronin and his mouthpiece, Francis Chisholm, are one's knowledge and use of the fundamentals of tolerance, humility, charity, and kindness. Where creeds divide, deeds of love and sympathy unite.

Like the great Victorians from whose rich tradition they spring, Cronin's characters, according to his modest moral aims, are unmistakably "good" or "bad." The reader knows as soon as he meets them that Aunt Polly, Nora Bannon, Mr. Chia, Dr. Willie Tullock, and Bishop McNabb are "good." One also can be reasonably sure that these people will endure their share of misfortune. The reader can find in these characters a schooling in generous humanity. Also easily recognizable are the unsympathetic characters: Bishop Mealey, Father Kezer, Mrs. Glennie, and Monsignor Sleeth. The reader always knows where he stands with Cronin.

This contrast between the "good" and the "bad" is apparent especially through the comparison of Francis Chisholm and his lifelong associate, Anselm Mealey, who lacks the feeling and innate spirituality of his friend, but who uses a certain veneer and his commanding appearance to get himself elevated to the bishopric. As a picture of the worldly priest, Mealey is eloquent in his sermons, popular with the women of the parish, and especially assiduous in those good works which gain him the approbation of his superiors. He attracts large donations, makes many converts, and fights the outward battles of the Church. He is even willing to capitalize on a "miracle" that proves to be no miracle at all.

Francis Chisholm, on the other hand, is the dissenter, the man who is different and therefore doomed to disappointment and failure in the eyes of the world. Through him, however, Cronin celebrates a central conviction: the significance—in possibility and promise, in striving if not in attainment—of tolerance and compassion and of encouragement for those striving to be true to their aspirations. Francis wins the priesthood the hard way: Being plain, outspoken, and unprepossessing in appearance, he never gets far in the Church. While Mealey attends to the social affairs of the

Church, Francis works with the poor and lonely. While Mealey complies with all of the Church's teachings, Francis speaks his mind. Christlike yet human, Francis believes in tolerance rather than dogma, and he holds humility above pride and ambition.

It is doubtful that a book has ever been more timely. Appearing as it did when most of the world was at war, and with most writers preoccupied with that topic, a book with religion as its background was most refreshing. When religion is presented logically and unpretentiously, as in *The Keys of the Kingdom*, without mawkishness or condescension, it is sufficiently novel to make the reading public take notice. In this atmosphere and with these attributes, Cronin's most popular novel achieved its immense success.

The Green Years · Until *The Green Years*, most of Cronin's attention had been focused on the absurdities and complications of the adult world. In *The Green Years*, however, Cronin set himself the added difficulty of working within the limited consciousness of a small child while at the same time avoiding the sentimentalities of so many books about childhood written for adults. To accomplish all of this Cronin takes his hero quite seriously, and he often describes his experiences with the same gravity as Robert, the protagonist, would view them. What is more, the novel consists of a grown man's remembered experience, for the story is told in retrospect of a man who looks back to a particular period of intense meaning and insight. "Our purpose," the author says, "is to reveal [the young Robert] truthfully, to expose him in all his dreams, strivings and follies." This double focus—the boy who first experiences, and the man who has not forgotten—provides for the dramatic rendering of a story told by a narrator who, with his wider, adult vision, can employ the sophisticated use of irony and symbolic imagery necessary to reveal the story's meaning.

The Green Years is a story of initiation, of a boy's quest for knowledge. The plot covers a period of ten years (1902-1912) and falls into three sections of nearly equal length as the hero progresses from innocence to perception to purpose. In the early chapters, Robert's innocence is expressed as a mixture of bewilderment and ignorance. The opening establishes with Proustian overtures the desolation which haunts him upon his arrival at his new home, Levenford, with his new "mama," Grandma Leckie: "I was inclined to trust Mama, who, until today, I had never seen before and whose worn, troubled face with faded blue eyes bore no resemblance to my mother's face." Robert's sensitivity to his new surroundings is apparent in his acute perception of details. At the dinner table, Papa says "a long, strange grace which I had never heard before." Robert has difficulty managing "the strange bare-handled knife and fork," does not like the cabbage, and finds the beef "terribly salty and stringy." He wonders why he is "such a curiosity" to all these people. The feeling of "being watched" is an experience that is repeated and a notion that reverberates throughout the novel. Suggested here is his continual need to perform for others and to be evaluated by others. Robert is the typical uncomprehending child caught in an uncomfortable situation. Lonely, imaginative, and isolated, he lacks the understanding necessary for evaluation and perspective.

Robert's gradual development into a perceptive young man functions, in large part, as a kind of organizing principle in the novel, uniting the common interest of a variety of disparate characters. These figures include Papa and Mama Leckie, Uncle Murdock, and Adam Leckie—all of whom are caught by marked shifts in their lives: illness, the death of those close to them, the breakup of careers, and the discovery of new opportunities. To compensate for this unhappy environment, Robert turns in part to nature and literature. His appreciation of nature, for example, may be attributed to his friend, Gavin Blair, in whom he discovers the companionship he craves. Like the companions of so many of Cronin's protagonists, Gavin is intelligent, gifted, and handsome. Particularly appealing to Robert is Gavin's "inner fibre, that spiritual substance for which no words suitable can be found."

While Cronin makes it clear that there is great comfort in all this, he also shows that this friendship initiates a problem that haunts Robert for much of the novel: a weakness for idealism. For Cronin, the great struggle of youth coming to maturity is the search for reality. This process involves disillusionment and pain. Robert endures a great deal of anguish each time one of his illusions is destroyed, but these disillusionments are necessary if he is to achieve intellectual and emotional independence. Once he must fight with his best friend, Gavin, to stop the taunts of his fellow classmates. At night, he is terrified by his grandmother's tales of Satan. He witnesses Gavin's death and on the same day fails the important Marshall examinations. All of this contributes to his temporary loss of faith in himself and his God.

Helping to shape Robert's purpose and philosophy is Alexander Gow, the one character with whom Robert feels secure. Robert quite naturally takes to Gow, with his apocryphal tales of the Zulu War, his eye for the ladies, his orotund views of human frailty, and his love for drink. Gow possesses "those faint ennobling virtues—never to be mean, always kind and inspiring affection." He defends Robert's right to Catholicism and to an education. Robert sees him as the reader sees him: erratic, not always dependable, yet, as one reviewer wrote, "still with an unquenchable zest for experience, an insatiable hunger for vital and beautiful things, an instinctive understanding of the human heart, especially a heart in trouble or in extreme youth."

In retrospect, *Hatter's Castle, The Stars Look Down, The Citadel, The Keys of the Kingdom,* and *The Green Years* fall into a pattern, illustrating Cronin's recurring themes. Each of the five novels features a protagonist who has glimpses of values beyond the reach of his environment and who must struggle to achieve them. All five novels focus with dramatic force on the essential evil of injustice: the personal suffering that is the real reason for hating such injustice. Cronin's humanitarian sympathies, his reaction against political, social, and religious injustice in his time, led him to a philosophical position somewhat akin to Thomas Carlyle's. He believed that it is man's responsibility to work, to prove his worth in whatever social stratum he happens to find himself.

Dale Salwak

Other major works
PLAY: *Jupiter Laughs,* pr., pb. 1940.
NONFICTION: *Report on First-Aid Conditions in British Coal Mines,* 1926; *Report on Dust Inhalation in Haematite Mines,* 1926; *Adventures in Two Worlds,* 1952 (autobiography).

Bibliography
Bartlett, Arthur. "A. J. Cronin: The Writing Doctor." *Coronet* 35 (March, 1954): 165-169. This readable, entertaining piece provides biographical details concerning Cronin's transition from life as a doctor to life as a writer.
Cronin, Vincent. "Recollection of a Writer." *Tablet* 235 (February 21, 1981): 175-176. One of Cronin's surviving sons writes a moving appreciation of his father with

biographical details and a discussion of *Hatter's Castle* through *The Spanish Gardener.* His novels were both "indictments of social injustice" and expressions of "a deep religious faith." From the latter stemmed "the warm humanity which gave his novels a worldwide appeal." Quotes from two messages of sympathy sent to the family.

Davies, Daniel Horton. *A Mirror of the Ministry in Modern Novels.* New York: Oxford University Press, 1959. This perceptive piece compares and contrasts the portrayal of a Protestant missionary in W. Somerset Maugham's "Rain" and Cronin's *The Grand Canary* and *The Keys of the Kingdom.*

Frederick, John T. "A. J. Cronin." *College English* 3 (November, 1941): 121-129. One of the earliest important considerations of Cronin's reputation in the light of his flaws as a writer. Discusses *Hatter's Castle, The Grand Canary, The Citadel, The Stars Look Down,* and *The Keys of the Kingdom.* Judges Cronin's novels to suffer from a lack of humor, an absence of stylistic grace, an obvious construction, and some feeble characters. On the positive side, finds a "deliberate choice of fictional material of the highest value and importance, unquestionable earnestness of purpose and—most important of all—positive evidence of capacity for self-criticism and for growth."

Fytton, Francis. "Dr. Cronin: An Essay in Victoriana." *Catholic World* 183 (August, 1956): 356-362. This important discussion covers the man behind the novels and his religious thinking since his return to the faith. Divides the works into two groups: those before *The Keys of the Kingdom* (which grow in quality) and those after (which descend in quality).

Salwak, Dale. *A. J. Cronin.* Boston: Twayne, 1985. The only published book-length study of Cronin, offering a full introduction to his life and works. After a discussion of his life as a doctor and his transition to that of a writer, examines each of Cronin's novels and concludes with an assessment of his career. Supplemented by a chronology, notes, a comprehensive bibliography (listing primary as well as secondary sources with brief annotations), and an index.

_____. *A. J. Cronin: A Reference Guide.* Boston: G. K. Hall, 1982. This annotated bibliography is an indispensable research tool for those interested in tracing the judgments passed on Cronin, the writer and the man, by his English and American readers from 1931 until his death in 1981. The annotations are descriptive, not evaluative, and are fully indexed, and the introduction traces the development of Cronin's literary reputation.

Daniel Defoe

Born: London, England; 1660
Died: London, England; April 26, 1731

Principal long fiction · *The Life and Strange Surprizing Adventures of Robinson Crusoe, of York, Mariner, Written by Himself,* 1719; *The Farther Adventures of Robinson Crusoe: Being the Second and Last Part of His Life,* 1719; *The History of the Life and Adventures of Mr. Duncan Campbell, a Gentleman Who, Tho' Deaf and Dumb, Writes Down Any Stranger's Name at First Sight, with Their Future Contingencies of Fortune,* 1720; *The Life, Adventures and Pyracies of the Famous Captain Singleton,* 1720; *Memoirs of a Cavalier: Or, A Military Journal of the Wars in Germany, and the Wars in England, from the Year 1632 to the Year 1648,* 1720; *The Fortunes and Misfortunes of the Famous Moll Flanders, Written from Her Own Memorandums,* 1722; *The History and Remarkable Life of the Truly Honourable Col Jacque, Commonly Call'd Col Jack,* 1722; *A Journal of the Plague Year: Being Observations or Memorials of the Most Remarkable Occurrences, as Well Publick as Private, Which Happened in London, During the Last Great Visitation in 1665,* 1722 (also known as *The History of the Great Plague in London*); *The Fortunate Mistress: Or, A History of the Life and Vast Variety of Fortunes of Mademoiselle de Beleau, Afterwards Call'd the Countess de Wintselsheim, in Germany, Being the Person Known by the Name of the Lady Roxana, in the Time of King Charles II,* 1724 (also known as *Roxana*); *The Memoirs of an English Officer Who Serv'd in the Dutch War in 1672, to the Peace of Utrecht in 1713, by Capt George Carleton,* 1728 (also known as *A True and Genuine History of the Last Two Wars* and *The Memoirs of Cap George Carleton*).

Other literary forms · Although Daniel Defoe is mainly remembered as the author of *The Life and Strange Surprizing Adventures of Robinson Crusoe, of York, Mariner, Written by Himself,* more commonly known as *Robinson Crusoe,* he did not begin to write fiction until he was fifty-nine. The earlier part of his writing career was spent primarily in producing essays and political pamphlets and working for strongly partisan newspapers. He also wrote travel books, poetry (usually on political or topical issues), and biographies of rogues and criminals.

Achievements · Defoe's principal contribution to English literature is in the novel, and he has been called the first English novelist. The extent of his contribution, however, has been debated. A contemporary of Defoe, Charles Gildon, wrote an attack on *Robinson Crusoe,* criticizing, in part, inconsistencies in the narrative. Such problems are not infrequent in Defoe's long and episodic plots. Nevertheless, the reader of almost any of Defoe's works finds himself in a real and solid world, and Defoe's constant enumeration of *things*—the layettes for Moll's illegitimate children, the objects she steals, even her escape routes through London—has earned for Defoe a reputation as a realist and for his style the label "circumstantial realism." To see Defoe as a photographic realist, however, is also to see his limitations, and some of his critics argue that the formlessness of his novels shows his lack of the very shaping power that belongs to great art. Further, even his circumstantial realism is not of the visual sort: Once Moll has named an object, for example, she rarely goes on to describe

Library of Congress

it in such detail that the reader may visualize it.

In the late twentieth century, Defoe's novels underwent a reassessment, and critics started to see him as more than a mere assembler of objects. Although these critics diverge widely in their interpretation of his techniques, they do agree that Defoe consciously developed the themes and used his narratives to shape these themes, all of which center around the conflict between spiritual and earthly values. Instead of viewing Defoe as a plodding literalist, some critics see a keen irony in his work: Moll's actions and her commentary on those actions, they argue, do not always agree. Thus, the reader is allowed to cultivate a certain ironic detachment about Moll. While few readers would judge Defoe to be a deeply psychological novelist, this double perspective does contribute to a rudimentary analysis of character. Others see a religious vision in his works, one that underwrites an almost allegorical interpretation of his novels: The ending of *Robinson Crusoe*, the killing of the wolves, is seen as Crusoe slaying his earthly passions. While such a reading may seem forced, one should perhaps remember that John Bunyan was a near contemporary of Defoe—he even preached at Morton's Academy at Stoke Newington while Defoe was a student there—and that readers in his time were accustomed to reading allegorically.

Part of the fascination—and achievement—of Defoe may well lie in the tension between realism and allegory that informs his work. Using natural dialogue and a kind of realistic detail, he can yet go beyond these to create events and characters which are, finally, mythic.

Biography · Daniel Defoe was born in the parish of St. Giles, London, the son of James Foe, a Dissenter and a tallow-chandler. (Only after the age of forty did Defoe change his last name, perhaps to seem more aristocratic.) The date of his birth is conjectural: In 1683, he listed his age on his marriage license as twenty-four, but since his sister, Elizabeth, was born in 1659, it is probable that Defoe was born the next year. Not much is known of his early childhood, but his education was certainly important in molding his interests. Being a Dissenter, Defoe was not allowed to attend Oxford or Cambridge; instead, he went to a dissenting academy presided over by the Reverend Charles Morton. While offering a study of the classics, the academy also stressed modern languages, geography, and mathematics, practical subjects neglected at the universities. This interest in the practical seems to have stayed with Defoe all his life: When his library was sold after his death, the advertisements listed "several hundred Curious, Scarce Tracts on . . . Husbandry, Trade, Voyages, Natural History, Mines, Minerals, etc." Defoe's appreciation of the objects and processes by which one is enabled to live in the world is obvious: After making a table and chair, Crusoe reflects that "by stating and squaring everything by reason and by making the most rational judgment of things, every man may be in time master of every mechanic art."

Although his father intended him for the ministry, Defoe became a merchant after leaving school and probably traveled on the Continent as part of his business. In 1684, he married the daughter of another dissenting merchant, and she brought him a considerable dowry. Defoe's fortunes seemed to be rising, but in 1685, he was briefly involved in the duke of Monmouth's rebellion, a Protestant uprising. Although he escaped the king's soldiers, this event illustrates his willingness to espouse dangerous political causes: Three former schoolmates who joined the rebellion were caught and hanged. While his affairs seemed to prosper during this time, there were disquieting lawsuits—eight between 1688 and 1694, one by his mother-in-law, whom he seems to have swindled—that cast doubt on both his economic stability and his moral character. In fact, by 1692 he was bankrupt, a victim of losses at sea and his own speculations. Defoe's character is always difficult to label; while the lawsuits show his unsavory side, he did make arrangements after his ruin to repay his creditors, which he seems to have done with surprising thoroughness.

Defoe then began building a brick factory on some land that he owned in Tilbury. This enterprise went well and, with William and Mary on the throne, Defoe could praise the government with a clear conscience. He admired William's religious toleration, foreign policy, and encouragement of English trade. He wrote several pamphlets supporting William's policy of containing Louis XIV's political aspirations, a policy not always popular in England. When William's followers from Holland were harassed by the English, Defoe wrote *The True-Born Englishman: A Satyr* (1701), a long poem arguing that the English are themselves a mixed race who cannot afford to deride other nationalities.

With the accession of Queen Anne of England in 1702, the Dissenters—and Defoe—suffered serious political grievances. Fiercely loyal to the Church of England, Anne looked with disfavor on other religious groups, and bills were introduced to limit the freedom of Dissenters. While both houses of Parliament debated the Occasional Conformity Bill in 1702, a bill that would have effectually prevented Dissenters from holding political office, Defoe published "The Shortest Way with the Dissenters," an ironic pamphlet urging the government to annihilate this group entirely. At first it was taken at face value and applauded by the High Church party but, when its irony was perceived, a warrant was issued for Defoe's arrest, and he went into hiding.

Fearful of imprisonment and the pillory, Defoe sent letters to Daniel Finch, second earl of Nottingham, the secretary of state, trying to negotiate a pardon: He would raise a troop of horses for the government at his own expense; he would volunteer to fight—and possibly die—in the Netherlands. Nottingham was inflexible, however, and when Defoe was found, he was imprisoned in Newgate, the scene of Moll's incarceration. Two months later, he was fined two hundred marks, forced to stand in the pillory three times, imprisoned at the queen's discretion, and forced to provide sureties for his good behavior for the next seven years. This experience helps, perhaps, to explain Defoe's later political views, which seemed to his contemporaries based on expediency rather than conviction: In a letter to a friend, he said that, after Newgate, he would never feel himself maligned if called a coward. When Defoe describes Moll's stay in prison, he knows whereof he speaks.

How long Defoe might have remained in Newgate at the queen's discretion cannot, of course, be known; certainly the government showed no sign of releasing him during the summer nor in the fall. He appealed to Robert Harley, a man destined to take Nottingham's place when the latter had been dismissed by the queen. After leisurely negotiations—perhaps to render Defoe more grateful when his pardon finally did come—Harley obtained Defoe's release in November, 1703, the queen even going so far as to send money to Mrs. Defoe and another sum to Defoe to settle his debt.

Harley continued to be influential in Defoe's life; indeed, popular opinion seems to have been that Defoe prostituted himself, abandoning all political ideals for Harley. Still, it is hard to imagine how a forty-three-year-old ruined businessman, with a wife and seven children to support, could begin life over if not with the help of a powerful ally. Defoe's letters to Harley also suggest that Harley sometimes kept him short of funds on purpose, perhaps to make him more compliant. In any case, Defoe's career was definitely the writing of political pamphlets—usually in favor of Harley's policies—and he also edited and wrote most of *A Weekly Review*, which ran from 1704 to 1713. Perhaps Defoe's most significant work for Harley was the establishment of a spy system in England to determine what the national sentiment was for the government. This project, which was Defoe's own idea, began in 1704 when Harley sent him on a preliminary reconnaissance trip through the country. This was the first of several such trips, including one to Edinburgh, Scotland, in 1706, to determine local opinion about the proposed union of the English and Scottish parliaments. On all these trips, Defoe had to assume fictitious identities, and he seems to have relished this subterfuge; it is perhaps significant that Defoe's characters usually are forced to assume many varied disguises in the course of their eventual lives. Even Defoe's tracts and pamphlets bear witness to his fascination with assuming various roles: One critic has estimated that Defoe created eighty-seven personae in these works.

After Harley's political decline and Queen Anne's death, Defoe continued to work for the government, characteristically, in a role requiring deception. Pretending to be a Tory out of favor with the government, he obtained a job on *Mist's Weekly Journal*, one of the most influential Tory papers. In this way, he was able to temper the writing so that its attacks on the government became less virulent. Defoe's shadowy activities are difficult to follow, but it seems that he was also performing the same service to the government on other papers: *Dyer's News-Letter*, *Dormer's News-Letter*, and *Mercurius Politicus*. Defoe's easy transition from Harley's Tory government to the succeeding Whig regime angered many people, who claimed that he had no principles. Defoe's reply, difficult to counter, was always that he was working for moderation, no matter on which side.

Only toward the end of his life did Defoe begin to write prose fiction: *Robinson Crusoe* (1719) and its sequels: *The Life, Adventures and Pyracies of the Famous Captain Singleton* (1720), *The Fortunes and Misfortunes of the Famous Moll Flanders, Written from Her Own Memorandums* (1722), *A Journal of the Plague Year* (1722), *The History and Remarkable Life of the Truly Honourable Col Jacque, Commonly Call'd Col Jack* (1722), and *The Fortunate Mistress* or *Roxana* (1724). Even after completing this enormous output, he continued to produce biographies of criminals and imaginary biographies of soldiers and sailors.

To all appearances, Defoe seemed to embark on a comfortable old age; Henry Baker, his son-in-law, reported that he had retired from London to a handsome house in Stoke Newington, where he lived a leisurely life, growing a garden, pursuing his studies, and writing. In 1730, however, Defoe vanished from his home and, in a rather cryptic letter to Baker, wrote about his "Load of insupportable Sorrows," a "wicked, perjur'd, and contemptible Enemy," and the "inhuman dealing of my own son" who reduced his "dying Mother to beg . . . Bread at his Door." The enemy seems to have been Mary Brooke, the wife of one of Defoe's former creditors. Although Defoe appears to have paid Brooke–at least Brooke's executor accepted Defoe's story– Brooke died before destroying his record of the debt and his wife was determined to collect it. Once again, Defoe was being hounded by a creditor. His reference to his unnatural son is a bit more puzzling but may show that he had transferred most of his money and property to his son to keep it out of Mary Brooke's hands; if so, his son seems to have abused the trust placed in him. Defoe died in April, 1731, while hiding in a lodging house in Ropemaker's Alley.

Although Defoe's colorful life almost calls too much attention to itself–some critics have tried to deduce his exact birthdate by events in his characters' lives–it is hard not to see a link between the elements of disguise and trickery in so many of his novels and his own eventful life, spent, in large part, in fabricating identities for himself in his government work. Like his character Moll Flanders, Defoe had personal experience with Newgate, and his biographies of criminals and rogues show a fascination with the inventive powers that allow one to thrive in a treacherous world. In this respect, Defoe and his characters seem to have a great deal in common: They are all survivors in an often hostile environment. This sense of alienation may also have a link with Defoe's religion, a creed that was sometimes tolerated but rarely encouraged by the Crown.

Analysis · Although *A Journal of the Plague Year* is not Daniel Defoe's first work of fiction, it does offer an interesting perspective from which to examine the novels. Purporting to be a journal, one man's view of a period in a city's history, it shows especially well the nexus between realistic reporting and imaginative invention that is the hallmark of Defoe's novels.

A Journal of the Plague Year · Defoe himself lived through one seige of the plague, and although he was only five years old when the disease swept through London, he presumably would have retained some recollections of this catastrophic event, even if only through conversations he would have heard in his family. He also refers frequently to the mortality list, drawing on actual documents of the time to give his narrative a sense of reality. In spite of the realistic foundations of the work, however, its imaginative–not to say fantastic–elements outweigh its realism. Defoe, in fact, often shows a surprising interest in the occult or grotesque for one who is supposedly forging the realistic novels in English. Dreams and premonitions often assail his characters: Crusoe's dream of the angel, Moll's telepathic contact with her Lancashire husband, Roxana's precognitive vision of the dead jeweler. The utter incomprehensibility of the plague takes this work far beyond cause-and-effect realism.

Perhaps the main thing to consider in *A Journal of the Plague Year* is the narrator, who, like many of Defoe's characters, is divided spiritually: He must decide whether to flee London or stay and trust God's divine providence. Like Crusoe, H. L. in times of stress opens the Bible randomly and applies its words to his immediate situation. A problem with theme–often Defoe's weakness–immediately arises, for while the passage that he finds in the Bible convinces him to stay, by the end of the novel he has decided that flight is the only sensible option. His stay in the city is not developed as a moral flaw, however, although given the religious concerns of the novel it seems as though it should be: Some critics even see him guilty of overstraining God's providence. This view seems inconsistent with the overall sympathetic character of H. L., and one feels that Defoe is not, perhaps, completely in control of his theme.

Even more significant for theme is the origin of the plague. H. L., a sensible, levelheaded man, insists that the plague's cause is natural; he is just as insistent, however, that God has used natural means to bring about the plague. In fact, he makes frequent biblical references which, if not providing specific emblematic types for the plague, do give it a resonance beyond that of a mere disease. Thus, the narrator's insistence on seeing all the horrors of the plague for himself, even though he admits he would be safer at home, has led some critics to see his curiosity as a desire to understand God's workings directly. Again, one encounters an awkward thematic problem. Is H. L. really curious about God's wisdom, or is his seeming inability to stay home simply a narrative necessity? There would, after all, be no journal without an eyewitness. Like many thematic problems in Defoe's works, this only becomes one in retrospect; H. L.'s emphasis on the particulars he describes can be so interesting—even if gruesome—that it is not until the reader has finished the book that these problems surface.

Two episodes from this work show how effective Defoe can be with detail. The first involves H. L.'s journey to the post office. Walking through silent and deserted streets, he arrives at his destination, where he sees "In the middle of the yard . . . a small leather purse with two keys hanging at it, with money in it, but nobody would meddle with it." There are three men around the courtyard who tell H. L. that they are leaving it there in case the owner returns. As H. L. is about to leave, one of the men finally offers to take it "so that if the right owner came for it he should be sure to have it," and he proceeds to an elaborate process of disinfection. This episode, on the surface merely straightforward description, is fraught with drama and ambiguity.

While it is realistic that the streets be deserted as people take to the safety of their houses, the silence lends an eerie backdrop to this scene. Furthermore, the men's motivations are hardly straightforward. Are they leaving the purse there out of honesty or are they fearful of contamination? Are they simply playing a waiting game with one another to see who leaves first? Does one man finally take the purse to keep it for the owner or for himself? Finally, why does he have all the disinfecting materials, including red-hot tongs, immediately available? Was he about to take the purse before H. L. arrived? H. L.'s remarks about the money found in the purse—"as I remember . . . about thirteen shillings and some smooth groats and brass farthings"—complete this episode: The particularity of the amount is typical of Defoe's realism, and H. L.'s hesitant "as I remember" also persuades the reader that he is witnessing the mental processes of a scrupulously honest narrator. In fact, this whole passage is so effective that one tends to overlook an internal inconsistency: Early in the paragraph H. L. says that the sum of money was not so large "that I had any inclination to meddle with it," yet he only discovers the sum at the end of this episode. Defoe is prone to narrative slips of this kind but, like this one, they are usually unimportant and inconspicuous.

Another vivid episode concerns H. L. going to check on his brother's house while he is away. Next to the house is a warehouse, and as H. L. approaches it, he finds that it has been broken into and is full of women trying on hats. Thievery is by no means uncommon during the plague, although the women's interest in fashion does seem bizarre. What is remarkable about this description, however, is its ambience: Instead of grabbing the hats and fleeing, the women are behaving as if they are at a milliner's, trying on hats until they find those that are most becoming. This scene shows Defoe ostensibly writing realistically, but in fact, he is creating a picture that borders on the surreal.

A Journal of the Plague Year does not always achieve the degree of success that these two episodes display; much of the book is filled with descriptions of the cries and lamentation the narrator hears as he walks the streets. Even horror, if undifferentiated, can become monotonous, and Defoe does not always know how to be selective about details. One device that he employs to better effect here than in his other works is the keeping of lists. Defoe's characters often keep balance sheets of their profits and expenditures, and while this may indicate, as Ian Watt contends, Defoe's essentially materialistic bias, these lists often seem examples of the crudest form of realism. In *A Journal of the Plague Year*, however, the mortality lists scattered throughout are rather more successful and provide almost a thudding rhythm to what is being described: God's terrible visitation.

Robinson Crusoe · *Robinson Crusoe*, like *A Journal of the Plague Year* and much of Defoe's fiction, is based on a factual event: Alexander Selkirk, a Scottish sailor, lived for four years on the island of Juan Fernandez until he was rescued in 1709. Defoe supplemented accounts of Selkirk's adventures with travel books: Richard Hakluyt's *Voyages* (1589), William Dampier's *New Voyage Round the World* (1697), and Robert Knox's *An Historical Relation of Ceylon* (1681). Nevertheless, it is as fiction—not a pastiche of other people's books—that *Robinson Crusoe* engrosses the reader. Since the story centers around one character, it depends on that character for much of its success, and critics have tended to divide into two groups: those who see Crusoe as the new middle-class economic man with only perfunctory religious feelings, and those who see him as a deeply spiritual person whose narrative is essentially that of a conversion experience. The answer, perhaps, is that both views of Crusoe coexist in this novel, that Defoe was not sure in this early work exactly where his story was taking him. This ambiguity is not surprising since the same problem surfaces in *The Fortunes and Misfortunes of the Famous Moll Flanders* (more popularly known as *Moll Flanders*); it was not until *Roxana* that Defoe seems to have worked out his themes fully.

The opening frame to Crusoe's island adventure provides a logical starting point for examining his character. Writing in retrospect, Crusoe blames his shipwreck and subsequent sufferings on his "propension of nature" which made him reject his father's counsel of moderation and prompted him to go to sea. His father's speech seems to echo the idea of a great chain of being: Crusoe's life belongs to the "middle state," and he should not endanger himself by reckless acts. If Crusoe's filial disobedience seems trivial to modern readers, it was not to Defoe: His *The Family Instructor, in Three Parts* (1715) and *A New Family Instructor* (1727) make clear how important the mutual obligations of parents and children are. Crusoe himself, recounting his exile from the perspective of old age, talks about his father in biblical terms: After Crusoe's first shipwreck he is "an emblem of our blessed Saviour's parable, [and] had even killed the fatted calf for me." When Crusoe reflects, then, on his sinful and vicious life, the reader has to accept Defoe's given: that Defoe's early giddy nature is a serious moral flaw.

Even with this assumption, however, the reader may have problems understanding Crusoe's character. Throughout the novel, for example, there are images of prison and capture. This makes sense, for the island is both a prison and, if the reader believes in Crusoe's conversion, a means of attaining spiritual freedom. Crusoe himself is imprisoned early in the novel by some Moors and escapes only after two years (which, like many long stretches of time in Defoe's novels, are only briefly summarized) with a boy named Xury, a captive who soon becomes Crusoe's helpmate and friend. Once Crusoe is free, however, he sells Xury willingly and misses him only when his plantation grows so large that he needs extra labor. Indeed, it is indicative of his relations with other people that, when Crusoe meets Friday, Friday abases himself to Crusoe, and Crusoe gives his own name as "Master." Perhaps one should not expect enlightened social attitudes about slavery or race in an eighteenth century author. Even so, there seems pointed irony–presumably unintended by Defoe–in Crusoe gaining his freedom only to imprison others; Crusoe's attitude does not seem sufficient for the themes and imagery that Defoe himself has woven into this work.

Crusoe does not behave appreciably better with Europeans. When he rescues Friday and his father, he also rescues a Spaniard who, with a group of Spaniards and Portuguese, has been living peaceably with Friday's tribe. Crusoe begins to think about trying to return to civilization with the Europeans and sends the Spaniard back to Friday's tribe to consult with the others. Before he returns, however, a ship with a mutinous crew arrives on the island: Crusoe rescues the captain and regains control of most of the mutineers. They leave the worst mutineers on the island and sail off for civilization; Crusoe apparently gives no thought to the Spaniard, who will return to the island only to find a motley collection of renegades. Defoe may, of course, simply have forgotten momentarily about the Spaniard as his narrative progressed to new adventures, but if so, this is an unfortunate lapse because it confuses the reader about character and, therefore, about Crusoe's humanity.

Another problem, this time having to do with theme, occurs at the end of the novel. After being delivered to Spain, Crusoe and another group of travelers set out to cross the Pyrenees, where they are beset by fierce wolves. They manage to escape, and Crusoe returns to England, marries, has three children, travels back to his island, and continues having adventures, which, he says, "I may perhaps give a farther account of hereafter." One might argue that the adventures after he leaves the island are anticlimactic, although some critics try to justify them on thematic grounds, the killing of the wolves thus being the extermination of Crusoe's earthly passions. The question remains whether the narrative can bear the weight of such a symbolic–indeed, allegorical–reading. The fact that the sequels to *Robinson Crusoe* are merely about external journeys–not internal spiritual states–shows, perhaps, that Defoe was not as conscious an allegorist as some critics imagine.

Given these thematic problems, it may seem odd that the novel has enjoyed the popularity it has over the centuries. In part, this may simply be due to the element of suspense involved in Crusoe's plight. On one level, the reader wonders how Crusoe is going to survive, although the minute rendering of the day-to-day activities involved in survival can become tedious. Of more interest are Crusoe's mental states: His fluctuating moods after he finds the footprint, for example, have a psychological reality about them. Further, the very traits that make Crusoe unappealing in certain situations lend the novel interest; Crusoe is a survivor, and, while one sometimes wishes he were more compassionate or humane, his will to endure is a universal one with which the reader can empathize.

Aside from the basic appeal of allowing the reader to experience vicariously Crusoe's struggles to survive, the novel also offers the reader a glimpse of Crusoe's soul; while some of Crusoe's pieties seem perfunctory, Defoe is capable of portraying his internal states in sophisticated ways. For example, early in his stay he discovers twelve ears of barley growing, which convinces him "that God had miraculously caused this grain to grow without any help of seed sown and that it was so directed purely for my sustenance on that wild miserable place." Two paragraphs later, however, "it occurred to my thoughts that I had shook a bag of chicken's meal out in that place, and then the wonder began to cease; and I must confess, my religious thankfulness to God's Providence began to abate too. . . ." The mature Crusoe who is narrating this story can see in retrospect that "I ought to have been as thankful for so strange and unforeseen Providence as if it had been miraculous; for it was really the work of Providence as to me" that God allowed the seed to take hold and grow. Here the reader finds Defoe using a sophisticated narrative situation as the older Crusoe recounts—and comments upon—the spiritual states of the young Crusoe. Indeed, one problem in the novel is determining when Crusoe's egocentric outlook simply reflects this early unregenerate state of which his mature self would presumably disapprove, and when it reflects a healthy individualism in which Defoe acquiesces. Perhaps Crusoe is most appealing when he is aware of his foibles—for example, when he prides himself on building a gigantic canoe, only to find that he cannot possibly transport it to water.

Colonel Jack · If *Robinson Crusoe* shows an uneasy balance between egocentricity and spiritual humility, materialism and religion, Defoe's novel *The Life, Adventures and Pyracies of the Famous Captain Singleton*, more commonly known as *Captain Singleton*, displays what Everett Zimmerman calls a "soggy amalgam of the picaresque and Puritan." This problem reappears in *The History and Remarkable Life of the Truly Honourable Col Jacque, Commonly Call'd Col Jack*, known to readers simply as *Colonel Jack*. Jack's motives are often suspect. When he becomes an overseer in Virginia, for example, he finds that he cannot whip his slaves because the action hurts his arms. Instead, he tells the slaves they will be severely punished by an absentee master and then pretends to have solicited their pardon. Grateful for this mercy, the slaves then work for Jack willingly and cheerfully. While Jack describes this whole episode in words denoting charity and mercy, the reader is uneasily aware that Jack is simply playing on the slaves' ignorance. It is method rather than mercy that triumphs here.

Moll Flanders and **Roxana** · The confusion in *Captain Singleton* and *Colonel Jack* between expediency and morality can also be found in *Moll Flanders* and, to a lesser extent, in *Roxana*. What makes these latter novels enduring is the power of their central characters. Both Moll and Roxana bear many children, and although they manage to dispose of their offspring conveniently so that they are not hampered in any way, their physical fertility sets them apart from Defoe's more sterile male heroes. This fertility may, of course, be ironic—Dorothy Van Ghent calls Moll an Earth Mother but only insofar as she is a "progenitrix of the wasteland"—but it adds a dimension to the characters that both Jack and Singleton lack. One also feels that Defoe allows his female characters greater depth of feeling: Each one takes husbands and lovers for whom they have no regard, but Moll's telepathic communication with her Lancashire husband and Roxana's precognitive vision of the jeweler's death imply that both of these women are involved deeply in these relationships, even though Roxana manages to use the jeweler's death as a way of rising in the world by becoming the Prince's mistress. Defoe's heroines may mourn their losses yet also use them to their advantage.

Another difference between the female and male protagonists is that neither Moll nor Roxana descends to murder, whereas Defoe's male picaros often do. Although Moll can occasionally rejoice when a criminal cohort capable of exposing her is hanged, she feels only horror when she contemplates murdering a child from whom she steals a necklace. Similarly, while Roxana may share an emotional complicity in Amy's murder of her importunate daughter, she explicitly tells Amy that she will tolerate no such crime. *Roxana* also seems to have more thematic unity than Defoe's other novels: Instead of advocating an uneasy balance between spiritual and material values, *Roxana* shows a tragic awareness that these are finally irreconcilable opposites. Roxana, although recognizing her weaknesses, cannot stop herself from indulging in them, and her keen awareness of what she calls her "secret Hell within" aligns her more with John Milton's Satan than with Defoe's earlier protagonists.

If Defoe begins to solve the thematic problems of his earlier novels in *Moll Flanders* and *Roxana*, he does so through fairly dissimilar characters. Moll equivocates and justifies her actions much more than does Roxana; when she steals the child's necklace, she reflects that "as I did the poor child no harm, I only thought I had given the parents a just reproof for their negligence in leaving the poor lamb to come home by itself, and it would teach them to take more care another time." She also shows a tendency to solve moral dilemmas by the simple expedient of maintaining two opposing moral stances simultaneously. When she meets a man at Bartholomew Fair who is intoxicated, she sleeps with him and then robs him. She later reflects on his "honest, virtuous wife and innocent children" who are probably worrying about him, and she and the woman who disposes of her stolen goods both cry at the pitiable domestic scene Moll has painted. Within a few pages, however, she has found the man again and taken him as her lover, a relationship that lasts for several years.

Moll seems to see no conflicts in her attitudes. Her speech also shows her ability to rationalize moral problems, and she often uses a type of equivocation that allows her to justify her own actions. When a thief is pursued through a crowd of people, he throws his bundle of stolen goods to Moll. She feels herself free to keep them "for these things I did not steal, but they were stolen to my hand."

Contrary to the character of Moll, Roxana recognizes her failings. After her first husband leaves her in poverty, her landlord offers to become her lover. Although he has a wife from whom he is separated, he argues that he will treat Roxana in every way as his legal wife. Throughout their life together, Roxana distinguishes between their guilt: The landlord, she says, has convinced himself that their relationship is moral; she, however, knows that it is not and is thus the greater sinner.

Indeed, Roxana is portrayed in much greater psychological depth than is Moll; one measure of this is the relationship between Roxana and her maid, Amy. While Defoe's characters often have close friends or confidants—Friday in *Robinson Crusoe*, the midwife in *Moll Flanders*, Dr. Heath in *A Journal of the Plague Year*—it is only in *Roxana* that the friend appears in the novel from the beginning to the end and provides an alter ego for the main character. When Roxana is deciding whether to take the landlord as her lover, for example, Amy volunteers several times to sleep with him if Roxana refuses. Once the landlord and Roxana are living together, Roxana decides to put Amy into bed with the landlord, which she does—literally tearing off Amy's clothes and watching their sexual performance. By the next day, the landlord's lust for Amy has turned to hatred and Amy is suitably penitent. The logical question is why Roxana does this destructive deed, and the answer seems to be that, since she herself feels intense guilt at sleeping with the landlord, she wants to degrade Amy and the landlord as well.

Amy, similarly manipulative, is less passive than Roxana. At the end of the novel, Susan, one of Roxana's daughters, appears, guesses her mother's identity, and begs Roxana to acknowledge her. Amy's suggestion is that she kill Susan, who alone can reveal Roxana's past, having been, unknowingly, a maid in her mother's household when Roxana had many lovers. Roxana recoils from this idea although she admits that Amy "effected all afterwards, without my knowledge, for which I gave her my hearty Curse, tho' I could do little more; for to have fall'n upon Amy, had been to have murther'd myself. . . ." Some critics argue that Roxana actually acquiesces in Susan's murder, even though she forbids Amy to do it; her statement that to fall upon Amy would be to destroy herself does lend credence to this view. Amy, perhaps, acts out the desires that Roxana will not admit, even to herself.

In fact, both *Moll Flanders* and *Roxana* seem to hint at an irrational perverseness in their characters that explains, in part, their crimes. At one point after beginning her life as a thief, Moll actually tries to earn her living with her needle and admits that she can do so, but temptation makes her return to crime. She appears to enjoy living outside the law, no matter how much she may talk of her fears of Newgate. Similarly, she once steals a horse simply because it is there; she has no way to dispose of it, but the irrational impulse in her that leads her to crime causes her to commit this theft anyway. Defoe is not given to high comedy, but the picture of Moll leading the horse through the streets, wondering how she is ever going to rid herself of it, is a memorably comic scene. The frequent irrationality of Moll's behavior seems reiterated in the actions of *Roxana*; without Moll's self-justifying rationalizations, however, Roxana becomes a tragic figure who knows that her behavior is wrong but cannot stop it. About halfway through the novel, for example, she meets a Dutch merchant, who helps her out of some difficulties; she sleeps with him, but, when he proposes marriage, she refuses him on the grounds that marriage is a kind of slavery for women. Actually, she fears that he is trying to take over her fortune. When he answers this unspoken objection, promising not to touch her wealth, she is left in the uncomfortable position of having to admit that her initial reluctance was based solely on financial considerations, or else continuing her spirited defense of female freedom. Moll chooses the latter option, arguing until the merchant admits defeat. After she is left alone, Roxana regrets her decision and wishes the merchant back, arguing that no "Woman in her Senses" would ever behave as she did. In these two novels, Defoe seems to be exploring the nature of evil, and it is seen repeatedly as an irrational drive that can deprive its victims of free choice.

In fact, *Roxana* is noteworthy for the ambiguously dark atmosphere that pervades the novel, even apart from Roxana's actions. Although *Moll Flanders* touches on incest, madness, and murder, these seem to be the understandable results of understandable causes: If you do not know your mother, you may marry your brother; if your brother-husband discovers your identity, he may go mad with grief; if you steal from a child, you may contemplate murder to cover up your crime. In *Roxana*, however, many of the characters seem motivelessly malignant, obscurely evil. The midwife whom the Prince hires for Roxana seems so murderous that Roxana has him dismiss her, yet there has been no suggestion in the novel that the Prince intends Roxana harm. On the contrary, he seems delighted with her pregnancy and even spends some time with her during labor. The sexual promiscuity found in *Moll Flanders* turns to sexual perversion in *Roxana*: Roxana's final lover before she goes to live with the Quaker disgusts her "on some Accounts, which, if I cou'd suffer myself to publish them, wou'd fully justifie my Conduct; but that Part of the Story will not bear telling. . . ."

Even the Quaker is an ambiguous figure. Although strictly truthful–Roxana states several times that the woman will not tell a lie–she hardly seems above reproach: She shows a surprising adeptness at bringing together Roxana and her former lover; she knows how to disguise the smell of alcohol on one's breath; she says at one point that she is almost tempted to abandon her sober Quaker attire and wear Roxana's Turkish costume, although the costume by this time has come to be an emblem of Roxana's sinful life.

Perhaps Defoe's darkening vision can best be seen by comparing the conclusions of *Moll Flanders* and *Roxana.* After a life of crime–by which she becomes quite wealthy–Moll is finally caught and sent to Newgate. Sentenced to die, she is instead transported, but not before meeting Jemmy, her Lancashire husband, who has been a highwayman and who also ends up in Newgate. They leave for America together, and since they have enough money to pay the captain of the ship handsomely, they are treated like gentry on their voyage. Once in America, they prosper, only returning to England at the end of the novel, presumably repentant but certainly wealthy from their life of crime.

The uneasy balance of religion and roguery in *Moll Flanders*–Moll's pieties interspersed throughout the work sometimes sound as perfunctory as Crusoe's–shifts in *Roxana*, where Defoe's character finally realizes that one cannot reconcile sin and prosperity in the easygoing synthesis that Moll seems to achieve. The novel ends with Susan's death and Amy's desertion; the final paragraph tells the reader that Roxana and her husband prospered for a while but that a "Blast from Heaven" finally destroyed her tranquility and she ended her days miserably. The abruptness of this conclusion makes for an unsatisfactory ending, but at least it does show Defoe solving the thematic problems inherent in all his earlier novels: Roxana recognizes a higher power but is unable to obey it. Instead of having the best of two worlds–prosperity and religion–she is doomed by a just providence which punishes her unrepentance.

If, like Defoe's heroes and heroines, the reader is given to keeping balance sheets, he could summarize easily Defoe's weaknesses and strengths. On a basic level, Defoe is often slipshod in his handling of narrative: At one point Moll tells the reader how many lovers she has had in her life, but Moll's list of lovers falls far short of the number she mentions in her own narrative. More serious are the thematic problems that Defoe seems to solve only in his final novel. Finally, his realism is quite crude in some places; descriptions of objects assail the reader without having any sensuous reality to them. To Defoe's credit, he is able to establish a convincing conversational tone for most of his characters, and they often have an energy which far exceeds their function as counters through whom Defoe can manipulate his episodic plots. When reading Defoe, however, one does not tend to think in terms of balance sheets. In his best works, the problems in Defoe's writings are so far masked by the vitality of his fiction as to be unnoticeable. Like all artists, Defoe has the ability to make his readers suspend disbelief.

Carole Moses

Other major works

SHORT FICTION: *A True Relation of the Apparition of One Mrs. Veal,* 1706.

POETRY: *The True-Born Englishman: A Satyr,* 1701.

NONFICTION: *An Essay upon Projects,* 1697; *The Shortest Way with the Dissenters,* 1702; *The History of the Union of Great Britain,* 1709; *An Appeal to Honour and Justice,* 1715; *The Family Instructor, in Three Parts,* 1715; *A General History of the Robberies and Murders of the Most Notorious Pyrates,* 1724-1728 (2 volumes); *A New Voyage Round the World by a Course*

Never Sailed, 1724; *A Tour Thro' the Whole Island of Great Britain,* 1724-1727 (3 volumes); *The Complete English Tradesman,* 1725-1727 (2 volumes); *The Four Years Voyages of Capt George Roberts,* 1726; *A New Family Instructor,* 1727; *Augusta Triumphans: Or, The Way to Make London the Most Flourishing City in the Universe,* 1728; *A Plan of the English Commerce,* 1728.

MISCELLANEOUS: *The Novels and Miscellaneous Works of Daniel Defoe,* 1840-1841 (20 volumes; Walter Scott, editor); *Romances and Narratives by Daniel Defoe,* 1895 (16 volumes; George Aitken, editor); *The Shakespeare Head Edition of the Novels and Selected Writings of Daniel Defoe,* 1927-1928 (14 volumes).

Bibliography

Backscheider, Paula R. *Daniel Defoe: Ambition and Innovation.* Lexington: University Press of Kentucky, 1986. Argues for Defoe's conscious artistry, seeing a consistency of outlook throughout his writing. Places him at the beginning of the English novelistic tradition and maintains that the historical novel is among his inventions. A fine survey of Defoe's entire oeuvre, including many pieces generally ignored.

_____. *Daniel Defoe: His Life.* Baltimore: The Johns Hopkins University Press, 1989. Excellent, detailed biography of Defoe. Sets the man and his writings in his political, social, and economic milieu. Includes a full bibliography of Defoe's writing and an extensive bibliography (thirty pages) of works about him from the eighteenth century through the 1980's.

Blewett, David. *Defoe's Art of Fiction: "Robinson Crusoe," "Moll Flanders," "Colonel Jack," and "Roxana."* Toronto: University of Toronto Press, 1979. In Defoe's letters and nonfiction, Blewett finds a worldview that sees the individual as isolated in an indifferent or hostile universe. Shows how four of Defoe's novels artfully voice this outlook. An epilogue considers Defoe's contribution to the development of prose fiction.

Hunter, J. Paul. *The Reluctant Pilgrim: Defoe's Emblematic Method and Quest for Form in "Robinson Crusoe."* Baltimore: The Johns Hopkins University Press, 1966. Examines *Robinson Crusoe* to understand not only that work but also the nature of the early English novel. Looks at the way Defoe used Puritan ideas, especially as they were expressed in seventeenth and early eighteenth century tracts.

Lund, Roger D., ed. *Critical Essays on Daniel Defoe.* New York: G. K. Hall, 1997. Essays on Defoe's domestic conduct manuals, his travel books, his treatment of slavery, his novels, and his treatment of the city. Includes an introduction and index, but no bibliography.

Novak, Maximillian E. *Defoe and the Nature of Man.* London: Oxford University Press, 1963. Traces the sources of Defoe's ideas about natural law and then discusses how Defoe demonstrates those views in *Robinson Crusoe, Moll Flanders, Colonel Jack,* and *Roxana.*

_____. *Realism, Myth, and History in Defoe's Fiction.* Lincoln: University of Nebraska Press, 1983. A collection of previously published essays by a leading Defoe scholar. Treats various aspects of Defoe's artistry: the psychological realism of *Roxana,* the use of history in *A Journal of the Plague Year* and *Memoirs of a Cavalier,* and myth-making in *Robinson Crusoe.*

Richetti, John J. *Daniel Defoe.* Boston: Twayne, 1987. A good general introduction to Defoe, with three of the seven chapters devoted to the novels. Includes a useful selective, annotated bibliography.

Spaas, Lieve, and Brian Stimpson, eds. *"Robinson Crusoe": Myths and Metamorphoses.*

New York: St. Martin's Press, 1996. Explores many aspects of the seminal novel. Includes bibliographical references and an index.

Sutherland, James. *Daniel Defoe: A Critical Study*. Cambridge, Mass.: Harvard University Press, 1971. An excellent overview of all of Defoe's work. Offers commonsensical readings of the works and provides helpful historical and biographical background as well as a useful bibliography for further study.

Watt, Ian. *The Rise of the Novel: Studies in Defoe, Richardson, and Fielding*. Berkeley: University of California Press, 1957. Discusses *Robinson Crusoe, Moll Flanders,* and Defoe's contribution to the realistic novel. Relates Defoe's fiction to the social and economic conditions of the age.

West, Richard. *Daniel Defoe: The Life and Strange, Surprising Adventures*. New York: Carroll & Graf, 1998. West covers all aspects of Defoe: not only the journalist, novelist, satirist, newsman, and pamphleteer, but also the tradesman, soldier, and spy. Written with considerable flair by a journalist and historian of wide-ranging experience.

Walter de la Mare

Born: Charlton, Kent, England: April 25, 1873
Died: Twickenham, Middlesex, England; June 22, 1956

Principal long fiction · *Henry Brocken*, 1904; *The Return*, 1910; *The Three Mulla-Mulgars*, 1910 (reprinted as *The Three Royal Monkeys: Or, The Three Mulla-Mulgars*, 1935); *Memoirs of a Midget*, 1921; *At First Sight: A Novel*, 1928.

Other literary forms · Walter de la Mare was a prolific author of poetry, short stories, and nonfiction. Like his novels, de la Mare's poetry and short fiction range from works written explicitly for children (for which he is best remembered) to works intended for adults. Poetry collections such as *Songs of Childhood* (1902) and *A Child's Day: A Book of Rhymes* (1912) reveal his understanding of the pleasures and frustrations of childhood, an understanding that made *The Three Mulla-Mulgars* a favorite with children. De la Mare's poetry for adults embodies his belief that human beings live in two coexistent worlds: the world of everyday experience and the world of the spirit, which is akin to dreaming.

Dreams and the nature of the imagination are frequent themes in both his fiction and his poetry. These and other interests are more explicitly revealed in his essays and in his work as an editor. Not much given to analysis, de la Mare was primarily an appreciative critic. Of the anthologies he edited, *Behold, This Dreamer!* (1939) is perhaps the most revealing of the influences that shaped his work.

Achievements · De la Mare published only five novels, one of which, *At First Sight*, is more a long short story than a true novel. His fiction is metaphorical and resembles his poetry in its concerns. Much of what he wanted to communicate in his writing is best suited to short works, and therefore his novels are haphazardly successful. In spite of the difficulties of the novels of de la Mare, his contemporary critics in general had a high regard for him as a novelist. Edward Wagenknecht, an important historian of the novel, ranked *Memoirs of a Midget* as one of the best twentieth century English novels. Indeed, in his essay on de la Mare in *Cyclopedia of World Authors* (1958), Wagenknecht emphasizes *Memoirs of a Midget* at the expense of de la Mare's other writings.

De la Mare's novels, however, were not as widely read in their time as his poetry and short fiction, and today they are seldom read at all. The lack of modern attention to de la Mare's novels is caused less by any absence of merit than by the predictable drop in reputation which many authors undergo in the literary generation after their deaths. Although his novels are unlikely to regain their popularity with a general readership, serious students of twentieth century English literature will almost certainly return to de la Mare's novels as his generation's writings are rehabilitated among scholars.

Biography · No full-length biography of Walter de la Mare has as yet been published. He was, by the few published accounts of those who knew him, a quiet and unpretentious man. One can reasonably infer from the absence of autobiographical material from an otherwise prolific writer that he was a private man. He seems to have lived his adventures through his writing, and his primary interests seem to have been of the intellect and spirit.

He was born in 1873 to James Edward de la Mare and Lucy Sophia Browning de la Mare, a Scot. While attending St. Paul's Cathedral Choir School, Walter de la Mare founded and edited *The Choristers' Journal*, a school magazine. In 1890, he entered the employ of the Anglo-American Oil Company, for which he served as a bookkeeper until 1908. During these years, he wrote essays, stories, and poetry, which appeared in various magazines, including *Black and White* and *The Sketch*. In 1902, his first book—and one of his most lastingly popular—was published, *Songs of Childhood*, a collection of poetry. He used the pseudonym "Walter Ramal," which he also used for the publication of the novel *Henry Brocken* in 1904, then dropped. He married Constance Elfrida Igpen in 1899, with whom he had two sons and two daughters. His wife died in 1943.

De la Mare's employment at the Anglo-American Oil Company ended in 1908, when he was granted a Civil List pension of a yearly one hundred pounds by the British government. Thus encouraged, he embarked on a life of letters during which he produced novels, poetry, short stories, essays, one play, and edited volumes of poetry and essays. These many works display something of de la Mare's intellect, if not of his character. They reveal a preoccupation with inspiration and dreams, an irritation with Freudians and psychologists in general (too simplistic in their analyses, he believed), a love of romance, and a love for the child in people. The works indicate a complex mind that preferred appreciation to analysis and observation to explanation.

Analysis · Walter de la Mare's novels are diverse in structure, although unified by his recurring themes. *Henry Brocken* is episodic, with its protagonist moving from one encounter to another. *The Return* has all the trappings of the gothic, with mysterious strangers, supernatural events, and unexplained happenings. *The Three Mulla-Mulgars* is a children's story, with a direct narrative and a clear objective toward which the novel's actions are directed. *Memoirs of a Midget* is Victorian in structure and is filled with incidents and coincidences; it emphasizes character over the other aspects of novel-writing. *At First Sight: A Novel* is really a long short story, what some might call a novella; its plot is simple, the problem its protagonist faces is straightforward, and it has only the barest attempt at a subplot.

Henry Brocken · Early in his literary career, de la Mare concluded that there were two ways of observing the world: inductive and deductive. Induction was a child's way of understanding his environment, through direct experience, whereas deduction was associated with adolescents and adults—the environment was kept at an emotional and intellectual distance. De la Mare believed that reality is best understood in relation to the self and best interpreted through imagination; childlike—as opposed to *childish*—observation is subjective, and childlike imagination can make and remake reality according to the imaginer's desires. Henry Brocken, the eponymous protagonist of de la Mare's first novel, is such a childlike observer. Critics are often confused by his adult behavior; they fail to understand that Brocken is intended to be childlike rather than childish.

Dreams are a part of the human experience that can be made and remade according to the subjective dictates of the self; de la Mare believed that dreams revealed a truer reality than that which is found in the waking experience. Given de la Mare's beliefs, Brocken's use of dreams to meet with famous literary characters seems almost natural. Brocken is able to converse with characters from the works of such authors as Geoffrey Chaucer, Jonathan Swift, and Charlotte Brontë. The characters are often living lives that were barely implied in their original author's works. Jane Eyre, for instance, is with Rochester long after the conclusion of Brontë's *Jane Eyre* (1847). *Henry Brocken* is about imagination and what it can do to reality. Great literary characters can seem more real than many living people. De la Mare represents this aspect of the imaginative response to literature by showing

Library of Congress

characters maturing and changing in ways not necessarily envisioned by their creators. Chaucer's Criseyde, for example, is not only older but also wiser than in *Troilus and Criseyde* (c. 1385). What is imagined can have a life of its own, just as dreams can be more alive than waking experience.

The Three Mulla-Mulgars · *The Three Mulla-Mulgars* seems to be an interruption in the development of de la Mare's themes of imagination, dreams, and reality. In it, three monkeys–called "Mulgars"–search for the Valley of Tishnar and the kingdom of their uncle Assasimmon. During their travels, the three–Nod, Thimble, and Thumb–have adventures among the various monkey species of the world and encounter danger in the form of Immanala, the source of darkness and cruelty. Although a children's story, and although humorous and generally lighthearted, *The Three Mulla-Mulgars* contains the spiritual themes typical of de la Mare's best work. Nod, although physically the weakest of the three monkeys, is spiritually gifted; he can contact the supernatural world in his dreams and is able to use the Moonstone, a talisman; Immanala is essentially a spiritual force; it can strike anywhere and can take any form; it can make dreams–which in the ethos of de la Mare are always akin to death–into the "Third Sleep," death. The quest for the Valley of Tishnar is a search for meaning in the Mulla-Mulgars' lives; their use of dreams, a talisman, and their conflict with Immanala make the quest spiritual as well as adventurous.

The Return · *The Return* represents a major shift in de la Mare's approach to fiction, both long and short. Before *The Return*, he presented his iconoclastic views in the guise of children's stories and allegories–as if his ideas would be more palatable in inoffensive fantasies than in the form of the adult novel. In *The Return*, de la Mare took an important step toward his masterpiece, *Memoirs of a Midget*, by creating a novel featuring adult characters with adult problems.

The Return seems gothic on its surface. Arthur Lawford, weak from a previous illness, tires while walking in a graveyard. He naps beside the grave of Nicholas

Sabathier, a man who committed suicide in 1739. Lawford awakens refreshed and vigorous, but to his dismay he discovers that his face and physique have changed. Later, a mysterious stranger, Herbert Herbert, reveals that Lawford resembles a portrait of Sabathier, and Herbert's sister Grisel becomes a powerful attraction for Lawford–she seems to be an incarnation of the lover who may have driven Sabathier to kill himself. The plot, when examined by itself, seems trite and melodramatic, yet de la Mare makes the events frightening, in part because he imbues the novel with genuine metaphysical questions and in part because he believes in his story.

Belief is always a problem in fiction, particularly fantastic fiction. Part of what makes hackwork poor literature is insincerity in the author; the author does not believe that his work is valid, important, or worthy of belief. De la Mare clearly believes that the love story in *The Return* is important, that the novel's themes are valid, and that its events can be believed. His sincerity endows the novel's events with poetic power. Thus, the question of Lawford's identity becomes disturbing for the reader: De la Mare is saying that no one's identity is certain. Soon after Lawford's physical metamorphosis, his speech takes on a dual sound, as if he and Sabathier were speaking simultaneously. His conversations with Grisel are discussions between the corporeal Lawford and Grisel and between Sabathier and his past love.

In *The Return*, de la Mare's notions about the human spirit being part of two coexistent worlds are made graphic. Lawford becomes a citizen of everyday reality and of the greater reality of the spirit. He can see the world out of time, past and present; he battles both corporeal and supernatural foes; he is at once Sabathier and an ordinary, middle-aged Englishman. Although a part of two realities, he is accepted by neither. His friends and neighbors want him jailed or locked up in a madhouse; Grisel tells him that he cannot have her, although she shares his love, because he is not free of the burdens of his old world. The dilemma of Lawford, trapped as he is between the two worlds, is representative of the human condition: Everyone is trapped between two realities because everyone, whether he chooses to recognize it or not, is spiritual as well as physical. So thick with double meanings and disturbing confusions is *The Return* that its almost too convenient resolution–on All Angels Eve, the night on which Sabathier had committed suicide, Lawford is freed of Sabathier's spiritual tug–is a relief. Lawford is free to pretend that what he sees is all that exists, and so is the novel's reader.

Memoirs of a Midget · Greeted from its publication with praise for its characterization and graceful prose, *Memoirs of a Midget* is generally regarded by critics as de la Mare's masterpiece. The novel allows multiple readings; most critics readily recognize de la Mare's unusually successful development of a character's point of view, and they note the subtlety of his social commentary, but they often fail to recognize the novel's informing purpose. The story is simple on its surface. Miss M., also known as Midgetina, is a perfectly formed midget. The novel describes her childhood and emergence as an adult. Her point of view as a small adult is carefully created. The bulk of the novel is devoted to her twentieth year, during which she confronts her selfhood and comes to understand that there is a world of the spirit that is greater than the physical one in which she is a social amusement.

The novel has a Victorian flavor, and many of the characters have a Dickensian vitality. One of the most memorable characters is Mr. Anon, a misshapen hunchback who is only a little taller than Miss M. Mr. Anon transforms Miss M. from a social manipulator into a thoughtful person. He loves her–probably, he says, because she is one of the few people close to his size. His ugliness is repulsive, and Miss M. wants to keep him as a friend, but not as a lover. She joins a circus in order to become independent and quickly becomes a main attraction. In order to save Miss M. from possible recognition when Mrs. Monnerie, Miss M.'s former patroness, attends the circus, Mr. Anon takes her place in a pony-riding act. He is thrown from the pony and later dies in Miss M.'s arms. Some critics contend that at Mr. Anon's death Miss M. finally loves him. What is probable is that she believes that his inner self–his spirit–is beautiful and more real than his ugly physical form. Later, Miss M. disappears from a locked room. Her housekeeper, Mrs. Bowater, who commands the only entrance and exit to the room, hears a male voice from within, even though no one had entered through the door. Upon investigation, Mrs. Bowater finds a note which reads "I have been called away."

The character of Miss M. is well suited to de la Mare's purposes. She is small and treated like a child by other characters, and thus her perspective is like that of a child. Reared in seclusion by indulgent parents, she emerges into society with much of her childlike ability to experience the world inductively still intact. She is an adult with an adult's thinking capacity, enabling her to understand as well as know the world. She is an excellent vehicle for de la Mare's ideas about the nature of the human spirit. She observes the best and worst in people, and she sees that the unhappiest people are those who see the world as something to be manipulated, who take without giving. Mr. Anon gives all he has without expectation of receiving what he wants, Miss M.'s love. *Memoirs of a Midget* is more than a story of a social outcast's view of society; it is a depiction of spiritual conflict and revelation.

De la Mare was a seeker, a questioner, and an observer; the endings of his novels are suggestive but provide few answers. A skilled and demanding craftsman, he never failed to entertain his readers, but he employed his storyteller's gift in the service of the lifelong spiritual quest which animated all of his works.

Kirk H. Beetz

Other major works

SHORT FICTION: *Story and Rhyme: A Selection*, 1921; *The Riddle and Other Stories*, 1923; *Ding Dong Bell*, 1924; *Broomsticks and Other Tales*, 1925; *Miss Jemima*, 1925; *Readings*, 1925-1926 (2 volumes); *The Connoisseur and Other Tales*, 1926; *Told Again: Traditional Tales*, 1927; *Old Joe*, 1927; *On the Edge*, 1930; *Seven Short Stories*, 1931; *The Lord Fish*, 1933; *The Nap and Other Stories*, 1936; *The Wind Blows Over*, 1936; *Animal Stories*, 1939; *The Picnic*, 1941; *The Best Stories of Walter de la Mare*, 1942; *The Old Lion and Other Stories*, 1942; *The Magic Jacket and Other Stories*, 1943; *The Scarecrow and Other Stories*, 1945; *The Dutch Cheese and Other Stories*, 1946; *Collected Stories for Children*, 1947; *A Beginning and Other Stories*, 1955; *Ghost Stories*, 1956.

PLAY: *Crossings: A Fairy Play*, pr. 1919.

POETRY: *Songs of Childhood*, 1902; *Poems*, 1906; *The Listeners and Other Poems*, 1912; *A Child's Day: A Book of Rhymes*, 1912; *Peacock Pie: A Book of Rhymes*, 1913; *The Sunken Garden and Other Poems*, 1917; *Motley and Other Poems*, 1918; *Flora: A Book of Drawings*, 1919; *Poems 1901 to 1918*, 1920; *Story and Rhyme*, 1921; *The Veil and Other Poems*, 1921; *Down-Adown-Derry: A Book of Fairy Poems*, 1922; *Thus Her Tale*, 1923; *A Ballad of Christmas*, 1924; *Stuff and Nonsense and So On*, 1927; *Self to Self*, 1928; *The Snowdrop*, 1929; *News*, 1930; *Poems for Children*, 1930; *Lucy*, 1931; *Old Rhymes and New*, 1932; *The Fleeting and Other Poems*, 1933; *Poems 1919 to 1934*, 1935; *This Year, Next Year*, 1937;

Memory and Other Poems, 1938; *Haunted,* 1939; *Bells and Grass,* 1941; *Collected Poems,* 1941; *Collected Rhymes and Verses,* 1944; *The Burning-Glass and Other Poems,* 1945; *The Traveller,* 1946; *Rhymes and Verses: Collected Poems for Young People,* 1947; *Inward Companion,* 1950; *Winged Chariot,* 1951; *O Lovely England and Other Poems,* 1953; *The Complete Poems,* 1969.

NONFICTION: *Rupert Brooke and the Intellectual Imagination,* 1919; *The Printing of Poetry,* 1931; *Lewis Carroll,* 1932; *Poetry in Prose,* 1936; *Pleasures and Speculations,* 1940; *Chardin, J.B.S. 1699-1779,* 1948; *Private View,* 1953.

EDITED TEXTS: *Come Hither,* 1923; *The Shakespeare Songs,* 1929; *Christina Rossetti's Poems,* 1930; *Desert Islands and Robinson Crusoe,* 1930; *Stories from the Bible,* 1930; *Early One Morning in the Spring,* 1935; *Animal Stories,* 1939; *Behold, This Dreamer!,* 1939; *Love,* 1943.

Bibliography

Atkins, John. *Walter de la Mare: An Exploration.* Folcroft, Pa.: Folcroft Library Editions, 1973. A brief but useful analysis of de la Mare's works.

Duffin, Henry Charles. *Walter de la Mare: A Study of His Poetry.* Freeport, N.Y.: Books for Libraries Press, 1969. The first full-length critical study of de la Mare's poetry. Unfortunately the repetition and effusive style detract from the main points of criticism.

Hopkins, Kenneth. *Walter de la Mare.* London: Longman, 1954. A brief but excellent overview of de la Mare. Includes a bibliography.

McCrosson, Doris Ross. *Walter de la Mare.* New York: Twayne, 1966. Focuses on his novels as being the clearest statement of de la Mare's vision, giving particular emphasis to his imagination and dreams. McCrosson hopes to correct the popular notion that de la Mare is primarily a children's author. A helpful study, in part because there is so little modern criticism on de la Mare.

Reid, Forrest. *Walter de la Mare: A Critical Study.* St. Clair Shores, Mich.: Scholarly Press, 1970. An important study of de la Mare that discusses both his prose and his poetry. Also focuses on the later tales, which Reid divides into various groups according to themes, including six tales of the supernatural.

Wagenknecht, Edward. *Seven Masters of Supernatural Fiction.* New York: Greenwood Press, 1991. See the chapter on Walter de la Mare, which includes a brief biographical sketch and discusses his fiction in the context of the English literary tradition. Wagenknecht deals with both the short and the long fiction, providing a succinct overview of de la Mare's body of work in prose.

Whistler, Theresa. *Imagination of the Heart: The Life of Walter de la Mare.* London: Duckworth, 1993. A good biography of de la Mare. Includes bibliographical references and an index.

Charles Dickens

Born: Portsmouth, England; February 7, 1812
Died: Gad's Hill, near Rochester, England; June 9, 1870

Principal long fiction · *Pickwick Papers*, 1836-1837 (originally pb. as *The Posthumous Papers of the Pickwick Club*); *Oliver Twist*, 1837-1839; *Nicholas Nickleby*, 1838-1839 (originally pb. as *The Life and Adventures of Nicholas Nickleby*); *The Old Curiosity Shop*, 1840-1841; *Barnaby Rudge: A Tale of the Riots of '80*, 1841; *Martin Chuzzlewit*, 1843-1844 (originally pb. as *The Life and Adventures of Martin Chuzzlewit*); *Dombey and Son*, 1846-1848 (originally pb. as *Dealings with the Firm of Dombey and Son, Wholesale, Retail, and for Exportation*); *David Copperfield*, 1849-1850 (originally pb. as *The Personal History of David Copperfield*); *Bleak House*, 1852-1853; *Hard Times*, 1854 (originally pb. as *Hard Times for These Times*); *Little Dorrit*, 1855-1857; *A Tale of Two Cities*, 1859; *Great Expectations*, 1860-1861; *Our Mutual Friend*, 1864-1865; *The Mystery of Edwin Drood*, 1870 (unfinished).

Other literary forms · All of Charles Dickens's novels were published in bound form after serialization, the Oxford edition being the most complete modern collection. A prolific writer, Dickens also published a number of other works. He founded and edited the periodicals *Master Humphrey's Clock* (1840-1841), *Household Words* (1850-1859), and *All the Year Round* (1859-1870), in which many of his essays, collaborative works, and Christmas stories were originally published. Some of the essays have been collected: *Sketches by Boz* (1836), for example, comprises Dickens's periodical contributions from 1833 to 1836, and *The Uncommercial Traveller* (1860) reprints essays from *All the Year Round*. In addition to the Christmas stories, Dickens published five Christmas books, all collected in 1852. He recorded his travel experiences as well: *American Notes* (1842) depicts his first American tour, and *Pictures from Italy* (1846) is a collection of essays first printed in the *Daily News*. Finally, the texts of his public readings have appeared, along with reprints of his dramatic productions. Many of Dickens's works have been anthologized and adapted for stage and screen, and the definitive Pilgrim Edition of his letters, *The Letters of Charles Dickens*, was completed in 1995.

Achievements · Known for his biting satire of social conditions as well as for his comic worldview, Dickens began, with *Pickwick Papers*, to establish an enduring novelistic reputation. In fourteen completed novels and countless essays, sketches, and stories, he emerged as a champion of generosity and warmth of spirit, those human traits most likely to atrophy in an industrialized society. In his own day, he appealed to all levels of society but especially to the growing middle class, whose newfound literacy made them educable to eradicate the social evils they themselves had fostered. Dickens was extremely popular in the United States, despite his ongoing attack on the lack of an international copyright agreement, an attack directed in part against the Americans who had a financial stake in pirated editions of his works.

Above all, Dickens appealed to his readers' emotions, and through them, to an awakened social sense. To be sure, Dickens's sentimentality offends as many modern

251

readers as it pleased Victorian ones. Indeed, the twentieth century reader may study his novels primarily for the enjoyment of his craft, but to do so is to ignore Dickens's purpose: to argue on the side of intuition against materialism, as Angus Wilson puts it, or on the side of the individual against the system, as Philip Hosbaum has commented. In his facility for comic language, for example, Dickens created the unforgettable Sairey Gamp, Flora Finching, and Alfred Jingle, whose manic lingo creates worlds with a preposterous logic of their own, but such lingo is sometimes a shield for a warm heart and sometimes an indicator of fragmentation and despair. The reader also finds that Dickens's attacks on certain social institutions, such as the Poor Law in *Oliver Twist* or the Court of Chancery in *Bleak House*, are actually attacks on universal human evils—the greed, hypocrisy, and lust for power that lead to dehumanization and make, for example, a "species of frozen gentleman" out of Mr. Dombey instead of a warm, affectionate human being.

Biography · Born on February 7, 1812, in Portsmouth, on Portsea Island, England, Charles Dickens was the son of John Dickens, a Naval Pay Office employee, and Elizabeth Barrow, the daughter of the Naval Conductor of Moneys. John Dickens's largely unsuccessful struggle to gain middle-class respectability was hampered not only by his parents' career in domestic service, but also by the disgrace of his father-in-law, who left the country to avoid the consequences of a petty embezzlement. John Dickens's seaport life left a lasting impression on his son to be recorded partly in Rogue Riderhood's river activities in *Our Mutual Friend*, and partly in metaphor, as in *Dombey and Son*, where the running of the river into the ocean represents the passage of life into immortality. John Dickens's improvidence and inevitable bankruptcy is reflected in the impecunious but absurdly hopeful Mr. Micawber and, more abstractly, in Dickens's ambiguous attitude toward wealth, which he viewed as a highly desirable tool but worthless as a gauge of human value, as in *Our Mutual Friend*, in which money is equated with an excremental dust heap. An inordinate number of his deserving characters acquire wealth fortuitously: Oliver Twist, the parish boy, finds his near relatives; Nicholas Nickleby becomes clerk to the generous Cheerybles; and Esther Summerson comes under the protection of the well-to-do Jarndyce.

Childhood associations were incorporated into his stories as well. His nurse, Mary Weller, by her own dogmatic adherence, inculcated in him a distaste for Chapel Christianity; his childhood taste for theatricals blossomed into a lifelong fascination. (In fact, in 1832, only illness prevented him from auditioning at Covent Garden.) Perhaps no other circumstance, however, had so profound an effect on Dickens as his father's imprisonment in the Marshalsea for bankruptcy, well chronicled in *David Copperfield.* John Forster, Dickens's friend and biographer, records the author's bitterness at being put to work at Warren's Blacking Factory. Even worse than the degradation of the job for the young Dickens was the feeling that he had been abandoned. While his period of employment in the factory could be measured in months, the psychological scars lasted for the rest of Dickens's life, as witnessed by his novelistic preoccupation with orphans and adopted families: Oliver Twist, Amy Dorrit, Pip, Little Nell—all abandoned in some sense and forced into precocity, some, in effect, reversing roles with their parents or guardians to become their protectors.

At the age of fifteen, Dickens was apprenticed as a law clerk in Doctor's Commons, certainly the source of his profound dislike for the pettifoggery exhibited in the Jarndyce case in *Bleak House.* He then became a reporter in Parliament, and, at the age of seventeen, fell in love with Maria Beadnell, the daughter of a banking family

who discouraged the attentions of the impoverished young man. This experience, as well as his unsuccessful marriage to Catherine Hogarth, daughter of the editor of the *Morning Chronicle*, contributed much to his alternate idealization of women (such as Dora in *David Copperfield*) and mockery of their foibles.

At the time of his marriage, Dickens had been writing a serial for Robert Seymour's sporting drawings–a work that became *Pickwick Papers* upon Seymour's suicide. Dickens's success came quickly: He became editor of *Bentley's Miscellany* (1836), and in February, 1837, *Oliver Twist* began to appear, one month after the birth of the first of his ten children. Before *Oliver Twist* had finished its serial run, Dickens had begun

Nicholas Nickleby, in which he drew on his dramatic interests to create the Crummles provincial acting company. Then, in 1840, Dickens arranged to edit *Master Humphrey's Clock*, which became a vehicle for both *The Old Curiosity Shop* and *Barnaby Rudge* (the story of the 1780 Gordon riots). Some of his immense creative energy came from the early happiness of his marriage, but some also came from an effort to forget the death of his beloved sister-in-law Mary, who died in his arms when she was seventeen.

This period of activity ended in 1842 with a six-month visit to the United States. In letters, in *American Notes*, and in *Martin Chuzzlewit*, Dickens reveals his double vision of America. Welcomed in Boston by such literati as Henry Wadsworth Longfellow, Dickens moved from the cultivated bluestocking milieu into a furious newspaper war that was battling over the lack of an international copyright agreement. Dickens came to believe that while democracy did exist in such model factory towns as Lowell, Massachusetts, America's much-vaunted freedom was an excuse for vulgarity on one hand and hypocrisy on the other. He was appalled at the conditions of slavery in St. Louis and dismayed by the flat stretches of the Great Plains and by the ever-present concern for partisan politics, money, and power. All of these he satirized bitterly in the American section of *Martin Chuzzlewit*.

At home again, he installed his sister-in-law Georgina in her lifelong role of housekeeper to counter what he judged to be Catherine's growing indolence, surely symptomatic of their growing disillusionment with each other. Two years later, he began publication of *Dombey and Son*, his first planned novel. His next, the autobiographical *David Copperfield*, contains advice by the novel's heroine, Agnes, that he applied to his own life: "Your growing power and success enlarge your power of doing good." In March, 1850, Dickens founded *Household Words*, a periodical that featured short stories, serialized novels, poetry, and essays. Dickens and his writers published exposés of hospitals, sanitary conditions, political affairs, education, law, and religion, all expressed in a characteristically fanciful style. In these years, Dickens was engaged in amateur theatricals, partly to raise money to endow an impoverished actors' home. Between 1852 and 1857, he wrote three novels: *Bleak House*, his experiment in first-person narration; *Hard Times*, an attack on utilitarianism; and *Little Dorrit*, a semiautobiographical work. Becoming more and more estranged from his wife, he engaged in a strenuous and highly popular series of readings from his works, again bringing his dramatic talent into play. In June, 1858, he published a much-criticized apologia for his marital separation; then, chafing at the restrictions imposed on *Household Words* by the publishers, Edward Chapman and William Hall, Dickens severed the connection and began *All the Year Round*, a new periodical of the same type.

His liaison with the actress Ellen Ternan continued in this period, during which he wrote *A Tale of Two Cities*, *Great Expectations*, and *Our Mutual Friend*, his last completed novel. He undertook another exhausting series of public readings, his reenactment of Nancy's murder in *Oliver Twist* proving the most demanding. In 1867, he left for a successful tour of the United States. He continued public readings until the end of his life.

Dickens died at Gad's Hill, near Rochester, on June 9, 1870, and is buried in Westminster Abbey. His last unfinished novel, *The Mystery of Edwin Drood*, appeared posthumously.

Analysis · The "Dickens World," as Humphrey House calls it, is one of sharp moral contrast, a world in which the self-seeking—imprisoned in their egotism—rub shoulders with the altruistic, freed from the demands of self by concern for others; a world in which the individual achieves selfhood by creating a "home" whose virtues of honesty and compassion are proof against the dehumanizing "System": a world in which all things are animate and where, indeed, metaphors for moral perversity take lives of their own, like the miasma of evil that hangs above the houses in *Dombey and Son.*

Many of Charles Dickens's most memorable characters are those whose language or personality traits are superbly comic: Sairey Gamp, the bibulous nurse in *Martin Chuzzlewit*, with her constant reference to the fictitious Mrs. 'Arris; Flora Finching, the parodic reincarnation of a stout, garrulous Maria Beadnell in *Little Dorrit*; and Turveydrop, the antediluvian dandy Beau Brummel in *Bleak House.* To provide characters with distinguishing traits is, of course, a dramatic device (to see red hair and a handkerchief is to be reminded of Fagin, and knitting, of Mme DeFarge); more important, however, such traits carry a moral resonance. While Dickens's villains grow more complex as his writing matures, most share an overriding egotism that causes them to treat people as things. Perhaps that is why things become animate; in a world in which human traits are undervalued, objects achieve a life and controlling power of their own. The miser Harmon disposes of Bella Wilfer in *Our Mutual Friend* as if she were a property to be willed away; the convict Jaggers creates a "gentleman" out of Pip in *Great Expectations*; both Carker and Dombey see Edith as a valuable objet d'art in *Dombey and Son.*

Dickens's later heroes and heroines are characterized by their movement toward self-actualization. In the early novels, Rose Maylie, Mr. Brownlow, Tom Pinch, Nicholas Nickleby, and even Pickwick represent compassionate but stereotyped models. Later, however, Dombey is thawed by his daughter Florence's love; Eugene Wrayburn, the blasé lawyer, is humanized by Lizzie Hexam; and Bella Wilfer gives up self-seeking for John Rokesmith. Some, however, must go through the reverse process of acquiring self-assertiveness. Florence Dombey is such a one; only by fleeing her father's household and establishing a family of her own can she achieve perspective. Amy Dorrit is another; she must grow up and then willfully become as a child again for the benefit of Arthur Clennam, who needs to be convinced of his worth. Esther Summerson is yet a third; persuaded of her worthlessness because of her illegitimacy, she must learn a sense of self-worth before she can marry Allan Woodstone.

Many of the heroes and heroines are tested by touchstone figures, such as Smike, Jo, Mr. Toots, Maggie, and Sloppy—unfortunates whose lack of mental capability or personal disfavor provide a test for altruism. Many of Dickens's child characters serve a similar purpose, from Oliver Twist and his famous request for more gruel to the itinerant Little Nell.

All of the characters are subject to the effects of the "System," in whatever shape it takes: Dotheboys Hall and the Gradgrind's school, the Circumlocution Office, the middle-class complacency of Podsnappery, the unsanitary conditions of Tom All Alone's, or the financial shenanigans of Montague Tigg's Anglo-Bengalee Disinterested Loan and Life Insurance Company. Far worse are the hypocrisy of Pecksniff, the concupiscence of Gride, the utilitarianism of Gradgrind, and the lovelessness of Estella, but all are personal evocations of the evils of the "System." Even as early as *Oliver Twist*, Dickens seemed to recognize that no one individual could rectify evil; as Stephen Marcus comments, "*Pickwick Papers* is Dickens's one novel in which wickedness, though it exists, is not a threat. The unfortunate and the deprived . . . have only to catch a glimpse of Pickwick in order to be renewed, for this is the world of the 'good heart,' that thaumaturgic resource of spirit." When Nicholas breaks up Dotheboys Hall by whipping Squeers, all that one can do is succor the runaways; when the law is befogged by obscurities as in the Jarndyce case, all one can do is provide a warm, loving household. This, in fact, seems to be Dickens's solution, for despite his call for reforms, he was, at heart, a conservative, more likely to help Angela Burdett-Coutts set up a home for "fallen women" and to campaign against public executions than to lead riots in the streets. Dickens, then, might say with Voltaire's Candide, "Let us cultivate our garden."

Nicholas Nickleby · *Nicholas Nickleby*, an ebullient novel loosely patterned after such picaresque models as Henry Fielding's *Tom Jones* (1749), is ostensibly an attack on the abusive Yorkshire schools that served as repositories for unwanted children. It is, as well, a depiction of Dickens's theatrical concerns, a condemnation of greed, a mystery story, and a conventional romance. To be sure, as Bernard Bergonzi points out, it has been criticized for its lack of a tightly woven plot as well as for its lack of a "significant moral pattern"; nevertheless it stands as the first of Dickens's full-scale, complex novels.

Dickens went to some trouble to establish the realistic fabric of the novel. Dotheboys Hall is modeled on William Shaw's notorious Bowes Academy, and the generous Cheeryble brothers, who give employment to the titular hero, mirror the merchants William and Daniel Grant. More important than the realistic antecedents, however, is what they represent: The schoolmaster Squeers and the Cheerybles are at opposite moral poles. Indeed, Nicholas's encounter with Dotheboys, his self-defense against Squeers, and his decision to "adopt" the enfeebled and mistreated Smike are preparation to confront his uncle Ralph, whose ungenerous nature is paradigmatic of moral usury. Even Nicholas's accidental joining with the Crummleses and their Infant Phenomenon is a way for him to act out his confrontation with pasteboard sword, for certainly, despite Crummles' benevolence, the closed world of the theater betrays as much selfishness as the world Nicholas eventually joins.

As Angus Wilson suggests, the foe that Nicholas confronts is more complex than generally recognized. Ralph, driven by the desire for money, is also driven by a desire for power. His belittlement of his clerk, Newman Noggs, is comically reflected in Miss Knag's spitefulness and in Mr. Lillyvick's patronizing attitude toward his relatives, and more seriously in Arthur Gride, the miser who charily serves an old wine—"liquid gold"—on his wedding day, and in Walter Bray, who affiances his daughter Madeline to Gride for a retirement stipend. Ralph is powerless, however, against generosity. Cast off by his uncle, Nicholas, like a hero in a French comedy of manners, rescues his sister Kate from the unwelcome advances of Sir Mulberry Hawk, one of Ralph's procurers; he is befriended by Noggs, with whose help he eventually rescues Madeline; and he is given a livelihood by the Cheerybles. In setting up a home for his mother, sister, and Smike, Nicholas establishes a center of domestic harmony independent of his uncle's world yet connected to that of the Cheerybles, who inculcate similar homely virtues in their business. Indeed, as Nicholas gathers friends around him, Ralph is slowly denuded of his power. Both plot strands meet in the Gride/Bray association, where Ralph faces a double loss, material and psychological: Not only does Gride's loss of valuable deeds spell the beginning of Ralph's financial downfall, but Ralph's scheme to marry Madeline to Bray is also foiled by his nephew, against whom he feels growing resentment.

Nicholas's circle of friends thus comes to dominate Ralph's circle of power. Ralph's bankruptcy is, moreover, symbolic of spiritual bankruptcy, for his ultimate ignominy is discovering that Smike, whom he had persecuted in an attempt to wound Nicholas, is his own son. That the enfeebled boy turned to Nicholas for help is, for Ralph, a final, inescapable bitterness. As Ralph's wheel of fortune reaches its nadir, he hangs himself, cursing the hope of the New Year which brings to Nicholas a marriage and a new family.

Martin Chuzzlewit · Partly the product of Dickens's 1842 trip to America, *Martin Chuzzlewit* takes as its theme the effects of selfishness. Some critics, such as Barbara Hardy, find this theme to be fragmented, insofar as the characters are so isolated that their moral conversions produce no resonance. Critic John Lucas locates the flaws not only in narrative sprawl and faulty timing but also in Dickens's indecision as to "whether he is writing a realistic study or a moral and prescriptive fable." The fabular element is indeed strong. Young Martin is a developing hero whose American experiences and the selflessness of his companion Mark Tapley bring him to recognize his flaws, while his father, Old Martin, serves in his wealth and eccentricity as a touchstone for cupidity. In studying the cumulative effects of selfishness, Dickens portrays a number of family groups and also presents an effective psychological study of a murderer.

Pecksniff, ostensibly an architect and Young Martin's teacher, is the root of hypocrisy in the novel. He imposes on the gullible Tom Pinch; he raises his daughters, Charity and Mercy, to be spiteful and thoughtless; he tries to seduce Martin's fiancé, then accuses Tom of the action; and he attempts to influence Old Martin to disinherit his grandson. Like Molière's Tartuffe, Pecksniff only appears to be virtuous. His assistant, Tom Pinch, is the reader's surrogate; honest, consistent, and generous, Pinch is exiled from Pecksniff's house and goes to London, where he is aided by John Westlock, a former pupil who has come into his inheritance. Tom's household, where he installs his sister Ruth (rescued from being a governess to a highly inconsiderate family), is in direct contrast to Pecksniff's in its innocent, loving companionship. Other family groups appear as contrasts as well, not the least being that of Anthony Chuzzlewit, brother to Old Martin. Anthony's miserly ways have inculcated in his son Jonas so grasping a nature that Jonas attempts to poison his father. Another kind of family group may be seen at Todgers' Commercial Boarding House, where the Pecksniffs stay and where Mercy, eventually married to the brutal Jonas, finds understanding from Mrs. Todgers. The association between young Martin and Mark Tapley may be contrasted with that between Pecksniff and Pinch, for Mark moves from the character of servant to that of friend. While Mark's Pollyannaish attitude—that one must be "jolly" under all circumstances—has annoyed many critics, he is a descendant of the comedy of humors and serves as an important antidote to Martin's selfishness. In setting Martin's conversion (a purgative illness) in the swamps of America, Dickens suggests that hypocrisy, greed, and false pride are not simply manifestations of the British social milieu but flourish even in the "City of Eden," which that worshiper of freedom, Major Hannibal Chollop, praises so highly.

Jonas, on the other hand, undergoes no such conversion, although Mercy fills a role similar to that of Mark. As an investor in a pyramid scheme, the Anglo-Bengalee Company, he is blackmailed into procuring Pecksniff as an investor by Montague Tigg, who is privy to Jonas's poisoning scheme. Fearing exposure, Jonas murders Tigg. Dickens's portrayal of the murderer's frame of mind is exceptional, accompanied as it is by a study of Nadgett, the self-effacing paid informer who shadows Jonas like conscience itself. Even more telling is the disclosure that the deed was unnecessary, for Anthony, who had discovered his son's scheme and foiled it, is said to have died of a broken heart.

The regrouping that occurs at the end when Old Martin confesses his own kind of selfishness, that of suspicion of others, is a reestablishment of an extended family and a casting out of Pecksniff as a kind of scapegoat. Martin and Mary, Ruth Pinch and John Westlock are affianced; only Tom Pinch, hopelessly in love with Mary, remains unwed, to be a source of financial support for Pecksniff and Charity, who cadge small amounts from him. In the final analysis, Dickens has performed an "anatomy of selfishness" that is especially powerful because some of his characters have exhibited moral development. To be sure, Old Martin's pretended subservience to Pecksniff and final revelations may be seen as contrivances making possible a *deus ex machina* ending; yet, for all their artificiality, the conversions seem as true in spirit as do Jonas's terrified and cowardly maunderings.

Dombey and Son · *Dombey and Son* is considered to be the first novel of Dickens's maturity. Indeed, as John Butt and Kathleen Tillotson point out, it is the first for which he worked out a complete plot outline; therefore, the subplots are controlled, and a fully orchestrated set of symbols emerges. Importantly, John Lucas notes that *Dombey and Son* presents the social panorama of the new, industrialized England, allowing "patterns of behavior and language to suggest connections more deeply insistent than blood-ties."

In this story of a middle-class merchant prince who must learn to place heart above head, Dickens produces one of his most moving and powerful studies of childhood, not only in Florence, the neglected daughter, but also in Paul, whom Dombey regards as a small version of himself. Paul is portrayed as an "old fashioned" boy, one who astonishes his father by asking what money is. Unlike Oliver Twist, who seeks to find a way into society, Paul runs counter to its expectations, resisting his father's attempt to make him into a grown-up before he has been a child. Alive to the world of the imagination, Paul is left untouched by Blimber's educational establishment, described as a hothouse where young minds are forced to produce before their time. Mr. Toots, one of Dickens's divine fools, is intellectually blasted by the process but retains a sweetness of soul that adds poignancy to his comic diction.

When Paul dies in Florence's arms, Dickens illustrates his pervasive water imagery in a masterly way. Paul, rocked gently out to sea in a flood of divine love, has come "to terms with the watery element," as noted by Julian Moynihan; only by close association with the sea is anyone in *Dombey and Son* saved from an atrophying of the affections. Paul's death is but one step in the education of Dombey, whom it initially hardens rather than softens: Dombey blames all of those Paul loved–Polly Toodle, his wet nurse; Walter Gay, one of Dombey's clerks in love with Florence; and Florence herself–for alienating Paul's affections. Another important step comes from Dombey's second marriage, which is to Edith Granger, a young widow put on the marriage market by her Regency mother, the artificial Mrs. Skewton. Bought for her accomplishments and ability to bear sons, Edith sets her will against Dombey's, determined to scorn his material success. She elopes with John Carker, the manager to whom Dombey had entrusted not only his domestic troubles but also his business affairs. Outraged, Dombey strikes Florence when she tries to comfort him. Florence runs away, taking refuge with a friend of Walter's uncle. Edith eventually runs away from Carker, for her motive was not adultery but vengeance. Carker, while trying to escape from the pursuing Dombey, is hit by a train. As Marcus notes, the railroad is Dickens's "great symbol of social transformation" as well as Carker's nemesis.

That Florence takes refuge with Captain Cuttle, a friend of Walter's uncle, shows the way in which the ocean theme is invoked even in a comic way, for Captain Cuttle is a peg-legged, Bible-quoting sea dog, yet he proves to be a tenderhearted surrogate father to Florence. Her affiancement to Walter, who, at Dombey's instigation, has been sent to the West Indies and shipwrecked, is another blow to Dombey, for it allies him not only with a class he shuns but also with an individual he believes had stolen his son's affections.

The last step in the education of Dombey is the failure of his business, largely through Carker's machinations. Left alone in his empty mansion to be pitied by Miss Tox, an old-maid figure whose ridiculousness, like Captain Cuttle's, is belied by her warmth of heart, Dombey meditates on the remembered figure of his daughter. His contemplation of suicide is interrupted, however, when Florence unexpectedly returns. For Dickens, Florence serves as the model of Christian, womanly behavior, of unselfish self-abnegation that, founded upon love, redeems her father. She returns because, as a mother, she can imagine what desertion by a child would be like.

The story of Dombey was a powerful parable for the middle classes, for whom, Dickens believed, overconcentration on such firms as Dombey and Son led to dehumanization, to a buying and selling not of goods but of people. That Paul's old-fashioned, loving nature could evoke responses in such unlikely quarters as in the pinched and spare Miss Tox or in the schoolmarmish Cornelia Blimber, or that Florence could melt both the disdainful Edith and her hardhearted father, is testimony to Dickens's optimism. In keeping with the theme, all of the characters, no matter how comic, are invariably treated as more than comic elements. Mr. Toots and his fascination with the boxer, the Game Chicken; Miss Tox's futile hope to become Mrs. Dombey; the straitlaced Mrs. Pipchin; and the seaman's caricature, Captain Cuttle himself, are integrated with the plot and ranged on the side of heart.

Little Dorrit · While *David Copperfield* is considered to be Dickens's autobiographical novel par excellence, *Little Dorrit* explores some of the same themes through the metaphor of the imprisonment that had so deep an effect on the Dickenses' family fortunes. Critical opinion ranges from Angus Wilson's comment that the "overcomplicated plot" weakens the imprisonment/release theme, to Lionel Trilling's assessment that the novel is "one of the most profound . . . and most significant works of the nineteenth century." In *Little Dorrit,* imprisonment has many facets. The initial and end scenes are set in the Marshalsea, where William Dorrit, imprisoned like Dickens's father for debt, has set up a social circle whose obsequiousness and class consciousness is simply a reflection of the society outside the prison. The resemblance suggests, in fact, that the large, self-seeking society without is itself a prison, for even when William Dorrit is freed by a legacy (as was John Dickens), he carries the taint of the Marshalsea with him, attempting to conform to social conventions so rigid that they dehumanize him, and hiring the "prunes and prisms" Mrs. General to tutor his daughters. That Dorrit, in ill health, should break down at Mrs. Merdle's state dinner to babble about the prison, is indicative that he has never, indeed, left it but has merely called it by different names.

Some prisons are built to contain those like Blandois, an evocation of the evil principle; others are less obvious, like the workhouse, for example, where old Nandy lives, or Bleeding Heart Yard, whose tenants are imposed upon by the patriarchal landlord Casby, or the Circumlocution Office—an accurate representation of the futile motions of a government bound by red tape. People, as well, create their own prisons: Miss Wade, for example, writes "The History of a Self-Tormentor"; Flora Finching is an "embodiment of romantic love that persists against all reason and propriety," as Wilson calls her; even Cavalletto is sequestered by his inability to speak English fluently. Amy, or Little Dorrit, is held in bondage not only by her selfless love for her father but also by her neurotic refusal to be anything but a child. Her sister Fanny willfully contracts a marriage with the dandified Edmund Sparkler, a marriage that guarantees her social respectability at the price of a fool for a husband. Fanny's prison becomes even smaller when her father-in-law, Mr. Merdle, commits suicide before his financial chicanery is discovered; without the emollient of money, Fanny spends her days in social battle with her mother-in-law, leaving her children in Little Dorrit's care.

For Arthur Clennam, to return home to his mother's house is to return to imprisonment, where the walls are walls of the spirit, built of her unforgiving nature and her Calvinism that judges by the letter, not by the spirit of the ethical law. Clennam, however, carries his prison with him in the form of diffidence, for it is a lack of self-confidence that prevents him from proposing to Pet Meagles and almost prevents him from believing in the redeeming love of Little Dorrit herself (whom Lionel Trilling sees finally as "the Paraclete in female form"). In the end, he deliberately takes responsibility for his friend Doyce's financial trouble and is imprisoned in William Dorrit's old room. It is fitting that Amy should tend him there, for just as she held the key of affection to lead her father from the prison of self, so she holds the key of love that frees Clennam. In this respect, she radically differs from Clennam's mother, who, knowing that Arthur Clennam is her husband's illegitimate child, takes her vengeance accordingly.

Clearly, in *Little Dorrit*, the individual is both the jailer and the jailed, the cause of suffering and the sufferer; perhaps nowhere else does Dickens so emphasize the intertwined fates of all humans. At this stage in his life, when he was actively involving himself in a number of projects and coming to understand that his marriage was failing, Dickens's view of the human condition had little of the sunny hope exhibited, for example, in *Pickwick Papers*, or little of the simplistic interpretation of motivation found in *Nicholas Nickleby*. Indeed, the last lines of the novel sound a quiet note; Little Dorrit and Clennam go down into the midst of those who fret and chafe as if entering a prison; their only hope is "a modest life of usefulness and happiness." Their ability to quell the "usual uproar" seems severely limited.

Our Mutual Friend · For J. Hillis Miller, "*Our Mutual Friend* presents a fully elaborated definition of what it means to be interlaced with the world." In this last completed novel, Dickens has indeed relinquished the idea that evil or, in fact, the redemption of society resides in any one individual or institution. The Poor Law in *Oliver Twist*, the effects of education in *Nicholas Nickleby*, and the law itself in *Bleak House* represent abuses that are manifestations of a larger illness permeating society. This view, which Dickens begins to develop in *Little Dorrit*, is clear in *Our Mutual Friend*. From the violent, repressed sexuality of the schoolmaster Bradley Headstone to the cool indifference of Eugene Wrayburn, who would despoil Lizzie Hexam to satisfy a whim, all society is affected with a kind of moral (and financial) selfishness that was a matter of parody in *Martin Chuzzlewit*. Even the heroine, Bella Wilfer, becomes, as she calls herself, a "mercenary little wretch," consciously weighing her desire for a wealthy marriage against love for John Rokesmith. The exuberance of subplotting evident in Dickens's early novels is again evident here, although in this case he provides a more disciplined framework, giving the reader not only a central symbol—money (represented as an excremental dust heap) inherited by the Boffins from the miser John Harmon—but also a central character, the enigmatic John Rokesmith, Harmon's son and therefore rightful heir to the fortune.

The central plot that devolves from a single generous act—the Boffins returning to Rokesmith his inheritance—is illustrative of the title, whose significance Arnold Kettle explores in terms of the mutuality of relationships, insofar as the activities of Rokesmith/Harmon interweave all social levels, from Wegg and Venus to the Podsnaps. The novel, moreover, contains elements of the masquerade in *Martin Chuzzlewit* as well as the motif of educating the affections in *Dombey and Son*. Boffin pretends to be a miser and Rokesmith an impoverished clerk to convince Bella that grasping for wealth deadens the heart. Her happy marriage is contrasted with that of her mother, whose perpetual toothache, tender temperament, and mortuary-like deportment minister to her pride but not to the comfort of her family. Indeed, other marriages in the book are hardly preferable: The nouveau-riche Veneerings, who make good friends of strangers in order to entertain them at a sumptuous board, are one example; another is the Lammles, who, sadly deceived in their original estimate of each other's wealth, set out to defraud the world. Likewise, the Podsnaps, an embodiment of the solid, tasteless, and pretentious middle class, are concerned not, for example, with the emotional state of the much-repressed Georgiana but rather with their place on the social scale, and they are therefore willing to entrust her to the Lammles, whose intention it is to procure her in marriage for the moneylender "Fascination Fledgeby."

The novel is about the use and misuse of childhood as well. It offers a panoply of unnatural parents, among them Jesse Hexam, who forces Lizzie to dredge corpses from the Thames, and the bibulous "Mr. Dolls," whose crippled daughter Fanny ("Jenny Wren") is a dolls' dressmaker. There are adoptive parents as well—some, like the Lammles, shamming affection to benefit themselves; others, like Lizzie, mothering her selfish brother Charley; or Riah, giving Lizzie fatherly protection; or Betty Higden, showing kindness to her diminutive boarders. The prime example is, of course, the Boffins, who nurture a series of children, young and old, beginning with John Harmon, for whom their kindness created a home in his father's cold house; then Bella, who they felt had been harmed by the dictates of Harmon's will, being, as she was, ceded in marriage to a stranger; then Johnny, the orphan who dies; and finally, Sloppy, an idiot foundling. Their adoption of Sloppy, an unprepossessing individual, is the key to the series, for Sloppy is another of Dickens's touchstone figures.

The subplot which runs parallel to the education of Bella is that of Lizzie Hexam's wooing by Eugene Wrayburn. While Bella originally refuses Rokesmith because of his supposed poverty, Lizzie evades Wrayburn because of his wealth, fearing that she will become his mistress rather than his wife. Again, while Bella can accept Rokesmith's proposal without knowing his true identity, Lizzie flees Wrayburn to a factory town (perhaps an evocation of Lowell, Massachusetts, where Dickens visited on his American tour). Even Bella's moment of bravery, in which she relinquishes all hope of inheriting the Boffins' money in favor of defending Rokesmith, whose dignity she thinks Boffin is maligning, has a parallel, albeit on a more earthy level; Lizzie rescues Wrayburn from the murderous attack of Headstone, thereby putting to use the skills she had learned when working with her father. Wrayburn's proposal of marriage to her is his recognition that financial and class standing are irrelevant in matters of the heart.

It is, in fact, their marriage that is central to the "trial" scene at the end of the novel, in which the Veneerings convene their friends to pass judgment on Wrayburn's action. Mr. Twemlow, a minor character with romantic notions and little apparent strength of character, nevertheless rises to the occasion, as he had in agreeing to help warn the Podsnaps that their daughter was in danger of a mercenary scheme. He asserts, with finality and against the general disparagement, that if Wrayburn followed his "feeling of gratitude, of respect, of admiration and affection," then he is "the greater gentleman for the action." Twemlow's voice is clearly not the voice of society; rather, it is the voice of the heart, and it is to him that Dickens gives the closing word.

Patricia Marks

Other major works

SHORT FICTION: *Sketches by Boz*, 1836; *A Christmas Carol*, 1843; *The Chimes*, 1844; *The Cricket on the Hearth*, 1845; *The Battle of Life*, 1846; *The Haunted Man*, 1848; *Reprinted Pieces*, 1858; *The Uncommercial Traveller*, 1860; *George Silverman's Explanation*, 1868; *Christmas Stories*, 1871.

PLAYS: *The Strange Gentleman*, pr. 1836; *The Village Coquettes*, pr., pb. 1836; *Mr. Nightingale's Diary*, pr., pb. 1851 (with Mark Lemon); *No Thoroughfare*, pr., pb. 1867 (with Wilkie Collins).

NONFICTION: *American Notes*, 1842; *Pictures from Italy*, 1846.

CHILDREN'S LITERATURE: *A Child's History of England*, 1852-1854; *The Life of Our Lord*, 1934.

EDITED PERIODICALS: *Master Humphrey's Clock*, 1840-1841; *Household Words*, 1850-1859; *All the Year Round*, 1859-1870.

Bibliography

Ackroyd, Peter. *Dickens.* New York: HarperCollins, 1990. British novelist and biographer Ackroyd is famous for immersing himself in the milieu of his subjects. He tried to incorporate all extant material on Dickens's life. The biography is written with a novelist's flair, opening with a set piece that places the reader squarely at the scene of the great Victorian's deathbed.

Connor, Steven, ed. *Charles Dickens.* London: Longman, 1996. Part of the Longman Critical Readers series, this is a good reference for interpretation and criticism of Dickens.

Davis, Paul B. *Charles Dickens A to Z: The Essential Reference to His Life and Work.* New York: Facts on File, 1998. An excellent handbook for the student of Dickens.

Epstein, Norrie. *The Friendly Dickens: Being a Good-natured Guide to the Art and Adventures of the Man Who Invented Scrooge.* New York: Viking, 1998. An interesting study of Dickens. Includes bibliographical references, an index, and a filmography.

Flint, Kate. *Dickens.* Brighton, England: Harvester Press, 1986. Looks at paradoxes within his novels and between his novels and his culture. Includes a select bibliography and an index.

Hawes, Donald. *Who's Who in Dickens.* New York: Routledge, 1998. The Who's Who series provides another excellent guide to the characters that populate Dickens's fiction.

Hobsbaum, Philip. *A Reader's Guide to Charles Dickens.* Syracuse, N.Y.: Syracuse

University Press, 1998. Part of the Reader's Guide series, this is a good manual for beginning students.

Kaplan, Fred. *Dickens: A Biography.* New York: William Morrow, 1988. Kaplan's biography is nearly as detailed and lengthy as one of Dickens's own novels. *Dickens* is a fairly straightforward account of the novelist's life. With the exception of an opening scene detailing Dickens's attempt in 1860 to thwart future biographers by making a bonfire of his correspondence, the biography proceeds more or less directly from Dickens's birth to his death with few diversions—and no introductory matter whatsoever.

Newlin, George, ed. and comp. *Every Thing in Dickens: Ideas and Subjects Discussed by Charles Dickens in His Complete Works, A Topicon.* Westport, Conn.: Greenwood Press, 1996. A thorough guide to Dickens's oeuvre. Includes bibliographical references, an index, and quotations.

Smith, Grahame. *Charles Dickens: A Literary Life.* New York: St. Martin's Press, 1996. A strong biography of Dickens.38S

Arthur Conan Doyle

Born: Edinburgh, Scotland; May 22, 1859
Died: Crowborough, England; July 7, 1930

Principal long fiction · *A Study in Scarlet*, 1887; *The Mystery of Cloomber*, 1888; *The Firm of Girdlestone*, 1889; *Micah Clarke*, 1889; *The Sign of Four*, 1890; *Beyond the City*, 1891; *The Doings of Raffles Haw*, 1891; *The White Company*, 1891; *The Great Shadow*, 1892; *The Refugees*, 1893; *The Parasite*, 1894; *The Stark Munro Letters*, 1895; *The Surgeon of Gaster Fell*, 1895; *Rodney Stone*, 1896; *The Tragedy of the Koroska*, 1897 (also as *A Desert Drama*); *Uncle Bernac*, 1897; *A Duet, with an Occasional Chorus*, 1899, revised 1910; *The Hound of the Baskervilles*, 1901-1902; *Sir Nigel*, 1906; *The Lost World*, 1912; *The Poison Belt*, 1913; *The Valley of Fear*, 1915; *The Land of Mist*, 1926.

Other literary forms · In his lifetime, Arthur Conan Doyle was far better known for his short stories than for his novels. Until he became interested in science fiction (a medium he found better suited to shorter fiction) after 1900, Doyle concentrated his creative energies on his novels, those works he felt posterity would judge him by, and took a purely monetary interest in the short-story format. Ironically, contemporary readers and critics continue to value the Sherlock Holmes short stories and largely ignore Doyle's historical novels.

One of the most prolific in an era of prolific authors, Doyle also dabbled in the theater. The most commercially successful of his dramas was the stage version of *Sherlock Holmes* (pr. 1899), starring William Gillette. Doyle frequently financed his own plays, such as the violent and realistic *The Fires of Fate* (pr. 1909, from his novel *The Tragedy of the Koroska*), a dramatization of a river-pirate raid on a party of English tourists in Egypt, an adventure based—like so many of Doyle's works—on his own experiences.

Doyle's nonfiction was largely polemic. The course of the British involvement in the Boer War was chronicled and defended in his *The Great Boer War*, written in 1900, and *The War in South Africa: Its Causes and Conduct* (1902). His efforts at defending government policy, as well as his own medical service during the war, were largely responsible for his knighthood. He also wrote extensively about other causes: the reform of the divorce laws, the denial of the vote for women, the abolition of ostrich-feather hats. He reserved his greatest energy, however, for his popularizing and propagandizing of spiritualism, a doctrine with which he had toyed from his youth and to which he became devoted after the death of his oldest son in World War I. Indeed, the last fifteen years of his life were spent in furthering the spiritualist cause through writings and lectures.

Achievements · "Come, Watson. The game's afoot." Few words by any author evoke a clearer picture in the public's mind. Individuals who have never read a Sherlock Holmes story can immediately conjure up a vision of two distinctive figures leaving the fog-shrouded entrance to 221-B Baker Street: Sherlock Holmes, tall and skeletal, pale from his sedentary existence and haggard from his addiction to cocaine, wearing his famous deerstalker cap; Dr. Watson, short and stolid, though limping from an old bullet wound, one hand nervously hovering over the pocket that holds his trusted revolver. Indeed, few, if any, imaginary addresses have received the bulk of mail which continues to be sent to Holmes's Baker Street apartment; few fictional characters have been the subject of even a single "biography," let alone the great number of books which purport to document the life of Sherlock Holmes; and certainly few authors have cursed the success of one of their creations as much as Doyle did that of Sherlock Holmes.

Library of Congress

When the young Portsmouth physician first wrote down the name of "Sherringford Hope," soon changed to "Sherlock Holmes" in honor of the American writer Oliver Wendell Holmes, he did not dream of fame or literary immortality but merely of some means of augmenting his income, for he had a wife as well as a younger brother and an impoverished mother to support. In fact, as soon as *A Study in Scarlet* had been sent off to a prospective publisher in early 1887, Doyle was hard at work on *Micah Clarke*, the novel he felt would represent "a door . . . opened for me into the Temple of the Muses." Two years later, Doyle wrote the second Holmes novel, *The Sign of the Four*, as a jeu d'esprit after a convivial dinner with Oscar Wilde, an unlikely admirer of *Micah Clarke*, and James Stoddart, the editor of *Lippincott's Monthly Magazine*, who challenged both Doyle and Wilde to supply him with suitable mystery manuscripts. Doyle's real interest at this time was in the completion of his "masterpiece," the historical novel *The White Company*, and its acceptance for serialization in the *Cornhill Magazine*, beginning in January, 1891, seemed to him a far better harbinger of literary fame.

The unexpected success of Sherlock Holmes stories as they appeared in *Strand Magazine* in the early 1890's quickly established Doyle's reputation, in the opinion of Greenough Smith, the literary editor of that magazine, as the greatest short-story writer since Edgar Allan Poe, but he continued to churn out a seemingly endless series of historical and semi-autobiographical novels, most of which are read today only by scholars. The commercial success of these novels (*The Firm of Girdlestone*, *Beyond the City*, *The Great Shadow*, *The Refugees*, *The Parasite*, *The Stark Munro Letters*, *Rodney Stone*, *Uncle Bernac*, and *Sir Nigel*, among others), of his numerous collections of short stories, of his occasional ventures into drama, and of his essays and pamphlets on social and political issues (such as reform of the divorce laws and the conduct of the Boer War), all depended in large part on Doyle's popularity as the creator of Sherlock Holmes. Yet throughout his life, he never saw the stories and novels featuring Holmes and Watson as much more than potboilers. Even the famous "resurrection" of Holmes in 1903 was an attempt to capitalize financially on the success of the London opening of the play *Sherlock Holmes*, starring William Gillette. Doyle saw his real life's work, up until he became a propagandist for spiritualism at the end of his life, as writing fiction which would amuse and distract "the sick and the dull and the weary" through the evocation of the heroic past.

Biography · The idealization of the past served other purposes for Arthur Conan Doyle, who had been born into genteel poverty in Edinburgh on May 22, 1859, and named for King Arthur: It gave him a model to live by and to instill in his sons, and it diverted him from the disappointments of life which frequently threatened to overwhelm him. From his earliest childhood, his mother, Mary Doyle, the daughter of a lodging-house keeper who believed herself a descendant of the Plantagenets, indoctrinated her oldest son in tales of his aristocratic ancestry and the virtues of medieval chivalry. Doyle's father Charles, although employed throughout his son's childhood as a municipal architect in Edinburgh, was the youngest son of a highly gifted and artistic family. Charles Doyle's father John Doyle was the talented caricaturist "H. B."; his maternal uncle Michael Edward Conan was an artist as well as the art and drama critic and Paris correspondent for *Art Journal*; his brother Richard was a graphic artist for *Punch* and later an illustrator for John Ruskin, Charles Dickens, and William Makepeace Thackeray; another brother Henry was a painter before becoming director of the National Gallery of Ireland; a third brother James was a famous mid-Victorian portrait painter. Charles Doyle himself, who had suffered since early childhood from epilepsy and emotional disturbances, supplemented his salary with sketches of famous criminal trials and illustrations of fairy tales and historical romances. By the time his older son reached adulthood, Charles Doyle had descended through alcoholism into incurable insanity, retreating from a world he found uncongenial to his artistic temperament.

Mary Doyle necessarily became the central figure in her children's lives and continued to be so after they grew up. When Doyle first considered killing off Sherlock Holmes in November, 1891, his mother convinced him not to do so, thus reprieving the famous detective for a year. She also supplied her son with ideas for the Holmes stories. Throughout his childhood, Doyle's mother managed the practical necessities of life for an improvident husband and eight children on £180 per year and also instilled a vision of the ideal gentleman into her oldest son. In contrast to his father's instability and impracticality, Doyle grew into the epitome of the Victorian male: respectable, decent, cautious, thrifty, stolid. Only his writing—with its predilection for the codes of chivalry and honor and its preoccupation with a romantic past and his later obsession with spiritualism—betrayed the influences of Doyle's belief in his descent from kings and his father's retreat into a world of fantasy.

Doyle's family was Catholic, and he was educated first at a Catholic preparatory school and then at Stonyhurst, the foremost Jesuit educational institution in England. He hated both, finding Stonyhurst rigid, backward, superstitious, narrow, and, above all, dull. Unpopular with the masters because of his frequent protests against physical punishment, Doyle survived his school days because of his ability at games, his preeminence among his schoolmates, and his aptitude at diverting himself through reading and writing about a more glorious and exciting past. In his five years at Stonyhurst, he had no formal holidays but managed one visit to his uncle Richard Doyle in London, where the highlight of his stay was a visit to the Chamber of Horrors at Mme Tussaud's on Baker Street. During this period, he began to read the short stories of Poe, which later influenced him through their fascination with the macabre as well as through the characterization of Poe's intellectual detective, M. Auguste Dupin, who was one of the models for Sherlock Holmes. When Doyle entered Stonyhurst, the Jesuits had offered free tuition if he would train for the priesthood; fortunately, his mother refused the offer for him in spite of the advantages such an arrangement would have held. Ironically, the reactionary atmosphere at Stonyhurst contributed to his loss of faith, a faith he would not regain until his adoption of spiritualism forty years later.

Leaving school, Doyle found himself with three choices: the priesthood, law, or medicine. His loss of faith ruled out the first alternative, his lack of influential connections the second, so he entered Edinburgh University to study medicine in 1877. Although he was once again not a particularly brilliant student, he was deeply influenced by two of his professors, Dr. Joseph Bell, who became a prototype for Sherlock Holmes, and Dr. Andrew Maclagan, an instructor of forensic medicine, who served as a model for Professor Challenger in Doyle's later science-fiction novels. The School of Medicine at Edinburgh formed both the setting and the subject of his early and happily forgotten novel *The Firm of Girdlestone.*

His university days were punctuated with two spells as a ship's surgeon. The first voyage was aboard the *Hope,* an Arctic fishing boat. The seven-month-long trip was one of the highlights of Doyle's life. Seemingly indifferent to the bloody spectacle of the slaughter of whales and seals, he remembered only the sense of adventure and camaraderie among the crew. After graduation, he took a similar job aboard the passenger ship *Mayumba* on a voyage to the Gold Coast. This trip was in stark contrast to the first. Passengers and crew were struck down with tropical fevers that the young doctor was unable to treat. This experience so depressed Doyle that he gave up his plans for a career as a ship's surgeon and took up a position as an assistant to a doctor who turned out to be incompetent. When Mary Doyle objected to this association, her son left his employer and went to Portsmouth, where he opened his first practice.

Since the first years of his practice were not prosperous, Doyle returned to writing to occupy his time and to supplement his earnings. He also began to toy with an interest in the supernatural that is reflected in his later fiction and in his obsession with spiritualism. He attended his first séance in 1879 and worked on a number of bizarre stories. His poverty was such (he earned only about fifty pounds a year from his writing, and not much more from his practice) that his nine-year-old brother Innes, who was living with him at the time, had to usher patients into his surgery. His mother sent sheets and other household necessities from Edinburgh.

One of Doyle's greatest strokes of good fortune was the death of a patient. When a young boy collapsed of meningitis, then an incurable illness, outside his office, Doyle took the patient in and nursed him until his death. The boy's mother was so grateful for the doctor's solicitude, if not his medical skill, that she introduced Doyle to her daughter Louise (Touie) Hawkins. The young couple was married on August 6, 1885, and Touie Doyle became the perfect Victorian wife. Not only was she gentle, undemanding, and industrious, but also she possessed a small yearly income which nicely supplemented her husband's earnings. The Doyles eventually had two children, Mary Louise and Alleyne Kingsley, before Touie developed consumption, the disease which doomed her to an early death and Doyle to years of celibacy.

Doyle's *Beyond the City* and *A Duet, with an Occasional Chorus* chronicle their married life. *Beyond the City* is set in Upper Norwood, the London suburb to which they moved in 1891, and details the days of their early married life: quiet afternoons spent bicycling together, equally quiet evenings with Touie sewing and her husband reading or writing. *A Duet*, written after Touie's fatal illness had been diagnosed, is silly and sentimental but ends with the deaths of the main characters in a train crash. Although Doyle remained devoted to assuring his wife's happiness until her death in 1906, he had fallen in love again in the mid-1890's. How much the fictionalized death of Touie in *A Duet* may have represented wish fulfillment remains conjecture.

The 1890's were years of contradiction for Doyle. His rise to literary prominence was paralleled by great personal distress. Although he had enjoyed moderate success as an author beginning with the publication of *A Study in Scarlet* in 1887, he still doubted that he could support his family by his pen. Early in 1891, he and Touie went to Austria, where he attempted to study ophthalmology; unsuccessful in this, he returned to England and moved his wife and daughter to London, where he set up a practice that drew even fewer patients than the one in Portsmouth. He had arrived back in England at a fortuitous moment for his career as a writer, however, as *Strand Magazine* had decided to bolster its circulation by abandoning the traditional serial novel for a series of short stories featuring a continuing character. Hearing of this, Doyle decided to revive his Sherlock Holmes character. In less than two weeks, he wrote two more Holmes stories, "A Scandal in Bohemia" and "The Red-Headed League," which were immediately accepted by Greenough Smith, the literary editor of *Strand Magazine*. With Sidney Paget as illustrator, the two stories were instant and enormous successes. Doyle found himself an overnight celebrity.

This, however, was not the type of literary fame for which Doyle had hoped. Although he continued to turn out Holmes stories for *Strand Magazine*, he worked more diligently on two new novels, *The Refugees*, another historical tale, and *Beyond the City*. By November, 1891, just five months after Holmes first appeared in *Strand Magazine*, his creator had decided to end the detective's life. Only the influence of Mary Doyle and the temptation of the one thousand pounds *Strand Magazine* was offering for a new series to run throughout 1892 made Doyle reconsider.

The second Holmes series confirmed Greenough Smith's opinion that Doyle was among the masters of the short-story form. Doyle himself found the format tedious; he always thought up the solution to the mystery first and then concocted the story in such a fashion as to obscure the true outcome from the reader as long as possible. His real affinity was for the historical novel, which he felt comfortable in writing and which he felt represented the true and highest purposes of art. In 1892, *The Great Shadow*, another example of his fondness for this genre, was published. It was extremely popular only because its author was the creator of Sherlock Holmes.

The continued ill health of Doyle's wife (her tuberculosis was finally diagnosed in 1893) required frequent journeys to the Continent. Churning out a story a month to meet his commitment to *Strand Magazine*, concerned about Touie's health, constantly on the move, unhappy with the format in which he was forced to write, Doyle became more and more dissatisfied with his literary detective. If he did not exactly grow to hate Sherlock Holmes, he found the process of inventing new adventures for him more and more distasteful. He informed *Strand Magazine* that Holmes's final case, recorded in "The Final Problem," would appear in their December, 1893, issue. No entreaties or offers of higher payments would change his mind. After the account of Holmes's death was published, more than twenty thousand *Strand Magazine* readers canceled their subscriptions.

With Sherlock Holmes seemingly permanently out of his life, Doyle devoted himself to a renewed interest in the psychical research of his youth and to public affairs. Since his wife's illness precluded sexual intercourse, Doyle's writings of this period reverted to his earlier preoccupation with a connection between sex and death. The 1894 novel, *The Parasite*, deals with the relationship between Professor Gilroy, a Holmesian figure who has retreated to the world of the intellect, and Helen Penclosa, a beautiful clairvoyant. At first a skeptic, Gilroy becomes increasingly obsessed with the beautiful young woman until, unable to withstand the passion that has made him lock himself in his own room, he rushes to her flat and makes love to her. Overcome immediately by guilt, he flees from her room, only to discover later that she has mesmerized him and forced him to rob a bank. As his obsession grows, Gilroy is dismissed from his post at the university and becomes increasingly erratic in his behavior. The more unstable Gilroy becomes, the weaker Penclosa grows, her power obviously transferring itself into his mind. In a moment of madness, Gilroy attempts to murder his fiancé, then decides to free himself by killing Penclosa. When he arrives at her flat, he finds her already dead and himself returned to sanity.

The public Doyle, however, continued to be the respectable man of affairs. Another historical novel, *Rodney Stone*, the story of a Regency dandy who becomes a "man" in the end, appeared in 1896. *Round the Red Lamp*, a collection of ghost stories Doyle wrote for his children, was published in 1894. He continued his travels in search of renewed health for Touie, journeying back and forth to Switzerland and spending the winter of 1896-1897 in Egypt.

In private, Doyle was increasingly troubled by the complications of his love for Jean Leckie, to whom he was originally attracted because of her descent from the Scottish hero Rob Roy. Although he confessed his love for Jean to his mother and other family members, he resisted all their advice that he divorce Touie. Vowing never to consummate his relationship with Jean until Touie's death, he instructed his family never even to hint of the affair to his wife. His "code of honor" as a gentleman mandated that he cherish and protect Touie at the cost of his own happiness. Jean, with whom he had never and would never quarrel, agreed. They continued to see each other, but Touie was kept ignorant of her husband's love for another woman. Doyle and Jean even waited the requisite year of mourning after Touie's death before they were finally married in 1907.

Although he had returned to an English setting for *Rodney Stone*, Doyle was fascinated by the events of the French Revolution and the Napoleonic Wars. In 1896 and 1897, after a spell in Egypt as a war correspondent during the Sudanese War, he published *The Exploits of Brigadier Gerard*, the first of a series of stories about the picaresque hero to appear in novel form. He also wrote *Uncle Bernac*, another Napoleonic novel, and *The Tragedy of the Koroska*, a melodrama about his adventures with paddleboat bandits in Egypt.

In the late 1890's and the first years of the new century, Doyle increasingly turned to the horror story. One particular story, "Playing with Fire," published in 1900, combined his interest in psychic phenomena with his love for animals and suggested that animals, too, survive the grave. "The King of Foxes" (1903) dealt with Jean Leckie's favorite sport, foxhunting, in a bizarre and macabre form. To make money and to forestall another dramatist from seizing on the idea, he adapted the character of Sherlock Holmes for the American stage, emphasizing that the play which would make William Gillette famous was not a new adventure but related events that had occurred before Holmes's "death."

The outbreak of the Boer War in October, 1899, gave Doyle the outlet he needed for his interest in public affairs. He first attempted to enlist and then accepted the position of senior surgeon with John Longman's private field hospital. He saw his service at Bloemfontein in 1900 as that of a medieval knight seeking to help those less fortunate than he. His heroic efforts with inadequate equipment, his propaganda pamphlet *The War in South Africa: Its Causes and Conduct,* and later his history of the war, *The Great Boer War,* combined to win him his knighthood in 1902.

While in South Africa, Doyle had read of the story of the Cabell family, which was haunted by a ghostly hound. He saw in this the germ of a new Holmes novel, and *The Hound of the Baskervilles* was duly published in 1901-1902. He was still not committed to reviving Holmes from beneath the Reidenbach Falls and insisted once again that *The Hound of the Baskervilles* was an earlier adventure only now coming to light. Although he continued to write horror stories, he was unable to resist the financial lure of more Holmes tales, and, consequently, in October, 1903, the first adventure of the "resurrected" Sherlock Holmes appeared.

During the last two decades of Doyle's life, his fame and finances were assured by the popularity of Sherlock Holmes. His private life, after his marriage to Jean Leckie and the birth of their three children, was that of an Edwardian paterfamilias. With the exception of *Sir Nigel,* he finally abandoned the historical novel in favor of science fiction. Politically reactionary, Doyle nevertheless was respected for his warnings about the outbreak of World War I. His greatest preoccupation, however, was with the cause of spiritualism; his final "conversion" to absolute belief in the phenomenon which had fascinated him for years resulted from the deaths of his brother Innes and oldest son Kingsley during World War I. To the end of his life, he was convinced that he was in frequent touch with the spirits of his loved ones and thus devoted all the proceeds from his novels and lectures to the "cause." In the early 1920's, he once again announced Holmes's departure, this time to honorable retirement as a bee-keeper on the Sussex Downs. Doyle brought him back only once, in a 1924 story written expressly for Queen Mary's Dollhouse. His literary reputation suffered be-cause of his involvement in spiritualism, and his excellent science-fiction novels, many of which rival those of Jules Verne, were ridiculed by the critics more for their author's peculiarities than for their own lack of merit. Doyle died on July 7, 1930; his wife Jean claimed to receive a spirit message from him less than twenty-four hours later. His epitaph, however, looked back to earlier decades, to the little boy named after King Arthur who had resolved to live his life according to knightly ideals: "STEEL TRUE/BLADE STRAIGHT."

Analysis · Arthur Conan Doyle's epitaph can also serve as an introduction to the themes of his novels, both those that feature actual medieval settings and those that center on Sherlock Holmes. Doyle's central character is always the knight on a quest, living and battling according to chivalric ideals. Micah Clarke, Alleyne Edricson, and Sir Nigel Loring all engage in real battles; Sherlock Holmes combats villains on behalf of distressed young women and naïve and frightened young men; Professor Chal-lenger takes on the unknown: a prehistoric world, the realm of the spirit, the threatened extinction of life on Earth.

Micah Clarke · Doyle's first historical novel, *Micah Clarke,* is set in seventeenth century England against the background of Monmouth's Rebellion. As he always did in his historical fiction, in which he intended to portray the actual conditions of life at the time the novels were set, he paid meticulous attention to actual detail. In the Sherlock Holmes stories, Doyle seems not to have cared whether Dr. Watson's old war wound was in his shoulder or his knee, whether the good doctor's Christian name was John or James, whether there were one or two Mrs. Watsons, but his period novels show none of this casualness. For *Micah Clarke*, the author had carefully explored the area around Portsmouth, where most of the action takes place. He also did careful research into the dress, customs, and speech of the era. Indeed, it was its "mode of speech" that caused both Blackwoods and Bentley, Ltd. to reject the novel; this same period diction makes the novel extremely slow going for the modern reader.

Like most of Doyle's characters, those in *Micah Clarke* are modeled on real individuals. Micah Clarke, the gallant young man fighting zealously for a lost cause, is largely based on young Doyle himself, protesting hopelessly at Stonyhurst against outmoded courses of study, unfair punishments, and censorship of his letters home. Ruth Timewell, the cloyingly sweet young heroine, depicts the quiet, meek Touie Doyle, who at the time the novel was written represented her husband's ideal of womanhood. In spite of the critical acclaim *Micah Clarke* received when it was originally published, few people would consider it the stirring tale of adventure that its author did, although parts of it, especially the description of the climactic Battle of Sedgmoor and the portrait of the evil Judge Jeffreys, retain some interest for the modern reader.

The White Company · *The White Company*, Doyle's second venture into the historical genre, and its companion piece, *Sir Nigel*, have worn slightly better. Like its predecessor, *The White Company* is distinguished by its scrupulous re-creation of the entire spectrum of life in fourteenth century England. Once again, Doyle's preoccupation with noble causes is reflected in the interests of his characters, members of a small but dedicated mercenary company who set off for the Continent to fight for England during the Hundred Years War.

The hero of *The White Company*, after whom Doyle later named his eldest son, is Alleyne Edricson, a landless young squire who leaves the monastery where he has been reared with his two companions, the lapsed monk Hortle John and the former serf Samkin Aylward, to join the White Company under the command of Sir Nigel Loring. Alleyne, his friends, his leader, and later his prince represent a microcosm of English society in the Middle Ages, depicting an idealized vision of the English character and contrasting with that of the country's main enemies: the French, the Spanish, and the Germans. Departing from his usual historical accuracy, Doyle presents the Germans as the worst foes of the English, reflecting his own late-Victorian perspective. Alleyne and his friend are mercenaries who live by their wits, but their fighting, looting, and pillaging are always conducted according to the rules of the chivalric game. At the end of the novel, Alleyne wins his knighthood, his inheritance, and his lady fair in the person of Sir Nigel's daughter Maude. The virtues Sir Nigel embodies and Alleyne learns are those that Doyle taught his own sons: sympathetic treatment of social inferiors, courtesy and respect for women, and honesty in financial dealings.

The novel is particularly interesting for its two main themes: the rise of the English middle class and of English patriotism. *The White Company* depicts a world where individuals are judged not by their birth but by their accomplishments, in much the same manner as Doyle rose from poverty to affluence through his own efforts. The book, however, also reflects its author's belief that the English character was the best in the world; Doyle clearly insists that the language, history, customs, and beliefs of England are far superior to those of any other nation.

The Sherlock Holmes novels · At first glance, the four Sherlock Holmes novels (*A Study in Scarlet, The Sign of the Four, The Hound of the Baskervilles, The Valley of Fear*) might seem to have little in common with Doyle's historical fiction. A closer look, however, shows that whatever the surface differences, the author's underlying concerns and prejudices are the same. Indeed, Sherlock Holmes can be seen as a knight-errant who ventures forth from Baker Street on a series of quests. In the earlier novels and stories, he battles dragons of crime on behalf of individuals. Mary Morstan in *The Sign of the Four* is the epitome of a damsel in distress. In Holmes's later adventures, both the suppliants and the dragons are different. There is an increasing tendency for those seeking Holmes's assistance to be representatives of the government itself or, as in "The Illustrious Client," a person no less exalted than King Edward VII himself, and for the villains to be international criminals or even foreign governments.

Holmes's relationship with Dr. Watson reflects that of a knight and his squire. The detective and his intellect operate according to the rules of detection which Holmes has himself established at the beginning of *The Sign of the Four*, rules analogous to the chivalric code, and squire Watson accompanies Holmes as much to learn how to conduct himself according to these rules as to assist in the solution of the crime. Dull, plodding, faithful Watson may never win his spurs, but at least he wins the hand of Mary Morstan.

The Holmes novels also exhibit Doyle's characteristic xenophobia. With the possible exception of Moriarty, who, after all, is an international rather than an English criminal, the villains Holmes contends with frequently are foreigners or else the crimes he deals with have their origins in foreign or distant events. *A Study in Scarlet* is a story of the revenge exacted for a crime committed in the mountains of Utah twenty years earlier. The novel's "victims" are in fact villains who have mistreated an old man and a young girl, those most deserving of protection, and so deserve their own deaths, while its "villain" is a just avenger who is saved from the gallows by a "higher judge" and dies with a smile upon his face as if looking back on a deed well done. The crime in *The Sign of the Four* similarly has its origins years before in India, and its victims also turn out to have brought their doom upon themselves. Rodger Baskerville, the father of Stapleton the naturalist, who perpetrated the hoax in *The Hound of the Baskervilles*, had fled to South America before his son was born. As in the fictional press report at the end of *A Study in Scarlet*, Doyle appears eager to distance the true Englishman from responsibility for crime.

Although Doyle himself favored his historical fiction while the public preferred the Sherlock Holmes adventures, the author's finest works have largely been ignored. *The Lost World, The Poison Belt*, and *The Land of Mist* are novels which belong to a series of science-fiction works featuring the eccentric Professor George Edward Challenger. By the time *The Lost World* was published in 1912, Doyle was already becoming a figure of fun among the intelligentsia because of his ardent defense of psychic phenomena and his reactionary political views. The critics' disdain for this series unfortunately affected its popularity, and there has been a consequent tendency to overlook them as examples of Doyle's literary skill at its finest.

The Lost World · *The Lost World* resulted from Doyle's interest in prehistoric footprints near his home in the New Forest. After he made casts of the prints, he consulted with zoologist Edwin Ray Lankester and came away with the idea for the novel. *The Lost World* is narrated by Edward Dunn Malone, a journalist who comes to act as a Watson-like chronicler of the exploits of Professor Challenger, an eccentric scientist with a great physical resemblance to Arthur Conan Doyle. After knocking Malone down the stairs at their first meeting, Challenger recruits him for a proposed expedition to South America in search of a prehistoric monster believed to exist on a plateau in the Amazon River basin.

Doyle's penchant for realistic description deserts him in *The Lost World.* His details are fifty years out of date; he instead presents a fantastically imaginative vision of the unexplored jungle wilderness. The beauty of the jungle vanishes as the explorers reach the historic plateau. With almost surrealistic horror, Doyle depicts the filthy, fetid nesting ground of the pterodactyls and the dank and dirty caves of the ape-men who inhabit the plateau. A marvelous comic ending has Challenger revealing the results of the expedition to a skeptical London audience of pedants by releasing a captured pterodactyl over their heads.

The characterization in *The Lost World* is among Doyle's finest achievements. The members of the expedition are well balanced: the eccentric and pugnacious Challenger, the naïve and incredulous Malone, the cynical and touchy Summerlee, and the great white hunter Lord John Roxton. The one woman in the novel, Malone's fiancé Gladys, bears no resemblance to the Ruth Timewells and Lady Maudes of Doyle's earlier work. She is spunky and independent, refusing to marry Malone until he has done something worth admiring, and in his absence marrying someone else because she decides money is a more practical basis for marriage than fame.

The series retains its high quality in *The Poison Belt,* but the subsequent related works are less consequential. In *The Land of Mist,* Challenger becomes a spiritualist convert when the spirits of two men whom he believes he has killed return to tell him of his innocence. "When the World Screamed," one of the stories in *The Maracot Deep and Other Stories* (1929), reverts to the morbid sexuality of *The Parasite.* When Challenger attempts to drill a hole to the center of the earth, the world turns out to be a living female organism. When Challenger's shaft penetrates the cortex of her brain, she screams, setting off earthquakes and tidal waves.

Few of Doyle's writings from the last decade of his life are read by other than specialists, dealing as they do with the propagation of spiritualism. The canon of his fiction can thus be said to have ended with science-fiction novels. These novels too all deal with Doyle's characteristic themes and concerns. Challenger and Maracot uncover hidden truths about the nature of the past, the present, the future, and life after death much in the same way as Sherlock Holmes discovered the truth about human nature in the course of his investigation of crime. The historical fiction had sought to explore the truth about a specialized human nature, that of the archetypal Englishman, in the same manner. Even the obsession with spiritualism that cost him his credibility among intellectual circles was but another example of Doyle's lifelong search for the truth about human existence.

In whatever guise he portrayed that search, Doyle never deviated from the devotion to the ideals that had been instilled in him in childhood and which were recorded on his gravestone: "STEEL TRUE/BLADE STRAIGHT." Similarly, all his literary protagonists embodied these same ideals: a devotion to truth and a belief in the rightness of their cause. Few other authors have managed to create such a coherent body of work as did Arthur Conan Doyle, and fewer have matched the content of their work so closely to the conduct of their lives.

Mary Anne Hutchinson

Other major works

SHORT FICTION: *Mysteries and Adventures*, 1889 (also as *The Gully of Bluemansdyke and Other Stories*); *The Captain of Polestar and Other Tales*, 1890; *The Adventures of Sherlock Holmes*, 1892; *My Friend the Murderer and Other Mysteries and Adventures*, 1893; *The Great Keinplatz Experiment and Other Stories*, 1894; *The Memoirs of Sherlock Holmes*, 1894; *Round the Red Lamp: Being Fact and Fancies of Medical Life*, 1894; *The Exploits of Brigadier Gerard*, 1896; *The Man from Archangel and Other Stories*, 1898; *The Green Flag and Other Stories of War and Sport*, 1900; *The Adventures of Gerard*, 1903; *The Return of Sherlock Holmes*, 1905; *Round the Fire Stories*, 1908; *The Last Galley: Impressions and Tales*, 1911; *One Crowded Hour*, 1911; *His Last Bow*, 1917; *Danger! and Other Stories*, 1918; *Tales of the Ring and Camp*, 1922 (also as *The Croxley Master and Other Tales of the Ring and Camp*); *Tales of Terror and Mystery*, 1922 (also as *The Black Doctor and Other Tales of Terror and Mystery*); *Tales of Twilight and the Unseen*, 1922 (also as *The Great Keinplatz Experiment and Other Tales of Twilight and the Unseen*); *Three of Them*, 1923; *The Dealings of Captain Sharkey and Other Tales of Pirates*, 1925; *Last of the Legions and Other Tales of Long Ago*, 1925; *The Case-Book of Sherlock Holmes*, 1927; *The Maracot Deep and Other Stories*, 1929; *The Final Adventures of Sherlock Holmes*, 1981; *Uncollected Stories: The Unknown Conan Doyle*, 1982.

PLAYS: *Foreign Policy*, pr. 1893; *Jane Annie: Or, The Good Conduct Prize*, pr., pb. 1893 (with J. M. Barrie); *Waterloo*, pr. 1894 (also as *A Story of Waterloo*); *Halves*, pr. 1899; *Sherlock Holmes*, pr. 1899 (with William Gillette); *A Duet*, pb. 1903; *Brigadier Gerard*, pr. 1906; *The Fires of Fate*, pr. 1909; *The House of Temperley*, pr. 1909; *The Pot of Caviare*, pr. 1910; *The Speckled Band*, pr. 1910; *The Crown Diamond*, pr. 1921.

POETRY: *Songs of Action*, 1898; *Songs of the Road*, 1911; *The Guards Came Through and Other Poems*, 1919; *The Poems: Collected Edition*, 1922.

NONFICTION: *The Great Boer War*, 1900; *The War in South Africa: Its Causes and Conduct*, 1902; *The Case of Mr. George Edalji*, 1907; *Through the Magic Door*, 1907; *The Crime of the Congo*, 1909; *The Case of Oscar Slater*, 1912; *Great Britain and the Next War*, 1914; *In Quest of Truth, Being a Correspondence Between Sir Arthur Conan Doyle and Captain H. Stansbury*, 1914; *To Arms!*, 1914; *The German War: Some Sidelights and Reflections*, 1915; *Western Wanderings*, 1915; *The Origin and Outbreak of the War*, 1916; *A Petition to the Prime Minister on Behalf of Roger Casement*, 1916(?); *A Visit to Three Fronts*, 1916; *The British Campaign in France and Flanders*, 1916-1919 (6 volumes); *The New Revelation*, 1918; *The Vital Message*, 1919; *Our Reply to the Cleric*, 1920; *Spiritualism and Rationalism*, 1920; *A Debate on Spiritualism*, 1920 (with Joseph McCabe); *The Evidence for Fairies*, 1921; *Fairies Photographed*, 1921; *The Wanderings of a Spiritualist*, 1921; *The Coming of the Fairies*, 1922; *The Case for Spirit Photography*, 1922 (with others); *Our American Adventure*, 1923; *My Memories and Adventures*, 1924; *Our Second American Adventure*, 1924; *The Early Christian Church and Modern Spiritualism*, 1925; *Psychic Experiences*, 1925; *The History of Spiritualism*, 1926 (2 volumes); *Pheneas Speaks: Direct Spirit Communications*, 1927; *What Does Spiritualism Actually Teach and Stand For?*, 1928; *A Word of Warning*, 1928; *An Open Letter to Those of My Generation*, 1929; *Our African Winter*, 1929; *The Roman Catholic Church: A Rejoinder*, 1929; *The Edge of the Unknown*, 1930; *Arthur Conan Doyle on Sherlock Holmes*, 1981; *Essays on Photography*, 1982; *Letters to the Press*, 1984.

TRANSLATION: *The Mystery of Joan of Arc*, 1924 (Léon Denis).

EDITED TEXTS: *D. D. Home: His Life and Mission*, 1921 (by Mrs. Douglas Home); *The Spiritualist's Reader*, 1924.

Bibliography

Baring-Gould, W. S. *Sherlock Holmes of Baker Street: A Life of the World's First Consulting Detective.* New York: Bramhall House, 1962. A "biography" of Doyle's most popular creation, Sherlock Holmes. Based upon the Sherlock Holmes stories and numerous secondary sources. A chronological outline of Holmes's life as created by Baring-Gould is also included.

Booth, Martin. *The Doctor, the Detective, and Arthur Conan Doyle: A Biography of Arthur Conan Doyle.* London: Hodder & Stoughton, 1997. A good survey of the life of Doyle.

Carr, John Dickson. *The Life of Sir Arthur Conan Doyle.* New York: Harper & Brothers, 1949. Well researched and written by a distinguished mystery writer, this is a highly readable biography. Carr had access to Doyle's personal papers and enjoyed the cooperation of Doyle's children. A good place to begin further study.

Edwards, Owen Dudley. *The Quest for Sherlock Holmes: A Biographical Study of Arthur Conan Doyle.* New York: Barnes & Noble Books, 1983. Concentrates on the first twenty-three years of Doyle's life in an attempt to unravel the influence of various forces in his early life on his writing, such as his early love of history and Celtic lore, the impoverished and Catholic Edinburgh of his youth, and his alcoholic father.

Green, Richard Lancelyn. *A Bibliography of A. Conan Doyle.* New York: Oxford University Press, 1983. Provides a massive (712-page) bibliography of all that Doyle wrote, including obscure short pieces. Illustrated and containing a seventy-five-page index, this book includes a list of more than one hundred books of biographical, bibliographical, and critical interest for the study of Doyle.

Higham, Sir Charles. *The Adventures of Conan Doyle: The Life of the Creator of Sherlock Holmes.* New York: W. W. Norton, 1976. A popular biography which attempts to establish a link between Doyle's detective fiction and events in his own life, such as his use of actual criminal cases, the mental collapse of his father, and his interest in spiritualism. Indexed and illustrated. Includes a bibliography.

Jann, Rosemary. *The Adventures of Sherlock Holmes: Detecting Social Order.* New York: Twayne, 1995. Part of Twayne's Masterwork Series, this slim volume is divided into two parts, the first of which places the great detective in a literary and historical context, followed by Jann's own reading of Arthur Conan Doyle's Sherlockian approach to detective fiction. In addition to a selected bibliography, Jann's book includes a brief chronology of Doyle's life and work.

Kestner, Joseph A. *Sherlock's Men: Masculinity, Conan Doyle, and Cultural History.* Brookfield, Vt.: Ashgate, 1997. Discusses the theme of masculinity in Doyle's fiction. Includes bibliographical references and an index.

Orel, Harold, ed. *Critical Essays on Sir Arthur Conan Doyle.* New York: G. K. Hall, 1992. Including both evaluations by Doyle's contemporaries and later scholarship—some of it commissioned specifically for inclusion in this collection—*Critical Essays* is divided into three sections: "Sherlock Holmes," "Other Writings," and "Spiritualism." Harold Orel opens the collections with a lengthy and comprehensive essay, which is followed by a clever and classic meditation by Dorothy L. Sayers on "Dr. Watson's Christian Name." Also included are pieces by such literary lights as George Bernard Shaw, Max Beerbohm, and Heywood Broun.

Ross, Thomas Wynne. *Good Old Index: The Sherlock Holmes Handbook, a Guide to the Sherlock Holmes Stories by Sir Arthur Conan Doyle: Persons, Places, Themes, Summaries of all the Tales, with Commentary on the Style of the Author.* Columbia, S.C.: Camden House, 1997. An excellent manual for followers of Doyle's Holmes stories.

Symons, Julian. *Conan Doyle: Portrait of an Artist.* New York: Mysterious Press, 1979. This biography is particularly useful, as it tries to present Doyle as much more than the creator of Sherlock Holmes. Only 135 pages, it contains 122 illustrations, a chronology of Doyle's life, and a bibliography of his writings.

Margaret Drabble

Born: Sheffield, England; June 5, 1939

Principal long fiction · *A Summer Bird-Cage*, 1963; *The Garrick Year*, 1964; *The Millstone*, 1965 (pb. in U.S. as *Thank You All Very Much*); *Jerusalem the Golden*, 1967; *The Waterfall*, 1969; *The Needle's Eye*, 1972; *The Realms of Gold*, 1975; *The Ice Age*, 1977; *The Middle Ground*, 1980; *The Radiant Way*, 1987; *A Natural Curiosity*, 1989; *The Gates of Ivory*, 1991; *The Witch of Exmoor*, 1997.

Other literary forms · Margaret Drabble has combined literary scholarship with her career as a novelist. She wrote a short critical study of Willliam Wordsworth, *Wordsworth* (1966), and edited a collection of critical essays about Thomas Hardy, *The Genius of Thomas Hardy* (1975). Over the years, she has edited or written introductions for most of Jane Austen's works for various publishers, including *Lady Susan* (1974), *The Watsons* (1974), and *Sanditon* (1974). She also edited Thomas Hardy's *The Woodlanders* and Emily Brontë's *Wuthering Heights* and *Poems*. In 1989, she published her Gareth Lloyd Evans Shakespeare Lecture at Stratford-Upon-Avon as *Stratford Revisited: A Legacy of the Sixties*. She has written two major biographies: *Arnold Bennett* (1974) and *Angus Wilson* (1995). Her literary travelogue *A Writer's Britain: Landscape in Literature* was published in 1979.

Drabble has had a long-standing connection with drama. Her works include *Bird of Paradise* (1969), a stage play; *A Touch of Love* (1969), a screenplay based on her novel *The Millstone*; and *Laura* (1964), a play for television. She has written political essays, including *Case of Equality* (1988). She is well known for editing the fifth edition of *The Oxford Companion to English Literature* (1985, revised 1995). Drabble has written a fair number of short stories, as yet uncollected and only partially available to American audiences. Finally, Drabble has also written a book for children, *For Queen and Country: Britain in the Victorian Age* (1978).

Achievements · Drabble's novels charm and delight, but perhaps more significantly, they reward their readers with a distinctively modern woman's narrative voice and their unusual blend of Victorian and modern structures and concerns.

Although there seems to be critical consensus that Drabble has, as Bernard Bergonzi has said, "devised a genuinely new character and predicaments," the exact nature of this new voice and situation has not been precisely defined. Bergonzi sees the new character as an original blend of career woman and mother, yet Drabble's career woman begins to appear only in her seventh novel, *The Realms of Gold*. Her earlier, yet equally freshly portrayed heroines are often not mothers, as, for example, Sarah in *A Summer Bird-Cage*, or Clara in *Jerusalem the Golden*. Most of the mothers who precede Frances Wingate in *The Realms of Gold* can in no way be considered career women. Rose Vassiliou in *The Needle's Eye* does not work; Rosamund Stacey in *Thank You All Very Much* works only sporadically to support her baby, and her job can hardly be considered a career.

Other critics have claimed that the new voice involves an unprecedented acquaintance with the maternal attitude toward children. This is the voice Erica Jong pre-

Jerry Bauer

dicted would emerge once mother-hood was no longer thought to be incompatible with literary artistry. In fact, only three Drabble novels can be said to contain this voice: *Thank You All Very Much, The Ice Age,* and *The Middle Ground;* yet all the novels seem to present something original in their female point of view.

Female characters have illuminated literature for more than a thousand years, but until recently they have appeared as secondary figures. The female has been present, but her point of view and voice have been lacking. Drabble seems to be able to evoke not only the female point of view but also the cadence of the female voice. Her ear for speech rhythms is exceptional, and each central female character has a distinct speech pattern and cadence. This is, of course, more intensely true in the first-person narratives of Drabble's earlier novels, but it is also true of her later novels in which the heroine's interior life is rendered by an omniscient narrator who mimes her speech in order to discuss her feelings and thoughts. Perhaps Drabble's artistry in portraying the sound of the female voice is among her most significant accomplishments, more simple and more complex than the evocation of a maternal career woman or of the mother-child bond.

Drabble has also begun to experiment with the return of the outspoken omniscient narrator. Drabble's rediscovery of an old literary technique seems timely rather than regressive. She does not embed the characters in the amber of the narrator's point of view, preventing them from dramatizing themselves. Drabble's omniscient narrator gives the reader a sense of place, a sense of location and history, without forcing the characters to bear the burden of carrying all that perception in their minds. It frees the characters to notice only what they perceive within the confines of their personalities, for there is a narrative voice to create the density of the social and physical scene.

The narrator's involvement in place and history has important thematic implications for Drabble's fiction. She departs from the prevalent modern emphasis on the centrality of the individual sensibility, reaching back instead to the tradition of two authors she admires, Arnold Bennett and George Eliot. She explores modern fragmentation as a function, to some extent, of human choice. She explores the consequences of choosing to submit to centrifugal forces as opposed to struggling against them in an effort to be true to one's roots.

This original blend of a deep concern for society's conventions and origins and an unusually sensitive evocation of the individual female sensibility gives Drabble's works their particular flavor.

Biography · Margaret Drabble was born into a family that at once reflects the breakup of old patterns and the power of conventions, which may account for her receptiveness to both aspects of modern England. Her parents, John Frederick Drabble and Kathleen Marie (Bloor) Drabble, were the first of their families to attend a university. The results of her parents' upward mobility were both creative and destructive. Her father became a barrister and then a judge; her mother suffered the dislocations which attend such rapid social changes. She became an atheist and thus estranged herself from her fundamentalist parents. Drabble says that her mother was released from the harshness of her religious training when, as a young woman, she read George Bernard Shaw. As she turned the pages she had a revelation that there was no God. "One could say," says Drabble, "that that was a revelation from God not to worry about him because it was going to drive her mad if she did." Drabble's mother struggled against clinical depression until her death.

Drabble herself is the second of three daughters. Her sisters are Dr. Helen Langdon, a scholar, and Susan Duffy, a novelist, whose pen name is A. S. Byatt. She also has a brother, Richard J. B. Drabble. She attended a Quaker boarding school in York, The Mount School, and then read English at Newnham College, Cambridge, where she finished among the top of her class. In 1960, in the week that she finished at Cambridge, she married Clive Swift.

Swift was an aspiring actor who worked with the Royal Shakespeare Company. In the early years of their marriage, Drabble spent much of her time having three children, writing novels, and acting bit parts and understudying for the Royal Shakespeare Company. While she was writing *The Garrick Year*, she understudied Imogen in *Cymbeline*, played a fairy in *A Midsummer Night's Dream*, and had a bit part in *The Taming of the Shrew*. Drabble separated from her husband in 1972; their divorce became final in 1975.

For many years, Drabble lived in the North London village of Hampstead. Her novels have won many prizes: the John Llewelyn Rhys Memorial Award (1966), the James Tait Black Memorial Book Prize (1968), the Book of the Year Award from the Yorkshire *Post* (1972), and the E. M. Forster Award of the American Academy of Arts and Letters (1973). She is a member of the National Book League and served as its chair from 1980 to 1982. During the 1980's she devoted much of her efforts to revising the *Oxford Companion to English Literature* for its fifth edition. She was made a Commander of the Order of the British Empire (CBE) in 1980. Drabble has received honorary D.Litt. degrees from many universities: Sheffield, Manchester, Keele, Bradford, Hull, East Anglia, and York. She has lectured in the United States at such educational institutions as Purdue University and Carleton College. She was made an Honorary Fellow of the Sheffield City Polytechnic in 1989. In 1982, Drabble married the biographer Michael Holroyd. They settled in the Notting Hill district of London and at Porlock Weir, Somerset.

Analysis · Margaret Drabble's novels begin as female arias in the bel canto style, predominantly elaborate embellishments on a simple series of events relative only to the first-person narrator, events that reflect a brief but formative time in the narrator's life. The early novels deal with the lives of rather ordinary middle-class girls and, but for their sensitivity and subtlety of insight, come dangerously close to being considered women's magazine fiction. The later novels are more complex, exploring the delicate webs of social interconnections and covering longer periods of time in which the convergences of many lives upon one another effect subtle and not so subtle changes.

Both the early and later novels express concern with finding the legitimate sources of growth and development.

A Summer Bird-Cage · Drabble's distinctive narrative voice is clear in her first novel. Sarah Bennett, a recent college graduate, is the protagonist of *A Summer Bird-Cage*, but figures mainly as a witness to her sister Louise's marriage. From her older sister's mistakes, Sarah learns about her own attitude toward the future. The novel begins as Sarah returns from Paris to attend Louise's marriage to Stephen Halifax, a boring, trendy, wealthy, satirical novelist. Louise is a stunning and exciting raven-haired beauty, yet Sarah cannot understand why she is marrying the bloodless Stephen Halifax. Sarah and her friends attempt to puzzle this out through the progress of the novel, especially as it becomes increasingly obvious that Louise has been having an affair with a very attractive actor, John Connell. In the end, Sarah learns directly from Louise what was obvious all the while: Louise married Stephen for his money. Rather than seeming anticlimactic, this knowledge solidifies Sarah's growing understanding of what fidelity and betrayal are about. Despite its socially sanctioned position, the marriage Louise has contracted is in fact adulterous because it is a betrayal of her heart and affections. The technical adultery is an act of faith.

Louise divorces Stephen to take her chances with John, and Sarah ends the novel with a forged bond of affection with Louise. Sarah is thus prepared for the return of her boyfriend, Francis, from America. Having observed Louise, Sarah realizes that fidelity to her vow to marry Francis is not as important as waiting to see if in fact their relationship has its roots in truth. Sarah will only marry if the action follows from an authentic feeling.

Jerusalem the Golden · In her fourth novel, *Jerusalem the Golden*, Drabble experimented for the first time with omniscient narration, maintaining an ironic distance from her protagonist. Clara Maugham, a provincial girl from Northam, a small town in the north of England, is that young woman all too familiar in fiction, the woman whose capacities for development are greater than the opportunities presented by her narrow circumstances. In general, such a character is often created by writers who have escaped the clutches of small minds and tight social structures; an identity of author and character is usually suspected. The character becomes a vehicle through which the author gets back at the tormentors of his or her youth; the character finds dazzling fulfillment in the city.

Clara Maugham, then, comes out of this tradition, but does not lead the reader into the usual pitfalls. Drabble considers the problems of leaving one's roots for fuller possibilities. As impoverished as it may be, one's heritage provides the individual with a foothold in reality. Hence, the title of the novel is a mocking one. It alludes to the utopian dream that emerges from a hymn to which Clara is attracted as a school girl:

> Jerusalem the Golden
> With Milk and Honey blest
> Beneath thy contemplation
> Sink heart and voice oppressed.
> I know not, oh, I know not
> What social joys are there
> What radiance of glory
> What light beyond compare.

For Clara, the mysteries of ecstasy counterpoint the threadbare, wretched, familiar world. For her there is nothing in between, and she leaves Northam only to find a sham Jerusalem in London.

Clara begins life believing that she is doomed to be as her mother is, a woman without hope who remarks that when she is dead the garbage collector can cart her off. Mrs. Maugham is a jealous, inconsistent woman who verbally snipes at her neighbors behind her lace curtains because of their concern for their proprieties, and then she outdoes them in cheap ostentation. Rejecting such a life, Clara finds hope in literary images. Metaphors provide avenues of escape, as in the hymn. So too does a children's story that makes a deep impression on her, *The Two Weeds*. The story presents the choices of two weeds. One decides on longevity at the cost of a miserly conservation of its resources, growing "low and small and brown"; the other longs for intensity, the spectacular but short life, and puts its efforts into fabulous display. Each weed achieves its goal. The small, plain one survives, as it had hoped. The magnificent, attractive weed is plucked and dies happily at the bosom of a lovely girl. What impresses Clara about this story is the offer of any possibility other than the low road of mere survival. Little by little, Clara chooses the mysteries of ecstasy.

Clara has to make her way to these mysteries by rejecting a more moderate course, thus losing real opportunities to grow and succeed. Her intellect is widely despised by the good people of Northam, although it is valued by some of her teachers, who fight to attach her to their subjects. She is also revered by a boy named Walter Ash, who values culture and comes from a family tradition which stresses intellectual stimulation. Clara is cynical about her teachers' admiration; she does not value their esteem. She allows Walter to go out with her, but has little regard for him. She ultimately rejects him, thinking, "I shall get further if I'm pulled, I can't waste time going first."

This cryptic remark makes sense only in the light of her choices in London, to which she goes on scholarship to attend Queens College. By chance, she meets Clelia Denham at a poetry reading. This meeting drives her to an instinctual attachment to the girl and subsequently to her family, especially Clelia's brother Gabriel, with whom she has an affair. Although her attachments to the Denhams "pull her," and she does not need to "go first," it is questionable whether they take her anywhere. Indeed, the Denhams provide her the accoutrements of ecstasy. The life she leads with them, however, having torn herself away from her unsatisfactory family, is not one that she builds herself. It is one that envelops her in a "radiance of glory."

The Denhams are rich, and their money is old. Their family house is exquisitely done in tile, fireplaces, pictures, and mirrors, old, good things. Outside the house is a terraced garden that to Clara is the original Eden. The Denhams themselves are good-looking people who dress well and speak cleverly. Mrs. Denham is a writer known professionally as Candida Grey. Mr. Denham is a lawyer. Magnus, the oldest boy, is a rich capitalist. Gabriel is in television, and Clelia works in a chic art gallery.

To the detached eye, the Denham children seem smothered by this "good life." The oldest child, no longer living in the Denham house, has gone crazy. Clelia is startlingly infantile. She speaks in all situations as if to a close relative, never using tact or discretion. Although twenty-seven years old, she lives at home, seemingly unable to establish herself on her own as wife, mother, or career woman. The job she holds in the gallery is purely decorative, one she obtained through family connections, and on which she could never support herself. Her extremely chic room contains her childhood toys as part of the decor. Clara interprets their presence as

Notable British Novelists

part of Clelia's enviable sense of continuity with a happy childhood. Unfortunately for both Clelia and Clara, they are the sign of a childhood that has never ended.

Gabriel is married and lives with his wife and children in one of those fashionable sections of London that are emerging from slum conditions. He has a good job with Independent Television and makes a good salary. He and his wife, Phillipa, make stunning personal impressions. When Clara visits the couple, however, she is appalled to find that their home is in a state of chaos. The house is potentially as beautiful as others in the neighborhood which have been renovated, but nothing has been done to it. The floors are pitted and worn, the walls are badly in need of paint, the ancient wallpaper hangs in tatters, and the rooms are poorly lit. The kitchen is a war zone in which the litter of cracking plaster vies with expensive cooking equipment. Phillipa is unable to provide food for her family or any kind of supportive attention to the children. Gabriel is unable to organize a life of his own, so dependent is he on the glorious life of his mother and father's house. Gabriel becomes obsessively attracted to Clara and dreams of a *ménage à trois* between them and Clelia.

Magnus is an industrial mogul, a bachelor who becomes parasitically and emotionally attached to Gabriel's women. At first in love with Phillipa, when he senses the affair between Gabriel and Clara he begins an erotic flirtation with Clara. Clara gives herself over emotionally to all the Denhams, and sexually to the brothers Magnus and Gabriel. She feels little for them, or anyone, but the lust for inclusion in a beautiful life. She acts out increasingly more elaborate scenes with them, climaxed by a visit to Paris with Gabriel. During this journey, a flirtation between Clara and Magnus sends Gabriel back to the hotel where he and Clara are staying. Clara outdoes him by leaving him sleeping to miss his plane while she returns to London alone. Once there, she discovers that her mother is dying of cancer.

Clara visits her mother but there is no feeling between them. Returning to London, her connections to her childhood severed, she finds that the affair with the Denhams is just beginning. Despite the seemingly decisive break in Paris, Clara is now well into Denham games. Her future is to be composed of "Clelia, and Gabriel and she herself in shifting and ideal conjunctions." There is no mention of the development of her intellect or talents.

Clara, at last, contemplates her victory: her triumph over her mother's death, her triumph over her early life, her survival of all of it. "Even the mercy and kindness of destiny she would survive; they would not get her that way, they would not get her at all." These final words are fully ironic: Clara has not triumphed over anything. She is a victim of her own fear of life. Her evasion of a nebulous "them" is a type of paranoid delusion which amounts to a horror of life. Clara has been true to her need to expand, but false to what she is. The outcome is not a joyous one. She has achieved a perverse isolation in a bogus, sterile Jerusalem.

The Waterfall · The same themes are explored in Drabble's next novel, *The Waterfall.* Though rendered in the first person by the central character, Jane Grey, *The Waterfall* is a highly ironic, fearfully complex exploration of the question which informs *A Summer Bird-Cage* and *Jerusalem the Golden*: To what must one be true? There is a vast variety of claims on one's fidelity, and these claims frequently pull in different directions. Shall one be true to one's family? One's religion? One's friends? One's heart? One's sexuality? One's intellect? Even from the simple personal perspective, Drabble arrives at an impasse from which the protagonist herself cannot reckon her obligations or even the main issue deserving of her attention.

Jane Grey begins her story giving birth, overwhelmed, that is, by her biology, shaped and determined by her gender, her flesh, her sexuality. This is confirmed by her statement to her husband, Malcolm, who has left her before the birth of their second child, "If I were drowning, I couldn't reach out a hand to save myself, so unwilling am I to set myself up against my fate."

Jane Grey is a woman who does not give allegiance to anything that requires conscious choice. She cannot sustain a marriage, a career, or any affiliation that calls for directed will. She is faithful only to what takes her, overwhelms her, leaving her no choice—her sexuality. Thus, she can be a mother, but not a wife. She can be a lover, but not a companion. The result is that she becomes the adulterous, almost incestuous lover of James, her cousin Lucy's husband. This comes about in a way that can be seen as nothing less than a betrayal of a number of social norms.

Because Jane has been deserted by Malcolm, Lucy and James alternate visits to assist her. Lucy, who has been like a sister to Jane, initiates these visits without Jane's request. Jane's breaking of her marriage vows and her betrayal of Lucy is not as uncomplicated as Louise's affair with John in *A Summer Bird-Cage*. Louise has violated nothing more than the law; Jane has violated the bonds of her heart, since Lucy has been so close to her, and the bonds of family and morality, as well as the bonds of law and ethics. Nevertheless, there is a fidelity in Jane's choice. She and James, whose name is deliberately the male reflection of hers, are, in being overwhelmed by each other, satisfying the deepest narcissistic sexuality in each other. It is, of course, true that in so doing they create social limbo for their mates and children, and for themselves.

Their adultery is discovered when they are in an automobile accident. James's car hits a brick, although he is driving carefully, as they begin a weekend outing together with Jane's children. The car turns over; only James is hurt, but he recovers almost fully. Jane and James continue with their ordinary life. Neither Malcolm nor Lucy exacts any payment from them. The lovers meet when they can. The novel ends with their only full weekend together after the accident. Jane and James climb the Goredale Scar, one of England's scenic wonders. They are there because someone described it so enthusiastically to Jane that it became her goal to see it herself. The Scar is the quintessential female sexual symbol, a cavernous cleft in the mountains, flushed by a waterfall and covered by a pubic growth of foliage. Drabble then sends the lovers back to their hotel room to drink Scotch inadvertently dusted by talcum powder, which leaves a bad taste in their mouths. They have been faithful in their own minds to a force validated by nature.

The Needle's Eye · *The Needle's Eye*, regarded by many readers as Drabble's finest novel, takes its title from Jesus' proverbial words to a rich young man: "It is easier for a camel to go through the eye of a needle, than for a rich man to enter into the kingdom of God" (Matthew 19:24). At the center of the novel are Simon Camish, a barrister from a poor background who would seem to have regretfully gained the world at the expense of his soul, and Rose Bryanston Vassiliou, a rich young woman who compulsively divests herself of the benefits of her inheritance but is not fully enjoying her flight into the lower classes.

Rose, a pale, timid girl, had created a tabloid sensation by marrying out of her class. Her choice was the disreputable, seedy, sexy Christopher Vassiliou, son of Greek immigrants whose pragmatic financial dealings are not solidly within the boundaries of the law. Rose sought to escape from the evils of wealth through

Christopher, one of the downtrodden. Much to her consternation, however, Christopher is not a "happy peasant." He detests poverty, legitimately, and associates it not with virtue but with humiliation and deprivation, both of which he has endured.

Christopher's dream is to make something of himself. This dream is only strengthened by the birth of their three children, for whom Christopher wants "only the best." He sees in Rose's war on wealth nothing but perverse self-destructiveness. His fury vents itself in physical abuse. Frail, pale Rose is equally adamant in the protection of her children's future. To her mind, "the best" means freedom from possessions. Again Rose and Christopher become figures of tabloid fantasy, this time in a dramatic divorce case.

Rose is working out her divorce settlement when she meets Simon. Simon is introduced to the reader on the same night that he is introduced to Rose; the reader first sees him in a store, buying liquor. Simon feels estranged from the lower-class types who frequent and staff the store. Soon thereafter, this isolation is established as a sharp discontinuity in Simon's life, for he has risen from these ranks. He has been pushed upward by a mother embarrassed by the meanness of her lower-class life and determined that her son will have what she never had. Ironically, the essential gap in his mother's life is also left unfilled in Simon's; that is, the need for warmth and affection. Simon tried to marry into an inheritance of warmth and wealth by his alliance with what he thought was a good-natured girl of the comfortable upper-middle class, Julie Phillips. Their marriage, however, only revealed her fear and insecurity, her essential coldness. What Simon had mistaken for warmth was merely superficial brightness, a by-product of the Phillipses' affluence.

Rose and Simon have attempted to gain what each personally lacked through marriage, as if one could graft onto oneself a human capacity with a wedding ring. Such marriages are doomed to failure. Also doomed has been Rose's attempt to meet human needs with "filthy lucre." She has given a huge portion of her inheritance to a schoolhouse in a lonely, little-known part of Africa. Within months, the school was demolished in the chaos of a civil war, along with approximately one hundred children. Rose does not attempt to deny the futility of what she has done.

Simon and Rose strike up a professional acquaintance, casually, it seems, because Christopher has begun some devious maneuvers to get his children away from Rose. As he becomes increasingly involved in helping Rose, Simon realizes that he is in love with her. Rose reveals but a few of her feelings on this issue, but does indicate the joy she takes in his company. While Rose and Simon are chasing around after Christopher, who appears to be in the process of abducting the children and taking them out of England, Simon finally tells Rose that, were they at liberty, he would marry her. He blurts out this sentiment as they are walking in a woodland setting. The moment of his revelation finds them in sudden confrontation with a dead stoat, hanging grotesquely in front of them, a dried-up little corpse. According to the narrator, this is "a warning" to Simon and Rose.

The satisfaction that Rose and Simon might find together is based on their shared concern for their obligations and duties. To turn to each other, a temptation for both of them, would be a betrayal of the very basis of their attraction to each other, as it would necessitate shirking their responsibilities. It is the grace in them that understands commitments beyond the self. Understanding this, Simon and Rose remain friends; Christopher and Rose are reunited. Rose has achieved a modus vivendi with Christopher, who goes to work for her father. There is no fully articulated happiness, but a kind of integrity exists at the heart of Rose's and Simon's arrangement.

In the novel's final tableau, Rose is looking at a vandalized lion outside a second-rate British edifice called the Alexandra Palace. The lion's plaster head is broken, revealing a hollow inside. It has been spray-painted red with the name of a local gang, but Rose decides that she likes it. Although beginning life as an anonymous, mass-produced piece of kitsch, the lion has been worn into something unique: "it had weathered into identity. And this she hoped for every human soul." Rose's final wish accepts the uniqueness of life, the beauty of its mere being. She rejects the vision of a life that is continually being held up to an intellectual ideal, by which standards the lion, like her life, is an awful mess.

Drabble has said in an interview that, had she written *The Needle's Eye* after her husband left her, she might have altered Rose's destiny; perhaps she meant that Rose might have been sent off with Simon, after all. Perhaps these words reveal something of the personal Drabble, but they are a betrayal of the novel. The delicacy of Simon and Rose's poise in front of the dead stoat and the final image of the lion resist second thoughts.

The Realms of Gold · Drabble has called *The Realms of Gold* her only comedy. It is the most elaborately plotted of her novels, and Drabble has observed that comedies are permitted such carefully structured plots. Perhaps Drabble defends her plot to excuse herself for pivoting the outcome of her story on the delay in the mail of a postcard, consciously parodying the tragic turn of William Shakespeare's *Romeo and Juliet* (1595-1596), when Romeo's letter from Friar Laurence is delayed. Unlike the passion of Romeo and Juliet, however, the passion of the lovers in *The Realms of Gold*, Frances Wingate and Karel Schmidt, is not "too swift, too unadvised." Frances and Karel are survivors, and it is for this reason that true love is possible.

The novel begins in a hotel room. Frances is on tour, lecturing about her discovery of an ancient city, Tizouk. One evening, in a fit of loneliness, she writes a postcard to Karel, whom she capriciously rejected six months previously. She now regrets her gesture. Impulsively, she writes on the card, "I miss you. I love you." Bothered when she receives no response to her card, she is ignorant of the fact that her card has not been delivered, having been mislaid by the European mail system. Frances is distraught, but carries on as mother to her four children, as a professional, and as a member of her family.

Karel, too, carries on, thinking hopelessly about Frances, his lost love, puzzled by her rejection of him, suffering at the hands of his deranged wife and his students at the polytechnic, where he is a lecturer in history. Both wife and students continually take advantage of Karel's patience and good nature, and he, not quite understanding why, allows them to victimize him.

Karel and Frances's professional interests, history and archaeology, bring to the novel the long view of continuity. This view is partially what sustains Karel and Frances, whose families cannot or will not support them. Karel has been cut off from his family by the horrors of history. He is Jewish, the only member of his immediate family to survive World War II. Frances, on the other hand, has a large family, but it is wracked with odd and self-destructive behavior: alcoholism, suicide, depression. Frances's family is composed of two estranged branches, isolated from each other by an ancient quarrel—that no one can remember—between two brothers. During the course of the novel, the branches are reconciled. The healing begins when Frances discovers her cousin David, of whom she has never before heard. She meets him professionally at a UNESCO conference in Adra.

The conference has taken Frances away from England at a particularly crucial time in the life of her family. In Tockley, in the English midlands, an old lady discovered dead of starvation turns out to be Frances's estranged great-aunt. As Frances's family is a prominent one, there is a scandal about this shocking neglect of a family member. Frances is called home from the conference and discovers another lost cousin, Janet Bird, the last person to see their great-aunt alive.

Meanwhile, Frances's cousin David is surprised at the conference by the arrival of Karel, who, finally receiving the delayed postcard, flies heedlessly to join Frances at the conference and must be escorted by David back to Tockley. The upshot of these and more complications is the marriage of Karel and Frances and the reunification of Frances's family.

Frances and Karel synthesize stability and freedom; their marriage triumphantly asserts the victory of human freedom through history, continuity, and culture. The horrors of history present in both the Nazi persecution of the Jews, Frances's blighted family history, and the evidence of child sacrifice which Frances has found in her ancient city Tizouk, do not lead to a rejection of continuity but to the passion to grow through it and outlive the evil it contains.

The major image of the novel incarnates the comic attitude necessary if one is to lay hands on that hard-won treasure known as life. Shortly before Frances had rejected Karel, causing the long separation that was to end in Tockley, Frances and Karel were enjoying a holiday together. Endeavoring to spend a pleasant day in the country, they had driven their car into the mud, resulting in the bespattering of their persons in a most unromantic way. In the midst of their predicament, they heard a strange, almost ominous sound. An investigation turned up hundreds of frogs simply honking away in a drainage pipe in a ditch. Frances and Karel were flooded with affection and amusement at this gratuitously joyous spectacle. The image of it never leaves them and becomes a sustaining force during their ordeal of separation. Perhaps this is Drabble's best image of a realistic optimism in a very flawed world, joy spontaneously uttered from a muddy ditch.

The Ice Age · In *The Ice Age*, Drabble considers the problem of survival within a dying tradition. England is enduring an ice age: Its social structure is collapsing. In a brilliantly dark vision, Drabble surveys the challenge this poses to personal resources.

As the novel begins, a reckless real estate speculator, Len Wincobank, is serving time in Scratby Open Prison for fraud. Len's technically innocent accomplice, Maureen Kirby, is wondering how to fit the pieces of her life back together again. A teenage girl, Jane Murray, daughter of an extremely beautiful former actress, Alison Murray, is on trial in the remote Communist country of Wallachia. Anthony Keating, a charming author of musical comedies turned real estate speculator, is recovering from a heart attack and the collapse of his financial empire.

All the characters are suffering through imprisonment in England. It is a time in which Max and Kitty Friedman are the victims of an IRA terrorist attack as they are having an anniversary dinner. England is plagued with degenerate youth, frightening in what it portends for the future. Jane Murray is an angry, shallow child, seemingly incapable of love or of true civility. Anthony Keating finds two young squatters on the empty floor of his former home. The girl is a heroin addict, pregnant and in labor. The boy is drunk and stoned, unable to summon assistance for the girl. Anthony's chance visit to his old house means that the girl will get to the hospital, but she will die and her baby will be born suffering from prenatal heroin addiction.

Through the gloom of England's dark night, Drabble feels her way toward dawn, steadfastly refusing to deny the value of principle because history is suffering temporarily from chaos. She paints a damning picture of a contemporary of Anthony, Mike Morgan, a comedian who pointlessly and viciously ridicules his audience because he mistakes a bad patch for the end of coherence. She also, however, defends the human being as a flexible, creative source of energy not be be trapped within rigidities of principle.

Alison Murray emerges as the polar opposite to Mike Morgan. She too is a doomed soul, because as England flails about, she has chosen the sterility of a noble perfection over the struggles of possibility. Alison's choice has been to devote herself to her brain-damaged daughter Molly rather than to her normal daughter, Jane. Molly can never develop and grow, despite Alison's martyrdom, and Jane is wild and sullen as a result of her displacement. Drabble shows that Alison's choice is at least as bad as Mike's, leading directly to her own misery and indirectly to Jane's self-imposed troubles in Wallachia. Alison's choice also leads indirectly to Anthony Keating's downfall.

Anthony, Alison's lover, goes to Wallachia to escort Jane home when the authorities suddenly decide to return her to England. A civil war erupts, randomly freeing Jane and trapping Anthony. He is mistaken for a British spy and remanded to a Siberian-style forced labor camp.

Between the extremes of Mike Morgan and Alison Murray lies the possibility of working one's way back to continuity by keeping the spirit free. The major examples of such survival in the novel are Maureen Kirby and Anthony Keating. Maureen is a lower-class girl, sexy rather than beautiful, who falls somewhat short of conventional morality. Hardly a person who eschews extremes, Maureen has been the partner of Len Wincobank in his whirlwind financial spree. She has also temporarily retreated into her own selfish, protected world when Len is imprisoned, but she is resilient. In a striking narrative device, Drabble looks into the future at the end of the novel, coolly summarizing the fates of her characters. Maureen is projected as a woman of the 1980's who ultimately marries well and becomes a model to young women. Her coarse-grained vitality and common sense lack the charm of Alison's elegant self-immolation, but it radiates the warmth of survival.

Anthony Keating, in his frozen Wallachian prison, the ice age of England made palpable, turns also toward life in the only way that is available to him. He becomes enthralled with watching birds, symbols of his spirit which, despite everything, remains untrammeled.

At the close of the novel, the state of the nation is given a good prognosis. It will recover, asserts the narrator. Anthony has come to terms. Len will surely go on to further development and a financial comeback. Maureen's trajectory is in ascent, but, asserts the narrator, Alison Murray will never recover. The doom of Alison Murray strongly suggests that her kind of retreat from possibility is the worst prison of all, subject to no reprieve or amelioration. Here Drabble seems to have found the limits of what critics have called her conservatism. Cutting off from one's roots to rise in the world brings peril, denying one's context in order to acquire more brings suffering; these may reveal the flaws in the liberal dream. The ultimate horror, however, would seem to be turning away from growth, regardless of the reason.

The Radiant Way · In her novels of the 1980's–*The Middle Ground, The Radiant Way,* and *A Natural Curiosity*–Drabble continued to work in the manner of *The Realms of*

Gold and *The Ice Age.* Her intrusive narrators continued to reflect on the nature of fiction and to make arch asides to the reader. All three of these novels center on well-educated characters of the upper middle class whose domestic concerns are intertwined with larger social issues.

The Radiant Way, A Natural Curiosity, and a long novel published in 1991, *The Gates of Ivory,* form a trilogy that follows a number of characters through the 1980's and beyond. Not only is *The Gates of Ivory* a long book, it is also a demanding one. It moves from England to Thailand and back and seems to take as its subject not only the state of England but also the state of the world. In the book's opening sentence, Drabble understandably wonders whether it is a novel at all.

There is no doubt that the first two books in the trilogy are novels. As *The Ice Age* had shown Britain's suffering during a Labour government, so these novels show national life under Margaret Thatcher. At the center of the novels are three women friends: Liz Headleand, a psychotherapist; Alix Bowen, an idealistic social worker; and Esther Breuer, a mysterious art historian who focuses on minor figures of the Italian Renaissance. The title *The Radiant Way* refers both to a book that Liz's husband, Charles, read as a boy and to a television documentary he made in the 1960's. It also provides the novel's double-edged central symbol: the radiant personal sun of achievement that many of its youthful characters once envisioned and a radiant national future of justice and harmony. The novel's other pervasive symbol is a web–a vast and complicated web of interconnections in which the characters live.

The novel begins at Liz's New Year's Eve party in the last minutes of 1979. The 1980's get off to a bad start when Charles announces that he is leaving her. Things get worse nationally as relations between social classes deteriorate and as the gap between the North and South of England widens. Alix, the most political of the three friends, finds that her efforts to help the underprivileged not only bear no fruit but also lead to horrible violence. She loses faith in her husband's old-fashioned lower-class values and is content to sift through the papers of an old poet. Liz finds herself enmeshed in a personal web with her sister, Shirley Harper, unhappily married back in their home in the North of England, and with their mother, Rita. The Dickensian secret that Rita Ablewhite keeps is one of even more interrelationships.

A Natural Curiosity · By means of a loosely constructed narrative that shifts from plot thread to plot thread, *A Natural Curiosity* enables readers to follow the stories of the three women up to the point where *The Gates of Ivory* begins. In *A Natural Curiosity,* Liz and her former husband try to discover what has happened to a friend of theirs who is being held hostage. Liz also worries about the fate of another friend, a novelist named Stephen Cox. (The story of Stephen Cox will form the backbone of the plot of *The Gates of Ivory.*) Alix, now living in the North, visits the murderer who was introduced in the previous novel and brings him books. In order to try and understand him, she tracks down and confronts his unpleasant father and even more unpleasant mother. Shirley Harper is more prominent in this book; she finds herself free for the first time in her adult life and flees to Paris and a wild affair. Liz and Shirley find that the Ablewhite family mysteries deepen and go in new directions; these lead in turn to new revelations and new energy. Drabble's narrative voice is more intrusive than ever.

Martha Nochimson, updated by George Soule

Other major works

PLAY: *Bird of Paradise*, pr. 1969.

SCREENPLAYS: *Isadora*, 1969 (with Melvyn Bragg and Clive Exton); *A Touch of Love*, 1969.

TELEPLAY: *Laura*, 1964.

NONFICTION: *Wordsworth: Literature in Perspective*, 1966; *Arnold Bennett: A Biography*, 1974; *A Writer's Britain: Landscape in Literature*, 1979; *The Tradition of Women's Fiction: Lectures in Japan*, 1982; *Case of Equality*, 1988; *Stratford Revisited: A Legacy of the Sixties*, 1989; *Angus Wilson: A Biography*, 1995.

CHILDREN'S LITERATURE: *For Queen and Country: Britain in the Victorian Age*, 1978.

EDITED TEXTS: *Lady Susan; The Watsons; Sanditon*, all 1974 (by Jane Austen); *The Genius of Thomas Hardy*, 1975; *The Oxford Companion to English Literature: New Edition*, 1985, rev. ed. 1995; 6th ed. 2000.

Bibliography

Bokat, Nicole Suzanne. *The Novels of Margaret Drabble: This Freudian Family Nexus*. New York: Peter Lang, 1998. Part of the Sexuality and Literature series, this volume examines the sexual and psychological backgrounds of Drabble's characters.

Creighton, Joanne V. *Margaret Drabble*. New York: Methuen, 1985. This slim volume begins with an introductory overview, followed by a chronological survey of Drabble's novels through *The Middle Ground*. Creighton argues that Drabble, with such contemporaries as John Fowles and Muriel Spark, has gradually changed her approach to fiction, "challenging the conventions and epistemological assumptions of traditional realistic fiction, perhaps in spite of herself." Includes notes and a bibliography.

Hannay, John. *The Intertextuality of Fate: A Study of Margaret Drabble*. Columbia: University of Missouri Press, 1986. Drabble's characters sometimes think they are fated when their lives seem to imitate the patterns (or intertexts) of stories they have read. As a result, Drabble's references to other stories are not decorations but serious allusions to the myths that shape the novels. Accidents and coincidences often signal that an intertext is in operation.

Myer, Valerie Grosvenor. *Margaret Drabble: A Reader's Guide*. New York: St. Martin's Press, 1991. Myer usefully identifies allusions, sets historical and literary contexts, and summarizes critical opinions.

Rose, Ellen Cronan, ed. *Critical Essays on Margaret Drabble*. Boston: G. K. Hall, 1985. An important collection of essays and a useful introduction to Drabble's career.

_____. *The Novels of Margaret Drabble: Equivocal Figures*. Totowa, N.J.: Barnes & Noble Books, 1980. Rose's study seeks to "acknowledge and applaud [Drabble's] feminist vision and encourage her to give it freer rein in the future." Drabble's first three novels are discussed together in the opening chapter, while each of her next five novels (through *The Ice Age*) is given a separate chapter. Includes a list of works cited and endnotes for each chapter.

Rubenstein, Roberta. "Fragmented Bodies/Selves/Narratives: Margaret Drabble's Postmodern Turn." *Contemporary Literature* 35 (Spring, 1994): 136-155. Rubenstein treats Drabble's novels of the 1980's and 1990's and shows how they are fragmented in postmodern ways.

Sadler, Lynn Veach. *Margaret Drabble*. Boston: Twayne, 1986. Acknowledging that Drabble both "exasperates and delights" her, Sadler offers a balanced and readable appraisal. A very brief biographical sketch is followed by a chronological survey of Drabble's novels through *The Middle Ground*, with a coda on "Drabble's Reputation." Includes notes and an extensive bibliography, both primary and secondary; entries for secondary sources are annotated.

Soule, George. *Four British Women Novelists: Anita Brookner, Margaret Drabble, Iris Murdoch, Barbara Pym—An Annotated and Critical Secondary Bibliography*. Lanham, Md.: Scarecrow, 1998. An analysis and evaluation of most of the critical books and articles on Drabble through 1996.

Talwar, Sree Rashmi. *Woman's Space: The Mosaic World of Margaret Drabble and Nayantara Sahgal*. New Delhi: Creative Books, 1997. A comparative study of Indian writer Sahgal and Drabble, exploring the effects of feminism on the writers.

Daphne Du Maurier

Born: London, England; May 13, 1907
Died: Par, Cornwall, England; April 19, 1989

Principal long fiction · *The Loving Spirit*, 1931; *I'll Never Be Young Again*, 1932; *The Progress of Julius*, 1933; *Jamaica Inn*, 1936; *Rebecca*, 1938; *Frenchman's Creek*, 1941; *Hungry Hill*, 1943; *The King's General*, 1946; *The Parasites*, 1949; *My Cousin Rachel*, 1951; *Mary Anne*, 1954; *The Scapegoat*, 1957; *Castle Dor*, 1962 (with Arthur Quiller-Couch); *The Glass-Blowers*, 1963; *The Flight of the Falcon*, 1965; *The House on the Strand*, 1969; *Rule Britannia*, 1972.

Other literary forms · In addition to her many novels, Daphne du Maurier wrote and edited biographies, collections of letters, travel books, plays, and short stories. Her biographical works include *Gerald: A Portrait* (1934), the life story of her actor father; *The du Mauriers* (1937), the inside story of her famous family of actors, dramatists, and novelists; and *Young George du Maurier: A Selection of His Letters, 1860-67* (1951), a selection of her caricaturist-novelist grandfather's letters. She earned a place among playwrights with *The Years Between* (1945) and *September Tide* (1949). Her travel book *Vanishing Cornwall* (1967) described the rugged coastal area of southwestern England, where she set so many of her novels and stories. Often weaving elements of the supernatural into her tales of mystery and romance, du Maurier produced several notable volumes of short stories, including *Echoes from the Macabre* in 1976 and *Classics from the Macabre* in 1987.

Achievements · The theatrical quality of du Maurier's novels is evidenced by the frequency and reported ease with which her works were adapted for the big screen. Alfred Hitchcock directed film versions of *Jamaica Inn*, in 1939, and her best-selling gothic novel *Rebecca*, in 1940. The latter won an Academy Award for Best Picture. Paramount filmed *Frenchman's Creek* in 1944. Universal Pictures released a film adaptation of *Hungry Hill* in 1947, for which du Maurier herself wrote the first draft of the screenplay. *My Cousin Rachel* became a Twentieth Century Fox production in 1952, and Metro-Goldwyn-Mayer released *The Scapegoat* in 1959. Hitchcock turned her story "The Birds" into a highly successful motion picture in 1963. Her story "Don't Look Now" became a hit film in 1973. *Rebecca* won an award from the American Booksellers' Association in 1939. In 1969, du Maurier was named a Dame Commander of the Order of the British Empire.

Biography · Daphne du Maurier was born to a theatrical family. Her father, Gerald, was an actor and manager; her mother, Muriel Beaumont, was an actress. Du Maurier was educated in both England and France. Plagued from childhood by feelings of self-doubt and inadequacy, she turned to writing to achieve the solitude she desperately craved. She preferred fantasy to reality and shunned social engagements. She began writing stories and poems in her teens. By the time she was in her twenties, she was selling regularly to magazines such as *The Bystander* and the *Sunday Review*.

She wrote her first novel, *The Loving Spirit*, when she was only twenty-two years old. This romantic family saga earned both critical acclaim and best-seller status. It so impressed a major in the Grenadier Guards that he arranged a meeting with its author. The two soon developed an attachment, and in 1932 du Maurier married the Major Frederick Arthur Montague Browning, whom she called Tommy. He later earned the rank of lieutenant general, became Chancellor of the Exchequer in the household of Princess Elizabeth, and became treasurer to the Duke of Edinburgh. The couple had three children: daughters Flavia and Tessa and son Christian. Browning died in 1965.

In 1943, du Maurier fulfilled a childhood dream and moved into Menabilly, a seventy-room manor house in Cornwall that inspired Manderley, the eerie setting for *Rebecca.* She adored the reputedly haunted house, asserting that it whispered its secrets to her in the solitude of midnight. Never one for social life, she preferred solitary walks in the woods to bustling cities and glittering social gatherings. Family life was seldom serene, with du Maurier's troubled and erratic spirit manifesting itself in frequently problematic ways, while Browning was plagued with psychological problems and poor physical health, both associated with his chronic abuse of alcohol.

A rocky marriage was only one of this writer's torments. Her biographer, Margaret Forster, asserts that du Maurier's stories and novels reflected severe emotional turbulence. Du Maurier had, Forster said, a stifling relationship with her father, a complicated extramarital affair, and a lesbian relationship with actress Gertrude Lawrence. The details of daily life troubled her, and she frequently retreated from family and friends to find solace in make-believe. Twice she faced plagiarism charges and endured the agonies of court hearings as a result of claims that she had stolen the second-wife theme used in *Rebecca.* Although she was acquitted in both instances, the publicity wearied and shamed her, and she grew increasingly reclusive in later life.

Analysis · Du Maurier came naturally by her dramatic bent. Having eschewed a career in acting, she turned instead to writing, creating the settings of her novels as a vivid stage upon which her melodramas could unfold. Most often, she wrote about what she knew: the craggy, tempestuous coasts and climate of Cornwall. With the playwright's flare, she elicited as much suspense from her setting as from her characters and plots. Du Maurier yearned to write light romance, but it was not in her nature. "I may determine to write a gay, light romance. But I go for a walk on a moor and see a twisted tree and a pile of granite stones beside a deep, dark pool, and *Jamaica Inn* is born," she told *Current Biography* in 1940. Du Maurier's readers can only be glad for the writer's solitary walks, for *Jamaica Inn* and the writer's many other haunting novels and stories rank among the finest spine-tingling page-turners ever written. Her books contain passion, jealousy, evil, and murder, with surprise heaped upon surprise.

While du Maurier's works may not probe the depths of human experience, they create worlds and peoples which haunt long after the book is finished. Du Maurier believed in her own brand of predestination, a reincarnation of the human spirit. Evil is inevitable in her view, but not insurmountable. Yet people are, by their very nature, condemned to a vision that exceeds their grasp. Her interest in character took a backseat to her fascination with personality types symbolic of abstract qualities of good and evil. She told Barbara Nichols in an interview for *Ladies Home Journal*: "I am not so much interested in people as in types—types who represent great forces of good or evil. I don't care very much whether John Smith likes Mary Robinson, goes to bed with Jane Brown and then refuses to pay the hotel bill. But I *am* [emphasis in original] passionately interested in human cruelty, human lust, and human avarice—and, of course, their counterparts in the scale of virtue."

Although critics have complained about her melodrama, plot contrivances, shallow characterization, romanticism, sentimentality, vague motivations, and moralizing, such commentary probably misses the point. Du Maurier's unfailing appeal to her readers is fundamental: She tells a good story, and she tells it well. Unsurpassed as a teller of gothic tales tinged with horror or the supernatural, she is worth studying if only for her pacing, which moves from plot twist to plot twist with consummate ease. A romance writer in the best sense of the label, she creates engaging heroines blessed with immense inner strength. Her heroes establish the model for modern romances: dark of complexion, dark of spirit, silent, enigmatic, harboring some unspeakable secret. Her settings evoke the foreboding ambience of Cornwall's precipitous cliffs and misty moors, the perfect backdrop for the dramatic events that so astonish and delight her readers.

Rebecca · Among the most memorable opening lines in English literature is the first sentence of du Maurier's best-known work, *Rebecca*: "Last night I dreamt I went to Manderley again." In a landscape of words, du Maurier takes her readers to Manderley to hear the rustle of leaves, smell the flowers in the garden, luxuriate in the opulence of the estate's drawing room. As ominous waves pound the Cornish coast, the dark tale unfolds. Maxim de Winter, the brooding, detached master of Manderley, marries in haste while abroad and brings his new bride home to Cornwall. The new Mrs. de Winter (whose given name is never revealed) recounts her tale entirely in flashback, compelling the reader to stay with her as the reason for her departure from Manderley is slowly brought to light.

What begins as a Cinderella story—this young girl of modest means swept off her feet by a wealthy, powerful gentleman—soon turns sinister. The narrator is haunted by the lingering influence of Maxim's first wife, Rebecca, who died in a sailing accident. Yet Rebecca's presence is perpetually felt; even the name of Rebecca's boat, *Je reviens* (French for "I return"), suggests its owner will not depart, either in body or in spirit. Manderley itself seems keeper of Rebecca's mystique, with its forbidden halls, haunted rooms, and secret passages accidentally discovered. Beautiful, witty, flirtatious, and strong, Rebecca looms large—her power all the greater, even as a memory, for its contrast to the reticent nature of de Winter's diffident, second bride. The narrator imagines she can hear Rebecca calling to the dogs and Rebecca's evening dress rustling on the stairs. The housekeeper, Mrs. Danvers, exhibits fierce loyalty to the first Mrs. de Winter and sullen contempt for the second. Cruelly, she plots to displace the narrator from Manderley and drive a wedge between its master and mistress.

The ensuing labyrinth of deceptions, betrayals, and revelations spellbinds readers and proves that the new Mrs. de Winter is not without resources. Determined to uncover the truth and break free of Rebecca's legacy, she counters the housekeeper's wicked lies and her husband's silent brooding with a resolute search for the truth. In a surprise ending, she rises whole and victorious, her nightmare ended and justice served. Manderley was great and corrupt, just as was Max's dead wife. Readers find it satisfying to learn that love can be deep and enduring enough to overcome an adversary as powerful as Rebecca.

Jamaica Inn · Critics praised *Jamaica Inn* as a tale nineteenth century adventure writer Robert Louis Stevenson would have been proud to write, and du Maurier admitted it was similar to—and inspired by—*Treasure Island.* The rain-swept Cornish coast in raw

November portends danger, but orphan Mary Yellan is determined to keep the promise she made to her dying mother, to make her home with her victimized Aunt Patience and brutish Uncle Joss. Working at the dilapidated Jamaica Inn, where thieves and smugglers come to divide their spoils and pirates plot their next raids, Mary discovers a secret about her father's death. Alone and afraid, Mary feels a sexual (although not romantic) attraction to Jem Merlyn, Joss's younger brother and a domineering ruffian not above violence. In the background lurks the mysterious vicar of Altarnum, who hides a few secrets of his own. With its twisted motives, midnight crimes, smugglers, and secrets, this is du Maurier at her best. Although depicting a rather pessimistic view of the plight of women as helpless and subservient, the fast-paced adventure gains fresh popularity with each new generation of readers who discover it.

The House on the Strand · In du Maurier's penultimate novel, *The House on the Strand,* the narrator Dick (the last among five du Maurier books featuring a male protagonist) travels back to fourteenth century England, his journeys made possible by an experimental drug concocted by his scientist friend and mentor, Magnus. A stereotypic "nice guy," Dick marries an American who is already mother to two sons. Dick is no fan of women (including his wife), judging the feminine point of view trivial and restrictive, but he changes his mind when he becomes entranced with Isolda, a woman of the fourteenth century saddled with a faithless husband. Dick develops as a pathetic character who longs for perceived glories of the past but can find no fulfillment in any epoch, past or present. Combining historical fact with psychological analysis, the book paints the same haunting atmosphere so apparent in du Maurier's earlier works, this time using the Kilmarth house in Cornwall and its rich history as both setting and theme. Dick's unwillingness to be pulled away from his time travels reflects du Maurier's own total immersion in her fantasy worlds. When writing, she lost herself in the lives of her characters, finding real life little more than a distraction and an annoyance.

Faith Hickman Brynie

Other major works

SHORT FICTION: *Come Wind, Come Weather,* 1940; *Happy Christmas,* 1940; *The Apple Tree,* 1952; *Kiss Me Again, Stranger,* 1952; *Early Stories,* 1955; *The Breaking Point,* 1959; *The Treasury of du Maurier Short Stories,* 1959; *Not After Midnight,* 1971; *Echoes from the Macabre,* 1976; *The Rendezvous and Other Stories,* 1980; *Classics from the Macabre,* 1987.

PLAYS: *The Years Between,* pb. 1945; *September Tide,* pb. 1949.

NONFICTION: *Gerald: A Portrait,* 1934; *The du Mauriers,* 1937; *Young George du Maurier: A Selection of His Letters, 1860-67,* 1951; *The Infernal World of Branwell Brontë,* 1960; *Vanishing Cornwall,* 1967; *Golden Lads: Anthony Bacon, Francis and their Friends,* 1975; *The Winding Stair: Francis Bacon, His Rise and Fall,* 1976; *Growing Pains: The Shaping of a Writer,* 1977 (pb. in U.S. as *Myself When Young: The Shaping of a Writer,* 1977); *The Rebecca Notebook and Other Memories,* 1980; *Letters from Menabilly: Portrait of a Friendship,* 1994 (Oriel Mallet, editor).

Bibliography
Block, Maxine, ed. *Current Biography: Who's News and Why: 1940.* New York: H. W. Wilson, 1940: 262-264. Up close and personal with the novelist at the beginning of her career, including insights into her involvement with the war effort.

Breit, H. "Talk with Lady Browning." *New York Times Book Review*, March 16, 1952, p. 25. A glimpse into the character of du Maurier in her maturity.

Cook, Judith. *Daphne: A Portrait of Daphne du Maurier.* London: Bantam Books, 1991. Good insights into the woman and the author.

Du Maurier, Daphne. *Letters from Menabilly: Portrait of a Friendship.* Edited by Oriel Malet. New York: M. Evans, 1994. A selection of Du Maurier's correspondence during the middle part of her life.

Forster, Margaret. *Daphne du Maurier: The Secret Life of the Renowned Storyteller.* New York: Doubleday, 1993. A candid, meticulous, and riveting biography, prepared with cooperation of the du Maurier family after du Maurier's death.

Horner, Avril, and Sue Zlosnik. *Daphne du Maurier: Writing, Identity and the Gothic Imagination.* New York: St. Martin's Press, 1998. An evaluation of du Maurier's fiction from historical, cultural, geographic, and female gothic literary perspectives.

Kelly, Richard Michael. *Daphne du Maurier.* Boston: Twayne, 1987. A solid introduction to the author's works. Includes index and bibliography.

Leng, Flavia. *Daphne du Maurier: A Daughter's Memoir.* Edinburgh: Mainstream, 1994. A good biography of du Maurier written by her daughter.

Lawrence Durrell

Born: Julundur, India; February 27, 1912
Died: Sommières, France; November 7, 1990

Principal long fiction · *Pied Piper of Lovers*, 1935; *Panic Spring*, 1937 (as Charles Norden); *The Black Book*, 1938; *Cefalû*, 1947 (republished as *The Dark Labyrinth*, 1958); *Justine*, 1957; *Balthazar*, 1958; *Mountolive*, 1958; *Clea*, 1960; *The Alexandria Quartet*, 1962 (includes previous 4 novels); *Tunc*, 1968; *Nunquam*, 1970; *Monsieur: Or, The Prince of Darkness*, 1974; *Livia: Or, Buried Alive*, 1978; *Constance: Or, Solitary Practices*, 1981; *Sebastian: Or, Ruling Passions*, 1983; *Quinx: Or, The Ripper's Tale*, 1985; *The Avignon Quintet*, 1992 (includes previous 5 novels).

Other literary forms · Lawrence Durrell was a prolific writer in many genres. As a successful poet, he published many books, including *Ten Poems* (1932); *Bromo Bombastes* (1933); *Transition: Poems* (1934); *A Private Country* (1943); *Cities, Plains, and People* (1946); *On Seeming to Presume* (1948); *Deus Loci* (1950); *The Tree of Idleness and Other Poems* (1955); *Private Drafts* (1955); *Selected Poems* (1956); *The Ikons and Other Poems* (1966); *The Red Limbo Lingo* (1971); *Vega and Other Poems* (1973); and *Collected Poems 1931-1974* (1980). He wrote three plays in verse, *Sappho* (pr. 1950), *An Irish Faustus* (pb. 1963), and *Acte* (pr. 1964). He also published travel books such as *Prospero's Cell* (1945), *Reflections on a Marine Venus* (1953), *Bitter Lemons* (1957), *Sicilian Carousel* (1977), and *The Greek Islands* (1978). His essays and letters were published in *A Key to Modern British Poetry* (1952), *Art and Outrage* (1959), *Lawrence Durrell and Henry Miller: A Private Correspondence* (1963, George Wickes, editor), and *Spirit of Place* (1969, Alan G. Thomas, editor). His publisher apparently persuaded him to identify one of his books, *White Eagles over Serbia* (1957), as being "for juveniles." He translated Greek poetry by C. P. Cavafy, George Seferis, and others, as well as *The Curious History of Pope Joan* (1954; revised as *Pope Joan: A Romantic Biography*, 1960) by Emmanuel Royidis. He published widely in periodicals as various as *Mademoiselle*, *Quarterly Review of Literature*, *New Statesman*, *T'ien Hsia Monthly of Shanghai* and *Réalités*, and he edited anthologies of poetry and collections of letters. He also spent some time working on the screenplay for the 1963 film *Cleopatra*. His last book, a nonfiction work entitled *Caesar's Vast Ghost: A Portrait of Provence*, appeared in 1990.

Achievements · Although Durrell was highly respected as a poet and travel writer, it is generally agreed that his greatest accomplishments were his *The Alexandria Quartet* and *The Avignon Quintet*. There is little doubt that Durrell's place in twentieth century literature rests on these extraordinary works. Throughout his career, Durrell had a sensuous, ornate, and lyrical style that sometimes degenerated into overwriting–a tendency to which he freely admitted. In his best books, however, the style reflected his Mediterranean surroundings of Greece, Egypt, or Provence, France. Influenced by Henry Miller but by no means an imitator of him, Durrell appealed to so-called literary tastes beginning with *The Black Book*. Yet the popularity of *The Alexandria Quartet* seems to be the result of the blend of an exceptional style with an exotic setting and characters, wit, and exciting plot elements such as murder, conspiracy, and unrequited love. *The Avignon Quintet* has these same elements and is no less a literary triumph for its lack of public acclaim.

Biography · Lawrence George Durrell was born in Julundur, India, on February 27, 1912, to Lawrence Samuel Durrell, an English engineer who built the Tata Iron and Steel Works, and Louise Florence "Dixie" Durrell, of Irish heritage. Both his parents' families had been in India for some time. When the boy was very young, the Durrells moved to Kurseong, near the Himalayas, so that the elder Durrell could accept a three-year contract on a mountain railway to Darjeeling. The sight of the mountains made a strong impression on the boy, so much so that he once described his childhood in a letter to Henry Miller as "a brief dream of Tibet." While in Darjeeling, he began his education at the College of St. Joseph and received the first encouragement for his writing from a Belgian priest, Father Joseph De Guylder.

At twelve, Durrell was sent to England with his brother Leslie "to get the hall-mark," as his father said, of a public school education. He attended St. Olave's and St. Saviour's Grammar School, where he developed his lifelong interest in Elizabe-than writers, and later entered St. Edmund's School in Canterbury. Despite several attempts, he was never admitted to Cambridge University and would later write of his life in England, "That mean shabby little island . . . wrung my guts out of me and tried to destroy anything singular and unique in me."

The death of his father left Durrell with a small income, which he used to move to Bloomsbury in order to become a writer. During his Bloomsbury years, Durrell held a number of odd jobs, including jazz pianist and composer, race-car driver, and real-estate agent. During this period, he also met his first wife, Nancy Myers, a student at the Slade School, with whom he ran a photo studio for a time. At nineteen, he met John Gawsworth in a café after fleeing from an upstairs window during a police raid on the Blue Peter Night Club, where Durrell was playing piano. Awed by Gaws-worth's personal knowledge of many famous authors, he became his friend, and though they often disagreed on literary matters—Gawsworth was a very conservative poet who admired the literature of the 1890's and had little respect for W. H. Auden and Stephen Spender—Gawsworth helped him to get his first poems published. *Ten Poems* was published in 1932 under the pseudonym "Gaffer Peeslake" by Caduceus Press, founded by Durrell, his wife, and George Wilkinson.

Durrell began his first novel, *Pied Piper of Lovers*, while he and Nancy lived for a year in a Sussex cottage with George and Pam Wilkinson. After the Wilkinsons immigrated to Corfu, Greece, Durrell lived with his mother, sister, and two brothers in Bournemouth, where they received glowing letters from the Wilkinsons. Excited by the idea of the warm climate, Durrell left his novel under consideration at Cassell's and departed for Corfu. When the rest of his family followed a few weeks later, they bore the news that the book had been accepted, confirming Durrell in his notion to take up writing as a profession, though very few copies of the book would sell. The residence in Corfu had two important results for him. First, it began his long associa-tion with Greece, its poetry, and language; and second, he discovered *Tropic of Cancer* (1934) by Henry Miller.

The latter was probably the most significant development in the young Durrell's career. He wrote a letter of praise to Miller, who responded warmly, saying that the letter was the most intelligent he had yet received from a Briton about his book. By 1936, Durrell was clearly under the influence of Miller, apologizing for his second novel and engrossed in writing *The Black Book*. The next year, Durrell announced that he was the "first writer to be fertilized by H. M." and sent *The Black Book* to Miller, who paused in the writing of *Tropic of Capricorn* (1939) to type out (with Anaïs Nin) three copies to be sent to Herbert Read, T. S. Eliot, and Jack Kahane. Kahane published it in Paris, and Eliot endorsed it as "the first piece of work by a new English writer to give me any hope for the future of prose fiction." Durrell visited Paris, and Miller later visited Corfu, solidifying a friendship which would last until the latter's death, despite Durrell's forthright, often scathing, reviews of Miller's later works.

The war interrupted Durrell's idyllic life in Corfu. He moved to Athens in 1940, where he worked for the British Embassy, and then was posted to the Institute of English Studies in Kalamata. While in Athens he met George Katsimbalis and George Seferiades ("Seferis"), both of whose works he would later translate. In 1941, he was forced to escape the Nazi invasion with Nancy and their daughter Penelope Berengaria in an old caïque bound for Crete. From Crete, they went on to Egypt, where Durrell served as a foreign press service officer for the British Information Service. Nancy and Penelope spent the war in Palestine, and the marriage deteriorated, resulting in a divorce in 1947, when Durrell married Eve Cohen, a dark-eyed Alexandrian woman who may have partly inspired the character of Justine.

Happy to escape from Egypt, Durrell lived for a time on Rhodes, then in Argentina and Yugoslavia, disliking both places. In the early 1950's, he left Yugoslavia for Cyprus, where he bought a home, taught school, and, during the developing civil war, became Public Relations Officer for the British government. His second marriage deteriorated early in his stay on Cyprus, but by 1956, he had completed *Justine*, the first novel of *The Alexandria Quartet*. Late that year, he moved on to Dorset with Claude-Marie Vincenden, later to become his third wife, where he worked on *Bitter Lemons*, a book drawing on his experiences in Cyprus.

Financially exhausted, but unable to live away from the Mediterranean area for very long, Durrell and Claude began to look for a home in the Midi. Virtually overnight, he became a world-renowned author when *Justine*, *Bitter Lemons*, *White Eagles over Serbia*, and *Esprit de Corps* were published in 1957. He was translated into numerous foreign languages and could devote his entire time to writing. With his favored mode of work being intense days of some fourteen hours of writing, he allegedly produced *Justine* in four months, *Balthazar* in six weeks, *Mountolive* in twelve weeks, and *Clea* in eight.

For thirty years or so, Durrell lived a settled life in Provence, with occasional travel. On March 27, 1961, he and Claude were married, and in 1966, they moved into a larger house in Sommieres to accommodate their guests, Claude's children by a previous marriage, Penelope, and their daughter Sappho-Jane. After a period of declining health, Claude died on New Year's Day, 1967. In 1973, Durrell married Ghislaine de Boysson, but by 1986 his fourth marriage was finished. The five novels of *The Avignon Quintet* appeared between 1974 and 1985 to mixed reviews, but there is no question that this thirteen-hundred-page sequence is a tour de force of the first order.

Lawrence Durrell died on November 7, 1990, at the age of seventy-eight in his home in Provence. His literary reputation, which rests chiefly on *The Alexandria Quartet*, is higher on the Continent and in the United States than in Great Britain.

Analysis · Lawrence Durrell's first novel, *Pied Piper of Lovers*, is a story of life among the bohemians at Bloomsbury. It was sufficiently dismal to provoke a publisher to advise him to offer *Panic Spring* under the pseudonym of Charles Norden, so that the latter, a slightly better book, would not be associated with its predecessor. *Panic Spring* has been described as being influenced by, even imitative of, the works of Aldous Huxley; even as it was published, Durrell was writing an apology to Henry Miller for his "new and facile novel." In essence, Durrell's early career was characterized by a search for a paradigm or form for his talent, a search that ended with his discovery of *Tropic of Cancer.*

The Black Book · The impact of Miller's novel on the young Durrell was enormous. A comparison of his earlier works with his third novel, *The Black Book*, reveals a dramatic transformation. His creative impulses have been freed. As he described it in 1959, *The Black Book* is "a two-fisted attack on literature by a young man in the thirties," taking its aggressive intent from Miller's all-out assault on the literary establishment. The narrator, Lawrence Lucifer, recounts his experiences in a seedy London hotel from the perspective of his life on Corfu. In the hotel, he finds the diary of Herbert Gregory, which overlaps with his own experiences. There are numerous other characters and much obscurity as to the details of time and event. There is a great deal of erotic content, both homosexual and heterosexual, as the characters betray and cuckold one another. The novel's themes are revealed not through a carefully constructed plot but through a series of scenes, reminiscences, and vignettes.

Durrell later wrote in the 1959 introduction to the second edition of *The Black Book*:

> With all its imperfections lying heavy on my head, I can't help being attached to it because in the writing of it I first heard the sound of my own voice, lame and halting, perhaps, but nevertheless my very own.

In it, the reader finds the first cry of Durrell's literary voice, his exotic characters, his sensual and sensuous prose, and his experiments with narrative time. When it was published, T. S. Eliot (among others) was perspicacious enough to recognize the voice of a major new talent. Had Durrell ended his career with *The Black Book*, it would most likely be forgotten. Burdened with an excessively baroque style, it is of interest chiefly because of its place in his career.

The Dark Labyrinth · *Cefalû*, Durrell's next novel (reissued as *The Dark Labyrinth* after *Justine* had assured Durrell a place in twentieth century literature), can be viewed in much the same way as *The Black Book.* In it, he seems to be discovering himself, experimenting, finding the form and style which would achieve maturity in *The Alexandria Quartet.* One also sees a tugging away from Miller's influence—only a few years later, Durrell would write a scathing indictment of Miller's *Sexus* (1949)—and a reversion to the influence of Aldous Huxley that had been so apparent in *Panic Spring.* *The Dark Labyrinth* has extensive allegorical elements, reminiscent of Huxley: The characters are trapped in a labyrinth in Crete, and each finds in the maze that for which he or she has been looking. The book was written quickly—which is not unusual for Durrell—and seems rather derivative in structure, though the writing itself often attains his characteristic brilliance.

The Alexandria Quartet · The four novels which compose *The Alexandria Quartet* are collectively one of the greatest achievements in the modern novel. Like many modern works, *The Alexandria Quartet* often seems to be about the creation of fiction. Darley, the narrator of *Justine* and *Balthazar*, is a novelist, as are two other characters. Diversity in point of view is regularly exploited through the use of diaries, letters, and recounted experiences. Truth becomes subjective and layered. The characters' knowledge is limited to what they perceive, and numerous questions are left unanswered.

The Alexandria Quartet is also an examination of love in the modern world as the characters pass through convoluted interrelationships. Sex and love, like art, become ways of glimpsing underlying truths, of developing one's knowledge of reality. Durrell has also stated that *The Alexandria Quartet* consists of four parts because he was attempting to produce a novelistic version of Albert Einstein's universe. Relativity (or subjectivity) thus appears as a justification for the exploitation of point of view, for the questionable reliability of narrators, and for an exploration of time and memory. Durrell, however, is careful, despite the modern and postmodern objectives of *The Alexandria Quartet*, to hang all the theory on a generous structure of narrative. There are a number of stories of betrayal, murder, love, devotion, and tragedy intertwined, and although they are elusive, they make the tetralogy accessible in a way that many "experimental" works are not, without compromising the artistic integrity of the work.

Finally, Durrell's extraordinary prose, his poetic, lyrical, and erotic use of language, elevates *The Alexandria Quartet* above most modern fiction, although this talent was manifest as early as *The Black Book*, provoking Miller to write "You are *the* master of the English language." Some critics have regarded Durrell's prose as excessive, overdone, a flamboyant collection of purple clichés and Victorian decadence. Yet, in each of his major works, and especially in *The Alexandria Quartet*, it is difficult to imagine a prose style without his deliberate rhythms and cadences that would be suitable to his themes and extraordinary settings.

The chief characters of *The Alexandria Quartet* may be loosely based upon people Durrell had known. Darley has a number of characteristics in common with the author: They are both novelists; three women (up to the writing of the novel) have played a major part in both their lives; and they have held similar jobs. Other resemblances between other characters and certain "real people" might be noted, but these would only contribute to the thematic question of how reality is transformed by experience, recollection, and novelization. The whole question adds another layer to the multiple levels among which the tetralogy moves.

Justine is one of the most haunting characters in the tetralogy. Born in Alexandria, she is a dark, beautiful Jewess with an intense sexuality and an obscure background. She runs the gamut of sexual pleasure and is seen from a variety of viewpoints, including the romanticized memories of Darley's love, the cynical stance of the novelist Pursewarden, and the *roman à clef* of her first husband, Arnauti. Though not really in love with Nessim Hosnani, a Copt, she marries the devoted Egyptian on the condition that he help her find her kidnapped child. Nessim becomes involved in gunrunning into Palestine because of his hatred of the English. Narouz–Nessim's harelipped, violent, and earthy brother–becomes a force in the second and third volumes of the tetralogy. Balthazar, a physician, gives his name to the second volume, which he also partly narrates, though he is present throughout the books. A mystic homosexual, he seems to know most of the other characters' secrets, and his illuminations of Darley's perceptions provide new insights into the situations. Mountolive is a diplomat who has an affair with Leila Hosnani, Nessim's mother, who later contracts smallpox, loses her beauty, and engages in a lengthy correspondence with Mountolive, who falls in love with Pursewarden's blind sister, Liza.

Alexandria, with its convoluted intrigues, gradually wears away the English confidence of the diplomat as Nessim and others betray him as he investigates the circumstances of Pursewarden's suicide. Clea is a superstitious artist, beloved of Narouz, lover of Justine, Dr. Amaril, and eventually, Darley. With blonde hair and blue eyes, Clea's northern European beauty contrasts with Justine's Mediterranean beauty.

Even this short summary of the characters reveals the complexity of the story line of *The Alexandria Quartet*, and there are even more characters who play important roles: Scobie, the transvestite who becomes a saint; Cohen, who plots to liberate Palestine; Dr. Amaril, who loves the noseless Semira; Mnemjian, the dwarf barber; Pombal, involved in espionage; Capodistria of the great sexual prowess; and Toto de Brunel, who is murdered with a hatpin, probably by mistake. A complete list of characters would number more than one hundred.

Alexandria itself has often been discussed as playing a characterlike role in the tetralogy. Like James Joyce's Dublin, Marcel Proust's Paris, and William Faulkner's Yoknapatawpha County, the landscape exhibits a crucial influence upon the characters, determining their behavior. Sometimes characters seem to be mere expressions of some element of the landscape, appearing and disappearing into the textures of Alexandrian life, just as the "reality" of Scobie is absorbed into the legend of "El Scob." Alexandria is mysterious, full of deception and treachery. There are always murderous undercurrents, such as when Justine suspects Nessim's plans to kill Darley at the duck shoot and when Toto is murdered at the masked ball, probably in Justine's place. Even Narouz's frustration at being unable to satisfy his love for Clea seems to explode out of his harpoon gun after his death, the accident nearly causing her to drown when her hand is staked to a sunken ship.

A brief discussion of *The Alexandria Quartet* can hardly do justice to the complexity of the work. With no ostensible intention of making a moral statement, Durrell's foremost intention was the creation of a work of art which reflected the relativistic sensibility of the modern world, yet he carefully maintained an absorbing plot to serve as a skeleton on which to flesh out his musings on love, sex, art, writing, memory, and time. Although Durrell celebrates life in a way many contemporary artists do not, *The Alexandria Quartet* also reveals ambiguities and darknesses. The tetralogy cannot be reduced to story, theme, or message. Its lush writing becomes a sensory experience of a world with overlapping, often conflicting layers of reality.

Tunc* and *Nunquam · *Tunc* and *Nunquam*, the pair of novels which followed *The Alexandria Quartet*, have much in common with the tetralogy, despite the great difference in subject matter. Felix Charlock invents a computer, named Abel, which can recall or predict virtually anything. Charlock soon finds himself under contract to a huge conglomerate headed by Julian Merlin, a mysterious character who seems to control, through business connections, most of the people in the world. To join Merlin is to be assured of comfort but also to give up individual freedom. *Tunc* and *Nunquam* contain Durrell's usually rich selection of characters, including the neurotic Benedicta, Julian's sister; Iolanthe, a prostitute-become-film-star; and Caradoc, a wordplaying architect.

In style, *Tunc* and *Nunquam* are similar to *The Alexandria Quartet*, despite the science-fiction *mise-en-scène*. When Merlin creates a robotic duplicate of Iolanthe, which can hallucinate eating and other bodily functions even though it does not do these things, Charlock comes to identify with the robot's quest for freedom, seeing in it his own struggle to remain an individual despite his absorption into Merlin's world. This thematic concern with individual freedom in the contemporary world does not play a large part in *The Alexandria Quartet*, but *Tunc* and *Nunquam* exhibit the tetralogy's themes of time, space, art, love, and sex, as well as a masterful use of language.

The Avignon Quintet · With the five novels that constitute *The Avignon Quintet* (*Monsieur: Or, The Prince of Darkness*; *Livia: Or, Buried Alive*; *Constance: Or, Solitary Practices*; *Sebastian: Or, Ruling Passions*; and *Quinx: Or, The Ripper's Tale*), Durrell recapitulates the themes of a lifetime with self-conscious exuberance, like a magician putting on his show for the last time. Shifts of viewpoint are kaleidoscopic in effect: bright, dazzling, patterned, but ambiguous as to meaning. He presents two novelists, Aubrey Blanford and Robin Sutcliffe, who explore the theme of novel writing to a fare-thee-well. Durrell creates two different fates for each of these characters, as if his world suddenly split in two and his personae lived out opposing potentialities. Duality is rife in *The Avignon Quintet*, as one can see from the double titles of each novel.

There is one underlying idea, however, that permeates everything: entropy, the tendency for orderly systems to dissolve in anarchy and death. Taking the period from 1938 to 1945, with the whole of World War II occurring in *Constance*, Durrell shows entropy at work in Europe under the impact of Nazism, entropy in the failure of Western rationalism to stem the "deathdrift" of society or individuals, and entropy in the breakdown of personality in the forms of insanity and suicide. Against entropy, Durrell poses the forces of love and art. Yet even these succumb to chaos and death.

As an author, Durrell is like the "Lord of Misrule," the comic king of festival, in *The Avignon Quintet*. His world is one in which social disorder reigns amid drinking and feasting. In fact, *The Avignon Quintet* describes celebrations and banquets frequently, often at the end of a novel, and often with something sinister at their cores. Durrell's comic tone and exuberance just barely conceal a deeply pessimistic outlook, like gallows humor.

The Provence town of Avignon is the geographical and spiritual center of the quintet. With its dual legacy, very much present in these novels, of having been the center of Catholicism and of the heretical Knights Templar in the Middle Ages, Avignon represents the opposing pulls of reason and mysticism, West and East, and life and death on the characters. Egypt stands for the East, for Gnostic mysticism (linked with the Templar heresy), and for death throughout *The Avignon Quintet*. Geneva is the site of safety and reason during World War II, an outpost of civilized Western values in an era turned savage and suicidal. Each locale—Avignon, Egypt, and Geneva—has its own distinct flavor and ambiguity, and each is fully realized artistically. Durrell's unique descriptive prose and his use of vignette and narrative event are matchless in creating the feel of place.

Most of the main characters are on a quest of sorts: some for love (Blanford, a novelist; Constance, a psychoanalyst; Chatto, a consul), some for sexual adventure (Livia, Prince Hassad), some for wealth (Lord Galen, Smirgel), some for revenge (Quatrefages, Mnemidis), and some for a sacrificial death at the hands of a Gnostic cult (Piers de Nogaret, Sebastian Affad). Several of these private quests are subsumed under one last, collective quest: the search for the lost Templar treasure, hidden centuries ago in a labyrinth of caves near the Roman aqueduct at Avignon, caves mined with explosives by Austrian sappers in the closing days of World War II. On a Friday the 13th, Blanford and Constance enter the caves, following a group of intoxicated revelers from a banquet at which Death has just appeared. The inconclusive end of this quest for treasure hints strongly that some poor fool set off the dynamite, sending *The Avignon Quintet* into the silence of extinction.

In the end, three aspects of life matter to Durrell: love as the means to truth, art as the mirror of truth, and a joyful acceptance of both life and art as the final consummation of truth. By facing down entropy, his own and his world's, Durrell achieved a rare and disturbing kind of wisdom.

J. Madison Davis

Other major works

SHORT FICTION: *Esprit de Corps: Sketches from Diplomatic Life*, 1957; *Stiff Upper Lip: Life Among the Diplomats*, 1958; *Sauve qui peut*, 1966; *The Best of Antrobus*, 1974; *Antrobus Complete*, 1985.

PLAYS: *Sappho*, pr. 1950; *An Irish Faustus*, pb. 1963; *Acte*, pr. 1964.

POETRY: *Quaint Fragment: Poems Written Between the Ages of Sixteen and Nineteen*, 1931; *Ten Poems*, 1932; *Bromo Bombastes*, 1933; *Transition: Poems*, 1934; *Proems: An Anthology of Poems*, 1938 (with others); *A Private Country*, 1943; *Cities, Plains, and People*, 1946; *Six Poems from the Greek of Sekilianos and Seferis*, 1946 (translation); *The King of Asine and Other Poems*, 1948 (translation of George Seferis); *On Seeming to Presume*, 1948; *Deus Loci*, 1950; *Private Drafts*, 1955; *The Tree of Idleness and Other Poems*, 1955; *Selected Poems*, 1956; *Collected Poems*, 1960; *Penguin Modern Poets 1*, 1962 (with Elizabeth Jennings and R. S. Thomas); *Beccaficio Le Becfigue*, 1963 (English; includes French translation by F. J. Temple); *Selected Poems 1935-63*, 1964; *The Ikons and Other Poems*, 1966; *The Red Limbo Lingo: A Poetry Notebook for 1968-70*, 1971; *On the Suchness of the Old Boy*, 1972; *Vega and Other Poems*, 1973; *Collected Poems 1931-1974*, 1980.

NONFICTION: *Prospero's Cell*, 1945; *A Landmark Gone*, 1949; *A Key to Modern British Poetry*, 1952; *Reflections on a Marine Venus*, 1953; *The Curious History of Pope Joan*, 1954 (translation, revised as *Pope Joan: A Personal Biography*, 1960); *Bitter Lemons*, 1957; *Art and Outrage*, 1959; *Lawrence Durrell and Henry Miller: A Private Correspondence*, 1963 (George Wickes, editor); *Spirit of Place: Letters and Essays on Travel*, 1969 (Alan G. Thomas, editor); *The Big Supposer: Dialogues with Marc Alyn/Lawrence Durrell*, 1973; *Sicilian Carousel*, 1977; *The Greek Islands*, 1978; *Literary Lifelines: The Richard Aldington-Lawrence Durrell Correspondence*, 1981; *The Durrell-Miller Letters, 1935-1980*, 1988; *Caesar's Vast Ghost: A Portrait of Provence*, 1990; *Lawrence Durrell: Conversations*, 1998 (Earl G. Ingersoll, editor).

CHILDREN'S LITERATURE: *White Eagles over Serbia*, 1957.

Bibliography

Adams, Robert M. *After Joyce: Studies in Fiction After "Ulysses."* New York: Oxford University Press, 1977. A look at modern and postmodern fiction, tracing James Joyce's influence from the 1920's through the mid-1970's. A bit sketchy and patronizing on Durrell.

Bowker, Gordon. *Through the Dark Labyrinth: A Biography of Lawrence Durrell.* London: Sinclair-Stevenson, 1996. A good biography of Durrell. Includes bibliographical references and an index.

Fraser, George S. *Lawrence Durrell.* London: Longman, 1970. A perceptive pamphlet-length study of Durrell's major literary output up to 1970, tracing the themes and plot of *The Alexandria Quartet* with admirable clarity. Contains a select bibliography.

Friedman, Alan W., ed. *Critical Essays on Lawrence Durrell.* Boston: G. K. Hall, 1987. A stimulating collection covering many aspects of Durrell's work. Concentrates on his important fiction, including *The Avignon Quintet*.

Kaczvinsky, Donald P. *Lawrence Durrell's Major Novels: Or, The Kingdom of the Imagination.* London: Associated University Presses, 1997. An excellent discussion of Durrell's seminal works.

MacNiven, Ian. *Lawrence Durrell: A Biography.* London: Faber and Faber, 1998. Written with Durrell's cooperation, MacNiven has extraordinary access to both his subject and his papers (including notebooks and letters). MacNiven's interviews with Durrell's friends and lovers are integrated into a probing look at the sources of his writing. Includes illustrations, chronology, family tree, and notes.

Moore, Harry T., ed. *The World of Lawrence Durrell.* Carbondale: Southern Illinois University Press, 1964. A landmark collection of early critical essays on Durrell by eminent scholars and writers, a reminiscence by Henry Miller, and letters to and from Durrell.

Pinchin, Jane LaGoudis. *Alexandria Still: Forster, Durrell, and Cavafy.* Princeton, N.J.: Princeton University Press, 1976. A study of how a seedy Egyptian port was transformed by three writers of genius, and by Durrell in particular, into a place of imagination, mystery, and romance. Includes a fine bibliography.

Weigel, John A. *Lawrence Durrell: Revised Edition.* Boston: Twayne, 1989. Weigel updates his 1965 edition to cover both the work Durrell produced after 1965 and the criticism of his work after that date. Includes chronology, notes, and annotated bibliography.

Maria Edgeworth

Born: Black Bourton, England; January 1, 1767
Died: Edgeworthstown, Ireland; May 22, 1849

Principal long fiction · *Castle Rackrent*, 1800; *Belinda*, 1801; *Leonora*, 1806; *Ennui*, 1809; *The Absentee*, 1812; *Vivian*, 1812; *Patronage*, 1814; *Harrington*, 1817; *Ormond*, 1817; *Helen*, 1834.

Other literary forms · Like a number of late eighteenth century and early nineteenth century authors, Maria Edgeworth did not intend to become a novelist but began writing extended prose fiction as an outgrowth of other kinds of literary production. Her first works were children's tales, usually short and always with a clear and forcefully advanced didactic thesis—a few titles suggest the nature of the themes: "Lazy Laurence," "Waste Not, Want Not," "Forgive and Forget." Many of these stories were assembled under the titles *The Parent's Assistant: Or, Stories for Children* (1796, 1800) and *Moral Tales for Young People* (1801), the first of which encompassed six volumes, while the second filled five volumes.

These tales were written largely at the behest of Edgeworth's father, Richard Lovell Edgeworth, who was a deeply committed moralist and is still considered a notable figure in the history of education in England and Ireland. Both father and daughter collaborated on many of the stories, as they did on most of what Maria Edgeworth wrote. As a sort of commentary on the short fictions and certainly as an adjunct to them, the essays on education collected in *Essays on Practical Education* (1798) were designed to advance the liberal but moralistic theories on child rearing that the elder Edgeworth had imbibed in part from Jean-Jacques Rousseau and had transmitted to his daughter. Richard Edgeworth's credentials for such a piece of writing were perhaps enhanced by the fact that he fathered no fewer than twenty-two children with four wives.

Apart from further essays (again, chiefly written either in collaboration with her father or under his watchful eye) on education, morals, Ireland, and culture, Edgeworth's primary emphasis was on fiction, usually of novel length (her "novels" range in length from the quite short *Castle Rackrent*, merely one hundred pages, to *Belinda*, which extends to almost five hundred pages). The only other form she attempted—one in which, like many nineteenth century authors, she had no publishing success—was the drama. The plays were composed essentially for the pleasure of the family, as were the first drafts of the majority of the fictions; the volume containing the best of them, *Comic Dramas in Three Acts* (1817), is now almost universally unread.

Achievements · During her long lifetime, Edgeworth helped to make possible the Victorian novel. Reared with a rich background in the high achievements of Henry Fielding, Samuel Richardson, and Tobias Smollett, she began to write at a time when female novelists were just beginning to be accepted; a few of them, such as Fanny Burney and Elizabeth Inchbald, managed to attain some popularity. The novel of manners was the prevailing genre produced by these "lady writers." It had affinities with the lachrymose novel of sensibility (the classic example of which, *The Man of*

Feeling, was penned in 1771 by a man, Henry Mackenzie), and the tight focus and excessively delicate feelings exhibited in this form limited its appeal and artistic possibilities. It fell to Jane Austen to instill clever and penetrating satire, along with a much greater sense of realism in regard to human behavior, and to Maria Edgeworth to extend its bounds of character depiction, to include persons of the lower classes, and to broaden its range: Men are seen at the hunt, in private conference, and in all manner of vigorous activity unknown in Austen's fiction.

Edgeworth is, of course, bound to be compared with Austen, to the former's derogation; there can be no doubt that the latter is the greater novelist, from an artistic standpoint. This judgment should not blind the reader to Edgeworth's accomplishment. As P. N. Newby observes in *Maria Edgeworth* (1950), though "Jane Austen was so much the better novelist," yet "Maria Edgeworth may be the more important." Her significance rests chiefly on two achievements: She widened the scope of the "female" novel (the emphasis on female sensibility in her work is considerably less than in Austen's novels, though it can be detected); and, as Newby remarks, in her careful and detailed treatment of Ireland and its people, she "gave dignity to the regional subject and made the regional novel possible." Today, readers tend to take for granted the insightful historical works of, for example, Sir Walter Scott; they often do not realize that, had it not been for Edgeworth, Scott might not have attempted the monumental effort that he began in *Waverly* (1814), in whose preface he gives Edgeworth full credit for inspiring him to essay the regional fiction in which his work became a landmark. It has also been claimed that such disparate figures as Stendhal and Ivan Turgenev were influenced by Edgeworth's sympathetic treatment of peasants. Some critics and literary historians have gone so far as to claim for her the title of the first intelligent sociological novelist in English literature. More than any author up to her time, Edgeworth revealed human beings as related to, and partially formed by, their environment.

Biography · January 1, 1767, is usually accepted as the birth date of Maria Edgeworth; but, in *Maria Edgeworth: A Literary Biography* (1972), Marilyn Butler asserts that Maria herself "seems to have considered 1768 correct, and the Black Bourton records on the whole support her." This is one of the few uncertainties in a life dedicated to family, friends, and literature. Edgeworth was born in England, the child of Richard Lovell Edgeworth (an Anglo-Irish gentleman with extensive estates in County Longford, about sixty miles from Dublin) and his first wife, Anna Maria Elers Edgeworth, who died when Maria was five years old. By all accounts, Maria got along well with her three siblings, two sisters and a brother (another child died before she was born), and with her father's next three wives and her seventeen half brothers and half sisters, most of whom she helped to rear. The general harmony in the Edgeworth household may be seen as all the more remarkable when one considers that Richard Edgeworth's last wife, Frances Anne Beaufort Edgeworth (with whose family Maria became quite friendly), was a year or two younger than Maria.

Much of this impressive concord can be credited to Richard Lovell Edgeworth, a man of enormous confidence and personal force. He took the not untypical eighteenth century view that, as the father in the household, he was the lord and master in a literal sense. Fortunately, he was a benevolent master. Although he believed firmly that he knew what was best for all his wives and children, what he believed to be best was their relatively free development, confined only by his sense of what was morally right and socially proper. Maria evidently accepted her father's guidance to the point of seeking and welcoming his advice. Richard Edgeworth had such confidence both in the good sense of his children and in his own principles of education, which were patterned after those of his eccentric friend, Thomas Day (author of the once-famous novel of education, *Sandford and Merton,* 1783-1789), that he informed his family of the reasons for nearly all of his decisions, and certainly for the important ones. The most important of these was his resolve to settle on his family estate in Ireland (he had been living in England for a number of years, having left Ireland about 1765; and Maria had visited Ireland only briefly, in 1773). One reason for the election to live in Ireland—Edgeworth could have afforded to stay in England, since he received rents from his Irish property—was that Richard Edge-

worth was convinced by his reading and by the course of national affairs (one feature of which was the harsh economic treatment of Ireland because of the great expense incurred by England in its war with the American colonies) that Ireland could be one of the best and most productive areas in the British Empire.

   To achieve the goal of proper estate management, a subject that was to engage the interest of Maria Edgeworth for the rest of her life, her father had to revolutionize the way in which his lands and tenants were cared for. The salient aspect of the change was a greater concern for genuine productivity and less for high rents. He was quite successful, partly because of the help of his adoring and sensible daughter. The estate and the family survived riots, famines, and the very real threat of a French invasion of Ireland during the Napoleonic campaigns. From the time the Edgeworth family relocated to Edgeworthstown, in 1782, until her death, Maria Edgeworth lived in the family homestead—the constancy of her residence there being broken by only a few trips to England, France, and Scotland, and brief visits to other countries on the Continent. During these sojourns, she managed to become acquainted, largely through her father's influence, with some of the leading thinkers and artists of the day, notably Sir Walter Scott, with whom she formed a warm personal friendship and for whom she had a great admiration, which was reciprocated. Edgeworth was one of the first readers to recognize that the anonymously published *Waverly* was the work of "the Wizard of the North."

   While visiting France in 1802, Edgeworth met the Chevalier Abraham Nicolas Clewberg-Edelcrantz, a Swedish diplomat to whom she was introduced in Paris. For this somewhat shy, very small, not particularly attractive woman, the encounter was extraordinary. Edelcrantz was not handsome, and he was forty-six years old. On the positive side, he was very intelligent and quite well educated, a fact that appealed to Edgeworth. Although evidently astounded and pleased by Edelcrantz's proposal of marriage, she was wise enough to realize that his devotion to Sweden, which he could not think of leaving as his home, and hers to Ireland posed an absolute barrier to any happiness in such a union. Richard Edgeworth was apparently in favor of the marriage, but he did nothing to persuade Maria to accept the Swede, and he received her decision with equanimity.

Apart from helping her father to manage the estate—managing it herself almost single-handedly after his death in 1817—and looking after the family, Edgeworth devoted herself almost exclusively to writing. Some of her novels began as very short tales written (usually on a slate, so that erasures and improvements could be made readily) for the entertainment of the younger members of the family circle. Richard Edgeworth, though, persuaded her to take her writing seriously. This she did for some fifty years, until shortly before her death in 1849, by which time she had become respected and, to a degree seldom achieved by a female author, famous.

Analysis · The novels of Maria Edgeworth are, to the modern reader, an odd combination of strengths and weaknesses. This phenomenon is not really very strange, given the times in which she lived and the progress of fiction writing in the early nineteenth century. The work of all the novelists of that period may be considered strongly flawed and yet often unexpectedly effective (Sir Walter Scott is the obvious example, but the same might even be said of much of the work of Charles Dickens). What is perhaps more surprising is that Edgeworth herself was aware of the defects of her work. She knew, for example, that her writings were didactic to an often annoying degree. Her father, who had a great deal to do with her conviction that fiction should aim to elevate the morals of its readers, even comments on the fact in one of his prefaces to her novels and claims that a severe attempt had been made to subdue the moralistic features. By modern standards, the attempts never fully succeeded in any of Edgeworth's novels.

One reason for the "failure" is simply the prevalence of the late eighteenth century belief that behavior can be modified by edifying reading and that character can be formed and, possibly more important, reformed by acts of the will. Those of Edgeworth's tales titled with the name of the central character, such as *Ormond, Belinda*, and *Vivian*, are thus the stories of how these young people come to terms with society and their responsibilities: in short, how they grow up to be worthy citizens. The concept itself is not ludicrous; literature is replete with studies of the ways in which young people come of age successfully. What is distressing in Edgeworth's "moral tales" (and those of many other writers of the era) are the improbable turns of plot such as those by which poor but honest people are suddenly discovered to be heirs to great properties, those believed to be orphans are revealed as the offspring of noble houses, and so forth. This sort of device has a long history in both fiction and drama, but it is especially dismaying in a work that is otherwise, and by clear intention, realistic. The distracting and hardly credible process by which Grace Nugent, in *The Absentee*, is proved legitimate so that Lord Colambre can in good conscience marry her (the moral logic behind his reluctance to wed her, blameless as she is for the situation of her birth, may repel modern readers who are not familiar with the depth of the eighteenth century conviction concerning the influence of a flawed family background), is needlessly detailed. Such a device also intrudes on a story that is otherwise filled with convincing details about estate management (and mismanagement) in Ireland and fairly realistic studies of the lives of the common people.

Richard Edgeworth was blamed, perhaps unjustly, for the excess of didacticism in his daughter's novels (it is surely no accident that the only work lacking such material, *Castle Rackrent*, was her most popular title and is today her only novel still read); some of the tiresome passages of "uplifting" commentary do sound as if they came from his eloquent but ponderous pen, as in Belinda's comment in a letter, "Female wit sometimes depends on the beauty of its possessor for its reputation; and the reign of beauty is proverbially short, and fashion often capriciously deserts her favourites, even before nature withers their charms." To his credit, however, Richard Edgeworth is now known to have done a great deal to provide his daughter with ideas for stories and plot sequences. Perhaps the most important artistic flaw to which the younger Edgeworth pleaded guilty was a lack of invention, and critics over the decades have noticed that she depends to excess on details and facts, many of which she collected from her own family's records and memoirs. The rest she gathered by direct (and penetrating) observation, as in the realistic farm scenes in the Irish tales and the believable pictures of society gatherings in London and Paris. One of the most obvious indications of Edgeworth's failure to devise plots artfully is her reliance on the retrospective strategy of having a character reveal his or her background by telling it to another. Certainly, the review of her own life that Lady Delacour provides for Belinda is not without interest and is necessary to the story; yet it seems cumbersome, appearing as it does in two chapters that occupy more than thirty pages near the opening of the novel.

The two types of novels that Edgeworth wrote—the Irish tales and, as the title of one collection indicates, the *Tales of Fashionable Life* (1809-1812)—manifest the poles of her thematic interest. She believed, as did her father, that Ireland could benefit and even prosper from a more responsible aristocracy, landowners who lived on their property and saw that it was fairly and efficiently managed. In her three best Irish tales, *Castle Rackrent, The Absentee,* and *Ormond,* Edgeworth underlines the virtues of fair play with tenants, caution in dealing with hired estate managers (the wicked Nicholas Garraghty, in *The Absentee,* should be warning enough for any proprietor), and close attention to details of land and equipment. The years that Edgeworth spent aiding her father at Edgeworthstown bore impressive fruit in her grasp of the problems and difficulties faced by owners of large estates.

Because the sectarian, political, and economic problems that faced Ireland have tended to persist into the present, while the aspects of fashionable life have not, the "society" novels in Irish literature are almost unknown by the reading public today. In any case, Edgeworth was much more intellectually involved in the politics and social problems of her homeland than she was in the vagaries and evils of society life in big cities. Much as she believed that a great deal can be learned about the proper way to live one's life by observing society closely, she was personally never so involved in that topic as she was in such concerns as the injustices created by absentee landlords and the abuse of tenants by land agents hired by the absentees and given enormous power. Thus, while Belinda, Vivian, and Helen do hold some interest for the reader, their problems and challenges are dated. The modern reader has difficulty taking seriously the follies of Vivian, who manages to misjudge nearly everybody in the novel, leading to his not unexpected demise, which is sad but far from tragic. The peculiarities of King Corny in *Ormond,* however, as when it is revealed that he is elevating the roof of his large house so that he can construct attics under it, help to provide the reader with a more substantial grasp of the great power, the tendency toward eccentricity, and the frequent good-heartedness of Irish estate owners. Edgeworth usually dealt with events and conditions in the fairly recent past; as such, she can be considered a historical novelist. Her emphasis on what can be viewed as an international theme, however (the relationship between English, as well as Irish, characters and attitudes), is thought by many to be the most significant aspect of her novels. Critics have even suggested that her treatment of the topic prefigures the more detailed analyses by Henry James.

Edgeworth appeared on the literary scene at the best possible moment for her career and the future of the English novel. Her own records designate the amounts that she was paid by her publishers for each major work, and the list of payments is, by the standards of the time, impressive. For example, the minor novel *Patronage* earned Edgeworth £2,100, at that time an enormous sum. The influence that she had on the course of the historical and regional novel is proof of her little-known but vital contribution toward the development of the English novel.

Castle Rackrent · In his introduction to the Oxford English Novels edition of *Castle Rackrent* (1964), George Watson claims for this unusual book the distinction of being "the first regional novel in English, and perhaps in all Europe." Certainly, the work is a tour de force, all the more impressive because it was, by most accounts, achieved virtually by accident. Richard Edgeworth had on the estate a steward named John Langan. His opinions and mode of expression so struck Maria Edgeworth that she began to record his comments and became an able mimic of his dialect and turns of speech. Her letters to her father's sister, Mrs. Margaret Edgeworth Ruxton, one of her favorite correspondents, inspired this sympathetic lady to encourage her niece to develop the material into a story. Thus was born Maria Edgeworth's only substantial piece of fiction written during Richard Edgeworth's lifetime in whose composition he evidently did not play a part.

Edgeworth claimed that only the narrator was based on a real-life person, Langan; some scholars have suggested that one or two other characters might have been fashioned after people known to her. An example is the entertaining character Sir Condy Rackrent, who may have been broadly patterned on Edgeworth's maternal grandfather. However great or small its basis in real life, the novel has the air of reality about it. The actions and the motivations ring true to life. *Castle Rackrent* is often praised for its lack of an obtrusive moral emphasis, but it would be a mistake to read the novel as having no message. The decline and fall of the Rackrent family is the story of irresponsibility and extravagance, an unfortunately common phenomenon in the history of Irish landowners.

The narrator, Thady Quirk, commonly called "honest Thady," tells the dismal but occasionally humorous tale of the several masters under whom he has served: Sir Patrick O'Shaughlin, who drinks himself to death early in the story; Sir Murtaugh Rackrent, who dies in a paroxysm of anger over a legalistic contretemps; Sir Kit Rackrent, who dies in a duel over the controversy stemming from his indecision regarding the choice of a new wife, when his first spouse seems on the point of death; and Sir Conolly Rackrent, whose narrative is longer than the tale of the first three owners of Castle Rackrent. Another innovative aspect of the novel, besides the use of such an authentic narrator, is the consistent employment of dialect. The text is not difficult to read, but many of the expressions are not easily comprehensible to a reader unfamiliar with the Irish speech and mores of that era. Wisely, Edgeworth—with her father's help—appended a glossary which explains, occasionally in needless detail, many of Thady's locutions and references. That Thady opens his memoir on a Monday morning might have little special significance unless the reader is informed by the glossary that "no great undertaking can be auspiciously commenced in Ireland on any morning but *Monday morning.*"

Perhaps the chief appeal of the work to the modern reader lies in the personality of Thady and in the folkways he embodies. On the first page, he tells of his "great coat," which poverty compels him to wear winter and summer but which is "very handy, as I never put my arms into the sleeves, (they are as good as new,) though come Holantide next, I've had it these seven years." The extraordinary loyalty of Thady to a family that seems not to deserve such fidelity is both exasperating and admirable. Thady is not, however, overcome with emotion when unfortunate circumstances arise. Though he cannot recall the drinking habits of Sir Patrick without the brief aside, "God bless him!," he speaks of a shocking event at the funeral with relative calm: "Happy the man who could get but a sight of the hearse!–But who'd have thought it? Just as all was going on right, through his own town they were passing, when the body was seized for debt. . . ." Thady is moved enough to call the creditors "villains," but he swiftly moves on with his tale: "So, to be sure, the law must take its course–and little gain had the creditors for their pains." The old man spends more time on the legal implications of the seizure than on the event itself. This passage displays Edgeworth's understanding of the contentious element in the Irish personality and the formidable grasp of the law that even poorly educated people often had. Indeed, lawsuits and legal technicalities abound in Edgeworth's fiction.

Thady's almost eccentric equanimity and generous nature are further revealed when, after Sir Kit has gambled away virtually all the assets of the Rackrent estate, including the good will of his wealthy wife, the old retainer remarks, "the Castle Rackrent estate was all mortgaged, and bonds out against him, for he was never cured of his gaming tricks–but that was the only fault he had, God bless him!" Further, Thady seems untroubled by the confinement of Sir Kit's wife for seven years in her apartments (an incident based on the actual imprisonment of a Lady Cathcart, in 1745, who was kept locked up by her husband for a much longer period), apparently lost in admiration of the fierce temper of his master, which not only caused the drastic action but also discouraged anyone from asking him about it.

The first part of *Castle Rackrent* is entitled "An Hibernian Tale." It is indeed very "Hibernian," but no more so than the story of Sir Conolly Rackrent, whom Thady refers to as "ever my great favorite, and indeed the most universally beloved man I had ever seen or heard of." Condy's chief attractions are a good nature and a propensity to spend excessively. Both of these qualities contribute to the further impoverishment of the estate, a condition that he does little to alleviate. Even his marriage to the daughter of a wealthy landowner on a nearby estate (who promptly disinherits his offspring as soon as he learns of the wedding, thus frustrating even this halfhearted attempt to repair the Rackrent fortunes) is a matter of chance: Condy, who actually loves Thady's pretty but fortuneless grandniece, Judy M'Quirk, flips a coin to determine whether he will propose to Judy or the moneyed Isabella.

Despite the disinheritance, Sir Condy is fond of Isabella; when financial disaster looms, he attempts to provide her with a generous allotment in his will. The closing of the novel exposes another theme that may be derived from the plot. The villain who buys up Sir Condy's debts and brings on his personal ruin is Thady's own son, the self-serving Jason. Edgeworth possibly had in mind to make some point about the difference between the single-minded loyalty and honesty of the older generation and the selfish heartlessness of the younger. Even the attractive Judy, when Thady suggests that she might become the next mistress of Castle Rackrent (Isabella has had an accident from which Thady believes she will die), tells him there is no point in marrying a poor man; she has evidently set her sights on Jason, much to Thady's dismay.

Typically, the novel ends with a lawsuit. Lady Condy, after her husband's death from drinking, sues for the title to the estate. Thady does not know how the suit will end, and he seems not to care: "For my part, I'm tired wishing for any thing in this world, after all I've seen in it." With this touching close to what is considered Edgeworth's best novel, the reader may well believe that the author has provided the opportunity for a greater understanding of those elements of Irish culture and history that impelled her to devote a lifetime of study to them.

The Absentee · During Edgeworth's lifetime, *The Absentee* was probably her most influential work. The central problem addressed in the novel is that of the absentee landlords, who left the management of their often vast Irish estates in the hands of inept and frequently unscrupulous agents. These agents robbed the landlords as well as the tenants, but the indifferent landowners took little interest in the lands so long as the rents were paid on time. As Edgeworth makes eminently clear by the contrast between the sensible and benevolent Mr. Burke, one of Lord Clonbrony's agents, and the other, Nicholas Garraghty, who is scheming and dishonest, not all agents were bad; the trouble was that the owners had no accurate way of knowing, since they were almost never on the scene.

The hero of this novel, Lord Colambre, is the son of Lord and Lady Clonbrony; it is around this unbelievably virtuous and somewhat stuffy young man that the several subplots and themes are centered. Each subplot is designed to underline an obvious theme, and Colambre is a vital, if artificial, unifying element in a novel whose general absence of unity is disquieting. The main plot line has to do with the Clonbronys, who live in London because Lady Clonbrony believes that high society is indispensable to her happiness (typically, the other members of the "smart set" find her pretensions ridiculous; Edgeworth explores a number of opportunities to satirize the false values of such people). Lord Clonbrony would not mind returning to the family estate, and he realizes that remaining away may be ruinous, since he is already in considerable debt. Lord Colambre visits his father's lands in disguise, where he identifies the problem and recognizes the virtues and evils of the two agents. After vigorous efforts to repay his father's debts, he saves the situation and persuades his mother to return to Ireland. A related theme concerns the actions that Colambre will not take in order to pay the debts—chiefly, he will not marry for money, a time-honored method of acquiring funds in a short time. Edgeworth offers several illustrations of the folly of such a practice, though perhaps to the modern reader her emphasis on the legitimacy of the birth of Grace Nugent, Colambre's cousin, as a criterion for his proposing to her may seem artificial and even essentially immoral. Interestingly, when Miss Nugent (who has been unaware of the "disgrace") learns of the reason for Colambre's erstwhile restraint, she fully agrees that it would have been improper for him to offer marriage when her birth seemed under a cloud. Through an unlikely and tiresome concatenation of circumstances and accidents, the problem is solved: It is proved that Grace's birth was legitimate, and the marriage is approved, even by Lady Clonbrony, who for most of the story has been trying to persuade her son to wed the wealthy Miss Broadhurst.

The Absentee is filled with flat characters created in the heroic mold, most of whom befriend Colambre and impress him with a variety of sensible insights: the positive aspects of life in Ireland; the joys and satisfactions of the quiet country life (the O'Neill family, tenants on the Clonbrony estate, underline this point; they, too, are so honest and good-hearted as to be difficult to accept); the emptiness and falseness of "society"; and the great importance of taking responsibility and performing one's duty well. *The Absentee* emphasizes two aspects of Edgeworth's philosophy of life. She fully accepted the eighteenth century conviction that the class structure of society was inevitable and proper, and she wholeheartedly believed in the primacy of duty (a word iterated by her father as the chief element of a worthy life) as everyone's first responsibility. Thus, in *The Absentee* there is an interesting mingling of liberal attitudes toward the rights of the peasants and conservative views regarding the propriety of aristocratic privilege.

At the close of a long and complicated reticulation of plot lines, Edgeworth had the clever notion of ending the story simply and even humorously (there is an unfortunate paucity of humor in this novel) by completing the tale through the device of a letter written by an Irish coach-driver to his brother, who currently lives in England, telling him of the happy return of the Clonbronys to the estate and the upcoming marriage of Colambre and Grace, and urging him to come back to Ireland, since "it's growing the fashion not to be an Absentee." *The Absentee* lacks the humor and directness of *Castle Rackrent*, but it makes its thematic points forcefully, and in Sir Terence O'Fay, Edgeworth has created a revealing, rounded portrait of an interesting Irish type: a good-natured wastrel who is no one's enemy but his own. His function in the plot is minimal, but he displays some of the most engaging features of the Irish personality.

Ormond · Unlike *The Absentee*, whose title indicates that the subject is a general phenomenon, *Ormond*, as its title suggests, is about the development of a single individual. The novel is based on the view that young people can change their character by learning from their experiences and exerting their will. Although Harry Ormond is not exactly Rousseau's "noble savage," he is clearly intended to be the image of an untutored, raw personality, full of fine possibilities that must be cultivated to be realized. During the long, complex advance of the story, this is just what happens.

The lad has been reared by an old friend of his father, who died in India, a minor aristocrat named Sir Ulick O'Shane, who believes that educating the boy would be a waste of time, since he is destined to be a poor dependent for life. The contrast between Harry Ormond and Ulick's own son, Marcus, a formally educated but weak and ineffective youth, is one of several that give the novel a sense of polarity. Ulick is contrasted with his cousin, Cornelius O'Shane, the King Corny who takes over the care of Harry when he is forced to leave Ulick's estate after a shooting incident; Dora O'Shane, the daughter of Corny, with whom for a while Harry believes himself to be in love, is seen as quite different from the modest and highly moral Florence Annaly, whom he does love and finally marries; White Connal, Dora's first suitor, is, even by his name, contrasted with his brother, Black Connal, who ultimately is the man who marries Dora.

Harry Ormond is placed in the care of a succession of older men, and from each he learns things that help him grow into a responsible and sensitive man. Ulick teaches him some of the complexities of business and helps him to understand the difficulty of judging character in another; King Corny instructs him in the need for bold action and in the excellences to be found in the primitive personality; Dr. Cambray, a clergyman, starts Harry on his formal education; and, while staying with the Annaly family, Harry perceives the delights of a well-ordered life in a well-regulated family, something he has never before experienced.

The essence of the book, apart from Ormond's development into a mature person, is his ultimate winning of the girl he truly loves. His material dependence is easily (and, again, incredibly) solved by the discovery that his father has left him a fortune. His only real problem, then, is to pass a series of moral tests created by Edgeworth to prove that he is a worthy, responsible man. The novel is marked by a number of traditional devices, such as the timeworn "While Sir Ulick is drinking his cup of cold coffee, we may look back a little into his family history," which is done for some six and a half pages. Frequent references to Ormond as "our hero" remind the reader that this is his story and that Harry is to be thought of as heroic, no matter what mistakes he makes (and he does blunder now and then, usually on the side of excessive credulity). The author does not hesitate to intrude into the story, to proclaim ignorance ("What he said, or what Florence answered, we do not know"), or to move the plot along with phrases such as "We now go on to," or "We now proceed to." *Ormond* is thus in many ways a traditional novel of the period, but it achieves a level of social criticism—of French society (a number of scenes are set in Paris) as well as of English and Irish ways—seldom found before William Makepeace Thackeray in the history of the English novel. This tale, unlike *The Absentee*, is also enlivened by humor.

Edgeworth's novels are unfortunately little read today, except by students of the English novel. Aside from plainly revealing the significant lines of tradition and transition from the eighteenth century to the nineteenth century novel, her work is enjoyable in itself. Nowhere else can one find such a lively and fairly balanced picture of the life and values found in the Ireland and England of the late Georgian period.

Fred B. McEwen

Other major works

SHORT FICTION: *The Modern Griselda,* 1805; *Tales of Fashionable Life,* 1809-1812; *Tales and Miscellaneous Pieces,* 1825; *Garry Owen: Or, The Snow-Woman, and Poor Bob, the Chimney-Sweeper,* 1832; *Tales and Novels,* 1832-1833, 1848, 1857 (18 volumes), 1893 (10 volumes), 1893 (12 volumes); *Orlandino,* 1848; *Classic Tales,* 1883.

PLAY: *Comic Dramas in Three Acts,* pb. 1817.

NONFICTION: *Letters for Literary Ladies,* 1795; *An Essay on the Noble Science of Self-Justification,* 1795; *Practical Education,* 1798 (also known as *Essays on Practical Education;* with Richard Lovell Edgeworth); *A Rational Primer,* 1799 (with Richard Lovell Edgeworth); *Essay on Irish Bulls,* 1802 (with Richard Lovell Edgeworth); *Essays on Professional Education,* 1809 (with Richard Lovell Edgeworth); *Readings on Poetry,* 1816 (with Richard Lovell Edgeworth); *Memoirs of Richard Lovell Edgeworth Esq.,* 1820 (vol. 2); *Thoughts on Bores,* 1826; *A Memoir of Maria Edgeworth,* 1867 (Francis Edgeworth, editor); *Archibald Constable and His Literary Correspondents,* 1873; *The Life and Letters of Maria Edgeworth,* 1894 (Augustus J. Hare, editor); *Chosen Letters,* 1931 (F. V. Barry, editor); *Romilly-Edgeworth Letters,* 1813-1818, 1936 (Samuel H. Romilly, editor); *Letters from England,* 1813-1844, 1971 (Christina Colvin, editor).

CHILDREN'S LITERATURE: *The Parent's Assistant: Or, Stories for Children,* 1796 (3 volumes), 1800 (6 volumes); *Early Lessons: Harry and Lucy, I and II; Rosamond, I-III; Frank, I-IV and Other Stories,* 1801 (with Richard Lovell Edgeworth); *Moral Tales for Young People,* 1801; *The Mental Thermometer,* 1801; *Popular Tales,* 1804; *Continuation of Early Lessons,* 1814; *Rosamond: A Sequel to Early Lessons,* 1821; *Frank: A Sequel to Frank in Early Lessons,* 1822; *Harry and Lucy Concluded,* 1825; *Little Plays for Children,* pb. 1827; *The Purple Jar and Other Stories,* 1931.

Bibliography

Bilger, Audrey. *Laughing Feminism: Subversive Comedy in Frances Burney, Maria Edgeworth, and Jane Austen.* Detroit: Wayne State University Press, 1998. Part of the Humor in Life and Letters series, this volume reveals feminist traits of these eighteenth century writers.

Butler, Marilyn. *Maria Edgeworth: A Literary Biography.* Oxford, England: Clarendon Press, 1972. Does a good job of balancing Edgeworth's personal and working life. Her large family was very important to her and seems to have provided sources for her novels. Devotes much space to establishing how her father, Richard Lovell Edgeworth, was a major influence in her life. Also focuses on Edgeworth's contemporary reputation, placing her as an important member of the literary milieu of her day. The bibliography and index are extensive. Includes three interesting appendices on her siblings and publication information regarding her novels.

Gilmartin, Sophie. *Ancestry and Narrative in Nineteenth-century British Literature: Blood Relations from Edgeworth to Hardy.* Cambridge, England: Cambridge University Press, 1998. Examines familial relationships in Edgeworth's works. Includes bibliographical references and an index.

Harden, O. Elizabeth McWhorter. *Maria Edgeworth.* Boston: Twayne, 1984. Attempts to dispel critical myths about Edgeworth, such as her father's negative influence over her, but does not always succeed. While trying to take an open-minded approach, Harden often treats Edgeworth and her contemporaries, such as Jane Austen, in highly conventional ways; for example, Harden's distinctions between Austen and Edgeworth in the last chapter are too simplistically polar. Provides a short biography and is divided into chapters based on Edgeworth's intended audiences, starting with children, moving to adolescents, and ending with adults, which is more useful than a purely chronological treatment. The bibliography is helpful given the limited number of works dealing with Edgeworth, even including chapters in books not specifically about her.

_____. *Maria Edgeworth's Art of Prose Fiction.* The Hague: Mouton, 1971. While this book treats Edgeworth's works simply, giving little more than plot summary and some approving comments for each novel, it is useful because it runs through her canon of fiction work by work, discussing them chronologically. The bibliography is good, including biographies, works containing important contemporary comments, mentions of Edgeworth in general works, contemporary reviews and notices, fiction technique studies, and general criticism and background. A good starting place for a study of Edgeworth.

Hollingworth, Brian. *Maria Edgeworth's Irish Writing.* New York: St. Martin's Press, 1997. See especially the chapters on *Castle Rackrent* and *Ormond.* Includes detailed notes and bibliography.

Hurst, Michael. *Maria Edgeworth and the Public Scene: Intellect, Fine Feeling, and Landlordism in the Age of Reform.* Coral Gables, Fla.: University of Miami Press, 1969. Takes an interesting and fresh approach to Edgeworth, looking at her attitudes toward Irish reform in the early nineteenth century. Sees her as a moderate who wanted improvement for the lower classes of society but no fundamental change in the upper classes. Historically based and not especially literary, focusing on political events and Edgeworth's opinion of them. Since these events took place fairly late in her life, Edgeworth is seen as an older, possibly more political woman, and Hurst argues that since her father was dead, her opinions at this time were probably more fully her own than those she voiced during his life.

Kowaleski-Wallace, Elizabeth. *Their Fathers' Daughters: Hannah More, Maria Edgeworth, and Patriarchal Complicity.* New York: Oxford, 1991. What does it mean for a female writer to identify with her father? This is the question Kowaleski-Wallace explores, devoting several chapters to Edgeworth's life and work. Includes detailed notes but no bibliography.

McCann, Andrew. *Cultural Politics in the 1790's: Literature, Radicalism, and the Public Sphere.* New York: St. Martin's Press, 1999. Discusses the political and social views of Edgeworth and such writers as Mary Wollstonecraft Shelley and William Godwin.

George Eliot

Mary Ann Evans

Born: Chilvers Coton, England; November 22, 1819
Died: London, England; December 22, 1880

Principal long fiction · *Adam Bede,* 1859; *The Mill on the Floss,* 1860; *Silas Marner,* 1861; *Romola,* 1862-1863; *Felix Holt, the Radical,* 1866; *Middlemarch,* 1871-1872; *Daniel Deronda,* 1876.

Other literary forms · George Eliot's three early stories, "The Sad Fortunes of the Reverend Amos Barton," "Mr. Gilfil's Love Story," and "Janet's Repentance," originally published in *Blackwood's Magazine,* were collected as *Scenes of Clerical Life* in 1858. She wrote two other stories, "The Lifted Veil," also published in *Blackwood's Magazine* in 1859, and "Brother Jacob," published in *Cornhill* in 1864. *The Impressions of Theophrastus Such,* a miscellany of sketches and essays, was published in 1879. Eliot's poetry does not achieve the high quality of her prose. Most notable examples are *The Spanish Gypsy* (1868), a verse drama, and *The Legend of Jubal and Other Poems* (1874). Eliot wrote more than seventy periodical essays and reviews; the most comprehensive collection is Thomas Pinney's *Essays of George Eliot* (1963). Eliot translated David Friedrich Strauss's *Das Leben Jesu* as *The Life of Jesus Critically Examined* (1846) and Ludwig Feuerbach's *Das Wesen des Christentums* as *The Essence of Christianity* (1854). Her translation of Benedictus de Spinoza's *Ethics* (1677) has never been published.

Achievements · Eliot's pivotal position in the history of the novel is attested by some of the most distinguished novelists. Reviewing *Middlemarch* in 1873, Henry James concluded, "It sets a limit, we think, to the development of the old-fashioned English novel"; *Middlemarch* does, indeed, take what James calls the panoramic novel—"vast, swarming, deep-colored, crowded with episodes, with vivid images, with lurking master-strokes, with brilliant passages of expression," seeking to "reproduce the total sum of life in an English village"—to an unsurpassed level of achievement. Eliot was also an innovator. In the words of D. H. Lawrence, "It all started with George Eliot; it was she who put the action on the inside," thus giving impetus to the rise of the psychological novel, where the most significant actions derive from the motives of the characters rather than from external events. Eliot's work is, then, both the culmination of the panoramic Victorian novel as practiced by Charles Dickens and William Makepeace Thackeray and the beginning of the modern psychological novel as practiced by James, Lawrence, and many others.

More than anyone else, Eliot was responsible for making the novel, a genre which had traditionally been read primarily for entertainment, into a vehicle for the serious expression of ideas. Few novelists can equal Eliot's depth of intellect or breadth of learning. Deeply involved in the religious and philosophical ferment of her time, Eliot was probably the first major English novelist who did not subscribe, at least nominally, to the tenets of Christian theology. Nevertheless, her strong moral commitment, derived from her Evangelical Christian heritage, led her to conceive of the novel as an instrument for preaching a gospel of duty and self-renunciation.

Moral commitment alone, however, does not make a great novelist. In addition, Eliot's extraordinary psychological insight enabled her to create characters who rival in depth and complexity any in English or American fiction. Few novelists can equal her talents for chronicling tangled motives, intricate self-deceptions, or an anguished struggle toward a noble act. She creates a fictional world that combines, in a way unsurpassed in English fiction, a broad panorama of society and psychological insight into each character.

Biography · The woman known to countless readers as George Eliot–a name she did not use until she was nearly forty–was born on November 22, 1819, and christened Mary Ann Evans, the third child of Robert Evans and his second wife Christina Pearson. Evans, a man of extraordinary competence and unimpeachable integrity, worked as a general overseer of Arbury Hall, the seven-thousand-acre estate of the Newdigate family in Warwickshire. A shy and homely girl, Eliot excelled as a student in nearby boarding schools. Under the influence of a favorite teacher, Maria Lewis, the strict and conventional adherence to the Church of England which she learned from her parents acquired an overlay of pious Evangelicalism.

After her mother's death and her father's retirement, Eliot and her father moved to a new home outside Coventry. She soon established a close and lasting friendship with Charles and Cara Bray and Cara's sister Sara Hennell. Her conversations with the Brays, who were Unitarians and whose views of religion were more intellectual than those with which Eliot had been acquainted, accelerated the process of religious questioning that she had already experienced. At Bray's suggestion, she began to translate *Das Leben Jesu*, a key work of the German theologian David Friedrich Strauss. Strauss, by applying the methods of scientific research and criticism to the Bible, questioned the divinity of Christ. Eliot's work on this translation, published anonymously in 1846, completed the destruction of her religious orthodoxy.

Following the death of her father in 1849 and a brief stay in Switzerland, Eliot moved to London, where she began to write for the *Westminster Review*. The fact that, while in Switzerland, she began to spell her name Marian suggests her awareness of a new and different life ahead of her.

Although the *Westminster Review* was nominally edited by John Chapman–a man with whom Eliot may have been romantically involved–Eliot assumed most of the responsibilities of editorship and was, especially after Chapman bought the periodical in January, 1852, virtual editor. Her work with the *Westminster Review* placed her near the center of the intellectual life of Victorian England and brought her into contact with many of the prominent thinkers of the time.

One of the persons whom Eliot met at this time was George Henry Lewes, who later became her common-law husband. A man of unusual versatility, Lewes had written novels, a blank-verse tragedy, a history of philosophy, and many periodical articles on a variety of subjects. He was, with Thornton Leigh Hunt, coeditor of a weekly newspaper called *The Leader*.

Lewes, Hunt, and Lewes's wife Agnes subscribed to the notion that passions could not be restricted by social conventions; thus, when Agnes, after bearing Lewes four sons, delivered a fifth son who had been fathered by Hunt, Lewes quietly registered the child as his own. By the time Agnes bore a second child fathered by Hunt, however, Lewes no longer considered her his wife, although he continued to support her and to be on friendly terms with her and Hunt, with whom he continued to work

on *The Leader.* Victorian laws made divorce virtually impossible and prohibitively expensive; the fact that Lewes had accepted Hunt's child as his own precluded his citing adultery as possible grounds.

Under the circumstances, Eliot and Lewes had the choice of living together in a common-law marriage or not living together at all. They chose the former, and on July 20, 1854, traveled to Germany as husband and wife. Eliot wrote to her friends to explain her new status and to ask that from henceforth they address her as Marian Lewes.

Although the couple had no children, their relationship was in many respects a model Victorian marriage. They lived happily together until Lewes's death in 1878; with their writing, they supported not only themselves but also Lewes's four sons and Agnes and her children by Hunt. Lewes's sons appeared to regard Eliot with great affection. In other respects, however, the irregularity of their relationship cut Eliot off from much of the social life of the time, since only the most courageous Victorian women dared risk their own respectability by calling on her. Eliot's family, especially her brother Isaac, also cut her off, condemning her relationship with Lewes as adulterous.

Encouraged by Lewes, Eliot published her first work of fiction, "The Sad Fortunes of the Reverend Amos Barton," in *Blackwood's Magazine* in January, 1857. Because Eliot wished to protect her standing as an editor and reviewer and because she feared that her unconventional marriage to Lewes would prejudice the reception of her fiction, she published under the pseudonym George Eliot. Encouraged by the favorable reception of these stories and protected by Lewes from adverse criticism, Eliot published her first full-length novel, *Adam Bede*, in 1859.

For the next two decades the chief events in Eliot's life were the publications of her novels—*The Mill on the Floss, Silas Marner, Romola, Felix Holt, Middlemarch*, and *Daniel Deronda*. Of these novels, only *Romola*, a meticulously researched historical novel set in fifteenth century Florence, was less than successful; the others won Eliot both an enthusiastic popular audience and critical recognition as the major English novelist of her time.

As the success of Eliot's novels and the continuing acceptance of Lewes's articles and books also brought considerable prosperity, the Leweses' life together was punctuated by trips to various parts of England and the Continent and by a series of moves to houses in more attractive parts of London. In November, 1878, only a few months after they moved to a long-sought-for house in the country, Lewes died.

Devastated by the loss of the emotional support that Lewes provided, on May 6, 1880, Eliot married John Cross, who, although twenty years younger than she, had long been a close friend and frequent visitor to the Lewes household. In the eyes of her sternly conventional brother Isaac, this marriage conferred respectability; he wrote to his sister for the first time since 1854 to offer his "sincere congratulations." Their marriage, though happy, was brief: Eliot died in December, 1880.

Analysis · Discussions of George Eliot's fiction are likely to begin by quoting chapter 17 of *Adam Bede*, in which she makes one of the most persuasive statements of the creed of the realistic novelist to be found in nineteenth century literature. Indicating that she is seeking that "rare, precious quality of truthfulness that I delight in [in] many Dutch paintings," she goes on to state the need for "men ready to give the loving pains of a life to the faithful representing of commonplace things—men who see beauty in these commonplace things, and delight in showing how kindly the light of heaven falls on them." Through the truthful and sympathetic rendering of a fictional world no better than the actual one "in which we get up in the morning to do our daily work," novelists should win the reader's sympathy for "the real breathing men and women, who can be chilled by your indifference or injured by your prejudice, who can be cheered and helped onward by your fellow-feeling, your forbearance, your outspoken, brave justice." These statements suggest that Eliot conceived of fiction as a moral force, not because it is didactic in any narrow sense, but because it inculcates in the reader an attitude of sympathy for his or her fellow people, which in turn leads to everyday acts of justice and compassion that lighten the burden of the human lot. Fiction, then, performs one of the functions that is commonly associated with the church as a Christian community by reminding readers of Christ's second commandment, that they love their neighbors as themselves.

Indeed, although Eliot's belief in Christian theology waned when she was in her twenties, her devotion to the major elements of Christian morality as she understood them remained steadfast throughout her life and provided the moral framework for her fiction. Her practice as a novelist eventually goes beyond her statement in *Adam Bede* in both complexity and subtlety, but this statement remains as the foundation of her creed as a novelist.

As her career developed, Eliot's characters became complex moral paradigms that could serve her readers as both examples and warnings. The highest moral achievement of her characters is renunciation of their own claims to happiness in order to minister to the needs of others, sometimes less deserving, whose lives impinge on theirs. The act of renunciation involves acknowledgement of the claims of community and often provides a sense of continuity with the character's past or traditions. Conversely, the characters whom Eliot condemns most severely are those who evade their responsibilities by a process of self-delusion or self-indulgence, avoiding hard choices and hoping that chance will deliver them from the consequences of selfish actions. Characters are often moved toward renunciation by others who act as "messengers"–almost secularized angels–to guide them; their acts of renunciation and sense of community are often associated with the sacraments of baptism or communion. The process of egotistical self-indulgence, on the other hand, is often associated with a sexual relationship that is clearly inappropriate, although not necessarily illicit. Later in her career, Eliot treated the difficulty of finding an arena for purposeful life in the England of her time, but she never abandoned her intense commitment to individual moral responsibility.

Adam Bede · Eliot's first full-length novel, *Adam Bede*, is built on two pairs of contrasting characters, one male and one female. Adam, a carpenter of consummate skill, is a model of rectitude and self-discipline whose only flaw is his intolerance of any weakness in others. Contrasting with Adam is Arthur Donnithorne, a well-intentioned young landowner whose moral weakness causes the principal catastrophe of the novel. There is a similar contrast between the two major female characters: Dinah Morris, a self-effacing Methodist preacher whose primary concern is doing what she can for others, and Hetty Sorrel, a young farm girl whose kittenish appeal conceals a hard core of egotism. The fact that both Adam and Arthur love Hetty intensifies the contrast between them. Adam, captivated by her charms, admires her as a paragon of femininity without ever perceiving her indifference to him. Arthur, without really intending to, takes advantage of Hetty's self-deluding dreams of being a wealthy landowner's wife to indulge in an affair with her. Frightened when she discovers that she is pregnant, Hetty runs away from home in a vain attempt to find Arthur, who has gone to rejoin his regiment. After her baby is born, she abandons it in a forest, where it dies of exposure. When she is arraigned for child murder, she appears hard and indifferent until Dinah moves her to repentance. Although Arthur succeeds in obtaining a pardon that saves Hetty from hanging, the young woman disappears from the story and, like the overwhelming majority of fallen women in Victorian fiction, dies. The somewhat improbable marriage of Adam and Dinah provides the happy ending that the contemporary audience expected.

The melodramatic aspects of *Adam Bede* tend to obscure, especially in summary, Eliot's primary concerns in the novel. Most conspicuously, the relationship between Arthur and Hetty is not simply a trite story of a sexual encounter between a wealthy young man and a simple farm girl; the sexual aspect of their relationship is less important than their self-delusion, self-indulgence, and egotism. Both characters embody moral issues that Eliot returned to again and again in her career: Arthur is attractive, likable, and well-intentioned, but he lacks both strength of purpose and self-knowledge. Intending to break off his relationship with Hetty, he finds himself contriving meetings with her; dreaming of being a model landowner, he comes near to destroying the happiness of his best tenants. Hetty's flaw is even more damaging: Although she appears to be a creature of simple charm with the "beauty of young frisking things, round-limbed, gambolling, circumventing you by a false air of innocence," her egotism makes her indifferent to almost everything except her own beauty and her self-deluding dreams.

Similarly, Dinah's success in leading Hetty to repentance is a prototype of much more complex processes that occur in later novels, when characters who have greater potential for moral growth than Hetty are enabled to develop that potential. Dinah's willingness to take on responsibility for sympathetically ministering to the needs of people around her—a moral virtue Eliot lauds above all others—has to be learned by Adam, whose own stalwart rectitude causes him to scorn weakness in others. His success in learning sympathy is symbolized by his acceptance of a meal of bread and wine in an "upper room" the morning of Hetty's trial—one of several instances in Eliot's fiction where objects associated with a Christian sacrament are used to suggest the establishment of a sense of community.

Although it is a major achievement for a first novel, *Adam Bede* pales in comparison to Eliot's later fiction. Eliot's depiction of the self-deception and egotism of Arthur and Hetty looks ahead to the fuller development of this theme in later novels, but neither the characters nor their situation provides the opportunity for the depth of psychological insight Eliot shows later. Similarly, Arthur's last-minute rescue of Hetty from the very foot of the gallows is reminiscent of the clichés of nineteenth century melodrama and seems almost pointless in the light of Hetty's immediate disappearance from the story and her early death. The marriage of Adam and Dinah caters too obviously to the Victorian taste for this kind of conventional "happy ending" and seems inconsistent with the earlier description of Dinah. Adam himself is too idealized a character to be convincing.

Many minor characters, however, demonstrate Eliot's impressive gift for characterization. Mr. Irwine is the first of several Eliot clergymen who are virtuous but hardly spiritual; Mrs. Poyser's pungent sayings indicate Eliot's humor; and Adam's mother Lisbeth combines maternal love with grating querulousness and self-pity.

The Mill on the Floss · More than any of Eliot's other novels, *The Mill on the Floss*, her second novel, focuses on a single character: Maggie Tulliver. Considered one of Eliot's most complex creations, Maggie embodies both the tendency toward self-indulgence that Eliot condemns elsewhere and the earnest desire for moral achievement by renunciation of one's own happiness that is the hallmark of the characters of whom Eliot appears to approve most highly.

These conflicting tendencies in Maggie, although evident in the long childhood section of the novel, assume their full significance when Maggie begins a series of secret meetings with Philip Wakem, the crippled son of a lawyer whom Maggie's father regards as a mortal enemy. In some respects, these meetings are innocent enough: Philip and Maggie are both lonely, as Philip is set apart by his physical handicap and Maggie is isolated by her family's financial distresses, and their conversations provide them with companionship they find nowhere else. More significantly, however, Maggie's meetings with Philip are wrong in that they require her to deceive her family and because they would, if discovered, add to her father's already overflowing cup of grief and bitterness. Although the standard of conduct that Maggie is being asked to meet seems almost pointlessly rigid, Eliot makes it clear that Maggie errs by not meeting it. When Maggie's narrowly righteous brother Tom discovers the meetings and harshly puts a stop to them, even Maggie feels that the "sense of a deliverance from concealment was welcome at any cost."

Maggie's failure to meet the standards of conduct required of her has much more serious consequences when she allows herself to go away with Stephen Guest, a young man who is virtually engaged to her cousin Lucy. Although Maggie rejects Stephen's offer of marriage, their apparent elopement causes a scandal that prostrates Lucy and bitterly divides Maggie's family. Tom is especially adamant in condemning her.

Maggie is a character who is sometimes almost painful to read about, for she has too little self-discipline to avoid slipping into actions that she knows to be wrong and too sensitive a conscience not to feel acutely the consequences of her errors. The ideal of conduct that she longs for and ultimately achieves when she decides to reject Stephen's second proposal of marriage is expressed by passages marked in an old volume of St. Thomas à Kempis that is in a package of books given to Maggie in the depths of the Tullivers' poverty. Reading the words "Forsake thyself, resign thyself, and thou shall enjoy much inward peace," Maggie seems to see "a sudden vision" and feels this "direct communication of the human soul's belief and experience . . . as an unquestioned message."

Maggie is spared further conflict by the melodramatic conclusion of the novel. A flood gives her the opportunity to demonstrate her love for Tom by rescuing him from the mill. Maggie and Tom are briefly reconciled; then a floating mass of machinery bears down on their boat, drowning them both. Their epitaph–"In death they were not divided"–suggests a harmony that Maggie hungered for but seldom achieved in life.

The collision that results in the drowning of Maggie and Tom is, in fact, a kind of *deus ex machina* employed to achieve a resolution for Maggie that would be hard to envision otherwise. More intelligent and gifted than any of the other women in the novel, Maggie would hardly have found the fulfillment in marriage that appears to be the only resource for the women of the village, especially since marriage to Philip would have brought her into irreconcilable conflict with Tom and marriage to Stephen could only have been achieved at the cost of Lucy's happiness. Finally, since Maggie's sensitive compassion has conflicted with Tom's narrow dogmatism throughout the novel, it seems unlikely that their reconciliation could have been permanent. Even the renunciation she learns about in Thomas à Kempis seems to offer more a model of resignation than a pattern for a fruitful and fulfilling life. In the melodramatic ending, therefore, the issues raised by the novel finally remain unresolved.

As in *Adam Bede*, Eliot's brilliant creation of minor characters is one of the finest achievements of the novel. Especially noteworthy are the Dodson sisters, Maggie's aunts, who embody the common qualities of a proud and clannish family, and yet have traits which clearly distinguish them according to their age, degree of prosperity, and individual temperament.

Silas Marner · Eliot's third and most perfectly constructed novel, *Silas Marner*, embodies her complex moral vision with the precision of a diagram. Like *Adam Bede*, the novel is built on morally contrasting characters, but Silas Marner and Godfrey Cass reveal with much greater clarity than any of the characters in the earlier novel Eliot's concern with the moral patterns of renunciation and self-indulgence.

In a sort of prologue to the main action of the novel, Silas, a linen weaver who is a member of a pious religious sect in a large industrial city, is accused of stealing church funds by a close friend who actually stole the money. When a trial by lots sponsored by the sect declares Silas guilty, he loses faith in God and humanity and flees to a distant country village, where he isolates himself from the community and finds solace in constant weaving, like a "spinning insect."

Through years of weaving, Silas accumulates a hoard of gold coins which become the only object of his affections. When his gold is stolen by Godfrey Cass's irresponsible brother Dunstan, Silas is utterly devastated, until Godfrey's daughter by a secret marriage toddles into his house after her mother dies of exposure and an overdose of laudanum. The presence of this child, whom Silas rears as his own, restores the contact with his fellow men and women that Silas had lost; Eliot compares the girl to the "white-winged angels" that "in old days . . . took men by the hand and led them away from the city of destruction."

Almost every act that Silas performs in relation to the loss of his gold and the rearing of the child takes on near-symbolic significance. His spontaneous turning to the men assembled at the village tavern when his gold is stolen and to the New Year's assemblage at the Cass house when he finds the child suggest an instinctive searching for community. His heeding the parish clerk's admonition not to accuse the innocent after his gold is stolen and his choice of his younger sister's "Bible name" of Hepzibah (shortened to Eppie) for the child suggest the reestablishment of ties to his past. Most particularly, his acceptance of lard cakes with I. H. S. pricked on them from his kindly neighbor Dolly Winthrop provides a secularized communion that suggests that ties between human beings and God may be replaced in importance by ties between individuals, as Eppie has replaced the white-winged angels of older days. It may also be significant that Silas spends Christmas in lonely isolation, while Eppie comes to his house on New Year's Eve.

Similarly, Godfrey embodies the consequences of a self-indulgent avoidance of one's responsibilities. Prevented by his secret marriage to the dissolute mother of Eppie from marrying Nancy Lammeter, he weakly trusts to chance, "the god of all men who follow their own devices instead of obeying a law they believe in," to somehow relieve him of the consequences of his actions. Godfrey has none of the malice of his younger brother Dunstan; nevertheless, his anxiety is so great that his "one terror" when Silas comes to his house with Eppie is that his wife might *not* be dead. He sees that the child is his, but fails to acknowledge her, salving his conscience by giving Silas a half-guinea when he finds that Silas has determined to keep her.

The chance that has relieved Godfrey of the consequences of his secret marriage eventually brings retribution. His marriage to Nancy is childless, and when Dunstan's body is discovered with Silas's long-lost gold, Godfrey finally tells Nancy that Eppie is his child. Their plan of relieving their childlessness by adopting Eppie comes to nothing when Eppie tells them that she can only think of Silas as her father. With poetic justice that even Godfrey recognizes, the man who admits that he "wanted to pass for childless once" will now "pass for childless against my wish."

Middlemarch · *Middlemarch* is unquestionably Eliot's finest achievement as a novelist. Whereas *Silas Marner* presented the moral patterns of renunciation and self-indulgence with unparalleled clarity, *Middlemarch* explores them with profound subtlety and psychological insight. The vast scope of *Middlemarch*–it is more than twice the length of *Adam Bede* or *The Mill on the Floss*–gives Eliot room for a panoramic view of provincial life, and her focus on the upper middle class and gentry gives her an opportunity to deal with characters whose experience is wider and whose motives are more sophisticated and complex than those of many of the characters in the early novels. In this "Study of Provincial Life," as the novel is subtitled, Eliot explores the familiar moral territory of renunciation and self-indulgence by developing four more-or-less-distinct plot lines: The most important of these concern Dorothea Brooke and Tertius Lydgate, but Fred Vincy and Nicholas Bulstrode also claim a substantial amount of Eliot's attention.

This vast novel is unified not only by Eliot's moral concerns and by various cross-connections among the plot lines, but also by a pervasive theme of reform. The implied contrast between the climate for "far-resonant" action that existed when a "coherent social faith" allowed St. Theresa to find "her epos in the reform of a religious order" and the time of the novel, which ends "just after the Lords had thrown out the Reform Bill [of 1832]," suggests the difficulty of achieving meaningful action in the fragmented world of contemporary England. More than any previous novel, *Middlemarch* explores the moral achievements and failures of individuals against the background of an entire society, a society which does not provide many opportunities for people to put their best talents to use.

These issues are perhaps most fully embodied in Dorothea Brooke, a young heiress with "a nature altogether ardent, theoretic and intellectually consequent" who is "struggling in the bands of a narrow teaching, hemmed in by a social life which seemed nothing but a labyrinth of petty courses, a walled-in maze of small paths that led no whither." Seeking a way to give her life consequence and purpose, she marries Edward Casaubon, a desiccated pseudoscholar, whom she naïvely thinks of as a John Locke or a John Milton, a "winged messenger" who can guide her along the "grandest path." She soon discovers that Casaubon is not a great man, but a rather pathetic egotist, who is morbidly sensitive to real or imagined criticism of his work, pettishly jealous of Dorothea's friendship with his nephew Will Ladislaw, and incapable of offering her any real affection. She also learns that his projected work, grandly entitled a "Key to All Mythologies," is nothing but a monumental collection of trivia, already rendered obsolete by superior German scholarship. Nevertheless, Dorothea prepares to promise her husband, who is suffering from a "fatty degeneration of the heart," that she will continue his work after his death, a sacrifice from which she is saved by his timely demise.

Like Dorothea, Tertius Lydgate finds his ambitions for significant achievement frustrated by social pressures, but unlike Dorothea he adds to his difficulties by a tendency toward heedless self-indulgence. His well-intentioned plans for medical reform are jeopardized by his lack of sensitivity to the feelings of both patients and other practitioners and by his regrettable involvement with Nicholas Bulstrode, an unpopular but powerful leader in community affairs. More important, he shackles himself by marriage to Rosamond Vincy, the beautiful and self-centered daughter of the mayor of Middlemarch. This marriage, which Lydgate slips into more or less intentionally, blights his hopes of success. He gets heavily into debt as both he and Rosamond carelessly incur expenses on the unconsidered assumption that they ought to live well. Rosamond, utterly unwilling to make any sacrifices, simply blames him for their problems.

These two plot lines come together when Dorothea, deeply moved by Lydgate's marital and financial problems and eager to clear him from blame in a scandal involving Bulstrode, offers to call on Rosamond. She finds Rosamond in what appears to be a compromising tête-à-tête with Will, whom she had come to love since

Casaubon's death. Deeply distressed by what she assumes about Will's conduct, she nevertheless forces herself to "clutch [her] own pain" and think only of the "three lives whose contact with hers laid an obligation on her." Feeling "the largeness of the world and the manifold wakings of men to labour and endurance," she compels herself to make a second visit. She has some success in reconciling Rosamond to Lydgate and finds that Will's conduct was indeed blameless.

Although Dorothea's renunciation of herself has the unexpected result of opening the way for her marriage to Will, she never achieves her potential as a latter-day St. Theresa, "for the medium in which [her] ardent deeds took shape is forever gone." Her "full nature" spends itself "in channels which had no great name on earth" but which nonetheless bring benefits to her fellow men and women. Lydgate, who allowed himself to slip into marriage with the paralyzingly egotistical Rosamond, achieves financial success as a society doctor but "always regarded himself as a failure; he had not done what he once meant to do."

The other two plot lines, although less important than those centering on Dorothea and Lydgate, afford Eliot opportunity to round out her study of provincial life. Fred Vincy, who is Rosamond's brother, overcomes his tendency to fritter away his money in casual pleasures when he realizes the distresses that his failure to pay a debt will cause the Garth family, who represented security for him, and recognizes that Mary Garth will not marry him unless he undertakes a worthwhile career. The plot line centering on Nicholas Bulstrode, although the least extensive of the four, contains some of Eliot's most perceptive explorations of self-delusion. Bulstrode, who had gathered a fortune dealing in stolen goods before coming to Middlemarch, aspires to leadership in the community as a banker and as an Evangelical Christian. Although he assiduously conceals his former life, he is no simple hypocrite, but an ambitious man who aims at "being an eminent Christian," capable of deluding himself even in his prayers. His lifetime habit of confusing his own desires with God's will comes to a climax when he allows his housekeeper to administer brandy to an alcoholic former associate who has been blackmailing him—a treatment which, although common at the time, has been forbidden by Lydgate. Only after the man dies does Bulstrode discover that the former associate has already revealed Bulstrode's long-guarded secrets in his drunken ramblings.

Although the principal themes of *Middlemarch* are developed primarily in the four major plot lines, the novel's extraordinary richness of minor characters is surely one of its outstanding features. Mr. Brooke, Dorothea's uncle, is one of Eliot's supreme comic creations, a man "of acquiescent temper, miscellaneous opinions, and uncertain vote." Caleb Garth, "one of those rare men who are rigid with themselves and indulgent to others," is a model of sturdy rectitude. Mrs. Bulstrode's loyal support of her guilty husband and her acceptance of "a new life in which she embraced humiliation" is one of Eliot's finest passages. The list could be continued almost at will, amply justifying the claim of the novel's subtitle to be a "study of provincial life."

The subtitle is also appropriate in that it calls attention to Eliot's recognition, more fully expressed in this novel than in any of the earlier ones, of the ways in which the circumstances of society limit her characters' options. Dorothea achieves the ideal of self-renunciation that earlier characters have striven for, but the conditions of her life prevent her from achieving her potential; Lydgate fails not only because of his ill-advised marriage, but also because the community views his eagerness to advance his medical practice with suspicion and prejudice. Conditions of society, as well as moral flaws, frustrate the ambitions of even the worthiest characters.

Daniel Deronda · *Daniel Deronda*, Eliot's final novel, emphasizes the search for purpose more than the ideal of renunciation. Eliot continues her examination of egotism and self-indulgence, but these themes are muted with pathos in the portrayal of Gwendolen Harleth. In subject matter, Eliot also takes another step or two up the social ladder, dealing in this novel with the wealthy upper middle class and aristocracy.

The protagonist, Daniel Deronda, is such a paragon at the beginning of the novel that he has little need of the lessons in renunciation that Eliot's other protagonists must learn. Handsome, well-educated, and generously supported by Sir Hugo Mallinger, Deronda is only concerned with finding something purposeful to do with his life. His only burden is the assumption that he is Sir Hugo's illegitimate son. His discovery of a cause to which he can dedicate himself proceeds by easy stages. His rescue of Mirah, a Jewish singer who is preparing to drown herself, prompts his interest in Judaism. He succeeds in reuniting Mirah with her terminally ill brother Mordecai, a visionary Jewish mystic. When Mordecai sees Deronda from a bridge, which he describes as "a meeting place for spiritual messengers," he assumes that Deronda has been sent to bring him "my new life—my new self—who will live when this breath is all breathed out." Finally, Deronda discovers that he is actually the son of a distinguished Jewish singer who had asked Sir Hugo to bring him up as an Englishman. The discovery that he is Jewish enables him to marry Mirah, take up the torch from the dying Mordecai, and dedicate himself to the "restoration of a political existence to my people, giving them a national center, such as the English have." (In assigning this cause to Deronda, Eliot anticipated the Zionist movement by some twenty years and, indeed, gave powerful stimulus to the movement for the development of a Jewish national state.)

In Gwendolen Harleth, Eliot examines again the anatomy of egotism. Concerned only with her own comforts, Gwendolen rules imperiously over the household of her twice-widowed mother, Mrs. Davilow. Gwendolen's manifest dislike of men and her habit of sleeping in her mother's bedroom suggest sexual frigidity. Nevertheless, she is on the verge of marrying Henleigh Grandcourt, Sir Hugo's nephew and heir, when she discovers that Grandcourt has had four children by a mistress who deserted her own husband and whom Grandcourt still supports. An invitation to visit Germany with some family friends allows Gwendolen to evade a decision, but when her family loses its fortune, she decides on marriage rather than having her mother live in painfully reduced circumstances while she is forced to take the ignominious position of governess.

Gwendolen's motives in marriage are intriguingly mixed. To be sure, she is essentially egotistical and assumes that she will be able to control her husband. The family's dismal prospects after their catastrophic financial losses inevitably influence her. She is especially concerned for her mother, the one person for whom she feels genuine affection. Nevertheless, she also suffers an agony of guilt in her sense that her marriage has deprived Grandcourt's illegitimate children of any claim to his wealth.

Once they are married, the ruling hand is entirely Grandcourt's. Gwendolen bears his elegantly polite sadism with proud reserve, but is inwardly tormented by dread that her fear and hatred of her husband may drive her to some desperate act. When he drowns, perhaps because she fails to throw him a rope, she is overwhelmed with guilt. Desolated by the marriage of Deronda, whom she has turned to as a moral guide and mentor, she takes solace in Deronda's admonition that she "may live to be one of the best of women," although, as she adds in a final letter to Deronda, "I do not yet see how that can be."

Although Gwendolen's willingness to accept suffering scourges her egotism and brings her to a prospect of redemption that Rosamond Vincy glimpses only briefly, *Daniel Deronda* is in most ways Eliot's bleakest novel. An air of futility hangs like a pall over most of the characters; without a tradition of commitment to some place or purpose, they lack a future also. Mrs. Davilow moves from one rented house to another, and the estates passed down to Sir Hugo from the time of William the Conqueror will finally be inherited by Grandcourt's illegitimate son. Jewish characters such as Mirah's father and Deronda's mother wander over Europe, rejecting even an obligation to their own children. Only the dedication to art of Herr Kelsmer, a German musician, and the acceptance of Mordecai's dream of a national Jewish homeland by Deronda provide a sense of purpose or direction, and these vocations are ones from which most of the characters are inevitably excluded. Except in unusual cases, it appears that even the desire to renounce oneself may not be efficacious. The very circumstances of modern life work against moral achievement.

Erwin Hester

Other major works
SHORT FICTION: *Scenes of Clerical Life*, 1858.
POETRY: *The Spanish Gypsy*, 1868; *The Legend of Jubal and Other Poems*, 1874.
NONFICTION: *The Impressions of Theophrastus Such*, 1879; *Essays of George Eliot*, 1963 (Thomas Pinney, editor); *The Journals of George Eliot*, 1998 (Margaret Harris and Judith Johnston, editors).
TRANSLATIONS: *The Life of Jesus Critically Examined*, 1846 (with Mrs. Charles Hennell; of D. F. Strauss's *Das Leben Jesu*); *The Essence of Christianity*, 1854 (of Ludwig Feuerbach's *Das Wesen des Christentums*).

Bibliography
Beer, Gillian. *George Eliot*. Brighton, England: Harvester Press, 1986. One of a number of feminist readings of Eliot. Concentrates on her engagement with contemporary feminist issues in her fiction and the tensions between her life and her art set up by gender. Contains a full bibliography and an index.
Brady, Kristin. *George Eliot*. New York: St. Martin's Press, 1992. Includes chapters on Eliot as icon, on her life as a woman writer, and on her major novels and poetry. Argues that in spite of Eliot's major status, obviating the customary feminist call for a reevaluation, her work is still susceptible to a feminist rereading. Includes bibliography and index.
Haight, Gordon. *George Eliot: A Biography*. New York: Oxford University Press, 1968. Still the basic biography of Mary Ann Evans, making full use of her letters. A very large index is provided.
Hardy, Barbara. *The Novels of George Eliot: A Study in Form*. London: Athone Press, 1959. This study has retained its relevance in the continuing discussion of Eliot's fiction, dealing particularly with attempts to shape tragedy out of fiction. Plot, characterization, setting, imagery, and voice are dealt with separately but then focused into a discussion of Eliot's construction of the moral individual.
Hughes, Kathryn. *George Eliot: The Last Victorian*. London: Fourth Estate, 1998. A standard biography of Eliot, good for the general reader. Includes bibliographical references and an index.
Hutchinson, Stuart, ed. *George Eliot: Critical Assessments*. East Sussex, England: Helm

Information, 1996. Volume 1 consists of biography, nineteenth century reviews, and responses; volume 2 contains perspectives from 1900-1970 on Eliot's work; volume 3 provides critical essays on individual works; volume 4 includes perspectives from the 1970's on.

Karl, Fred. *George Eliot: Voice of a Century.* New York: W. W. Norton, 1995. While Karl's biography does not supersede Haight's, it does draw on valuable new archival material and on feminist criticism.

Pangallo, Karen L., ed. *The Critical Response to George Eliot.* Westport, Conn.: Greenwood Press, 1994. Provides sections divided into articles on individual novels as well as a separate section on general responses to Eliot's novels. The selection encompasses both the responses of Eliot's contemporaries and later generations of critics. Includes a bibliography and index.

Pinion, F. B. *A George Eliot Companion.* Basingstoke, England: Macmillan, 1981. Not only is this volume a mine of information on Eliot's life and work, but it also seeks to rehabilitate some of her neglected later fiction. Includes appendices and an index.

Shaw, Harry E. *Narrating Reality: Austen, Scott, Eliot.* Ithaca, N.Y.: Cornell University Press, 1999. Explores the technique of the three authors. Provides bibliographical references and an index.

Henry Fielding

Born: Sharpham Park, Somersetshire, England;
April 22, 1707
Died: Lisbon, Portugal; October 8, 1754

Principal long fiction · *An Apology for the Life of Mrs. Shamela Andrews*, 1741; *The History of the Adventures of Joseph Andrews, and of His Friend Mr. Abraham Adams*, 1742; *The History of the Life of the Late Mr. Jonathan Wild the Great*, 1743, 1754; *The History of Tom Jones, a Foundling*, 1749; *Amelia*, 1751.

Other literary forms · Henry Fielding's literary output, besides his novels, can be categorized in three groups: plays, pamphlets and miscellaneous items, and journals. In addition, the publication of his three-volume *Miscellanies* (1743) by subscription brought together a number of previously published items, as well as new works, including the first version of *The History of the Life of the Late Jonathan Wild the Great*, commonly known as *Jonathan Wild*, and an unfinished prose work, "A Journey from This World to the Next."

Fielding's dramatic works, many presented with great success at either of London's Little Theatre in the Haymarket or the Drury Lane Theatre, include ballad opera, farce, full-length comedy, and adaptations of classical and French drama. Most are overtly political in theme. Because of their contemporary subject matter, few have survived as viable stage presentations, although *The Covent Garden Tragedy* (1732) was presented by The Old Vic in London in 1968. Fielding also wrote a number of prologues, epilogues, and monologues performed in conjunction with other dramatic pieces.

The pamphlets and miscellaneous items which are currently attributed to Fielding, excluding those for which he merely wrote introductions or epilogues, are "The Masquerade" (1728), a poem; *The Military History of Charles XII King of Sweden* (1740), a translation; "Of True Greatness" (1741), a poem; "The Opposition: A Vision" (1741), a poem; "The Vernoniad" (1741), a poem; "The Female Husband" (1746); "Ovid's Art of Love Paraphrased" (1747); "A True State of the Case of Bosavern Penlez" (1749); "An Enquiry into the Causes of the Late Increase in Robbers" (1751); "Examples of the Interposition of Providence in the Detection and Punishment of Murder" (1752); "A Proposal for Making an Effectual Provision for the Poor" (1753); "A Clear State of the Case of Elizabeth Canning" (1753); and *The Journal of a Voyage to Lisbon*, published posthumously (1755).

Fielding edited and made major contributions to four journals: *The Champion* (November 15, 1739-June 1741; the journal continued publication without Fielding until 1742); *The True Patriot* (November 5, 1745-June 17, 1746); *Jacobite's Journal* (December 5, 1747-November 5, 1748); and *The Covent-Garden Journal* (January 4-November 25, 1752).

Achievements · Fielding's lasting achievements in prose fiction—in contrast to his passing fame as an essayist, dramatist, and judge—result from his development of critical theory and from his aesthetic success in the novels themselves. In the preface to *The History of the Adventures of Joseph Andrews, and of His Friend Mr. Abraham Adams*, more commonly known as *Joseph Andrews*, Fielding establishes a serious critical basis for the novel as a genre and describes in detail the elements of comic realism; in *Joseph Andrews* and *The History of Tom Jones, a Foundling*, popularly known as *Tom Jones*, he provides full realizations of this theory. These novels define the ground rules of form that would be followed, to varying degrees, by Jane Austen, William Makepeace Thackeray, George Eliot, Thomas Hardy, James Joyce, and D. H. Lawrence, and they also speak to countless readers across many generations. Both, in fact, were translated into successful films (*Tom Jones*, 1963; *Joseph Andrews*, 1978).

Library of Congress

The historical importance of the preface results from both the seriousness with which it treats the formal qualities of the novel (at the time a fledgling and barely respectable genre) and the precision with which it defines the characteristics of the genre, the "comic epic-poem in prose." Fielding places *Joseph Andrews* in particular and the comic novel in general squarely in the tradition of classical literature and coherently argues its differences from the romance and the burlesque. He also provides analogies between the comic novel and the visual arts. Thus Fielding leads the reader to share his conception that the comic novel is an aesthetically valid form with its roots in classical tradition, and a form peculiarly suited to the attitudes and values of its own age.

With his background in theater and journalism, Fielding could move easily through a wide range of forms and rhetorical techniques in his fiction, from direct parody of Samuel Richardson in *An Apology for the Life of Mrs. Shamela Andrews*, to ironic inversion of the great man's biography in *Jonathan Wild*, to adaptation of classical structure (Vergil's *Aeneid*, c. 29-19 B.C.) in *Amelia*. The two major constants in these works are the attempt to define a good, moral life, built on benevolence and honor, and a concern for finding the best way to present that definition to the reader. Thus the moral and the technique can never be separated in Fielding's works.

Joseph Andrews and *Tom Jones* bring together these two impulses in Fielding's most organically structured, brilliantly characterized, and masterfully narrated works. These novels vividly capture the diversity of experience in the physical world and the underlying benevolence of natural order, embodying them in a rich array of the ridiculous in human behavior. Fielding combines a positive assertion of the strength of goodness and benevolence (demonstrated by the structure and plot of the novels) with the sharp thrusts of the satirist's attack upon the hypocrisy and vanity of individual characters. These elements are held together by the voice of the narrator—witty, urbane, charming—who serves as moral guide through the novels and the world. Thus, beyond the comic merits of each of the individual novels lies a collective sense of universal moral good. The voice of the narrator conveys to the reader the truth of that goodness.

Although the novels were popular in his own day, Fielding's contemporaries thought of him more as playwright-turned-judge than as novelist. This may have been the result of the low esteem in which the novel as a form was held, as well as of Fielding's brilliant successes in these other fields. These varied successes have in common a zest for the exploration of the breadth and variety of life—a joy in living—that finds its most articulate and permanent expression in the major novels.

Today Fielding is universally acknowledged as a major figure in the development of the novel, although there is still niggling about whether he or Richardson is the "father" of the British novel. Ian Watt, for example, claims that Richardson's development of "formal realism" is more significant than Fielding's comic realism. Other critics, notably Martin Battestin, have demonstrated that Fielding's broader, more humane moral vision, embodied in classical structure and expressed through a self-conscious narrator, is the germ from which the richness and variety of the British novel grows. This disagreement ultimately comes down to personal taste, and there will always be Richardson and Fielding partisans to keep the controversy alive. There is no argument, however, that of their type—the novel of comic realism—no fiction has yet surpassed *Joseph Andrews* or *Tom Jones.*

Biography · Henry Fielding was born April 22, 1707, in Sharpham Park, Somersetshire, to Edmund and Sarah Fielding. His father, an adventurer, gambler, and swaggerer, was a sharp contrast to the quiet, conservative, traditional gentry of his mother's family, the Goulds. In 1710, the family moved to Dorset, where Fielding and his younger brother and three sisters (including the future novelist Sarah Fielding) would spend most of their childhood on a small estate and farm given to Mrs. Fielding by her father, Sir Henry Gould.

The death of Fielding's mother in April, 1718, ended this idyllic life. Litigation over the estate created a series of family battles that raged for several decades. In 1719, Fielding was sent to Eton College, partly because the Goulds wanted him influenced as little as possible by his father, who had resumed his "wild" life in London, and partly because he disliked his father's new, Catholic wife. Remaining at Eton until 1724 or 1725, Fielding made many friends, including George Lyttleton and William Pitt. At Eton he began his study of classical literature, a profound influence on his literary career.

Few details are known of Fielding's life during the several years after Eton. He spent a good deal of time with the Goulds in Salisbury, but he also led a hectic, boisterous life in London, spending much time at the theater, where the popular masquerades and burlesques influenced him greatly. His visits to the theater stimulated him to try his own hand at comedy, and in February, 1728, *Love in Several Masques,* based on his own romantic adventures of the previous year, was performed at Drury Lane.

In March, 1728, Fielding enrolled in the Faculty of Letters at the University of Leyden (Netherlands), where he pursued his interest in the classics. In August, 1729, at the age of twenty-two, he returned to London without completing his degree.

It is clear from his literary output in the 1730's that Fielding was intensely involved in theatrical life. From 1730 through 1737 he authored at least nineteen different dramatic works (as well as presenting revivals and new productions of revised works), most with political themes, at both the Little Theatre in the Haymarket and the Drury Lane. In addition to writing ballad opera, full-length comedies, translations, and parodies, Fielding was also producing, revising the plays of other writers, and managing theater business. He also formed a new, important friendship with the artist William Hogarth.

His theatrical career came to an abrupt halt (although a few more plays appeared in the 1740's) with the passage of the Licensing Act of 1737, which resulted in the closing of many theaters. Fielding's political satire offended Prime Minister Sir Robert Walpole and had been part of the motivation for the government's desire to control and censor the theaters.

In addition to this theatrical activity with its political commentary, Fielding found time from 1733 to 1734 to court and marry Charlotte Cradock of Salisbury. Charlotte's mother died in 1735, leaving the entire estate to the Fieldings and alleviating many of the financial problems caused by the legal disputes over the estate in Dorset. The couple moved from London to East Stour the same year, although Fielding regularly visited London, because he was manager, artistic director, and controller-in-chief of the Little Theatre. The first of their three children, Charlotte, was born April 17, 1736.

Fielding's relentless energy (and desire to add to his income) compelled him to begin a new career in late 1737, whereupon he began to study law at the Middle Temple. He became a barrister on June 20, 1740, and spent the next several years in the Western Circuit. During this service he became friends with Ralph Allen of Bath. He remained active in the practice of justice, as attorney and magistrate, until he left England in 1754.

Fielding continued to involve himself in political controversy, even while studying law. He edited, under pseudonyms, *The Champion*, an opposition newspaper issued three times a week, directed against Prime Minister Walpole (a favorite subject of Fielding's satire). Later he would edit *The True Patriot* in support of the government during the threat of the Jacobite Rising, *Jacobite's Journal*, and *The Covent-Garden Journal*.

From theater to law to journalism, Fielding had already charged through three careers when the first installment of Richardson's *Pamela* appeared on November 6, 1740. Deeply disturbed by the artificiality of the novel's epistolary technique, and appalled by its perversion of moral values, Fielding quickly responded with *An Apology for the Life of Mrs. Shamela Andrews*, often referred to as *Shamela*, an "antidote" to *Pamela*. Although published anonymously, Fielding's authorship was apparent and created ill feelings between the two authors that would last most of their lives.

The success of *Shamela* encouraged Fielding to try his hand at a more sustained satire, which eventually grew into *Joseph Andrews*. In 1743 he published, by subscription, the *Miscellanies*, a collection of previously published works, and two new ones: an unfinished story, "A Journey from This World to the Next," and the first version of *Jonathan Wild*.

Although the mid-1740's brought Fielding fame, success, and money, his personal life was beset with pain. He suffered continually from gout, and Charlotte died in November, 1744. In the following year he became involved in the propaganda battles over the Jacobite Rising. On November 27, 1747, he married his wife's former maid, Mary Daniel, and some sense of peace and order was restored to his private life. They would have five children.

While forming new personal ties and continuing strong involvement in political issues, Fielding was preparing his masterwork, *Tom Jones*. He also took oath as Justice of the Peace for Westminster and Middlesex, London, in 1748, and opened an employment agency and estate brokerage with his brother in 1749. His last novel, *Amelia*, was not well received, disappointing those readers who were expecting another *Tom Jones*.

The early 1750's saw Fielding's health continue to decline, although he remained active in his judgeship, producing a number of pamphlets on various legal questions. In June of 1754, his friends convinced him to sail to Lisbon, Portugal, where the climate might improve his health. He died there on October 8, 1754, and is buried in the British Cemetery outside of Lisbon. *The Journal of a Voyage to Lisbon*, his last work, was published one year after his death.

Analysis · Analysis and criticism of Henry Fielding's fiction have traditionally centered on the moral values in the novels, the aesthetic structure in which they are placed, and the relationship between the two. In this view, Fielding as moralist takes precedence over Fielding as artist, since the aesthetic structure is determined by the moral. Each of the novels is judged by the extent to which it finds the appropriate form for its moral vision. The relative failure of *Amelia*, for example, may be Fielding's lack of faith in his own moral vision. The happy ending, promulgated by the *deus ex machina* of the good magistrate, is hardly consistent with the dire effects of urban moral decay that have been at work upon the Booths throughout the novel. Fielding's own moral development and changes in outlook also need to be considered in this view. The reader must examine the sources of Fielding's moral vision in the latitudinarian sermons of the day, as well as the changes in his attitudes as he examined eighteenth century urban life in greater detail, and as he moved in literature from *Joseph Andrews* to *Amelia*, and in life from the theater to the bench of justice.

As is clear from the preface to *Joseph Andrews*, however, Fielding was equally interested in the aesthetics of his fiction. Indeed, each of the novels, even from the first parody, *Shamela*, conveys not only a moral message but a literary experiment to find the strongest method for expressing that message to the largest reading public. This concern is evident in the basic plot structure, characterization, language, and role of the narrator. Each novel attempts to reach the widest audience possible with its moral thesis. Although each differs in the way in which Fielding attempts this, they all have in common the sense that the *how* of the story is as important as the *what*. The novels are experiments in the methods of moral education—for the reader as well as for the characters.

This concern for the best artistic way to teach a moral lesson was hardly new with Fielding. His classical education and interests, as well as the immediate human response gained from theater audiences during his playwriting days, surely led him to see that fiction must delight as well as instruct. Fielding's novels are both exemplars of this goal (in their emphasis on incidents of plot and broad range of characterization) and serious discussions of the method by which to achieve it (primarily through structure and through narrative commentary).

The direct stimulation for Fielding's career as novelist was the publication of Samuel Richardson's *Pamela*, a novel that disturbed Fielding both by its artistic ineptitude and by its moral vacuousness. Fielding was as concerned with the public reaction to *Pamela* as he was with its author's methods. That the reading public could be so easily misled by *Pamela*'s morals disturbed Fielding deeply, and the success of that novel led him to ponder what better ways were available for reaching the public with his own moral thesis. His response to *Pamela* was both moral (he revealed the true state of Pamela/Shamela's values) and aesthetic (he exposed the artificiality of "writing to the moment").

Sermons and homilies, while effective in church (and certainly sources of Fielding's moral philosophy), were not the stuff of prose fiction; neither was the epistolary presentation of "virtue rewarded" of *Pamela* (nor the "objectively" amoral tone of Daniel Defoe's *Moll Flanders*, 1722). Fielding sought a literary method for combining moral vision and literary pleasure that would be appropriate to the rapidly urbanizing and secular society of the mid-eighteenth century. To find that method he ranged through direct parody, irony, satire, author-narrator intrusion, and moral exemplum. Even those works, such as *Jonathan Wild* and *Amelia*, which are not entirely successful, live because of the vitality of Fielding's experimental methods. In *Joseph Andrews* and *Tom Jones*, he found the way to reach his audience most effectively.

Fielding's informing moral values, embodied in the central characters of the novels (Joseph Andrews, Parson Adams, Tom Jones, Squire Allworthy, Mr. Harrison) can be summarized, as Martin Battestin has ably done, as Charity, Prudence, and Providence. Fielding held an optimistic faith in the perfectibility of humanity and the potential for the betterment of society, based on the essential goodness of human nature. These three values must work together. In the novels, the hero's worth is determined by the way in which he interacts with other people (charity), within the limits of social institutions designed to provide order (prudence). His reward is a life full of God's provision (providence). God's providence has created a world of abundance and plenitude; man's prudence and charity can guarantee its survival and growth. Both Joseph Andrews and Tom Jones learn the proper combination of prudence and charity. They learn to use their innate inclination toward goodness within a social system that ensures order. To succeed, however, they must overcome obstacles provided by the characters who, through vanity and hypocrisy, distort God's providence. Thus, Fielding's moral vision, while optimistic, is hardly blind to the realities of the world. *Jonathan Wild*, with its basic rhetorical distinction between "good" and "great," and *Amelia*, with its narrative structured around the ill effects of doing good, most strongly reflect Fielding's doubts about the practicality of his beliefs.

These ideas can be easily schematized, but the scheme belies the human complexity through which they are expressed in the novels. Tom Jones is no paragon of virtue, but he must learn, at great physical pain and spiritual risk, how to combine charity and prudence. Even Squire Allworthy, as Sheldon Sacks emphasized in *Fiction and the Shape of Belief* (1964), is a "fallible" paragon. These ideas do not come from a single source, but are derived from a combination of sources, rooted in Fielding's classical education; the political, religious, and literary movements of his own time; and his own experience as dramatist, journalist, and magistrate.

Fielding's familiarity with the classics, begun at Eton and continued at the University of Leyden, is revealed in many ways: through language (the use of epic simile and epic conventions in *Joseph Andrews*), through plot (the symmetry of design in *Tom Jones*), through theme (the importance of moderation in all the novels), and through structure (the relationship of *Amelia* to Vergil's *Aeneid*). The preface to *Joseph Andrews* makes explicit how much Fielding saw in common between his own work and classical literature. His belief in the benevolent order of the world, especially illustrated by country living, such as at Squire Allworthy's estate (Paradise Hall), is deeply rooted in the pastoral tradition of classical literature. These classical elements are combined with the beliefs of the latitudinarian homilists of the seventeenth and eighteenth centuries, who stressed the perfectibility of humankind in the world through good deeds (charity) and good heart (benevolence).

While Fielding's thematic concerns may be rooted in classical and Christian thought, his literary technique has sources that are more complex, deriving from his education, his own experience in the theater, and the influence of Richardson's *Pamela*. It is difficult to separate each of these sources, for the novels work them into unified and original statements. Indeed, *Joseph Andrews*, the novel most closely related to classical sources, is also deeply imbued with the sense of latitudinarian thought in its criticism of the clergy, and satire of Richardson in its plot and moral vision.

The London in which Fielding spent most of his life was a world of literary and political ferment, an age of factionalism in the arts, with the Tory wits (Jonathan Swift, Alexander Pope, John Gay, John Arbuthnot) allied against Colley Cibber, the poet laureate and self-proclaimed literary spokesman for the British Isles. Swift's *Gulliver's Travels* (1726) and Gay's *The Beggar's Opera* (1728) had recently appeared; both were influential in forming Fielding's literary methods—the first with its emphasis on sharp political satire, the second with the creation of a new literary form, the ballad opera. The ballad opera set new lyrics, expressing contemporary political and social satire, to well-known music. Fielding was to find his greatest theatrical success in this genre and was to carry it over to his fiction, especially *Jonathan Wild*, with its emphasis on London low life and its excesses of language.

It was a time, also, of great political controversy, with the ongoing conflicts between the Tories and Jacobites about the questions of religion and succession. Prime Minister Walpole's politics of expediency were a ripe subject for satire. Fielding's career as journalist began as a direct response to political issues, and significant portions of *Joseph Andrews* and *Tom Jones*, as well as *Jonathan Wild*, deal with political issues.

These various sources, influences, and beliefs are molded into coherent works of art through Fielding's narrative technique. It is through the role of the narrator that he most clearly and successfully experiments in the methods of teaching a moral lesson. Starting with the voice of direct literary parody in *Shamela* and moving through the varied structures and voices of the other novels, Fielding's art leads in many directions, but it always leads to his ultimate concern for finding the best way to teach the clearest moral lesson. In *Tom Jones* he finds the most appropriate method to demonstrate that the world is a beautiful place if man will live by charity and prudence.

Shamela · The key to understanding how *Shamela* expresses Fielding's concern with both the moral thesis and the aesthetic form of fiction is contained in the introductory letters between Parsons Tickletext and Oliver. Oliver is dismayed at Tickletext's exuberant praise of *Pamela* and at the novel's public reception and popularity. The clergy, in particular, have been citing it as a work worthy to be read with the Scriptures. He contends that the text of *Shamela*, which he encloses, reveals the "true" story of Pamela's adventures and puts them in their proper moral perspective. By reading Oliver's version, Tickletext will correct his own misconceptions; by reading *Shamela* (under the guidance of the prefatory letters), the public will laugh at *Pamela* and perceive the perversity of its moral thesis.

Shamela began, of course, simply as a parody of Richardson's novel, and, in abbreviated form, carries through the narrative of the attempted seduction of the young serving girl by the squire, and her attempts to assert her virtue through chastity or marriage. Fielding makes direct hits at Richardson's weakest points: His two main targets are the epistolary technique of "writing to the moment" and the moral thesis of "virtue rewarded" by pounds and pence (and marriage).

Fielding parodies the epistolary technique by carrying it to its most illogical extreme: Richardson's technical failure is not the choice of epistolary form, but his insistence on its adherence to external reality. Shamela writes her letters at the very same moment she is being attacked in bed by Squire Booby. While feigning sleep she writes: "You see I write in the present tense." The inconsistency of Pamela's shift from letters to journal form when she is abducted is shown through Fielding's retention of the letter form throughout the story, no matter what the obstacles for sending and receiving them. He also compounds the criticism of Richardson by including a number of correspondents besides Shamela (her mother, Henrietta Maria Honora Andrews, Mrs. Jewkes, Parson Williams) and including various complications, such as letters within letters within letters.

Fielding retains the essential characters and key scenes from *Pamela*, such as Mr. B's hiding in the closet before the attempted seduction, Pamela's attempted suicide at the pond, and Parson Williams's interference. For each character and scene Fielding adopts Richardson's penchant for minute descriptive detail and intense character response to the event; he also parodies the method and seriousness of the original by revealing the motives of the characters.

The revealing of motives is also Fielding's primary way of attacking the prurience of Richardson's presentation, as well as the moral thesis behind it. He debunks the punctilio (decorum) of the central character. Shamela's false modesty ("I thought once of making a little fortune by my person. I now intend to make a great one by my virtue") mocks Pamela's pride in her chastity; the main difference between them is Shamela's recognition and acceptance of the mercenary motives behind her behavior and Pamela's blindness to her own motivation. Richardson never examines the reliability of Pamela's motivations, although he describes her thoughts in detail. Fielding allows Shamela to glory in both her ability to dupe the eager Squire Booby and her mercenary motives for doing so. The reader may, as Parson Oliver wants Tickletext to do, easily condemn Shamela for a villain but never for a hypocrite.

Fielding also attacks Richardson's refusal to describe the sexual attributes of his characters or to admit the intensity of their sexual desires, particularly in the case of Pamela herself. Pamela always hints and suggests—and, Fielding claims, wallows in her suggestiveness. Fielding not only describes the sexual aspects directly, but exaggerates and reduces them to a comic level, hardly to be taken sensually or seriously. *Shamela* quickly, fully, and ruthlessly annihilates the moral thesis of "virtue rewarded" through this direct exaggeration. Fielding does not, however, in his role as parodist, suggest an alternative to *Pamela*'s moral thesis; he is content, for the time, with exposing its flaws.

This first foray into fiction served for Fielding as a testing ground for some of the rhetorical techniques he used in later works, especially the emphasis on satiric inversion. These inversions appear in his reversal of sexual roles in *Joseph Andrews*, the reversal of rhetoric in the "good" and "great" in *Jonathan Wild*, and the reversal of goodness of motive and evil of effect in *Amelia*. Fielding's concern to find a rhetorical method for presenting a moral thesis was confined in *Shamela* to the limited aims and goals of parody. He had such success with the method (after all, he had his apprenticeship in the satiric comedy of the theater), that he began his next novel on the same model.

Joseph Andrews · Like *Shamela, Joseph Andrews* began as a parody of *Pamela*. In his second novel, Fielding reverses the gender of the central character and traces Joseph's attempts to retain his chastity and virtue while being pursued by Lady Booby. This method of inversion creates new possibilities, not only for satirizing Richardson's work, but for commenting on the sexual morality of the time in a more positive way than in *Shamela*. The most cursory reading reveals how quickly Fielding grew tired of parody and how *Joseph Andrews* moved beyond its inspiration and its forerunner. Even the choice of direct narration rather than epistolary form indicates Fielding's unwillingness to tie himself to his model.

Most readers agree that the entrance of Parson Adams, Joseph's guide, companion, and partner in misery, turns the novel from simple parody into complex fiction. Adams takes center stage as both comic butt, preserving Joseph's role as hero, and moral guide, preserving Joseph's role as innocent.

Adams's contribution is also part of Fielding's conscious search for the best way to convey his moral thesis. The narrative refers continually to sermons, given in the pulpit or being carried by Adams to be published in London. These sermons are generally ineffectual or contradicted by the behavior of the clergy who pronounce them. Just as experience and the moral example of Adams's life are better teachers for Joseph than sermons—what could be a more effective lesson than the way he is treated by the coach passengers after he is robbed, beaten, and stripped?—so literary example has more power for Fielding and the reader. Adams's constant companion, his copy of Aeschylus, is further testament to Fielding's growing faith in his exemplary power of literature as moral guide. In *Joseph Andrews*, narrative art takes precedence over both parody and sermon.

Fielding's concern for method as well as meaning is given its most formal discussion in the preface. The historical importance of this document results from both the seriousness with which it treats the formal qualities of the novel and the precision with which it defines the characteristics of the genre, the "comic epic-poem in prose." The seriousness is established through the careful logic and organization of the argument and through the parallels drawn between the new genre and classical literature (the lost comic epic supposedly written by Homer) and modern painting (Michelangelo da Caravaggio and William Hogarth).

Fielding differentiates the comic epic-poem in prose from contemporary romances such as *Pamela*. The new form is more extended and comprehensive in action, contains a much larger variety of incidents, and treats a greater variety of characters. Unlike the serious romance, the new form is less solemn in subject matter, treats characters of lower rank, and presents the ludicrous rather than the sublime. The comic, opposed to the burlesque, arises solely from the observation of nature, and has its source in the discovery of the "ridiculous" in human nature. The ridiculous always springs from the affectations of vanity and hypocrisy.

Within the novel itself, the narrator will continue the discussion of literary issues in the introductory chapters to each of the first three of four books: "of writing lives in general," "of divisions in authors," and "in praise of biography." These discussions, although sometimes more facetious than serious, do carry through the direction of the opening sentence of the novel: "Examples work more forcibly on the mind than precepts." Additionally, this narrative commentary allows Fielding to assume the role of reader's companion and guide that he develops more fully in *Tom Jones*.

While the preface takes its cue from classical tradition, it is misleading to assume that *Joseph Andrews* is merely an updating of classical technique and ideas. Even more than *Shamela*, this novel brings together Fielding's dissatisfaction with Richardson's moral thesis and his support of latitudinarian attitudes toward benevolence and charity. Here, too, Fielding begins his definition of the "good" man in modern Christian terms. Joseph redefines the place of chastity and honor in male sexuality; Parson Adams exemplifies the benevolence all people should display; Mrs. Towwowse, Trulliber, and Peter Pounce, among others, illustrate the vanity and hypocrisy of the world.

The structure of the novel is episodic, combining the earthly journey and escapades of the hero with suggestions of the Christian pilgrimage in John Bunyan's *The Pilgrim's Progress* (1678-1684). Fielding was still experimenting with form and felt at liberty to digress from his structure with interpolated tales or to depend on coincidence to bring the novel to its conclusion. The immediate moral effect sometimes seems more important than the consistency of rhetorical structure. These are, however, minor lapses in Fielding's progression toward unifying moral thesis and aesthetic structure.

Jonathan Wild · In *Jonathan Wild*, Fielding seems to have abandoned temporarily the progression from the moral statement of parody and sermon to the aesthetic statement of literary example. *Jonathan Wild* was first published in the year immediately following *Joseph Andrews* (revised in 1754), and there is evidence to indicate that the work was actually written before *Joseph Andrews*. This is a reasonable assumption, since *Jonathan Wild* is more didactic in its method and more negative in its moral vision. It looks back toward *Shamela* rather than ahead to *Tom Jones*.

Jonathan Wild is less a novel, even as Fielding discusses the form in the preface to *Joseph Andrews*, than a polemic. Critic Northrop Frye's term, "anatomy," may be the most appropriate label for the work. Like other anatomies–Sir Thomas More's *Utopia* (1516), Swift's *Gulliver's Travels*, and Samuel Johnson's *Rasselas, Prince of Abyssinia* (1759)–it emphasizes ideas over narrative. It is more moral fable than novel, and more fiction than historical biography, altering history to fit the moral vision.

More important, it was Fielding's experiment in moving the moral lesson of the tale away from the narrative (with its emphasis on incident and character) and into the rhetoric of the narrator (with its emphasis on language). Fielding attempted to use language as the primary carrier of his moral thesis. Although this experiment failed–manipulation of language, alone, would not do–it gave him the confidence to develop the role of the narrative voice in its proper perspective in *Tom Jones*.

Fielding freely adapted the facts of Wild's life, which were well known to the general public. He chose those incidents from Wild's criminal career and punishment that would serve his moral purpose, and he added his own fictional characters, the victims of Wild's "greatness," expecially the Heartfrees. Within the structure of the inverted biography of the "great" man, Fielding satirizes the basic concepts of middle-class society. He differentiates between "greatness" and "goodness," terms often used synonymously in the eighteenth century. The success of the novel depends on the reader's acceptance and understanding of this rhetorical inversion.

"Goodness," characterized by the Heartfrees, reiterates the ideals of behavior emphasized in *Joseph Andrews:* benevolence, honor, honesty, and charity, felt through the heart. "Greatness," personified in Wild, results in cunning and courage, characteristics of the will. The action of the novel revolves around the ironic reversal of these terms. Although Wild's actions speak for themselves, the ironic voice of the narrator constantly directs the reader's response.

Parts of *Jonathan Wild* are brilliantly satiric, but the work as a whole does not speak to modern readers. Fielding abandoned the anatomy form after this experiment, recognizing that the voice of the narrator alone cannot carry the moral thesis of a novel in a convincing way. In *Jonathan Wild*, he carried to an extreme the role of the narrator as moral guide that he experimented with in *Joseph Andrews*. In *Tom Jones*, he found the precise balance: the moral voice of the narrator controlling the reader's reaction through language and the literary examples of plot and character.

Tom Jones · In *Tom Jones*, Fielding moved beyond the limited aims of each of his previous works into a more comprehensive moral and aesthetic vision. No longer bound by the need to attack Richardson nor the attempt to define a specific fictional form, such as the moral fable or the comic epic-poem in prose, Fielding dramatized the positive values of the good man in a carefully structured narrative held together by the guiding voice of the narrator. This narrator unifies, in a consistent pattern, Fielding's concern for both the truthfulness of his moral vision and the best way to reach the widest audience.

The structure of *Tom Jones*, like that of *Joseph Andrews*, is based on the secularization of the spiritual pilgrimage. Tom must journey from his equivocal position as foundling on the country estate of Squire Allworthy (Paradise Hall) to moral independence in the hellish city of London. He must learn to understand and control his life. When he learns this lesson, he will return to the country to enjoy the plenitude of paradise regained that providence allows him. He must temper his natural, impetuous charity with the prudence that comes from recognition of his own role in the larger social structure. In precise terms, he must learn to control his animal appetites in order to win the love of Sophia Western and the approval of Allworthy. This lesson is rewarded not only by his gaining these two goals, but by his gaining the knowledge of his parentage and his rightful place in society. He is no longer a "foundling."

Unlike the episodic journey of *Joseph Andrews*, *Tom Jones* adapts the classical symmetry of the epic in a more conscious and precise way. The novel is divided into eighteen books. Some of the books, such as 1 and 4, cover long periods of time and are presented in summary form, with the narrator clearly present; others cover only a few days or hours, with the narrator conspicuously absent and the presentation primarily scenic. The length of each book is determined by the importance of the subject, not the length of time covered.

The books are arranged in a symmetrical pattern. The first half of the novel takes Tom from his mysterious birth to his adventures in the Inn at Upton; the second half takes him from Upton to London and the discovery of his parentage. Books 1 through 6 are set in Somerset at Squire Allworthy's estate and culminate with Tom's affair with Molly. Books 7 through 12 are set on the road to Upton, at the Inn, and on the road from Upton to London; the two central books detail the adventures at the Inn and Tom's affair with Mrs. Waters. Books 13 through 18 take Tom to London and begin with his affair with Lady Bellaston.

Within this pattern, Fielding demonstrates his moral thesis, the education of a "good man," in a number of ways: through the narrative (Tom's behavior continually lowers his moral worth in society); through characters (the contrasting pairs of Tom and Blifil, Allworthy and Western, Square and Thwackum, Molly and Lady Bellaston); and through the voice of the narrator.

Fielding extends the role of the narrator in *Tom Jones*, as teller of the tale, as moral guide, and as literary commentator and critic. Each of these voices was heard in *Joseph*

Andrews, but here they come together in a unique narrative persona. Adopting the role of the stagecoach traveler, the narrator speaks directly to his fellow passengers, the readers. He is free to digress and comment whenever he feels appropriate, and there is, therefore, no need for the long interpolated tales such as appeared in *Joseph Andrews*.

To remind his readers that the purpose of fiction is aesthetic as well as moral, the narrator often comments on literary topics: "Of the Serious in Writing, and for What Purpose it is introduced"; "A wonderful long chapter concerning the Marvelous"; "Containing Instructions very necessary to be perused by modern Critics." Taken together, these passages provide a guide to Fielding's literary theory as complete as the preface to *Joseph Andrews*.

Although in *Tom Jones* Fielding still schematically associates characters with particular moral values, the range of characters is wider than in his previous novels. Even a minor character, such as Black George, has a life beyond his moral purpose as representative of hypocrisy and self-serving.

Most important, *Tom Jones* demonstrates Fielding's skill in combining his moral vision with aesthetic form in a way that is most pleasurable to the reader. The reader learns how to live the good Christian life because Tom learns that lesson. Far more effective than parody, sermon, or moral exemplum, the combination of narrative voice and literary example of plot and character is Fielding's greatest legacy to the novel.

Lawrence F. Laban

Other major works

PLAYS: *Love in Several Masques*, pr., pb. 1728; *The Temple Beau*, pr., pb. 1730; *The Author's Farce, and The Pleasures of the Town*, pr., pb. 1730; *Tom Thumb: A Tragedy*, pr., pb. 1730 (revised as *The Tragedy of Tragedies*, pr., pb. 1731); *Rape upon Rape: Or, Justice Caught in His Own Trap*, pr., pb. 1730 (also known as *The Coffee-House Politician*); *The Letter-Writers: Or, A New Way to Keep a Wife at Home*, pr., pb. 1731; *The Welsh Opera: Or, The Grey Mare the Better Horse*, pr., pb. 1731 (revised as *The Grub-Street Opera*, pb. 1731); *The Lottery*, pr., pb. 1732; *The Modern Husband*, pr., pb. 1732 (five acts); *The Old Debauchees*, pr., pb. 1732; *The Covent Garden Tragedy*, pr., pb. 1732; *The Mock Doctor: Or, The Dumb Lady Cur'd*, pr., pb. 1732 (adaptation of Molière's *Le Médecin malgré lui*); *The Miser*, pr., pb. 1733 (adaptation of Molière's *L'Avare*); *Don Quixote in England*, pr., pb. 1734; *The Intriguing Chambermaid*, pr., pb. 1734 (adaptation of Jean-François Regnard's *Le Retour imprévu*); *An Old Man Taught Wisdom: Or, The Virgin Unmask'd*, pr., pb. 1735; *The Universal Gallant: Or, The Different Husbands*, pr., pb. 1735 (five acts); *Pasquin: Or, A Dramatic Satire on the Times*, pr., pb. 1736; *Tumble-Down Dick: Or, Phaeton in the Suds*, pr., pb. 1736; *Eurydice: Or, The Devil's Henpeck'd*, pr. 1737 (one act); *Eurydice Hiss'd: Or, A Word to the Wise*, pr., pb. 1737; *The Historical Register for the Year 1736*, pr., pb. 1737 (three acts); *Miss Lucy in Town*, pr., pb. 1742 (one act); *The Wedding-Day*, pr., pb. 1743 (five acts; also known as *The Virgin Unmask'd*); *The Fathers: Or, The Good-Natured Man*, pr., pb. 1778 (revised for posthumous production by David Garrick).

NONFICTION: *The Journal of a Voyage to Lisbon*, 1755.

TRANSLATION: *The Military History of Charles XII King of Sweden*, 1740.

MISCELLANEOUS: *Miscellanies*, 1743 (3 volumes).

Bibliography

Battestin, Martin C. T*he Moral Basis of Fielding's Art: A Study of Joseph Andrews*. Middletown, Conn.: Wesleyan University Press, 1959. An important study arguing that in *Joseph Andrews* Fielding presents an allegory of the conflict between vanity and true Christian morality. Like John Bunyan's *The Pilgrim's Progress*, the novel traces the movement from the sinful city to the redemptive countryside. Sees the story of Mr. Wilson not as a digression but as a central expression of the novel's theme.

Battestin, Martin C., with Ruthe R. Battestin. *Henry Fielding: A Life*. London: Routledge, 1989. *The Sunday Times* voted this work one of the four best biographies of the year. Based on fourteen years' research, this detailed biography replaces Wilbur L. Cross's *The History of Henry Fielding* (1918, New York: Russell & Russell, 1945) as the definitive story of Fielding. Includes a useful bibliography of Fielding's writings.

Bloom, Harold, ed. *Henry Fielding*. New York: Chelsea House, 1987. Essays on Fielding's major novels, his anti-Romanticism, and his uses of style, history, and comedy. Includes chronology and bibliography.

_____, ed. *Henry's Fielding's "Tom Jones."* New York: Chelsea House, 1987. Essays on the style and structure of the novel, with an introduction by Bloom succinctly detailing the history of criticism of the novel and Fielding's handling of Squire Western. Includes a chronology and bibliography.

Johnson, Maurice. *Fielding's Art of Fiction: Eleven Essays on "Shamela," "Joseph Andrews," "Tom Jones," and "Amelia."* Philadelphia: University of Pennsylvania Press, 1961. Johnson writes in his introduction, "I want to suggest how, in his fiction, Fielding attempted vigorously and cheerfully to define the good life, within the severe limitations set by Fortune, society, and man's own errant nature" (pages 16-17). These eleven pieces provide a good critical survey of Fielding's fiction.

Mace, Nancy A. *Henry Fielding's Novels and the Classical Tradition*. Newark: University of Delaware Press, 1996. Examines the classical influence on Fielding.

Pagliaro, Harold E. *Henry Fielding: A Literary Life*. New York: St. Martin's Press, 1998. Part of the Literary Lives series, this is an excellent, updated biography of Fielding. Provides bibliographical references and an index.

Rivero, Albert J., ed. *Critical Essays on Henry Fielding*. New York: G. K. Hall, 1998. A good collection of essays about Fielding's major novels. Includes bibliographical references and an index.

Sacks, Sheldon. *Fiction and the Shape of Belief*. Berkeley: University of California Press, 1964. Posits three categories of fiction: satire, apologue, and novel. Argues that, because Fielding uses characters to demonstrate his moral stance, his works are novels, but that his various digressions, providing more overt moral lessons, are apologues.

Stoler, John A., and Richard D. Fulton. *Henry Fielding: An Annotated Bibliography of Twentieth-Century Criticism, 1900-1977*. New York: Garland, 1980. After listing a number of major Fielding bibliographies and various editions of his works, this bibliography provides a comprehensive, annotated list of secondary works. Arrangement is by title, so students seeking material on a specific work, such as *Tom Jones*, can quickly find what they need.

Watt, Ian. *The Rise of the Novel: Studies in Defoe, Richardson, and Fielding*. Berkeley: University of California Press, 1957. While praising Fielding's "wise assessment of life," Watt believes that Fielding's novelistic techniques reject verisimilitude for the sake of the moral. Hence, Watt sees Fielding's approach as a fictional dead end. Contains some useful observations about Fielding's plots and language.

Ford Madox Ford

Ford Madox Hueffer

Born: Merton, England; December 17, 1873
Died: Deauville, France; June 26, 1939

Principal long fiction · *The Shifting of the Fire*, 1892; *The Inheritors*, 1901 (with Joseph Conrad); *Romance*, 1903 (with Conrad); *The Benefactor*, 1905; *The Fifth Queen*, 1906; *Privy Seal*, 1907; *An English Girl*, 1907; *The Fifth Queen Crowned*, 1908; *Mr. Apollo*, 1908; *The "Half Moon,"* 1909; *The Nature of a Crime*, 1909 (serial), 1924 (book; with Conrad); *A Call*, 1910; *The Portrait*, 1910; *The Simple Life Limited*, 1911; *Ladies Whose Bright Eyes*, 1911; *The Panel*, 1912; *The New Humpty-Dumpty*, 1912; *Mr. Fleight*, 1913; *The Young Lovell*, 1913 (also known as *Ring for Nancy*); *The Good Soldier*, 1915; *The Marsden Case*, 1923; *Some Do Not . . .* , 1924; *No More Parades*, 1925; *A Man Could Stand Up*, 1926; *The Last Post*, 1928; *A Little Less Than Gods*, 1928; *When the Wicked Man*, 1931; *The Rash Act*, 1933; *Henry for Hugh*, 1934; *Vive le Roy*, 1936; *Parade's End*, 1950 (includes *Some Do Not . . .* , *No More Parades*, *A Man Could Stand Up*, and *The Last Post*).

Other literary forms · Ford Madox Ford was an extremely prolific author, working in virtually every literary form. His children's stories and fairy tales include *The Brown Owl* (1891); *The Feather* (1892); *The Queen Who Flew* (1894); *Christina's Fairy Book* (1906); and the pantomime *Mister Bosphorus and the Muses* (1923). His volumes of poetry include *The Questions at the Well* (1893, as Fenil Haig); *Poems for Pictures* (1900); *The Face of the Night* (1904); *From Inland and Other Poems* (1907); *High Germany* (1911); *Collected Poems* (1913); *On Heaven, and Poems Written on Active Service* (1918); *A House* (1921); *New Poems* (1927); and *Collected Poems* (1936). Ford, who is acknowledged with Joseph Conrad as coauthor of the novels *The Inheritors* and *Romance*, may have had some hand in the composition of a number of Conrad's other works during the decade from 1898 to 1908. Ford's biographical, autobiographical, and critical works include *Ford Madox Brown* (1896); *Rossetti* (1902); *Hans Holbein, the Younger* (1905); *The Pre-Raphaelite Brotherhood* (1907); *Ancient Lights* (1911); *The Critical Attitude* (1911); *Henry James* (1913); *Thus to Revisit* (1921); *Joseph Conrad: A Personal Remembrance* (1924); *The English Novel* (1929); *Return to Yesterday* (1931); *It Was the Nightingale* (1933); and *Mightier Than the Sword* (1938). During the last years of his life, Ford served as professor of comparative literature at Olivet College in Michigan and prepared his final book, a massive critical history of world literature, *The March of Literature* (1938). His history and travel books include *The Cinque Ports* (1900); *Zeppelin Nights* (1916); *Provence* (1935); and *Great Trade Route* (1937). Collections of essays include *The Soul of London* (1905); *The Heart of the Country* (1906); *The Spirit of the People* (1907); *Women and Men* (1923); *A Mirror to France* (1926); *New York Is Not America* (1927); and *New York Essays* (1927). Several volumes Ford classified simply as propaganda, including *When Blood Is Their Argument* (1915) and *Between St. Dennis and St. George* (1915). Ford also edited *The English Review* and later *The Transatlantic Review* and wrote much ephemeral journalism.

Achievements · It is generally agreed that Ford's *The Good Soldier* is one of the masterpieces of modernism, a major experimental novel of enormous historical and artistic interest. His tetralogy *Parade's End,* composed of *Some Do Not . . . , No More Parades, A Man Could Stand Up,* and *The Last Post,* is also a key work in the modernist revolution, more massive than *The Good Soldier,* more sweeping in its treatment of historical change, but less daring in its formal innovations. After these five novels, there is a considerable drop in the quality of Ford's remaining fiction. The historical trilogy concerning Henry VIII (*The Fifth Queen, Privy Seal,* and *The Fifth Queen Crowned*) is cited by some critics as meriting serious reading. Scattered among his many volumes, works such as *A Call* reward the reader with surprisingly high quality, but most of the lesser books are all too obviously potboilers.

Ford was equally at home in the English, French, and German languages, and he contributed to the cosmopolitan and polyglot texture of European modernism. As an editor of influential literary magazines, he recognized and encouraged many writers who have since become famous. His collaboration with Joseph Conrad in the 1890's corresponded with Conrad's most productive artistic period, but whether Conrad's achievements were stimulated by Ford's collaboration or accomplished in spite of Ford's intrusion is still under debate. Ford also exercised a considerable influence on Ezra Pound during Pound's early London years. Later, after World War I, Ford was associated with all the prominent writers of the Parisian Left Bank: James Joyce, Ernest Hemingway, Jean Rhys, and others.

Ford's achievement, then, was as a man of letters whose diverse contributions to modern literature—particularly as an editor and as a champion of modernist writers— far transcended his not inconsiderable legacy as a novelist.

Biography · Ford Madox Hermann Hueffer was born in what is now London on December 17, 1873; he was named for his maternal grandfather, the pre-Raphaelite painter Ford Madox Brown (1821-1893). Brown had two daughters: The elder married William Michael Rossetti (brother to the poet Dante Gabriel Rossetti); the younger daughter, Catherine, married the German journalist Francis Hueffer, music critic for the London *Times,* who wrote many books and had a serious scholarly interest in Richard Wagner, Arthur Schopenhauer, and Provençal poetry. Ford was born to this couple and grew up in an intellectual hothouse of painters, musicians, artists, and writers with advanced ideas. His family expected him to be a genius, which led him to acquire, early in his life, a sense of inadequacy and failure. Ford tended later to falsify information in his biography and to have difficulty separating reality from fantasy in his recollections. He attended the coeducational Praetorius School in Folkestone, apparently an institution with very modern ideas of education. One of his schoolmates there was Elsie Martindale, a young woman whom he married against her parents' wishes in 1894. Perhaps this elopement by the impetuous young lovers shows Ford's tendency to play out in reality the conventions of courtly love, a subject of intense study by Ford's father and a preoccupation of the author himself in all his fiction, evident even in his final book, the critical survey *The March of Literature.* Ford and Elsie did not, however, find passionate love a practical way to attain long-term happiness or stability.

In September, 1898, Edward Garnett introduced Ford to Joseph Conrad, now recognized as one of the greatest English-language novelists, even though his native tongue was Polish. Ford, like Conrad, was multilingual, and, at least to some degree, he helped Conrad with the niceties of the English idiom. The two would often write in French, then translate the work into English. By the spring of 1909, however, Ford and Conrad had quarreled and were never again closely associated. They acknowledged that they collaborated on *The Inheritors* and *Romance*, although Ford must have had at least some slight hand in many of Conrad's fictions written between 1898 and 1909. In fairness, the reader should note that Ford, too, must have had his ideas and his style permanently shaped to some degree by his collaboration with the older, more worldly master, Conrad.

Conrad had married an Englishwoman, Jessie George, in 1896, and he lived in a settled and respectable way with her until his death in 1924. At least in part, Conrad's breach with Ford stemmed from Jessie's dislike for what she regarded as Ford's ever more outrageous sexual behavior. In 1903, Ford had an affair with his wife's sister, Mary Martindale. Throughout his fiction, Ford replays similar real-life issues of passion, adultery, and their tawdry consequences. Thomas C. Moser in *The Life in the Fiction of Ford Madox Ford* (1980) maintains that Ford's writing follows a cyclical pattern, with each outburst of creativity triggered by the introduction of a new love into his life: Elsie Martindale, Mary Martindale, Arthur Marwood, Violet Hunt, Brigit Patmore, Jean Rhys, Stella Bowen, and Janice Biala. Moser's thesis is a bit too neat to be completely convincing, but its outline suggests the generally messy personal life that Ford must have been living while writing his voluminous works.

Analysis · From his association with Conrad, his study of Henry James and of the rise of the English novel, and his knowledge of French literature, Ford Madox Ford developed his notion of *literary impressionism*, which is central to an understanding of his masterpiece, *The Good Soldier*. Ford's clearest statement of his theory of literary impressionism is found in *Joseph Conrad: A Personal Remembrance*. Literary impressionism, Ford says, is a revolt against the commonplace nineteenth century novel, or "nuvvle," as he calls it. The impressionist novel should not be a narration or report, but a rendering of impressions. Rather than following a linear plot, giving one event after another as they occur, the impressionist novel enters the mind of a storyteller and follows his associated ideas in a tangled stream of consciousness, so that vivid image becomes juxtaposed to vivid image, skipping across space and time in a collage of memory and imagination. The impressionist novel takes as its subject an *affair*, some shocking event which has already happened, and proceeds in concentric rings of growing complication as the storyteller cogitates. The focus of the novel is internal rather than external. The reader must focus on the storyteller's mental processes rather than on the events themselves. The impressionist novel is limited to the mind of the storyteller, and so is finally solipsistic. The novel refers to itself, so that the reader can never "get out of" the storyteller's limited mentality and judge whether he is reliable or unreliable, perhaps merely a madman telling a tale which has no connection whatever to reality. Limited and unreliable narration, time-shifts, fragmentation of details torn from the context in which they occur, verbal collages of such fragments in configurations produced by the narrator's association of ideas, defamiliarization of the commonplace—all these are characteristics of Ford's best work.

The traditional nineteenth century English novel depended on the convention of the linear plot. The process of reading from page one to the end of the text was generally assumed to correspond to the passage of time as one event followed another in the story, so that the hero might be born on page one, go to school on page fifty, commit adultery or consider committing adultery on page one hundred, and meet his just reward in the concluding pages of the book. In *The Good Soldier*, Ford Madox Ford rejected this linear structure and substituted for it the "affair": A shocking set of events has already occurred before the book begins, and the narrator weaves back and forth in his memories related to the affair. Gradually, in concentric circles of understanding, the reader learns the complicated situation underlying the superficial first impressions he or she may have formed. The drama of the story shifts from the events of the tale to the process of the telling; such stories necessarily contrast first appearances with deeper "realities" revealed in the narration.

The Good Soldier · *The Good Soldier* concerns two married couples: Arthur Dowell (the narrator) and his wife Florence (Hurlbird) Dowell and Edward Ashburnham and his wife Leonora (Powys) Ashburnham. The events of the story take place between August, 1904, and August, 1913, a nine-year period throughout most of which the two couples are the best of friends, living the life of the leisured rich at European spas, in elegant, cultivated idleness. There is an elegiac tone to this work, reflecting the autumn sunshine of the Edwardian era and a way of life which would be brutally wiped out with the outbreak of World War I.

The texture of the novel invites the reader to consider the conflict between appearance and reality. For most of the nine-year period of the action, Arthur Dowell believes that his wife is suffering from a heart ailment which confines her travels and requires her to be shut in her room under peculiar circumstances from time to time. He subsequently learns, however, that her heart is sound and that these arrangements are necessary to allow her to commit adultery, first with a young man named Jimmy and later with Edward Ashburnham himself. Dowell imagines Ashburnham to be a model husband, only gradually learning that he has engaged in a series of affairs and that his wife does not speak to him except when required to do so in public. This novel is like a hall of mirrors, and any statement by the narrator must be doubted.

Because readers are accustomed to novels with linear plots, the novel is more easily understood if the plot is rearranged into the customary linear sequence of events. Edward Ashburnham is from an ancient Anglican landholding family who owns the estate Branshaw Teleragh. As the novel opens, he has recently returned from serving as a military officer in India and arrives at the health spa, Bad Nauheim, in Germany, where he meets the Dowells for the first time. Although he appears to be brave, sentimental, and heroic, like the knights in ancient romances, the reader learns that he has been involved in a series of unfortunate affairs with women. His parents arranged his marriage to Leonora Powys, a convent-educated Catholic girl, whose impoverished family had an estate in Ireland. Religious and temperamental differences soon cause their marriage to cool. While riding in a third-class carriage, Edward tries in a blundering way to comfort a servant girl and is arrested for sexual misbehavior in what is called the Kilsyte case. This misadventure leads him for the first time in his life to consider himself capable of bad conduct. His next affair involves a short-lived passion for a Spanish dancer, La Dolciquita, who demands cash for spending a week with him at Antibes. Reckless gambling at the casino, combined with the direct expenses of La Dolciquita's passion, substantially deplete Edward's inherited fortune. His wife, Leonora, makes herself the guardian of his estate and sets out to recover their financial losses. She demands that he take a military post in India for eight years and doles out his spending money carefully while squeezing his tenants and lands back in England for as much profit as possible.

In India, Edward finds his next woman, Mrs. Basil, whose husband, a brother-officer, allows the affair to continue in order to blackmail Edward. Eventually, Mrs.

Basil's husband is transferred to Africa so that she can no longer stay with Edward. Edward then makes an alliance with Mrs. Maidan, also the wife of a junior officer. Mrs. Maidan has a heart condition and accompanies the Ashburnhams to Bad Nauheim for treatment. On the day that the Dowells and the Ashburnhams first meet, Leonora Ashburnham has found Mrs. Maidan coming out of Edward's bedroom in the hotel. Enraged, Leonora has slapped her and, in doing so, entangled her bracelet in Mrs. Maidan's hair. Florence Dowell, in the hall, sees them struggling there and comes to help. Leonora lamely explains that she has accidentally caught her bracelet in Mrs. Maidan's hair, and Florence helps them get untangled, as the sobbing Mrs. Maidan runs to her room. That evening, Leonora Ashburnham insists on sitting at the Dowells' dinner table in the hotel so as to prevent any gossip about that day's events in the hallway. Mrs. Maidan soon commits suicide, leaving Edward free to form a liaison with Florence Dowell herself.

Edward's ward, Nancy Rufford, is being educated in the same convent where Leonora went to school. As Nancy grows to a mature woman, Edward becomes attracted to her, but he is caught in the conflict between love and honor. He desires Nancy, but he is honor-bound not to violate his sacred trust to protect her. After Florence Dowell learns of Edward's affection for Nancy (along with some other distressing developments), she too commits suicide. Edward remains firm, however, and refuses to take advantage of his ward or corrupt her, even when she openly offers herself to him. He arranges for her to be sent to her father in Ceylon. On her voyage there, she cables from Brindisi a cheerful note implying that she feels no sorrow about leaving him. Edward then commits suicide with a penknife, and Nancy goes insane when she hears of his death. His widow, Leonora, marries a rabbitlike neighbor, Rodney Bayham, while Arthur Dowell is left as the proprietor of the Branshaw Teleragh estate, where he nurses the insane Nancy Rufford.

From the exterior, to those who know him only slightly, Edward Ashburnham appears almost superhumanly noble, the ideal of the British country gentleman and good soldier. If the reader believes all that is alleged about him, he is quite the contrary, a raging stallion, recklessly ruining every female he meets. The superficial goodness is merely a veneer masking his corruption. All the other characters, as well, have two sides. Florence Dowell, the respectable wife, has had an affair before her marriage to Arthur with the despicable Jimmy and may have married simply to get back to her lover in Europe. She certainly does not hesitate to become Edward Ashburnham's mistress and commits suicide when she learns in a double-barreled blow that Edward is attracted to Nancy Rufford and that the man in whose house she committed adultery with Jimmy is now talking with her husband in Bad Nauheim. Leonora is purposeful in trying to manage her husband's estate economically, but she is cruel and unloving. The reader can easily imagine that her husband would be driven to seek other company. Arthur Dowell, the narrator himself, is stupid, lazy, and piggish.

Since the story is told entirely from the point of view of Arthur Dowell, and since his is a limited intelligence, the reader can never entirely trust his narration as reliable. Dowell may assert on one page that a character is noble, yet show the reader in a hundred ways that the character is despicable. The reader is caught in the web of Dowell's mind. Clearly, Dowell sometimes does not tell the "truth"; but since the total work is fiction, the reader is not simply confronted with a conflict between appearance and reality but with the status of competing fictions. Is Edward a noble knight or a despicable roué? The story evaporates into the impressions in Dowell's mind. What

Dowell thinks or believes *is* the truth at that moment in the fiction. It could be seriously argued that Edward, Leonora, and Florence have no external "reality" at all, that they are simply the imaginings of the sickly Dowell as he tells or dreams his story. This approach may shock readers of conventional fiction, who are accustomed to reading a novel as if the characters were real people, yet all characters in every fiction are simply projections of the author's creative imagination.

Parade's End · Ford's massive tetralogy, *Parade's End*, consists of four separate novels: *Some Do Not . . .* ; *No More Parades*; *A Man Could Stand Up*; and *The Last Post*. The main theme of these works repeats a major concern of *The Good Soldier*, the destruction of the Tory gentleman. Edward Ashburnham in *The Good Soldier* belongs to the same class as Christopher Tietjens, the protagonist of *Parade's End*. Both are said to have been modeled on Ford's friend Arthur Marwood, who collaborated with Ford in publishing *The English Review*. Ashburnham is the landowner of Branshaw Teleragh, whereas Tietjens's family owns the Groby estate. Both feel an obligation to their dependents and take seriously their stewardship over the land. Both are highly altruistic in certain areas but are tormented by the conflict between their sexual impulses and what is considered proper or honorable behavior. They are Tory gentlemen, landowning, relaxed in manner, Anglican in religion, physically vigorous, classically educated, generous, virile, and possessed of a worldview in which man's place in the universe is clearly defined. Such men are assailed on all sides by women, by modern commercial industry, by Catholics and Jews, by fascists and communists, and finally by the internal contradictions of their own characters. World War I smashed that class of Tory landholding gentlefolk once and for all, in an externalization of that internal battle.

Because the books are a kind of verbal collage, creating a palimpsest of memory and imagination, weaving backward and forward through the minds of characters who are frequently under stress and incapable of reporting events without distorting them, the linear plot of the tetralogy is difficult to summarize. The first novel, *Some Do Not . . .* , opens with Christopher Tietjens traveling in a railway carriage. His destination, unknown to him at the time, is the future world, the wasteland created by World War I and the destruction of the comfortable Tory universe into which he was born. His wife, Sylvia, has a child of whom he is perhaps not the true father, and she has run away with another man to Europe. Christopher meets an attractive young woman named Valentine Wannop. In the course of the tetralogy, Valentine replaces Sylvia as Tietjens's mate. The war, when it breaks out, is a terrifying expression of the conflict already implied in the mind of Christopher. In *No More Parades*, Christopher sees the men on the battlefield harassed by infidelity at home. The combat scenes in the next volume, *A Man Could Stand Up*, include ones in which Christopher is buried in a collapsed trench under fire, fights desperately to free his companions, and then is demoted for having a dirty uniform. At the end of this book, Valentine and Christopher come together in a nightmare party celebrating the end of the war. The final volume in the tetralogy, *The Last Post*, is composed of a series of dramatic monologues in which the reader learns that the estate has passed to other hands and that the Groby elm, signifying the Tietjenses' ownership of the land, has been cut down.

Ezra Pound suggested that Ford's contribution to modern literature could be measured less by reference to any given works than by "the tradition of his intelligence." While most of Ford's many novels have been consigned to oblivion, *The Good*

Soldier and *Parade's End* testify to his manifold gifts as a man of letters and as a godfather to the modernists.

Todd K. Bender

Other major works

POETRY: *The Questions at the Well*, 1893 (as Fenil Haig); *Poems for Pictures*, 1900; *The Face of the Night*, 1904; *From Inland and Other Poems*, 1907; *Songs from London*, 1910; *High Germany*, 1911; *Collected Poems*, 1913; *Antwerp*, 1915; *On Heaven, and Poems Written on Active Service*, 1918; *A House*, 1921; *New Poems*, 1927; *Collected Poems*, 1936.

NONFICTION: *Ford Madox Brown*, 1896; *The Cinque Ports*, 1900; *Rossetti*, 1902; *The Soul of London*, 1905; *Hans Holbein, the Younger*, 1905; *The Heart of the Country*, 1906; *The Pre-Raphaelite Brotherhood*, 1907; *The Spirit of the People*, 1907; *Ancient Lights*, 1911 (published in the United States as *Memories and Impressions*, 1911); *The Critical Attitude*, 1911; *Henry James*, 1913; *When Blood Is Their Argument*, 1915; *Between St. Dennis and St. George*, 1915; *Zeppelin Nights*, 1916; *Thus to Revisit*, 1921; *Women and Men*, 1923; *Joseph Conrad: A Personal Remembrance*, 1924; *A Mirror to France*, 1926; *New York Is Not America*, 1927; *New York Essays*, 1927; *No Enemy*, 1929; *The English Novel*, 1929; *Return to Yesterday*, 1931 (autobiography); *It Was the Nightingale*, 1933 (autobiography); *Provence*, 1935; *Great Trade Route*, 1937; *Mightier Than the Sword*, 1938; *The March of Literature*, 1938.

CHILDREN'S LITERATURE: *The Brown Owl*, 1891; *The Feather*, 1892; *The Queen Who Flew*, 1894; *Christina's Fairy Book*, 1906; *Mister Bosphorus and the Muses*, 1923.

Bibliography

Bender, Todd K. *Literary Impressionism in Jean Rhys, Ford Madox Ford, Joseph Conrad, and Charlotte Brontë*. New York: Garland, 1997. Examines style and technique in the four authors. Includes bibliographical references and an index.

Cassell, Richard A., ed. *Critical Essays on Ford Madox Ford*. Boston: G. K. Hall, 1987. In his introduction, Cassell reviews Ford criticism, which he believes becomes more laudatory and perceptive after 1939. Though there are essays dealing with Ford's romances, poetry, and social criticism, the bulk of the book focuses on *The Good Soldier* and *Parade's End*. Also valuable are contributions by literary figures such as Graham Greene, Ezra Pound, and Conrad Aiken. Well indexed.

_____. *Ford Madox Ford: A Study of His Novels*. Baltimore: The Johns Hopkins University Press, 1961. The first three chapters (biography, aesthetics, literary theory) are followed by close readings not only of the major works (*The Good Soldier, Parade's End*) but also of neglected minor fictional works, particularly *Ladies Whose Bright Eyes, The Rash Act*, and *Henry for Hugh*. Also includes helpful discussions of Joseph Conrad's and Henry James's influence on Ford.

Green, Robert. *Ford Madox Ford: Prose and Politics*. Cambridge, England: Cambridge University Press, 1981. Unlike earlier studies which applied New Criticism to Ford's work, Green's analysis places Ford within his historical context and identifies his political beliefs. Asserts that Ford drew no firm line between fiction and nonfiction, treating such works as *Ancient Lights* and *Henry James* as important in themselves and glossing over Ford's major fiction, *The Good Soldier* and *Parade's End*. Also contains a chronological bibliography of his work as well as an extensive yet selected bibliography of Ford criticism.

Huntley, H. Robert. *The Alien Protagonist of Ford Madox Ford*. Chapel Hill: University of North Carolina Press, 1970. Focuses on the Ford protagonist, typically a man whose alien temperament and ethics produce a conflict with his society. After extensive treatments of neglected novels (*An English Girl, A Call, The Fifth Queen*), concludes with an entire chapter devoted to *The Good Soldier*, which is discussed in terms of Ford's historical theories.

Judd, Alan. *Ford Madox Ford.* Cambridge, Mass.: Harvard University Press, 1991. A very readable, shrewd biography. However, this major university press includes no source notes and only a brief bibliographical note.

Leer, Norman. *The Limited Hero in the Novels of Ford Madox Ford.* East Lansing: Michigan State University Press, 1966. After defining "heroism" in Ford's thought, Leer discusses the early novels and the ineffectual hero before an extended analysis of *The Good Soldier* and *Parade's End.* Leer sees a decline in Ford's post-1929 fiction, but praises Ford's travel books of the same period. A first-rate bibliography of secondary sources is also included.

MacShane, Frank, ed. *Ford Madox Ford: The Critical Heritage.* London: Routledge & Kegan Paul, 1972. An invaluable collection of reviews and responses, gleaned from literary journals, to Ford's fiction and poetry. Includes an 1892 unsigned review of *The Shifting of the Fire,* as well as essays by such literary greats as Theodore Dreiser, Arnold Bennett, Ezra Pound, Conrad Aiken, Christina Rossetti, H. L. Mencken, Graham Greene, and Robert Lowell. There are reviews of individual novels, essays on controversies in which Ford was embroiled, and general studies of Ford's art.